8/09

Archaeology in America

Archaeology in America
An Encyclopedia

Volume 2
Midwest and Great Plains/Rocky Mountains

Francis P. McManamon, General Editor
Linda S. Cordell, Kent G. Lightfoot,
and George R. Milner, Editorial Board

GREENWOOD PRESS
Westport, Connecticut • London

Library of Congress Cataloging-in-Publication Data

Archaeology in America : an encyclopedia / Francis P. McManamon, general editor ; Linda S. Cordell, Kent G. Lightfoot, and George R. Milner, editorial board.
   v. cm.
 Includes bibliographical references and index.
 Contents: v. 1. Northeast and Southeast — v. 2. Midwest and Great Plains/Rocky Mountains — v. 3. Southwest and Great Basin/Plateau — v. 4. West Coast and Arctic/Subarctic.
 ISBN 978–0–313–33184–8 (set : alk. paper) — ISBN 978–0–313–33185–5 (v. 1 : alk. paper) — ISBN 978–0–313–33186–2 (v. 2 : alk. paper) — ISBN 978–0–313–33187–9 (v. 3 : alk. paper) — ISBN 978–0–313–35021–4 (v. 4 : alk. paper)
 1. United States—Antiquities—Encyclopedias. 2. Excavations (Archaeology)—United States—Encyclopedias. 3. Historic sites—United States—Encyclopedias. 4. Archaeology—United States—Encyclopedias. 5. Canada—Antiquities—Encyclopedias. 6. Excavations (Archaeology)—Canada—Encyclopedias. 7. Historic sites—Canada—Encyclopedias. 8. Archaeology—Canada—Encyclopedias. I. McManamon, Francis P. II. Cordell, Linda S. III. Lightfoot, Kent G., 1953– IV. Milner, George R., 1953–
  E159.5.A68 2009
  973.03—dc22   2008020844

British Library Cataloguing in Publication Data is available.

Library of Congress Catalog Card Number: 2008020844
ISBN: 978–0–313–33184–8 (set)
       978–0–313–33185–5 (vol. 1)
       978–0–313–33186–2 (vol. 2)
       978–0–313–33187–9 (vol. 3)
       978–0–313–35021–4 (vol. 4)

First published in 2009

Greenwood Press, 88 Post Road West, Westport, CT 06881
An imprint of Greenwood Publishing Group, Inc.
www.greenwood.com

Printed in the United States of America

The paper used in this book complies with the Permanent Paper Standard issued by the National Information Standards Organization (Z39.48–1984).

10 9 8 7 6 5 4 3 2 1

Cover: Monks Mound, the main earthen architecture monument at Cahokia Mounds State Historic Site, Illinois, just east of St. Louis, Missouri. Cahokia Mounds is a World Heritage Site. For a related essay, see John E. Kelly, "Cahokia Mounds State Historic Site—World Heritage Site: Center of the Mississippian World."

CONTENTS

About the Editorial Board and *About the Contributors* can be found in volume 4.

VOLUME 2: MIDWEST AND GREAT PLAINS/ROCKY MOUNTAINS

MIDWEST LIST OF ENTRIES

GREAT PLAINS/ROCKY MOUNTAINS LIST OF ENTRIES

Midwest Region

KEY FOR MIDWEST REGIONAL MAP

1. Kimmswick site, Mastodon State Historic Site
2. Carrier Mills Archaeological District
3. Graham Cave State Park
4. Indian Knoll, Carlston Annis, and other Archaic shell midden sites
5. Koster
6. Modoc Rock Shelter
7. Isle Royale National Park
8. Adena Mound
9. Robbins Mounds
10. Middle Woodland mounds, Pere Marquette State Park
11. Grave Creek Mound Site Historic Site
12. Hopewell Culture National Historical Park
13. Edwin Harness Mound
14. Hopewell
15. Newark Earthworks State Memorial
16. Marietta Earthworks
17. Serpent Mound State Memorial
18. Alligator Mound
19. Fort Ancient State Memorial
20. Flint Ridge State Memorial
21. Seip Mound State Memorial;
22. The Trempealeau Lakes Mound Group
23. Effigy Mounds National Monument
24. The St. Louis and East St. Louis Mound Groups
25. Giant City State Park
26. Angel Mound State Historic Site
27. Aztalan State Park
28. Cahokia Mounds State Historic Site
29. Dickson Mounds
30. Range
31. Kincaid
32. Mill Creek chert quarries
33. Powers Fort
34. Towosahgy State Historic Site
35. Jonathan Creek Village
36. Wickliffe Mounds State Park and Research Center
37. Sand Lake
38. Norris Farms 36 Cemetery
39. Lonza-Caterpillar
40. Pea Ridge National Military Park
41. South Park Village
42. Mammoth Cave National Park
43. Fort St. Joseph
44. New Philadelphia
45. The Lincoln Home National Historic Site
46. Wilson's Creek National Battlefield
47. Red Wing Area Oneota sites
48. Thunder Bay National Marine Sanctuary48
49. Fathom Five National Marine Park
50. Alger Underwater Preserve
51. Fort Michilimackinac
52. Marquette's St. Ignace Mission
53. Rock Island sites
54. Grand Village of the Illinois (Zimmerman)
55. Gainey
56. Napoleon Hollow
57. Anderson Mound, Mounds State Park
58. Miamisburg Mound
59. Nobles Pond
60. Pictured Rocks National Lakeshore
61. Sleeping Bear Dunes National Lakeshore
62. Pollack Earthworks, Indian Mound Reserve
63. Wright Mounds
64. C & O Mounds

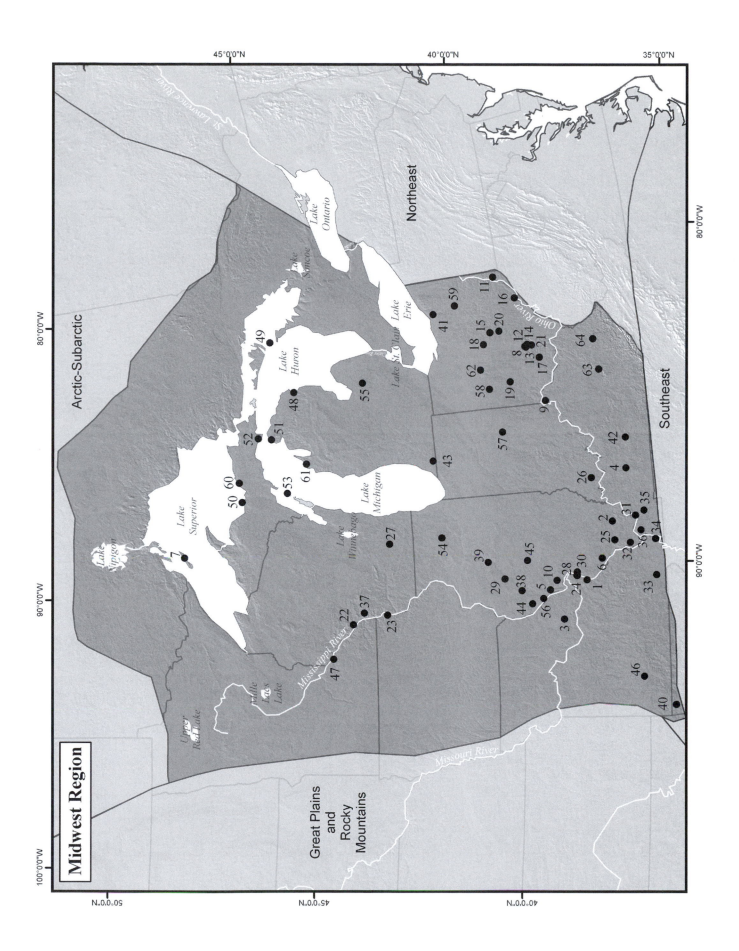

INTRODUCTION

This section of *Archaeology in America* includes essays about archaeological sites in the Midwest region of North America. This region is defined roughly by the eastern borders of Ohio and Kentucky, and the western boundary of West Virginia; the southern borders of Kentucky and Missouri; and the western portions of Missouri, Iowa, and Minnesota. To the north the region includes the drainages of the Great Lakes of Erie, Huron, Michigan, a portion of Ontario, and Superior (one essay covers historic shipwrecks and historic economic and settlement developments related to shipping in the Great Lakes).

The dominant geomorphological features of the northern half of the Midwest are the Great Lakes. These bodies provided a relatively easy means of waterborne communication in ancient and historic times. Resources here were used for thousands of years (see, e.g., the description of ancient copper mining in the essay on Isle Royale in Lake Superior). In its southern half, the Midwest is characterized by the valley of the Mississippi River and two of its main tributaries, the Missouri from the west and the Ohio from the east. The environments and resources that humans have exploited in these two sections of the region are so distinctive that we have included separate essays in this section on the Great Lakes and on the riverine environments of the region.

Ancient earthen architecture is a well-known constituent of the archaeological record of the Midwest. In the nineteenth century the ancient earthen mounds, enclosures, and other architectural earthworks encountered by European Americans moving into the region led to the development of fanciful legends of ancient mound builders. The myth of the mound builders was finally put to rest at the end of that century through systematic archaeological research by early scientists at the Smithsonian Institution (the essay by Hawley summarizes this historical episode). In the Ohio River valley, centered in what is now southern Ohio and adjacent Kentucky, about 2,500 years ago the human groups began to create earthen monuments as part of burial ceremonies (Milner's essay on earthen architecture provides many details of this and subsequent architectural developments). The culture of the time is called Adena by modern archaeologists, based on one of the early sites of this period that was studied. The conical earthen mortuary mounds these people constructed to bury their dead are a distinctive part of the archaeological record of their ancient culture.

A few hundred years later another major ancient culture, referred to today as the Hopewell, developed in the same area. The Hopewell people constructed complex assemblages of earthen architectural monuments in linear and more complicated geometric shapes (see, e.g., the essays on Hopewell Culture National Historical Park, Newark Earthworks State Memorial, and Serpent Mound State Memorial). In the lower Midwest, substantial earthen architecture was also being created, mostly burial mounds.

By the beginning of the second millennium AD, the most notable earthen architecture consisted mainly of platform mounds, some of them quite tall, on which structures of political and ritual importance were constructed. These mounds were frequently arranged in groups surrounding large open plazas. In association with these developments, highly structured agricultural societies emerged in the central Mississippi valley. Along with the intensive focus on agriculture, political, ritual, technological, and stylistic concepts developed and were integrated into a cultural complex that reached its height at the Cahokia site in the American Bottom area, near present-day St. Louis (see especially the introductory essay by Brose and the essays on Cahokia, Angel Mounds, and the Range site).

The Midwest region also contains many interesting historic period sites related to early European exploration and trade, the ultimate development of urban centers and industrialization, and the historic wave of immigration. Essays on a "free black" site (New Philadelphia, Illinois), President Lincoln's Springfield (Illinois) home, and the Civil War battlefields at Wilson's Creek, Missouri, and Pea Ridge, in extreme northwest Arkansas fill out our examination of Midwest historic period archaeology.

We have focused these essays on the most important and interesting archaeological sites and topics in the Midwest region. Readers can learn more about these sites, and others as well, by using the additional sources of information and references listed at the end of each essay. More articles, books, Web sites, museum information, and other sources are available to those who want to learn more about these fascinating places and subjects. In many cases, the sites can be visited as parts of national, state, local, or other public parks.

The articles in the Midwest section of *Archaeology in America* include thirteen general essays on various topics that cover the ancient and historic time periods. The general essays are followed by forty-six essays on specific archaeological sites or related groups of sites in a particular region. These more specific essays are arranged in roughly chronological order.

ENTRIES FOR THE MIDWEST REGION

ANCIENT AND HISTORIC PERIOD ARCHAEOLOGY OF THE MIDWEST

INTRODUCTION AND SCOPE

In this overview the Midwest region is constrained by the western prairies of Minnesota, Iowa, and Missouri. To the south, this region is bounded by the confluence of the Mississippi and the Ohio rivers and the latter's southern tributaries that drain the Appalachian plateau in West Virginia and northern Kentucky. Encompassing the entire Lake Michigan basin, to the north and east this region also covers the drainages of Lakes Superior, Huron, Erie, and the western portion of Lake Ontario, thus including significant portions of southern Ontario province. Although this region was often considered a coherent "American" region, and treated as such by early seventeenth-century French explorers, since the mid-eighteenth century the area has been politically separated into British Canada and the United States along the watercourses that once united it. More important, this region has seldom shown similar region-wide prehistoric patterning. Only episodically in ancient times was it swept by a single new technology, a broad stylistic horizon marker, or an iconic system of structured exchange. These phenomena were likely of greater significance to the region's recent archaeologists than to its ancient occupants.

During the sudden cooling and subsequent long, episodic warming conditions of the Paleoindian and Archaic periods, from 13,000 to 1500 BC, a number of cultural groups with technologically and stylistically similar adaptations settled into the river valleys of the Midwest as these gradually dried, warmed, and filled with modern biota. In the upper Great Lakes northern groups modified technologies, adapting to differing ecologies as they created ephemeral archaeological sites with their occupations and activities across favored locations in a kaleidoscope of ecological change with many unique biotic associations, responding to changing lake levels, shifting stream connections, and fluctuating water tables.

During the more variable climate regimes of the Late Archaic and Woodland periods, from 1500 BC to AD 750, most of the cultural groups who occupied the prairies drained by the upper Mississippi and lower Missouri rivers, as well as some groups in the Ohio River basin or occupying the upper Great Lakes, participated in three overlapping waves of social exchange. Although some exchanged materials were similar across space and time, the patterns of use and disposal differed, and the materials and the meanings assigned to them by the limited participants varied dramatically at any single time and throughout the millennia.

Finally, the climatic warming and then cooling of the late prehistoric and/or Mississippian period, from AD 850 to the end of the sixteenth century, saw the rise and then the fall of complex agriculturally based cultures that were integrated with other cultures in the Southeast through iconographic ritual and social exchange. This Midwestern cultural complex grew from a center at Cahokia in the American Bottom, where the Missouri, Illinois, and Ohio rivers join the Mississippi, and spread along the floodplains and bluffs of the lower Missouri River valley, much of the upper Mississippi River valley, and along the Ohio River valley to the Scioto River in Ohio. Lying beyond these socially complex hierarchical Mississippian sites was an interactive cultural zone showing every variety of frontier experiment from Cahokia-influenced independent hierarchical town and temple complexes to apparently fortified trading centers, to less socially complex and less hierarchical upper Mississippian cultural complexes, many of which continued along the ecological and social trajectories of their Woodland ancestors despite adopting aspects of Mississippian technology or style. Beyond these lay more diffuse non-Mississippian cultures scattered at arable or favored fishing locations amidst less occupied areas along the northern lakes or in the sheltered river valleys of the Appalachian uplands. During this period, many of these outlying cultural groups in the Great Lakes or the Ohio River valley interacted with their eastern neighbors, the Iroquoian groups of Ontario and New York, or with mid-Atlantic Algonquian populations in the upper Potomac and Roanoke river drainages. Many populations in the upper Mississippi and Missouri river valleys moved out onto the Great Plains as specialized farmers or later as nomadic hunters while many minimally hierarchical groups abandoned the lower Ohio sometime after AD 1500. Finally, the varying cataclysms of the historic period swept into this Midwest region directly and indirectly from every direction but the west.

THE FIRST OCCUPANTS

The earliest occupations of this region left a surprisingly rich scatter of early Paleoindian fluted projectile points, variants of the widespread but short-lived Clovis technology.

Based on the densities of early sites and find locations and the manufacture of most tools from a few selected lithic sources, Paleoindians appear to have moved into the region from the Southwest, reaching eastern Ohio sites such as the thoroughly excavated but plowed Nobles' Pond and the sealed Paleo Crossing site at Dague Farm by 10,250 BC. After 9500 BC people moved north to the shores of newly drained, often ice-fronted ancient Great Lakes in Minnesota, Wisconsin, Michigan, and Ontario. Although these occupants lacked many small blade and core techniques, the extreme resharpening of Clovis and Clovis-like Gainey points as well as the intra-site distributions of numerous small scrapers suggest that they initially made seasonal hunting-party forays into the Great Lakes. Only later did larger permanent populations move from Illinois or Ohio regions to the north.

The stratified Kimmswick site in eastern Missouri had Clovis points associated with the remains of mastodon. In north central Ohio the deep Sheriden Cave site with a suite of radiocarbon dates from around 9500 BC yielded sealed deposits with Paleoindian points and ground sloth, as well as a number of extant species. Paleoindian points and extinct fauna occurred at the undated Boaz mastodon site in southern Wisconsin. However, in south central Michigan and northern Ohio a number of sites without artifacts dated between 10,000 and 7500 BC yielded unusual assortments of particular fall-killed mastodon bones, suggesting Paleoindians cached meat in frozen bogs. Somewhat later Paleoindian projectile points with projecting "eared" bases or constricted midsections were associated with the remains of barren ground caribou in the southeast Michigan Holcomb site and at the Fisher site among others in Ontario, all on shorelines of ancestral Lake Huron at 9000 BC. In southern Iowa, central Missouri, Illinois, Indiana, and east central Ohio, Clovis points have been recovered where open grasslands with oak and poplar were intermixed with more general forests on rolling hills or along river corridors. On the prairie edge in northwest Iowa, the stratified Cherokee Sewer site revealed a sequence of late Paleoindian Agate Basin style lanceolate points in association with modern bison in levels dated 6600 BC, and at the Renier site similar large late Paleoindian lanceolate points accompanied a cremation burial on the Lake Michigan shore of Wisconsin.

FILLING THE MODERN ECOSYSTEMS

Early Archaic notched and lanceolate-shaped projectile point sequences occur at 8000 BC in reused, seasonally occupied archaeological sites in large rock shelters overlooking wide river floodplains, such as the basal layers at Modoc in southern Illinois, Raddatz in southern Wisconsin, and Graham Cave in Missouri. Differing notched and bifurcated-base points from 7600 through 3500 BC were revealed in deeply buried strata at the St. Albans site, along the lower Kanawha River in West Virginia. Numerous plains-like nonfluted,

stemmed, and lanceolate-style Late Paleoindian points as well as southeastern-style notched and bifurcated-base points that resembled Early Archaic points came from farm fields in Ohio, Michigan, and Indiana. It is possible that the variability of these late Paleoindian stone tool assemblages reflect different regional social populations. However, despite the number of well-dated and stratified Early through Middle Archaic cave and floodplain sites in the southern and western portions of the Midwest, there are remarkably few of either in the upper Great Lakes or Appalachian plateau regions to the north and east.

By 7500 BC, as the prairie fingered eastward with the onset of a period of climatic warming, the open grasslands in south central Illinois were being used by cultural groups using both expanding stemmed and barbed points. At the same time, corner-notched and side-notched projectile points were being used in forested areas. It is not clear whether this different distribution of projectile point forms indicates different activities being pursued by the same cultural group, or different cultural groups using different point styles. According to sealed and dated short-duration components at archaeological sites such as Modoc in Illinois and Graham, Pigeon Roost, Arnold, Rogers, and the upper levels of Missouri's Dalton site, the period from about 7500 to 5500 BC produced levels with a variety of point hafting styles along with gravers, drills, scrapers, chipped-stone pulper-planers, chopper/chopping tools, and adzes. Such tools were also found in deeply buried open sites such as Phillips Spring in Missouri and Koster and Napoleon Hollow in Illinois. People from the Late Paleoindian through the Middle Archaic time periods adopted similar diffuse hunting and gathering economies with small game predominating but with increasing reliance on seeds and nuts. At Koster, horizons dated 6600–4300 BC showed an unbroken technological continuity, with each extensive sealed soil layer showing different activity clusters that contained one of several types of points. Similar situations at other Illinois and Mississippi river valley sites suggest that some changes in lithic tool styles were functional and not simply related to change over time.

Farther north, the ecologically dynamic regions of eastern Wisconsin, Michigan, southern Ontario, and northern Ohio yield numerous projectile points that seem to be chronologically diagnostic of Late Paleoindian and Early or Middle Archaic occupations between 7500 and 2500 BC. Other small sites and surface collections from fossil beach ridges, river bluffs, or interfluvial divides contained only a few similar Plano- or Archaic-style projectile points and few sites provided radiometric dates or were accompanied by tools that indicated Middle or Late Archaic time periods. A few rare larger sites, such as the Late Paleoindian McConnell chert quarry workshop, showed technological specialization precluding stylistic lithic variability.

In the absence of large sealed and well-dated sites, some archaeologists argue against any local Paleoindian-Archaic continuity. Their reasoning is that Great Lakes Paleoindians were so strictly adapted to large-game hunting that rising lakes, which quickly flooded boreal forests, led to abandonment of the region from 7000 to 2500 BC. Later immigrations from the western Great Lakes and Appalachians, they suggest, repopulated this part of the region.

From the Middle through Late Archaic, a time period of essentially modern climates, the southern Midwest displayed a similar series of cultural complexes, each becoming increasingly dense by exploiting reliable resources within stable, regionally bounded ecosystems, and each engaging in limited nonessential exchange with one or more of its neighbors. Such "Midcontinent Archaic" phases include the Riverton culture along the Wabash River and the Helton and Koster site phases in the lower Illinois River valley; the Black Earth and Faulkner sites in southern Illinois; the deeply stratified Middle to Late Archaic occupations along the Falls of the Ohio region of Indiana and Kentucky as well as the thoroughly studied Carlson Annis, BT-5, and Indian Knoll sites along Kentucky's Green River; the McCain, Bluegrass, and other French Lick phase sites in southern Indiana; the Maple Creek and McWhinney phase sites in the central Ohio River valley; and the Dunlap phase sites of central and eastern Ohio. Also during this period, solution caves across the region were first explored and then exploited by local groups to obtain workable sedimentary rock, crystal, and several physiologically active mineral salts.

Middle to Late Archaic sites were thoroughly integrated with the local resource base. In southern Illinois, the Middle Archaic (4000–3000 BC) Black Earth site near Carrier Mills was a year-round, economically diverse settlement whose biotic remains and artifacts suggest a concentrated population. Across the trans-Mississippi prairies of Missouri, Iowa, and Minnesota, regional Middle and Late Archaic cultures shared many mid-continent Archaic material styles but alternated seasonal bison hunting farther west with diffuse resource collecting from small camps along the river valleys. They buried their dead with ground stone and bone tools and the occasional copper tool or projectile point from the Great Lakes region. Multi-seasonal exploitation of aquatic mollusks supported large Middle and Late Archaic groups along the Green and Kentucky rivers, for whom detailed study of associated artifacts reveals surprising biophysical and demographic details. Most of these domestic sites included a similar suite of igneous ground-stone woodworking and seed-processing implements; several varieties and sizes of stemmed and notched knives and spear or dart points; and a rich variety of tools and ornaments made of local bone, antler, and shell.

The more northerly Great Lakes populations shifted site locations to maximize seasonally diffuse resources. Most of the data comes from sites where spawning fish provided reliable large-group sustenance, although most of the year was likely spent hunting deer and turkey and collecting nuts from small shelters and upland campsites along connecting lake and river systems. In northern Michigan and Wisconsin, as early as 2500 BC, a number of social units supplemented their use of chipped points, knives, scrapers, and ground and polished woodworking tools and ornaments made of local stone with tools and ornaments cut, folded, and cold-hammered out of Lake Superior copper. Some copper was painstakingly freed from in situ outcrops, such as those on Isle Royale in Lake Superior, but perhaps as frequently the copper came from cobbles or boulders incorporated into the glacial deposits scattered across the Great Lakes states.

Many of the Late Archaic sites yielded individual or group burials in pits scattered across shell midden or site features, in discrete isolated cemeteries, or in low mounds. Burials were accompanied by engraved bone bodkins, *atl atl* hooks, and flutes; turtle shell rattles; beads, tubes, palettes, and cups cut from marine shell; rolled beads, pins, and celts of native copper; and ornaments and tool and weapon handles of colorful stone from a few Midwestern sources. However, the well-used southern Illinois bifacial points and knives scattered across the central prairie states and the many Ohio flint points found in archaeological sites throughout the lower Great Lakes suggest fluid social unit composition rather than extensive long-distance exchange per se, and the limited mortuary offerings document intra-regional status differences and inter-regional contact but were not significant economic factors.

Also during this time period, farther east, from central Illinois to Ontario, individual and group cremations and burials covered with red ocher were accompanied by caches of unused stemmed or notched blades of local chert or Indiana hornstone. Some had birdstones, tubular pipes, and gorgets of Michigan and Ontario slate; small axes and rolled beads of native copper; and beads or gorgets of marine shell and pyrite, hematite, or galena crystals from the upper Mississippi River valley. Along the drainage divide between the Ohio River and the Great Lakes, similar burials with cut wolf jaw masks, engraved bird skulls, and perforated mammal canines were placed in glacial kames and ridges where reuse of some sites created mounds. Recent studies suggest small family group-to-group exchange of finished artifacts with no local physical reworking. While indicating development of lineage territoriality in the Midwest, this spectacular Late Archaic exchange was of limited economic significance.

THE SOCIOLOGY OF RITUAL EXCHANGE AND BURIAL

By the Early Woodland period (ca. 1000 BC) a localized pattern of diffuse hunting, fishing, and gathering had become established throughout the Midwest. In broad river valleys the growth of sunflower, chenopod, goosefoot, and marsh elder was encouraged, if not deliberately cultivated, to obtain starchy and oily seeds, and by 500 BC a variety of squash was being planted and cultivated by human groups. But several cold periods during a generally cool climatic episode miti-gated reliance on local harvesting. Where dense populations strained resources from seasonal subsistence, intergroup collaboration became structured by individual and family ritual exchange.

Native copper tools and ornaments, large ornaments of marine shell, and large caches of exotic chert and flint blades along with tubular and effigy pipes of exotic material were recovered from elite burials where larger groups constructed large ceremonial structures. Through time there was an increase in the number and size of circular earthworks and burial mounds. Mortuary offerings included shell, mica, and pipestone from mid-Atlantic and Appalachian groups, geometric objects, ornaments or small tools of Great Lakes copper and hematite, or central Mississippi Valley galena. Flat steatite-tempered south Atlantic ceramics that appeared in southern Ohio River tributaries by 850 BC were soon replaced by local clay-tempered "Fayette Thick" copies. At the same time, thick incised and smoothed "Black Sands" bowls similar to earlier Mid-south ceramics were made at small sites in the central and upper Mississippi River valley, and thick cord-marked, grit-tempered Northeastern-looking jars appeared in central Ohio, Indiana, and Michigan and southern Ontario. These early "Marion Thick" or "Vinette I" ceramics followed the distribution of red ocher–covered cremation sites that also contained triangular cache blades of New York and southeastern Ontario chert.

By 500 BC these patterns had coalesced in two regional traditions. Morton complexes in Illinois had group burials in log crypts within groups of mounds at seasonally reoccupied sites on major river terraces. Red ocher was liberally used to cover or decorate the dead in burials and some of the skeletons, but not all show cranial deformation similar to that seen in Adena peoples further east. Ceramics showed local technology and morphology but carried decorative motifs from the lower Mississippi valley. The few goods included with individual burials or left as isolated caches included copper beads, Illinois and Indiana flint blades, gorgets of marine shell, and fragments of hematite and galena. At the same time, burial elaboration also was occurring in the discontinuous concentrations of Adena ritual sites along the Scioto and Ohio river valleys, where a few related individuals were cremated and placed in log- or clay-lined pits below small mounds, all within a circular house, or, as at the Kentucky Peter Village site, in an open corporate structure. These interment structures were burned as part of burial rituals and mounded over with earth. Some sites, such as the Adena and Miamisburg Mounds in Ohio, the Anderson Earthworks in Indiana, Grave Creek Mound in West Virginia, and the Robbins and Mt. Horeb Mounds in Kentucky, showed several styles of grave and mortuary treatment and numerous episodes of accretion. Grave goods, generally left with only a few individuals in any mound, included cut animal teeth and jaws, some as masks; gorgets of polished Appalachian slate or

native copper; occasionally fully carved tubular pipes of stone from Ohio, Ontario, or the mid-Atlantic; and caches of points and blades of Ohio Flint Ridge flint or Pennsylvania jasper. Cloth-wrapped celts or points, bracelets and beads of Lake Superior copper, crescents of Appalachian mica, and fossil shark teeth from the mid-Atlantic or gulf coast occurred rarely, as did limestone palettes with complex zoomorphic engravings used as fabric stamps.

From these two centers, one vector of exchange ran north from Illinois into Minnesota, Wisconsin, and southwest Michigan, thence to western Ontario and upper Michigan, while Adena-like mortuary artifacts appeared at northeastern Ohio, Ontario, and Quebec sites along Lakes Huron, Ontario, and Erie. Beyond the Potomac, late Adena iconography and a few artifacts, some of Ohio Valley materials, were found with individuals in local sites on the Delmarva peninsula. The suggested population dispersal eastward remains unsupported by biophysical analysis and is less probable than irregular and non-ideological individual or family exchange with a few Ohio Valley people. By 200 BC, the related ceramic innovations had spread across the northern Great Lakes from both east and west, and the thick eastern Saugeen ceramics showed more complex decorative motifs than the better-made western Nokomis or North Bay ceramics. The consistent exchange of local materials over time and the broad participation in similar social rituals at many sites suggest that these connections were more than occasional southern excursions to "cottage country."

Yet throughout this region in the Early Woodland there were distinctions between the societies that participated in exchange and the larger number of societies that did not. In addition, there were status distinctions among and within the involved groups marked by material and by regionally restricted rituals, quite different from the Late Archaic. Despite increased long-distance exchange, Early Woodland Midwestern groups marshaled less corporate energy than coeval Southeastern groups.

VARIED MIDDLE WOODLAND SOCIAL RELATIONS OF THE MIDWEST AND GREAT LAKES

Although the Midwest had long, warm, and moist summers with short, mild winters from 300 BC to AD 536, no Middle Woodland economy was committed to agriculture. Around AD 150, maize ultimately from Mexico was introduced to the Midwest, probably along the Red River–Mississippi River–Ohio River route that brought other weird and wonderful material to eastern Hopewell sites. The rare maize cobs or kernels recovered from a few ceremonial and domestic sites in Ohio and Illinois represent occasional gardening at best, and several native and tropical seed plants continued to be intensively harvested. Collecting acorns, nuts, and shellfish, hunting deer and turkey, and fishing structured the seasonal locations of most Middle Woodland sites, whose overall material culture and domestic architecture seem to have changed little over the millennium between 250 BC and AD 650. Raw materials and the styles of domestic artifacts were also regional, although exotic materials from the upper Great Lakes, the Gulf of Mexico, the south Atlantic coast, the farthest Missouri Valley, and the south Appalachian Piedmont were used in mortuary rituals along with new, pan-regional icons. The regional foci for these cultural patterns were the Havana culture of central Illinois and, somewhat later and far more spectacular, the Hopewell culture of southern Ohio.

In Illinois and Indiana, incised Havana and Crab Orchard pottery developed from earlier local ceramics and became common in small river terrace villages. It was found in the few associated early Havana mortuary mounds constructed in stages, during each of which a burial structure was built upon a prepared floor on which intense fires had been burned. Family groups buried in subfloor tombs had personal possessions and a few exotic goods or iconographic ceramics included with them as grave goods. More plentiful, if smaller and less complex, Middle Havana traditional mounds served several larger "village" middens on bluffs and terraces. Unique mounds yielded a headless roseate spoonbill and sets of headless adult skeletons, adult skulls, and whole pots. However, most contained a few reburials with few grave goods, including "Classic Hopewellian" pottery vessels. Smaller and later mounds were constructed over single subfloor pit cremations or burials with few status distinctions or individual accumulations of goods; for example, at many mounds one or two individuals had a mica mirror or an Ohio-style effigy pipe, not always of Ohio pipestone. There were cut carnivore or human teeth and jaws, a few copper or exotic stone ornaments, many rubbed fragments of Missouri galena, and numerous bracelets or necklaces of local and marine shell beads and pearls. Caches of local chert points were frequent, with a few points of obsidian or Knife River chalcedony from the upper Missouri River, and a few points of Ohio Flint Ridge.

Episodic Havana exchange occurred with Crab Orchard cultures in the Wabash valley. At one bluff-top mound group all burials had fabric-wrapped or plain copper celts or awls, cut animal jaws, conch dippers, or effigy pipes, although in nearby mounds males were buried with tool kits only. In a nearby bluff-edge cemetery, caches of local tools and jars along with fragments of earlier Havana pottery were associated with burials. The late Rutherford Mound had strong Havana influence, with many reburials on prepared surfaces having pipes and flint blades from Ohio. Along the lower Ohio, above the Wabash, the large third-century AD Mann site earthworks were surrounded by small mounds with subfloor tomb burials and few grave goods. The domestic areas yielded Indiana Hornstone points; cores and bladelets of Ohio Flint Ridge, obsidian, and quartz crystal; cut copper and mica sheets and scrap; shark teeth; galena fragments; and nearly 100 fire-fragmented clay human figurines. Local Crab Orchard ceramics abounded, but some pots displayed classic Hopewell motifs and some had the form and complicated stamped motifs of earlier cultures in the Deep South.

Havana ceramics and a few objects occurred in the Trempealeau Mound group in Wisconsin, in related sites in southeast Minnesota, at sites in eastern Iowa and Missouri, and along the Missouri River to the Renner site at Kansas City. Havana styles and rituals were adopted at a few sites up the Illinois and Kankakee rivers to the Lake Michigan shore and to the Muskegon and Grand River Norton Mounds in western Michigan, and thence to the small mounds at the large reoccupied Schultz fishing site near Saginaw Bay. The demography and health of these Havana populations did not differ much from their Archaic ancestors', and the various local populations were genetically distinct and stable. Most Havana individuals received mound burial and the burial goods, although the ritual patterns of the peripheral Havanoid mound sites, from Kansas to Michigan, showed similar but differing frequencies than those in Illinois: all of these related sites qualitatively differed from Ohio Hopewell.

The best-known Ohio Hopewell sites were the large ceremonial mound and earthwork complexes of the Miami, Scioto, and Muskingum river valleys, which stimulated considerable nineteenth-century speculation. Despite older settlement models derived from Mesoamerican precepts, recent excavations demonstrate that in Ohio large and complex earthwork centers are nestled amidst arrays of domestic architecture and activities, only some of which appear to be seasonally or ritually restricted. Recent excavations continue to reveal a surprising number of adjacent small domestic camps and hamlets, as well as a few similar domestic and/or workshop sites in nearby drainages. The sites, usually on river floodplains, consist of a few subrectangular single-post houses for minimally extended families practicing general hunting and gathering with some limited gardening of local seed plants. They contain little of the exotic material and few of the artifacts or elaborate ceramics found with burials.

Ohio earthworks of this time period included defensive-looking hilltop enclosures such as Fort Ancient or the Pollack Earthwork; immense Euclidean geometric forms, such as Hopewell, Liberty/Harness, Seip, Mound City, Newark, Hopeton, and Portsmouth; flat-topped rectangular mounds, such as those at Marietta and Cedar Bank; and long walled roadways, some apparently random, some running from mound complexes to rivers, and some running for tens of kilometers between sites. These sites displayed an unusual range of variability in their ritual and mortuary behavior, the nature and distributions of the exchanged goods they contained, and in the sizes, configurations, and numbers of earthworks and mounds. Critical studies now suggest that these reflected social and subregional differences rather than temporal change, and many of the larger sites were used over several generations. Since the mid-1970s it has been known that large sites such as Hopeton, High Banks, and Newark were constructed to align activities with 18.6-year lunar cycles, and newer studies have guided excavations that reveal the social significance of the sequences and materials that compose the earthworks walls themselves.

Some mounds included sequences of activities that took place in large structures or rooms of various shapes, which were destroyed as part of the ceremony or buried in place. In Ohio a few mounds had scores of burials, yet there were many mounds with no burials. It appears that many members of the local group did not receive mound burial. Among those who did, there were vast disparities in the quality and quantity of mortuary treatment and accompanying material. Marine shell was cut into cups and dippers, often stained by dark liquids. There were copper awls, bracelets, celts, and axes wrapped in dyed fabrics, copper-wrapped river cane panpipes, gorgets, headdresses, silhouetted respoussé animals, antler headwear, and large copper breastplates with geometric cutouts. There were also wooden earspools and buttons covered with copper, Ontario silver, or meteoric iron foil. The many mirror-like mica discs and copper artifacts found outside of mounds suggest they were used in lunar or solar rituals associated with the earthworks. Appalachian mica was also cut into geometric and zoomorphic silhouettes and into headless, limbless human torsos as well as heads and hands. Similar images were translated to carved-bone musical instruments and to carved and modeled clay and stone pipes. Half of all Ohio effigy pipes that have been recovered and studied were used, broken, and finally concentrated in two isolated mound caches in separate earthworks. The remaining half of the known effigy pipes accompanied dozens of individuals in disparate mounds. In addition, new chemical element analyses contradict the long-held assumption that these pipes were made from nearby Ohio Pipestone sources.

There were significant changes in the intensity and the nature of exotic goods used during the first and the second episodes of intense Ohio Hopewell ceremonial exchange, between 100 BC and AD 150, followed by a "revival" around AD 300. The early exchange of mica came to be balanced by exchange in locally reworked Yellowstone obsidian, cut and polished grizzly bear claws and canine teeth, and blades of Knife River chalcedony from Missouri River tributaries. Acquisition of Great Lakes hematite, Mississippi River valley galena, and worn crystals from Quebec, Ontario, northern Ohio, and the Carolina Piedmont predominated in the earlier period, while there were fewer shark, alligator, or gar teeth and more marine or local shell, pearl, and mother-of-pearl beads in the later revival. The distributions of these materials in time and social space and their disposition in often peripheral or non-ceremonial contexts suggest a shift to individual or small group exchange from the earlier large lineage activity—a situation reflected in mound and earthwork constructions

Changes in external exchange partners also occurred. During the Early Havana phase, around 100 BC, Illinois/Indiana chert and Havana ceramics were found at sites along the lower Mississippi River valley that shared similar ritual structures. There was little to no Ohio Hopewell influence in the Lake Erie drainage basin or in the upper Ohio River valley, despite, or perhaps due to, their proximity to New York and Ontario groups that participated in Ohio exchange. However, during the later Hopewell episode, around AD 350, Hopewell pottery, Ohio effigy pipes, copper-wrapped earspools and panpipes, and Flint Ridge blades or cores appeared at sites in eastern Tennessee, Alabama, Georgia, and along the gulf coast—all of which have distinctly non-Hopewellian ceremonial systems and structures.

In the upper Great Lakes, from Manitoba and northern Minnesota, east around Lake Huron, to the St. Lawrence River valley of southern Ontario and New York, small Northern Tier Middle Woodland camps and large mounds spanned the period from 250 BC to AD 500. These camps and mounds had a clinal distribution of Laurel to Saugeen to Point Peninsula culture with ceramics, rituals, and exotic ceremonial objects influenced by the Havana tradition and related to the Ohio Hopewell. In this region of unreliable horticulture and thin, seasonal resources, groups consisted of small mobile bands who exchanged material from group to group along the lakes and rivers they traveled. These bands seasonally concentrated for social and economic exchange and community-building rituals where shoal-spawning fish or wild rice could be obtained in abundance.

Large and small Laurel, Saugeen, and Point Peninsula mounds contained burials or cremations along with local ceramics and clay-plastered human skulls. Many of these mounds held well-made tool or shell-stamped pottery and chipped-stone notched or stemmed points of local or Illinois flint, and most included a limited selection of the following: basket and fur-wrapped copper axes, awls, and beads; tubular pipes of Ohio pipestone; out-sized, hafted, corner-notched knives of local chert; and caches of triangular blades and stemmed points of local and exotic cherts, taconites, and flints. At Dunn Farm, near Sleeping Bear Dunes, south of Mackinac Strait, a fourth-century reused pit contained a cremation with charred wild rice. Evidence of wild rice harvesting also comes from the series of Point Peninsula mounds along Ontario's Trent waterway, where the few Hopewell artifacts of copper and locally available silver foil–covered panpipes were found with remains of children. Unlike most regions of the Midwest, along the northern lakes the people who participated in Middle Woodland exchange were not surrounded by larger areas occupied by nonparticipants.

Yet here, too, where artifacts from mortuary offerings acquired through exchange tied Havana and Hopewell sites together despite economic and social differences, there appear to have been several distinct temporal and geographic patterns. Only in some regions were the exotic artifacts accompanying burials systematically related to age or sex. Few mounds or even mound groups contained all potential status classes, and although great concentrations existed, they were not restricted to specific sources or artifact types, nor were they associated with the same types of social groupings as found in more southern Middle Woodland societies. Despite the near identity of some objects, ritual goods often took different roles among various groups with whom they were exchanged. Only limited ceremonial sets of artifact types, not ideographic structure, were shared. No single Middle Woodland exchange network operated across 1,500 kilometers and 750 years.

LATE WOODLAND LOCAL ECONOMIC INITIATIVES

Between AD 500 and 900 the shift from long, warm summers and cool, short winters to increasingly cooler and wetter winters and drier summers was more pronounced in the northern Great Lakes and western prairies than in the lower Great Lakes or major river valleys. Just as most Midwestern Middle Woodland populations had done, their early Late Woodland descendents spent much of the year in small, seasonal, multi-family villages growing squash, sunflower, and other native seed plants; hunting deer and turkey; gathering acorns and nuts; or fishing. Seed plants were much less important in the north, but fishing and hunting over large and diverse environments offered most mobile groups enough seasonal resources for self-sufficiency. Indeed, if the relative absence of diagnostic materials accurately reflects population distributions, then throughout the Midwest there were large unoccupied areas between coherent cultural territories for significant times in a Late Woodland period that persisted locally until European contact. With relatively minor differences in early ceramics and sacred or secular architecture, after AD 900 very different social and economic patterns developed across the Midwest, and these began at its northeastern periphery.

Unlike the conservative Late Woodland ceramic traditions in the southern Midwest, after AD 700, across the estuaries and bays of Lake Erie and western Lake Ontario, ceramics elaborately decorated with styles derived from New York's Northern Tier late Middle Woodland traditions were used by fishing, hunting, and gathering lineages who occasionally cultivated plants for their starchy seeds. Between the eighth and eleventh centuries, that late Point Peninsula—influenced complex had grown to represent two related but distinguishable developments: a Western [Lake Erie] Basin tradition and an eastern Princess Point tradition. New excavations with detailed radiometric dating, botanical analyses, and human biophysical data confirm that by AD 800 the peoples of these related traditions in the Lake Erie/western Lake Ontario region had begun growing the short-season Northern Flint maize that would later structure Mississippian societies.

Because any critical shift in scheduling procurement would have been fraught with social uncertainty, a new reliance on maize agriculture must have occurred where, during planting and harvesting seasons, sufficient locally available resources could be relied on without the need to relocate population aggregates. That early adoption must have been preceded by a period during which 180-day-germinating maize, like that present in Hopewell ceremonial contexts, was being planted in an environment with variable spring and fall weather and occasionally had to be harvested early, so that shorter-season mutations could be selected as a new cultivar. The fish-laden shores of Lake Erie and westernmost Lake Ontario are among the few places in the Eastern Woodlands to meet all of these conditions. Ultimately, even the Late Woodland societies throughout the Mississippi, lower Ohio, and the Illinois river valleys came to rely on this short-season maize, however, prior to AD 950 their village and mortuary sites reflect an economy so dominated by hunting and gathering and small native seed exploitation as to be called "terminal Middle Woodland."

Yet if the general economy in the riverine Midwest was little changed, there was a withering of style and motif for ceremonial ceramics after AD 600. Most Late Woodland ceramics, even in burial mounds, were simple open jars. The dozen relatively plain cord-marked ceramic styles of the local Late Woodland complexes carried their few technical or stylistic regional Middle Woodland distinctions along with the bulk of their material culture. This trend was accompanied by a loss of both stylistic complexity and technical competence in the stone and bone artifact styles as well.

Just as ceramic continuities persisted in some regions, so did mound construction, although few Late Woodland societies maintained the complexity of Middle Woodland rituals. From the mouth of the Missouri River into northern Wisconsin, from AD 600 to the end of the fourteenth century, small horticultural villages occupied the Mississippi and Missouri river bluffs and the eastern river floodplains of the prairies. Along adjacent river bluffs large groups of small circular, elliptical, and linear mounds were mixed with low effigy mounds in the shapes of various animals (e.g., birds). Many of these were built over a single subfloor pit containing a few flexed and/or bundle burials or, rarely, cremations with cord-marked ceramic jars occasionally decorated with trailed or engraved swirled lines, triangular arrow points of local flints, and a few bone tools, although some adults had strands of local shell beads.

In southern Missouri, Illinois, and Kentucky, coeval rock-shelters and upland campsites were reoccupied to exploit seasonal subsistence resources, but whether the plant resources were cultivated or collected is unknown. There was a shift to status-free group burials with little exchanged material in stone mounds along river bluffs, and some of the most egalitarian and largest stone mounds are assigned to the early Late Woodland period. These Late Woodland groups in the central Ohio and middle Mississippi valleys occupied permanent small planned villages of generally square houses, but they appear to have been no more committed to maize agriculture than others. The economic insularity of the period is reflected by the simplification of ceramic decorative technique and motif everywhere save along the southern margins of the central Mississippi valley.

MISSISSIPPIAN EMERGENCE, EXPANSION, AND DECLINE

By AD 950, from southwest Missouri north to the Sponeman site in the American Bottom, burials were being placed in accretional platform earth lodges and substructure flat-topped pyramids. Diverse mortuary treatments began to show vastly differing investments of social and biomechanical energy, and artifacts of gulf coast shell or lower Mississippi valley ceramics, along with the iconography carried on these media, marked a few significantly differing intra-group roles and social statuses. Most other burials of all sex and age classes contained strands of marine shell beads.

Between AD 950 and 1000, highly structured hierarchical societies based on intensive agricultural economies emerged in the central Mississippi valley among local Late Woodland populations. Along with the intensive maize agriculture and the common beans added to their diet, political, ritual, technological, and stylistic concepts, ultimately of Mesoamerican derivation, came to be integrated into a new Mississippian cultural complex that reached its apogee at the Cahokia site in the American Bottom, at the boundary of the upper central Mississippi valley.

The largest and most hierarchically complex Midwestern site, the Cahokia complex consisted of scores of substructure and burial mounds constructed and used by the few thousands of lineage-stratified families who occupied the site over a dozen or so generations between AD 1000 and 1350. From Cahokia, finished ceremonial artifacts and a variety of material for production of artifacts symbolic of Mississippian control were exchanged to and from all directions; perishable subsistence items may also have moved in these networks but are difficult to detect archaeologically. In many ways, Cahokia was emblematic of what have been called Mississippian chiefdoms.

These Mississippian chiefdoms relied on controlling the rituals of exchange and warfare and the redistribution of maize. They flourished in the floodplains during the long warm and moist summers of the Medieval Warm climatic episode, from AD 900 to 1250. During this period Mississippian social systems expanded by borrowing and imitation, by ritual conversion and structured exchange, by conquest, and possibly by emigration and colonization. Although smaller and more ephemeral than Cahokia, by AD 1200 there were hierarchically structured Mississippian town-and-temple agricultural centers throughout the southeast, from the Caddoan country to the south Georgia coast. Across the southern Midwest smaller, and even briefer, secondary Mississippian systems appeared along the lower Ohio at the Kincaid and Angel mound complexes in Indiana and Illinois, at the Wycliff and Jonathan Creek sites in Kentucky, across

the Mississippi at the St. Louis mound group, and in Powers phase towns and platform mounds such as Lilbourne and Towosahgy in Missouri.

Among these highly diverse and fiercely independent Midwestern centers there was some economic exchange and considerable sharing of ritual and iconography akin to relations among Classic Greek cities of the fourth century BC. Not even Cahokia's most socially stratified burials, those excavated from Mound 72 at the site, commanded more than the ritual symbolism of regional tribute. Yet by AD 1450, a century after the onset of the Little Ice Age, most Late Mississippian or Late Woodland geographic complexes abandoned outlying territory and constricted into a limited number of major sites, most in a defensive posture. This was accompanied by a shift in exchange among elite members to emphasize elaborate and exotic ceremonial objects reflecting Mesoamerican symbols of mythic and corporate power. Across the continent, the distribution of these artifacts in mortuary contexts suggests their use as symbols for maintaining structured relationships of politically active participants among and within deteriorating Mississippian societies.

In the upper Midwest when Cahokia was rising to prominence, there was a burst of major earthwork construction, extreme status-differentiated burial, and geographic expansion. Mississippian towns and smaller platform burial mounds developed to the immediate north of Cahokia in the central Illinois River valley and Spoon River complex. Much farther north, at the mid-thirteenth-century Aztalan site in central Wisconsin, a plethora of Mississippian ritual architecture and exotic artifacts appeared in a large, fortified site with local Late Woodland domestic goods. Elsewhere along the northern and eastern peripheries of this greater Mississippian core, by AD 1300 less hierarchically structured tribal societies displayed economies that mixed agriculture with hunting and fishing. Social burial even in the regions peripheral to secondary Mississippian societies changed to large group cemeteries, many with evidence of altered or mutilated secondary burials. The only consistent evidence for extra-regional exchange in these societies consisted of locally remanufactured artifacts of gulf coast and mid-Atlantic coast shell and native copper ornaments, especially beads and pins. These appear to continue individual or lineage exchange, and few artifacts displayed iconic or ritual images that would have had local significance.

CAHOKIAN SPIN-OFFS

Between AD 1100 and 1250 Late Woodland groups along the Missouri and upper Mississippi rivers had rather simple economies and material culture, despite the presence of a few Mississippian technical and stylistic innovations. Chief among these was maize agriculture and, after 1150, the cultivation of beans and tobacco, possibly introduced from more southerly Early Mississippian sites. But most of these Oneota sites consisted of a few oval single-family houses along river terraces where farming of maize, sunflower, and squash, but fewer native plants, from winter through early summer alternated with fall bison hunting. Especially across the northern prairies, only a few Mississippian technological and iconographic styles were adopted, and limited exchange of raw materials occurred, so many related Oneota cultural groups retained most of the social and economic patterns of their woodland forbears and their Great Lake woodland neighbors. After AD 1350 some of these people moved into large, permanent agricultural villages with semi-subterranean extended-family houses spread up the Missouri and Iowa river valleys far into the plains, where, as the historic Mandan, Arikara, and Hidatsa, they developed a symbiotic economy with newly arrived nomadic hunters.

After 1450 most of the late Oneota groups farming the east central Midwestern prairies on both sides of the Mississippi River valley retained fluid and nonhierarchical economies that superseded Cahokia's declining influence, although retaining and reinterpreting Mississippian symbols and ceremonies. These groups are written about in the early French journals as the forbears of the central Algonquian speakers who will be recorded by later European visitors or Euro-American settlers as Sauk-Fox, Kickapoo, or a tribe of the Illini confederacy. On the west bank they appear as some of the Siouan-speaking Iowa, Missouri, or Oto tribes. After European guns and horses appeared, Dakota groups to the north and Pawnee groups to the south abandoned the typical Oneota mixed economy and moved onto the high plains on a year-round basis to join other bison-hunting nomadic tribes.

To the north and east of Mississippian farmers and the south or southwest of the broad band of Late Woodland hunters and fishers, other proto-Algonquian- and Siouan-speaking groups shared ceramic technology and style with more agriculturally committed upper Mississippian villages of the Blue Earth and Oneota complexes of Minnesota and Wisconsin; the Fisher and related Huber complexes of north central Illinois and Indiana; and the Moccasin Bluff complex of southwest Michigan, who during the thirteenth century had moved north as far as sustenance by means of stick-and-hoe horticulture in ridged-field and corn hill gardens on the broader river valleys of Iowa, Wisconsin, or Michigan would allow. Farther north still, the Carcajou Point complexes of eastern Wisconsin in less arable Great Lakes regions—the Red Wing area of Minnesota, near the long-used catlinite quarries and adjacent to the prairies—represented different upper Mississippian adaptations from those of their Late Woodland neighbors and retained some Mississippian ritual imagery well into the historic period. Indeed, each region of the upper Great Lakes adopted from its southerly Mississippian neighbors different new styles of shell-tempered ceramics and equally identifiable new patterns of gardening and social village life.

The northeastern Mississippian influences culture appeared in the lower Miami River valley about AD 1100 as the Fort Ancient tradition. It spread up the Miami and Little Miami rivers to the Madisonville, Anderson, and Sun Watch sites and into the Scioto River valley, where sites such as Baum and Feurt abut classic Hopewell mounds. Egalitarian burials occurred in small flat-topped mounds or in cemeteries ringing the plaza of palisade-surrounded circular villages. Burials show the overwhelming importance of maize in the diet. It was early Fort Ancient peoples who between 1100 and 1250 constructed the enigmatic egg-in-mouth Serpent Mound overlooking Ohio Brush Creek, as well as several smaller stone serpent and sun gnomons at other sites over the next few centuries. Isotopic analyses reveal that occupants of Fort Ancient sites had more maize in their diets than individuals buried in such significant Mississippian sites as Angel Mounds at the same period. Yet Fort Ancient displays little ritual or social control of exchange, despite the occasional Mississippian iconography on ceramics or marine shell from the lower Ohio valley and later from the upper Tennessee River. The latest Fort Ancient sites were concentrated along the lower Miami and central Ohio river valleys. There, several European trade goods match seventeenth-century radiometric dates. At least some of these peoples appear in the historic records as Shawnee.

By the twelfth century, Fort Ancient influences occurred in the Oliver complex at the heads of the White, White Water, and Maumee river systems in Indiana, where a complex dominated by thumbnail scrapers and triangular Madison points was accompanied by grit-tempered and then shell-tempered, cord-marked ceramic jars with trailed and incised curvilinear guilloches and a few loop handles. From these locations, by the fifteenth century, Fort Ancient ceramic styles and technology spread north into the Lake Erie estuaries of the Maumee and Sandusky rivers and eventually through southeast Michigan and north to Saginaw Bay.

Coeval Fort Ancient sequences developed in the major river valleys of southern Ohio, southeast Indiana, and northern Kentucky. Mississippian influences are found in the upper Ohio River valley as well as in eastern Fort Ancient ceramic styles and technology and some mortuary material.

BEYOND THE MISSISSIPPIAN PALE

After AD 600, across the Great Lakes–Ohio valley region and into New York, societies had continued to bury individuals in shallow pits covered by low mounds, sometime digging pits that intruded into classic Ohio Hopewell mounds. In addition to local ceramics, burials of adults or children were accompanied by caches of chert blades, copper and tubular beads from south Atlantic or gulf coast shells, local clay or stone elbow pipes, and a variety of bone and antler tools, including harpoons. Rarely, males were buried with galena nodules and quartz crystals from Missouri and Arkansas or trophy skulls and skull plaques. In the central Ohio River valley, individuals were buried in low accretional mounds with locally acquired personal tools and ornaments. Through most of this region after AD 1100, burial was in large cemeteries of simple pit burials with few, mostly personal ornaments of native copper or Atlantic coast shell. However, by AD 1000, there was a dramatic revival of the level of social hierarchies and annual or semi-annual mortuary ceremonies, and the first fortified sites appeared. Perhaps these changes were related to the introduction of the bow and arrow sometime between AD 650 and 850, which occasioned a revolution in both the equipage and in the practice of hunting and armed conflict.

In the upper Great Lakes, fish were still more reliable than crops, and much of life remained little changed from what it had been through past millennia. After AD 600 there were continual and gradual subregional shifts in the overall shapes and decoration on jars. Clam River ceramics were made by scaffold-burying horticulturalists in the uppermost Mississippi River valley. To their east, canoeing clans left their Black Duck and Juntunen pottery in archaeological sites across Wisconsin and northern Michigan to the east of the Lake Huron shore. It is increasingly difficult to distinguish the early Adawa from the related Ontario Iroquois ceramics that are found in the year-round lineage-based agricultural villages of Ontario after AD 1300.

Nearly all lower Great Lakes littoral sites after AD 950 are small, scattered, seasonally occupied camps of two or three circular houses on river bluffs, on old beach ridges inland, and on islands and peninsulas across the lakes. Most of these small sites have only an occasional pit with fragmentary cremations or a few human limb bones. Some sites had a few bundle burials or, rarely, burials in anatomical disarray with missing (or extra) skull plaques. Most of the populations received eventual burial at one of a very few enormous pan-regional cemeteries. These sites represented the major cemetery between AD 1050 and 1250 for several generations whose annual needs, even with limited cultivation of Eastern Flint maize, required catchments encompassing major portions of one of the lower Great Lakes' drainage basins. A seasonal visit to one of the vast cemeteries would have been a cultural and community renewal ceremony at which respect for dead relatives, current fishing stories, and future mates were exchanged. For such populations, spatial and economic associations beyond those of the extended family shift on an annual or seasonal basis, and the social meanings of material culture signify participation in the entire Western Basin tradition population and only secondarily signify membership in one of the current, economically effective families. After AD 1150, the ceramics of this latest Western (Lake Erie) Basin tradition diverge into those of the southeastern Michigan Young tradition and those of the north central Ohio Sandusky tradition. However, the late Princess Point complexes of Ontario appear to have been replaced after 1200 by proto-Iroquoian social and stylistic patterns (if not peoples) derived from New York.

In northern Ohio from AD 900 to 1250, lakeside and inland sites contained a few reoccupied single-family houses. Hunting and fishing along with local nuts or seeds were more important than squash or corn. Between 1250 and 1450, ceramic innovations from Fort Ancient and Sandusky cultures to the west and Iroquoian traditions to the east coalesced into a Whittlesey tradition dependent on maize and squash agriculture supplemented by fishing and small game hunting. However, after 1450, Whittlesey people fled the lakeshore and concentrated in a few year-round ditch- and embankment-protected villages on high promontories overlooking arable floodplains. Deep storage pits in multi-family longhouses were filled with corn, and a few sites had beans and squash. Hunting became focused on elk, raccoon, turkey, and deer. Cemeteries yielded mutilated bodies, and some Indian Hills and Allegheny River ceramics appeared along with a few Mid-south Mississippian artifacts. No European material has been found in Whittlesey sites, which suggests depopulation between 1620 and 1640, just as village horticultural societies who had occupied central and eastern Ohio and the West Virginia panhandle since AD 900 abandoned those areas of fewer than 160 frost-free days after 1500.

The latest prehistoric Sandusky tradition sites in north central Ohio were small ditch- and embankment-protected agricultural villages whose Indian Hills ceramics had flared rims decorated by rows of stamped appliqués, strap handles, and effigy faces. In the lower Maumee River valley, glass beads and scrap brass of European derivation have been found at the large river bluff palisaded Indian Hills site, with its cemeteries, wattle-and-daub rectangular houses, and central plaza confirmed as early seventeenth century by carbon-14 dates for the type site and for the small seasonal sites on larger Miami River islands. Early French documents suggest that Indian Hills and Sandusky people were pushed into southern Michigan as the *Attistaeronon* or "Nation of Fire," later called Mascouten or Potawatomi, while the Eastwall complex of northeast Ohio was part of the Neutral Indians that the Jesuits in 1638 noted as living on Lake Erie's south shore. Between these groups, the remnants of the Whittlesey tradition moved south into the upper Ohio valley after 1656 and, a generation later, into the Carolina Piedmont, where the English called them Tutelo.

In the upper Great Lakes portions of northern Michigan and Wisconsin, northeastern Minnesota, and the Manitoulin to Rainy River districts of Ontario, climatic changes from 1350 to the early seventeenth century put a premium on social patterns that minimized economic risk. Increasingly, Juntunen and Ontario Iroquois-influenced or affiliated groups readopted the cultural ecologies of the Middle Woodland. Cultural interfingering and stylistic blurring occurred where straits and rapids favored by spawning fish became loci for alternating group aggregations in spring and fall. With the onset of the cold season during this unusually cold climatic episode, fragmented populations moved into annually shifting, hitherto lightly occupied headwaters interior areas. With the renewed importance of social territorial markers, large circular earthworks were built, and some were later incorporated into the traditional mythologies of new immigrants or into rituals borrowed from new affinal members of the heterogeneous groups who came to be known by early seventeenth-century French explorers and traders as Ojibwa or Adawa clans.

Throughout the region, as climate worsened, most Mississippian-related groups ensured that economic redistribution from agricultural fields paralleled development of minimal hierarchies for settlement, warfare, ideology, and status. Where widespread aquatic resources provided a reliable fallback for agriculture, some coeval non-Mississippian groups retained nonhierarchical social segments and thus were able to form strong but temporary economic collaborations with similar groups in diverse habitats. Both these minimally centralized Mississippian-derived organizations and the regionally flexible Iroquois-like organizations were able to survive the cultural pressures of the rapidly chilling Little Ice Age by either displacing or incorporating their neighbors from frontier zones.

A different fate awaited more structurally conservative and therefore less polarized Midwestern groups, such as the Whittlesey, Monongahela, Caiborne-Wellborn, and Kentucky Fort Ancient as well as many of the Oneota complexes from southern Wisconsin and northern Illinois and Indiana, and the Moccasin Bluff and Wolf cultures of southern Michigan. Having failed to adopt strong social mechanisms capable of resisting fission or for ensuring regional collaboration, as evenly mixed agriculture became unreliable, these groups were forced to rely on increasingly restricted productive areas. Thus, pitted against each other with traditions of tribal autonomy approximating anarchy, these were among the first societies to succumb to the consequences of European contact with their neighbors.

THE END OF PREHISTORY

History arrived in the early seventeenth century with explorers, soldiers, missionaries, and colonists, whose earliest reports followed a century or more of biological and social chaos as European-generated and then European-carried disease, warfare, and population displacements distorted and then obliterated existing aboriginal economic, social, and religious patterns. Across the Midwest, from the Great Lakes down the Mississippi valley, ephemeral political and military alliances and disadvantageous trading relationships were first brokered by the French and English and then imposed and maintained by Americans. Few aboriginal exchange relationships survived the contact era in the Midwest, as corporate aboriginal exchange shattered and clan or individual acquisition by exchange became more concerned with the distant area that had become Birmingham, England, than with the nearer area that would become Birmingham, Alabama. The end of effective aboriginal occupation was marked by individually beneficial but corporately represented exchanges of land rights in order to clear debts on used hardware, firearms,

and spirits, and finally for food or evanescent American political influence.

Early, indirect evidence of the demographic effects of French and British involvement with the shifting native groups has come from the seventeenth-century Rock Island and Apostle Islands sites in Wisconsin. Later trade with these acculturated tribal groups is evident at Bois Forte Ojibwe near International Falls, Minnesota, and Pickawillany, Ohio, just as the new American nation's nineteenth-century conflict with native groups is documented at Boonesboro, Kentucky, and at the Fallen Timbers Battlefield in northwest Ohio and Fort Wayne, Indiana. The rise and travails of early nineteenth-century American religions and utopian communities is present in the Kirtland, Ohio, and Nauvoo, Illinois, Mormon Temples as well as at the Gnadenhutten-Zoar Village in Ohio and at the Mt. Pleasant Shaker Village in Kentucky. The later history of nineteenth-century American industrial developments is captured in archaeological excavations of the potteries of East Liverpool or the Franklin Glass Works in eastern Ohio, the Mines of Spain in Iowa, the northern Michigan Fayette Iron Furnace and Calumet Copper Mines and Lumbering Camps, or at numerous archaeological sites along the routes of the mid-nineteenth-century Ohio Canal and the Michigan-Illinois Canal. These canals connected the Great Lakes and the Midwest with the eastern states and led to the growth of such midwestern cities as St. Louis, Missouri; Detroit, Michigan; Cincinnati and Cleveland, Ohio; and Covington and Louisville, Kentucky. There archaeology conducted to meet federal guidelines during the renovation of urban centers has corrected and amplified the history of America's immigrants. So too, archaeology at the Lincoln Home and New Philadelphia Free Black sites in southern Illinois, the Underground Railroad sites along the Ohio River, and Missouri's Wilson's Creek National Battlefield has revealed new facts regarding the Civil War era.

Underwater archaeology now represents the new frontier in understanding how the connections of natural resources and manufacturing industries created what became known across the world as the "American System." It is a story for which much of the information lies deep below those Great Lakes, whose waters, as Melville noted in *Moby Dick*, could be as dangerous and storm-lashed as any ocean and had "claimed full many a midnight ship with all her shrieking crew."

Further Reading: Brose, David S., C. Wesley Cowan, and Robert Mainfort, eds., *Societies in Eclipse: Archaeology of the Woodland Indians 1400–1750* (Washington, DC, and Tuscaloosa: Smithsonian Institution Press and University of Alabama Press, 2002); Brose, David S., and N'omi B. Greber, eds., *Hopewell Archeology: The Chillicothe Conference* (Kent, OH: Kent State University Press, 1979); Cantwell, Anne-Marie, Lawrence Conrad, and Jonathon E. Reyman, eds., *Aboriginal Ritual and Economy in the Eastern Woodlands: Essays in Honor of Howard Dalton Winters,* Illinois State Museum Scientific Papers XXX and Kampsville Studies in Archaeology and

History, No. 5 (Kampsville, IL: Center for American Archaeology, 2004); Farnsworth, Kenneth, and Thomas Emerson, eds., *Early Woodland Archaeology*, Kampsville Seminars in Archaeology, No. 2 (Kampsville, IL: Center for American Archaeology, 1986); Halsey, John, ed., *Retrieving Michigan's Buried Past: An Archaeology of the Great Lakes State*, Cranbrook Institute of Science Bulletin No. 64 (Bloomfield Hills, MI: Cranbrook, 1999); Lepper, Bradley T., *Ohio Archaeology: An Illustrated Chronicle of Ohio's Ancient American Indian Cultures* (Columbus, OH: Orange Frazer, 2005); Marquardt, William H., and Patty Jo Watson, *Archaeology of the Middle Green*

River Region, Kentucky, Institute of Archaeology and PaleoEnvironmental Studies Monograph 5 (Gainesville: University of Florida, 2005); Melville, Herman, *Moby Dick*, Modern Library Giant Edition (New York: Random House, 1930); Smith, Bruce D., ed., *Rivers of Change: Essays on Early Agriculture in Eastern North America*, 2nd ed. (Washington, DC: Smithsonian Institution, 2002); Trigger, Bruce, ed., *Handbook of North American Indians*, Vol. 15: *The Northeast* (Washington, DC: Smithsonian Institution, 1978).

David S. Brose

HISTORY OF ARCHAEOLOGY
IN THE MIDWEST

The history of archaeology in the Midwest largely coincides with an interest in the ancient mounds and earthworks in the region. Also of interest historically is the question of the antiquity of humans in the region and in America. Federal involvement in archaeology in the 1920s and 1930s, through the National Research Council and then archaeology associated with "back to work" relief programs of the Great Depression and New Deal, resulted in the development of a coherent body of methods, an interest in problems of cultural classification and chronology, and a growing political confidence by the profession. Following World War II, additional sources of funding came from reservoir and other archaeological salvage programs, which with the passage of several important preservation laws led to the development of cultural resource management (CRM). At the same time, interest in theoretical issues deepened. To an extent, Midwest archaeology shared in these changes and continues to be a vital field of study.

THE MOUND BUILDERS

A major impetus in the development of archaeology in the eastern United States was the thousands of enigmatic mounds and earthworks, some of remarkable size and complexity, dotting the landscapes of the Ohio and Mississippi River valleys. The presence of these mounds and earthworks was noted during the initial land surveys in the Ohio River valley in the mid-1780s, and they continued to be found as the new American republic expanded westward.[1] As with no other archaeological phenomena, these ancient architectural constructs focused the attention of scholars, then mostly natural historians with broad

interests in a host of natural and cultural phenomena, as they mapped, dug, pondered, and argued about the mounds.

By the late eighteenth century there were already two competing views of who constructed the mounds: the Mound Builders, a mysterious elder race, or, more prosaically, the ancestors of the Native American peoples. The latter is exemplified in Thomas Jefferson's excavation of a mound in Virginia in the early 1780s, after which he concluded that it was the work not of some vanished race but of ancestors of the local Native Americans. Others such as J. H. McCulloch, who based his knowledge on his Ohio excavations in the early 1800s, concurred with Jefferson. So, too, did Samuel G. Morton, whose study of hundreds of crania exhumed from mounds demonstrated their close affinity to historic Native Americans. Albert Gallatin, formerly Jefferson's secretary of treasury and a noted linguist, weighed in on the matter in an 1836 summary of the mound work done in the Ohio River valley and reasoned that Native Americans created the mounds.

On the other side of the question, popular writers, such as Josiah Priest, continued to promulgate the more fanciful Mound Builder myth. Exactly who the Mound Builders were or from whence they came remained open questions to such individuals and their readers. Among the suggestions put forth were Hindus, the Lost Tribes of Israel, Vikings, and Welshmen. The myth gained added credence from the work of Ephraim G. Squier and Edwin H. Davis, who were commissioned by the American Antiquarian Society in 1845 to study the problem. The men opened over 200 mounds, mostly in Ohio, and mapped numerous mound groups. Their report, *Ancient Monuments of the Mississippi Valley*, published in 1848 by the nascent Smithsonian Institution, broke new ground in its presentation of a staggering body of systematically collected data. Ultimately, however, they concluded that the mounds were likely the product of an extinct race, possibly with ties to Mexico.

---

[1]The French pushed into the upper and western Great Lakes region by the early 1600s but apparently left few descriptions of archaeological sites, although in 1673 Marquette and Joliet observed two large pictographs on a cliff along the Mississippi River near modern Alton, Illinois, and a few years later, in 1679, Father Nouvel described an abandoned Native American site near present-day St. Ignace, Michigan.

The Mound Builder myth may well have passed into obscurity but for Squier and Davis's monograph. Even as scholars such as Increase A. Lapham and Samuel Haven continued to argue against it, however, the myth took root in the nineteenth-century American psyche. The Smithsonian published Lapham's study of effigy mounds, *Antiquities of Wisconsin,* in 1855 and that of Haven, the first major synthesis on American archaeology, *Archaeology of the United States,* in 1856. A poignant example of the myth's persistence, however, is that the members of the Lapham Archaeological Society, formed in Milwaukee following Lapham's death in 1876, attributed the area's mounds not to Native Americans but to the Mound Builders!

In the years following the Civil War, mound researches were reported across the Midwest as far west as Kansas City. The Reverend Stephen Peet founded the *American Antiquarian and Oriental Journal,* providing the first national archaeology journal. The Peabody Museum's Frederick Ward Putnam made important excavations of mounds in Ohio, including the Great Serpent Mound, and also introduced stratigraphic excavation methods to the region. Through the turn of the century, a succession of scholars were devoted to the study of the sprawling mound complex known as Cahokia, leaving a number of important maps, other documents, and collections. (Attempts in the late 1800s to get the Illinois legislature to preserve the site failed; Warren King Moorehead finally accomplished that goal in the 1920s.) In Wisconsin, there was much debate about how the copper artifacts found in the state and adjacent areas were fabricated (i.e., smelting or annealing) and whether they suggested ties to Europe or had been made by the Mound Builders. The discovery of extensive source quarries around Lake Superior, some bearing evidence of great age, argued for local manufacture.

The era was also marked by several notorious hoaxes, including the Newark Holy Stones and the Davenport tablets, which were dug up by the Reverend Jacob Gass in Iowa in the late 1870s. Gass also purchased an elephant pipe and found another during one of his digs. The artifacts drew Gass and the Davenport Academy, whose members perpetrated the hoax, into sharp, face-saving conflict with the Smithsonian Institution.

In 1881, the newly formed Division of Mound Exploration of the Smithsonian Institution's Bureau of Ethnology was directed to settle the mound debate. Its director, John Wesley Powell, put Cyrus Thomas in charge of the operation. Thomas planned and implemented a long-term field program, which kept a small staff of field workers busy for the next decade mapping nearly 10,000 mounds throughout much of the eastern United States, although only a portion of these were explored. In 1894 the Smithsonian Institution issued the result of this work in a massive volume, *Report on the Mound Explorations of the Bureau of Ethnology.* In it, Thomas marshaled an array of data to demonstrate, conclusively to all willing to accept the evidence, that the Mound Builders and the Native Americans were one and the same. Often regarded as the capstone for the Mound Builder myth, it also solidified the dominance of the Smithsonian Institution as the preeminent anthropological institution in the country. Incidentally, Thomas and the Smithsonian Institution were not alone in their researches. Based out of St. Paul, Minnesota, businessman Alfred J. Hill hired Theodore H. Lewis to map mounds throughout the upper Midwest, northern Great Plains, and parts of Canada, forming the Northwest Archaeological Survey for this purpose. From 1881 until Hill's untimely death in 1895, Lewis documented over 17,000 mounds and hundreds of village sites in Minnesota, Wisconsin, Illinois, Iowa, Indiana, Michigan, and elsewhere. Hill's death and legal wrangling over control of the data by J. V. Brower, another well-known Minnesota archaeologist, left Lewis without access to his maps and notes, and he finally abandoned any hope of producing the report he and Hill had planned. Lewis, like Thomas, staunchly rejected the Mound Builder myth.

In the early republic, the Mound Builder myth lent an air of mysterious antiquity to the American landscape, offering the equivalent of Europe's ancient ruins; not unimportant when Americans struggled to overcome European notions of American inferiority. By the mid-1800s the myth articulated nicely with the doctrine of Manifest Destiny, which was first mentioned in the press in 1845, about the time that Squier and Davis began their mound investigations. Grounded in the idea of American exceptionalism, Manifest Destiny asserted the right of the American people, so clearly superior to their neighbors and, of course, the Native Americans, to lay claim to the continent. Because some argued that the Indians had wiped out the Mound Builders, the myth offered justification for equal treatment. Yet there were extenuating circumstances: even as Americans were entering the Ohio River valley, smallpox epidemics raged through the west, decimating or even wiping out entire populations. The catastrophic collapse of Native American populations led unwitting observers of the surviving remnants to conclude that the number of Indians was too small for them to have ever been capable of constructing so many mounds and earthworks.

THE ANTIQUITY PROBLEM

The other major question of nineteenth-century American archaeology arose out of the discovery of the European Paleolithic or Old Stone Age, which sparked intense interest in finding corresponding evidence for an American Paleolithic. By the early 1870s, the evidence was found, first in form of "rude" stone implements embedded in Pleistocene age gravels at Trenton, New Jersey, and then elsewhere. By the late 1880s, belief in an American Paleolithic was widespread. Even in the Midwest, where the matter remained of secondary importance to the question of who built the mounds, evidence for glacial age humans turned up. Indeed, as early as the 1830s Albert Koch claimed to have found associated mastodon bones and stone tools at several localities in Missouri. The mastodon theme continued into the 1870s, when claims were made of elephant-shaped (mastodon) effigy mounds in Wisconsin, and then there were the Reverend Gass's elephant pipes; these two claims also effectively intertwined the Mound Builder and antiquity questions. More credible, however, was the report of quartz tools at Little Falls, Minnesota, in 1884, also claimed as proof that humans occupied the area during the last glacial epoch. All of these were discounted by Smithsonian Institution experts, including William Henry Holmes, who proclaimed the quartz tools as of comparatively recent age. Holmes was at the forefront in the refutation of often ill-conceived proof for the American Paleolithic, such that by the 1890s the idea began to lose credence.

The matter did not die, however, and reports by archaeologists, geologists, paleontologists, and others of putatively ancient, that is, glacial age, sites kept the "Early Man" debate alive into the new century. Not until the 1926 discovery and subsequent validation of the co-occurrence of stone spearheads and extinct bison at Folsom, New Mexico, did the anthropological community come to accept that humans had been in the Americas at least since the end of the last ice age. In light of Folsom, archaeologists in the Midwest took a renewed interest in the antiquity question. Throughout the 1930s, Albert E. Jenks, a professor at the University of Minnesota, and his associates proposed several isolated skeletons and other sites as being late glacial in age. In 1937 Alonzo W. Pond heralded the Interstate Park Bison site in northwest Wisconsin, a bog deposit with the bones of extinct *Bison occidentalis*, as comparable in age to Folsom. Although not all of these finds were generally accepted, that there was an eastern Paleoindian tradition seemed evident. For instance, Henry C. Shetrone noted a number of fluted, Folsom-like points in the collections of the Ohio Historical Society. Similar points, referred to as "Folsomoid," were in fact found throughout the Midwest, although usually as surface finds, which tended to obscure an understanding of their age. At the Parrish site in northwest Kentucky, William Webb excavated deposits in 1938 that bore evidence of Paleoindian and later occupations.

A TIME OF CHANGE

Archaeology evolved throughout the nineteenth century, shifting from a natural history–based pursuit to a largely museum-based profession late in the century. By this time a small number of colleges and universities were teaching archaeology courses and, in some cases, offering degrees in anthropology. Nonetheless, archaeology in the eastern United States was very much a discipline in crisis, characterized by its haphazard methods, uneven reportage of results, and too little communication between field workers. In an effort to shake off the last vestiges of its antiquarian origins, in 1920 the Division of Anthropology and Psychology of the National Research Council established the Committee on State Archaeological Surveys (CSAS) with the goal of fostering a sense of professionalism in archaeology.

Over the next fifteen years, the committee worked to further this goal, partly through three influential conferences: the first in St. Louis in 1929, the second in Birmingham, Alabama, in 1932, and the last in Indianapolis in 1935. The meetings dealt with, respectively, preservation of the archaeological record, the advancement of chronology, and culture classification.

By the late 1920s and early 1930s, there was as yet no method to correlate the results of years of archaeological investigations either within or between regions. To remedy this, W. C. McKern, of the Milwaukee Public Museum, spearheaded an effort to effectively classify artifacts in a way that had cultural relevance. The result, born out of several years of intense discussion between McKern and a number of other archaeologists in the region, was the Midwestern Taxonomic Method (MTM). The method, in principle, allowed archaeologists to classify artifacts, using similarities and differences in the physical characteristics of the artifacts, into a hierarchy of groups, which in principle would facilitate comparisons between and among groups. In the southwest United States, classificatory systems were anchored in sound chronology, thanks to tree-ring dating. In the Midwest and elsewhere in the eastern United States, however, despite recognition since the 1830s that the mounds were built by different cultures at different time, there was still no means to establish absolute culture chronologies. Thus the MTM eschewed any concern with time.

During the 1950s, excavated stratigraphic sequences from such localities as Modoc Rockshelter in Illinois, Graham Cave in Missouri, Raddatz Rockshelter in Wisconsin, and from the Kentucky shell mounds, among others, were carefully dated with the newly developed C-14 method. The result of this and other such research was to close the temporal gap between Paleoindian and much later pottery-producing cultures and to outline a "deep history" of the native occupation of the region extending back 11,500 years. With a better grasp of chronology across the region, the MTM gave way to other means of ordering archaeological data that factored in time.

RELIEF ARCHAEOLOGY AND
THE DEVELOPMENT OF
AMERICAN ARCHAEOLOGY

If the 1920s and early 1930s were a time of change, the interval from the early 1930s to World War II was a period of expansion for American archaeology. The catalyst for this was, ironically, the Great Depression. On October 29, 1929, the U.S. stock market crashed, signaling the beginning of a global economic depression. The Hoover administration took a hands-off approach toward the economy, and with millions out of work, in 1932 Franklin D. Roosevelt was elected president. The new administration immediately sought to stimulate the economy and provide jobs, implementing a series of relief initiatives, including the Emergency Civil Works (ECW) in 1933, popularly known as the

Civil Conservation Corps (CCC) and the Federal Emergency Relief Administration (FERA). The short-lived Civil Works Administration (CWA) followed in 1934, and as the depression worsened, in 1935 the Work Progress (later Projects) Administration (WPA) was established. All the programs sponsored archaeological projects because the administration saw archaeology as one means of employing a mix of skilled and unskilled labor.

The first New Deal archaeology project, sponsored by FERA in Louisiana, demonstrated the efficacy of such programs, and other FERA, CWA, and WPA projects followed. Owing both to the high levels of unemployment and a climate favorable to year-round work, the largest percentage of relief archaeology projects were located in the Southeast. However, between 1934 and 1942 a number of projects were sponsored under various New Deal programs in Midwestern states. The most notable of these was in Kentucky, where under the aegis of the WPA, CCC, and Tennessee Valley Authority (TVA)—a multi-state program empowered to build dams and power plants and to improve navigation and flood control—many archaeology projects were conducted. In Indiana, major WPA excavations were conducted at Angel Mounds, while smaller projects in Illinois included work at the Murdock Mound near Cahokia and the University of Chicago's ongoing dig at Kincaid. Also in Illinois, CCC workers exposed portions of the inferred site of Fort de Chartes. CWA, FERA, and, later on, National Youth Administration funds were used for survey and surface collection of sites in Boone County, Missouri. FERA and WPA monies allowed for survey and excavation in Iowa, and in Minnesota CCC and WPA workers investigated both pre-contact Native American and Euro-American sites. Relief archaeology in Michigan and Wisconsin was more limited in nature, although CCC personnel excavated the Interstate Park Bison site and WPA funds were used to excavate the Fort Crawford I site. WPA funds were used in Ohio and West Virginia to various ends, but not for archaeology.

Field methods, initially haphazard and often improvised, gradually were standardized, in part as methods developed by the University of Chicago were disseminated through the network of relief projects. Beginning in 1925, the University of Chicago conducted annual field schools, notably in Joe Davies County in northwest Illinois, Fulton County in the central part of the state, and at Kincaid in southern Illinois. Under the overall direction of Fay-Cooper Cole, the field schools trained dozens of students, many of whom went on to become leaders in the profession. As relief projects fired up, particularly in the Southeast, many University of Chicago students found themselves directing crews, implementing the careful methods learned.

FEDERAL ARCHAEOLOGY AFTER WORLD WAR II
Relief-era projects were initially guided by Smithsonian Institution staff, but the early successes of these projects quickly shifted professional archaeology away from museums to academia. Moreover, a major benefit of relief archaeology was to impart to the profession a newfound coherence, not only in field methods but in political confidence, something that would be put to effective use in the years following World War II.

The profession's political maturation manifested directly in the Committee on the Recovery of Archaeological Remains, formed after the war to meet the newest threat to the nation's archaeological resources: the impoundment of hundreds of reservoirs and other flood control projects across the country. Because an estimated 80 percent of pre-contact Native American sites were located on or near river floodplains, the inundation of these areas constituted a major crisis. The means to meet the challenge was the Inter-Agency Salvage Program (IASP), of which included the River Basin Surveys (RBS), established by a series of agreements between the Smithsonian Institution and the National Park Service (NPS) and the construction agencies (i.e., U.S. Army Corps of Engineers and Bureau of Land Reclamation). By 1950 the NPS contracted directly with colleges, universities, and state historical societies.

The IASP operated for a total of twenty-four years, during which time personnel affiliated with the Smithsonian Institution and dozens of cooperating institutions surveyed over 500 proposed reservoir and related project areas. Although the largest single unit of the IASP was the Missouri River Basin project, investigations were made in forty-three states, including all of those in the Midwest. IASP-sponsored surveys were the first major federally funded archaeological projects ever conducted in Ohio and West Virginia, both states that had missed out on New Deal archaeology. Collectively, 20,000 previously unknown archaeological sites were recorded, and excavations were conducted at over 500 of those. The IASP integrated the use of power machinery to clear overburden from sites as well as aerial photography. In addition, they contributed to the development of historic sites archaeology, culture chronology, the study of human skeletal remains, animal bones, and even botanical remains from sites.

The early success of the IASP-RBS programs fostered the creation of other salvage archaeology programs, including pipelines and roads. Highway archaeology originated in the Southwest, but in 1956 Congress passed the Federal-Aid Highway Act, which proposed a fifteen-year nationwide highway construction program. As amended in 1959, the act permitted the use of federal funds for survey and excavation within highway rights-of-way. Implementation of the act was rendered uneven by widely differing state bureaucracies, interest by transportation agencies, and often the lack of personnel. Although the full effects of highway salvage were not generally felt until the 1960s and even 1970s, it would be hard to overestimate the impact of highway salvage in the Midwest. Especially notable have been a lengthy series of investigations in Illinois in the greater St. Louis area, where large-scale mechanical site clearing in the early 1960s and during the FAI-270 project in the 1970s and 1980s has revealed sites with complex and often long occupational histories containing innumerable houses and other structures, thousands upon thousands of storage and other subterranean features, and millions of artifacts. The investigations were instrumental in defining a cultural sequence for the area and have done much to fuel the ongoing debates about the size of the population and complexity of Cahokia.

CULTURAL RESOURCE MANAGEMENT

The political confidence gained through New Deal and RBS archaeology translated into the passage of important cultural resource legislation through the 1960s and early 1970s, including the National Historic Preservation Act (NHPA) of 1966, which was designed to protect historic buildings and archaeological sites, and culminating with the Archeological and Historic Preservation Act (AHPA), colloquially known as "Moss-Bennett" for the sponsoring legislators. The Moss-Bennett Act authorized federal agencies to expend up to 1 percent of the cost of federally funded projects for cultural resource investigations, thus finally ensuring the means to defray the costs of historic preservation and cultural resource projects. Thus, the salvage programs of the post–World War II years were modified into present-day cultural resource management (CRM), the goal of which is to locate and assess archaeological and other cultural properties (i.e., historic buildings, cultural landscapes, and sacred places) on public lands or that potentially would be impacted by federally funded projects. The results of these investigations are to be used to inform the decision-making process.

AHPA resulted in the privatization of CRM studies, which subsume archaeological studies for highway projects, pipeline and power transmission lines, cell phone towers, and a host of other public projects. For archaeology, the inception of CRM consulting firms in the mid-1970s and 1980s sparked intense debates, partly because of changes in theoretical concerns and the employment structure of American archaeology. Among others issues, significance— that is, what makes a site important—field methods, professional standards, and ethics were hotly debated. CRM has often been called a mixed blessing, but by the 1990s a majority of the archaeologists in the United States were involved, at least some of the time, in CRM. By some estimates, as many as 80 percent of the sites recorded in the archaeological site inventories of many Midwestern states have been recorded through CRM studies. Moreover, CRM investigations often have been remarkably interdisciplinary, drawing on the work of not only archaeologists, but geologists, paleoethnobotanists, and others. Historic sites archaeology has also benefited enormously from IASP and more recent CRM work, and across the Midwest sites ranging from forts, battlefields, mining sites, and industrial sites to rural farmsteads have been investigated.

THE CHANGING GOALS OF ARCHAEOLOGY

Concurrent with the development of IASP and the legislative bulwark of CRM in the 1960s, American archaeology was once again in a state of intellectual ferment. With chronological issues in hand, archaeologists such as Lewis R. Binford argued that archaeology should become scientifically more rigorous in not only its methods but in its underlying logic. Moreover, this "new archeology," as it was called, should address behavioral questions. As with earlier culture- and history-oriented archaeology of the 1920s through the 1950s, the new archeology evolved, and by the 1980s and 1990s a number of derivative, complementary, or rival theories jostled with it. Although the new archeology originated at the University of Michigan and, for a brief few years in the early 1960s was centered at the University of Chicago, archaeologists in the Midwest generally have been reluctant to embrace it or other theoretical positions. Archaeologists in this region continue to struggle, as elsewhere, with classification, chronology, and the many issues raised by the new archaeology and subsequent theoretical schools. Midwest archaeology continues to be a vital field of research.

Further Reading: Dunnell, Robert C., "Methodological Impacts of Catastrophic Depopulation on American Archaeology and Ethnology," in *Columbian Consequences*, Volume 3 of *The Spanish Borderlands in Pan-American Perspective*, edited by David H. Thomas (Washington, DC: Smithsonian Institution, 1991), 561–580; Fagette, Paul, *Digging for Dollars, American Archaeology and the New Deal* (Albuquerque: University of New Mexico Press, 1996); Finney, Fred A., ed., "The Archaeological Legacy of Theodore H. Lewis: Letters, Papers and Articles," *Wisconsin Archeologist* 87 (2006); Green, William, and John F. Doershuk, "Cultural Resource Management and American Archaeology," *Journal of Archaeological Research* 6 (1998): 121–167; Meltzer, David J., *Search for the First Americans* (Washington, DC: Smithsonian Books, 1993); O'Brien, Michael J., and R. Lee Lyman, *Setting the Agenda for American Archaeology: The National Research Council Archaeological Conferences of 1929, 1932, and 1935* (Tuscaloosa: University of Alabama Press, 2001); Schroeder, Sissel, "Current Research on Late Precontact Societies of the Midcontinental United States," *Journal of Archaeological Research* 12 (2004): 311–372; Silverberg, Robert, *Mound Builders of Ancient America: The Archaeology of a Myth* (Greenwich, CT: New York Graphic Society, 1968); Squier, Ephraim G., and Edwin H. Davis, *Ancient Monuments of the Mississippi Valley*, edited by David J. Meltzer (Reprinted, Washington, DC: Smithsonian Institution Press, 1998); Thiessen, Thomas D., *Emergency Archeology in the Missouri River Basin*, Special Report No. 2 (Lincoln, NE: Midwest Archeological Center, 1999).

Marlin Francis Hawley

CLIMATE AND NATURAL ENVIRONMENT OF THE GREAT LAKES AREA

INTRODUCTION

The pre-contact aboriginal culture history of the Great Lakes watershed, spanning approximately 11,000 years, cannot be fully understood without an appreciation of the natural environment in which this history took place. This was not a static environment for, just as today, climatic and subsequent plant and animal changes were continuous and occurred at various spatial and temporal scales. Native peoples responded to these changes in different ways. This discussion outlines the major environmental changes from the end of the last ice age to the period of European contact and highlights some of the factors that likely influenced human adaptation. It also examines how certain environmental changes have modified the archaeological record, concealing or destroying sites through processes such as inundation and erosion.

LATE PLEISTOCENE
Deglaciation and Glacial Lakes

Toward the end of the last ice age, known as the Wisconsinan glaciation, the continental glacier reached its maximum extent around 18,000 years ago, advancing as far south as Ohio, Indiana, and Illinois. Over millennia it had advanced in a south-southwesterly direction as a series of eight ice lobes that flowed through bedrock depressions corresponding to the modern Great Lakes basins. When the glacier began to melt, around 14,000 years ago, the lobes began to shrink and retreat, but at times they would either pause or even re-advance. In so doing, they laid down a complex landscape of recessional moraines and related glacial deposits. The melt-water that flowed from the glacier formed large, temporary lakes, first against the edge of the ice and later within the newly exposed basins of the Great Lakes. The shorelines of these lakes changed considerably, and sometimes relatively rapidly, as various outlets became available and were down-cut by erosion and as the entire Great Lakes basin began to rise and tilt in response to removal of the weight of the continental glacier. This process of gradual uplift, known as isostatic rebound, continues today. It was during the latter part of this period of deglaciation and glacial lake formation that the southern part of the Great Lakes watershed was first colonized by the Paleoindians about 11,000 years ago.

Some of the earlier glacial lakes, such as Lake Iroquois in the Ontario basin, had vanished centuries before the Paleoindians arrived. Others, such as glacial Lake Algonquin in the Huron-Michigan basin, were very important features of the Paleoindian landscape. Although the details of development vary from basin to basin, all share a similar overall sequence of lake level evolution. This begins with a period of early high-water stages above modern elevations, followed by a drop of the water plane well below modern elevations, a gradual refilling of the basin to modern levels, a brief and variable period of transgression above modern elevations, and eventual stabilization at or near the present. Most of these changes would have been imperceptible to Paleoindian and succeeding Archaic period hunter-gatherers, yet some may have been quite significant. For example, the relatively rapid drainage of the Huron-Michigan basin around 10,000 years ago would have significantly increased the land area of the Great Lakes watershed while reducing the distances and times necessary to circumnavigate or cross the lakes with watercraft. Unfortunately, much of the archaeological evidence that could shed light on how people adapted to these changes now lies deeply submerged.

Paleoclimate and Paleoecology

The changing climate of the Great Lakes region since the last glacial maximum can be reconstructed from a variety of data sources, such as differences in plant pollen deposits. Climate change is keyed to interactions between cold and dry arctic air masses in the north, warm and moist tropical air masses in the south, and Pacific-derived mild dry air in between. Predominant airflow may be either west to east or north to south, and air mass interactions move latitudinally along frontal zones. In the Great Lakes region, warm tropical air masses expanded south of the glacial ice sheet around 17,000 to 16,000 years ago, ultimately widening and extending northward as the effects of glacial ice diminished.

Regional reconstruction of vegetation change suggests latitudinal plant community zones at the peak of the last glaciation around 18,000 years ago, with a discontinuous tundra zone along the glacial margins, periodically broken by boreal forest and often invading the ice margin itself. Postglacial warming trends significantly impacted regional biotic communities until around 4000 BP, and plant adaptive and migration patterns were often complex. Consequently, changes in tree ranges were not necessarily step-like south to north shifts but rather were a complex interplay of competing tree species, especially in biotic transitional zones.

Clear trends in vegetation change are evident following deglaciation of the Great Lakes region. Newly opened areas in the south were initially dominated by tundra, but by about 14,000 BP spruce-dominated boreal forest began to expand northward, retreating along its southern margin with the mixed conifer–northern hardwood forest in pursuit. At the time of Paleoindian colonization around 11,000 years ago, the

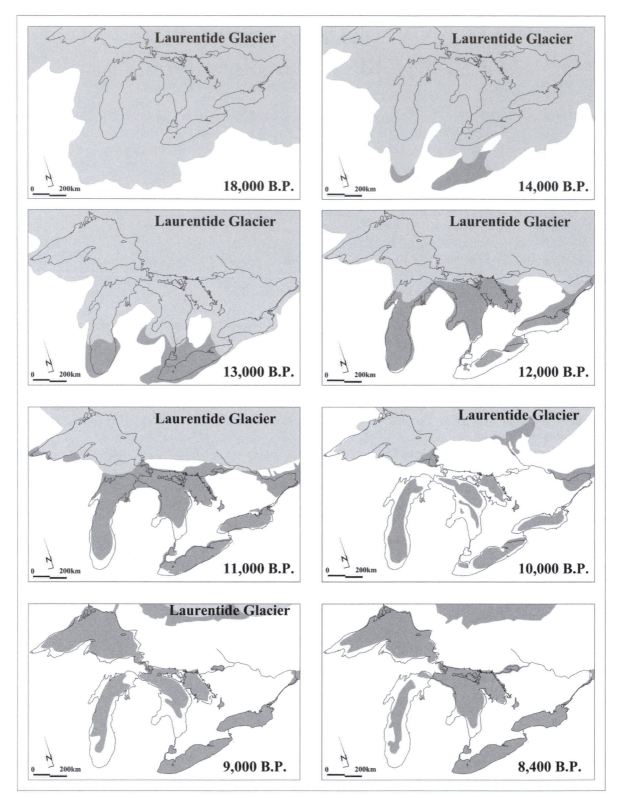

The shrinking of the Laurentide glacier.   [Robert I. MacDonald]

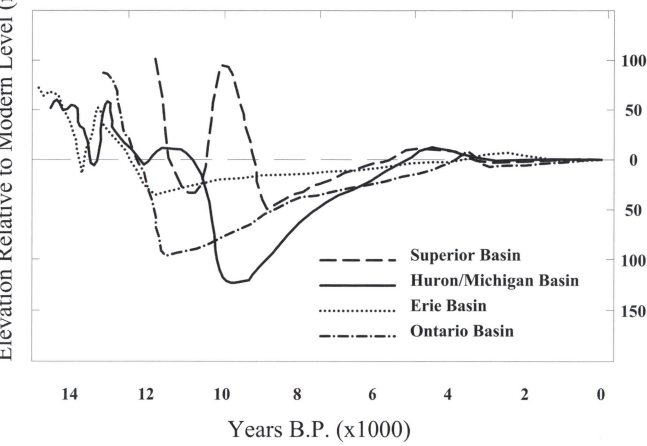

Great Lakes water level changes.   [Robert I. MacDonald]

vegetation of the Great Lakes area ranged from patches of tundra near the edges of the retreating glacier to extensive tracts of open parkland with scattered spruce groves and isolated trees, to closed-canopy boreal forest dominated by spruce and intermixed with pine, fir, hemlock, poplar, and ash. This developing landscape was likewise colonized by pioneering animal communities, including caribou and now-extinct mastodons and mammoths. Since tundra, spruce parkland, and boreal forest tend to be relatively less productive habitats than those that would develop later, the Paleoindian's lifestyle was highly mobile and likely primarily adapted to hunting large game supplemented by fishing and gathering.

EARLY HOLOCENE
Climate and Vegetation
Between 10,000 and 7,000 years ago, north-south atmospheric circulation replaced the primarily west-east pattern that had dominated while the continental glacier was extant.

Circulation patterns changed again as the Pacific air mass expanded northward and eastward across the mid-continent, reaching its maximum extent across the southern third of the Great Lakes between about 7,000 and 5,000 years ago. Regional temperatures peaked at this time, an interval known as the Holocene Climatic Optimum.

By about 10,000 years ago, boreal forest prevailed throughout most of the Great Lakes region. Spruce and pine often dominated, and oak both established itself regionally and, along with elm, became dominant in more southern areas within a broad zone of deciduous forest. Between about 8,000 and 7,000 years ago, during the Holocene Climatic Optimum, essentially modern plant and animal communities became established and began to be exploited by Middle Archaic hunting and gathering populations. By 6,000 years ago, the northern half of the region was dominated by mixed conifers and northern hardwoods; pine became dominant in the north, while oak dominated in the south along with other species

Late Pleistocene/Holocene temperature reconstruction.   [Robert I. MacDonald]

including beech, maple, poplar, and hemlock. Economically important nut-producing species such as hickory and walnut also became established. Deciduous forest expanded into southern Minnesota, central Wisconsin, and southern Michigan, although the southwestern parts of the region experienced the expansion of prairie grassland habitats and accompanying animal species. With the end of the Holocene Climatic Optimum and the onset of a slight cooling trend, there was a general southward displacement of vegetation communities. Although the prairie retreated 100–400 kilometers in the face of deciduous forest re-advance, it left patchy remnants across the southwestern Great Lakes.

The Evolving Great Lakes
The Superior basin was the last to be freed of glacial ice, and even as late as about 9500 BP a glacial re-advance blanketed parts of Michigan's Upper Peninsula. As it retreated beyond the Great Lakes watershed, the melting continental glacier formed other large glacial lakes. To the northwest was

glacial Lake Agassiz, estimated to have been larger than all the current Great Lakes combined. After 9,500 years ago, drainage from Lake Agassiz entered the Great Lakes basin. From then until drainage to Hudson Bay commenced around 8,000 years ago, Lake Agassiz contributed meltwater to the Great Lakes drainage basin. Unlike today, however, the primary outlet of the upper Great Lakes was not through the lower lakes and into the St. Lawrence River. Rather, it drained via an outlet at North Bay, Ontario, which flowed through Lake Nipissing and the Mattawa River to the Ottawa River. This situation continued until around 5,500 years ago, when the North Bay outlet rebounded to the same level as the southern outlets at Chicago and Port Huron. Thus, from about 9,500 to about 5,500 years ago, a major east-west drainage corridor existed across the northern part of the Great Lakes basin.

After 5,500 years ago, the North Bay outlet continued its rise, thereby initiating the current drainage regime from the upper Great Lakes through the lower Great Lakes via the St. Clair, Detroit, and Niagara rivers and ultimately to the St.

Lawrence River. Bedrock sills in these rivers initially brought the lake levels somewhat above modern levels, but their continued erosion lowered the water slightly below modern levels by around 4,500 years ago. This interval of high lake levels is known as the Nipissing Transgression, in reference to the former outlet at North Bay.

Aboriginal Land-Use Patterns

The post-Nipissing archaeological record (after about 4,500 years ago) gives us our first complete window into aboriginal land-use patterns since Paleoindian times, because settlement generally occurred above the Nipissing high-water mark. What this reveals is a pattern of small residential or special-purpose logistic camps linked to repeatedly occupied seasonal settlements at key landscape and resource points. The latter include important transportation nodes, for example, where major rivers meet or enter the Great Lakes, and/or important resource locations, such as chert outcrops, coastal wetlands, and fishing grounds. Some sites, such as the 20-hectare Peace Bridge site in Fort Erie, Ontario, exhibit multiple attractions to settlement and may even have had sufficient local resources to support year-round occupation. Many other major sites, spanning the Late Archaic to Late Woodland periods, highlight the fundamental significance of coastal and wetland habitats to aboriginal hunter-gatherers, for few other locations would have afforded the opportunity to sustain the increased population densities of seasonal band aggregation. The Schultz and Schmidt sites in the Saginaw Valley of Michigan exemplify how seasonal aggregation points may have been situated in order to maximize access to a radial network of both interior hunting and gathering camps and coastal camps focused on fishing and exploitation of rich wetland resources. Because similar land-use strategies had probably been in place since the modern flora and fauna were established during the Early Archaic period, it is believed that most major camps of the Early and Middle Archaic periods are now under water.

LATE HOLOCENE: LATER ADAPTATIONS IN THE MODERN GREAT LAKES

Since the end of the Nipissing Transgression, around 4,500 years ago, Great Lakes water levels have slowly responded to ongoing isostatic tilting, bedrock sill erosion, and other factors, ultimately attaining modern water-plane altitudes. Regional temperatures have diminished as predominantly north-south flow has returned and intensified, and the tropical air mass has re-expanded to the northwest. Pacific air masses continue to dominate the southern and western portions of the Great Lakes region. By around 4,000 years ago, during the Late Archaic, there is evidence of wild squash entering the region, with domestic squash present by around 3,000 years ago. This is the first evidence of regional horticulture, and it predates the onset of the ceramic-producing Woodland period by half a millennium.

Over the last millennium, several smaller climatic episodes have been identified across the northern hemisphere, including the Great Lakes region. These are the Medieval Climatic Optimum, from about 1,000 to 750 years ago, and the Little Ice Age, from about 400 to 100 years ago. Prior to about 1,500 years ago, during the Middle Woodland period, local populations intensified their reliance on the oily and starchy seed plants known as the Eastern Agricultural Complex along with aquatic animal and plant resources including wild rice. Ultimately, this led to the full adoption of maize, bean, and squash horticulture (large-scale gardening) and eventually agriculture across the southern tier of the Great Lakes region during the Late Woodland–Upper Mississippian time periods. This economic transformation occurred during the Medieval Climatic Optimum. Food production resulted in reduced mobility, increased aggregation and sedentism, shifts in settlement locations, and increases in population and social complexity. In the north, where indigenous agriculture incurred greater risk, there is evidence for either intensification on fall-spawning fish species, and/or symbiotic exchange relationships, both of which also greatly affected seasonal mobility, timing, and population size. The impact of the Little Ice Age on these societies, at or just prior to European contact in the sixteenth and seventeenth centuries, has yet to be systematically evaluated, although minor and/or local level perturbations in temperature can pose substantial risk to economies focused on domestic plants, particularly in climatically marginal locations, such as the Great Lakes region.

Further Reading: Delcourt, Paul A., and Hazel R. Delcourt, *Prehistoric Native Americans and Ecological Change* (Cambridge: Cambridge University Press, 2006); Holman, J. Alan, *Ancient Life of the Great Lakes Basin: Precambrian to Pleistocene* (Ann Arbor: University of Michigan Press, 1995); Lovis, William A., and Robert I. MacDonald, "Archaeological Implications of Great Lakes Paleoecology at the Regional Scale," in *Taming the Taxonomy*, edited by R. F. Williamson and C. M. Watts (Toronto, ON: Eastendbooks, 1999), 125–150; Karrow, Paul F., and Parker E. Calkin, eds., *Quaternary Evolution of the Great Lakes*, Geological Association of Canada Special Paper No. 30 (St. John's, NF: Memorial University of Newfoundland, 1985); Karrow, Paul F., and Barry G. Warner, "The Geological and Biological Environment for Human Occupation in Southern Ontario," in *The Archaeology of Southern Ontario to A.D. 1650*, edited by Chris J. Ellis and Neal Ferris, Occasional Publication No. 5 (London: Ontario Archaeological Society, , 1990), 5–35; Mason, Ronald J., *Great Lakes Archaeology*, rev. ed. (Caldwell, NJ: Blackburn Press, 2002); Monaghan, G. William, and William A. Lovis, *Modeling Archaeological Site Burial in Southern Michigan: A Geoarchaeological Synthesis* (East Lansing: Michigan State University Press, 2005).

William A. Lovis and Robert I. MacDonald

CLIMATE AND NATURAL ENVIRONMENT
OF THE MIDWEST RIVER VALLEYS

The Midwest Riverine region consists of the central Mississippi River valley and the lower reaches of the Missouri and Illinois river basins. Historically, the broad floodplains of these large rivers were heavily forested and interspersed with bottomland prairie. Bordering the valleys loess-covered bluffs connected the valleys to uplands that supported a mosaic of oak-hickory forests and tallgrass prairie. This is part of the southern Prairie Peninsula, that extension of the North American grassland that extended eastward from the Great Plains into Illinois and Indiana, with outliers into Ohio. The early historical record, prior to the transformation of the landscape by modern agriculture, only gives a snapshot of the environment that was the culmination of a dynamic process of change in the land and its biota (plants and animals) over the past several thousand years. The landscape history of relevance here is the Holocene, that is, the last 12,000 years of earth history following the end of the most recent glacial age.

The earliest aboriginal inhabitants of the Midwest Riverine region were present by the time of the Pleistocene-Holocene transition, that is, at the close of the glacial period, 13,000–11,000 years ago. This was a period of dramatic climatic and environmental change, as glaciers receded and arctic air, blocked earlier by the great ice sheets, flowed into the Midwest increasing effective precipitation and increasing seasonality. Changing climate (temperature and precipitation) led to a transition from spruce-dominated forests during the full glacial to a mosaic of conifer and deciduous forests during the transition to Holocene climates, and eventually to mesic deciduous forests during the early Holocene by 8200 BC.

The earliest people to occupy the Mississippi valley consisted of small mobile bands of hunters known as the Clovis culture or tradition, who hunted, among other animals, large game that would soon become extinct, such as mastodon, mammoth, and giant ground sloth. There is still debate among scientists on whether the rapid changes in the environment at the end of the glacial period or the Clovis hunters themselves were the principal cause of extinction of these large animals, collectively referred to as megafauna. Regardless of the cause, the Clovis hunters arrived at a time when the climate was rapidly warming with increased moisture, a time when the spruce forests were declining and being replaced by mesic deciduous species. Thus the Clovis hunters were occupying a dynamic landscape during which vegetation was changing and species were becoming extinct.

The warming trend was reversed, and a period of cooling prevailed again between 11,000 and 9700 BC, as glaciers to the north began to re-advance, and the trend of deciduous trees replacing conifer forests was halted. The Midwest Riverine area was still occupied by hunting and collecting people, now known as the Dalton culture or tradition, who were adapting to a landscape in which megafauna had become extinct. Whitetail deer populations, although not numerous, became the principal quarry of Dalton people. The climate began to warm again after 9700 BC. The warm, moist environment was ideal for the development of mesic deciduous forests of elm, ash, maple, and ironwood. This was the archaeological period known as the Early Archaic, and the time was the early Holocene. The fauna was modern, that is, the animals present were those species that occurred in the region historically. The mesic forests were closed, meaning that whitetail deer that prefer edge areas and open woodland were not as plentiful and many of the economically important nut-producing trees, such as hickory and oak, were not as abundant as they would become later in time. The early Archaic peoples adapted to these mesic forests by harvesting a variety of small mammals, especially tree squirrels, with lesser numbers of whitetail deer. Nuts they procured tended to be those that grow in denser and moister conditions, such as pecans. During this period these hunter-foragers utilized the uplands as well as the floodplains in their quest for food.

Around 7100 BC the climate warmed and became increasingly arid. This change was soon reflected in the vegetation as the density of trees declined, and more drought-tolerant species, such as oak, replaced the mesic taxa of the early Holocene. This was the period during which prairie initially expanded east of the Mississippi River as patches of grassland dotted the uplands. Within a few centuries, channels on the floodplain of the Mississippi River began to hold permanent, shallow flood-basin lakes that became hatcheries for several economically important species of fish. The evolution of the lake basins with their bounty of aquatic resources set apart for the first time the Midwest Riverine region from adjoining regions. This would have a profound impact on the evolution of native cultures in these major river valleys.

The climate again fluctuated between 5900 and 4350 BC, returning to more mesic conditions (with moderate moisture or rainfall) as prairie patches reverted to woodland. The climate reversal lasted slightly over 1,500 years, when the major onset of mid-Holocene warming and drying transpired, a time when prairie again expanded at the expense of forests and became the predominant vegetation on the uplands. For the first time, fire appears to have become a significant ecological factor, combining with the doughty climatic regime to expand the prairies to their maximum extent, well into Ohio. Although still speculative, the increase in fire was most likely caused by Native Americans. It was also during this period that flood-basin lakes formed in the flood channels along the Illinois River, a process that lagged behind their appearance in the Mississippi valley. As these productive bottomland lakes formed in the Illinois River valley, this major drainage system became one of the most productive fisheries in the New World. By the mid-Holocene, the Midwest Riverine region had become the "breadbasket" of reliable and sustainable aquatic resources for native hunters and foragers in the American midlands.

While the floodplains were becoming rich in aquatic resources, forests on the valley slopes and dissected uplands were transformed into another resource-rich environment for Native American populations. Two parallel trends contributed to forests yielding resources that were rich in protein and carbohydrates. Whitetail deer populations that were present but not numerous in the Late Glacial mixed conifer-hardwood forests and the relatively dense mesic forests of the early Holocene expanded significantly as optimal habitats for this animal evolved during the early mid-Holocene. Edge areas were created along prairie-forest borders, and with increased burning by native peoples, deer browse was increased dramatically. In addition, as the fire-tolerant and drought-resistant oak-hickory forest developed, acorn and nut mast production increased exponentially, providing a cold-season staple for whitetail deer. Thus, along with aquatic resources, deer became a principal meat staple for aboriginal populations.

The second trend was the increase in nut-bearing trees that produced mast (hickory nuts, walnuts, and acorns). Mast was not only important for whitetail deer and squirrels but also was a staple for human foragers. Frequent fires opened the woodland so that mast-producing trees, with less competition from surrounding trees, yielded optimal production. Technological advances allowed processing of large numbers of hickory nuts, thus providing another staple for the diet that was rich in fat and carbohydrates. The evolution of the floodplain lakes with their sustainable fisheries and the climatically linked vegetation change to mast-producing forests contributed directly to technological and settlement changes that made possible this bountiful harvest of aquatic and terrestrial resources.

After 3800 BC effective moisture increased, and within a few centuries climate had essentially reached modern conditions. The prairies persisted with the aid of frequent fires set by Native Americans. This was the period of experimentation with native plants during which wild plants were harvested for seeds and eventually domesticated. Four species, marsh elder, chenopod, squash, and sunflower were all domesticated in eastern North America and were grown and cultivated in the Midwest Riverine region.

Native cultures evolved from hunting and foraging societies to sedentary villagers. This evolutionary pathway eventually led to complex chiefdoms with large population centers based on maize horticulture, a crop introduced from Mexico that became important after AD 800. Climate change impacted horticultural societies when extended droughts led to catastrophic crop failures. Technological advances, trade networks, and food surpluses led to larger population aggregates, the largest being in the American Bottom just below the confluence of the Missouri and Illinois rivers with the Mississippi River. Cahokia, a Mississippian mound center that reached its zenith around AD 1100, and its immediately surrounding area may have attained a population of 10,000 or greater. This major population center developed during what is known as the Medieval Warm Period, between AD 800 and 1200.

After the warming of the four previous centuries, a cooling trend began that culminated in a prolonged cold period between AD 1300 and 1850, which became known as the Little Ice Age. This climatic downturn may have been one of several factors that led to the decline of Mississippian culture in the Midwest Riverine region, although the causes of this decline are still widely debated. Slightly later in time, the first Euro-Americans contacted Native peoples, carrying with them European diseases that would soon reach epidemic proportions.

The natural environment throughout the Holocene changed as climate fluctuated through periods of increased or decreased temperature and moisture. Environmental change created opportunities and limitations for Native American societies as they adapted to each new set of conditions. It was this interplay between culture and environment that created the evolutionary pathways along which human cultures developed over the past 12,000 years in the Midwest Riverine region.

Further Reading: Nelson, D. M., Feng Sheng Hu, E. C. Grimm, B. B. Curry, and J. E. Slate, "The Influence of Aridity and Fire on Holocene Prairie Communities in the Eastern Prairie Peninsula," *Ecology* 87(10) (2006): 2523–2536; RiverWeb: American Bottom Landing Site Web site, http://www.riverweb.uiuc.edu; Styles, B. W., "Aquatic Exploitation in the Lower Illinois River Valley: The Role of Paleoecological Change," in *Foraging, Collecting, and Harvesting: Archaic Period Subsistence and Settlement in the Eastern Woodlands*, edited by Sarah W. Neusius, Center for Archaeological Investigations Occasional Paper No. 6 (Carbondale: Southern Illinois University, 1986); Styles, B. W., and S. R. Ahler, "Changing Perspectives on the Archaic: Contributions from Modoc Rock Shelter," in *Mounds, Modoc, and Mesoamerica: Papers in Honor of Melvin L Fowler*, edited by S. R. Ahler, Scientific Paper No. 28 (Springfield: Illinois State Museum, 2000), 25–38.

R. Bruce McMillan

THE EARLIEST INHABITANTS OF THE MIDWEST

MIDWESTERN PALEOINDIANS

When we think of Midwestern pioneers, images of sturdy woodsmen and Conestoga wagons come to mind. But the true pioneers in the American Midwest arrived at least 13,000 years earlier. At a time when many Americans regard immigration with fear and anxiety, it is worth remembering that in the longest historical view we are all immigrants. This is as true of Native Americans as the rest of us, but their ancestors arrived much earlier and lived here much longer. There is no evidence in prehistoric North America of space invaders, Irish monks, or other subjects of fancy. Natives are truly the first Americans, and the archaeological manifestation of the earliest natives is called "Paleoindian" culture. (There is no acceptable general name for Native Americans. Some prefer "Indian," "native," or the neologism "First Americans." "Paleoindian" is common archaeological usage.)

Paleoindians and their Clovis culture reached North America, including the Midwest, as long ago as 13,000 years. This is the "Clovis First" view that many archaeologists continue to hold. Paleoindians were biologically modern humans; there is no evidence for Neanderthals or other earlier humans in the Americas. However, some now believe that people reached North America before 13,000 years ago, whether or not they were lineal ancestors of contemporary Natives. Paleoindians left abundant evidence of their presence in the North American Midwest, but not so their possible predecessors.

The archaeological record places severe limitations on the study of Paleoindians. No doubt these people had shelter, clothing, ornament, and tool of wood and bone. In the Midwest, however, most such objects did not survive long exposure, leaving in the archaeological record only imperishable artifacts and other remains, such as stone tools. Archaeologists must reconstruct the Paleoindian whole from these sparse fragments. To appreciate the challenge that confronts archaeologists, imagine a future archaeologist who contemplates twenty-first-century American society possessing just the odd scrap of metal from a 2002 Chevy, a few styrofoam containers for burgers, and some asphalt shingles.

THE SETTING

The Midwest is bordered by some of the greatest natural features of North America: plains to the west, Appalachians to the east, and the Great Lakes to the northeast. Through it flows the continent's greatest river, the Mississippi, and its Ohio and Missouri tributaries. Europeans "settled" North America because of, not despite, natives. Eighteenth- and nineteenth-century midwesterners contemplated a landscape that they mistook for an unspoiled wilderness. They marveled at the abundance of apparently unimproved nature that they encountered. Yet this abundance was as much the product of 13,000 years of careful, sophisticated native husbandry as it was the unimproved bounty of nature. In contrast, when Paleoindians reached the Midwest they had the benefit of no one's prior experience. The region lacked human landmarks, some animal species were unknown to the newcomers, and no one was there to impart knowledge or guidance for survival, let alone prosperity.

The Midwestern landscape was carved by successive glacial advances during the Pleistocene Epoch. The last advance, the Wisconsinan, covered almost all of Michigan and Minnesota, most of Wisconsin, and some of Ohio, Indiana, Illinois, and Iowa before retreating around 18,000 years ago. It left behind a landscape of rolling till plains, hilly moraines, and sandy outwash plains.

Arriving Paleoindians encountered a complex patchwork of habitats forged by glacial climate, topography, and soil. A massive glacier lay across the northern Midwest. Winters, obviously, were cold, and summers warm but short. When Paleoindians arrived, the Midwest's northern fringe was roughly comparable to modern tundra of northern Canada. Farther south were boreal and then deciduous forests not unlike Midwestern forests today. Paleoindians successfully colonized this unknown and forbidding landscape, responding to staggering environmental challenges and changes. Gradually, climates slowly shifted toward modern conditions. Yet from about 12,000–12,800 years ago, North America experienced an abrupt and rather severe cold, dry period. Paleoindians persevered in the Midwest during this "Younger Dryas" period.

Mammoths and mastodons inhabited the Midwest when people arrived. Paleoindians hunted or at least scavenged mastodons at places like the Kimmswick site and perhaps the Chesrow complex sites of southeastern Wisconsin. Mastodon State Historic Site, south of St. Louis, Missouri, displays evidence from Kimmswick. Visitors may view the locations from which many mastodon bones were mined and some excavated by archaeologists. The University of Wisconsin Museum of Geology in Madison displays the Boaz mastodon, found more than a century ago in southwestern Wisconsin, possibly with Paleoindian stone tools. To date, however, apart from Kimmswick the Midwest's many mastodon and mammoth sites have not yielded conclusive evidence that Paleoindians hunted these animals. In particular, archaeologists lack evidence of unquestioned stone tools in or very near the animal bones. Accordingly, archaeologists continue to debate the role that Paleoindians may have played in causing the extinction of these species.

PALEOINDIAN ARCHAEOLOGY AND CULTURE

Anyone can determine the approximate date of an old photograph from the style of hair, dress, or automobile that it shows. Archaeologists use similar logic and practice to identify successive phases of Paleoindian culture. The evidence is limited, so they pay special attention to imperishable chipped-stone tools. These often are mistakenly called "arrowheads," but in Paleoindian times they were the tips or "points" of spears.

Beginning about 13,000 years ago, Clovis is the earliest major Paleoindian phase recognized in western North America; Clovis fluted points occur in the Rocky Mountains and on the plains, even reaching the western Midwest. On the plains, Clovis is succeeded by Folsom, also present in the Midwest. Farther east, Great Lakes research defined the chronological series of later Paleoindian projectile point styles, first Gainey and then later phases, by a combination of fluted-point typology and glacial geology (dating sites from their location on geological features of known age). Technologically, Gainey represents something of a Clovis-Folsom hybrid, although it seems closer to Clovis. Parkhill and Cumberland are broadly similar to Folsom. Late Paleoindian Agate Basin, Dalton, and other point types are scattered widely, but apparently thinly, across the Midwest. A phase called Crowfield postdates Parkhill/Cumberland in the Great Lakes.

Hunter-gatherers, which the Paleoindians were, do not have permanent homes. Instead, they moved strategically across their territories, changing their activities according to their location; seasonal resources, such as available game; and other factors. Coshocton County, Ohio, and Silver Mound, Wisconsin, have workshops where Paleoindians quarried stone for use as tools. Public hiking trails crisscross the Silver Mound quarries. Temporary Paleoindian sites, whether hunting camps or residences, dot the Midwestern landscape. Some (e.g., Nobles Pond, Gainey, Paleo Crossing, Bostrom, Lincoln Hills, and Martens) are large enough that Paleoindians might have gathered there periodically to hunt caribou herds, exchange news, and just to socialize. Visit the McKinley Museum in Canton, Ohio, for a display on Nobles Pond that includes a replica caribou-skin tent of the sort that the site's occupants may have used, and stone tools found there.

Most large Midwestern Paleoindian sites are identified as Clovis/Gainey, based on point typology and glacial features. Later Parkhill/Cumberland evidence is less abundant, so perhaps Paleoindian populations actually fell, not rose, during this time period. Even now we know little about the details of Midwestern Paleoindian life, but later Paleoindians apparently ranged over smaller territories than their ancestors, perhaps because of the gradually if unevenly warming climate.

PRESERVING PALEOINDIAN EVIDENCE

Because the Midwest is plowed ground, it offers better prospects for collectors than do other regions. For a century and more, people accumulated large collections, many including Paleoindian tools. Most known prehistoric artifacts in the Midwest were found by lay people, and many now reside in trunks, cigar boxes, or display cases. Many such collections are lost to scientific study when they fall into the hands of heirs or others who lack the collector's passion for the past and respect for the evidence. Imagine the pages of medieval church records or Gutenberg Bibles torn out and sold because descendants did not appreciate their historical value. Something very similar is the fate of many Midwestern archaeological collections. Once lost to study, they can never be restored.

We can only wonder what Midwestern evidence was unearthed long ago but not recognized. Tantalizing hints are part of Midwestern folklore; most archaeologists know a farmer who knew a farmer who had a father who said that his grandfather had a friend who long ago found "spear points" with the fossils of a prehistoric beast. What, for instance, can we make of an Illinois collector's 1921 account that three fluted points "were found with a tooth as big as your fist," unless the tooth was a mastodon molar?

Losses are irretrievable, but parts of the Midwestern Paleoindian record remain to be discovered. Anyone, not just trained archaeologists, can help, provided only that they are responsible in their collection and documentation of the evidence and make it available to others who study Midwestern prehistory for scholarly or educational reasons. Anyone who has a collection of prehistoric artifacts, perhaps from a family farm, should accept the responsibility of arranging its permanent curation at a county, state, or university museum. Paleoindians probably were the first people in the Midwest; we owe it to them to preserve and study the evidence they left behind.

EXHIBITS

Much Paleoindian evidence probably languishes unrecognized and unrecorded in cigar boxes, but some is housed in museums. When most people think of archaeology, their minds run to pyramids and tombs. By comparison, Paleoindian sites are not nearly so massive or majestic. Most are merely clusters of stone tools in fields or forests that one could drive past or walk over without noticing them. Only Kimmswick and Nobles Pond, among major Midwestern Paleoindian sites, have associated exhibits. Fortunately, public museums such as the Illinois State Museum and major university museums include Paleoindian exhibits. Farther afield, one of the finest Paleoindian exhibits is at the Mashantucket Pequot Museum near Mystic, Connecticut.

Further Reading: Ellis, C. J., and D. Brian Deller, *An Early Paleo-Indian Site Near Parkhill, Ontario*, Paper No. 159 (Ottawa: Archaeological Survey of Canada, 2000); Lepper, Bradley T., "Pleistocene Peoples of Midcontinental North America," in *Ice Age Peoples of North America: Environments, Origins, and Adaptations of the First*

Americans, edited by R. Bonnichsen and K. Turnmire (Corvallis: Oregon State University Press), 362–394; Morrow, Juliet E., "The Organization of Early Paleoindian Lithic Technology in the Confluence Region of the Mississippi, Illinois, and Missouri Rivers," Ph.D. diss. (Washington University, 1997); Overstreet, David F., *Chesrow: A Paleoindian Complex in the Southern Lake Michigan Basin* (Milwaukee, WI: Great Lakes Archaeological Press, 1993);

Shott, Michael J., "Midwestern Paleoindian Context," in *The Earliest Americans: Paleoindian Sites in the Eastern United States*, edited by E. Seibert (Washington, DC: National Historic Landmarks Survey, U.S. Dept. of the Interior, National Park Service, 2005), available at www.nps.gov/history/archeology/PUBS/NHLEAM/index.htm.

Michael J. Shott

SETTLING DOWN IN THE MIDWEST: ANCIENT HUNTER-GATHERER SEDENTISM

The transition from the highly mobile way of life practiced by most hunter-gatherers to the more sedentary lifestyle associated with complex hunter-gatherers and horticultural-agricultural groups represents a major watershed in the social, economic, and political organization of human society. Evidence from a variety of eastern North American archaeological sites has provided important new insights on this major change in human adaptive strategies.

From the Late Pleistocene through the early part of the Middle Holocene (ca. 12,000–6,000 years ago), much of eastern North America was inhabited by small groups of highly mobile hunter-gatherers. These early people had relatively few material possessions—primarily the gear needed to obtain food, construct shelter, and make clothing. The locations of their activities are indicated by innumerable small, low-artifact-density sites scattered across the highly diverse eastern North American landscape. Site frequency, size, and distribution suggest that these early hunter-gatherers followed a very generalized settlement-subsistence strategy, not focusing on any one particular place or food source but rather exploiting the full range of the region's plant and animal communities.

Toward the end of the Middle Holocene (ca. 6,000 years ago), some eastern North American hunter-gatherer societies began to reorganize their settlement-subsistence strategies by decreasing their movement and exploiting smaller hunting territories or home ranges. Some archaeologists view this as a gradual transition from a generalized to a more specialized subsistence strategy made possible by the increased abundance of certain of food resources, particularly nuts. This shift in subsistence strategies brought with it a change in how groups organized themselves and moved about the landscape. Instead of moving the entire group from one resource-rich area to the next, most of the group stayed at one centrally located site, or "base camp," for an extended period. More distant resources were obtained by small task-specific groups that made short forays away from the base camp. Over time, these changes contributed to an increasingly sedentary way of life.

The primary archaeological indicator of this shift toward greater hunter-gatherer sedentism is the appearance of large, intensively occupied and long-term base camps toward the end of the Middle Holocene (ca. 6,000 years ago). Many of these sites were strategically situated adjacent to areas of abundant, diverse, and reliable food sources (e.g., lakes, swamps, rivers, and marshes). Many base camps are characterized by thick, dark refuse deposits, or "middens." The interpretation is that these deposits, containing abundant artifacts, features (hearths, storage facilities, structures, etc.), and food remains, indicate extended, or repeated, occupation of these locations. Some middens largely consist of shell, emphasizing the dietary significance of riverine shellfish, where available.

Not only did hunter-gatherers conduct life's basic activities at the base camp, such as tool manufacture and maintenance, food preparation and consumption, and caring for the young and elderly, but they were also places for ritual and social activities that included performing curing rituals, burying the dead, and interacting and trading with both local residents and visitors from distant lands. Ties with hunter-gatherers who lived far away are indicated by the presence of a few objects made from nonlocal materials— for instance, the marine shell and copper items found at some mid-continent sites. Over time, the repeated use of such economically important locations, combined with the site's ritual significance, meant that these spots became very important places on the hunter-gatherer cultural landscape. Not only were they the source of food, shelter, and clothing, but they also held the physical remains of multiple generations of ancestors.

Settlement data from throughout eastern North America suggests that although evidence for increased hunter-gatherer sedentism is widespread by the end of the Middle Holocene, it is not found everywhere. Apparently, some hunter-gatherers continued to follow a relatively mobile existence, much in the way of their ancestors. Such continuity may reflect the abundance and/or distribution of needed resources in particular places, or perhaps some groups were able to, or preferred to, remain mobile when such an option existed.

Archaeologists have investigated numerous excellent examples of sites having evidence for increased hunter-gatherer sedentism. Some are situated on low uplands overlooking the shallow lakes, swamps, and marshes of the interior riverine systems of central Kentucky (Carlston Annis, Chiggerville, Indian Knoll, KYANG), southern and central Illinois (Black Earth, Modoc Rock Shelter, Koster, Napoleon Hollow), and southern Indiana (Old Clarksville, Bluegrass, Crib Mound, McCain). Similar examples also are found in the Southeast—for example, in southern and western Tennessee (Eva, Anderson), eastern Georgia (Stallings Island), northern Alabama (Mulberry Creek, Bluff Creek, Long Branch), northern Louisiana (Poverty Point), and northern Mississippi (Walnut, Poplar). Sites showing similar evidence for increased hunter-gatherer sedentism occur along the south Atlantic and gulf coasts. Most of these are characterized by extensive linear to oval-shaped shell deposits situated along the margins of coastal plain rivers or overlooking vast coastal marshes and estuaries. Some of these shell middens date to as early as 4200 BP.

Evidence for increased sedentism found at these sites—rapid midden accumulation, numerous human burials, food storage facilities, more substantial habitation structures, and the long-distance exchange of nonlocal materials (e.g., marine shell and copper)—points to the emergence of relatively complex hunter-gatherer societies across much of eastern North America by the end of the Middle Holocene. Although the specific reasons for the strong relationship between sedentism and the emergence of cultural complexity are unclear, it probably is associated with more intensive use of local food source (along with the eventual development of horticulture), more extensive food storage capabilities, and more complex social, economic, and political organization.

In the past, many anthropologists assumed that a sedentary lifestyle was preferred over a highly mobile one, so it was only natural for hunter-gatherers to strive to be more sedentary. In contrast, many researchers now consider high mobility to be a very adaptive strategy, raising questions as to why some hunter-gatherers adopted a more sedentary existence.

Anthropologists have developed several possible explanations for this major transition in lifestyle, including environmental stress, resource abundance, population pressure, and social risk. The environmental stress argument is based on the assumption that reduced food resources resulting from climatic change made high mobility a less reliable option. In contrast, greater resource abundance allowed groups to stay in one place longer, encouraging greater sedentism. Increased population and competition for resources may have led to more circumscribed home ranges and, ultimately, reduced mobility. Finally, increased efforts to avoid risk may have required more food to meet the ritual demands of interacting and maintaining ties with other groups.

Although North America, including the Midwest region, was inhabited by people who pursued a hunter-gatherer lifestyle for much of its past, it is clear that these societies changed over time, adapting to differences in their physical and social worlds. The earliest hunter-gatherers consisted of small groups that maintained a high level of mobility, not staying in one place for very long. By the late Middle Holocene, about 6,000 years ago, some hunter-gatherer groups were starting to become much more sedentary, exhibiting many of the characteristics associated with later agricultural societies that inhabited eastern North American at the time of European contact.

Further Reading: Binford, Lewis R., "Willow Smoke and Dogs' Tails: Hunter-Gatherer Settlement Systems and Archaeological Site Formation," *American Antiquity* 45 (1980): 4–28; Brown, James A., "Long-Term Trends to Sedentism and the Emergence of Complexity in the American Midwest," in *Prehistoric Hunter-Gatherers: The Emergence of Cultural Complexity*, edited by T. Douglas Price and James A. Brown (Orlando, FL: Academic Press, 1985), 201–231; Crothers, George, and Reinhard Bernbeck, "The Foraging Mode of Production: The Case of the Green River Archaic Shell Middens," in *Hunters and Gatherers in Theory and Archaeology*, edited by George M. Crothers (Carbondale, IL: Center for Archaeological Investigations, 2004), 401–422; Hitchcock, Robert K., "Patterns of Sedentism among the Basarwa of Eastern Botswana," in *Politics and History in Band Societies*, edited by Eleanor Leacock and Richard Lee (Cambridge: Cambridge University Press, 1982), 223–267; Marquardt, William H., and Patty Jo Watson, eds., *Archaeology of the Middle Green River Region, Kentucky* (Gainesville: Florida Museum of Natural History, 2005); Price, T. Douglas, and James A. Brown, eds., *Prehistoric Hunter-Gatherers: The Emergence of Cultural Complexity* (Orlando, FL: Academic Press, 1985); Sassaman, Kenneth E., "The Cultural Diversity of Interactions among Mid-Holocene Societies of the American Southeast," in *Native American Interactions: Multiscalar Analyses and Interpretations in the Eastern Woodlands*, edited by Michael S. Nassaney and Kenneth E. Sassaman (Knoxville: University of Tennessee Press, 1995), 174–204; Stafford, C. Russell, "Structural Changes in Archaic Landscape Use in the Dissected Uplands of Southwestern Indiana," *American Antiquity* 59 (1994): 219–237.

Richard W. Jefferies

THE ORIGINS OF AGRICULTURE IN THE MIDWEST: THE EASTERN AGRICULTURAL COMPLEX

The Eastern Agricultural Complex is the name given to a group of ancient plant species that represents an independent development of agriculture within the interior of the United States beginning some 5,000 years ago. These plants appear to have been grown for their seeds as both starchy and high-oil additions to the prehistoric peoples' diet (and probably for use as greens as well). A small hard-shelled garden squash (*Cucurbita pepo* spp. *ovifera*), derived from a wild indigenous ancestor, was grown along with these prolific seed producers. In some areas the true bottle gourd (*Lagenaria siceria*) perhaps was also cultivated. Finally, charred seeds of the native tobacco (*Nicotiana rustica*), originally traded in from the American southwest, have been recovered from a few sites, suggesting that in some areas this crop had also been planted.

THE EASTERN AGRICULTURAL COMPLEX

The Eastern Agricultural Complex consists of five different plant species, including goosefoot or lambsquarters (*Chenopodium berlandieri*), erect knotweed (*Polygonum erectum*), maygrass (*Phalaris caroliniana*), little barley (*Hordeum pusillum*), sumpweed or marsh elder (*Iva annua*), and sunflower (*Helianthus annuus*). Only the sunflower remains in use as a significant crop today, while the remaining Eastern Agricultural Complex plants are represented by wild forms rather than the domesticated varieties. These early crop plants were all derived from wild weedy ancestors that were aggressive colonizers of recently disturbed soils along the floodplains and forests of the river valleys within the Midwest. They still can be found in such environments today.

These early crops fall into two basic groups: (1) plants that produce large amounts of small "starchy" seeds (seeds that are high in carbohydrates, similar to today's major crops of wheat or oats, for example), and (2) plants that produce larger seeds that are rich in fats and oils and have a higher protein amount than the members of the first group. Goosefoot, maygrass, and little barley fall into the first category. Two species of cultivated crops included in the Eastern Agricultural Complex were valued for their oily high-protein seeds: sunflower and sumpweed, a plant most likely unfamiliar to today's consumers.

Most of the Eastern Agricultural Complex species would not look like typical crop plants that we grow in our own gardens or farm fields. For example, goosefoot (named for the distinctive shape of this plant's leaves) is often considered a nuisance weed and can grow into large, almost bushy plants that reach 4–5 feet high and bear numerous almost invisible, nondescript green flowers. Goosefoot can be eaten as a "green" (like cooked spinach) when very young, but the leaves become bitter as the plant matures. The presence of thousands of charred seeds in archaeological sites suggests that its major importance was for its starchy seeds. However, there is a domesticated form of goosefoot still grown in remote areas of Central and South America called quinoa that has a very pale or white seed color and is cooked into an oatmeal-like meal. Quinoa is now being grown in a minor commercial way, and consumers can find it for sale in large health-food stores, touted as a healthy alternative to wheat or rice.

Erect knotweed has a similar growth pattern and prefers the same type of disturbed habitat as goosefoot. It may have been used in the same manner as goosefoot as well. Little barley, as the name suggests, is a North American distant cousin of the cultivated barley we know today ("modern" barley is original to the Near East). This native grass, however, is much smaller and less compact than the barley that we grow in our modern farm fields. Sumpweed looks like a smaller, stouter version of sunflower, and both species are similar in having a high-protein, fat-rich kernel encased in a hard outer seed coat (the shell often discarded by the birds that frequent our feeders today). In fact, the sunflower that was grown in prehistoric gardens is similar to the black high-oil seeds now sold as a major source of bird seed.

Archaeological evidence indicates that the smaller seeds of the Eastern Agricultural Complex were most likely parched or toasted, perhaps by tossing seeds and hot coals or heated rocks in baskets and containers. This action would abrade the tough outer seed coat, aiding in digestibility and enhancing taste. When toasted, for example, goosefoot tends to pop almost like miniature corn kernels. After this process, the seeds could be boiled like a gruel or ground into a flour. We find far fewer specimens of squash and sumpweed in archaeological sites, suggesting that they were processed, stored, or used in a manner different from the starchy seeds.

Finally, the earliest prehistoric squash in the Midwest was quite different from the thin-skinned, thick-fleshed varieties, such as summer squash or pumpkin, that currently grace our tables. This ancient yellow-flowered squash had a hard woody, warty outer rind, a thin bitter flesh, and numerous nutritious and tasty seeds. You can still find examples of this type of unique squash in supermarkets around early fall when they are marketed as "ornamental gourds"—the bright variegated green and yellow unusually shaped warty "gourds" seasonally sold are actually *Cucurbita pepo*. The woody rind has quite distinctive cells observable under high magnification, and numerous charred fragments of the rind have been

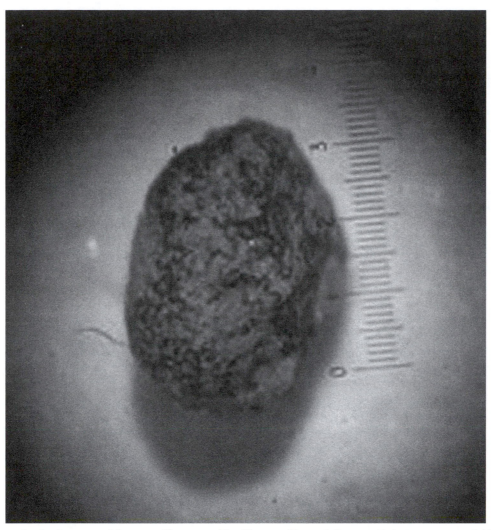

Microscope photograph of tobacco seed from an Ohio mound builder site (Brown's Bottom 1) dating to around AD 300. The seed is approximately 1 millimeter in length.   [DeeAnne Wymer]

recovered in archaeological sites. Evidence from well preserved sites, such as caves and rockshelters, suggest that this squash was grown both for use as containers and for the edible seeds.

EVIDENCE FOR PLANT DOMESTICATION

Evidence for domestication (plants so genetically changed that they need human help to survive) is difficult for researchers to determine for such ancient plants. Nonetheless, paleoethnobotanists (specialists who study plant remains from archaeological sites) can gain clues by studying charred seeds from archaeological soils as well as intact prehistoric plant bunches and baskets containing preserved seeds from the dry interiors of caves. Direct evidence of ingestion of the Eastern Agricultural Complex is also detectable in the preserved human coprolites (dried and

preserved feces) recovered in the deep cave systems of Kentucky and Tennessee.

Paleoethnobotanists detect changes indicating domestication of the Eastern Agricultural Complex plants by closely examining the size and shape of seed specimens as well as microscopic changes in the thickness of the outer protective seed coat. Squash domestication is determined by modifications in the rind (thickness and cell structure). For example, both sumpweed and sunflower reveal increasing seed size (especially length) over time, until archaeological recovered culturally modified specimens two to three times the size of their wild cousins. Goosefoot examples from archaeological sites, represented by tiny round black seeds the size of poppy seeds, reveal that the hard outer seed coat progressively becomes thinner and thinner, thus allowing for early germination and resulting in larger amounts of edible carbohydrates.

Erect knotweed, although not showing changes initially, does begin to show archaeological traces of a larger, thin seed-coated variety in sites dating to around 1,400 years ago. Finally, both maygrass and little barley tend to be found in archaeological sites outside their natural growth range today; maygrass, for example, is typically not found north of southern Kentucky under natural conditions, but it was fairly prominent in Ohio and Illinois sites 2,000 years ago. One final piece to the puzzle is that during time periods when these plants were grown as crops, it is not uncommon to find thousands of charred seeds of all five species, along with burned squash rind, in the soils from archaeological trashpits and earthovens—hence the use of the term "complex."

WHEN, WHERE, AND HOW THESE PLANTS BECAME DOMESTICATED

The first evidence for the beginning cultivation of the Eastern Agricultural Complex species appears in archaeological sites that date to around 4,000 to 5,000 years ago in the river valleys and rockshelters within Arkansas, Missouri, Tennessee, Kentucky, Illinois, and surrounding areas. The first plants that appear to have been grown include squash and sunflower (around 4,500 years ago), rapidly followed by the other Eastern Agricultural Complex members. Goosefoot, for example, has been recovered from a Kentucky rockshelter with evidence of its use as a garden plant dating to around 3,500 years ago, and sumpweed may have been domesticated around 4,400 years ago. Tobacco was a later addition found in a handful of sites beginning around 1,800 years ago. The prehistoric squash grown in ancient gardens, based on new archaeological and genetic evidence, seems to be derived from a small wild form of a native Ozark or a Texan squash and reveals domestication as early as 5,000 years ago.

Researchers still do not yet understand the process that led to such a dramatic shift in how ancient populations used plants or how they eventually came to craft a "human-created" environment (the garden plot). The evidence suggest that this process began thousands of years before we can actually see genetic changes in the Eastern Agricultural Complex seeds—probably around 6,000 to 8,000 years ago, when the climate was slightly warmer than today (called the Hypsithermal period). Humans during this time were attracted to the rich floodplain environments of the interior rivers, such as the Mississippi and Illinois rivers. It is in such environments that the wild, weedy ancestors of the later crops would have grown. For example, the scoured edges of floodplains is exactly the preferred habitat for sumpweed, and the wild small hard-shelled squashes grow along riverbanks, depending upon the rivers to transport their floating buoyant fruits (the hard "gourds"). Apparently, the close proximity of prehistoric humans with these plants, in a generally warmer and drier environment impacted by the Hypsithermal, led to people using these plants as a food source. This in turn set the stage for the changes that we later see as signs of genetic

changes indicative of true domestication and cultivation of the plants as crops.

Around 3,000 years ago in a few regions (such as Illinois, Ohio, and Kentucky) the Eastern Agricultural Complex species appear to be grown together in small garden plots as a minor component to the peoples' diet. In later Hopewell (so-called mound builder) sites around 2,000 years ago, especially in Ohio and Illinois, the complex appears to be an important component of the diet and habits of these remarkable populations. A handful of sites of this time period reveal that maize may have been grown in small amounts as a ceremonial plant (skeletal analysis indicates it was not part of their diet, however). A few specimens of native tobacco have been found in only a small number of Hopewell sites in Tennessee, Illinois, and Ohio. Tobacco had undoubtedly been grown for ritual purposes (this form of tobacco is extremely powerful in the impact of its nicotine and may have had interesting psychogenic properties).

CHARACTERISTICS OF EARLY GARDENS

Evidence from archaeological sites suggests that the Eastern Agricultural Complex reached its maximum importance in the diet and gardening of prehistoric populations from about 1,000 to 2,000 years ago (from approximately AD 100 to 800). It is not uncommon in sites of this time period to find thousands of charred seeds of most if not all of the five complex cultigens, along with squash rind and squash seeds. Many of the prehistoric settlements are located in areas that would have once supported a dense, rich hardwood forest. Thus, small patches of open space must have been created in these forests for use as garden plots. Most likely the gardens were placed very close to their settlements since hungry hordes of forest animals, such as raccoons and deer, could easily have devoured an unguarded plot.

Given the growth characteristics of the plants, the crops must have been planted together in the space in such a way to maximize the light and use of the soil nutrients. Perhaps the tall and bushy goosefoot and sunflower plants were located in the "back" of gardens so as to not cast a shadow on smaller plants—squashes, given their tendency to vine, could have been planted in and among the taller crops. Researchers do not know how long a single garden could have been used before the crops began to deplete the soil nutrients, but eventually new gardens had to be cleared in the surrounding forests. That this activity took place is supported by the discovery of the nuts and seeds of wild plants that probably re-colonized abandoned gardens. For example, hazelnut, raspberry, sumac, and elderberry specimens are found in quantities in sites from this time period that indicate they were heavily collected by the prehistoric populations. All of these plants are found today growing at the edges of forests and in clearings because they need more sunlight than could be found in undisturbed forests. Thus, if we went back in time some 2,000 years ago we would probably see small settlements within forests located next to an active garden and surrounded by recently abandoned gardens in different stages of re-growth. Within those abandoned gardens would have been shrubby hazelnut, raspberry thickets, and other fruit and berry plants that afforded easy picking for the human populations (and undoubtedly formed a temptation for deer and other animals thus perhaps increasing hunting success as well).

THE EMERGENCE OF MAIZE AGRICULTURE

Intriguingly, by AD 800 maize appears to begin to replace most of the Eastern Agricultural Complex crops. Some researchers suggest that it took a long period of time for maize to adapt to more northern climates, and other archaeologists note that perhaps maize could produce greater food yields for a growing population. By a thousand years ago beans (*Phaseolus vulgaris*) and new squash/pumpkin varieties enter eastern North America from the southwest and Mexico, and the classic "Three Sisters" (maize, beans, and squash) supplant the Eastern Agricultural Complex crops. In some regions, such as Illinois, some members of the starchy Eastern Agricultural Complex (such as goosefoot) may have been grown as a minor crop into the historic Contact period, while in other areas (such as Ohio) it appears that maize agriculture totally replaced the high-carbohydrate members of the complex.

A REMARKABLE STORY

The Eastern Agricultural Complex is the story of a rarity in the archaeological world—the emergence of a completely independently created food supply of domesticated plants. These domesticated plants are also unique in having their origins in the natural plant communities of the forested valleys of the interior rivers and floodplains of the Midwest. Most of the major food crops today, such as wheat, barley, oats, and maize, seem to derive from wild ancestors in more arid and open grasslands, whether in the New or the Old World. Finally, agriculture in eastern North America, including the Midwest, is also a story of food plants imported from other regions (maize and beans) eventually replacing a once thriving and successful local crop and gardening system in the interior Midwest. Archaeologists are only now beginning to truly explore the details of this narrative that unfolded over several thousand years.

Further Reading: Gremillion, Kristen J., ed., *People, Plants, and Landscapes: Studies in Paleoethnobotany* (Tuscaloosa: University of Alabama Press, 1997); Minnis, Paul E., ed., *People and Plants in Ancient Eastern North America* (Washington, DC: Smithsonian Books, 2003); Scarry, Margaret C., ed., *Foraging and Farming in the Eastern Woodlands* (Gainesville: University of Florida Press, 1993); Smith, Bruce D., *Rivers of Change: Essays on Early Agriculture in Eastern North America* (Washington, DC: Smithsonian Institution Press, 1992).

DeeAnne Wymer

ANCIENT EARTHEN ARCHITECTURE IN THE MIDWEST

When most people think about the original inhabitants of the Midwest, mounds immediately come to mind. Perhaps that is because mounds are such an obvious part of local landscapes and so many attractive artifacts have been found in them. Usually made of earth, but also of stone, they are widely but unevenly distributed across the Midwest. Mounds were constructed over a long period—mostly between 2,500 and 500 years ago—by Native American peoples who led very different ways of life and used the piles of earth or stone for correspondingly diverse purposes. In some places, earthen embankments (or earthworks) or, more rarely, stone walls were built as well.

Mounds come in various shapes and sizes. Most are circular or oval piles of earth with gently to steeply sloping sides and rounded tops. However, in some places they commonly take the form of long ridges, truncated pyramids with flat tops, or animal shapes. Earthworks include both irregular enclosures and various geometric forms. Some encompass less than an acre, whereas others are much larger, ranging up to a few dozen or more acres. Occasionally rocks were used as the primary construction material for mounds and platforms, as well as for small mortuary structures.

Mounds and earthworks were built by hand, one basketful at a time, typically of nearby dirt but also of specially selected colorful earth carried some distance to the construction site. Often soil was scraped from the ground immediately around a mound, as shown by dark organic-stained soil and large amounts of habitation-related debris. In some places large, deep holes (or borrow pits) were dug to get the necessary earth, with the largest such pits found at Cahokia in Illinois. Elsewhere, such as at the Great Circle at Newark in Ohio, soil was removed from ditches alongside the embankments, accentuating the visual impact of earthen ridges.

One reason so much is known about mounds is that they have long attracted the attention of archaeologists and the public alike. Mounds are obvious places to excavate, and they tend to yield more fine artifacts than do neighboring villages. More important, mounds and their contents have the potential to contribute significantly to our understanding of past societies. The differential treatment of the dead tells us much about relations among people with respect to age, sex, social group affiliation, and status within their communities. Skeletons provide information on the demographic structure of past populations, the health of these people, and their dietary intake. Buildings erected on some mounds—used for special purposes or as residences of high-ranking individuals—provide clues about the ritualistic, social, and political dimensions of life in the past.

MOUNDS

It is not known for certain when mound building began in the Midwest. That is because the earliest known mounds were little more than minor, perhaps even unintentional, modifications of natural knolls used for burial purposes. The first large mounds appeared in the second half of the first millennium BC. Mounds became more widely distributed, in some places quite common, around 2,000 years ago. That was also when many earthworks were being constructed, mostly in southern Ohio. Mounds continued to be an important feature of cultural landscapes from that point up to the historic period. Construction of by far the biggest of them all, Monks Mound at Cahokia, took place for the most part from the eleventh to the thirteenth centuries AD.

Equivocal signs of mound building date to as early as late Middle Archaic times (ca. 4500–3000 BC) in western Illinois. By the Late Archaic (ca. 3000 BC to the early first millennium BC), mounds were present in this area and in neighboring Missouri. These mounds, associated with burials, were low and barely modified existing topography, often situated on hilltops. Some mounds were purposeful mortuary-related constructions, as indicated by layers of rock laid down with human bones. Others might not have been intentional at all, the result of digging closely spaced graves on natural knolls and moving loose earth around in the process.

More mounds date to the Early Woodland period (spanning much of the first millennium BC), including the often impressive Adena mounds dating after about 500 BC in the middle Ohio River valley. Mounds classified as Adena are typically poorly dated, although some are known to have been built as late as the subsequent Middle Woodland period.

In central Kentucky, many Adena mounds occur on high ground in rolling countryside, as if scattered communities were intent on making an indelible mark on the landscape, presumably to indicate rights of access to the surrounding area. In many cases these mounds were built where a large wooden structure, sometimes many of them, once stood. The structures were not ordinary dwellings—they were much too large for that, and habitation-related debris is sparse—although their precise function is unknown. Thus, Adena mounds often were built in prominent spots where ritually

significant activities other than mound construction also took place.

Adena mound building usually took place in stages, with much of the earth added in the construction of new graves. These graves took various forms, but were typically large log-lined tombs for one or more people and were surrounded by low earthen embankments added to the existing mound. At Robbins Mound in Kentucky, layers of soil were periodically deposited to cover earlier construction episodes and associated graves. The result was a somewhat smoother surface on a mound with an otherwise irregular shape from earlier grave construction and a slumping of soil over old log tombs. Thus, this mound is best envisioned as a sequence of cemeteries, each sealed by a cap to prepare the way for more burials. The people interred in the Adena mounds represent but a small fraction of the deaths of those who would have lived nearby, and they may have been among the most important individuals in their communities in view of the elaborate tombs and the fine artifacts they contained.

By Middle Woodland times (ca. 200 BC–AD 400), mounds containing burials and impressive artifacts had become widespread. There was considerable variation within and between sites in the kinds of mortuary facilities present, how bodies were handled, and the artifacts placed with them. Nonetheless, regional patterning is detectable in common funerary procedures, with the two best-known mortuary practices occurring in Ohio and Illinois.

In southern Ohio, mounds often cover wooden structures consisting of one or more rooms that served as tombs. Within these structures were bodies treated in different ways—as simple inhumations, bundles of disarticulated bones, or cremations. Many artifacts, including those fashioned from copper, marine shell, and obsidian from distant sources, were placed with the dead or deposited as separate hoards. These structures were the scene of activities that went far beyond those needed for the simple disposal of bodies. Although it is not clear what the ceremonies were or who participated in them, they involved amassing great numbers of objects and disposing of them with the dead and as part of other ritualistically significant events.

In western Illinois along the Illinois River and the adjacent Mississippi valley, mounds often encompassed a centrally located and large log-lined tomb surrounded by simple inhumations. The central tombs had earthen walls, often made by piling soil around them, and were lined with logs. They typically held multiple individuals, represented by intact skeletons or bundles of bones, as well as fancy artifacts, sometimes large numbers of them. Central tombs were commonly used for lengthy periods, with earlier remains removed or stacked to one side to make room for new bodies. Many of these mounds were grouped together on hilltops overlooking adjacent river floodplains. Such prominent locations, which provided panoramic views of the surrounding countryside, are consistent with the idea of mounds marking rights of access to particular segments of resource-rich valleys.

Although the overwhelming majority of Middle Woodland mounds were used for burial, not all were used for that purpose. The flat-topped Capitolium at Marietta in Ohio, for example, was a platform upon which ceremonies that involved lighting fires took place.

During Late Woodland times (ca. AD 400–1000), burial mounds were built in many places, such as along the Illinois River, but they did not contain the impressive mortuary features and artifacts found in somewhat earlier mounds. Late Woodland burial mounds often grew through accretion as new burials—intact bodies or bone bundles, typically lacking the numerous and fine grave goods used earlier—were added. The eventual result was a circular to linear, but generally low, pile of earth.

Stone platforms and mounds, sometimes encompassing small mortuary-related structures with walls composed of loosely piled slabs, were also built in Late Woodland times. These mortuary-related constructions are best known in Missouri and adjacent west central Illinois, but they occur elsewhere as well.

Of all the mounds of this period, the ones that have received the most public attention are the so-called effigy mounds of Wisconsin and adjacent states that date from the eighth to the twelfth centuries. The term "effigy mound" comes from the piles of earth that take the shapes of real or mythical animals, with birds being a commonly occurring and easily recognized form. Many of them, however, are simply low domes or long ridges. Shallow depressions conforming to mound outlines, called intaglios, also occur. The effigy mounds tend not to contain very much, although burials are often located near the "animal's" heart. They tend to occur in groups of mixed shapes, often on locally high spots. Considering the distinctive mound shapes, their existence in groups in prominent locations, and the paucity of materials in them, the mounds probably served to signify various social groupings, perhaps marking places where they periodically met.

Mound building continued in many parts of the Midwest through the rest of the prehistoric period. Many of these mounds are classified as Mississippian (in the Midwest, mostly dating to ca. AD 1000–1400). Although Mississippian mounds were still used for burial purposes, many took on a different function, and their shape changed accordingly. These mounds included platforms with rectangular bases that supported wooden buildings. The buildings included residences for the most important people, charnel structures to hold the bones of illustrious ancestors, and other ritually and socially significant architecture, including sweat lodges at Cahokia.

Mississippian mounds also differ from those of earlier times in that many were incorporated as central elements of the layouts of principal settlements. Mounds commonly bordered centrally located open areas, or plazas, that were the focus of the surrounding community's attention. Chiefs in the most important settlements were literally elevated above all other members of their societies, and the charnel structures were reminders of their descent from prominent lineages with lengthy histories. Most major Mississippian settlements had only a few such mounds, perhaps only one. The site with by far the most mounds—over 100 of them—is Cahokia. It includes Monks Mound, which, at 100 feet, towered over everything else. In fact, more than half of the roughly 1,540,000 cubic yards of earth used in mound construction at Cahokia was put into this enormous mound.

EMBANKMENTS AND DITCHES

Earthworks of various shapes and sizes are much less common than mounds, and they are more restricted in their temporal and geographic distributions. The earliest earthworks are associated with Adena sites in the middle Ohio River valley, mostly in Kentucky and Ohio. The best known are small circular embankments, often accompanied by shallow ditches. A single gap was typically left in the embankment through which one could enter the circle. Mt. Horeb, on a hill in the rolling countryside of central Kentucky, is a fine example of such an earthwork. Excavations revealed a row of closely spaced soil stains where vertical posts were once located immediately inside the embankment and ditch. The interiors of many of these small circular earthworks are flat, and nothing visible has survived to the present day. Some earthworks, however, encircle mounds. These mounds are often small and take up only part of the enclosed area, although others, such as the Conus at Marietta, essentially fill the entire circle.

During Middle Woodland times, most earthworks were built in southern Ohio, but they occur elsewhere as well. They include irregular enclosures and take various geometric forms, most notably squares, circles, octagons, and parallel lines. Hilltops are occasionally surrounded by embankments, such as at Fort Ancient. These particular enclosures can be quite large with irregular outlines that conform closely to local topography. Geometric earthworks are also irregularly distributed. For example, many geometric enclosures, including Mound City, were located along the Scioto River in the vicinity of Chillicothe, Ohio. Here, as in other places, the great majority of the enclosures recorded in the nineteenth century have since disappeared as a result of modern land use.

Many enclosure walls contained gaps, sometimes plugged by small mounds. Other symbolically important features were located in the openings as well, such as the rock pavements and ponds identified at Fort Ancient. Various ritually and socially significant activities took place within the enclosures, the most obvious of which were funerary proceedings related to the structures and mounds. Other activities, however, also occurred, as indicated by several wooden buildings at Seip in Ohio that yielded fragments of nonlocal raw materials used to produce artifacts for mortuary and other ceremonial purposes. Thus, the embankments and ditches defined spaces used for special ceremonies, including but not limited to burials.

Walls of stone surround hilltops in a few places in southern Illinois and into Kentucky. They are generally poorly dated, although some are thought to be Middle Woodland and others Late Woodland. Dating these walls is a problem because their relationship to other, nearby cultural deposits, when such materials can be located, is typically unclear. There are also late prehistoric earthworks in the Great Lakes area. Little is known about them, although they too probably were mostly of ritual significance.

The vast majority of enclosures, regardless of when they were constructed or where they were located, were not defensive works, as is apparent from their size and the arrangement of ditches and embankments. Many were so large that it would have been impossible for a local population to fully man them. The arrangement of many ditches and embankments makes no sense if the intent was to erect a formidable defensive barrier. Gaps in some earthworks, such as those at Fort Ancient, are numerous enough that they would have made the walls unsuitable for military purposes.

The most notable exceptions are the earthen embankments around a few Mississippian towns, most notably Angel in Indiana and Aztalan in Wisconsin. These embankments, accompanied by stout wooden palisades with bastions, were clearly defensive in nature. For these communities, the threat posed by enemy warriors was sufficient to necessitate the construction of carefully laid out and strongly reinforced walls. Mississippian settlements encircled by embankments are unusual in the Midwest; most sites with walls had only wooden palisades, with no embankments or ditches.

ADVANTAGES OF EARTHEN MONUMENTS

One might well ask why so many groups built mounds over such a long period for quite different purposes. One reason has to be that mounds can create a strong impression in those who view them. Indeed, mounds continue to impress us today, despite the fact that their symbolic significance for the most part has been lost.

Mounds and earthworks also had other distinct advantages from the perspective of the builders. They could be made from material readily at hand, and only ordinary digging tools and baskets were required. It took no special skill to erect an imposing monument; anyone who could carry a basketful of earth could help. Mounds were cheap to build

in terms of labor costs, as indicated by digging and load-carrying estimates from experimental work and historical accounts. With several exceptions—most notably the geometric earthworks and effigy mounds—the final shape and dimensions of a particular form did not have to be determined at the outset. Mounds in particular could be used throughout the period during which they were constructed, with new stages added one after another. Moreover, how a mound was used could vary over time as the pile of earth grew and its shape changed.

Thus, it is by no means surprising that mounds were a critical part of the cultural landscape in so many places for such a long period of time. The earthworks were likewise important components of how people visualized and interacted with their surroundings. The enclosures delineated places that had great symbolic significance, though today we can identify only a few of the events that took place in and around them.

An Enduring Legacy

Individually and collectively, the mounds and earthworks that capture our attention encourage us to learn more about the many achievements of the Native Americans who built and used them for so many different purposes. Despite two centuries of destruction from urban development and agricultural practices, many of the mounds and earthworks remain prominent features of local landscapes and sources of community pride. They can still be seen as the centerpieces of the rural and city parks where these irreplaceable cultural resources are preserved for future generations to enjoy.

Further Reading: Abrams, Elliott M., and Ann Corinne Freter, eds., *The Emergence of the Moundbuilders* (Athens: Ohio University Press, 2005); Birmingham, Robert A., and Leslie E. Eisenberg, *Indian Mounds of Wisconsin* (Madison: University of Wisconsin Press, 2000); Brown, James A., "The Search for Rank in Prehistoric Burials," in *The Archaeology of Death*, edited by Robert Chapman, Ian Kinnes, and Klavs Randsborg (Cambridge: Cambridge University Press, 1981), 25–37; Fowler, Melvin L., *The Cahokia Atlas*, rev. ed. (Urbana: University of Illinois, Illinois Transportation Archaeological Research Program, 2003); Goldstein, Lynne G., "Landscapes and Mortuary Practices: A Case for Regional Perspectives," in *Regional Approaches to Mortuary Analysis*, edited by Lane A. Beck (New York: Plenum Press, 1996), 101–121; Mainfort, Robert C., and Lynne P. Sullivan, eds., *Ancient Earthen Enclosures of the Eastern Woodlands* (Gainesville: University Press of Florida, 1998); Milner, George R., *The Moundbuilders* (London: Thames and Hudson, 2004); Pacheco, Paul J., ed., *A View from the Core: A Synthesis of Ohio Hopewell Archaeology* (Columbus: Ohio Archaeological Council, 1996); Railey, Jimmy A., "Woodland Cultivators," in *Kentucky Archaeology*, edited by R. Barry Lewis (Lexington: University of Kentucky Press, 1966), 79–125.

George R. Milner

THE ORIGIN, ORGANIZATION, AND DEMISE
OF MIDWEST CHIEFDOMS

Between about AD 1000 and 1450, in what archaeologists term the Mississippian period, American Indians living in the Midwest developed new, complex social and political systems. These Mississippian societies differed from earlier groups because they had a political hierarchy with chiefs organizing several communities in an area rather than having people living in politically independent villages. There were social rankings and status differences between individuals in these chiefdoms such that higher social status was often inherited from one's kin group, in addition to being affected by individual skills and accomplishments. Although there was a range in scale, centralization, and complexity among the Mississippian chiefdoms in the Midwest during the Mississippian period, these societies allocated some centralization of authority in social and political elites. People were attracted to the places where these leaders lived because they were locations of community rituals and ceremonies, of feasts, and of mound building.

Today, the archaeological sites that remain as ruins of these chiefdom centers include Cahokia, East St. Louis, St. Louis, Wickliffe, Lilbourn, and Towosaghy in the central Mississippi River valley, Kincaid and Angel in the lower Ohio River valley, Larson in the Illinois River valley, and Aztalan in southeastern Wisconsin. Cahokia, located in a broad expanse of Mississippi River floodplain on the Illinois side of the river (opposite the city of St. Louis), was the largest of them all. With over 100 earthen mounds and associated settlement covering an area of some 5 square miles, Cahokia is unusual in that it developed earlier and became far larger than other Mississippian mound centers in the Midwest and Southeast. Because of its size and perceived influence, Cahokia has also dominated the archaeological literature on chiefdoms in this region, but it was not necessarily typical of Midwestern or Southeastern chiefdoms.

These Midwestern chiefdoms shared a number of features during the Mississippian period, such as the use of pottery tempered with crushed mussel shell and formed into a variety of vessel shapes, houses built to a rectangular floor plan and often with wall posts set into foundation trenches, flat-topped earthen mounds that supported buildings used as residences or temples, and domesticated crops of corn and squash farmed in river floodplain settings. Other characteristics indicative of chiefdom political organization or ranked social status, including settlements of different sizes and special burial treatment beyond age and gender distinctions, are more variable and often subject to dispute by specialists. Beyond the Mississippian chiefdoms to the northeast of the Ohio River, north of southern Wisconsin, and northwest of the Mississippi-Ohio-Missouri river confluence region were located Midwestern groups that archaeologists have termed Late Woodland, Fort Ancient, and

Oneota. These societies were contemporaneous with the Mississippian chiefdoms and showed some similarities in diets, foodways, material culture, and settlements, but the groups were smaller in scale and lacked the indications of hereditary chiefs and political hierarchies. Mississippian chiefdoms also developed in the Mississippi River valley and across the interior Southeast, and related Caddo societies were centered in and around the Red River valley.

Archaeologists working in the Midwest are asking key research questions, such as how are maize agriculture, population density, settled community life, and political organization interrelated in the societies that are termed Late Woodland, Oneota, Fort Ancient, and Mississippian? Other issues revolve around how neighboring societies interacted with one another at this time; specifically, how did migration, trade and exchange, and warfare affect cultural patterns across this region? Of great interest is why certain areas, including many of those where chiefdoms had once been located, were abandoned after AD 1450. Finally, there is concern with tracing relationships between the pre-contact American Indian societies and the historic period tribes that inhabited this area.

ORIGINS AND ORGANIZATION
OF MIDWESTERN CHIEFDOMS

Mississippian period chiefdoms in the Midwest developed a settled village way of life structured around farming, hunting, and fishing, all of which had deep roots in this region. Long before the emergence of these chiefdoms, the mid-continent had been an important center for the independent development of agriculture, ever since Native Americans began to domesticate a variety of plants for food here during the Late Archaic period (ca. 3000–1000 BC). Oily and starchy seeded plants such as sunflower, sumpweed, squash, gourd, and chenopod were cultivated for food (and tobacco was grown as a nonfood crop) by farmers from the Woodland period (1000 BC–AD 1000). Maize or corn, a starchy seeded plant food first domesticated in highland Mexico and later grown in the American Southwest, shows up rarely in Woodland period contexts in the Midwest and Southeast. Its transformation from an occasional (and perhaps ceremonial) food item to a staple crop at the beginning of the Mississippian period is one of the dramatic changes that occurred in these communities between AD 800 and 1000. The Mississippian period mound centers were typically located in river floodplain settings, where the cultivation of corn and native seeds was both feasible and productive. While growing a storable staple food crop was important to supporting large Mississippian period populations, these people also relied on a diverse array of seed crops, also grown in the floodplain soils, as well as other sources of food that included fish from floodplain lakes and rivers and deer and nuts that were plentiful in the uplands.

A reliable mix of plant and animal foods as well as knowledge of the local environment to predict their availability enabled American Indian communities to live a settled lifestyle during some times and places in the Archaic and Woodland periods. The construction of earthen mounds—important locations for rituals, mortuary ceremonies, and community identity—was one indication of the ways that these people altered their local landscapes, and mounds have considerable antiquity in the Midwest. But if villages occupied year-round and mound buildings were found earlier in this region, what was different about the Mississippian period communities? One new aspect was that the functions of mounds changed, with mounds used as earthen platforms to elevate important buildings, in addition to their use as mortuaries and as locations for important rituals. In addition, community and settlement patterns changed. In the American Bottom region of the central Mississippi River valley, people either moved away from their villages to larger towns/mound centers like Cahokia or dispersed to occupy small scattered "rural" farmsteads early in the Mississippian period. There were different kinds and sizes of settlements across the area. Mississippian sites in western Kentucky and the bootheel of Missouri were nucleated towns with mounds, plazas, and residences, often surrounded by fortification walls. Populations were increasing, and the social climate sometimes included competition and conflict.

The view that Mississippian culture was influenced by or derived from Mesoamerican societies far to the south in Mexico and Central America has been raised repeatedly. Some scholars look at Mississippian art or the use of mounds as building platforms arranged around open plazas and see similarities with Mesoamerican cultural patterns. Certainly maize and later beans were domesticated crops first found in Mesoamerica that eventually found their way to eastern North America, presumably by way of the Southwest. However, we do not find artifacts from the central Mississippi River valley in Mesoamerica or vice versa. The consensus view is that the Mississippian chiefdoms were indigenous developments in the Midwest and Southeast, and that similarities can be traced to common cultural roots of Indians across the Americas in the distant past, rather than to direct contacts.

Researchers once interpreted the appearance of so-called Mississippian traits in the Midwest as a migration or spread of people from the central Mississippi River valley at about AD 1000. They expanded in territory, dominating and conquering the local Woodland groups as they moved. Alternatively, outlying Mississippian mound centers such as Aztalan in southeastern Wisconsin were viewed as trading outposts or colonies from Cahokia. More recent interpretations have scaled back the reach or control of the Cahokia polity and its chiefs. Involvement in exchange relations did not necessarily

mean large-scale provisioning of a center, and emulation of ceremonies and material aspects of culture did not necessarily involve coercive control of an outlying region. Changes were occurring across the region after AD 1000, and populations were affected by developments around them as well as by more distant ones.

The interactions between neighboring societies took the form of warfare and alliances, trade, and exchange of information. These kinds of interactions are certainly found before the Mississippian period, but become a hallmark of these late prehistoric Midwestern chiefdoms. The exchange of utilitarian goods such as chipped-stone hoe blades and pottery vessels increased during this time, as did prestige goods made of marine shell, copper, and exotic stone. The social relationships between people and groups, both dependencies within chiefdoms and alliances between neighboring groups, could be seen in material form in exchanges of food and gifts.

The objects of shell, copper, stone, and pottery were sometimes elaborately decorated with motifs and symbols that hint at the shared ideology among the Native Americans living in the Midwest during this period. Recent scholarly research has interpreted layers of meaning in the art and iconography of the Midwestern Mississippian groups, in part through reference to historic period beliefs and traditional stories from Dhegiha-Siouan speakers such as the Osage, Quapaw, and Omaha and from Chiwere-Siouan and Winnebago speakers such as the Iowa, Missouri, and Ho-Chunk. The iconography in these objects is thought to refer to a world or cosmos that included both the natural and the supernatural, with figures portraying not ordinary people but mythic characters such as Morning Star/Red Horn/Birdman, Old Woman/Corn Mother, and Underwater Serpent-Panther/Piasa. All such symbols, in their various forms, were heavy with death, life, renewal, and fertility themes. This work points to the importance of Cahokia artists in the production of objects that were used locally and that circulated well beyond the region as objects of power, prestige, and display in ceremonial contexts. Often they were maintained as heirlooms. Eventually, many of these objects became incorporated into elite burial contexts.

DEMISE OF THE CHIEFDOMS IN THE MIDWEST

The chiefdoms in the Midwest, including the major center of Cahokia, declined prior to the contacts with Europeans. This is in contrast to Mississippian period chiefdoms in the Southeast, some of which were visited by the mid-sixteenth-century Spanish expedition led by Hernando de Soto. Since the demise of the Midwestern chiefdom polities pre-dated European contact, it is necessary to look at the other influences, conditions, and causes for the decline. One possibility is that subtle climate changes after AD 1400 altered growing conditions and made maize farming riskier in some areas of the Midwest. Alternatively, climate and vegetation changes may also have increased the availability of bison herds and drawn people westward toward the plains. Ecological degradation has been suggested, with large centralized populations in danger of over-using resources such as fertile soils, wood, and game. Political factors may have been to blame. A loss of confidence in the ruling elite or increasing demands for food and labor may have caused people to move away from mound centers, which may then have increasingly been used for mortuary and ceremonial functions rather than for residence.

The collapse of Cahokia is generally thought to have occurred by AD 1350, but it was preceded by a concentration of the elite in the ceremonial core of the mound center while ordinary residents began to move away to the surrounding uplands. During the thirteenth century, much of the monumental construction at Cahokia involved work on the bastioned palisade wall that encircled the central mounds and plaza complex, setting it off from the main residential areas of the community as well as signaling greater expectation of attacks. Interactions—warfare, alliances, and trade—with outside groups continued. Chiefly elites became more involved in the crafting of elaborate and ideologically laden goods of engraved shell and repoussé copper, most of which were exchanged away from Cahokia, displayed and circulated and heirloomed, and later deposited in elite mortuary contexts at Southeastern mound centers.

However, the collapse of the elite-focused political hierarchy and decentralization of population did not mean a collapse of culture or depopulation in many areas. Instead, Native American communities may have returned to the essentially egalitarian kin-based social and political structures with villages like those seen in earlier periods. The more centralized ranked chiefdom polities were relatively unstable and had individual histories of florescence and failure that occurred within the span of a few hundred years. Oneota communities to the north and west of the Mississippi River valley and Fort Ancient communities to the east in the Ohio Valley were more egalitarian societies with local village control, and these were more lasting sociopolitical structures in the Midwest region. These Oneota groups, contemporaneous with Mississippians but continuing after the decline in mound centers, increased hunting of bison in addition to their practice of agriculture. Some interaction continued, with ideas and goods moving between communities and regions as before. The

motifs that Oneota groups used to decorate their pottery were reminiscent of Mississippian designs, and stylistic similarities cover a broad region.

Who were the descendants of the people in these Midwestern chiefdoms? It is difficult to link the historic Indian populations who had known linguistic and cultural patterns with the more ancient precursors, including the Mississippian chiefdoms, known only from archaeology. However, there is support for the idea that central Mississippi River valley chiefdoms, including Cahokia, were related to Dhegiha-Siouan speakers or possibly to Chiwere-Siouan and Winnebago speakers. Comparisons and contrasts between Siouan cultural traditions and those of Muskogean speakers (Creek, Alabama, Choctaw, Chickasaw) and Caddoan speakers (Caddo), descendants of some of the Southeastern chiefdoms, is currently an active aspect of anthropological research.

Further Reading: Butler, Brian M., and Paul D. Welch, eds., *Leadership and Polity in Mississippian Society*, Center for Archaeological Investigations Occasional Paper No. 33 (Carbondale: Southern Illinois University, 2006); Emerson, Thomas E., and R. Barry Lewis, eds., *Cahokia and the Hinterlands: Middle Mississippian Cultures of the Midwest* (Urbana: University of Illinois Press and Illinois Historic Preservation Agency, 1991); Lewis, R. Barry, and Charles Stout, eds., *Mississippian Towns and Sacred Spaces: Searching for an Architectural Grammar* (Tuscaloosa: University of Alabama Press, 1998); Milner, George R., *The Cahokia Chiefdom* (Washington, DC: Smithsonian Institution Press, 1998); National Park Service, U.S. Department of the Interior, Archeology Program, *Ancient Architects of the Mississippi*, http://www.cr.nps.gov/archeology/feature/feature.htm (2007); Schroeder, Sissel, "Current Research on Late Precontact Societies of the Midcontinental United States," *Journal of Archaeological Research* 12(4) (2004): 311–372; Townsend, Richard F., ed., *Hero, Hawk, and Open Hand: American Indian Art of the Ancient Midwest and South* (New Haven, CT: Art Institute of Chicago and Yale University Press, 2004); Trubitt, Mary Beth D., "Mound Building and Prestige Goods Exchange: Changing Strategies in the Cahokia Chiefdom," *American Antiquity* 65(4) (2000): 669–690; University of Texas at Austin, College of Liberal Arts, *Texas beyond History: Caddo Fundamentals, Mississippian World*, http://www.texasbeyondhistory.net/tejas/fundamentals/miss.html (2003).

Mary Beth Trubitt

EUROPEAN EXPLORATION AND EARLY SETTLEMENTS

HISTORICAL OVERVIEW

The first Europeans to explore and inhabit the Midwest were the French in the early seventeenth century. Claims that the Norse visited the area earlier remain unsubstantiated. French exploration of the North American interior was staged from

the St. Lawrence River valley in an effort to expand the fur trade and locate a western passage to the Far East. Jesuit Father Jacques Marquette and Louis Jolliet descended the Mississippi River to the mouth of the Arkansas River in 1673, and less than a decade later (1682) René-Robert Cavelier

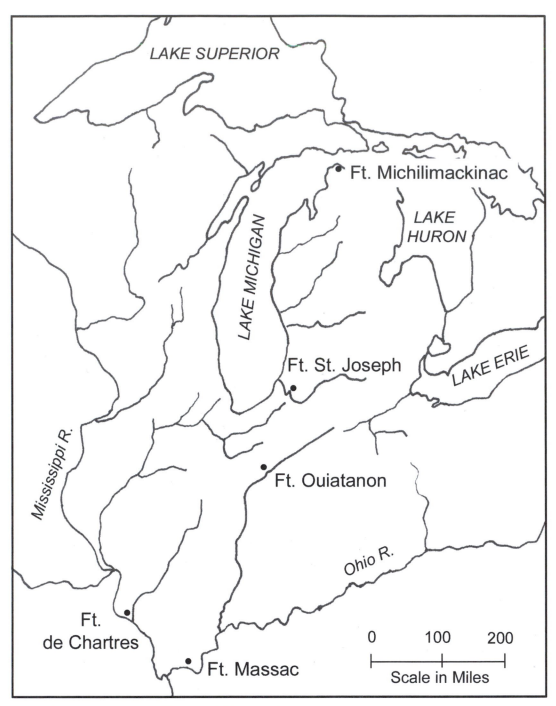

A map of the region showing major sites.   [Michael S. Nassaney]

sieur de La Salle continued to the Gulf of Mexico claiming the entire Mississippi watershed for the French Crown. After 1700 French policy was oriented toward the construction of fortifications along the many waterways that served as the arteries of this riverine empire. New France consisted of a series of linked settlements scattered in a broad arc from the North Atlantic maritime region (Acadia), down the St. Lawrence River valley to the Great Lakes (known as the *pays d'en haut* or Upper Country), into the Illinois Country to the lower Mississippi Valley. Major settlements in the Midwest, which included the Illinois Country and the western Great Lakes, consisted of missions, forts, and agricultural villages that reflected the religious, military, and commercial goals of the empire. At many of these sites, archaeologists have

The commemorative monument for French explorer Robert La Salle. [Michael S. Nassaney]

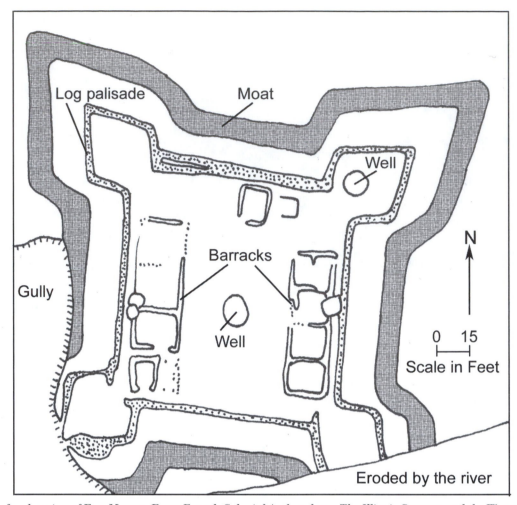

A line drawing of a plan view of Fort Massac. From *French Colonial Archaeology: The Illinois Country and the Western Great Lakes*. Copyright © 1991 by the Board of Trustees of the University of Illinois. Used with permission of the University of Illinois Press.

identified material evidence of the early explorers and settlers that provides insights into their activities and daily lives.

Although the French claimed an enormous territory that greatly exceeded that of the English, they had a much smaller population that remained dispersed. In an effort to contain the English along the Eastern Seaboard, the French allied themselves with the Native occupants of the region by creating mutually beneficial exchange relationships that were often reinforced through intermarriage. Priests, small contingents of soldiers, voyageurs (fur traders), habitants (farmers), and their households, which often included Indians and slaves, established settlements in what would become Michigan, Illinois, Indiana, and adjoining states throughout the eighteenth century until the French ceded their holdings in the interior of the continent to England in 1763 at the end of the Seven Year's War.

ARCHAEOLOGICAL APPROACHES
Archaeologists have employed documentary sources including maps and official correspondence to assist them in identifying the routes of exploration and the locations of early

settlements. Because Europeans in the Midwest were confined to a few locations prior to the first quarter of the eighteenth century, archaeological sites dating to this period are rare and limited to fortified outposts and mission churches. Relatively small sites of limited duration or those that experienced later developments have left few archaeological traces, making them difficult to find. Nevertheless, there has been considerable interest in examining material evidence of seventeenth- and eighteenth-century French activities in the region. Nineteenth-century antiquarians frequently collected artifacts from French colonial sites. Forts and sites associated with French explorers were frequently commemorated soon after. For example, monuments were dedicated to La Salle in St. Joseph (1902) and to Fort St. Joseph in Niles (1913), Michigan. Systematic investigations generally did not begin until the later half of the twentieth century, although Paul Maynard, a University of Chicago archaeologist, conducted excavations at former French colonial outposts in Illinois in the 1930s. About the same time, archaeologist George I. Quimby began to use museum

Reconstructed building at Fort Michilimackinac site.   [Mackinac State Historic Parks]

collections associated with sites that could be dated through documentary sources to establish a chronological framework for artifacts associated with the French presence in the western Great Lakes. Subsequent work at many sites was motivated by the need for information to assist in reconstruction and site interpretation, as at Fort Michilimackinac, where archaeological excavations began in 1959. In the 1970s other sites were investigated in compliance with federal legislation that mandated the identification, evaluation, and conservation of archaeological resources. More recent work is oriented to research questions that aim to examine similarities and differences in the French experience within a broader context of comparative colonialism.

In conjunction with written documents, archaeologists have used material remains to classify sites according to age and function in order to better understand settlements synchronically and diachronically. In addition to fortifications, there were trading centers, farmsteads, villages, churches, cemeteries, and production sites. Some archaeologists see these settlements as hierarchically organized in different levels from ports of entry and governmental centers down to regional and local distribution centers, thereby reflecting the flow of goods from France into the hands of consumers. Others have found it useful to distinguish sites that were engaged in the extraction and processing of natural resources such as furs from those that were engaged in the production of agricultural goods. Both of these activities occurred in the Midwest, and they have implications for the types of artifacts seen at different sites and how those sites were organized. In a society in which most people were illiterate and left no written records, archaeology can contribute to understanding the daily activities at these sites and the identities of their occupants.

ARCHAEOLOGICAL CONTRIBUTIONS

Archaeology has provided important information about early French exploration and settlement in the Midwest, particularly in regards to architecture, trade, subsistence practices, and social relationships. Most of the buildings associated with early settlement in the region were built of wood and, as a result, few have survived. Nevertheless, archaeologists have benefited from studying extant structures, insofar as they can provide insight into some of the styles represented in the archaeological record. Buildings, as might be expected, vary in their construction techniques, size, function, and contents.

French building styles derive from northwest France with modification in the St. Lawrence River valley. Most buildings were simple *poteau en terre*, or post-in-the-ground structures that were built by setting upright posts within a trench and filling the interstices with *bousillage* (a mixture of clay and straw) or *pierrotage* (a mixture of stone and mortar), then covered with white wash (a mixture of lime and water to protect the walls from the elements). Sometimes the wall posts would be set on a sill placed on a stone foundation (known as *poteau sur sole*). Rarely were horizontal timbers (*piece sur piece*) employed, although that is the method used for ecclesiastical buildings at Fort Michilimackinac. Building size was dependent upon function; most residences were about 5 × 6 meters, or roughly 16 × 20 feet. Some French buildings at Forts Massac (southern Illinois) and Michilimackinac (northern Michigan) consisted of barracks or row houses that had shared walls. Stone fireplaces and hearths with stick chimneys chinked with *bousillage* were often placed at the ends or corners of habitation rooms; spaces lacking a source of heat might have been used for storage.

Habitation, storage, and other special-purpose buildings have been identified in the archaeological record, although a building's function or the identity of its occupants is sometimes difficult to discern. For example, at Michilimackinac the powder magazine yielded a significant quantity of trade goods suggesting that it was used to hold not only armaments but also served as a storeroom for traders. Donald Heldman has noted that both commoners and privileged lived in *poteau en terre* structures, whereas those of means lived in somewhat larger buildings associated with high-status goods. They were located for protection from the prevailing northwesterly winds.

Many of the forts were constructed according to the principles of fortification developed by the seventeenth-century military strategist Sébastien Le Prestre de Vauban. His design employed bastions or projections at the four corners of a roughly square palisade to increase flank coverage so as to defend against an attack. Such a spatial configuration is evident in the shape of the palisade at Forts de Chartres, Massac, and Michilimackinac. Older, smaller, or more informal forts may not have taken advantage of this design. For instance, in 1695 the Iroquois were able to place their guns between the palisade posts at Fort St. Joseph, implying the appearance of the walls and the likely absence of any bastions. Nearly thirty years later (1721) Father Pierre Francois Xavier de Charlevoix described Fort St. Joseph as the commandant's house and a few other structures surrounded by a palisade in disrepair. The use of stone at Fort de Chartres and the placement of a moat at Fort Massac demonstrate further elaborations in the designs of French forts. Archaeological evidence also demonstrated that the palisade was enlarged at Michilimackinac to accommodate the growing fur trade.

Early explorers and settlers were forced by necessity to employ local raw materials of wood and stone in their constructions. Yet the French imported various goods for their own use and as gifts to maintain exchange relationships with their Native allies; distinguishing these in the archaeological record can be difficult. Trade lists confirm that the glass beads, thimbles, finger rings, guns, kettles, knives, hoes, axes, and other metal artifacts found at archaeological sites were desired by and often destined for Native groups. Indeed, many of these objects appear in contemporaneous Native American sites. Records also indicate that textiles and clothing were among the most frequently traded goods, although they seldom preserve archaeologically.

Objects associated with the fur trade are ubiquitous at many French sites in the region. For example, collections from Forts Michilimackinac, Ouiatanon, and St. Joseph include numerous glass beads, lead seals that were used to identify and secure the contents of bales and bolts of cloth, and baling needles to wrap bundles of furs. The scarcity of coinage recovered from these and other sites indicates that much of the exchange took the form of barter and credit. Services, as well as goods, were exchanged between the French and the Indians. The presence of a forge at Fort Ouiatanon and a concentration of over 100 gun parts at Fort St. Joseph point to the presence of a gunsmith who could repair guns and produce metal artifacts to fulfill Native needs.

The French imported significant quantities of goods to recreate their way of life on the frontier. Glass bottles, window-pane glass, refined earthenware ceramics, and objects of personal adornment such as cuff links, buckles, and brooches testify to the flow of goods. Yet supply lines were not always reliable, and people on the frontier often engaged in craft production to create their own commodities as well as goods needed for daily life. For example, many sites exhibit evidence of local production of musket balls or lead shot as indicated by the waste that results from pouring molten lead into a mold. Scraps of copper alloy metal are also frequently recovered. These derive from cutting sheet metal to make patches and rivets to repair worn out kettles. Trapezoidal pieces of copper alloy were also cut to shape to make tinkling cones—cone-shaped ornaments used to decorate clothing or leather bags.

Despite the importance of exchange for maintaining close alliances, the fur trade did not dominate all aspects of the French economy in the Midwest. The archaeological record shows that trade goods occur less frequently at sites in which habitants attempted to become self-sufficient, as among the settlements along the Mississippi River that produced a wheat surplus for New Orleans and Caribbean markets. Many of these sites, not coincidentally, included numbers of Indian and African slaves who were employed in agricultural tasks.

In order to ensure the success of the colony, the French Crown encouraged all settlements in New France to become self-sufficient. Given the range of ecological settings that the French inhabited, there was considerable diversity in their subsistence practices, and this is reflected in archaeological findings. With the implementation of fine screening in archaeological recovery, preserved ecofacts (plant and animal food remains, such as seeds and bones) have been recovered from sites in the Midwest.

Terrance Martin has compared the animal exploitation strategies at several French sites in the region. He noted that the differences in frequencies of animal remains reflect environmental setting, site function, and the degree of interaction between the French inhabitants of various posts and their Indian neighbors. Fort Michilimackinac exhibits a distinct pattern indicative of its setting in the Canadian biotic province that was not favorable to whitetail deer and other game animals. As a result, high proportions of lake trout and whitefish have been recovered archaeologically from several trash deposits, indicating their contribution to the diet.

The Laurens site, thought to be the first Fort de Chartres in the Mississippi Valley, was established just after 1718 and supported about sixty soldiers and a sizeable civilian population by the next decade. The faunal remains reflect a high proportion of domesticated animals, including cattle, pigs, and chicken, with lesser amounts of deer. Fish species were exploited from the main channel of the Mississippi River. Black bear bones also occur, supporting documents that indicate the French viewed bear oil as a delicacy, which they used for shortening and as a seasoning.

These very different patterns contrast further with Fort Ouiatanon, a local distribution center established in 1717 along the Wabash River that housed a small detachment of about a dozen marines and fewer than twenty French families. Here the animal assemblage is dominated by wild species, most notably deer. Although domesticated animals are present, they were used to supplement the predominantly wild animal diet. Martin also noted that several modified animal remains might reflect trade with local Indian groups, the presence of local Indians, or perhaps French accommodations to local Native customs. A similar pattern occurs at Fort St. Joseph, where excavations have yielded bone tools, antler gaming pieces, and high frequencies of wild animal remains.

Plant remains have not been as frequently recovered and analyzed in the region. Indian corn has been found at sites in which there was interaction with local Native groups, although it is not known whether the French actually practiced maize agriculture or merely acquired it in trade from the Indians. Old World domesticates have seldom been found at Midwestern sites, with the exception of rare occurrences of watermelon, peach, and wheat in the Mississippi Valley. This may represent a reliance on local plant food resources in much the same way that wild animal species were exploited.

In the process of accommodating to life on the frontier, the French interacted with a wide range of Native populations. These interactions are integral to understanding French immigrant life, and they left an indelible archaeological imprint. New France always had a demographic imbalance, with men vastly outnumbering women despite the Crown's efforts to encourage the emigration of women and the formation of stable nuclear families. For the many voyageurs and coureurs de bois (illicit fur traders because they lacked a license) who literally went into the woods to acquire furs and often lived only part-time in settled communities, unions to Native women were a practical option that served a mutual benefit. Moreover, such close relationships created intimate bonds that led to new cultural forms that were neither Native nor French, in a process referred to by anthropologists as ethnogenesis.

Archaeologists have begun to use archaeological evidence to gain insight into the creation, maintenance, and transformation of ethnic boundaries in the context of intense cultural interaction. French material culture studies indicate the mutual exchange of ideas and not one of French domination over local Native populations. For example, dietary practices often relied on local resources, particularly when Native spouses were collecting and preparing foods with which they were familiar. The low frequency of imported ceramics at some sites and among some households also suggests that new culinary practices were being adopted, although this may also reflect differences in social status. The ubiquity of smoking pipes on eighteenth-century sites points to the frequency of tobacco consumption, yet the presence of both imported white clay and locally made stone pipes at some sites suggest that these types were interchangeable and shared by French and Natives alike. Likewise, dress and personal adornment reflects the fluid social identities that were expressed through the adoption of traditionally Native styles in combination with French imports. For example, new forms of material culture, such as tinkling cones that were made of imported raw materials, were produced and used by both Native and French, reflecting their close interaction.

This is not to imply that the French merely absorbed Native societies, and social distinctions became erased. Just as ethnicity is expressed in the archaeological record, so too is gender and socioeconomic status. Work on gender roles at Fort Michimackinac by Elizabeth M. Scott has demonstrated that we cannot identify the presence of women in households by looking solely for evidence of activities because men, servants, or slaves might have performed activities attributed to women, such as food preparation. Alternatively, materials from clothing and sewing, such as buttons, buckles, cuff links, thimbles, awls, straight pins, and other accessories, can be associated with men and women of various socioeconomic and ethnic groups.

Finally, as in all consumer societies, people had differential access to resources in early French settlements. Even though a lack of currency or industries to invest in prevented the accumulation of great wealth, differences in material culture were sometimes tied to social status. For example, household inventories in the Illinois Country list silver and crystal goblets along with different quantities and varieties of personal goods, such as clothing, that are indicative of status. Likewise, objects that were costly to transport and acquire, such as windowpane glass and ceramics, may have been restricted in their distribution and served to demarcate persons of rank. Household size and location were also ways in which prosperous traders and officers set themselves apart from commoners. More work needs to be conducted in identifying high-status objects and comparing their presence within and between sites to understand how socioeconomic status was expressed on the frontier of New France and how it changed over the course of the eighteenth century.

PUBLIC EDUCATION AND PUBLIC OUTREACH

Information from several early French sites that were investigated for interpretive purposes is accessible to the public through museum collections, publications, videos, Web sites, and living history exhibits. By far, the best-known and most impressive French colonial archaeological site is Fort Michilimackinac. Over two-thirds of the site has been excavated since 1959, providing information that has been used to reconstruct fifteen buildings, many of which include interpretive exhibits. The site also employs living history interpreters during the summer months, when visitors can also view ongoing excavations. A similar reconstruction is open to the public at Fort de Chartres south of St. Louis. The results of investigations at Forts Ouiatanon and St. Joseph are also accessible to the public. Western Michigan University archaeologists under the direction of Michael Nassaney are currently investigating Fort St. Joseph, a mission-garrison-trading post complex established by the French in 1691. Artifacts from their excavations and interpretations are on display at the Fort St. Joseph Museum in Niles, Michigan.

Further Reading: Colonial Michilimackinac Web site, http://www.mackinacparks.com/parks/colonial-michilimackinac_7 (online March 2007); Harris, Richard Colebrook, ed., *The Historical Atlas of Canada, Vol. 1, From the Beginning to 1800* (Toronto, ON: University of Toronto Press, 1987); Heldman, Donald P., *Excavations at Fort Michilimackinac, 1976: The Southeast and South Southeast Row House*, Archaeological Completion Report Series No. 1 (Mackinac Island, MI: Mackinac Island State Park Commission, 1977); Martin, Terrance J., "Modified Animal Remains, Subsistence, and Cultural Interaction at French Colonial Sites in the Midwestern United States," in *Beamers, Bobwhites, and Blue-Points: Tributes to the Career of Paul W. Parmalee*, edited by James R. Purdue, Walter E. Klippel, and Bonnie W. Styles, Scientific Papers Vol. 23 (Springfield: Illinois State Museum 1991) 410–419; Nassaney, Michael S., "Identity Formation at a French Colonial Outpost in the North American Interior," *International Journal of Historical Archaeology* 12 (4) 2008 (in press); Quimby, George I., *Indian Culture and European Trade Goods* (Madison: University of Wisconsin Press, 1966); Stone, Lyle M., *Fort Michilimackinac 1715–1781: An Archaeological Perspective on the Revolutionary Frontier*, Publications of the Museum (Michigan State University in cooperation with Mackinac Island State Park Commission, 1974); Walthall, John A., ed., *French Colonial Archaeology: The Illinois Country and the Western Great Lakes* (Urbana: University of Illinois Press, 1991); Waselkov, Gregory A., *The Archaeology of French Colonial North America English-French Edition*, Guide to Historical Archaeological Literature No. 5 (Society for Historical Archaeology, 1997).

Michael S. Nassaney

CONTACT PERIOD CULTURE CHANGE, POPULATION DECLINE, AND MOVEMENT

The arrival of Europeans in North America would have a profound and lasting effect on native peoples across the continent. Change came later, of course, to those in the vast interior than it did to the indigenous groups along the Atlantic seaboard, where initial contact occurred. But because of the St. Lawrence–Great Lakes waterway, what we now consider the upper Midwest was reached by French explorers, missionaries, and fur traders decades before British influences extended across the Appalachian-Allegheny mountain barriers farther south in the latter half of the eighteenth century.

Even before Europeans made prolonged contact with aboriginal peoples of the Midwest, their colonial presence in the East was felt indirectly at those more remote locales. Subtle changes were slowly beginning to occur among far-flung native cultures when the French arrived (scholars refer to this transitional period immediately prior to face-to-face contact

as the "protohistoric"). Trade goods, such as glass beads, brass kettles, and iron knives, reached the western Great Lakes region by way of native middlemen in the fur trade and were readily adopted in place of traditional but less durable articles made of shell, clay, and stone. The immediate impact of those exotic materials was slight, perhaps, but their introduction even in limited numbers would have fostered a desire for more and prepared those distant tribes for full participation in the fur trade as the European presence moved farther into the interior.

European colonization of the East fostered greater competition among native groups, heightening levels of conflict and leading to the defensive coalescence of related groups into larger tribal entities. At the same time, various peoples increasingly involved in trade were drawn to settle in villages near seats of the European powers. Concentrated native populations also made them more susceptible to newly introduced European diseases, to which they had little resistance. Depopulation from epidemic illness in some cases proved devastating.

The French had their first brief encounters with peoples of the upper Great Lakes when Samuel de Champlain reached Lake Huron in 1615. Subsequent exploratory journeys west from French Canada, notably those of Étienne Brulé around 1622, Jean Nicollet in 1634, and others, acquainted the French with the more distant Great Lakes of Michigan and Superior, as well as the natives who lined their shores, principally bands of Algonquian speakers such as the Ojibwa. Not until the founding of Jesuit missions at several upper Great Lakes locations in the latter part of the seventeenth century, however, did the French begin to have a more dramatic influence on the cultures of this region.

French influence grew with the advent of key military installations, such as Fort de Baude at modern St. Ignace, Michigan (1683), Fort St. Joseph near modern Port Huron, Michigan (1686), and another fort by that same name near modern Niles, Michigan (1691). Thus, they were able to establish a strategic presence on two of the upper Great Lakes and on the Straits of Mackinac that connects them. That presence would become even more solidified during the opening decades of the eighteenth century with the establishment of influential fur-trading posts such as Michilimackinac, founded on the south side of the straits in 1715.

One of the best primary sources on the period of initial contact in the Midwest is the massive *Jesuit Relations*, first translated and published in English as a seventy-three-volume set (Thwaites 1896–1901). The *Relations* collected documents represent the annual reports that the heads of the Jesuit order in New France sent back to Paris detailing the experiences and observations of missionaries living among the natives of North America from 1610 to 1791. As such, they provide a unique and detailed firsthand written record of general conditions and memorable events throughout New France during that period. Like all eye-witness accounts, however, the *Jesuit Relations* do not necessarily present a true and comprehensive picture of the native cultures described. They have been shown to contain many inaccuracies, including basic errors of interpretation resulting from cultural misunderstandings and more overt misrepresentations of fact.

Archaeological research can provide a different perspective on the native cultures that Europeans encountered in the Midwest and, through continued interaction, forever changed. Although the archaeological record is an incomplete representation of the lives of those who occupied a particular site, it is also free of many of the inadvertent and purposeful biases that may be included, purposefully or inadvertently, in the written historic record. Relatively few early historic period native villages have been excavated in the Midwest compared with the great number that must have once existed; however, several important sites have been investigated. When compared with findings from earlier occupations of the region, the data derived from such archaeological sites can offer important insights into the effects of European contact on native culture.

MARQUETTE'S ST. IGNACE MISSION

The Huron Confederacy, from their traditional homeland east of Georgian Bay on the Great Lake that now bears their name, were ideally situated to serve as middlemen in the fur trade. That unique position proved to be a double-edged sword because they also suffered greatly as a consequence of that pivotal status. With their population already drastically reduced by the ravages of European disease, the Iroquois wars of 1649–50 proved to be devastating. In fact, some scholars have argued that the Huron were no longer a viable cultural entity afterward. Iroquois raiding parties decimated the Huron and drove many of those who eluded capture into what is now the American Midwest. The subsequent dispersal of the surviving Huron in the second half of the seventeenth century set off a chain reaction, much like the scattering of billiard balls, among neighboring groups, which affected traditional patterns of settlement over much of the region.

While some Huron groups fled south toward Lake Erie and present-day Ohio, the Tionontate (also known as the Petun) traveled westward as far as Wisconsin and relocated frequently in response to pressures from the Iroquois, the Sioux, and other groups. Pushed east again from the mission at Chequamegon on Wisconsin's Lake Superior shore, where they had sojourned after 1665, the Tionontate eventually settled near Father Marquette's mission at St. Ignace in 1671. They were able to resume their participation in the fur trade from that key location at the Straits of Mackinac until they were persuaded to move south soon after Antoine de La Mothe Cadillac founded the military garrison at Detroit in 1701.

The Marquette Mission site, also known as the St. Ignace Mission, has been the subject of numerous archaeological studies since 1971. The specific location of the mission and associated villages was not precisely known until a farmer clearing his field in 1877 happened upon tantalizing evidence. Soon thereafter, the Reverend Edward Jacker explored the site to confirm its supposed identity, and by the turn of the twentieth century a monument had been erected there and a city park set aside to commemorate the mission and Marquette's alleged grave.

The first professional archaeological investigations at the Marquette Mission, carried out under the auspices of the Mackinac Island State Park Commission in cooperation with Michigan State University in 1971 and 1972, sought basic information on the extent and character of the native occupation. A third season in 1973, funded by the Michigan History Division, focused on the remains of a native longhouse and other major cultural features. After a decade's hiatus, Michigan State University resumed research at the site in 1983 and carried out more intensive excavations over the next several years.

In contrast with prevailing thought, and in spite of the dynamic forces of change, archaeological evidence from the Tionontate village at the Marquette Mission site supports the interpretation that Huron cultural continuity was still strong through the end of the seventeenth century. Artifacts recovered at the site reveal not only the retention of some traditional items of material culture but also the adaptation of many European trade goods for traditional uses—for example, projectile points were flaked from broken bottle glass and objects used for personal adornment cut from brass kettles. Other findings related to subsistence practices and community settlement patterns also show that the Huron cultural identity persisted in the face of rapidly changing conditions. As Susan Branstner concluded in her study of the site, the Huron seem to have readily adopted exotic trade goods into their daily routine without becoming dependent on them. Furthermore, they incorporated elements of Christian ritual without wholly discarding their own belief system and traditions.

The importance of this site for illustrating the broad history of America was officially recognized in 1960 with its designation as St. Ignace Mission National Historic Landmark. Much of the Huron village site is still preserved in a city park, and some of the features discovered archaeologically have been partly reconstructed for public interpretation. In addition, the story the Ojibwa, who occupied this area after the departure of the Huron in the early nineteenth century, is told in a museum building on the property.

ROCK ISLAND

Another important Contact period archaeological site is located on the southwestern shore of Rock Island, one of several islands in the archipelago that extends toward Michigan's Upper Peninsula from Wisconsin's Door Peninsula and separates Green Bay from the rest of Lake Michigan. There are many references in historical documents about the French visiting villages occupied by various native peoples on islands in northern Lake Michigan during the seventeenth century, but the historical record is so vague and the possibilities so numerous that one could not determine with any certainty which island was meant in a particular account. René-Robert Cavelier de La Salle sailed his ship the *Griffon*, the first vessel of its kind on the western Great Lakes, as far as Green Bay, but it is unclear which of the islands he visited. Even Father Marquette may have passed Rock Island with his exploring partner, Louis Jolliet, as they entered Green Bay to take the Fox River upstream to the Wisconsin River prior to their descent of the Mississippi.

Unlike the Marquette Mission site, which could be readily identified with a known group once the site location was discovered, tribal associations of occupations at the excavated Rock Island sites were not immediately clear. Ronald J. Mason of Lawrence University conducted the initial survey within Rock Island State Park in 1969 and discovered three sites on the island's sandy southern shore. Two of them were predominantly prehistoric, but Rock Island Site II also clearly contained substantial evidence from the early historic period, which was to become the subject of extensive study over the next four summers. Continued research revealed that Rock Island Site II was stratified with soil layers representing four distinct historic occupation periods. The analytical challenge was to determine which Native American groups were associated with each stratum of the multi-component site (a site with multiple occupations represented in different layers of archaeological material).

Analysis of the material remains and documentary sources led to the conclusion that Period 1 represents an initial occupation of the site by a band of Potawatomi between 1641 and 1650–51. Mason believes that the Period 2 occupation commences on the heels of the first and lasted only two years, during which a palisade was built to enclose the village site. Comparison of the artifacts in this stratum, particularly clay potsherds, with materials derived from other sites in the upper Great Lakes, suggest that the principal occupants at this time were of Huron-Petun-Ottawa ethnicity.

The third historic period occupation at Rock Island Site II is believed to have been of much longer duration (ca. 1670–1730) and is again attributed to the Potawatomi chiefly on the basis of distinctive ceramics found in the midden deposits. Period 4, the final native occupation of the site discernible from the archaeological record, occurred much later (1760–70). It appears to have been associated with the Ottawa. Furthermore, the recovery of considerable numbers of European goods associated with this occupation period indicates that the inhabitants were then fully engaged with the fur trade.

Mason points out that the prehistoric record of native occupation on Rock Island goes back at least as far as the Middle Woodland and perhaps earlier. Episodic settlement over 1,000 years of prehistory shows that the resources of this and other islands in the archipelago crossing the mouth of Green Bay attracted native peoples long before the incursions of Europeans into the Midwest. The burgeoning fur trade, however, most certainly enhanced the strategic importance of this locality through the early historic period, and increasing pressures of the fur trade doubtless affected the movements of those groups that would sequentially occupy the south shore of Rock Island.

GRAND VILLAGE OF THE ILLINOIS

Located on the north bank of the Illinois River, between the towns of LaSalle and Ottawa, Illinois, is the site of the Grand Village of the Illinois—also known as the Zimmerman site, so named after a former landowner. Designated Old Kaskaskia Village National Historic Landmark in 1964, the village site derives its historical importance by virtue of the fact that Marquette and Jolliet stopped here in 1673 with their exploration party while returning from the lower Mississippi River to Lake Michigan. Within sight of the distinctive landform called Starved Rock, where La Salle and Henri de Tonti would establish their Fort St. Louis a decade later, the village then consisted of some seventy-three cabins of Kaskaskia Indians, a branch of the great Illinois Confederacy. Occupied by various peoples before and after that historic visit, the archaeological site is now protected from the threat of agricultural practices and commercial development and preserved by the Illinois Historic Preservation Agency.

This important site was initially the subject of a single season of excavations carried out as a joint endeavor of the University of Chicago and Illinois State Museum in 1947. This early archaeology was formally reported by James A. Brown in 1961, using field records kept by the original excavators. The 1970s saw three more seasons of archaeological work under the auspices of the LaSalle County Historical Society. With a team of archaeologists, more intensive investigations were carried out after state acquisition in 1991 and continuing through 1996. In combination, these studies enlighten our understanding of Native American life in the Midwest during and immediately before the early historic period.

Like many historic period Native American villages, archaeological evidence indicates that the Grand Village of the Illinois was occupied periodically before the arrival of Europeans. Indeed, a major component of the site is associated with the Heally phase, which roughly dates to the second half of the thirteenth century. Although it cannot be shown that the historic period occupants were descendants of those who occupied the site in prehistory, Brown notes that there are substantial differences between the prehistoric and historic assemblages at the site. Cultural features, such as houses and storage pits, appear to differ in shape and size, and subsistence activities seem to shift from one that involved a balance between agriculture and individual small-animal hunting, including a dependence on shell fish, to a strategy that focused more on the communal hunting of bison.

The documentary record also bears witness to the cultural dynamics of the early historic period at this locale. Brown notes that by the time La Salle and Tonti arrived on the scene, the village that Marquette and Jolliet had visited had attracted several related tribal groups to establish themselves nearby. Thus, in less than a decade the expanded community had grown to some 500 households, constituting a population that may have included between 6,000 and 9,000 persons.

History records that in the fall of 1680 an Iroquois raiding party destroyed the Grand Village, routing its occupants, and the site for the most part was abandoned for several years thereafter. After La Salle and Tonti completed Fort St. Louis at Starved Rock, the French solicited tribes to engage with them in the fur trade, and a smaller community of about 300 households was reestablished at the old village site with several subgroups of the Illinois represented. Indeed, the fort drew many other tribal entities, such as the Miami and Shawnee, to settle in the vicinity. The native community could not be sustained after the death of La Salle in 1687, however,

and the occupants dispersed a few years later with the abandonment of Fort St. Louis.

SUMMARY
Other Contact period archaeological sites have been excavated in the Midwest, but the three discussed here are particularly useful in illustrating the dynamic forces at work during the early historic period. Native groups frequently moved across the vast Midwest woodlands in response to the shifting circumstances, needs, and alliances of the fur trade, as well as in concert with the increasing hostilities among intensely competing tribes. Those same pressures resulted in the coalescence of some related Native groups into larger tribal entities. Although warfare certainly was a factor in bringing about population decline and movement among many Native American groups, newly introduced diseases had an even more dramatic effect on Native mortality rates. The scourge of smallpox was especially dreadful, as major epidemics occurred in the region at intervals well into the eighteenth century. At the first encounter with Europeans, the Illinois people were estimated to exceed 10,000 in number, spread across a sizable territory. When they officially ceded the last of their lands in 1832, after many decades of decline, the Illinois occupied a single village of a few hundred individuals.

The ubiquitous presence of European-made artifacts on native village sites of the early historic period provides testimony to the cultural changes that were occurring, gradually at first but with increasing intensity over time. This is not to say that native cultural identity did not survive the influences at play, for evidence indicates that many traditional practices persisted well into the post-colonial era. Nor were such forces of change directed only at the aboriginal peoples, for the European intruders, in adapting to their new and often hostile environment, underwent similar changes and selectively embraced certain aspects of native culture.

Subsequent implementation of federal Indian policies, particularly after the Civil War, effected far more dramatic changes among native peoples, including forced removal from their historical homelands and assimilation efforts designed to suppress traditional culture. Nevertheless, lineages descendant from Midwestern tribal groups of the early historic period continue to this day. Some, like the Ojibwa, continue to have a significant presence in the upper Great Lakes region, whereas descendants of the Illinois kin groups endure among the Peoria Nation of Oklahoma, and the Huron live on as members of the Wyandot Nation of Kansas or the Wyandotte Nation of Oklahoma.

Further Reading: *American Indians in Illinois*, Web site with information about Grand Village of the Illinois and related sites, http://www.museum.state.il.us/muslink/nat_amer/post/; Branstner, Susan M., "Tionontate Huron Occupation at the Marquette Mission," in *Calumet and Fleur-de-Lys: Archaeology of Indian and French*

Contact in the Midcontinent, edited by John A. Walthall and Thomas E. Emerson, eds. (Washington, DC: Smithsonian Institution Press, 1992), 177–201; Brown, James A., ed., *The Zimmerman Site: A Report of Excavations at the Grand Village of Kaskaskia, LaSalle County, Illinois* (Springfield: Illinois State Museum, 1961); *Jesuit Relations and Allied Documents 1610–1791*, http://puffin.creighton. edu/jesuit/relations/; *Marquette Mission Site—St. Ignace Michigan*, Michigan State University Department of Anthropology Web site, http://anthropology.msu.edu/marquettemission//MarquetteMission. html/; Mason, Ronald J., *Great Lakes Archaeology* (New York: Academic Press, 1981); Mason, Ronald J., *Rock Island: Historical Indian Archaeology in the Northern Lake Michigan Basin* (Kent, OH: Kent State University Press, 1986); Rohrbaugh, Charles L., Lenville J.

Stelle, Thomas E. Emerson, Gregory R. Walz, and John T. Penman, *The Archaeology of the Grand Village of the Illinois: Report of the Grand Village Research Project, 1991–1996; Grand Village of the Illinois State Historic Site (11LS13), LaSalle County, Illinois*, Illinois Transportation Archaeological Research Program, Research Paper No. 60 (Urbana: Department of Anthropology, University of Illinois, 1998); Tanner, Helen H., ed., *Atlas of Great Lakes Indian History* (Norman: University of Oklahoma Press, 1987); Thwaites, Reuben Gold, ed., *The Jesuit Relations and Allied Documents*, 73 vols. (Cleveland: Burrows Bros., 1896–1901); Trigger, Bruce G., ed., *Handbook of North American Indians*, Volume 15, *Northeast* (Washington, DC: Smithsonian Institution Press, 1978).

Vergil E. Noble

HISTORIC PERIOD URBAN ARCHAEOLOGY IN THE MIDWEST

The Midwest is a blanket of small towns and metropolises alike that has long been home to a wide range of industries, commercial agriculture centers, and transportation corridors essential to the nation. The "heartland" has often fancied itself a paragon of American values revolving around its rural heritage and middle-class white values. However, much of the Midwest's history is told in the many culturally diverse towns and cities that developed in the nineteenth century, and their stories represent an array of industrial working experiences, urban neighborhood spaces, and social diversity not often identified within Midwestern stereotypes. Historical archaeologists have been systematically examining Midwestern cities since the 1960s, and although this archaeology is almost universally in the narrowly disseminated cultural resource management literature, a rich archaeological record has been amassed of the complexity of Midwestern urban life.

Many scholars see the Midwest in a broad form like that envisioned by Frederick Jackson Turner, who in 1921 defined the "Middle West" as a province stretching from Pittsburgh and Buffalo in the east to St. Louis and Cincinnati to the south, to Kansas City and St. Paul in the west, placing Chicago at the region's spatial and social heart. The notion of a relatively cohesive region known as the Midwest has firm historical and legal roots in the Northwest Territory. The 1787 Northwest Ordinance defined the terms under which all of the United States' lands west of Pennsylvania could be admitted as full states, which settled a variety of eastern states' claims on the territories. The sparsely occupied Northwest territories covered the full range of what became Ohio, Indiana, Illinois, Michigan, and Wisconsin as well as the eastern half of

Minnesota, all of which entered the union between 1803 (Ohio) and 1858 (Minnesota). The Northwest Ordinance provided a concrete blueprint for organizing statehood in the Midwest by setting up schools, defining a governance system, and rejecting enslavement, all moves meant to lay the foundation for a commercial economy in a region that was originally most closely associated with rural life and agricultural production.

EARLY MIDWESTERN URBANIZATION

Prior to the Northwest Ordinance, the Midwest was simply a frontier. Before the American Revolution the Midwest was explored and lightly colonized by the French beginning about 1615, but they gave up their claims to a scatter of posts throughout the region in 1763 as part of the settlement ending the French and Indian Wars. Relatively little archaeological research has focused on this earliest settlement phase in Midwestern cities. Original settlements were small and constructed mainly of wood. Where these original settlements developed into historical urban centers, the remains of the earlier occupations have been destroyed or buried by subsequent historical developments, making archaeological investigation impossible, or at least difficult.

One of the earliest European sites in the region was Fort St. Anthony, which soon became known as Fort Snelling and is today located in the Twin Cities of Minneapolis–St. Paul, Minnesota. American troops built a fort beneath the bluffs overlooking the confluence of the Minnesota and Mississippi rivers in 1820, and from here they secured the fur trade and monitored relations between the Dakota and Ojibwe. The fort

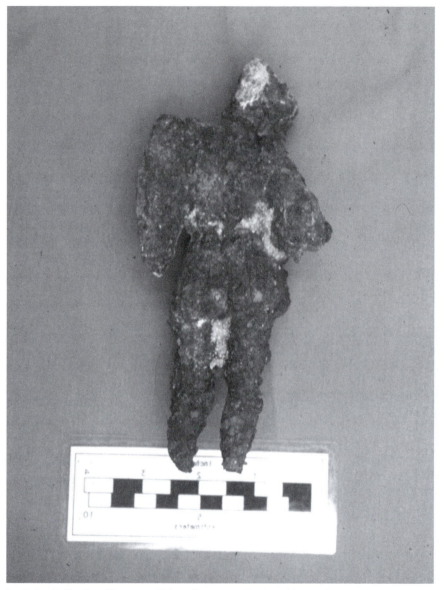

An iron angel found at the John P. Parker House and Foundry site in Ripley, Ohio.   [Photo courtesy of Robert A. Genheimer]

remained an operating military base until its closure in 1946. Excavations were first conducted at the site in 1957, so this was one of the region's earliest historical archaeology projects. In 1965 thirteen years of excavations began at the fort, which became part of a state park that reconstructed the long-time fort based on archaeological findings.

Urbanization came slow to the Northwest Territory, with most cities emerging in the early nineteenth century and not really expanding significantly until the mid-nineteenth century. Much of the Midwest's urban expansion was spurred by northeastern growth, particularly the Erie Canal's completion in 1825. The canal's completion transformed cities such as Chicago, Milwaukee, and Minneapolis by linking the upper Midwest to the northeast and fostering transportation links

that fed immigrants into the heartland. The population of Detroit, for instance, increased fourfold in the decade between 1830 and 1840 and tripled yet again in the following decade. At almost the same moment, the first city charters were struck in Cleveland (1836), Milwaukee (1836), and Chicago (1837). Cities on the Great Lakes were ideally situated for massive immigration, industrial production, and shipping, so all expanded quite rapidly in the mid-nineteenth century.

THE URBAN MIDWEST AFTER 1850
Most historical archaeology in the Midwest has focused on the period after the region's rapid mid-nineteenth-century urbanization, and many of the studies from this period focus on

residential life among industrializing urbanites. For instance, archaeology was conducted in 1982 on working-class Detroit residents' diet and foodways in the final quarter of the nineteenth century. Mark C. Branstner and Terrance J. Martin examined ceramic and faunal assemblages and found very little variability among households, including unskilled manual laborers as well as more skilled tradesmen. However, the appearance of ceramic homogeneity contrasted significantly with faunal assemblages, which displayed considerable variation in the animal species eaten and meat costs. Branstner and Martin concluded that the more affluent households favored more costly beef cuts, more marginalized households were consuming higher quantities of fish, and in contrast to other Detroit sites there were no food remains reflecting importation, such as Atlantic shellfish. Similar questions on consumption patterns have been addressed elsewhere in the region. For instance, in Louisville, Kentucky (directly across the state line from Indiana), M. Jay Stottman excavated nearly 50,000 artifacts from a pair of privies and a cesspool vault dating from the period 1860 to 1890. Stottman examined how proximity to Louisville's busy mercantile district and wharf provided residents access to an especially wide range of goods, complicating simple notions of status and the linking of conspicuous consumption and social class.

A Chicago project conducted by Jane Eva Baxter and Scott Demel examined a working neighborhood of a similar period in Chicago. Rather than focus on the material details of everyday life, Baxter and Demel focused on the industrial spaces in which laborers worked, arguing that many nineteenth-century laborers spent more of their time in factories than they actually spent at home. Baxter and Demel examined the Pullman Community on the city's far South Side, where George Pullman's railroad car manufacturing plant and factory town were built in 1880. Among their most interesting finds was that flowering plants appear to have been intentionally planted around the factory during its operation, undermining the commonplace stereotype of workers alienated to their laboring spaces.

Several ambitious neighborhood-wide archaeological projects have been conducted in Midwestern cities. In 1997, for instance, a salvage project was conducted in St. Paul, Minnesota, examining three of the city's historic period brothels and a neighboring saloon in the surrounding red-light district. In operation from 1888 through 1929, nearly 14,000 artifacts were associated with the brothel and a neighboring saloon privy. The archaeological material culture suggests a clear divide between the everyday domestic lives of prostitutes and the public representations of bordello customers' experiences, and the reports' authors suggest—based upon comparative study with other, similar sites—that there may be some regional differences in how the Minnesota bordellos were run.

Quite a few Midwestern projects have examined industrialization, some as early as the antebellum period, and there is an especially rich record of ceramic manufacturing in the

urban Midwest. For instance, in Louisville the Lewis Pottery Company was established in 1829 with the aspiration of competing with British ceramic producers. However, in 1837 the firm was absorbed by the Indiana Pottery Company, which was run by former British potter James Clews. Archaeological investigations showed that the pottery discarded a significant volume of stoneware wasters and that the firm experimented with the production of a refined earthenware approximating the English-produced Queensware. Directly across the river from Cincinnati in Covington, Kentucky, Robert Genheimer directed excavations along a three-block section of the riverfront that included a mid-nineteenth-century pottery with two updraft "beehive" kilns. Chamber pots were the most common vessel type in the waster deposits, and Rockingham-type and clear-glazed mugs were recovered along with banded bowls and mugs. Excavations from about 1854 to 1870 at Caldwell and McCumber Pottery in Arrow Rock, Missouri, focused on a community whose population changed radically around emancipation, including many African American residents. In other parts of the Midwest some archaeologists have examined lighter industry, which was typically based in residents' yards. For instance, during construction of Minneapolis's Federal Reserve Bank in 1994, archaeologists excavated an early neighborhood that contained several archaeological examples of light industries including a harness shop and brewery as well as supporting businesses such as a saloon. Archaeologists were interested in the timing for the shift from outhouses to plumbing among these laborers. They found that most houses changed over to plumbing in the mid-1880s, and their privies contained very few parasites.

AFRICAN AMERICAN ARCHAEOLOGY IN THE URBAN MIDWEST

The Underground Railroad has well-documented connections that ran throughout the Midwest, but much of the route tended to skirt major cities and has left relatively little clearly documented archaeological data. However, Robert Genheimer conducted an archaeological survey at the John P. Parker House and Foundry site in Ripley, Ohio, outside Cincinnati, which has strong links to the Railroad. Parker was born enslaved in 1827 and purchased his freedom at age 18, when he moved to Ripley and established a foundry. As he later detailed in a series of interviews, Parker became a conductor on the Underground Railroad. Genheimer conducted testing on behalf of the Cincinnati Museum Center and identified extensive evidence for foundry materials as well as fires that had destroyed structures in the lot during the nineteenth century. Over 10,000 artifacts were recovered, including an iron angel likely cast in Parker's foundry.

Many studies have examined the African American experience in the urban Midwest, where African Americans migrated in large quantities from emancipation onward. Some of the region's urban newcomers arrived during enslavement. In Pike County, Illinois, for example, a now-rural area was once the ambitious plan for a city outlined by a free African American named Frank McWorter. McWorter moved to Pike County in 1830 and began laying out the proposed settlement, "New Philadelphia." But the hopeful city had only about 160 residents in 1865; and McWorter's ambitious plan for an African American city eventually was undone when railroad lines bypassed the community, leading to its dissolution in 1885. Archaeological excavations indicate that the frontier town's homes were quickly filled with stylish consumer goods, complicating easy distinctions between urban and rural consumption, and remains of an African American school house and a resident's sewing assemblage were identified.

Under the direction of Timothy Baumann, a series of projects focused on African American life have been conducted in the St. Louis area. In addition to research conducted in west central Missouri at Arrow Rock, Baumann directed archaeological research in the multicultural neighborhood of Old North St. Louis that included a significant African American community. Incorporated in 1816, the neighborhood became home to waves of African Americans around emancipation, and more followed at the turn of the century and then again during World War II. Baumann's work examined relationships between African American and German American neighbors. In a region that became home to immigrants from a range of points in Europe and the South, the St. Louis project is one of the few archaeological excavations to wrestle with a multicultural history and examine it in light of twentieth-century urban renewal. Baumann recently began a study of the Scott Joplin State Historic Site in St. Louis that will conduct archaeology as part of a broad interdisciplinary project to examine varying perspectives and different ethnic histories of life along the color line.

In Indianapolis, Indiana, Paul Mullins has examined the city's near Westside and the historically African American community known as Ransom Place. The project uses archaeological excavations, oral historical research, and public interpretation to probe the confluence of African American culture, business and consumption, and race and racism in Indiana's capital city. The community included homes, businesses, and a variety of social institutions from the mid-nineteenth century onward. In the nineteenth century African Americans lived alongside virtually every European immigrant group in the area. By the early twentieth century, however, Ransom Place and the neighborhoods were predominately African American, as residential segregation seized the Midwest, and they remained so until the community was completely displaced by urban renewal projects. The archaeological project examines the material evidence for these historic neighborhoods now erased by urban expansion. The investigations are examining how archaeology can illuminate the contemporary heritage of racially based urban renewal.

There are exciting possibilities for archaeological studies of twentieth-century Midwestern urbanization and the very recent past, and several projects have examined the period. In Chicago, for example, Scott Demel and Jane Eva Baxter have conducted excavations along the city's lakefront at the Field Museum, examining a vast quantity of landfill material representing virtually every possible type of material culture from the late nineteenth century onward. Baxter and Demel used stratigraphic analysis to document the systematic patterns of filling engineers developed to expand the lakefront beginning around the turn of the twentieth century.

CONCLUSION

As in many other regions, there has been no synthesis of archaeological findings that has established particularly clear regional distinctions. Instead, much of the scholarship remains confined to sources that are not printed in large quantities, so the Midwestern urban archaeological studies remain somewhat disconnected from each other. Clearly there are opportunities to study issues that crosscut the entire region, such as immigration and labor, which have received some archaeological attention. This also is true for examinations of the complex relationship between urban centers and rural agriculture. These potential overarching topics may eventually be drawn in very interesting ways in regional analyses of the Midwest region. Yet in a region that has witnessed historic archaeology for a rather brief period, there is still a foundation for the specific studies that are needed to build upon.

Further Reading: Baumann, Timothy E., "'Because That's Where My Roots Are': Searching for Patterns of African-American Ethnicity in Arrow Rock, Missouri," Ph.D. diss. (University of Tennessee, Knoxville, 2001); Baxter, Jane Eva, and Scott Demel, "The Archaeology of the Pullman Community: An Ongoing Collaboration in Industrial Archaeology," paper presented at the annual meeting of the Society for Industrial Archaeology (Milwaukee, WI: 2005); Branstner, Mark C., and Terrance J. Martin, "Working-Class Detroit: Late Victorian Consumer Choices and Status," in *Consumer Choice in Historical Archaeology*, edited by Suzanne Spencer Wood (New York: Plenum, 1987), 301–320; Clouse, R. A., "Fort Snelling, Minnesota: Intrasite Variability at a Nineteenth Century Military Post (United States Army)," Ph.D. diss. (University of Illinois, Urbana-Champaign, 1997); Demel, Scott, and Jane E. Baxter, "Creating Urban Spaces in Early Chicago: The Archaeology of Chicago's Lakefront," paper presented at the annual meeting of the Society for American Archaeology (Milwaukee, WI: 2003); Genheimer, Robert A., "Underground at the Underground Railroad: Testing at John P. Parker's House and Foundry Site in Ripley, Ohio," *Ohio Archaeological Council Newsletter* 13(2) (2001): 13–19; Mullins, Paul R., "Racializing the Commonplace Landscape: An Archaeology of Urban Renewal along the Color Line," *World Archaeology* 38(1) (2006): 60–71; New Philadelphia Web site, University of Maryland Center for Heritage and Resource Studies http://www.heritage.umd.edu/CHRSWeb/New%20Philadelphia/2005report/3h.htm (online 2005); Stottman, M. Jay, "Consumer Market Access in Louisville's 19th Century Commercial District,"

Ohio Valley Historical Archaeology Journal of the Symposium on Ohio Valley Urban and Historic Archaeology 15 (2000): 8–19; Stradling, Diana, and J. Garrison Stradling, "American Queensware—The Louisville Experience 1829–1837," in *Ceramics in America*, edited by Robert Hunter (Hanover and London: Univer-

sity Press of New England, 2001), 162–185; *Washington Street Residential District Site, From Site to Story: The Upper Mississippi's Buried Past,* http://www.fromsitetostory.org/tcm/21ra0032wsrd/21ra0032wsrd.asp (online 1999).

Paul R. Mullins

UNDERWATER ARCHAEOLOGY IN THE GREAT LAKES

The Great Lakes provided a natural corridor for the exploration, colonization, and development of both the United States and Canada, connecting the Atlantic Ocean with the heartland of North America. The areas surrounding the Great Lakes were interconnected by sea-lanes long before a system of roadways and railroads were effectively established. Abundant natural resources, inexpensive land, and a nonhostile national border encouraged westward expansion and the development of lakefront communities early in the nineteenth century (Lusardi 2007, 13). The maritime history of Thunder Bay, a large embayment on the western shore of Lake Huron in northeast Michigan, is unique in its details though not unlike many other small communities that border the Great Lakes. The area around Thunder Bay was settled and developed to exploit natural resources, and whether it was limestone or taconite, grain or lumber, fish or coal, similar areas throughout the Great Lakes area developed where resources were abundant and their means of extraction and transportation via commercial shipping was facilitated.

Over 10,000 ships have been lost in the Great Lakes in the last 330 years. Countless other submerged cultural resources—everything from inundated prehistoric landscapes to modern aircraft, pilings and shoreline structures to fishnet stakes, isolated artifacts to huge piles of dredge spoil and historic trash—exist on the lake bottom. Because of the fresh, cold water, much of this archaeological record is well preserved. Shipwrecks, in particular, are often found completely intact and many still have their masts standing and artifacts in place. The popularization of scuba diving in the 1960s made these shipwrecks and other resources available for exploration, but it also facilitated unchecked looting and vandalism at the shipwreck sites (Thompson and Lusardi 2004, 30–31). Consequently, the National Park Service, State of Michigan, Parks Canada, and even local communities such as Hamilton, Ontario, recognized the need to protect submerged cultural resources and established a system of underwater preserves and marine protected areas beginning in the 1970s. Legislation was adopted at the state and federal levels making it illegal to disturb or recover artifacts from shipwrecks or on bottomlands without a permit. Today history is being protected for everyone to enjoy, and facilities such as

the Great Lakes Maritime Heritage Center in Alpena, Michigan, are providing the entire community with access to these incredible resources.

Humans have occupied the southern shores of the Great Lakes since the last glacial retreat, some 11,000 years ago (Shott and Wright 1999, 63). Prehistoric peoples, however, probably did not arrive in the areas surrounding Thunder Bay until the Late Archaic period (5,000–2,500 years ago). Although the Great Lakes' water levels were considerably different from what is seen today, native peoples hunted and camped along the shorelines, near river mouths, and around sinkholes now submerged in the lake to take advantage of the area's abundant natural resources (Pott 1999, 359–360). Archaic time period fishing equipment found in upper Great Lakes archaeological sites includes bone and copper fishhooks, gorges and spears, and notched pebble net sinkers (Cleland 1982). Large-scale fishing and lake travel began during the Woodland period (2,500–500 years ago) when indigenous peoples recognized the value of water transportation, and today their technologies and traditions often reflect this maritime connection. Michigan's first mariners navigated small open boats, particularly dugout and bark canoes, which provided an effective means for trade and communication, as well as platforms for hunting, fishing, and gathering aquatic resources from the region's biologically rich wetlands (Pott 1999, 359).

Native mariners considered the Great Lakes a potential hazard centuries before European contact. Many of the Late Woodland period shale discs found near the mouth of Thunder Bay River, today exhibited at the Besser Museum of northeast Michigan, were incised with symbols recognizable in Algonquian mythology, and the figure of Me-she-pe-shiw is well represented. A panther that lived beneath the waters of Lake Huron, Me-she-pe-shiw was believed to cause storms with immense, deadly waves with the thrash of its tail. Native travelers were mindful to sacrifice dogs or tobacco to appease Me-she-pe-shiw before beginning long voyages across Thunder Bay (Cleland et al. 1984, 236–239). Ah-ne-mi-ke, or thunderbird, is also featured on the discs and was believed to generate thunder by flapping its wings and throwing lightning bolts at malevolent water creatures (Haltiner 2002, 131).

Historic shipwreck the *Florida*, located in Thunder Bay, Michigan.   [Thunder Bay National Marine Sanctuary, National Oceanic and Atmospheric Administration]

Adrien Jolliet was likely the first European to see Thunder Bay during his paddle along the eastern shore of Lake Huron in 1669 (Tongue 2004, 7). In August 1679, René-Robert Cavelier La Salle constructed the 45-ton *Griffin* in the Niagara River above the falls to explore and colonize the upper lakes. On his upward journey, La Salle became perhaps the first European to experience the wrath of Thunder Bay. According to chronicler Father Louis Hennepin, a violent storm was encountered there, and all took to their knees in prayer—save the pilot, who instead "did nothing all that while but curse and swear against M. La Salle, who as he said had brought him thither to make him perish in a nasty lake, and lose the glory he had acquired by his long and happy navigations on the ocean" (Hemming 1992, 3; Quaife 1944, 30). *Griffin* was lost with all hands in northern Lake Michigan the following month, becoming the first of thousands of historic craft to go down in the upper Great Lakes.

Seafaring traders, trappers, and missionaries followed in *Griffin*'s wake, adopting or exchanging Native American technologies, often using bark canoes and dugouts (Feltner and Feltner 1991, 11; Halsey 1990, 13). Although the Straits of Mackinac (which link Lake Huron and Lake Michigan), only 90 miles northwest of Thunder Bay, saw extensive colonial activity, French and English travelers merely passed by Thunder Bay. No colonial vessels have been reported lost in the area, and no historic terrestrial sites pre-dating the 1830s have been discovered in Alpena County. The earliest losses of colonial vessels in the vicinity of Thunder Bay occurred when the British sloop *Welcome* from Fort Mackinac was lost in the straits in 1781 (Feltner and Feltner 1991, 48) and the warship HMS *Hope* became stranded on the south shore of Drummond Island in 1804, some 56 miles north of Alpena, the main town on Thunder Bay. Other colonial vessels and British and American warships were lost in Lake Ontario and Lake Erie. The earliest reported shipwrecks in Thunder Bay are distinctly American and date from the 1830s to the 1850s.

Alpena's first Euro-American residents, fishermen from the Detroit area, built seasonal shanties on the shores of Thunder Bay in the mid-1830s. The fishermen utilized Mackinaw boats, small two-mast sailing craft that could easily navigate the shoals surrounding the approaches to the bay islands. The boats were eventually replaced by steam tugs that could extract immense quantities of fish from the lake, primarily through gill netting. Net stakes were driven by the thousands into the lake bottom, so many that coast surveyors began plotting them on charts as hazards to navigation. A handful of fishing vessels were lost in Thunder Bay, including the Mackinaw boat *Equator* (1880) and the tugs *Aimee* (1880) and *William Maxwell* (1908). Most small vernacular fishing craft saw their demise as rotting hulks dragged ashore and stripped, or abandoned in out-of-the-way places along the shorelines of the Great Lakes.

By the 1850s businessmen seeking to exploit the area's virgin white pine forests as a source of lumber arrived in Thunder Bay. The lumber industry was booming, as it was the product used primarily to construct cities and towns across the region. Two sawmills commenced operation in 1859 and over 1 million feet of logs soon filled Thunder Bay River. The schooner *Meridian* carried the first cargo of lumber from Alpena (Boulton 1876, 10–11). The preferred method of transporting large quantities of lumber and other bulk cargoes with minimal expense was a system comprising a steam barge that towed between three and six schooners in consort. Most Great Lakes schooners after 1870 were actually tow barges no longer intended to be self-propelled, and it was not uncommon for a steam barge and consorts to haul between 1.5 and 2 million feet of lumber per trip (Bazzill 2007, 40–41).

Hundreds of vessels engaged in the lumber trade were lost throughout the Great Lakes, and both steam barges and schooners appear in Thunder Bay's archaeological record. The 127-foot, two-mast wooden schooner barge *John F. Warner* probably became the first total loss at the mouth of Thunder Bay River when it wrecked in October 1890. The lumber cargo was recovered from the *Warner*, and the hulk was moved to the waterfront south of town and abandoned at Alpena's first of several ship graveyards (*Alpena Weekly Argus*, 10/22/1890, 3). The steam barge *Shamrock* was also wrecked while engaged in the lumber trade. Built as the schooner *John W. Hanaford* in 1875, the 146-foot vessel was equipped with an engine the year before it sank at Alpena, in June 1905. It was later removed and abandoned south of town only a few hundred feet from the *Warner* wreck site. The shipwreck graveyard today is easily accessible to beginning divers, snorkelers, and kayakers.

Alpena's lumber boom, like many across the region, ended nearly as quickly as it began. Widespread deforestation and overuse of a slowly regenerating resource silenced the saws, and one by one the mills closed. Today evidence of this once thriving industry can be seen throughout Thunder Bay. Wooden pilings used to support docks, wharfs, and bridges occur by the thousands on the river and lake bottom. Cribs and abutments for dams and bridges, cables, pipes, and other cross-river structures, general refuse, sunken logs, slab wood, and dredge spoil were deposited across the maritime landscape.

The beginning of the twentieth century witnessed the widespread abandonment of vessels engaged in the rapidly declining lumber trade. Ship graveyards developed wherever vessels could be disposed of for easy retrieval or perpetual decay, and giant graveyards around major ports such as Sarnia, Ontario, contain dozens of intentionally abandoned vessels. Whitefish Point, 2½ miles east of Alpena, served as a graveyard for F. W. Gilchrist's schooner barge fleet, which was abandoned when he moved his sawmill operations to Oregon. In 1902 the *S.H. Lathrop* was stripped and run up onto the point, where "her old 'bones' will be allowed to bleach on the shore of the bay" (*Alpena Argus*, 5/14/1902, 5). In 1903 both the *Light Guard* and *Knight Templar* were placed at Whitefish

Point after being stripped, thus ending Gilchrist's "Red Line" that "carried lumber the value of which is fabulous" (*Alpena Evening News*, 7/23/1903, 4). All three schooner barges were canal size, 136 to 143 feet in length, and large sections of hull representing at least two of them can be viewed in 3 to 7 feet of water adjacent to miscellaneous wreckage, including a centerboard, rudder, and a small metal duck boat, at Whitefish Point.

In 1899 John Monaghan convinced area lumber barons that his experiments with a process for making limestone into cement would provide Alpena with a new industry. All the necessary ingredients were locally available for the manufacture of fine Portland cement, including high-grade limestone, marl, shale, and clay (Haltiner 1986, 51). The Alpena Portland Cement Company was organized and stone quarrying commenced east of Alpena. With cement production fully under way and a deep water channel facilitating lake access, the Huron Transportation Company was formed to solve the problem of delivering bulk product from Alpena to plants throughout the Great Lakes. In 1915 company president S. T. Crapo revolutionized the method of shipping cement in a ship's hold rather than in individual cloth sacks. Self-unloading machinery was installed on the 292-foot steamer *Samuel Mitchell*, and in September 1916 the ship transported from Alpena the first load of bulk cement ever carried by a self-unloading vessel (*Alpena News*, Special 2007 Supplement, 5).

Stone-carrying vessels were not without their mishaps and several were lost in Thunder Bay. Built by well-known shipwright James Davidson at West Bay City, Michigan, in 1888, the 288-foot wooden steam barge *William P. Rend* sprung a leak in a storm while in tow of the tug *Harrison* and grounded on a shoal north of the river mouth in September 1917 (*Alpena News*, 9/25/1917, 4). Attempts to remove the 2,323-ton vessel from the reef were futile, and the ship and its limestone cargo were abandoned in place (Stonehouse 1992, 35–36). The wreck is largely intact and its upright sides come to within a few feet of the water surface. A large boiler is located near the stern, and the wooden hull is heavily reinforced with iron strapping.

The 218-foot wooden bulk freighter *Oscar T. Flint* burned to the waterline on Thanksgiving Day 1909 and sank 4 miles from the mouth of Thunder Bay River. The *Flint*, bound for Duluth with a cargo of Kelley's Island limestone and a deck load of barreled salt, was at anchor when it caught fire. The barge *Nellie Redington*, in tow of the *Flint* with 800 tons of limestone on board, managed to escape the inferno (*Alpena Argus Pioneer*, 12/1/1909, 1). The wreck was an immediate threat to navigation, and in May the following year it was struck by the steamer *McLouth*, which was leaving the bay loaded with cement (*Alpena Evening News*, 5/25/1910, 4). Government contractors blew the wreck to pieces, and its heavily damaged machinery and twisted steel strapping remain on site. The *Flint* nonetheless remains a popular diving attraction because of its proximity to Alpena, shallow

depth, and embellishment with other shipwrecks' artifacts, including anchors and a windlass in 1993.

Stone carriers continued to be lost in the lakes. The 308-foot steel whaleback *Clifton*, built as *Samuel Mather* in 1892 and converted to a self-unloader in 1923, went down with twenty-eight souls in September 1924. The pilothouse and floating wreckage were found southeast of Thunder Bay, although the wreck has not yet been located. *Clifton* represented a type of craft truly unique to the Great Lakes. Whalebacks, invented in 1888 by Captain Alexander McDougall, were steel-hulled bulk carriers with rounded decks and long, snout-like bows resembling the hulls of early submarines. Only forty-one were constructed, most before 1893, when it was discovered that the design of their rounded decks and narrow hatches made unloading bulk cargo difficult. The 623-foot, 10,000-ton, electrically driven propeller ship *Carl D. Bradley*, a Rogers City stone carrier, was lost in November 1958 southwest of Gull Island in Lake Michigan with thirty-three crewmen. The 588-foot, 8,000-ton steel bulk carrier *Cedarville*, another Rogers City vessel, went down in the Straits of Mackinac after colliding with the Norwegian *Topdalsfjord* in May 1965 with ten lives. Perhaps the most famous bulk carrier lost in the Great Lakes was the 729-foot steamer *Edmund Fitzgerald*, which sank with all hands in Lake Superior in November 1975.

The same Devonian limestone outcrops prized by the cement industry were responsible for the majority of shipwrecks in Thunder Bay and surrounding areas of Lake Huron. Particularly dangerous rock outcrops creating "wreck traps" occur at Black River, South Point, North Point Reef, Thunder Bay Island, Middle Island, and Presque Isle. Through the centuries, hundreds of vessels hit the rocks in heavy seas, under conditions of limited visibility, or as a result of pilot error. Most vessels could be salvaged, repaired, and put back into service; however, of the 200 historic losses reported in northeast Michigan, one-third resulted from stranding, while the remainder were caused by foundering, collisions, fire, intentional abandonment, and other, miscellaneous factors.

The United States government recognized the area's hazards to navigation, and federal attempts to reduce the number of shipwrecks off Thunder Bay began early in the nineteenth century. A series of lighthouses were constructed beginning in the 1830s along the shores of Lake Huron to protect and rescue mariners in distress, and the first lighthouse on Thunder Bay Island was erected in 1831 (Tongue 2004, 12–14). Others followed, with lights established at Old Presque Isle (1840), Sturgeon Point (1869), Presque Isle Point (1870), the mouth of Thunder Bay River (1875), Forty Mile Point (1894), and Middle Island (1905). A series of lifesaving stations were likewise provided in the 1870s at Sturgeon Point, Thunder Bay Island, and Middle Island.

Despite improvements to navigation, countless ships still failed to reach their destinations. The earliest reported loss in Thunder Bay occurred when the paddle wheel steamer *New*

Orleans ran aground west of Sugar Island on June 15, 1849. Fishermen from Thunder Bay and Sugar islands rescued the passengers and crew, and most of the cargo and machinery were later recovered. In addition to *New Orleans*, two other early paddle wheelers, *Benjamin Franklin* (1850) and *Albany* (1853), met their demises on Thunder Bay Island and Presque Isle, respectively. All three vessels were extensively salvaged and little remains but the lower hull structure, although *Franklin's* shafts, boilers, and machinery remain on the lake bottom.

The quintessential workhorses of the day, schooners sailed the lakes by the thousands in the late nineteenth century, and dozens were lost in and around Thunder Bay. The two-masted vessels *Kyle Spangler* (1860), *Persian* (1868), and *E.B. Allen* (1871) and the three-masted *Cornelia B. Windiate* (1875), *Lucinda Van Valkenburg* (1887), and *Typo* (1899) represent a class of schooners typical of the late nineteenth century known as canalers. Designed with dimensions to allow passage through the Welland Canal connecting Lake Erie and Lake Ontario, the hulls were configured as nearly as possible to fit the locks' dimensions. Even the bowsprits were hinged to maximize hull length and thus carrying capacity. All of these vessels, with the exception of *Windiate*, were sunk as result of collisions with other vessels in the busy shipping lanes off Alpena.

Smaller schooners, usually involved in more local endeavors, are also found at Thunder Bay. *Maid of the Mist* (1878), for example, was contracted to haul cedar posts from Alpena County to Detroit when it washed ashore in a gale at Huron Beach. The 15-year-old schooner was involved in a dozen mishaps before its ultimate demise, and evidence of large-scale repair is preserved in the archaeological record. Larger than canal-size schooners, the 156-foot *Fame* (1887) and *Ishpeming* (1903), 178-foot *Nellie Gardner* (1883), and 185-foot *American Union* (1894) are giant vessels that wrecked in shallow water, their large drafts likely contributing to their unfortunate ends.

Schooners are not the only sailing craft found on the lake bottom. The three-masted bark *Ogarita* went down in 1905. Built by C. W. Lent of Conneaut, Ohio, in 1864, *Ogarita* burned and sank when its cargo of 1,200 tons of coal ignited off Thunder Bay Island. The two-masted brigantine *John J. Audubon* (1854) is located not far from its collision mate, the two-masted schooner *Defiance*. *Audubon*, still with a deck load of railroad iron, sits upright in 170 feet of water.

Steamers and their tows also are well represented in the archaeological record, particularly on North Point Reef, a geologic feature that extends over 1 mile from shore and rises to depths as shallow as 5 feet. The wooden lumber steamer *Galena* went ashore on North Point carrying 272,000 feet of lumber on September 24, 1872, and quickly broke apart. Much of the machinery, furniture, and crew's possessions were removed from the wreck, and the engine was later salvaged for use in another vessel. Wreckage tentatively identified as

originating from *Galena* lies intermingled with materials from later losses, including three ships that went aground on North Point during a blinding snowstorm on November 28, 1904. The wooden lumber steamer *B.W. Blanchard* ran aground while towing the schooner barges *John T. Johnson* and *John Kilderhouse*. *Blanchard* and *Johnson* were completely wrecked, while the *Kilderhouse* was eventually recovered. The vessels carried a combined load of 2 million feet of lumber valued at $28,000. The greater portion of the lumber was recovered, and the boilers and machinery of the *Blanchard* were removed from the wreck the following year.

Early steam propellers, bulk and package freighters, and lumber hookers have also been found in and around Thunder Bay, including *James Davidson* (1883), *Monohansett* (1907), *William P. Thew* (1909), *F.T. Barney* (1868), *Florida* (1897), *Grecian* (1906), *Montana* (1914), *Norman* (1895), and *Portsmouth* (1867). Many of these wrecks are popular dive destinations because of their structural integrity or unique circumstances of loss. *Florida*, for example, collided with the *George W. Roby* off Middle Island, was nearly cut in half, and went down with a cargo of 50,000 bushels of wheat, 1,451 barrels and 3,150 sacks of flour, syrup, barrels of whiskey, and a full upper load of package freight, much of which remains on site. The steel-hulled bulk freight steamer *Grecian*, a Globe Iron Works creation from 1891, stranded at Detour then foundered in Thunder Bay while under tow southbound for repairs. Two large steel tanks known as canalons were sunk and fastened to *Grecian's* stern by hardhat divers intending to raise the vessel in 1909. The tanks exploded when filled with air and remain attached to the crippled wreck.

Perhaps the most tragic accident in Thunder Bay occurred in August 1865, when the passenger freighter *Pewabic* was run into and sunk by its sister vessel *Meteor*, with the loss of life estimated to be between 30 and 125 people. No explanation for the collision has ever been offered. Weather conditions were favorable and the vessels were in sight of one another for several miles before impact. Though injured, *Meteor* was able to continue to Sault Ste. Marie after rescuing many passengers from the water. *Pewabic*, built by Peck and Masters of Cleveland, went down with several hundred tons of valuable copper and iron ore in its hold. Search and salvage efforts began almost immediately, though the wreck was not discovered until June 1897. Much of the cargo was recovered from 180 feet of water using armored divers, submersible bells with manipulator arms, and bucket cranes, though at great cost; several divers perished on the wreck from drowning or decompression illnesses (*Alpena News*, 7/12/197, 3). Today the wreck is visited by technical divers and remotely operated vehicles.

Even with the twentieth century's more accurate charts and advanced positioning and lifesaving equipment, modern freighters still occasionally sank in Lake Huron. *Isaac M. Scott* went down with all hands during the infamous storm of

1913, when eight vessels and 194 seamen perished in Lake Huron alone. *Scott* sits upside down on the lake bottom like several of its contemporaries (Hemming 1992, 77, 137). *D.R. Hanna* (1919), *W.C. Franz* (1934), *Viator* (1935), and *Monrovia* (1959) all went down as a result of collisions in the busy shipping lanes off Thunder Bay. The German freighter *Nordmeer*, Thunder Bay's newest large shipwreck, ran up on a shoal and stuck fast in 1966. Attempts to free the vessel failed, and in a few harsh winter seasons ice all but destroyed the steel vessel. A salvage barge involved in the recovery of deck machinery and scrap steel from *Nordmeer* sits on the bottom near the larger wreck (*Alpena News*, 7/11/1975, A1).

Although perhaps not as romanticized as passenger vessels, paddle wheelers, or sailing craft, barges also played an important role in Great Lakes maritime history. The 309-foot *Lake Michigan Car Ferry Barge No. 1* was built in 1895 by James Davidson to haul twenty-eight rail cars on four tracks across the decks. It was converted to a tow barge before sinking with a deck load of lumber and 200 crates of live chickens in November 1918. *Barge No. 83* (1941) foundered northeast of Thunder Bay Island with well drilling machinery and sheet piling. "Scanlon's Barge" (unknown date of loss) sank off North Point with a derrick crane on board, and the "Carbide Barge" (unknown date of loss) and a "Dump Scow" (ca. 1930) also foundered in heavy seas with unsalvaged deck equipment still in place. Barges were also intentionally sunk to serve functions other than hauling cargo. The U.S. Coast Guard, for example, grounded a wooden spud barge on North Point in the 1930s to serve as the foundation of a pier for loading vessels with supplies and equipment for Thunder Bay Island (Feltner and Stock 1983, 21). The barge is partially submerged and also served as the entry point for a submarine telephone cable extending from the mainland to the islands.

Maritime heritage is ingrained in the residents of the Great Lakes area. A deep sense of stewardship for the numerous shipwrecks, submerged cultural resources, and lighthouses led to the establishment of historic preservation societies and marine protected areas in the United States and Canada beginning in the 1970s. Isle Royale National Park, Pictured Rocks and Sleeping Bear Dunes National Seashores, and Fathom Five National Marine Park are federally managed parks containing numerous submerged cultural resources. Because virtually every type of watercraft used on the Great Lakes is represented in Thunder Bay's archaeological record, the bay became one of eleven state underwater preserves in Michigan nearly thirty years ago. Thunder Bay was further designated as a National Marine Sanctuary in October 2000, becoming the first of its kind located in a freshwater environment, and only the second after USS *Monitor* off the North Carolina coast expressly created for the protection of maritime heritage resources (Thompson and Lusardi 2004, 30–31).

All of Thunder Bay's shipwrecks are accessible to the public, and diving and visitation are encouraged.

Remember, however, that all wrecks are protected by state and federal laws that prohibit the removal or disturbance of artifacts without a permit. Mooring buoys are seasonally placed on many of the heavily visited sites to prevent anchoring damage. A variety of dive charters, glass bottom boat tours, and kayak rental agencies exist around the Great Lakes, particularly at Thunder Bay, at the Alger Underwater Preserve in Munising, and in the Straits of Mackinac. The Great Lakes Maritime Heritage Center in Alpena, Michigan, as well as dozens of other maritime museums across the region, bring the shipwreck experience to nondivers through outreach and education programs, telepresence, and interactive exhibits. For more information about Great Lakes shipwreck preserves and exhibits readers can visit the Web sites and other information sources listed below.

Further Reading: *Alpena Argus Pioneer*, weekly publication, Alpena, Michigan (12/1/1909); *Alpena Evening News*, daily publication, Alpena, Michigan (7/23/1903, 5/25/1910); *Alpena News*, daily publication, Alpena, Michigan (9/25/1917, 7/12/1974, 7/11/1975, Special 2007 Supplement); *Alpena Weekly Argus*, weekly publication, Alpena, Michigan (10/22/1890, 5/14/1902); Bazzill, Dina M., *The Missing Link between Sail and Steam: Steambarges and the Joys of Door County, Wisconsin* (Greenville, NC: East Carolina University, 2007); Boulton, William, *Complete History Alpena County, Michigan* (Alpena, MI: Argus Books and Job Rooms, 1876); Cleland, Charles E., "The Inland Shore Fishery of the Northern Great Lakes: Its Development and Importance in Prehistory," *American Antiquity* 47(4) (1982): 761–783; Cleland, Charles E., Richard D. Clute, and Robert E. Haltiner, "Naub-Cow-Zo-Win Discs from Northern Michigan," *Midcontinental Journal of Archaeology* 9(2) (1984): 235–250; Fathom Five National Marine Park of Canada Web site, http://www.pc.gc.ca/amnc-nmca/on/fathomfive/index_e.asp; Feltner, Charles E., and Jeri Baron Feltner, *Shipwrecks of the Straits of Mackinac* (Dearborn, MI: Seajay, 1991); Feltner, Charles E., and Stanley J. Stock, "Shipwrecks of Thunder Bay, Part I," *Chronicle: The Quarterly Magazine of the Historical Society of Michigan* 19(3) (1983): 16–21; Halsey, John R., *Beneath the Inland Seas: Michigan's Underwater Archaeological Heritage* (Lansing: Michigan Department of State, 1990); Haltiner, Robert E., *The Town That Wouldn't Die: A Photographic History of Alpena, Michigan from Its Beginnings through 1940* (Traverse City, MI: Village Press, 1986); Haltiner, Robert E., *Stories the Red People Have Told, and More: A Testimonial to N.E. Michigan's "Long-Ago People"* (Alpena, MI: Robert E. Haltiner, 2002); Hemming, Robert J., *Ships Gone Missing: The Great Lakes Storm of 1913* (Chicago: Contemporary Books, 1992); Lusardi, Wayne R., "Northeast Region: Thunder Bay National Marine Sanctuary," in *Fathoming Our Past: Historical Contexts of the National Marine Sanctuaries*, edited by Bruce G. Terrell (Silver Spring, MD: U.S. Department of Commerce. National Marine Sanctuary Program, 2007), 12–15; Michigan Underwater Preserves Web site, http://www.michiganpreserves.org/; Pott, Kenneth R., "Underwater Archaeology in Michigan," in *Retrieving Michigan's Buried Past: The Archaeology of the Great Lakes State*, edited by John R. Halsey (Bloomfield Hills, MI: Cranbrook Institute of Science, 1999), 359–367; Quaife, Milo M., *The American Lake Series: Lake Michigan*

(Indianapolis, IN: Bobbs-Merrill, 1944); Shott, Michael J., and Henry T. Wright, "The Paleo-Indians: Michigan's First People," in *Retrieving Michigan's Buried Past: The Archaeology of the Great Lakes State*, edited by John R. Halsey (Bloomfield Hills, MI: Cranbrook Institute of Science, 1999), 59–70; Stonehouse, Frederick, *A Short Guide to the Shipwrecks of Thunder Bay* (Alpena, MI: Thunder Bay Underwater Preserve, 1992); Thompson, Kate, and Wayne R. Lusardi, "Lessons beneath the Waves: Maritime Heritage Revealed through Shipwrecks," *Current: The Journal of Marine Education* 20(3) (2004): 30–34; Thunder Bay National Marine Sanctuary Web site, http://thunderbay.noaa.gov/; Tongue, Stephen D., *Lanterns and Lifeboats: A History of Thunder Bay Island* (Alpena, MI: Sarge, 2004).

Wayne R. Lusardi

KIMMSWICK PALEOINDIAN SITE

Mastodon State Historic Site, Missouri

Early Paleoindian Hunters and Their Prey

The Kimmswick site, historically known as the Kimmswick Bone Beds, has a complex archaeological and paleontological history. The site is located in east central Missouri, approximately 32 kilometers (20 mi) south of St. Louis, on the eastern margin of the Ozark Highland physiographic province, or Salem Plateau. Karst topography has developed upon the unglaciated Salem Plateau, which is drained to the east by numerous tributaries of the Mississippi River. The Kimmswick site is situated at the confluence of two of these tributaries, called Rock and Black creeks, under a talus slope at the base of a limestone bluff approximately 2.4 kilometers (1.5 mi) west of the Mississippi River. The bedrock is mapped as Ordovician age Kimmswick limestone. The ancient vegetation of the region where the site is located included upland oak and hickory forest interspersed with bottomland prairie grasses.

The Kimmswick locality was initially referred to as Sulphur Springs, presumably because of a sulphur spring located about 0.4 kilometers (0.25 mi) from the site. Albert C. Koch was the first person to conduct an excavation at the site, but his publications contain limited information about his extensive excavations. Koch sold numerous fossil specimens he recovered from Kimmswick and other Missouri sites to various museums in the United States and overseas. It was after Koch's extensive excavations that Sulphur Springs became known as the Kimmswick Bone Beds.

Albert C. Koch was born in Germany in 1804 and immigrated to the United States when he was 22. Shortly after his arrival, he settled in St. Louis, where he set up a museum that housed his many fossil finds, along with other curiosities. Over a few short years, Koch compiled one of the most impressive fossil collections of the day, which included hundreds of mastodon teeth, cranial and postcranial elements, and the remains of deer, elk, giant ground sloth, and probably bison.

In 1897 amateur paleontologist C. W. Beehler resurrected interest in the Kimmswick Bone Beds by lecturing on and publicizing the site. He attracted the attention of a group of wealthy scholars in St. Louis known as the Humboldt Exploration Company, who eventually leased the site from the landowner for ninety-nine years. With financing from the Humboldt Exploration Company, plans were made to excavate the site to provide specimens for a museum in St. Louis. In 1900 Beehler initiated his excavations under the direction of J. W. Caldwell, secretary of the Humboldt Exploration Company. Beehler's museum was a small (60 ft by 40 ft) and simple wooden structure filled with fossils. Located less than a mile from a railroad linking St. Louis and New Orleans, it became very popular. Visitors included eminent archaeologists and paleontologists from across the United States.

On their way to the Afton Springs fossil locality in Oklahoma, De Lancey Gill and W. H. Holmes, then curator of anthropology at the Smithsonian Institution, visited with Beehler at the Kimmswick site for several days. During this time—in September 1901—they conducted minor excavations. Holmes returned to Kimmswick with Gerard Fowke in 1902 to conduct excavations at the site. It is uncertain what became of the excavated materials. It is not known what became of Beehler's museum and much of his collection. Four pieces of chipped-stone tools found at Kimmswick during Beehler's excavations are currently curated at the Field Museum of Natural History in Chicago. One is a resharpened Clovis projectile point (FMNH 205526) originally classified as an eastern Folsom, and the other is described as a knife (FMNH 205527). Along with the stone artifacts, the Field Museum collection from Kimmswick came with an affidavit of authenticity and association with extinct fauna signed by W. F. Parks, a dentist and well-known artifact collector from St. Louis who visited the site often during early 1900s excavations.

In 1905 a large lime kiln was built, and extensive limestone quarrying took place at the site. Although the lime kiln burned in 1938, the remains are still visible. A 10-by-14-meter concrete-slab remnant of the lime kiln covers a portion of the site today. Removal of large portions of the kiln in the 1950s and 1960s adversely affected areas of the site.

Following Beehler's work, a number of private excavations took place at the site, but all of these lack scientific records. However, in the early 1940s, the site again became the focus of scientific inquiry when Robert McCormick Adams, then a student of Fay Cooper Cole at the University of Chicago, conducted extensive, federally funded WPA (Works Progress Administration) excavations. Although much of Adams's documentation (artifacts, notes, maps, photographs) of his work at Kimmswick is deteriorated or missing, it is possible to form a general reconstruction of his excavations. The majority of cultural material recovered, including many faunal specimens, was apparently derived from disturbed contexts. The only artifact he recovered from an undisturbed context was an Early Archaic projectile point from a loess deposit overlying the Bone Bed. Adams never recovered any artifacts directly associated with Pleistocene fauna at Kimmswick, but he apparently believed the site had potential for providing such evidence.

In 1976 the site became part of the Missouri state park system and is located within Mastodon State Park. Archaeological and paleontological resources played a major role in the planning and development of the new park. In 1979 personnel from the Illinois State Museum (ISM) conducted contract archaeological investigations (survey and testing) for the Missouri Department of Natural Resources (MDNR). The purpose of their investigations was to locate and define cultural and paleontological resources in proposed development areas; to provide recommendations concerning mitigation and possible impact; to determine the physical context of and assess the integrity of the Bone Beds; and to provide information and specimens for a proposed interpretive center to be built in the park.

Fieldwork at Kimmswick was conducted in 1979, and preliminary laboratory processing and analyses were conducted in 1980. Kimmswick (23JE334) was one of five archaeological sites identified during the ISM survey. Testing of the Kimmswick site included hand excavation of about 52 square meters and nine backhoe trenches to define the stratigraphy. Bulk soil samples (50 cm by 50 cm) were collected in 10-centimeter levels from each hand-excavated unit for wet sieving. All artifact-bearing sediment was wet screened through 1/16-inch mesh, while sediments above and below the cultural horizons were dry screened through 1/4-inch mesh hardware cloth. With the test excavations of the Bone Beds, the project became an interdisciplinary research effort, with a host of prominent researchers providing their interpretations of various aspects of the site.

Seven strata were identified in the Kimmswick test excavations. The deepest of these were colluvial limestone gravels (B1 and B2). The upper zone, B2, is pedogenically altered and contains an E horizon (E). Bone from this zone, which was 10 to 50 centimeters thick, was not well preserved.

The age of the colluvium is uncertain. Several shallow ponds developed in the surface of the colluvial gravel and filled with overbank deposits and colluvium. Excavations indicate the presence of three ponds, each of which contains artifacts, megafaunal remains, and extant and extirpated microfauna. The deepest of the pond deposits is a bluish gray silty clay (C1), and the shallower pond deposits consist of olive green silty clay (C3). Silty colluvium characterized by sterile brown clay separates C1 and C3 pond deposits. The pond deposits were buried beneath a layer of silty colluvium that measures 50 centimeters thick and is characterized by brown clay. Diagnostic Clovis artifacts were recovered from both the C1 and C3 pond deposits. The proximal half of an Early Archaic St. Charles point base was recovered from the tan colluvium and alluvium (D) overlying the pond sediments. Based on their stratigraphic position and their artifact content, the pond deposits probably date to between 11,000 and 12,000 years BP. The overlying tan alluvium and colluvium are likely early Holocene in age, based on their correlation with the Rogers alluvium in western Missouri and the inclusion within of an Early Archaic artifact dated to between 9,400 and 9,000 BP at the Twin Ditch site in west central Illinois.

A diverse assemblage of extinct and modern fauna is associated with the Clovis horizon at Kimmswick. The remains of mastodon (*Mammut americanum*), peccary (*Mylophus nasutus*), and ground sloth (*Glosserium harlani*) were found in direct association with Clovis artifacts. In addition to these large taxa, the Clovis horizon contains the remains of white-tail deer, fish, amphibians, reptiles, birds, and small mammals. Mammalian fauna from the pond deposits include open woodland species, such as tree squirrels (*Scurius*), woodchucks (*Marmota*), thirteen-lined ground squirrels (*Spermophilus*), pocket gophers (*Geomys*), microtine rodents (*Microtus pennsylvanicus*), and bog lemmings (*Synaptomys cooperi*).

The smaller vertebrate assemblage comprises mostly isolated teeth, tooth fragments, and snake vertebrae. Russ Graham suggests that the microfauna of the pond deposits were accumulated by small carnivores, such as weasels. Faunal remains are concentrated in areas containing lithic artifacts. Elements of certain taxa (i.e., deer and turtle bones, unbroken adult and juvenile mastodon teeth, and ground sloth dermal ossicles) appear to be clustered or concentrated in certain areas at the site. Clovis artifacts and the Harlan's ground sloth dermal ossicles (microscopic bony plates found as a layer beneath the outer skin) were distributed around a circular concentration of manganese, which is interpreted as a possible hearth feature.

The distribution of ground-sloth ossicles is significant, for their occurrence without other ground-sloth skeletal elements suggests that the skin or skins of these animals were brought to the site. Graham and Kay argue that the distributions of micro-flakes are evidence of human activity areas. Micro-flakes are interpreted as primary refuse derived from tool manufacture, use (e.g., cutting, skinning, scraping), and maintenance (e.g., resharpening), and have not have been displaced appreciably by natural or cultural processes. Based on the lithic artifact assemblage, faunal associations, and site formation factors, the Clovis component at Kimmswick is interpreted as a mastodon-killing and -processing site with short-term habitation.

A total of eight finished chipped-stone artifacts have been formally analyzed by Marvin Kay. Two of these eight artifacts are specimen FMNH 205526, a bifacially flaked cutting implement, and FMNH 205527, a Clovis point. Both were reportedly found at Kimmswick in the early 1900s and are now curated at the Field Museum of Natural History in Chicago. Sediments adhering to the knife-like implement indicate that it was derived from stratum D, the Early Archaic zone. The Field Museum's Clovis point, however, had microscopically observable manganese and bonded secondary sediments adhering to its surface, which suggests it may have come from the same stratum from which Clovis artifacts were derived in 1979.

The remaining six artifacts (all recovered in the 1979 excavations) include a complete, finished Clovis projectile point (K-L22-32); biface fragment (L-24:6); a utilized flake (L-20:45) and a heavily resharpened Clovis point (K-H22-83) from stratum C3; a proximal fragment of a fluted preform (K-L24-6) from C1; and an alternately beveled biface tip and a proximal fragment of a St. Charles point from stratum D. Bulk soil samples yielded additional lithic artifacts, including micro-debitage and utilized flakes. In fact, the majority of debitage is less than 0.32 centimeters.

The Clovis artifact assemblage from the Kimmswick site contains a wide variety of lithic raw material for such a small collection. The complete finished point in the FMNH collections and the basal ear from the ISM excavations are both made of St. Genevieve chert. The heavily resharpened point is made of Fern Glen chert. The fluted-point manufacturing reject is made of Burlington chert. All of these materials are available within 60 kilometers of the site and are therefore considered local. The largest point in the assemblage is made of an unidentified oolitic gray chert. The debitage from the Clovis components was produced from the manufacture, use, and maintenance of tools at the site and is apparently of the same suite of raw materials used in the manufacture of formal tools (Marvin Kay, personal communication 1993).

Further Reading: Graham, Russell W., C. Vance Haynes Jr., Donald Lee Johnson, and Marvin Kay, "Kimmswick: A Clovis-Mastodon Association in Eastern Missouri," *Science* 213(1) (1981): 115–117; Graham, Russell W., and Marvin Kay, "Taphanomic Comparison of Cultural and Non-cultural Faunal Deposits at the Kimmswick and Barnhart Sites, Jefferson County, Missouri," in *Late Pleistocene and Early Holocene Paleoecology and Archaeology of the Eastern Great Lakes Region*, edited by R. S. Laub, N. G. Miller, and DW Steadman, *Bulletin of the Buffalo Society of Natural Sciences* 33 (1988): 227–240; Morrow, Juliet E., "The Organization of Early Paleoindian Lithic Technology in the Confluence Region of the Mississippi, Illinois, and Missouri Rivers," Ph.D. diss., Washington University, St. Louis, 1996.

Juliet E. Morrow

THE CARRIER MILLS ARCHAEOLOGICAL DISTRICT

Saline River Valley, Southern Illinois

Ancient Long-Term Activities at the Black Earth Site

Black Earth (11SA87), one of three large, intensively occupied sites in the Carrier Mills archaeological district, was located along the South Fork of the Saline River in southeastern Illinois. In the late 1970s, Southern Illinois University archaeologists excavated the sites, because the pending expansion of a large surface coal mine would ultimately destroy them. Black Earth, the largest and most complex site, consisted of three discrete middens collectively covering more than 43,000 square meters along a low ridge. Human activity at Black Earth extended from the Early Archaic period through the Mississippian period (ca. 7000 BC–AD 1600). Significantly, parts of the site were intensively utilized by late Middle Archaic hunter-gatherers at the end of the middle Holocene (ca. 4000–3000 BC).

The most archaeologically significant part of the Black Earth site, known as Area A, was located at its extreme western end, adjacent to an expansive shallow wetland. The following discussion focuses on that part of the site. Area A excavations revealed more than 1.5 meters of dark, organically rich, artifact-bearing midden. The midden's lowermost meter contained primarily late Middle Archaic (ca. 4000–2900 BC) artifacts, features, burials, and food remains.

A series of eight charcoal samples taken from the late Middle Archaic zone yielded uncalibrated radiocarbon dates ranging from $5,905 \pm 85$ to $4,860 \pm 85$ years ago, indicating a rapid rate of midden formation. The upper third of the midden also contained late Middle Archaic artifacts, but these were mixed with those of the site's later inhabitants.

The intensity of late Middle Archaic activity at Area A also is indicated by the midden's physical and chemical properties. For example, sand comprised nearly 50 percent of the midden, compared to only 5 percent of the off-site soil. This difference is due to the breakdown of literally tons of sandstone brought there to make tools and construct features. Also, wood ash from fires produced very high concentrations of calcium, potassium, and magnesium in the midden, creating very alkaline conditions. The midden's chemical and physical properties, combined with the rapid rate of midden formation, suggest that late Middle Archaic hunter-gatherers intensively utilized the Black Earth site on a recurring, if not year-round, basis.

Late Middle Archaic hunter-gatherers lived at Black Earth during a time when environmental conditions were somewhat drier and warmer than today. Plants that thrived in drier habitats, such as grasses and certain herbs, increased in coverage, while the distribution of species preferring more moist conditions, like many nut-bearing trees, decreased. For hunter-gatherers, drier conditions significantly increased the strategic importance of wetland habitats like those near Black Earth. This increased emphasis on wetland resources conforms to a much broader pattern seen in other parts of the North American mid-continent at this time.

Black Earth's late Middle Archaic inhabitants subsisted by hunting and collecting a wide variety of seasonally available plants and animals. Unlike in some parts of the mid-continent, archaeologists found no evidence for early attempts at plant cultivation or gardening. Hickory nuts, acorns, and walnuts were important plant foods, as were many different kinds of wild fruits, starchy seeds, roots, tubers, and rhizomes. Undoubtedly many other plants had important dietary roles but are not preserved in the archaeological record.

Site inhabitants also hunted the many animal species that lived in the surrounding forest and wetland habitats. They focused their efforts on the forest-edge species (whitetail deer, turkey, elk, rabbit, fox squirrel, and quail), of which the deer was by far the most economically important. The forests provided raccoons, opossums, gray squirrels, and now-extinct passenger pigeons. Of course, the extensive wetlands that surrounded Black Earth provided many species of fish, waterfowl, mammals, and reptiles not found in other parts of the region.

The variety and intensity of late Middle Archaic activities is reflected by the frequency and diversity of cultural features and artifacts. Project archaeologists identified more than 200 features, including two kinds of pits: clay, charcoal, and ash concentrations and baked clay hearths. The most common of these were small, shallow, basin-shaped depressions thought to be associated with food preparation involving both direct and indirect heat. Larger circular pits with straight to slightly tapering sides may have been used for storage. Few post molds were documented at Black Earth, probably because of the very dark midden soil that made features of all kinds difficult to detect. The few post molds that were identified intruded into the lighter colored soil below the midden.

The large and diverse flaked- and ground-stone artifact assemblage from Black Earth provides important insights on late Middle Archaic technology, economics, and mobility. Site inhabitants used chert to make all of their flaked-stone implements—projectile points, scrapers, drills, and so on. Most of this chert was collected locally, but some of it came from sources located 40 to 50 kilometers west of Black Earth, providing insights into the size of the territory exploited by late Middle Archaic hunter-gatherers. Most of their projectile points were side-notched varieties that included examples of the Matanzas, Big Sandy II, Godar, and Faulkner types. Side-notched hafted end scrapers were an important tool form, many of which appear to be made from recycled broken projectile points. Edge wear studies indicate that many of the hafted end scrapers were used to process dry animal hide—probably deer.

The late Middle Archaic tool kit also contained numerous kinds of ground-stone implements. Many tools were made from locally available sandstone (grinding stone and grinding slabs), most of which were probably used to process plant foods. In contrast, stone used to fashion some ground-stone tools, like grooved axes, *atl atl* weights, pestles, and plummets, was collected from more distant glacial deposits.

In addition to stone tools, Black Earth's highly alkaline soils helped preserve many kinds of bone and antler artifacts not represented on most hunter-gatherer sites due to poor preservation conditions. Late Middle Archaic hunter-gatherers used the bones and antlers of the whitetail deer to make many utilitarian or ornamental objects like awls, scrapers, fishhooks, chert-knapping implements, *atl atl* hooks and handles, beads, and cups. They made cups, bowls, and rattles from turtle shell, and they fashioned finely carved and engraved hairpins from long pieces of split deer bone. Some of the Black Earth pins are identical to those found at contemporary sites in other parts of the mid-continent. The shared ideas about how to carve and engrave these elaborate pins suggests that widely scattered hunter-gatherer groups interacted on a recurring basis. The few exotic items made from nonlocal materials, like copper or marine shell, found at Black Earth support the existence of regular intergroup contact and exchange through far-reaching late Middle Archaic social networks.

In addition to conducting many domestic activities at Black Earth, late Middle Archaic hunter-gatherers also performed rituals associated with the burial of their dead. Excavation and study of the more than 150 late Middle Archaic burials yielded important insights into hunter-gatherer nutrition, health, and social organization. Based on the percentage of the site excavated, Black Earth may have once held as many as 400 late Middle Archaic burials.

Approximately half of these deceased individuals were buried in a flexed position; most of the remaining ones were extended. Associated burial goods accompanied 27 percent of the deceased. These items consisted of both utilitarian objects (projectile points, axes, awls) and ornamental or ritual objects (shell beads and pendants, bone beads, carved and engraved hairpins, crystals). The late Middle Archaic mortuary program at Black Earth is indicative of an egalitarian society in which a person's social position was based on their age, gender, and personal accomplishments.

The overall health of Black Earth inhabitants was generally good compared to that of many other prehistoric groups. Once surviving a childhood characterized by high infant mortality (27 percent died in the first year), male and female life expectancies were 32 and 38 years, respectively. One woman lived in excess of 58 years. These life expectancies are not that different from those of some pre-industrial European societies.

While the Black Earth hunter-gatherers were generally healthy, they did experience a variety of broken bones and other injuries. Many of these injuries had healed, indicating that the people tended to survive these traumatic events. Arthritis was a common problem for most Black Earth adults, as it is for many people today. In addition, all adults and most of the children experienced severe tooth wear caused by chewing food containing tiny pieces of grit. Most of this highly abrasive material came from the stone tools that they used to prepare food.

The rate of midden accumulation, the presence of numerous features and burials, the high frequency and diversity of artifacts, and the evidence for participation in regional social networks suggest that the late Middle Archaic hunter-gatherer groups that inhabited Black Earth became increasingly complex during this time. Black Earth appears to have served as a base camp where at least part of the group lived on a multiseasonal or year-round basis.

The Black Earth site continued to be occupied by subsequent Late Archaic (3000–1000 BC) hunter-gatherers, but the dramatic decrease in midden formation suggests that the site did not hold the same economic and social importance as before. Several thousand years later (ca. 200 BC–AD 400), Black Earth became the focus of Middle Woodland activity, as indicated by the construction of more than 100 deep storage pits. It appears that Middle Woodland people picked Black Earth to construct their storage facilities because of the well-drained sandy soil attributable to Middle Archaic activities thousands of years earlier. Even later (ca. AD 1200), Late Prehistoric Mississippian farmers took advantage of the same organically enriched Middle Archaic midden by placing some of their agricultural fields there, as did some of southern Illinois's first African American and European American settlers. Clearly the activities of late Middle Archaic hunter-gatherers had a profound impact on the area's cultural landscape for thousands of years.

More recently the landscape on which the Black Earth site was situated has been drastically altered by mining activities that removed all traces of the site and its former inhabitants. However, several of the publications listed below provide good overviews of the site and the prehistoric Native Americans who once lived there.

Further Reading: Jefferies, Richard W., *The Archaeology of Carrier Mills: 10,000 Years in the Saline Valley of Illinois* (Carbondale: Southern Illinois University Press, 1987); Jefferies, Richard W., and Brian M. Butler, eds., *The Carrier Mills Archaeological Project: Human Adaptation in the Saline Valley, Illinois* (Carbondale, IL: Center for Archaeological Investigations, 1982); Jefferies, Richard W., and B. Mark Lynch, "Dimensions of Middle Archaic Cultural Adaptation at the Black Earth Site, Saline County, Illinois," in *Archaic Hunters and Gatherers in the American Midwest*, edited by James L. Phillips and James A. Brown (New York: Academic Press, 1983), 299–322; Price, Douglas T., and Gary M. Feinman, "Carrier Mills: A Middle Archaic Settlement in Southern Illinois," in *Images of the Past*, edited by Douglas T. Price and Gary M. Feinman (Boston: McGraw-Hill, 2005), 180–184.

Richard W. Jefferies

GRAHAM CAVE HISTORIC SITE

Missouri

Early Inhabitants and Activities at Graham Cave

Graham Cave is a large rock shelter formed beneath a dome of Ordovician-age St. Peter sandstone located in Montgomery County, Missouri. The cave overlooks the Loutre River valley just north of U.S. I-70, approximately 100 kilometers west of St. Louis. About 24 kilometers downstream from the site, the stream enters the Missouri River. Today the cave is preserved as the featured attraction of a state park that is named after the site and visited annually by thousands of tourists traveling the

Photo of Graham Cave taken around the time of initial excavation, ca. 1950. [American Archaeology Division, University of Missouri]

interstate corridor. Graham Cave has been designated a National Historic Landmark by the Secretary of the Interior. Visitors may walk into the entrance and stand beneath the overhang while viewing the stratigraphic exposures but are restrained from proceeding further by protective fencing erected by the Missouri Department of Natural Resources. This measure has been taken to preserve the culture-bearing deposits.

The cave is a spectacular feature on the local landscape. The large semi-elliptical entrance measures 18 meters wide and nearly an equal distance from the entrance to the back of the cave. From that point, one can crawl for another 9 meters. Using artificial light, one can see for another 4 to 5 meters to where the surface merges with the ceiling. The ceiling height near the entrance was only about 2.4 meters prior to excavation; however, after excavation a ceiling height of 5 meters was reached at the base of the archaeological deposits. When the cave was initially occupied by humans during the early Holocene, lighted floor space (about 740 sq. m) was approximately twice that available when first reported by Euro-American settlers.

The cave was first recorded by archaeologists in 1930, but it was not until two decades later that the first archaeological work at Graham Cave was conducted by the University of Missouri as part of an archaeological salvage operation. Work was initiated in late 1949, when it was discovered that the landowner was bulldozing deposits from in front of and within the entrance of the cave to create a livestock shelter and feed-lot. University of Missouri archaeologists, with the aid of volunteers from the Missouri Archaeological Society, carried out work at Graham Cave periodically over the next five years, excavating and recording the archaeological deposits before they were destroyed.

The 1950s work established the importance of Graham Cave as a site of significant antiquity, containing a cultural sequence that helped define the age and content of the Early Archaic in the midwestern United States. A second, more systematic effort was carried out in the late 1960s, after the site had been acquired for preservation and professional study by the Missouri Department of Natural Resources. In the summers of 1967 and 1968, Walter E. Klippel excavated two control squares, removing the sediment in 3-inch (7.6 cm) levels and paying particular care to avoid mixing material from the natural stratigraphic levels, meticulously segregating materials that were found in disturbed areas. All sediment was water screened through fine-scale mesh. This carefully controlled excavation provided more systematic data to better define the nature of the sedimentary sequence, which also provided insight into the contextual relationships of materials previously excavated under salvage conditions.

The 1960s research demonstrated that changes in the source and size of particles in the sediments were proxies for changing climatic conditions that prevailed through the early and mid-Holocene. The sediments were contained in four natural strata. The upper, most recent unit (Stratum I) had accumulated since Euro-American settlement and constituted debris left from farming operations and the use of the cave as a livestock shelter. Strata II and III, buried beneath the historic layer, were composed almost entirely of silt and clay-sized particles that were rich in cultural debris. The lowermost unit (IV), resting on bedrock, was composed of sand grains that had fallen from the cave ceiling.

This lower unit contrasted significantly with the upper, silt-laden zones. Radiocarbon dates suggest that Zone IV began accumulating in the early Holocene (ca. 11,500 years ago). Little sediment from outside the cave was deposited in the cave until after 10,000 years ago. At that time, an influx of windblown silt and clay particles began accumulating in the cave, with deposition peaking around 9,000 years ago and with periodic eolian episodes into the mid-Holocene. This depositional process was responsible for much of the sediment in both strata II and III. The sedimentary sequence at Graham Cave records the onset of mid-Holocene warming that affected vegetation patterns, a climatic trend that created patches of bare ground and hillslope erosion, the sources for the silts and clays transported by eolian (airborne) activity into the cave.

Graham Cave was occupied periodically throughout most of the Holocene. Cultural materials representing the entire Archaic sequence (Early, Middle, Late) and a Late Woodland phase were identified among the remains recovered from the cave. Earlier archaeological work at Graham Cave tended to focus on the Early and Middle Archaic components, partially because the upper strata were highly disturbed by rodent burrowing. The mixing of materials made it difficult to successfully attribute items to the appropriate Woodland or Archaic component.

Graham Cave was important to the archaeology of the 1950s because of the Early Archaic Dalton component. The early radiocarbon dates, which averaged to a date of approximately 9,500 years ago, suggested that these early Holocene foragers were living at Graham Cave just at the end of the climatic period known as the Younger Dryas. A variant of the Dalton point with a deeply concave base and long, longitudinal, thinning flake scar became known as the Graham Cave Fluted point. This projectile point form led several archaeologists of the 1950s to view Graham Cave as a site that connected the eastern Archaic cultures with early foraging groups of the eastern plains. Graham Cave also became known as the type site for a long, narrow, side-notched projectile point form that was named after the cave. Unfortunately, this Middle Archaic projectile point form came from disturbed contexts, where it was difficult to determine artifact associations.

The most significant contribution that Graham Cave research has made to American archaeology was derived from the work of Walter Klippel in the 1960s. Two test units were designed to control for disturbance and thus eliminate the problem of mixing, thereby ensuring the integrity of materials utilized in the analysis. Although Klippel's work did not recover a significant number of artifacts, it did provide sufficient numbers of faunal remains, as well as the opportunity to analyze the sedimentary sequence. This enabled him to identify and isolate changes in these two aspects of the archaeological record: cultural and paleoenvironmental. Klippel's research into these two aspects of the early archaeology of the region has made Graham Cave an important site for interpreting the cultural and environmental history of the midwestern United States.

The sequence at Graham Cave demonstrates adaptations of prehistoric foragers to changing environment conditions caused by the onset of mid-Holocene droughts. The mesic forests (forests in areas with ample rainfall) of the early Holocene were transformed into an open oak-hickory community, with periods when sparse vegetation led to hillslope erosion and increased eolian activity. It was during this mid-Holocene time period that much of the windblown sediment accumulated in the cave. A shift in subsistence strategy by the cave occupants from one that emphasized forest-adapted species (squirrels and raccoons) to forest-edge species (deer and cottontail rabbits) indicates an opening of the forest due to drier conditions. Therefore, Graham Cave is a key site along the southern border of the Prairie Peninsula that provides evidence that prehistoric peoples were forced to adapt to a changing landscape—one that was linked to mid-Holocene climatic warming.

Further Reading: Chapman, C. H., "Recent Excavations in Graham Cave," *Memoir of the Missouri Archaeological Society* 2 (1952): 87–101; Klippel, W. E., "Graham Cave Revisited: A Reevaluation of Its Cultural Position during the Archaic Period," *Memoir of the Missouri Archaeological Society* 9 (1971): 1–66; Logan, W. D., "Graham Cave, an Archaic Site in Montgomery County, Missouri," *Memoir of the Missouri Archaeological Society* 2 (1952): 1–86; McMillan, R. B., and W. E. Klippel, "Post-glacial Environmental Change and Hunting-Gathering Societies of the Southern Prairie Peninsula," *Journal of Archaeological Science* 8 (1981): 215–245; *23MT2—Graham Cave*, http://users.stlcc.edu/mfuller/Grahamcave.html.

R. Bruce McMillan

INDIAN KNOLL AND OTHER EARLY SITES

Kentucky

Ancient Sites in the Green River Valley

Indian Knoll is one of the largest and best known Archaic shell mound sites on the Green River in west central Kentucky. Between 5,600 and 4,600 years ago, prehistoric people living at Indian Knoll built up deep deposits of shell and other refuse at this spot. The deposits, referred to as midden, are made up of organically rich sediments; sandstone fragments (from cooking with hot rocks); immense numbers of shells from freshwater mussels and aquatic snails; animal bone; and carbonized fragments of nutshell and seeds. The deposits also contain large numbers of bone, stone, and shell artifacts.

Indian Knoll, however, is probably best known for the almost 1,200 human burials that archaeologists excavated there in the early twentieth century. Few burial populations have taught us as much about pre-agricultural hunter-gatherers in the Americas than Indian Knoll. Research at Indian Knoll also was instrumental in helping archaeologists define the pre-pottery Archaic period in eastern North America in the early 1940s.

The lower and middle Green River, a major tributary of the Ohio River, is known as the shell mound region of Kentucky. In addition to Indian Knoll, other important shell midden sites in the region include the Carlston Annis and Read sites in Butler County; the Chiggerville and Bowles sites in Ohio County; and the Ward and Kirkland sites in McLean County. Prehistoric people may have begun to live at these sites as early as 8,000 years ago. Based on radiocarbon dating, however, archaeologists think the most intensive occupation of the shell midden sites took place between 6,000 and 4,500 years ago.

In this part of its valley, the Green River is deeply entrenched in Pleistocene lake deposits. Freshwater mussels do not thrive in these kinds of habitats. However, in some spots, the river flows over buried sandstone bedrock. At these places, the river formed shallow, quickly flowing rapids or shoals. Until engineers dammed the river and dredged the shoals for boat traffic in recent times, many different kinds of river mussels lived in these shoals.

Prehistoric people gathered near these shoals to take advantage of the region's abundant natural food resources. Mussel shells are the most obvious food remains archaeologists have recovered from the Indian Knoll midden, but they have found many other kinds as well. Animals bones are abundant, especially those from whitetail deer, wild turkeys, numerous fish species, and aquatic turtles. Carbonized nutshells, particularly hickory and black walnut, also occur in large quantities.

Although a great deal of food processing and feasting took place at sites like Indian Knoll, it was undoubtedly also the location of numerous social and cultural activities. Clearly the burial of deceased members of the group was important. People of both sexes and all ages were buried at the site. It may be that feasting and offerings of food were important elements of the burial ceremony.

Archaeologists have not found evidence of an organized village layout, or of substantial structures or other permanent dwellings. This suggests that the Indian Knoll inhabitants did not live at the site year-round. Other than burial pits, they have found only clusters of rock, fire hearths, and prepared clay cooking surfaces.

Clarence B. Moore was the first archaeologist to study the Green River sites. Traveling by steamboat (the aptly named *Gopher*) up the river in 1915–16, he stopped at several sites, including Indian Knoll. With a crew of eight men, Moore dug up 298 burials at Indian Knoll in just twenty-three days.

Moore was not overly impressed with the artifacts that he found at Indian Knoll. However, the curiously shaped prismatic stones and hooked-antler artifacts found with numerous burials intrigued him. Moore knew that the prehistoric people responsible for the deposits at Indian Knoll belonged to an intensive fishing culture. Therefore he concluded that the prismatic stones, based on their form, were net spacers. He also reasoned that the hooked antlers were net-making implements used to weave fishing nets. He even conducted a bit of experimental archaeology to show that fishing nets could be made using these artifacts.

William S. Webb, cofounder of the University of Kentucky's Department of Anthropology, began major excavations along the Green River in the late 1930s. Webb's fieldwork, funded by New Deal "back to work" programs, such as the Works Progress Administration, continued on an impressive scale until the start of World War II. Indian Knoll was the largest excavation Webb conducted in Kentucky. His crews recovered some 55,000 artifacts and 880 burials from the site.

Following Webb's investigations, archaeologists did not return to Indian Knoll until the late 1990s. These researchers collected sediment samples across the site area by systematically coring the deposits. They wanted to examine the site's sediment structure and to collect charcoal samples for radiocarbon dating. Their work showed that, despite Webb's extensive excavations, portions of the site on the edge of the shell midden deposits remain intact. They also collected a sample of mussel shell from the site's surface. Mussel species are very good indicators of what the river was like at the time the prehistoric people lived at Indian Knoll.

Indian Knoll is situated on a natural levee in the broad Green River valley. It measures approximately 140 meters by 70 meters. Based on Webb's excavations, we know that the midden deposit measured between 1.5 and 2.5 meters thick at its deepest. Today the site is located some 200 meters from the right bank of the Green River (the river has migrated to the southwest since prehistoric times). When prehistoric people lived at Indian Knoll, the river flowed immediately adjacent to the site.

There is also an extensive backwater slough near the site that would have been a good place to catch fish and turtles. The mussel species identified from Indian Knoll, however, suggest that shellfishing took place in the main river channel, rather than in the backwater areas. Archaeologists know this because the mussels identified from the site are species that are common in large to medium-sized rivers with water depths of 0.9 to 2.4 meters and a swift current over sand and gravel.

Webb's excavation at Indian Knoll recovered more than 13,000 chert tools, 3,000 groundstone tools, 8,000 bone artifacts, 4,000 antler artifacts, and 25,000 shell artifacts. Tools made of flaked chert are mainly various types of spear points, drills, and scrapers. Ground-stone artifacts are predominantly grooved axes, hammerstones, and pestles. Bone artifacts are overwhelmingly awls or other pointed objects. The inhabitants of Indian Knoll commonly made fishhooks out of bone too. The most common deer antler artifacts are cut and drilled antler tines that the prehistoric hunters used as spear points. The most common shell artifacts are snail shell beads and flat, disc-shaped beads ground into shape on sandstone abraders. Archaeologists have documented a small number of marine conch shell artifacts and a few small copper artifacts from Indian Knoll. Neither marine shell nor copper is readily available in the Green River area. Prehistoric people would have traveled great distances to get these materials or traded with people living outside the region.

Webb took exceptional care excavating the human burials at Indian Knoll. His workers kept meticulous records of the position of each burial in the grave and of the kinds of artifacts present. They recorded a number of dog burials too, some of which were located in the same pit as their presumed human masters. The exceptionally well-preserved human remains from Indian Knoll have provided important information about a variety of topics related to these people's hunting, gathering, and fishing way of life. The topics include the demographic characteristics of the groups that used the site, the diseases and injuries they suffered from, and certain aspects of human growth and development.

The study of human remains and burial practices at Indian Knoll also provides us with a vibrant picture of life during this remote time. Most individuals were not buried with nonperishable grave goods. However, a few burials included grave items, such as shell and bone bead necklaces, intricately beaded sashes, decorated bone pins, turtle shell rattles, and pendants of shell, bone, and stone.

The most common burial items, however, were the curiously shaped prismatic stones and antler hooks that Moore had interpreted as net-making implements. By carefully excavating the burials and recording the context of each associated object, Webb demonstrated that these artifacts most probably were composite parts of *atl atls*, or throwing sticks. Among several burials, he documented the linear arrangement of an antler handle, a drilled stone or shell prismatic weight, and a socketed antler tine with a hooked end. The wooden shaft that would have held all the pieces together had long since decayed. Webb helped pioneer the use of careful excavation techniques and detailed field recording at Indian Knoll as a way of documenting specific spatial relationships among objects as the basis for interpreting how people used artifacts in prehistory.

Indian Knoll is a National Historic Landmark, and twenty-four shell midden sites in the Green River region have been listed on the National Register of Historic Places. All of these sites are on private property. Because these sites are vulnerable to illegal digging, information about their locations is restricted.

The William S. Webb Museum of Anthropology at the University of Kentucky has a small exhibit of Indian Knoll and related shell mound artifacts. The museum continues to host several researchers each year to study the collection.

Further Reading: Henderson, A. Gwynn, Sheldon R. Burdin, and Kary L. Stackelbeck, *Archaic Hunters and Gatherers of the Green River Valley*, Education Series No. 7 (Lexington: Kentucky Archaeological Survey, 2006); Marquardt, William, and Patty Jo Watson, eds., *Archaeology of the Middle Green River Region, Kentucky*, Monograph 5 (Gainesville: Institute of Archaeology and Paleoenvironmental Studies, Florida Museum of Natural History, 2005); Metropolitan Museum of Art, *Indian Knoll (3000–2000 B.C.)*, http://www.metmuseum.org/toah/hd/knol/hd_knol.htm; Moore, Clarence B., *The Tennessee, Green, and Lower Ohio Rivers Expeditions of Clarence Bloomfield Moore*, rev. ed., edited and with an introduction by Richard R. Polhemus (Tuscaloosa: University of Alabama Press, 2002); Morey, Darcy F., George M. Crothers, Julie K. Stein, James P. Fenton, and Nicholas P. Herrmann, "The Fluvial and Geomorphic Context of Indian Knoll, an Archaic Shell Midden in West-Central Kentucky," *Geoarchaeology: An International Journal* 17 (2002): 521–553; Webb, William S., *Indian Knoll*, reprinted ed. (Knoxville: University of Tennessee Press, 1974).

George M. Crothers

THE KOSTER, NAPOLEON HOLLOW, AND OTHER SITES

Lower Illinois River Valley, Illinois
Early Activities and Habitations of the Illinois Valley

Between Meredosia and the Mississippi River confluence (a distance of 112 kilometers), the Illinois River valley is deeply entrenched in Paleozoic limestone bedrock. The valley is on average 5.6 kilometers wide and demarcated by cliffs, some of which rise 61 meters above the floodplain. In deposits that are more than 30 meters thick, late Wisconsinan (ca. 20,000 years ago) Peoria silt (loess) mantles the bedrock. Intermittent and permanent streams have breached the valley wall and formed fans of redeposited upland sediment at the valley edge.

The Illinois River floodplain has generally aggraded during the Holocene, burying a substantial proportion of the Archaic-period (ca. 10,000–3,000 years ago) landscape. Archaic-period sites are found at the surface in the floodplain on late Wisconsinan and early Holocene landforms, but some—perhaps many—valley margin fans and floodplain sediments contain multiple buried Archaic-period components (Hajic 1990; Wiant et al. 2007).

At the Koster site (11GE4) in Greene County, Illinois, between 1969 and 1978, archaeologists documented thirteen distinct cultural horizons in a valley margin colluvial fan. The deepest horizon is 8.6 meters below the ground surface. Archaic-period components range in age from $8,730 \pm 90$ to $2,980 \pm 70$ years ago, and several correspond with periods of relatively stable surfaces. In general, tool diversity, the creation and use of facilities (e.g., hearths, basins, pits, and structures), and use of aquatic resources and seed-bearing plants increase over time. These trends are consistent with the development of an ever more sedentary lifestyle (Brown and Vierra 1983; Houart 1971).

The late Early Archaic Horizon 11 (ca. $8,480 \pm 110$ to $8,130 \pm 90$ years ago), was occupied repeatedly, perhaps seasonally. Stone and bone tools are concentrated around surface hearths, which appear to be the center of domestic activity. There is no evidence of structures. Diminutive projectile points suggest use of the spear thrower (*atl atl*), but larger ones are consistent with handheld spears and knives. The number and variety of ground-stone tools (e.g., adze, axe, mano, metate, and pestle) indicate a mature industry, the origins of which remain obscure. Animal remains are consistent with a broad-spectrum strategy, but hickory accounts for 96 percent of the nutshell. The placement of the remains of nine humans suggests designation of a specific burial area; most are interred outside of the living area. Also found in the settlement were the articulated remains of at least three domesticated dogs in graves.

Processing or storage pits and (arguably) structures appear in the early Middle Archaic Horizon 8C (ca. 7,000 years ago). The sheer number of artifacts ($n = 868$) and features ($n = 135$) and their distribution indicates a substantial base settlement during this time period. Hickory accounts for 92 percent of the nutshell, and animal remains suggest intense reliance on fewer resources, particularly mussels, fish, and whitetail deer.

Horizon 6 (ca. $5,720 \pm 75$ to $4,880 \pm 250$ years ago), is a meter-thick Middle Archaic midden with hearths, basins, pits, and perhaps house floors. The artifact assemblage consists of more than 4,000 lithic (chipped stone and ground stone) and bone tools that represent a wide range of activities. The well-preserved animal bone assemblage indicates a broad-based strategy that included hunting, fowling, fishing, and mussel collecting, with particular emphasis on aquatic resources. Hickory again accounts for most of the nutshell, but for the first time, an appreciable number of wild seeds were found.

Like Koster, the Napoleon Hollow site (11PK500) is an extensive, stratified, multi-component archaeological site. It is located in Pike County, Illinois, slightly northwest of Koster, at the mouth of Napoleon Hollow, a minor tributary of the Illinois River. Three geomorphic systems—the Illinois River floodplain, Napoleon Hollow Creek floodplain, and the steep slopes of the river and creek valleys—interface here and contribute sediments that coalesce and interfinger to create a series of aggrading landscapes. An Early Archaic component is present but undated. Middle and Late Archaic components range in age from 7,050 BP to 3,920 years ago and correspond to Koster site horizons. Similarities in deposition history of the Koster and Napoleon Hollow fans suggest synchronous development of colluvial fans in the lower reach of the Illinois River valley (Wiant et al. 1983). The sequence of cultural developments is also comparable; the duration of occupation increases through time. By 4,000 years ago, residents are cultivating marshelder (*Iva annua*), one of a suite of native plants cultivated in the Midwest prior to the arrival of maize.

The Campbell Hollow site (11ST144) is a 15-foot-thick, stratified, multi-component deposit in a colluvial fan on the north side of Campbell Hollow near the embouchure of a small tributary of the Illinois River in Scott County. Archaeologists discovered two components—both evidently brief, short-term encampments occupied during the late Early Archaic and Middle Archaic, respectively (Stafford 1985). As is the case with other short-term Archaic-period occupations, on-site activities were centered around hearths.

The Twin Ditch site (11GE146) consists of two stratified, shallowly buried Archaic occupation components in the Illinois River floodplain near the river's east bank. The deepest artifact-bearing component (Horizon 2) has produced the oldest substantial evidence of Early Archaic occupation in the region.

In 1980 archaeologists discovered Early Archaic artifacts—Agate Basin, Hardin Barbed, and LeCroy points—and Middle Archaic artifacts—Matanzas and other side-notched points—in sediment dredged from two drainage ditches in the Illinois River floodplain (Hassen and Hajic 1984). Subsequent excavations between 1987 and 1990 revealed two artifact-bearing strata on a shallowly buried paleogeomorphic surface called the Columbiana Surface. Horizon 2 artifacts include Dalton, Holland, St. Charles, and Thebes points. Radiocarbon assays of Horizon 2 charcoal samples range in age from 9,510 to 8,740 years ago (Morrow 1996, 347). Only a preliminary analysis of the artifact assemblage and plant and animal remains is available.

In addition to the hafted bifaces, the Twin Ditch lithic artifact assemblage includes chipped-stone adzes, end scrapers, side scrapers, gravers, retouched and utilized flakes, bifacial blanks, and debitage. Wood charcoal is common, but few other plant remains have been reported. Whitetail deer and fish dominate the faunal assemblage. Bird bone is common, and some small-mammal elements are also present. Systematic refitting of lithic debitage and analysis of retouched specimens suggest a series of short-term occupations centered on hearths, each perhaps representing a seasonally reoccupied base camp (Morrow 1996).

These sites provide a robust cultural and chronological framework of our understanding the Archaic period in the Illinois River valley and the Midwest. More important, they continue to inspire research into the interaction of human societies with one another and with nature during ancient times in America.

Further Reading: Brown, James A., and Robert K. Vierra, "What Happened in the Middle Archaic?" in *Archaic Hunters and Gatherers in the American Midwest*, edited by James L. Phillips and James A. Brown (New York: Academic Press, 1983) 165–195; Hassen, Harold, and Edwin R. Hajic, *Shallowly Buried Archaeological Deposits and Geologic Context: Archaeological Survey in the Eldred and Spanky Drainage and Levee District, Greene County, Illinois*, Cultural Resources Management Report 8 (St. Louis, MO: U.S. Army Corps of Engineers, 1984); Hajic, Edwin R., *Koster Site Archeology I: Stratigraphy and Landscape Evolution*, Research Series 8 (Kampsville, IL: Kampsville Archeological Center, 1990); Houart, Gail L., *Koster: A Stratified Archaic Site in the Illinois Valley*, Reports of Investigations 22 (Springfield: Illinois State Museum, 1971); Morrow, Toby A., "Lithic Refitting and Archaeological Site Formation: A Case Study from the Twin Ditch Site, Greene County, Illinois," in *Stone Tools: Theoretical Insights into Human Prehistory*, edited by George H. Odell (New York: Plenum Press, 1996) 345–373; Stafford, C. Russell, ed., *The Campbell Hollow Archaic Occupations: A Study of Intrasite Spatial Structure in the Lower Illinois Valley*, Research Series 4 (Kampsville, IL: Center for American Archeology, Kampsville Archeological Center, 1985); Wiant, Michael D., Edwin R. Hajic, and Thomas R. Styles, "Napoleon Hollow and Koster Site Stratigraphy," in *Archaic Hunters and Gatherers in the American Midwest*, edited by James L. Phillips and James A. Brown (New York: Academic Press, 1983), 147–164; Wiant, Michael D., Kenneth B. Farnsworth, and Edwin R. Hajic, "The Archaic Period in the Lower Illinois River Basin," in *Archaic Societies: Diversity and Complexity Across the Midcontinent*, edited by Thomas E. Emerson, Dale L. McElrath, and Andrew C. Fortier (Lincoln: University of Nebraska Press, 2007).

Michael D. Wiant

MODOC ROCK SHELTER

Randolph County, Illinois
Archaic Period Campsites

The sandstone bluff at the Modoc Rock Shelter provided shelter for Native American groups beginning in the early part of the Holocene (the current interglacial, which begins after the Wisconsin glacial period) for a time span of almost 8,000 years. Modoc Rock Shelter is located on the east side of the Mississippi River floodplain in southwestern Illinois, at the eastern edge of the Ozarks. Periodic floods from the Mississippi River and nearby Barbeau Creek buried the abandoned camps, creating 7.6 meters of layered archaeological and natural deposits. Modoc Rock Shelter is best known for campsites of the Archaic period, ranging in age from 8100 BC to 2550 BC. Woodland occupations are also present but have been largely destroyed by highway construction.

The shelter has a long history of interdisciplinary archaeological research. Archaeologists from the Illinois State Museum and the University of Chicago excavated here in the 1950s, and the Illinois State Museum and the University of Wisconsin returned to carry out additional work in the 1980s. The excavations uncovered stratified deposits with well-preserved hearths and other features, stone and bone tools, debris from the manufacture of stone tools, and food remains (animal bones, shells, and plant remains) that were protected from the elements by the rock overhang. A team of archaeologists, botanists, zoologists, and geologists studied these remains and the sediments to determine how the environment and Native American culture changed through time.

During the early part of the Archaic period (from about 8100 to 6950 BC), Native American groups camped here for short periods. They hunted whitetail deer, trapped tree squirrels, procured a diverse assortment of other animals, and gathered a variety of nuts (including pecans and walnuts) in dense forests dominated by elm and ash. Such foliage thrived in a wetter climate than today.

The representation of fish, primarily species associated with flowing waters, varied from slight to moderate, likely related to the specific season of occupation for the camps. The pattern of a relatively high representation of squirrels and other small mammals, a low representation of whitetail deer, and a wide diversity of nuts has been documented in the lower Illinois River valley, Missouri, and the mid-south. This pattern has been attributed to the closed forests and wetter conditions of the early part of the Holocene. The density of diversity of stone tools found in the assemblages is low to moderate and variable in these camps, again varying with the specific season and range of activities that took place. The camps appear to be associated with groups with great residential mobility.

During the middle part of the Archaic period, the climate became drier, prairies expanded, and the forest opened, perhaps aided by fires deliberately set by humans to increase the biotic productivity. Open forest and edge species, such as whitetail deer and hickories, likely increased due to the opening of the forest. By 6950 BC, the inhabitants of the shelter were making greater use of whitetail deer, fish, and thick-shelled hickory nuts than earlier occupants had. The technological innovation of stone boiling may have also contributed to increased representation of thick-shelled hickory nuts, because such an advancement would have made processing easier.

Backwater fish species appear in the deposits by 6950 BC, suggesting that flood-basin lakes were likely present in the Mississippi River floodplain by this time. By 6950 BC, the inhabitants of the shelter were making greater use of fish from backwater lakes than earlier peoples had. Exploitation of these productive, shallow flood-basin lakes increased through time in the central Mississippi River valley and became very important to the support of more sedentary occupations. From 6950 to 5700 BC, some groups lived at the shelter for longer periods of time and left behind greater densities and diversities of stone tool assemblages. Between 5700 and 3600 BC, the site was used primarily for longer-term occupations, and tool density and diversity are consistently high. Reliance on whitetail deer, fish, and thick-shelled hickory nuts continued, and the use of seeds from wild plants also increased. Increased reliance of whitetail deer, fish, and thick-shelled hickory nuts is a well-documented pattern for Middle Archaic sites in the Illinois and Mississippi river valleys.

A presumed decrease in residential mobility with the establishment of longer-term occupations (base camps), perhaps now sustained with logistical mobility, has also been suggested to explain the archaeological patterns observed at other sites in these large river valleys. Logistical mobility refers to situations where people spent much or all of the year in their main camps while smaller groups traveled from the base camp or village to forage or hunt for specific kinds of food as they became available. The increased use of aquatic resources with the development of flood-basin lakes, although not synchronous in the Mississippi and Illinois river valleys, is also an important pattern represented at Modoc Rock Shelter and other sites.

During the latest part of the Archaic period (from after 3600 to 2700 BC), groups used the shelter more intermittently and for more limited functions, locating camps there to hunt deer and other animals. The low diversity of stone tool assemblages found during this interval suggests that the range of activities was more limited and specialized than for Middle and early Late Archaic occupations. It appears that longer-term occupations were now established elsewhere.

Because of the excellent preservation of archaeological remains and the long history of research, Modoc Rock Shelter is listed on the National Register of Historic Places and is a National Historic Landmark. A kiosk at the site provides photographs and overviews of the excavations and interpretations of the record. Further information on this site can be obtained from the Illinois State Museum in Springfield.

Further Reading: Ahler, S. R., and B. W. Styles, "A Summary of Changes in Archaic Period Subsistence and Site Function at Modoc Rock Shelter," *Illinois Archaeology* 19(1–2) (1998): 110–154; MuseumLink: Native American Module, http://www.museum.state.il.us/muslink/nat_amer; Styles, B. W. and S. R. Ahler, "Changing Perspectives on the Archaic: Contributions from Modoc Rock Shelter," in *Mounds, Modoc, and Mesoamerica: Papers in Honor of Melvin L. Fowler*, edited by S. R. Ahler, Scientific Papers, No. 28 (Springfield: Illinois State Museum, 2000), 25–38; Styles, B. W., S. R. Ahler, and M. L. Fowler, "Modoc Rock Shelter Revisited," in *Archaic Hunters and Gatherers in the American Midwest*, edited by J. L. Phillips and J. A. Brown (New York: Academic Press, 1983), 261–297; Styles, B. W., and R. B. McMillan, "Archaic Faunal Exploitation in the Prairie Peninsula and Surrounding Regions of the Midcontinent," in *Archaic Societies of the Midwest*, edited by T. E. Emerson, D. McElrath, and A. Fortier (Lincoln: University of Nebraska Press, 2007).

Bonnie W. Styles

ISLE ROYALE NATIONAL PARK

Isle Royale, Lake Superior
The Oldest Prehistoric Copper Quarries

Isle Royale is renowned as the location of the oldest prehistoric copper-mining quarries and mines in North America. It is an island approximately 80 kilometers in length, located in the western end of Lake Superior—the largest, coldest, and deepest of the Great Lakes. Within the bedrock formations of the island are thin veins of relatively pure elemental copper metal. The mining pits on the island date as early as 4,600 years ago and were mined intermittently over many years, until as recently as the sixteenth century. The antiquity of the mines and their extent across the island gives them special significance. No other native copper deposits in eastern North America display such an extensive material record of prehistoric human exploitation. There are more than 200 individual archaeological sites within the national park, and more than a thousand prehistoric mining pits.

ENVIRONMENT AND CULTURE ON ISLE ROYALE

The environment of Isle Royale is a formidable one of cool temperatures, profound snowfall in the long winters, and brief, cool summers. It is a boreal environment with vegetation dominated by cedar and spruce forests, but with enclaves of deciduous birch and maple forests. Successful human adaptation to this environment required profound knowledge of food resources and their distributions. A range of fish species within Lake Superior and within the inland lakes of the island provided people with reliable sources of protein; trout and whitefish were two very important species. Other reliable human foods included berries, maple sugar, and a variety of small edible plants and greens. Birds, especially aquatic species such as ducks and geese, were seasonally plentiful. Researchers conclude that while rich in food resources, the island does not have as broad a range of food species as the mainland, and this fact affected human settlement.

Though the human occupancy of Isle Royale was more or less continuous over the past 4,500 years, most of the island's people were seasonal users of the island, rather than permanent residents. From time to time in the warmest parts of the year, occasional visitors to the island would arrive by canoe to mine and gather copper from the island's bedrock, and perhaps to fish in the nearshore waters. The mining pits are most closely associated with people from two time periods and cultural systems: that of the Late Archaic period (about 5,000 to 3,000 years ago) and that of the Terminal Woodland period (about 1,200 to 500 years ago). In both time periods, people

probably lived in small, extended-family groups and came to the island for short stays. Often, related families might camp and perhaps work together. Overall, the social and economic arrangements were those that anthropologists and archaeologists refer to as forager systems, dominated by political and decision-making practices that promoted independence among family groups. Such flexible systems were found throughout the challenging southern boreal forest environment of the central North American continent prior to occupation by historic period Euro-Americans during the past few hundred years.

The cultural groups of the Late Archaic are sometimes referred to as the Old Copper Culture, so named because their materials (tools and ornaments) include that metal in great quantities and in a wide variety of forms. During the Late Archaic period, the variety of objects made of copper was larger than at any other point in prehistory in this region. Some of these objects were likely traded among people of neighboring cultural groups. But these people also manufactured a wide range of other copper implements, some of which were used to make other tools and objects, especially wooden ones. The later terminal Woodland people collected a specialized set of food resources, which may have included a narrowed range of fish species and the addition of wild rice. In social and cultural terms, their adaptation, which focused upon small group autonomy and a seasonal round of activities related to resource collection, was similar to that of the earlier people, from whom they were probably descended. They did, however, make use of additional resources for creating material culture. They were pottery makers and show evidence of widespread trade in pottery and in other materials, such as lithics (stone tools and raw nodules of useful stone).

THE MINING EVIDENCE ON ISLE ROYALE

Although the earliest accounts of copper in the Lake Superior basin come from the explorer Jacques Cartier in the sixteenth century, firsthand observations of the pits were not reported until the early era of American mining (mid-nineteenth century). By the time of the first systematic geological surveys of the area (in the nineteenth century), researchers concluded that the prehistoric mines were dug by the Native Americans of the region. Archaeological research at the mines of Isle Royale began in the late nineteenth century. Among the first to document the mining activities of indigenous people on Isle Royale was William H. Holmes of the Bureau of American

W. H. Holmes cross-sectioning a prehistoric copper mine near Minong, Isle Royale, 1892. In front of Holmes are two piles of hammer stones typical of those associated with prehistoric mine workings.   [National Archives]

Ethnology, part of the Smithsonian Institution. Seeking to gather field information about the miners for an exhibition to be made at the Chicago World's Fair of 1893, he came to Isle Royale to excavate a pit near the Minong Ridge, on the north side of the island.

The mine that Holmes chose for excavation was originally about 3 meters deep and 7 meters in diameter. It had been impacted to some degree by more recent industrial mining activity. Holmes discovered ancient stone hammers and piles of wasted, crushed rock that had been systematically whacked away from the walls of the pit. Holmes also recorded that a nearby area of several square kilometers was extensively worked over by the prehistoric miners. There was no real evidence of tunneling through the rock; instead, the mines were shallow, irregular pits several meters directly upon the deposits of copper. This mining style resembled the quarrying of flint that Holmes had seen and investigated elsewhere in the eastern United States.

Another archaeological excavation was conducted in the 1950s by researchers from two Michigan universities. Archaeologists verified that the ancient mining pit was excavated to a depth of about 4.5 meters below surface by the prehistoric miners. Associated with the pit were stone hammers used to break apart the bedrock to free up the fragments of metal embedded in it. Tailings from mining (bits of bedrock cracked and fractured by the miners) filled the pit. This pit yielded charcoal and wood samples that were dated to an approximate age of 3,500–3,800 radiocarbon years ago. The general area near this excavated pit included about 200 other pits made by prehistoric mining activities.

The general pattern of the mining is that of broad, shallow pits on the surface systematically following the line of bedded copper deposits. The evidence suggests slow and laborious mining methods using only handheld stone hammers. The prehistoric miners dug down to intersecting fissures in the bedrock, cracking rock as they went and removing thin,

Prehistoric miners on Isle Royale used hammers to crack apart the local bedrock and extract copper metal. Upper hammer of unknown material exhibits a partial groove, chipped around the hammer to attach a flexible handle: length 16 cm, weight 0.69 kg. Hammer to the left is quartzite, fully grooved: length 7 cm, weight 0.23 kg. Bottom right hammer is broken from heavy use, with full groove: length 14 cm, weight 1.4 kg. Photos are at different scales.   [Michigan Technological University, Archaeology Laboratory, Accession Unit 00-4: Gabriel Collection, Isle Royale, and Drier Collection, Isle Royale. Photo: Larry Mishkar.]

sheet-like pieces of copper that measured a centimeter or two in thickness. Some researchers thought that setting fires might help weaken the rock and that the prehistoric miners might have done this firing intentionally, but the actual evidence for this practice is negligible. Today the typical prehistoric mining pit is filled with ash, broken rock bits, dead vegetation, water, and broken hammer stones. Tools of copper are very occasionally associated with the pits.

In 1963 researchers from the University of Michigan conducted the first systematic study of the mining pits, recording over a thousand ancient pits that were associated with mining hammers and veins of copper. To these researchers,

Copper from Isle Royale, Michigan. Left: ISRO-1793: copper knife or blade, Chippewa Harbor. Length is 11.4 cm. Right: ISRO-4405: curved awl or perforator, McCargoe Cove. Length is 4 cm. Bottom: ISRO-1849: specimen of unworked elemental copper. 4.8 × 5.3 cm. [National Park Service, Isle Royale National Park. Photo: Larry Mishkar.]

the mining evidence suggested many visits of small groups of miners to the copper-bearing areas over several thousands of years of small-scale mining activities. In the 1990s, researchers from the National Park Service surveyed the shorelines and developed areas of the island to create an inventory of archaeological sites within Isle Royale National Park. More than 200 habitation and camp sites were discovered in the park.

MANUFACTURING METHODS

Copper is a relatively soft metal that can be shaped with repeated hammering into a range of forms. The copper from Isle Royale, being relatively pure elemental copper, needed no processing at high temperatures to remove excess impurities.

A piece of copper of an appropriate size and shape would be chosen for work, then beaten into the desired shape with small hammers and mallets. Repeated slow heating and cooling in a wood fire (annealing), followed by episodes of skillful and patient hammering, yielded the finished shape of the tool. These cycles of heating, cooling, and hammering helped control the shaping process and avoided cracking the tool or ornament during manufacture. The artifacts were sometimes polished and ground to provide a finished appearance.

The prehistoric copper workers produced a wide variety of artifact forms. Many were tools for wood and skin working, but knives, spears, projectile points, and harpoons were also made. Delicate ornaments such as beads and pins were common.

LEARNING MORE ABOUT ISLE ROYALE

Isle Royale National Park is a United States biosphere reserve in which 99 percent of its lands are managed as wilderness. It includes many miles of remote hiking trails and is accessible by boat or by floatplane. Viewing the most extensive prehistoric mining pits requires hiking to areas near McCargoe Cove and the Minong Ridge at the north central portion of the island. Most of the interpretive activities relating to the natural environment of the park, including prehistoric and historic mining, are available at the centers of park management at Rock Harbor and at Windigo, where there are a variety of programs for visitors. The Rock Harbor area has a fine bookstore for maps and documents about island history and may include temporary

exhibits featuring various aspects of the history of the island's human occupations, including lighthouse keeping and commercial fishing.

Further Reading: Clark, Caven P., *Archeological Survey and Testing: Isle Royale National Park, 1987–1990*, Seasons (Lincoln, NE: National Park Service, Midwest Archeological Center, 1995); Griffin, James B., *Lake Superior Copper and the Indians: Miscellaneous Studies of Great Lakes Prehistory*, Anthropological Papers 17 (Ann Arbor: University of Michigan Museum of Anthropology, 1961); Martin, Susan R., *Wonderful Power: The Story of Ancient Copper Working in the Lake Superior Basin* (Detroit, Michigan: Wayne State University Press, 1999); National Park Service's Isle Royale Web page, http://www.nps.gov/isro (online January 2006).

Susan R. Martin

ADENA CULTURE EARTHEN ARCHITECTURE

Central and Eastern Ohio River Valley, Ohio
The Earliest Ancient Architecture in Ohio

Adena is the name given by archaeologists to societies that were the first to build earthen mounds and other types of earthworks, sometimes in combination, in a widespread and formal manner in the central and eastern portions of the Ohio River valley. These mounds, described as conical but often more dome-shaped in profile, are used to establish the time frame for the Adena in Ohio: between 1000 and 50 BC, although the period often is given a beginning date of 500 BC. Based on the conspicuous nature of these engineering accomplishments by Ohio's first tribal societies, these mounds and earthen (or sacred) circles are the touchstones for many people interested in the archaeology of the Midwest. Adena mounds can be found throughout the eastern half of the United States, but the Ohio valley was a center for building mounds, and some of the largest mounds and concentrations of them can still be found in the region. Large mounds often rose to a height of 20 meters, but the vast majority were far smaller. Some of the largest mounds and earthworks still evident and available to the public are the Miamisburg Mound in Ohio and the Anderson Mound in Indiana.

Viewing Adena mounds invariably leads the observer to ask who built them and why. These earthen mounds contain the skeletal remains of at least one intentional burial and often several individuals. Societies prior to the Adena are known to have buried some of their dead in natural hills, so burial in an elevated earthen feature was not new. Formalizing this burial

behavior in human-made mounds, however, was a new cultural behavior. Addressing the issue of who these people were and why they might expand upon this concept of elevated earthen burials leads us to consider the history and recent studies of Adena mounds.

The name Adena comes from the original mound excavated in 1901 by William Mills, an Ohio Historical Society archaeologist. The mound was located on the Adena estate, owned by then-Governor Worthington in Chillicothe, Ohio. The burials and exotic artifacts from this large mound were used in the initial definition of the Adena culture, which was at first conceived of as a single society. Excavations during the Great Depression years in the 1930s in portions of Ohio, Kentucky, West Virginia, and Indiana greatly added to the list of materials that identified and defined this archaeological culture.

Today the term "Adena" reflects a collection of similar societies that, to varying degrees, shared fundamental religious and societal characteristics. Through excavations of the mounds themselves, archaeologists observed variability in how people were buried. In some cases, mounds only had one single burial; in others, there were multiple burials. Some people were buried in simple fashion, laid on a sheet of bark; others were buried in costly log tombs. Some were cremated, while others were subject to excarnation—exposure to the elements prior to burial. Further, some individuals were buried with exotic artifacts, such as copper beads and seashells, while others were buried with no accompanying artifacts at all. Analyses have shown that both men and women, as well as children, were buried in these mounds.

The mounds themselves were built incrementally, with discrete layers of soil added over time to the initial mounded soil over the burial. Early excavators also often observed soil stains where a circle of wooden post remains often closely approximated the interior perimeter of the mound, as though a structure had existed but was removed before the earthen mound was built. It was once believed that these post outlines were domestic houses that were abandoned and removed with the death of the individual, the mound then being erected over the old post foundation. Today these post outlines, in part because of their size, are seen as the remnants of ritually important, rather than domestic, structures.

In the 1960s, efforts to create ever-expanded trait lists of artifacts were abandoned in favor of research aimed at understanding the dynamic environmental, demographic, and economic conditions that influenced decisions made by ancient societies within a systemic framework. Thus research gravitated away from mound excavations, which at the time were used mainly to augment trait lists. The research focus shifted to investigating the domestic areas and regional settlement patterns of the Adena.

Based on the recovery and analysis of seed and other plant remains from hearths, pits, and post remains within and near houses of the Adena period, it is now known that the antecedents of the Adena in Ohio began relying upon wild seed-bearing plants, such as goosefoot and marsh elder, principally between 1500 and 1000 BC—and, in a few areas, even earlier. The Adena eventually tinkered with these and other plant species to create formal gardens, a historical process that justifies calling the Adena the first gardeners in the Ohio valley. The Adena were not the first people to make pottery, but they certainly continued refining the tradition of making ceramics that aided in the preparing of foods, such as soups and stews. Although the first pottery forms were thick and tempered with grit, very gradual improvements in pottery allowed for an increasing ability to boil foods, thus leading to gruels on which to wean infants.

The Adena communities often are referred to as hamlets, occupied by about fifteen to twenty-five people. These hamlets were only seasonally occupied, but movement away from one's hamlet was hardly random. As populations continued to increase over time, and prime areas began to be settled by varied communities, the best spaces for living were repeatedly reoccupied by that same community. In the Hocking valley of southeastern Ohio, flat, elevated terraces that were desired as living spaces represented only about 5 percent of the lands within the entire valley—making living space itself, in the context of increasing population, a scarce resource. Special axes, or celts, were made for clearing trees, and it is likely that extended use of the best areas for living was part of the Adena pattern of settlement.

The Adena afford us the opportunity to consider Native American religion. In some of the mounds, gorgets (smoothed stone pendants worn around one's neck) were found, some of which have birds of prey carved on them. Although this is scant reflection on the richness of religious belief, it confirms the tradition of an animistic religion for the Adena—one founded on the spirituality of nature as an integral part of the living world.

The combination of these factors—increasing population size and density; involvement of gardening to supplement hunting and gathering; pottery manufacture for processing of foods; new technology for clearing and managing the forests; and the restriction of prime living spaces—gives us the context for mound construction. In many cases, the mounds are near communities; in other settings, they are between communities. Regardless, most archaeologists agree that some form of territoriality was established by the construction and placement of the mounds and earthworks as part of Adena culture. The placement of select individuals in conspicuous and visible mounds is seen in the context of a growing sense of limited access to the best domestic and economic spaces, especially when the group must leave the area for part of the year. The development of a sense of one's home territory is consistent with the development of distinctive social corporateness or identity that includes some but excludes others, being established among different groups during Adena times.

The mounds contain far fewer individuals than existed in any community. Where was everyone else buried? The best answer is that these other people were cremated in order to reduce their bones in size and strength, and then perhaps buried or dispersed at or near the community at which they were living. These types of remains would be quite difficult to find, if they survived as part of the archaeological record at all.

Mounds were not the only form of earthwork built by the Adena. Circles of earth, anticipating far larger-scale earthen architecture by the later Hopewell, also were constructed. Most of these were plowed down by historic period agriculture and are barely, if at all, visible. Adena circles were often centered by a low rise—like a baseball pitcher's mound—that is presumably where a speaker or leader once stood, orating to an audience. When the remains of Adena circles are viewed today, most observers imagine past people sitting on the low walls of the circle. However, originally, the walls rose several feet. More reasonably, these walls were intended to obscure the vision of those outside the enclosure, making these features a restricted enclosure for those assembled.

Adena mounds such as the Anderson or Miamisburg Mound are available to those interested in the Adena culture. The Anderson Mound, or the Great Mound, is in Mounds State Park, Anderson, Indiana. The Miamisburg Mound is the largest extant Adena mound in Ohio, rising to a height of 70 feet. It too is available for public viewing and is located in Miamisburg, Ohio.

Further Reading: Abrams, Elliot M., and AnnCorinne Freter, eds., *The Emergence of the Moundbuilders: The Archaeology of Tribal Societies in Southeastern Ohio* (Athens: Ohio University Press, 2005); Fagan, Brian M., *Ancient North America: The Archaeology of a Continent*, 4th ed. (London: Thames and Hudson, 2005); Lepper, Bradley T., *Ohio Archaeology* (Wilmington, Ohio: Orange Frazer, 2004); Milner, George R., *The Moundbuilders: Ancient Peoples of Ancient North America* (London: Thames and Hudson, 2004); Silverberg, Robert, *The Mound Builders* (Athens: Ohio University Press, 1986).

Elliot M. Abrams

ADENA CULTURE BURIAL MOUNDS AND EARTHWORKS

Kentucky

Two Thousand–Year-Old Earthen Architecture

The Adena mound is located in southern Ohio at Chillicothe (Mills 1902), and the early attempts to describe Adena culture were based on southern Ohio archaeological sites (Shetrone 1931; Greenman 1932). However, archaeological studies in Kentucky have been influential in establishing characteristics of the Adena culture, when it dated (ca. 350 BC–AD 250), and how it has been interpreted. The individual most responsible for this work in Kentucky was William S. Webb (1882–1964), professor of physics, archaeology, and anthropology at the University of Kentucky, who summarized his work in two important publications (Webb and Snow 1943; Webb and Baby 1957).

Webb's early work, including excavation in 1934 of the Adena Ricketts Mound with the biologist W. D. Funkhouser (Funkhouser and Webb 1935), was funded by National Research Council grants. In the late 1930s, Webb had enthusiastic government support (Milner and Smith 1986); the Kentucky excavations were funded by Depression-relief work projects under such New Deal programs as the Works Progress Administration and the Civilian Conservation Corps. Recognizing early (Webb and Funkhouser 1932, 418–419) that the proper excavation of burial mounds he would later call "Adena" required large field crews, Webb took the opportunity to completely and carefully excavate a series of Adena sites in what he and Funkhouser (1932, 417–419) had called their "Mound Area." These excavations have provided the clearest picture archaeologists have of Ohio valley Adena. By 1947 Webb and his associates had produced ten monographs on Adena sites (Milner and Smith 1986).

SITE DISTRIBUTION AND CHARACTER

Two types of Kentucky earthworks are considered Adena. Most important are the accretional burial mounds. These vary considerably in size from the small Auvergne Mound (Clay 1983), which may have contained a single interment and was less than three feet high, to the much larger Robbins Mound (Webb and Elliot 1942) which contained 100 burials and was 20.5 feet high. These mounds are concentrated in the Inner and Outer Bluegrass regions of Kentucky, including the Ohio River valley from above Louisville to Ashland on the West Virginia border. Burial mounds were generally located in the uplands on prominent high points and not in the river valleys. There are concentrations of burial mounds at the edge of the Inner Bluegrass in Montgomery County and along the Ohio in Mason and Boone counties, which may relate to long-established north and south overland trails.

Elsewhere, Adena mounds have been identified in the eastern Kentucky drainages of the Big Sandy and Licking rivers; however, there seem to have been few burial mounds on the rugged Cumberland plateau. Burial mounds were not important during the Woodland Period (ca. 800 BC–AD 900) in the western parts of the state.

The second category of Adena earthworks, in the same area, includes the perfect circle-and-ditch enclosures known as ceremonial circles (generally with an entrance from one of the cardinal directions) and the much rarer oval-and-ditch enclosures. Perhaps as many as twenty-five circles are known to exist, often occurring in pairs. Three have been excavated: Mount Horeb (Webb 1941b) and the Camargo group (Fenton and Jefferies 1991) in central Kentucky, and Biggs in northern Kentucky (Hardesty 1964). All have an exterior bank and interior ditch. At Mount Horeb, a screen of posts formed a circle immediately inside the ditch. At Biggs, a small burial mound had been constructed in the middle of the circle at a later date. Only one oval enclosure, Peter Village in Fayette County (Webb 1943; Clay 1987), is known to exist, although there may be others. In contrast to the circles, Peter Village seems to have been the location of nonritual activities.

A problem facing early workers was the nature of the villages and other nonmortuary sites used by the earthwork builders. It remains an important and debated issue, because extensive Adena domestic sites have not been identified.

Webb found pot shards in most mounds that he felt came from domestic areas near or below them. A competing interpretation (Clay 1983) proposes that this pottery may have been used in graveside feasting, and that the mound sites and the structures below them were used as ritual areas, not domestic "houses" (Clay 1998; Seeman 1986). There is abundant but scattered evidence that, despite their use of burial mounds and construction of enclosures, Adena groups lived in dispersed, short-term camps that provided temporary shelter but lacked substantial domestic architecture (Clay 1998, 13). This would reflect an economy based on hunting, foraging, and the incipient domestication of certain local plants but lacked extensive plant cultivation.

SMALL BUT SIGNIFICANT MOUNDS

Far more small mounds existed than large, and they have been destroyed by the relentless effects of over 200 years of agriculture; few have been excavated. The Auvergne Mound (Clay 1983) was only 3 feet high and covered a single interment in a simple, shallow pit that included the burial of a single individual. A cache of chert flakes was included in the grave, and the small mound covered the grave area completely. A post was erected to one side. At a later date, broken pots were scattered over the mound surface, representing vessels that had probably been used in graveside feasting, and the mound was expanded over the grave to its full size. Possibly five pots were used in this feast and may have come from several areas in the Bluegrass region, indicating the coming together of dispersed mourners after an interval to celebrate the death.

These small mounds reflect the basic raison d'etre of the burial mound, small or large. The mound was a visible monument that was used both as a cemetery and as a focus for mortuary ritual, which continued after burial and reinforced social bonds between scattered social groups linked through intermarriage (Clay 1998).

LARGE MOUNDS AND MOUND GROUPS

In the case of the large mounds, these same groups returned to the mound and added interments. As with the single events, these accretional burials were also accompanied by graveside ritual. In the Robbins mounds (Webb and Elliot 1942) in northern Kentucky, the Wright mounds in central Kentucky (Webb 1940), and the C&O mounds in the Big Sandy drainage of eastern Kentucky (Webb 1942), Webb has given us our best view of large Adena burial mounds and mound groups. In all, use of the locale as a burial structure was preceded by its use for other ritual purposes. The principal Robbins and Wright mounds (smaller mounds were also excavated at each site) are the largest burial mounds in the state, although exceeded in size by Adena mounds in West Virginia (Grave Creek) and Ohio (Miamisburg).

Below Robbins, and dating approximately 150 BC, was a circular structure of paired posts built before the mound and used for ritual activities not at first related to burial. In its center was a smaller circle containing the cremated remains of eleven individuals. This deposition of remains, which involved the interment of those who may have died elsewhere, began the use of the site for burial and the construction of a mound over it. Eighty-nine burials were added, each on simple bark beds in turn covered by bark, sometimes in log-lined tombs. The mound grew in size as these were covered with dirt. Artifacts buried with them included distinctive chert projectile points known as Robbins Points, rolled copper bracelets, and bodily ornaments cut from sheet mica.

If the pre-mound activities at Robbins were fairly simple, those below the larger Wright Mound, one of a group of three, were far more complex, although probably similar. This mound, with a carbon-14 date of AD 210, had a series of post circles below it, suggesting long use of the locality for ritual activities. Artifacts from the general site indicate that it had been used even earlier, during the Archaic period. At Wright the first burials were made in cribbed log tombs, which continued to be added (fourteen in all) as the mound grew in size, using a form of burial container far more elaborate than the simple pit beneath Auvergne or the bark beds of Robbins.

Eighteen of the twenty-one burials from the mound came from these tombs, which were left open for a period of time, forming accessible burial crypts (Brown 1979). It is possible that bodies were interred in them and the bones removed at a later date—or perhaps additional bodies were added before the crypt was finally sealed. The burial pattern at Wright suggests an increasing complexity of mortuary behavior over time. Indeed the mound is a very late Adena mound, and there are nearby interments, mounds, and earthworks more properly called Hopewell (Fenton and Jefferies 1991; Richmond and Kerr 2005). Some have suggested (Clay 2005) that the similarities between Adena and Hopewell are of such importance that Adena should no longer be viewed as a separate culture.

Webb excavated two mounds 1,200 feet apart at the C&O site, in eastern Kentucky. As at Wright, there were multiple post circles beneath both, suggesting a long history of ritual activity at this locality. Unlike at Robbins, none of the circles were the locus for the first burials, which initiated mound construction. The first burials were cremations mounded over with puddle clay. These were later mounded over with dirt as later interments were added in bark-lined pits and log tombs.

One mound also incorporated a late feature with a distinctly southern character: at an early stage, mound fill was shaped into a flat-topped platform. In addition pot shards in mound fill included those decorated with simple stamping, a form of decoration then in use at Hopewell sites in Ohio, using a clay paste. This suggests southern origins in the Appalachian uplands. In artifacts and the platform, these two mounds, with other sites near the Wright mound (Kerr and Richmond 2005; Fenton and Jefferies 1991), indicate connections with other groups north and south of the state. Like the Wright mound, the C&O mounds are probably late.

RECONSTRUCTING ADENA SOCIETY FROM THE MOUNDS

We can develop some idea of Adena society by trying to understand why individuals were buried in mounds, who they were, and what role they played in social groups. Webb thought that only special individuals were buried in specially prepared tombs within mounds, and he suggested further that the Morgan Stone Mound (1941a) was started on the death of a chief who was buried in the center of his circular house. Adding the evidence from the Robbins and C&O mounds, he later suggested that lower-class individuals were cremated and deposited at the base of mounds, while higher-class individuals were buried as inhumations, on bark beds and in log tombs (Webb and Snow 1943).

There is little to support the idea that those buried in the mounds (or deposited as cremations) were either special or lower-class. They are roughly evenly divided between men and women, and children are underrepresented. It is clear that not everyone who died got a mound burial. Mounds have traditionally been viewed as analogous to our private cemeteries, containing the deceased generations of a specific family. Under this view, the burial mounds are viewed as corporate cemeteries of specific social groups claiming territory as theirs, in the same manner that the historic pioneer family marked its claim on its farm.

A recent physical anthropological study (Taxman 1994, 84) indicates a high degree of genetic similarity between widespread Kentucky Adena burial populations, suggesting a "highly mobile free ranging population south of the Kentucky River" with substantial exchange and interaction among the groups living in the region. Building on this, it has been suggested (Clay 1998, 14) that Adena burial mounds may have been used by Native American groups as cooperative, not corporate, burial centers, where different groups who were allied through intermarriage buried their dead. As mentioned there is some evidence that burial was accompanied by graveside feasting (Clay 1983), during which hypothetically allied social groups worked out the consequences of the death of marriage partners through cooperative feast and ritual exchange. This interpretation is supported by the fact that, although burial mounds do occur on sites that seem to have a long history of ritual use, these mounds do not seem to be closely related to habitation sites. This fact may also explain why there are so few children buried in mounds: they may have been buried at the habitations and not at the cooperative mortuary centers.

Further Reading: Brown, James, "Charnel Houses and Mortuary Crypts: Disposal of the Dead in the Middle Woodland Period," in *Hopewell Archaeology: The Chillicothe Conference*, edited by David S. Brose and N'ome Greber (Kent, OH: Kent State University, 1979), 211–219; Clay, R. Berle, "Pottery and Graveside Ritual in Kentucky Adena," *Midcontinental Journal of Archaeology* 8(1) (1983): 109–126; Clay, R. Berle, "Adena Ritual Spaces," in *Early Woodland Archaeology*, edited by K. B. Farnsworth and T. E. Emerson, Kampsville Seminars in Archeology No. 2 (Kampsville, IL: Center for American Archeology Press, 1986), 581–595; Clay, R. Berle, "Circles and Ovals: Two Types of Adena Space," *Southeastern Archaeology* 6(1) (1987): 46–56; Clay, R. Berle, "The Essential Features of Adena Ritual and Their Implications," *Southeastern Archaeology* 17(1) (1998): 1–21; Clay, R. Berle, "Adena: Rest in Peace?" in *Woodland Period Systematics in the Middle Ohio Valley*, edited by Darlene Applegate and Robert C. Mainfort (Tuscaloosa: University of Alabama Press, 2005), 94–110; Fenton, James, and Richard Jefferies, "The Camargo Mound and Earthworks: Preliminary Findings," in *The Human Landscape in Kentucky's Past*, edited by C. Sout and C. K. Hensley (Lexington: Kentucky Heritage Council, 1991), 40–55; Funkhouser, William D., and William S. Webb, *The Ricketts Site in Montgomery County, Kentucky*, Reports in Anthropology and Archaeology No. 3 (3) (Lexington: University of Kentucky, 1935); Greenman, Emerson, "Excavation of the Coon Mound and an Analysis of the Adena Culture," *Ohio Archaeological and Historical Quarterly* 41 (1932): 366–523; Hardesty, Donald, "The Biggs Site: A Hopewellian Complex in Greenup County, Kentucky," *Probes* (University of Kentucky, 1964), 14–21; Mills, William C., "Excavations of the Adena Mound," *Ohio Archaeological and Historical Quarterly* 10 (1902): 452–479; Milner, George R., and Virginia G. Smith, *New Deal Archaeology in Kentucky: Excavations, Collections, and Research*, Occasional Papers in Anthropology, No. 5 (Lexington: University of Kentucky Program for Cultural Resource Assessment, 1986); Richmond, Michael D., and Jonathan P. Kerr, "Middle Woodland Ritualism in the Central Bluegrass: Evidence From the Amburgy Site, Montgomery County, Kentucky," in *Woodland Period Systematics in the Middle Ohio Valley*, edited by Darlene Applegate and Robert C. Mainfort (Tuscaloosa: University of Alabama Press, 2005), 76–83; Seeman, Mark, "Adena 'Houses' and Their Implications for Early Woodland Settlement Models in the Ohio Valley," in *Early Woodland Archaeology*, edited by K. B. Farnsworth and T. E. Emerson, Kampsville Seminars in Archeology No. 2 (Kampsville, IL: Center for American Archeology Press, 1986); Shetrone, Henry C., *The Mound Builders* (New York: Appleton, 1931); Taxman, Steven M., "Nonmetric Trait Variation in the Adena Peoples of the Ohio River Drainage," *Midcontinental Journal of Archaeology* 19(1) (1994): 71–98; Webb, William S., *The Wright Mounds, Sites 6 and 7, Montgomery County, Kentucky*, Reports in Anthropology and Archaeology No. 5, (Lexington: University of Kentucky, 1940), 6–134; Webb, William S., *The Morgan Stone Mound, Site 15, Bath County, Kentucky*, Reports in Anthropology and Archaeology No. 5(2) (Lexington: University of Kentucky, 1941a), 139–218; Webb, William S., *The Mount Horeb Site Earthworks, Site 1, and the Drake Mound, Site 11, Fayette County, Kentucky*, Reports in Anthropology and Archaeology No. 5(2) (Lexington: University of Kentucky, 1941b), 139–218; Webb, William S., *The C and O Mounds at Paintsville, Sites Jo2 and Jo9, Johnson County, Kentucky*, Reports in Anthropology and Archaeology No. 5 (Lexington: University of Kentucky, 1942), 297–372; Webb, William S., *The Riley Mound, Site Be15, and the Landing Mound, Site Be17, Boone County, Kentucky, With Additional Notes on the Mt. Horeb Site, Fa1, and Sites Fa14 and Fa15, Fayette County, Kentucky*, Reports in Anthropology and Archaeology No. 5 (Lexington: University of Kentucky, 1943), 582–672; Webb, William S., and Raymond Baby, *The Adena People No. 2.* (Columbus: Ohio Historical Society, 1957), 123; Webb, William S., and William D. Funkhouser, *Archaeological Survey of*

Kentucky, Reports in Anthropology and Archaeology No. 2 (Lexington: University of Kentucky, 1932); Webb, William S., and John B. Elliot, *The Robbins Mounds, Site Be3 and Be14, Boone County, Kentucky*, Reports in Anthropology and Archaeology No. 5(5) (Lexington: University of Kentucky, 1942), 377–499; Webb, William S., and

Charles E. Snow, *The Crigler Mounds, Sites Be20 and Be27, and the Hartman Mound Site, Be32, Boone County, Kentucky*, Reports in Anthropology and Archaeology No. 5 (Lexington: University of Kentucky, 1943): 505–579.

Rudolf Berle Clay

MIDDLE WOODLAND PERIOD ANCIENT EARTHEN MOUNDS

Lower Illinois River Valley, West Central Illinois
Trade and Horticulture in the Mid-Continent

The bluffs overlooking the lower 70 miles of the Illinois River before it enters the Mississippi River at Grafton, Illinois, are lined with hundreds of prehistoric mounds. Most of these mounds date to the Middle and Late Woodland periods (100 BC–AD 300 and AD 300–900, respectively).

BRIEF HISTORY OF MOUND RESEARCH IN THE LOWER ILLINOIS VALLEY

Prehistoric mounds were discovered almost immediately by the early nineteenth-century Euro-Americans settling in the lower Illinois valley. From the 1830s through the 1870s, casual excavations of the mounds were common—a Sunday afternoon picnic outing. In the late nineteenth century, several dedicated antiquarians—notably John G. Henderson, William McAdams and John Francis Snyder—published descriptions of their excavations of mounds along the Illinois River. The first professional archaeological investigations of the mounds were organized by Warren K. Moorehead of the Robert S. Peabody Museum of Archaeology in Andover, Massachusetts, and were conducted by a team led by Jay L. B. Taylor in 1927 and 1928. Between 1950 and 1975, Gregory Perino, primarily in the employ of the Gilcrease Museum of the Americas in Tulsa, Oklahoma, excavated dozens of mounds in the lower Illinois valley. In 1958 Stuart Struever, then a graduate student at Northwestern University, began a salvage excavation on Mound 9 at the Kamp site. In the 1950s, Struever established a nonprofit organization that eventually became the Center for American Archeology (CAA). Since 1970 mound research in the lower Illinois valley has been conducted through, or in association with, the CAA.

Archaeological conceptions of the mounds have changed over this span of time, as have the kinds of information extracted from them. For early archaeologists, the burials in the mounds were an invaluable source of artifacts (grave goods) for establishing regional chronologies. By the 1970s,

archaeologists had realized that the mounds and their burials could provide information on social organization and biological dimensions, such as health and genetic relatedness. More recently the religious and symbolic meanings of mounds, burial practices, and grave goods have interested archaeologists.

CURRENT INTERPRETATIONS OF MOUNDS IN THE LOWER ILLINOIS VALLEY

The Middle Woodland period in the American Midwest was largely contemporaneous with what has been termed the Hopewell phenomenon. Hopewell is characterized by the widespread exchange of a range of rare and/or foreign raw materials (for example, obsidian, copper, mica, and whelk and conch shells) and objects fashioned from them. The geographic extent of the exchange encompasses the region bounded by the Great Lakes, the Appalachians, the Gulf of Mexico, and the Great Plains. Construction of earthworks (primarily mounds, but also geometric shapes) was also shared across this region, as were the stylistic motifs of artifact form and decoration.

The Middle Woodland period is associated with the widespread adoption of horticulture (gardening) of native, starchy and oily-seeded plants and the development of ceramic pots for boiling these seeds to enhance their nutritional contribution. This revolution in subsistence led to the aggregation of populations into major river valleys or other locales that provided the kinds of soils and moisture regimes conducive to intensive horticulture. Middle Woodland participation in Hopewell and in the horticultural revolution varied greatly from region to region across the Midwest. The lower Illinois valley was one of the areas most dramatically transformed by these changes.

By the Early Woodland period, the lower Illinois valley largely had been abandoned by Archaic populations, but with the onset of the Middle Woodland period, people moved back into the valley. Populations eventually filled the valley and

Mounds 4 and 6 at the Elizabeth site.   [Douglas K. Charles]

expanded into the surrounding tributary valleys and upland areas. The Middle Woodland period and the Hopewell phenomenon ended, and the Late Woodland period began around this time.

The Hopewell phenomenon represents a period of intense social interaction along the lines of earlier Archaic practices, but involved more people, a broader geographic scale, and more material goods. During the Middle Woodland period, mound building and ceremonial exchange occurred in two places: on the margins of bluffs and in the floodplain. Since at least 4000 BC, Archaic populations living in the lower Illinois valley had gathered for exchange, ceremonies, and burial of their dead in these same two locations.

Local communities buried their dead and performed rituals at cemeteries located on the ridges along the edges of the bluffs, which loomed 60 to 90 meters (200 to 300 ft) above the river's floodplain. Neighboring communities would congregate on elevated ridges in the floodplain to exchange news and valuables, arrange marriages, and bury their dead.

During the Archaic period, the use of these two locations corresponded to changing levels of mobility. During times of

resource abundance and relative sedentism, the local bluff-top cemeteries predominated; when resources were more limited, more frequent residential moves were required, and the floodplain sites became anchoring points for the mobile, dispersed communities. Middle Woodland communities simultaneously—and more intensively—utilized both locations, reflecting the scale of the demographic transformation of the valley that was under way.

There were, in fact, three kinds of communities to which Middle Woodland people belonged, each incorporating larger and more widespread social relations. Day-to-day life was spent in residential communities of ten to twenty-five people living in small hamlets of one to three houses. The members of several nearby hamlets formed ceremonial communities that would gather together to bury their dead and perhaps perform other ceremonies at a bluff-top mound site (such as the Elizabeth site) overlooking the valley where they lived. Larger sustainable communities (that is, incorporating the 500 or more people necessary to maintain a viable mating pool) composed of surrounding groups that would periodically assemble at the floodplain mound sites (such as the Mound House site)

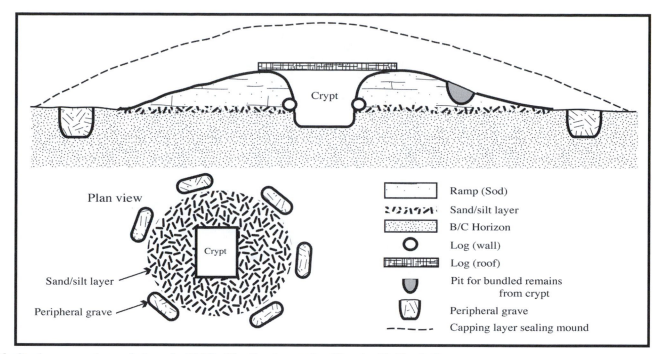

Idealized cross-section and plan of a Middle Woodland mound.   [Douglas K. Charles]

to exchange goods, arrange marriages, and bury high-ranking people in the mounds. The floodplain mounds are much larger than those found on the bluff tops, but they contain fewer burials and were probably more important as platforms or stages for ritual performances.

The internal structure of mounds was elaborate and incorporated important symbolism and meaning. Excavated mounds vary in their internal structure, but there tends to be a number of commonly recurring components. These elements include a central crypt, where bodies were temporarily housed during decomposition of the soft tissue; an earthen ramp composed of inverted blocks of sod that surrounded and formed the walls of the crypt; a layer of light-colored sand or sediment beneath the ramp; small graves in the ramp for the bundled bones of bodies processed in the crypt; and larger graves surrounding the ramp, where bodies not processed in the crypt were interred. When the mound was no longer used to process and bury the dead, it was covered by a layer of earth, forming the mounds as we see them now.

The structure and composition of the mounds appear to relate to a common southeastern Native American tripartite vision of the world: this world was a disk, with an upper world above and an underworld below. The structure and composition also relate to the widespread and very old Native American myth of the earth diver—an animal that dove beneath the waters covering the earth, retrieving some mud out of which the dry land expands. Among Plains tribes, sod was frequently used in ceremonies to represent

the mud brought up by the earth diver. Building the mound was a symbolic representation of the world and creation. The area where the mound was to be built was cleared of vegetation and topsoil, exposing the underworld. A circular layer of sediment represented this world, and the sky above was the upper world. On the layer of sediment, a ramp composed of sod—referencing the land in the earth diver story—was erected around a crypt. The dead were placed in the crypt—the center of the world—where their bodies melted into the underworld. Their dry bones were then gathered up and buried in the sod.

PLACES TO VISIT

Most of the bluff-top mounds are located on private land, but a number of mounds, including some partially excavated by William McAdams, can be seen along the hiking trails and elsewhere in Pere Marquette State Park, near Grafton, Illinois.

The Center for American Archeology in Kampsville, Illinois, has a visitor center with exhibits on the archaeology of the lower Illinois valley. The Kamp site, one of the floodplain ceremonial centers, is located about two miles north of Kampsville along Highway 100. The huge, tree-covered Mound 8 lies in the field to the east between the highway and the river. Mound 7, plowed down and under cultivation, is at a right angle (toward the highway) just to the north of Mound 8.

Artifacts from some excavated sites can be found at several museums: Moorehouse/Taylor excavations at the Robert S. Peabody Museum in Andover, Massachusetts; Perino excavations at the Gilcrease Museum of the Americas in Tulsa,

Cross-section of sod ramp in Mound House Mound 1 (blocks in scale = 1 cm).   [Douglas K. Charles]

Oklahoma; Center for American Archeology excavations at the Illinois State Museum in Springfield.

Further Reading: Buikstra, Jane, *Hopewell in the Lower Illinois Valley: A Regional Study of Human Biological Variability and Prehistoric Mortuary Behavior*, Northwestern University Archaeological Program, Scientific Papers No. 2 (Evanston, IL: Northwestern University, 1976); Buikstra, Jane E., Douglas K. Charles, and Gordon F. M. Rakita, *Staging Ritual: Hopewell Ceremonialism at the Mound House Site, Greene County, Illinois*, Kampsville Studies in Archeology and History No. 1 (Kampsville, IL: Center for American Archeology, 1998); Center for American Archeology Web site, http://www.caa-archeology.org; Charles, Douglas K., Steven R. Leigh, and Jane E. Buikstra, eds., *The Archaic and Woodland Cemeteries at the Elizabeth Site in the Lower Illinois Valley*, Kampsville Archeological Center Research Series 7 (Kampsville, IL: Center for American Archeology, 1988); Charles, Douglas K., Julieann Van Nest, and Jane E. Buikstra, "From the Earth: Minerals and Meaning in the Hopewellian World," in *Soils, Stones and Symbols: Cultural Perceptions of the Mineral World*, edited by Nicole Boivin and Mary Ann Owoc (London: UCL Press, 2004), 43–70; Farnsworth, Kenneth B., ed., *Early Hopewell Mound Explorations: The First Fifty Years in the Illinois River Valley*, Illinois Transportation Archaeological Research Program, Studies in Archaeology No. 3 (Urbana, IL: University of Illinois, 2004); Gilcrease Museum of the Americas Web site, http://www.gilcrease.org; Illinois State Museum Web site, http://www.museum.state.il.us; Pere Marquette State Park Web sites, http://dnr.state.il.us/lands/Landmgt/PARKS/R4/Peremarq.htm and http://www.greatriverroad.com/Pere/PereIndex.htm; Perino, Gregory, *Illinois Hopewell and Late Woodland Mounds: The Excavations of Gregory Perino 1950–1975*, Illinois Transportation Archaeological Research Program, Studies in Archaeology No. 4 (Urbana, IL: University of Illinois, 2006); Van Nest, Julieann, Douglas K. Charles, Jane E. Buikstra, and David Asch, "Sod Blocks in Illinois Hopewell Mounds," *American Antiquity* 66 (2001): 633–650.

Douglas K. Charles

THE EDWIN HARNESS MOUND

Ross County, South Central Ohio

The Liberty Earthworks—A Century of Studies

The Edwin Harness Mound was the largest of fourteen mounds associated with the Liberty Earthworks, located on the east bank of the Scioto River some 12 miles southeast of Chillicothe, Ohio. The mound was built in several stages over a large multi-room structure, a Big House that was partially dismantled prior to being ceremonially covered circa AD 300. The site is one of the relatively rare large multi-stage elongate mounds built by Ohio Hopewell peoples. The quantity, quality, and lavish intensity found in the concentrations of artifacts and structural remains left by these peoples sets them apart from contemporary groups scattered across eastern North America. A network of shared beliefs and practices involving the use of exotic materials and/or specific artifacts or architectural forms connected the geographically separate home territories. A common art style, with local variants, was carried out in a variety of media, including stone, clay, metals, bone, and other perishable materials.

In Ross County, the Harness Big House sheltered tombs, special artifact deposits, several large hearths, and numbers of small deposits of carefully cleaned up and redeposited debris from small ritual fires. The overall design of the Big House and the ground plan of the Liberty enclosures—a combination of a true square and generally circular elements—bear a close resemblance to similar features at the Seip Earthworks located in Paint Creek valley, a tributary of the Scioto, about 27 miles southwest of Chillicothe. The details of the funerary and other ceremonies conducted in the two Big Houses show local variations, as do the enclosure ground plans. However, the resemblances are more striking than the differences. For example, the pattern of the distribution of non-utilitarian copper objects in deposits or as grave inclusions among the sections of both Big Houses is similar, indicating common cultural ideas.

Excavations of the Edwin Harness site, as for many of the large classic Ohio Hopewell mounds, began in the early part of the nineteenth century and have continued intermittently. George Squier and Edwin Davis were the first; followed by local schoolboys and Frederick Putnam of the Harvard Peabody in 1885; and Warren K. Moorehead and William C. Mills of the Ohio Archaeological and Historical Society in 1897 and 1905, respectively. These excavations recovered the range of exotic materials associated with Ohio Hopewell, including copper, mica, obsidian, galena, and large marine shells. The collections are curated in Cambridge, Massachusetts, and Columbus, Ohio.

The 1976 excavations under the Ohio Archaeological Council and the 1977 continuation under the Cleveland Museum of Natural History obtained information that has allowed new interpretations of the archived artifacts and, except for Putnam's trench, incomplete excavation records. Analytic techniques and field equipment not available in 1905 provided details of the environment and dating of the site use. The post pattern of the Big House was identified, as were remnant elements of the symbols associated with the range of activities—including, but not limited to, funerary rituals that took place within and immediately adjacent to the Harness Big House.

The use of small-mesh screens and flotation techniques to process excavated materials by the most recent investigations yielded fragments from activities associated with the Big House that had not been collected previously. Small seeds, beads, small animal bone fragments, and other charred bits were sorted out. Small quantities of *Zea mays* (corn) were recovered—the first known in Ohio. The fragments, found in the remains of a small fire that burned on the building floor, indicate that when the Big House was in active use, corn was a special-purpose plant in the same sense as tobacco or other known ceremonially important plants. Corn became a major food crop in the central Ohio River valley many centuries after the Hopewell era.

Although the debris found at the site reflects specialized and public activities, it shows the use of relatively local resources. Scale fish, shellfish, and building materials were obtained from the river and the nearby hills. Deer, raccoon, turkey and other birds, and small mammals came from the woodland and edge areas. A study of the clays and temper used to make Harness ceramic vessels identified a direct connection to a contemporary site in Tennessee: a shard from a vessel made at Harness was found at the Icehouse Bottom site. The Appalachian plateau in eastern Tennessee and western North Carolina has many deposits of mica, a material found at Edwin Harness and other Hopewell sites.

In the first stage of mound construction, the three major sections, or rooms, were individually covered with loads of culturally sterile soils. Layers placed over these formed a single main mound sloping from 11 to 20 feet high. Two rings of flat sandstones were arranged on the eastern side of the mound, with a third on the western. Mills considered that many of these had been used to dig the soil used to build the mound. The last additions were thin layers that extended outward from the base of the mound. These layers were not apparent on the ground surface and unknown before the 1976–77 excavations.

The land where the Edwin Harness Mound once stood is a private working farm field and not open to the general public. Visitors are welcome at the museum and exhibits managed by the National Park Service at the Visitor Center for the Hopewell Culture National Historical Park located just north of Chillicothe. Five major sites are now protected in Hopewell Culture National Historical Park. Three sites are regularly open for visits: Mound City, Hopewell, and Seip. Special tours are arranged at times to visit Hopeton and High Bank.

Further Reading: Greber, N'omi B., "The Edwin Harness Big House," in *Ohio Archaeology: An Illustrated Chronicle of Ohio's Ancient American Indian Cultures*, by Bradley T. Lepper (Wilmington, OH: Orange Frazer Press, 2005), 132–134; Greber, N'omi, "Recent Excavations at the Edwin Harness Mound, Liberty Works, Ross County, Ohio," *Midcontinental Journal of Archaeology*, Special Paper No. 5 (Walnut Creek, CA: AltaMira Press, 1983); Greber, N'omi, "Two Geometric Enclosures in Paint Creek: An Estimate of Possible Changes in Community Patterns Through Time," in *Ohio Hopewell Community Organization*, edited by William Dancey and Paul Pacheco (Kent, OH: Kent State University Press, 1997), 207–230; Mills, William C., "The Explorations of the Edwin Harness Mound," *Ohio Archaeological and Historical Quarterly* 16 (1907): 113–193; Hopewell Culture National Historical Park Web site, http:/www.nps.gov/hocu.

N'omi B. Greber

GRAVE CREEK MOUND HISTORIC SITE

West Virginia
Grave Creek Mound

Grave Creek Mound, also known as the Mammoth Mound, is the largest Adena mound and the largest mound of its type in North America. The original site consisted of a conical earthen mound 65 feet in height and 240 feet in diameter, surrounded by a moat that was 910 feet long, 40 feet wide, and 4–5 feet deep. The Adena people began building it in the third century BC and completed it in the second century BC. The mound consists of 1.2 million cubic feet of earth weighing 57,000 tons. The mound's volume represents about 3 million basket loads of soil. The Adena people were basically hunters and gatherers who also practiced limited horticulture and lived in scattered hamlets. The most famous artifact associated with the mound is the Grave Creek Tablet, which played a major part in some of the most significant controversies in American archaeology.

Grave Creek Mound was the most prominent Native American feature on the upper Ohio valley landscape. It was a familiar landmark to early Euro-American settlers and travelers as they moved westward. The mound was first described by Nicholas Cresswell in 1775 and by many prominent travelers thereafter. The mound has been designated a National Historic Landmark.

Joseph Tomlinson, who was adamant about not having the mound excavated, originally owned the mound. Finally, in 1838, his son Jesse, the subsequent owner, authorized an excavation supervised by his nephew Abelard B. Tomlinson and Thomas Biggs. On March 19, 1838, the excavation began with the digging of a tunnel 4 feet off the ground into the north side of the mound. After two weeks of excavation, the tunnel reached 111 feet to the approximate center of the mound, where a log tomb with a male and a female skeleton was discovered. The male skeleton had a bar gorget with an expanded center and was surrounded with 650 bone and shell beads.

A shaft was started in the top of the mound, and a skeleton attributed to a later period was uncovered in the top 3 feet. Other skeletons and parts of skeletons were found near the top of the mound. Iron rods screwed together were sunk into the shaft to probe for additional burial vaults. At a depth of 34 feet, the probe struck a rock, which was dislodged. The rock sank 2 feet, signifying the existence of a second vault.

The second tunnel was started 34 feet up the side of the mound and slightly west of the first tunnel. The tunnel was low and narrow and much shorter than the first. On June 9, a second burial chamber containing one skeleton was reached

at the intersection of the shaft and tunnel. This burial contained 1,700 bone beads, 500 Marginella seashells, 5 copper bracelets, a quantity of square and rectangular pieces of mica, and a small, oval, flat, inscribed tablet of sandstone—the infamous Grave Creek Tablet. The total cost of the 1838 investigation was $2,500.

According to the original plan, the sides of the lower tunnel were lined with a brick arch. The lower burial vault was enlarged to 28 feet in diameter with a 9-foot ceiling. Ten additional skeletons were uncovered during this work. In the center of the vault was a brick column with a shelf at the base and wire cases where the artifacts and skeletons were displayed. The wet, damp room was lighted with twenty candles. A three-story frame observatory was built on the top of the mound. The first story was 32 feet in diameter, the second 26 feet, and the top 10 feet.

The museum was opened in May of 1839 with an admission charge of 25 cents (comparable to $5 in today's currency). The museum closed in 1846 due to a lack of patrons and customers.

The artifacts from the mound were typical of what would be found in some other Adena burial mounds. The copper bracelets from the Great Lakes area, the Marginella shell beads from the Gulf of Mexico, and the mica from the Carolinas provided evidence that the Adena participated in an extensive trade network. The Grave Creek Tablet, however, was unique. It was made of local sandstone and came from the upper burial chamber (the one with the single skeleton). The small, oval tablet had three rows of hieroglyphic-like characters cut into it. At first the tablet was accepted as genuine, but some archaeologists, including Ephraim George Squier, maintained that it was a fake. The distinguished ethnologist Henry Rowe Schoolcraft accepted it as genuine and was intrigued with how the individual characters corresponded with ancient alphabets. He eventually classified individual characters on the tablet as Ancient Greek, Etruscan, Runic, Ancient Gallic, Old Erse, Phoenician, Old British, and Celtiberic, concluding that the authors were Celts from Spain or Britain who came to America before Columbus.

While contemporary American archaeologists debated the authenticity of the tablet, Schoolcraft sent copies of the characters abroad. This resulted in several investigators providing outlandish translations. The first translation was provided in 1857 by a Frenchman, Maurice Schwab, and was submitted

Postcard published in 1910, from a drawing of Grave Creek Mound in 1850. Collection of the Division of Culture and History. [West Virginia Archaeological Society]

as "The chief of emigration who reached these places (or this island), has fixed these statutes forever." Andy Price wrote a fictional booklet in 1928 where he maintained the characters were distorted English letters that read "Bil Stumps Stone Oct 14 1838." The U.S. National Museum took Andy seriously and gave this as the correct interpretation for the inscription for many years.

One of the staunchest supporters of the authenticity of the tablet was the frontier historian and antiquarian Wills DeHass, who was also a physician from Wheeling. He supported the belief that the mounds were built by an older and more superior race than the Native Americans and used the tablet to support this position. Most contemporary archaeologists believe the tablet was a hoax.

E. Thomas Hemmings and the West Virginia Geological and Economic Survey undertook the only modern investigations of the Grave Creek Mound in 1975 and 1976.

Hemmings excavated as series of exploratory trenches to define the length, width, and depth of the moat at the site. He also drilled thirteen holes with a core-drilling rig to define the stratigraphy of the mound. Charcoal samples taken from three of the cores were combined and produced a radiocarbon date of 200 BC for the mean construction date. The stratigraphy identified in the core samples indicated that the mound was under more or less continuous construction, rather than having two main building phases.

All of the artifacts associated with the Grave Creek Mound, including the Grave Creek Tablet, have since disappeared. All of the skeletal material, except for one skull fragment, has also disappeared. The skull fragment was found at the Academy of Natural Sciences of Philadelphia and was eventually returned to the Delf Norona Museum. The tablet and many of the artifacts were last in the possession of Wills DeHass.

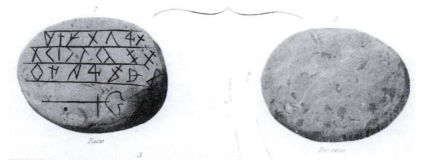

Grave Creek Tablet. From Norona (1998, 36). Drawn from the original by Capt. Seth Eastman in 1850.   [West Virginia Division of Archives/Archaeological Society]

Today the Delf Norona Museum, operated by the West Virginia Division of Culture and History, is located adjacent to the mound. A curation facility is being constructed in the museum that will house the West Virginia state archaeological collections.

Further Reading: Barnhart, Terry A., "Curious Antiquity? The Grave Creek Controversy Revisited," *West Virginia History* 46(1–4) (1986): 103–124; Grave Creek Mound Archaeology Complex Village, West Virginia Division of Culture and History Web site, http://www.wvculture.org/sites/gravecreek.html (online January 2006); Hemmings, E. Thomas, "Investigations at Grave Creek Mound 1975–76: A Sequence for Mound and Moat Construction," *West Virginia Archeologist* 36(2) (1984): 3–49; Norona, Delf, *Moundsville's Mammoth Mound*, Publications Series No. 1, reprint of 1962 ed. (Moundsville: West Virginia Archaeological Society, 1998).

Robert F. Maslowski

THE HOPEWELL SITE

Ross County, South Central Ohio

Excavations and Earthworks at the Namesake of an Ancient Culture

The Hopewell site stands out among pre-Columbian sites in North America. Its prominence can be attributed to the size and variety of its monuments and the numerous extraordinary artifacts recovered. Many of these artifacts were made of materials found far from the site, including copper from Upper Michigan, mica from the Appalachians, marine shell from the eastern coasts, and obsidian from the Rocky Mountains.

More than 3 miles of earthen embankments enclose more than 100 acres at the Hopewell site. The Great Enclosure, somewhat rectangular in shape, followed the edge of the terrace on the south, climbed 20 feet up onto the next terrace, dipped into and out of the ravines on the north, and turned south along a small creek to again reach the terrace edge, 30 feet above the floodplain of the North Fork of Paint Creek. Three walls joined the eastern side of the Great Enclosure to form a square, 850 feet on a side. Inside the Great Enclosure, a smaller, D-shaped enclosure surrounded a group of mounds, and a circular embankment was in the southeastern corner.

Forty mounds scattered inside and just outside the embankments ranged in size from very small to the huge Mound 25. The three segments of this largest mound stretched for the length of two city blocks (some 500 ft), and on the eastern side were three stories high (some 35 ft).

The oblong central segment was built over a group of wooden buildings that held burials and two deposits of thousands of artifacts. One deposit contained over 100 finely crafted obsidian bifaces, many 14 inches long. These are too large to be a practical tool. Their shiny, black surface was a marked contrast with the glittering silver mica that was part of an impressive public display before both broken and whole objects made of other exotic and local materials were placed in the deposit. Another deposit contained over 500 copper ear ornaments.

The buildings were torn down before the mound was built. Several generations made additions to the mound before it reached its final height. The two end segments covered large, empty plazas where many people could get together to participate in special public events, perhaps associated with adding layers to the central mound.

Even small mounds covered deposits of thousands of artifacts. Under Mound 2, more than 7,000 discs made of flint from Indiana were found. They were grouped by handfuls and placed in two layers separated by a layer of sand. Mound 11 covered a pile containing hundreds of pounds of obsidian chips left over from making the large bifaces, along with some smaller bifaces.

Three of the individuals buried in separate buildings covered by Mound 25 were accompanied by different styles of copper headdresses. These people were undoubtedly important in their society, but they were not kings, as they were called by early excavators. In contrast with the great public monuments, domestic sites are small and more difficult to find. No kingly mansions are known. Most mound burials were relatively simple.

The name of the site has been extended to identify the cultural remains of scattered independent groups of peoples living in eastern North America from about 200 BC to AD 400. These groups shared similar worldviews but interpreted these views in their own way. Each region also chose its own mix of hunting, gathering, and gardening to sustain the commitment to producing special artifacts and/or earthen monuments that expressed the local society's version of a strongly compelling worldview.

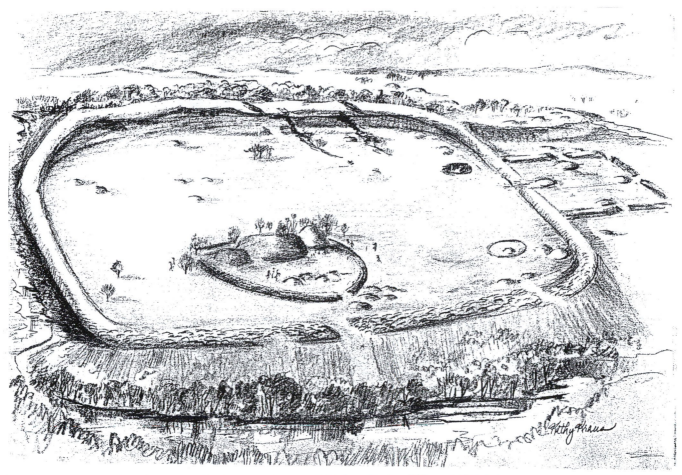

An artist's reconstruction of the Great Enclosure.   [Hopewell Culture National Historical Park]

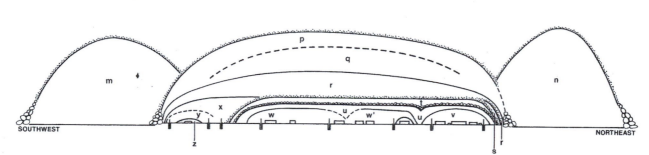

A sketch of an estimated profile, 25 feet north of center, Mound 25.   [N'omi B. Greber]

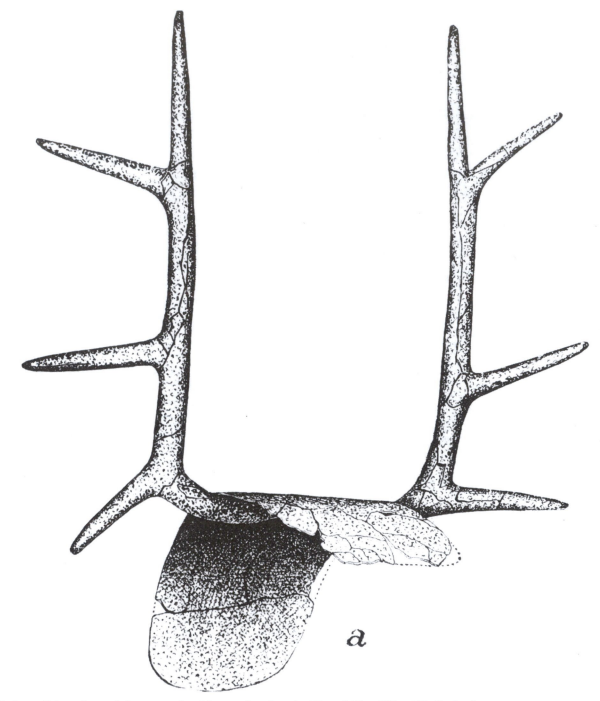

An artist's rendition of one of the copper headdresses found under Mound 25.   [N'omi B. Greber]

The Hopewell site is not typical of other contemporary sites, since it contains the entire range of burial and artifact types associated with the Hopewell phenomenon found across all sites. It is spectacular enough to deserve the honor.

Ephraim G. Squier and Edwin H. Davis conducted excavations at the site in 1845. Then it was called the Clarke site in honor of the landowner. Their map of the site and report of their work was included in the first volume published by the fledgling Smithsonian Institution in 1848. The artifacts recovered are now in the British Museum in London.

Warren K. Moorehead, working for Fredrick W. Putnam of Harvard, excavated in 1891–92 and named the site for

Mordecai Hopewell, who owned the site at that time. The artifacts recovered were displayed at the 1893 Chicago Columbian Exposition, where Putnam was director of the Department of Ethnology and Archaeology. These artifacts later became a part of the collections of the Chicago Field Museum. Examples of the fine artistic skills of the Hopewell artisans are now on exhibit in the Hall of the Ancient Americans and on the museum's Web site.

In the 1920s, Henry Shetrone of the Ohio Historical Society directed excavations. A sample of the materials recovered is on display at the Ohio Historical Center in Columbus. A virtual tour of a former exhibit and photographs of additional artifacts is on the society's Web site.

The Hopewell site itself is now part of Hopewell Culture National Historical Park and open to visitors. A bicycle trail crosses the site, and new visitor facilities and parking areas are being constructed. Directions to the site are available at park headquarters at the Mound City visitors' center and museum, north of Chillicothe on Route 104.

Recent geophysical remote-sensing work at the site by Jennifer Pederson, park archaeologist, led to the discovery a small, circular embankment within the Great Enclosure that had not been known before. She has also discovered pit features, dug centuries after AD 400, that show the longtime use of the site. Monitoring of the site showed that salvage work was required due to the continued erosion of the riverbank just beyond the Great Enclosure. In 2006 staff of the Midwest

Archaeological Center uncovered pit features in this area that were used in the Hopewell era. Also in 2006, Mark Lynott, director of the MWAC, studied the construction methods of a section of the major wall. Details of the 2006 work are on the MWAC Web site.

Further Reading: *First Ohioans*, http://www.ohiohistory.org/ archaeology (online May 2007); Greber, N'omi B., "A Commentary on the Contexts and Contents of Large to Small Ohio Hopewell Deposits," in *A View from the Core: A Synthesis of Ohio Hopewell Archaeology*, edited by Paul J. Pacheco, reprinted 2005 (Columbus: Ohio Archaeological Council, 1996), 150–173; Greber, N'omi B., and Katharine C. Ruhl, *The Hopewell Site: A Contemporary Analysis Based on the Work of Charles C. Willoughby*, 2nd printing (Washington, PA: Eastern National Parks and Monuments Assn., 2000); *Hopewell Archaeology: The Newsletter of Hopewell Archaeology in the Ohio River Valley*, Midwest Archaeological Center Web site, http://www.cr.nps.gov/mwac (online May 2007); Lepper, Bradley T., *Ohio Archaeology: An Illustrated Chronicle of Ohio's Ancient American Indian Cultures* (Wilmington, Ohio: Orange Frazer Press, 2005), 109–169; Milner, George R., *The Moundbulders: Ancient Peoples of Eastern North America* (London: Thames and Hudson, 2004), 54–96; Pederson Weinberger, Jennifer, "Ohio Hopewell Earthworks: An Examination of Site Use from Non-mound Space at the Hopewell Site," Ph.D. diss. (Ohio State University, 2006); Woodward, Susan L., and Jerry N. McDonald, *Indian Mounds of the Middle Ohio Valley* (Blacksburg, VA: McDonald & Woodward, 2002), 42–68.

N'omi B. Greber

HOPEWELL CULTURE NATIONAL HISTORICAL PARK

Ross County, South Central Ohio

The Mound City Group

The Mound City archaeological site—located on the Scioto River, a few miles north of Chillicothe in southern Ohio—is one of the most intriguing and significant mortuary sites in the Ohio Hopewell tradition of the Middle Woodland period (200 BC to AD 400). The site is so named because it consists of at least twenty-four burial mounds inside a low, roughly square earthen embankment with rounded corners that encloses 15.6 acres and has openings on the east and west sides. The embankment was constructed late in the site's history with soil from eight borrow pits around the perimeter. It was 4 feet tall in 1846, and burial mound heights at that time ranged from 1.5 feet to 17.5 feet. The density of mounds within this small geometric enclosure is 1.54 per acre—a high number compared to most other Hopewellian enclosures

in southern Ohio. For example, the nearby Hopewell Mound Group has only 0.19 mounds per acre.

Mound City served principally as a necropolis for distinguished people and their families in the local area during the second and third centuries AD. Some inhumations were placed in graves dug into the mounds sometime after AD 800, but all the Hopewellian burials at Mound City were cremations. The burial program was carried out within specially designed bent-pole structures, often referred to by archaeologists as charnel houses. At the end of the process, the charnel house was dismantled and covered with dirt, and another structure was erected nearby. Thus, during its period of use, the site consisted of one or more active charnel houses and a growing number of decommissioned structures buried, or

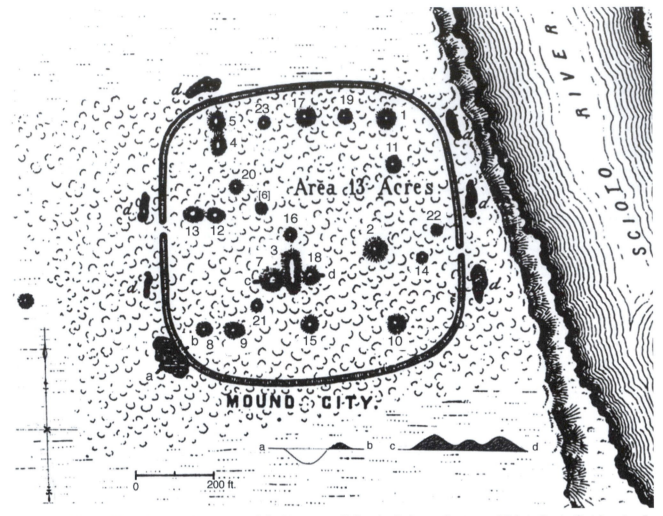

A portion of Plate XIX in *Ancient Monuments of the Mississippi Valley*, by Ephraim Squier and Edwin Davis (Smithsonian Institution, 1848) showing Mound City as it was in 1846.   [William S. Dancey]

being buried, under mounds of soil. It is thought that many communities supported the site, although only a fraction of the population was buried there.

The burial process entailed burning the deceased in a crematory basin and then moving the charred remains to a final resting place in another part of the charnel house. Most often the remains were deposited unceremoniously on the floor of the structure, but in some cases, they were placed in a specially prepared grave. Both ordinary and lavish burials might be covered by a low mound of soil. Upon decommissioning a charnel house, the crematory was covered with a low, pebble-capped mound, with tons of clay heaped over the footprint of the former structure and the cremation burials within it. Ultimately as many as three layers might be added before the mound was capped with a one-foot-thick layer of gravel. Thus it appears that human burial was a long-term investment for the Mound City Hopewellians.

While heralded in the mid-1800s as the archaeological find of the century, Mound City found itself in the way of

Camp Sherman, a World War I military training camp built in 1917. The site was almost completely obliterated during construction of the camp, but when the war ended, archaeologists from the Ohio State Museum salvaged what was left in 1920 and 1921 and reconstructed the mounds for tourism. The site became a national monument in 1923.

In the 1950s, it was discovered that most of the reconstructed mounds had been put in the wrong place. To correct this, an excavation program lasting 12 years (1963–75) was launched to re-excavate large parts of the site in hopes of finding more remaining traces of the leveled mounds in order to accurately construct reproductions of the original mounds. The program was successful, and today's reconstruction is faithful to the archaeological record as to exactly where the mounds originally stood.

Before looking at Mound City in greater detail, it is worth taking a bird's-eye view of the Scioto-Paint Creek region in which it is located. The region is at the southern margin of the glacial moraine that covers most of northern Ohio; the Pleistocene glacial ice was halted by the northern escarpment of the bedded sedimentary rock formations of the Appalachian plateau. The choice of the area for a WWI training camp was no accident. The terrain resembles that of France, where part of the war was being fought. During the period of Mound City's active use, the glacial terraces up and down the Scioto River were peppered with the farmsteads and hamlets of low-level food producers. Earthworks and burial mounds of various ages were embedded within the territories of these farming societies.

It is natural to assume that the Hopewellian burial grounds and earthworks were centering points for communal activities of all kinds, but minimal archaeological evidence exists of anything more than mortuary activities. Some of the sites, like Mound City, are clearly devoted primarily, if not exclusively, to mortuary ceremonialism, yet others, like Hopeton (located across the Scioto River from Mound City), have little evidence of burial mounds, if any. Therefore, these sites apparently were multi-functional, but in ritualistic, not economic, ways. With this thought in mind, it has been suggested that Mound City and Hopeton, contemporary for much of their life spans, were functionally paired to serve the surrounding communities with institutionalized burial space and bounded sacred places.

One of the truly fascinating things about Mound City is the nearly identical ground plan for its charnel houses. Except for the linear structure under Mound 13, they are oblong with entrances on two opposite sides, much like the embankment enclosing them. Post mold sizes and distributions suggest that benches and compartments were built around the outside wall to differing degrees. Each structure had a fired-clay, rectilinear crematory basin raised 6 inches to 1 foot above the floor and positioned near its center. Burials were placed along the edge of the benches and covered with clay and a thin layer of small pebbles. One or two of the burials in most units were given lavish treatment; they were placed in a prepared grave with special artifacts (e.g., sheets of mica, conch shell vessels, and artifact caches) deposited with the cremated bones. In most cases, an open area occurred between the crematory and the graves, making space for ritual activities.

Another interesting property of the site is the possible dependent relationships between at least two groups of adjacent charnel houses. In the first case, the 1960s fieldwork found that the structures under mounds 12 and 13 were conjoined, with one devoted to cremation and the other to burial. The second group consists of the structures under mounds 3, 7, and 13, near the center of the enclosure—three of the largest mounds in the group. Although not conjoined, these mounds also appear to have had complementary functions. For example, the Mound 7 charnel house contains a large number of cremations ($n = 13$), all of which have artifacts and several of which are in special graves, whereas the Number 3 structure, while having the largest floor plan (140 ft long) and three crematories, has but four floor-level cremations, only two of which

contain artifacts. In many ways, the burials and facilities of the central group suggest the resting place of a long line of related individuals of importance in the society—a grand old family.

The crematories in the Mound City charnel houses are much alike, except for their size. They are made of puddled clay and are rectangular in shape. The basins are trough-shaped or flat-bottomed, with low, steeply angled sides. There are two sizes: large (7.5–12.5 ft long and 4.5–8.4 ft wide) and small (4.5–7.5 ft long and 3–4.5 ft wide). Aside from one at the bottom of a pit measuring 30 feet by 40 feet and dug to 6 feet below the floor of Mound 7, all crematories are on the structure floor. In three cases, one was built on top of another, and in one case, they were conjoined. Almost all are described as reddened and cracked from the intensity of the cremation fire. Most of the cracks were mended, which strongly suggests that the facilities were used multiple times.

As with all Hopewellian mortuary sites, most grave goods at Mound City were made of materials from all over eastern North America, including marine shells from the Atlantic and Gulf coasts, obsidian from the Rocky Mountains, copper from the Lake Superior region, and mica from the southern Appalachian Mountains. Copper was hammered into many shapes, including a human effigy headdress, a human torso, and human hands. Long obsidian spear points, falcon copper cutouts, plain and effigy platform pipes, and a cache of 5,000 shell beads are a few of the outstanding artifacts from the site. All of the burial goods were expertly hand-crafted artifacts of exceptional artistic and social value and are thought to be associated with distinguished people in the community. Strong support for this idea comes from the small number of individuals ($n = 9$; 10%) whose cremated remains were buried in specially prepared graves accompanied by lavish artifacts.

The Mound City site is now the flagship site of the Hopewell Culture National Historical Park. It is located at 16062 State Route 104, Chillicothe, OH 45601. Information about the park can be found at the following Web site: http://www.nps.gov/hocu/index.htm.

Further Reading: Brown, James A., "Mound City and Issues in the Developmental History of Hopewell Culture in the Ross County Area of Southern Ohio," in *Aboriginal Ritual and Economy in the Eastern Woodlands: Papers in Memory of Howard Dalton Winters*, edited by Anne-Marie Cantwell, Lawrence A. Conrad, and Jonathan Reyman, Scientific Papers, Vol. XXX (Springfield: Illinois State Museum, 2004), 1–21; Cockrell, Ron, *Amidst Ancient Monuments: The Administrative History of Mound City Group National Monument/Hopewell Culture National Historical Park, Ohio* (Omaha, NE: National Park Service, 1999); Mills, William C., "Exploration of the Mound City Group," *Ohio State Archaeological and Historical Quarterly* 31 (1922): 423–584 (online at http://publications.ohiohistory.org); Squier, Ephraim, and Edwin Davis, *Ancient Monuments of the Mississippi Valley: Comprising the Results of Extensive Original Surveys and Explorations*, Smithsonian Contributions to Knowledge, Vol. 1 (Washington, DC: Smithsonian Institution, 1848).

William S. Dancey

NEWARK EARTHWORKS STATE MEMORIAL

Newark, Ohio

Astonishing Earthworks Architecture

The Newark Earthworks encompass a series of gigantic earthen enclosures and mounds planned and built around 2,000 years ago by the people who were part of the Hopewell culture. Originally the site included two large, circular enclosures, one of which was linked to an even larger octagon; an oval earthwork surrounding a dozen earthen mounds of varying size and shape; and a perfectly square enclosure, all interconnected by a network of parallel-walled "roadways." In addition, the site includes many smaller circular enclosures, a scattering of other mounds, and borrow pits, from which at least some of the soil used to build the earthen architecture was excavated. Across the South Fork of the Licking River are another square enclosure and a semicircular embankment crowning the top of a hill that overlooked the principal earthworks.

Excluding the additional square and the hilltop enclosure on the opposite side of the river, the Newark Earthworks cover more than 4 square miles (12 km^2). More than 7 million cubic feet (200,000 m^3) of earth was used in their construction. The technology used to build this monumental geometry was remarkably simple, consisting of little more than pointed digging sticks and baskets. On the other hand, these architectural marvels encode a sophisticated understanding of geometry and astronomy in their forms and alignments. For example, the circumference of the largest circle is equal to the perimeter of the square, and the area of the other large circle is equal to the area of the square. These sorts of relationships indicate the Hopewell people had a common unit of measure, considerable surveying skills, and the intent to establish esoteric connections between disparate elements of architecture. It further suggests that the separate components of the Newark Earthworks constituted some kind of unified composition in the minds of its creators.

Archaeologists refer to Newark and similar sites as "ceremonial centers," but we do not know the full range of activities engaged in by the people who built and used these places. They were not cities, for little evidence of domestic activities is found here. Nor are they fortifications, as some early European Americans believed. Hopewell shamans undoubtedly performed ceremonies at these sites, including mortuary rituals at particular locations. Nineteenth-century construction workers digging at the site of the largest burial mound at Newark found a small stone sculpture of a shaman wearing a bear's head and fur robe. This depiction appears to be holding a decapitated human head in his lap. Perhaps this was the head of an honored ancestor whose spirit the shaman was invoking.

The great earthworks at Newark and similar sites were not, however, simply memorials to the dead—they were centers for the living. They were social gathering places, religious shrines, pilgrimage centers, and even astronomical observatories.

Much of the Newark Earthworks has been destroyed by the growth of the modern city of Newark, but two major elements are preserved as islands of ancient grandeur within the twenty-first-century urban landscape. The Great Circle is a prodigious circular enclosure 1,200 feet (366 m) across. The walls of the Great Circle enclose an area of about 30 acres (12 ha). The circular wall varies in height from 5 to 14 feet (1–4 m) with a ditch or moat at the base of the wall inside the enclosure. The ditch varies in depth from 8 to 13 feet (2–4 m). The fact that the ditch is inside the wall rather than outside indicates it was not a defensive moat. If the ditch was intended to hold water, then perhaps it had ritual or symbolic significance.

The Great Circle was preserved initially when the community established the county fairgrounds on this site in 1854. Since 1933 it has been owned by the Ohio Historical Society and operated as an archaeological park.

The Octagon Earthworks consist of a circular enclosure connected to an octagon by a short section of parallel walls. The circular enclosure forms a nearly perfect circle 1,054 feet (321 m) in diameter and 20 acres (8 ha) in area. It deviates from a perfect circle of that diameter by less than 4 feet (1 m). The walls of the octagonal enclosure were each about 550 feet long (168 m) and from 5 to 6 feet (2 m) in height.

The citizens of Newark and Licking County purchased the Octagon Earthworks in order to preserve the site while providing the Ohio National Guard with a summer campground. By 1908 the National Guard had moved on to a different location, so beginning in 1910, the Newark Board of Trade began to lease the earthworks to Moundbuilders Country Club, and the site became a golf course. In the 1930s, the Newark Board of Trade was dissolved, and the property was deeded to the Ohio Historical Society. The society continues to lease the site to the same private country club.

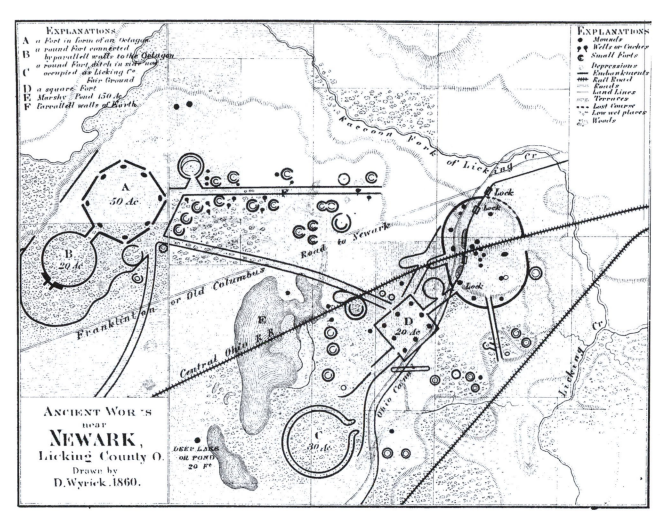

The Newark Earthworks as surveyed by David Wyrick in 1860. [1866 *Licking County Atlas*, Licking County, Ohio]

Ray Hively and Robert Horn, both of Earlham College, reported in 1982 that Octagon Earthworks incorporated alignments to the points on the horizon that mark the rising and setting of the moon throughout its complicated 18.6-year-long cycle. The only other Hopewell-built circle attached to an octagon is located near Chillicothe, 60 miles to the southwest. The circle at this site is identical in size to Newark's corresponding circle, and the Chillicothe earthwork incorporates the same alignments to the lunar cycle. These geometrical and astronomical connections lend credence to the idea that a formal road may have linked the two regions. The set of straight parallel walls that extended from the Octagon Earthworks to the southwest have been traced at least ten miles on a line pointing directly to Chillicothe. This Great Hopewell Road may have united these two great centers of Hopewell culture, both ritually and politically.

The Newark Earthworks are the largest and most complex of the great Hopewellian earthwork centers. Also, these monuments are located farther north than any other set of geometric earthworks. The confluence of Raccoon Creek and the South Fork of the Licking River was a rich environment and the high, flat glacial terrace there provided a broad canvas on which the Hopewell architects could lay out their masterpiece. A key reason for situating the Newark Earthworks in this particular valley, however, might have been the proximity of Flint Ridge. The rainbow-colored flint from Flint Ridge was highly prized by the Hopewell culture for the manufacture of chipped-stone tools. The Newark Earthworks may have served as the distribution center for this material.

The Newark Earthworks State Memorial is located about 25 miles east of Columbus, in Licking County, Ohio. For more information, see the Ohio Historical Society's Web

View of the moon rising at its northernmost point on the eastern horizon in perfect alignment with the axis of Newark's Octagon Earthworks.   [Image courtesy of The Center for the Electronic Reconstruction of Historical and Archaeological Sites (CERHAS), University of Cincinnati]

site at http://www.ohiohistory.org/places/newarkearthworks/index.cfm.

Further Reading: *Earthworks: Virtual Explorations of Ancient Newark, Ohio*, CD-ROM, University of Cincinnati, 2005, http://www.earthworks.uc.edu; Hively, Ray M. and Robert L. Horn, "Ohio Archaeoastronomy," in *Ohio Archaeology: An Illustrated Chronicle of Ohio's Ancient American Indian Cultures*, by Bradley T. Lepper (Wilmington, OH: Orange Frazer Press, 2005), 160–161; Lepper, B. T., "Tracking Ohio's Great Hopewell Road," *Archaeology* 48(6) (1995): 52–56; Lepper, B. T., "Ancient Astronomers of the Ohio Valley," *Timeline* 15(1) (1998): 2–11; Lepper, B. T., *People of the Mounds: Ohio's Hopewell Culture*, revised and reprinted (Fort Washington, PA: Eastern National Park and Monument Assn., 1999); Lepper, B. T., "The Newark Earthworks: Monumental Geometry and Astronomy at a Hopewellian Pilgrimage Center," in *Hero, Hawk, and Open Hand: American Indian Art of the Ancient Midwest and South*, edited by Richard V. Townsend and Robert V. Sharp (New Haven, CT: Art Institute of Chicago and Yale University Press, 2004), 72–81; Scarre, Chris, *Seventy Wonders of the Ancient World* (New York: Thames and Hudson, 1999).

Bradley T. Lepper

MARIETTA, OHIO

Washington County, Eastern Ohio
Early Historic Period Steps to Preserve Earthworks

The Marietta Earthworks, an ancient set of mounds and earthen embankment walls, were mapped in 1788 by Rufus Putnam, a director of the land-holding Ohio Company. Putnam led the group of New Englanders who established Marietta, the first permanent Euro-American settlement in the Northwest Territory of the fledgling United States. In a foresighted act, directors of the Ohio Company set aside portions of the earthwork to be preserved as common public land.

Located on the east bank of the Muskingum River near its conjunction with the Ohio, the earthworks included two nearly square enclosures, which together encompassed nearly 60 acres, and a finely graded passageway formed by high walls extending more than 650 feet from the larger enclosure toward the riverbank. Three flat-topped rectangular mounds, each flanked on two or more sides by ramps leading from ground level to the summit, were in the larger enclosure. A 30-feet-high conical mound surrounded by a low, circular wall and interior moat lay southeast of the smaller enclosure.

The directors favored classical names for the protected areas. The largest pyramidal mound became Quadranaou, the second-largest Capitolium. Conus was chosen for the conical mound, and Sacra Via for the graded way. Although eroded over the years, Quadranaou, now also known as Camp Tupper, is still a visible part of the landscape. The Washington County Library sits on top of Capitolium, and both are easily seen.

Clay from the walls of the Sacra Via was used for new constructions in the mid-nineteenth century. The trace of the graded way, now a street lined with Victorian houses, ends in Sacra Via Park on the bank of the Muskingum. Conus Mound, surrounded by a modern cemetery, remains the most intact. The other enclosure walls are not apparent today.

The diverse shapes seen in the elements of the earthworks have led to the attribution of the use of the site to different prehistoric cultures dating from 500 BC to late pre-Columbian times. The tall, conical mound has been assumed to be an Adena design—and the earliest element. The geometric nature of the two nearly square enclosures has led to a Hopewell assignment. In the 1840s, Dr. Samuel P. Hildreth found Hopewellian copper objects buried near the walls that are consistent with this interpretation. Many archaeologists and laymen considered the raised platform mounds to be examples of the temple mounds commonly built in the lower Ohio and Mississippi river valleys after AD 1000. Recent excavations at Capitolium Mound by the Cleveland Museum of Natural History recovered Hopewellian artifacts and features radiocarbon dated to circa AD 200, well within the Hopewell era. Though rare in Ohio, flat-topped mounds, likely Hopewellian in origin, occur at Ginther and Cedar Bank near Chillicothe in the central Scioto River valley. Radiocarbon dates place similar structures found in Tennessee and Alabama in Hopewell times.

In 1916 the Washington County Library, donated by Andrew Carnegie, was built on the top of Capitolium, some eight feet above street level. Memories of the 1913 flood that devastated much of Marietta made this a reasonable use for what was considered public land. In 1990 archaeological salvage excavations took place before an elevator for handicapped access was added to the library. The excavated area was restricted to the planned elevator shaft, where it impacted portions of two lobes that had been attached by the Hopewell builders to the central rectangular mound structure. As expected, no burials were found. Evidence of ceremonies and related activities that took place on specially prepared ancient floors atop the mound was uncovered. The floors were carefully covered with a mantle of soil after the activities were over. This type of decommissioning is typical for Ohio Hopewell ceremonial or ritual spaces.

The sequence at Capitolium is unusual in that a second upper floor was built on top of the earth and gravels that covered the lower floor. A few postholes and a small trench constructed on the upper floor intruded into the lower. Posts were removed, and in a classic Hopewell pattern, yellow and red clay pieces were used to refill the empty holes. No pattern in the placement of posts could be determined in the limited area excavated for the elevator construction. The final, upper strata of the two lobes were mounded on top of the flat horizontal layers, covering the upper floor in a complex sequence that included small burned areas. The appearance of the thin covering layers of gravel and earth seems to indicate that a relatively short time elapsed between the use of the lower and upper floors. Prehistoric artifacts encountered were typical Ohio Hopewell bladelets (thin, narrow, flint knives) and incised pottery shards. Historic nineteenth-century objects were included in the fill used for modern landscaping about the mound.

The recent investigation at Capitolium, along with studies at Pinson Mounds in Tennessee and the Walling site in Alabama, have added to our understanding about the types of ritual spaces associated with the Hopewell phenomenon shared by groups of people scattered across eastern North

America circa 100 BC to AD 400. The term "Hopewell" comes from the name of a major site in southern Ohio, and the term is frequently used to refer to contemporary cultures outside Ohio.

Striking examples of the remarkable cultural remains identified with Ohio Hopewell come from the Hopewell Mound Group in Ross County, where vast quantities of finely crafted artifacts, many of exotic materials, were recovered in 1891–92 and exhibited at the 1893 World's Columbian Exposition in Chicago. Many of the objects found at the Hopewell site were made of exotic raw materials not found in Ohio, including copper, mica, and obsidian. Whole and broken objects had been placed together in deposit within a multi-roomed wooden structure. This structure was found at the base of a huge mound that was about a city block long and three stories tall. More than forty other mounds and miles of enclosure walls complete the site.

Other culturally related groups of mounds and enclosures of varying shapes formed a human-engineered landscape in southern Ohio along the major tributaries of the Ohio River: the Muskingum, the Scioto, the Little Miami, and the Great Miami. The settlement pattern of domestic and public structures and the substance strategies are of current research interest.

Many mounds attributed to the Adena culture are also found in southern Ohio and in the wider area of the Ohio River drainage from the West Virginia panhandle to the falls at Louisville, Kentucky. The chronological and possible cultural relationships of Hopewell peoples to the Adena peoples in each local area are determined by the cultural changes found in the local historical sequence through the thousand-year time span circa 500 BC to AD 500. Geographically widespread cultural remains have been called Adena after a mound excavated in 1901–02 near Chillicothe in Ross County, Ohio. Commonly, single conical mounds are assumed to be Adena related.

In Marietta, Campus Martius Museum, which is owned by the Ohio Historical Society, contains information on the prehistoric earthworks and the historic New England founders of Marietta. The remnants of the earthworks are easily seen by walking in the historic district. A variety of other tourist activities are available.

Further Reading: Greber, N'omi B., "Chronological Relationships Among Ohio Hopewell Sites: Few Dates and Much Complexity," in *Theory and Practice in Modern Archaeology*, edited by Robert J. Jeske and Douglas K. Charles (Westport, CT: Praeger, 2003), 88–113; Greber, N'omi B., "Adena and Hopewell in the Middle Ohio Valley," in *Woodland Period Systematics in the Middle Ohio Valley*, edited by Darlene Applegate and Robert C. Mainfort (Tuscaloosa: University of Alabama Press, 2005), 19–39; Hildreth, Samuel P., "Pyramids at Marietta," *American Pioneer* (1843): 242–248; Ohio Historical Society Web site, http:/www.ohiohistory.org; Pickard, William H., "1990 Excavations at Capitolium Mound (33Wn13), Marietta, Washington County, Ohio: A Working Evaluation," in *A View From the Core*, edited by Paul J. Pacheco (Columbus: Ohio Archaeological Council, 1996), 274–285; Woodward, Susan L., and Jerry N. McDonald, *Indians Mounds of the Middle Ohio Valley* (Blacksburg, VA: McDonald & Woodward, 2002).

N'omi B. Greber

SERPENT MOUND STATE MEMORIAL

Adams County, Ohio

Serpent Mound: Ancient Naturalistic Architecture

Serpent Mound is the largest serpent effigy in the ancient world, extending for more than 396 meters (1,300 ft) along a bluff overlooking Ohio's Brush Creek. The mound was first described by Ephraim Squier and Edwin Davis, in their 1848 publication *Ancient Monuments of the Mississippi Valley*. At this time, the effigy was "upwards of five feet [1.5 m] in height by thirty feet [9 m]" wide at the base. At the head of the serpent, there is a large, oval embankment measuring 49 meters (160 ft) at its longest diameter. This embankment has been interpreted variously as an egg gripped in the gaping jaws of the serpent or as the serpent's eye. Originally, according to Squier and Davis, there was a "small circular elevation of large stones much burned" at the center of the oval, but it had been "thrown down and scattered" by some treasure-seeking vandal.

The bluff on which Serpent Mound is situated is now known to be a remnant of the inner portion of a geologically ancient meteorite impact crater that is about 8 kilometers (5 mi) in diameter. The bedrock formation that underlies the head of Serpent Mound, which is visible from the banks of Brush Creek, resembles a large serpent's head, so the selection of this particular bluff on which to build this singular effigy may have been inspired partially by the belief that a serpent spirit inhabited and was manifest in this natural feature.

The most comprehensive study of Serpent Mound and its environs was undertaken by Frederic Ward Putnam of Harvard University's Peabody Museum between 1887 and 1889. Putnam excavated portions of the effigy, three nearby burial mounds, and parts of the surrounding area. He identified a substantial habitation area on the bluff south of the effigy mound.

The Serpent Mound contained no artifacts, but Putnam reported that the base of the mound was, in places, composed of clay mixed with ashes. Two of the burial mounds contained artifacts and features now known to be associated with the Adena culture (ca. 800 BC–AD 100). The third mound, referred to as an elliptical mound, contained artifacts assignable to the Fort Ancient culture (ca. AD 1000–1550). The artifacts and features from the habitation area relate to both the Adena and Fort Ancient cultures.

In 1943, in his monumental study of the Fort Ancient aspect, James Griffin suggested Serpent Mound should be regarded as an Adena effigy based on its proximity to the Adena mounds and habitation remains. Yet a mound and habitation remains attributed to the Fort Ancient culture also occurred in close association to the Serpent. Moreover, serpent iconography is more prevalent in the art of the Mississippian and Late Prehistoric periods, which encompasses the Fort Ancient culture, than it is in the Adena culture of the Early and Middle Woodland periods.

In 1991 a team of avocational and professional archaeologists reopened one of Putman's trenches in the hope of finding the ash in the basal layer of the mound and obtaining a radiocarbon date that would resolve the uncertainty over its age and affiliation. Unfortunately, no ash layer was identified, but small fragments of charcoal recovered from soil samples yielded AMS radiocarbon dates of between AD 1025 and 1215, apparently establishing Serpent Mound as a Fort Ancient effigy mound. This attribution is consistent with a comparative analysis conducted by Robert Fletcher, which demonstrated many similarities between the iconography of Serpent Mound and representations of rattlesnakes on Mississippian engraved shell gorgets from the southeastern United States.

At the conclusion of his explorations, Putnam carefully restored the mounds; the Peabody Museum, having purchased the site in 1886, made it the first prehistoric site in North America to be preserved as a public archaeological park. The Peabody Museum operated the park until 1900, when it deeded the site to the Ohio Archaeological and Historical Society (now the Ohio Historical Society).

In the 1990s, various authors began to look for astronomical alignments at Serpent Mound. The head and the oval are aligned to the azimuth of the setting sun on the summer solstice. The three major coils of the serpent's body also may be aligned to the summer solstice sunrise, the equinox sunrise, and the winter solstice sunrise, respectively. This emphasis on a solar calendar also is consistent with a Fort Ancient cultural affiliation. Two linear stone embankments near the Anderson Village in Warren County, the Kern effigies 1 and 2,

belong to the Fort Ancient culture and may be serpent effigies, although they do not have the characteristic sinuosity of Serpent Mound. One is aligned to the summer solstice sunrise and the other to the summer solstice sunset.

Ohio's one other well-documented effigy mound, known as Alligator Mound, also yielded radiocarbon dates that place it in the Fort Ancient culture. If the Serpent and the so-called Alligator are less than a thousand years old, then it becomes reasonable to attempt to relate these effigies to the beliefs and traditions of the Native peoples whose cultural roots lie in the Eastern Woodlands.

There are two principal underworld spirits in the cosmology of many Eastern Woodlands tribes: the horned serpent and the underwater panther. Serpent Mound bears an obvious relationship to the powerful serpent spirit, and the iconography of the Alligator is plausibly related to the underwater panther. Indeed, Robert Hall has interpreted several similar and approximately contemporary effigy mounds from the upper Midwest as representations of the underwater panther.

There is ethnohistoric evidence that the Indians of the Great Lakes sometimes erected monuments for the worship of these underworld spirits. In 1827 there was a shrine to the underwater panther along the shores of Lake Huron in Thunder Bay, in northeastern Michigan. This shrine consisted of a cluster of twenty stones, including four large boulders. The local Indians identified this grouping of stones as the manitou and left offerings of tobacco, knives, pipes, and bits of old iron. Although none of the ethnohistorically documented shrines were sculpted effigies similar to either the Serpent or the Alligator, it is likely that Serpent Mound served as a similar shrine to the spirit of the underworld. Perhaps the circular, stone platform, formerly located in the eye of the serpent, was the altar on which offerings of supplication and thanksgiving were deposited and burned.

Interpretations that depend upon extrapolations from ethnographically documented oral traditions are problematic but are at least preferable to the numerous interpretations of Serpent Mound that have depended upon analogies derived from much further afield. Squier and Davis, for example, believed the oval enclosure at the Serpent's head represented an egg, and that it related to depictions of serpents swallowing eggs from Egypt, Greece, and Assyria. In 1900 the Reverend Landon West viewed the oval as an apple in the jaws of the biblical serpent, proposing that the mound marked the true location of the Garden of Eden. These interpretations illustrate the enduring power of this monumental rendering of a serpent and the extent to which our cultural preconceptions can influence our understanding of another culture's iconic imagery.

Serpent Mound is recognized by the United States as a National Historic Landmark. Serpent Mound State Memorial is located about 20 miles south of Bainbridge in Adams County, Ohio. For more information, see the Ohio Historical

Society's Web page regarding the Serpent Mound at http://www.ohiohistory.org/places/serpent.

Further Reading: Fletcher, Robert, Terry Cameron, Bradley T. Lepper, Dee Anne Wymer, and William Pickard, "Serpent Mound: A Fort Ancient Icon?" *Midcontinental Journal of Archaeology* 21(1) (1996): 105–143; Glotzhober, Robert C., and Bradley T. Lepper, *Serpent Mound: Ohio's Enigmatic Effigy Mound* (Columbus: Ohio Historical Society, 1994); Griffin, James B., *The Fort Ancient*

Aspect: Its Cultural and Chronological Position in Mississippi Valley Archaeology (Ann Arbor: University of Michigan Press, 1943); Lepper, Bradley T., "Great Serpent," *Timeline* 15(5) (1998): 30–45; Lepper, Bradley T., "Ohio's Alligator," *Timeline* 18(2) (2001): 18–25; Putnam, F. W., "The Serpent Mound of Ohio," *Century Magazine* 39 (1890): 871–888; Squier, Ephraim, and Edwin Davis, *Ancient Monuments of the Mississippi Valley*, Smithsonian Contributions to Knowledge, Vol. 1 (Washington, DC: Smithsonian Institution, 1848).

Bradley T. Lepper

THE FORT ANCIENT ARCHAEOLOGICAL TRADITION

Central Ohio River Valley, Ohio

Architecture and Sites of the Eleventh to Seventeenth Centuries

People of the Fort Ancient archaeological tradition lived in and near the central Ohio River valley between the eleventh and seventeenth centuries AD, and perhaps into the eighteenth. Remains of their villages, cemeteries, hunting camps, and ceremonial areas stretch from southeastern Indiana through southern Ohio and from northern Kentucky to western West Virginia. Although archaeologists have investigated Fort Ancient sites for a century and a half, they continue to make new—and sometimes surprising—discoveries, both by exploring recently located sites and by performing more sophisticated analyses of long-known ones and collections from past excavations.

From the tools and food remains they left behind, we know that Fort Ancient people raised, processed, and stored maize, beans, squash, and tobacco; gathered and used wild fruits and nuts; hunted deer, elk, bear, and turkey; gathered shellfish; and fished. They lived in farmsteads, hamlets, and villages that included houses, community structures, and storage pits (often encircling an open plaza). Many earlier Fort Ancient villages incorporated one or more burial mounds, but the later practice was to lay family members to rest in and around the houses where they had lived.

By the fourteenth century, Fort Ancient settlements and hunting camps were located along the Ohio and all its major tributaries in this region—from the Kentucky, Licking, Great Miami, and Little Miami rivers in the west to the Muskingum and Kanawha rivers in the east. Over time, larger settlements became more common, with preferred locations on or near the main river, rather than on the middle or upper reaches of tributaries.

Hundreds of Fort Ancient sites are known, many of which have been scientifically studied, mapped, and documented. Only a few can be visited today, but they provide a rich introduction to Fort Ancient landmarks and ways of life.

SERPENT MOUND, ADAMS COUNTY, OHIO, AND ALLIGATOR MOUND, GRANVILLE, OHIO

Southern Ohio is well known for the mounds and earthworks built by people of the Adena and Hopewell archaeological traditions between about 3,000 and 1,500 years ago. Ephraim Squier and Edwin Davis surveyed and described many of these mound features in the mid-nineteenth century during a pathbreaking project for the Smithsonian Institution, including some mounds that only recently have been demonstrated to have been built much more recently, during the Fort Ancient occupation of the area.

The well-known Serpent Mound, recognized as a National Historical Landmark, undulates nearly a quarter of a mile along a narrow plateau overlooking the Brush Creek valley in south central Ohio. Its head is aligned to the summer solstice sunset, and some of its coils may also have astronomical alignments. Excavations in the late nineteenth century by Frederic Ward Putnam of the Peabody Museum of Archaeology and Ethnology at Harvard University showed that the shape was defined by piling stones above a layer of clay and ashes. These, in turn, were covered first by a layer of yellow clay and then by soil to a height of 4–5 feet.

Putnam, who also investigated two nearby Adena burial mounds, attributed the Serpent Mound to that archaeological tradition. However, in 1991 a team of archaeologists reopened the mound and recovered charcoal that produced radiocarbon dates showing that the effigy was constructed 1,000–850 years ago, during early Fort Ancient times. This new evidence links the effigy mound to a third burial mound (also of the Fort Ancient times) and a nearby Fort Ancient village site.

Visitors can walk along this effigy and observe it from a viewing tower, as well as explore the surrounding 75-acre park, established by Putnam in 1889. The site museum

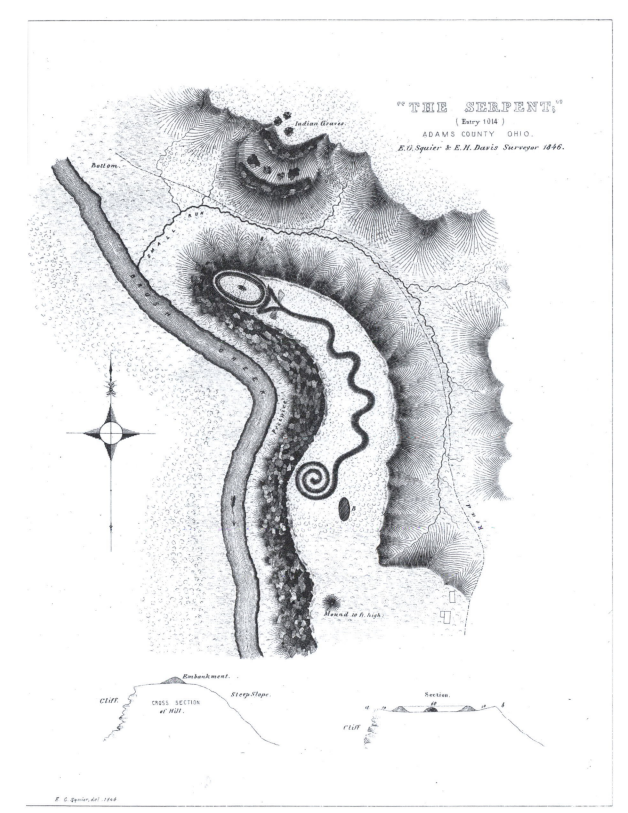

"The Serpent," Plate XXXV from *Ancient Monuments of the Mississippi Valley* by Ephraim G. Squier and Edwin H. Davis, 1848, republished 1998 by Smithsonian Institution Press.

An aerial photograph of the SunWatch Village reconstruction, 2004. Andy Sawyer, photographer. Courtesy SunWatch Indian Village/Archaeological Park. Used with permission.

provides an opportunity to learn more about the archaeology and geology of the site and region.

The 200-foot-long effigy mound that Squier and Davis called the Alligator—a four-legged creature with a long, curling tail—now is thought to represent a lizard or the mythical underwater panther. It sits on a bluff above the Raccoon Creek valley on a 0.6-hectare (1.5-acre) tract owned by the Licking County Historical Society, where it can be viewed today. Radiocarbon dates obtained in 1999 indicate that it was constructed 860–800 years ago, roughly contemporaneous with the Serpent Mound. Lizards and serpents are part of Fort Ancient symbolism, known from petroglyphs, appliqued effigies on pots, carved antler combs, effigy smoking pipes, engraved stones, and metal ornaments. The underwater panther is an awe-inspiringly powerful figure in Great Lakes area mythology.

These Ohio effigy mounds are also roughly contemporaneous with the famous midwestern effigy mounds, found by the hundreds in Wisconsin, Minnesota, Iowa, and Illinois and believed to date between 1,250 and 800 years ago. Like the Ohio mounds, these often were situated on high ground above resource-rich wetlands. They have been interpreted as markers of clan or corporate groups and of particular resources.

FORT ANCIENT STATE MEMORIAL, WARREN COUNTY, OHIO

A century ago, the Fort Ancient archaeological tradition was named after the impressive Fort Ancient State Memorial site, which encompasses 51 hectares (126 acres) of bluff-top land within 5,490 meters (18,000 ft) of earthen walls, which measure up to 7 meters (23 ft) high. Archaeo-astronomical features include four stone-faced mounds, plus U-shaped gaps in the walls that could be used to track solar and lunar alignments. Ironically we now know that the Fort Ancient earthwork was constructed between about 2,100 and 1,700 years ago, long before the culture that we refer to as the Fort Ancient tradition developed. But the same fine-tuned archaeological investigations that provided evidence for when the enclosure was constructed also showed that it continued to be used for at least a thousand years. People of the Fort Ancient tradition established villages nearby, and at least one—the South Fort Village—inside the enclosure.

Today's visitor can explore the entire enclosure, with its many vistas of the surrounding countryside and the Little Miami River 75 meters (245 ft) below. The Ohio Historical Society's museum at Fort Ancient interprets 15,000 years of Ohio valley history.

SUNWATCH VILLAGE, DAYTON, OHIO

About 750 years ago, contemporaneous with villages abutting the Fort Ancient site and with many other settlements across the central Ohio drainage area, a 1.2-hectare (3-acre), circular village surrounded by a palisade was established on the west bank of the Great Miami River just south of what now is Dayton, Ohio. For a few decades, up to 250 people lived there, farming in the fertile floodplain and hunting and fishing in adjacent forests and streams.

Their rectangular houses, averaging about 5 by 6 meters (16 by 20 ft) in size, formed a ring inside the palisade. In front of the houses were storage and refuse pits. Inside this domestic space was a ring of burials, most of which were covered by limestone slabs, and an open plaza. The village also included larger community buildings and sweat lodges, plus a massive cedar pole and four surrounding poles in the center of the plaza that, in alignment with important village structures, have been interpreted as an astronomical calendar complex.

SunWatch Village, originally named the Incinerator site, was discovered by landowners and collectors who observed numerous prehistoric artifacts in plowed fields and collected them from at least the 1930s onward. In the early 1970s, the site was threatened by the expansion of a city sewage treatment plant. Amateur archaeologists John Allman and Charles Smith alerted James Heilman, Dayton Museum of Natural History (now Boonshoft Museum of Discovery) curator of anthropology, and salvage excavations were initiated in hopes of recovering as much information as possible before the site was destroyed. As the importance of the site became evident, the city of Dayton cooperated in modifying the treatment plant project, and the land was set aside for research and public interpretation.

Seasonal excavations continued over decades, revealing the archaeological remains of over half of the village. Fine-grained research projects have investigated diet, building construction, relationships among households, and village social organization, as well as ritual aspects of the site. In 1988 an interpretive center and partial village reconstruction opened to the public. Today, visitors can learn about thirteenth-century life in the village through expanded museum displays, workshops and other special programs, and ongoing experimental archaeology, including reconstruction of houses and gardens and nearby restoration of native prairie.

MADISONVILLE SITE, MARIEMONT, OHIO

Toward the end of the fifteenth century, Fort Ancient people began to gather in larger communities located close to or directly along the Ohio River. Some of these areas, like the Clover and Buffalo sites in Cabell and Putnam counties, West Virginia; the Hardin Village site in Greenup County, Kentucky; and the Madisonville site in Hamilton County, Ohio, have produced small artifacts such as glass beads, ornaments made from European brass and copper, and small iron tools. The assemblages of artifacts can be dated to between about 1580 and 1650, before there is any historical record of Europeans reaching this region.

Madisonville, the site of a large late Fort Ancient village and cemetery, was known locally in the nineteenth century as the Pottery Field, due to the many shards and other artifacts found there. These artifacts had been helped to the surface by hogs rooting among the massive oak trees on the property. Physician Charles L. Metz and colleagues from the Madisonville Literary and Scientific Society sponsored excavations there between 1878 and 1881, which attracted the attention of Frederic Putnam. Putnam's Peabody Museum, in turn, sponsored a series of more professional archaeological excavations directed by Harvard University graduate students. By 1911 these excavations had explored much of the almost 2-hectare (about 5-acre) site. Techniques utilized, although adequate for their time, lacked modern controls, such as an excavation grid and fine screening of soil. Small-scale excavations carried out during the past two decades by the Cincinnati Museum of Natural History (now Cincinnati Museum Center) and contract archaeologists Gray and Pape Inc., together with radiocarbon dating of wood fragments and corn kernels, contributed to a more definitive occupation history and chronology for the site.

Situated on a bluff above the fertile Little Miami River floodplain about 8 kilometers (5 mi) upstream from the Ohio River, the Madisonville site was occupied and reoccupied over many hundreds of years. However, its most intensive settlement occurred during the late sixteenth and very early seventeenth centuries. It is the most completely excavated Fort Ancient village of this period, and among the most populous. The Madisonville Literary and Scientific Society and Peabody Museum excavations uncovered almost 1,400 burials and 1,000 large corn storage pits. Because few posthole patterns were recorded, little is known about house size and orientation. Structures seem to have been rectangular, with storage pits and burials interspersed in and around them. The village included two or more small plazas instead of a single large one, perhaps reflecting a more complex social organization than the earlier SunWatch settlement.

Like the people at SunWatch, Madisonville's residents grew maize, hunted, fished, and gathered shellfish and wild plant resources. Their village is the only Fort Ancient settlement known to have utilized bison, possibly hunted in the prairies farther west. Elk remains are also much in evidence. Along with deer, these large mammals were important sources of meat; hides; and bone and antler tools, musical instruments, and ornaments. Stone artifacts used at Madisonville ranged from triangular projectile points to hide scrapers to finely-made ax heads to a wide variety of smoking pipes. Food was stored and prepared in pots very similar in design to vessels used across the entire east-west extent of Fort Ancient territory—evidence supporting the hypothesis that people were visiting and intermarrying all along the central Ohio River valley during this period.

People from Madisonville appear to have traveled and received visitors from well beyond the Ohio valley. The large variety of nonlocal materials and artifacts found in the village indicate that its residents participated in exchange networks extending as far afield as the St. Lawrence valley, eastern Iowa, and northern Alabama—a surprisingly great distance. Such items include marine shell ornaments made in Tennessee and the broader Southeast; smoking pipes from Oneota people in the Midwest; Mississippian people in the Southeast, and Iroquoian people in the Northeast; and pottery in Mississippian, Oneota, and northern Ohio styles. European artifacts, while quite numerous, were not large or diverse, signaling indirect contact rather than sustained direct trade with European explorers. They include copper and brass scrap and small ornaments; blue glass beads; parts from iron-banded kettles traded in the St. Lawrence estuary by Basque fishermen during the late sixteenth century; and a brass Clarksdale bell, generally associated with mid-sixteenth-century Spanish expeditions in the Southeast. Using European brass and copper (probably obtained via

Iroquoian middlemen in Ontario and western New York), people at Madisonville seem to have been making and exchanging distinctive serpent-shaped ornaments that have been excavated there—and, in lesser numbers, at many contemporaneous sites farther west.

Today the location of this once-thriving community is noted by an historical marker and park pavilion near the Mariemont swim club in suburban Cincinnati.

Further Reading: Drooker, Penelope B., *The View from Madisonville: Protohistoric Western Fort Ancient Interaction Patterns*, Memoir 31 (Ann Arbor: Museum of Anthropology, University of Michigan, 1997); *Fort Ancient*, Ohio Historical Society Web site, http://www.ohiohistory.org/places/ftancien (online January 2006); Genheimer, Robert, ed., *Cultures Before Contact: The Late Prehistory of Ohio and Surrounding Regions* (Cincinnati: Ohio Archaeological Council, 2000); Heilman, James M., Malinda C. Lilias, and Christopher A. Turnbow, eds., *A History of 17 Years of Excavation and Research: A Chronicle of 12th Century Human Values and the Built Environment* (Dayton, OH: Dayton Museum of Natural History, 1988); Lepper, Bradley T., *Ohio Archaeology: An Illustrated Chronicle of Ohio's Ancient American Indian Cultures* (Wilmington, OH: Orange Frazer Press, 2005); *Serpent Mound*, Ohio Historical Society Web site, http://www.ohiohistory.org/places/serpent (online January 2006); SunWatch Indian Village/Archaeological Park Web site, http://sunwatch.org (online January 2006); Woodward, Susan L., and Jerry N. McDonald, *Indian Mounds of the Middle Ohio Valley: A Guide to Mounds and Earthworks of the Adena, Hopewell, Cole, and Fort Ancient People* (Blacksburg, VA: McDonald & Woodward, 2002).

Penelope B. Drooker

FORT ANCIENT STATE MEMORIAL AND POLLOCK EARTHWORKS

Southern Ohio

Ancient Hilltop Architecture and Enclosures

Southern Ohio was opened to Euro-American settlement after 1795, following the Treaty of Greenville, when the Shawnee and other tribes ceded ancestral lands to the United States of America. As the new settlers moved up the river valleys of what was then called the Northwest Territory, they encountered an extraordinary assemblage of earthworks built on the floodplains that were believed to be the architectural remnants of a past civilization. These sites consisted of linear earthen embankments constructed in a variety of geometric forms, including circles, squares, rectangles, octagons, ovals, and combinations thereof, frequently accompanied by one or more

mounds. They also discovered that certain elevated places, particularly hilltops and peninsular projections of bluffs above river valleys, were encircled with earth and stone walls. To them it was evident that a vanished race, which they labeled the "Moundbuilders," had constructed these ancient monumental architectural features and then had been driven out of the Ohio country by the invading ancestors of modern Native peoples. The Moundbuilder myth was an explanation that suited the need of the early settlers to disconnect what they regarded as the architecture of a noteworthy civilization from the unworthy peoples whom they were dispossessing of land.

As the results from archaeological investigations of sites in Ohio and elsewhere began to accumulate by the 1880s and 1890s, it became apparent that the prehistoric cultures could indeed be ancestrally linked to modern Indian peoples, and the Moundbuilder explanation for the origin of the enclosures was gradually discarded. In Ohio research at a large mound near Chillicothe and at an earthwork in the nearby Paint Creek valley enclosing over 100 acres and numerous mounds led to the identification and naming of the Adena and Hopewell cultures, respectively. As radiocarbon dates were added to the information gleaned from such sites by the 1950s, it became apparent the people of the Adena and Hopewell cultures had planned and constructed the vast majority of mounds and earthworks in Ohio.

The elevated sites, which have become known as hilltop enclosures, were widely considered to have been fortified places, analogous to the forts and castles of the European past, or at least as refuges of last resort. Many of their names reflect this: Fort Ancient, Fort Hill, Fortified Hill, Miami Fort, Carlisle Fort, West Carrolton Fort Works. A minority among the early antiquarians did, however, question this generic identification; Caleb Atwater, writing in the 1820s, compared many southwest Ohio elevated sites to the Greek and Roman practice of locating ceremonial sites on high hills. By the 1940s archaeologists had connected hilltop enclosures with the Hopewell culture and had begun to regard them as ceremonial sites. They particularly noted the many openings in their walls ("gateways") and their considerable size relative to the small populations expected to have inhabited the area, features that seemed to render them untenable as forts, although the nature of whatever "ceremonies" might have been held inside them remained unknown and the subject of speculation. The two hilltop sites that have been most intensively-examined are Fort Ancient and the Pollock Works. The archaeology of both suggests that they had long histories of development and use, and that their functional roles may have changed over time.

The Hopewell peoples of southern Ohio (ca. 100 BC to AD 350) are regarded by most archaeologists as having been organized at a tribal level of society, without hereditary institutional leadership. Their homesites have been found in small, clustered arrangements termed hamlets, from which they practiced what was essentially a hunting-gathering economy augmented by a horticulture focused on domesticated starchy- and oily-seed plants. Maize was not yet an economic species and has only been rarely encountered at Hopewell sites. They were in at least sporadic contact with people across much of the eastern United States, as demonstrated by their procurement, presumably through trade, of an array of imperishable materials whose source locations lay far from Ohio, including marine shell from the Gulf of Mexico, obsidian from Wyoming/Idaho, copper and galena from the upper Great Lakes, and mica and quartz crystal from the Carolinas. These substances were then fashioned into utilitarian and ritualistic artifacts, many of which were eventually deposited with their dead in mound burials (and thereby preserved for later archaeological discovery and interpretation). Many Ohio Hopewell burials were placed within charnel houses that held a hundred burials or more. These structures stood inside the earthwork enclosures and were eventually decommissioned by being burned and then covered with mounded soil. The combination of elaborate burials, beautifully crafted artifacts, and spectacular earthworks has ensured the Hopewell's place at the center of interest in Ohio archaeology.

FORT ANCIENT

The largest and most elaborate of the hilltop enclosures is Fort Ancient. Located in Warren County in southwest Ohio, it was the first archaeological site in the country to be designated a state park (in 1891). Serpent Mound was made a public park in 1886 by its private owner, the Peabody Museum of Harvard University, but it was not deeded to the state until 1900.

The Fort Ancient site consists of three connected sections, the North, Middle, and South forts, which together occupy over 100 acres on a long, peninsular landform situated more than 200 feet above the Little Miami River, connecting to uplands on the northeast. A pair of parallel walls extended a half mile from the northeast side of the North Fort and encircled a small mound. Although the parallel walls lay mostly outside the State Memorial's boundary and have been destroyed over the years by agriculture and residential construction, the other three sections of the fort enclosure are protected and in good condition. The embankments at Fort Ancient range from about 3 to 23 feet high and are penetrated by numerous gateways; authorities differ on the exact number, which ranges between sixty-seven and eighty-four, since erosion and intention can equally create openings. If all of the embankment segments could be placed end to end, they would stretch for about 3.5 miles.

Fort Ancient has been recognized as an enclosure for over 200 years and has been under intermittent archaeological investigation for 120 years. Excavations there have been conducted by L. M. Hosea, Warren Moorehead, William Mills, Richard Morgan, Patricia Essenpreis, Robert Connolly, this author, and others. These efforts have investigated site features that include several sections of the embankments, the interior ditches or ponds, mounds, stone pavements and circles, exterior terraces, and gateway complexes. A much more recent residential site of the Fort Ancient (late prehistoric) culture, located within the South Fort, has also been investigated. The site has been mapped on numerous occasions, by antiquarians, archaeologists, and engineers, sometimes in connection with archaeological projects but in other instances not. Although not all the excavation records and maps appear to have survived over the years, the site has received more archaeological attention than any other Hopewell site in Ohio—or probably anywhere else, for that matter.

From observations of soil stratigraphy in the embankments and the growing corpus of radiocarbon dates from the various excavation loci dug after 1980, it is now apparent that the site grew accretionally over several centuries. The size of its embankments increased, growing higher and wider as additional mantles of soil and stone were added in at least three (and probably more) stages of construction, along with the extent of the acreage that was gradually enclosed within its earthen walls. Since the excavations by Moorehead in the 1880s and 1890s, it has been suspected that the South Fort was built first, with the Middle and North forts and the parallel walls added sequentially later. Additionally, the embankments of the Middle and North forts show multiple construction stages. It has not yet been possible to correlate the construction stages throughout all four sections of the site because of both the size and complexity of the site and the limited amount of excavation done in the embankments.

The embankments of the South Fort closely follow the indented outline of the landform. This part of the site has what are considered to be two formal gateway complexes. The park roadway runs through the one that connects the South and Middle forts, known as the Great Gateway. This and the South Gateway are both marked by elevated rampways and large mounds located on both sides of their openings; both also have limestone pavements within their openings and down both sides of their embankments. The North Fort lacks an identical complex, but the gateway nearest to the exterior Twin Mounds has been considered to be comparably linked to them. Though not present within the opening itself, limestone pavement does fill the space between the parallel walls that originate at the Twin Mounds. The many other gateways in the three sections of the enclosure lead to naturally projecting spurs or open onto steep ravines, and are believed to have served other purposes than as avenues of formal entry. Some gateway openings may have facilitated astronomical observation.

The Middle Fort is bounded by steep ravines on both sides and low embankments, with curved walls inside that may have been intended to direct the flow of people to and from the North and South forts. The North Fort's embankments include the sections with the greatest dimensions, and along the north and east sides of the enclosure they are straight. Within the North Fort are four mounds, none of which contained burials, that form an almost perfect square measuring approximately 517 feet on a side.

Excavations in the early 1980s by Essenpreis outside the North Fort near the Twin Mounds detected multiple postmolds that were probably from several structures. When the museum built in 1967 inside the North Fort was scheduled to be rebuilt in the mid-1990s, the area to be affected by construction was archaeologically tested. There, for the first time at any hilltop enclosure, large-scale stripping revealed ten or more post structures arranged in an arc. Two of the structures were fully exposed and measured about 22 feet on a side. Apparently, these structures, which date to between the first

and fourth centuries AD, were associated with a range of both domestic and ceremonial activities. In 2005 remote sensing of several sections of the enclosure was performed prior to the initiation of erosion control measures. The data revealed the presence of a previously unknown circular earthwork in the North Fort. Large expanses of the enclosure—in fact, the majority of its acreage—remain untested, and it is tempting to speculate on what else may lie undiscovered within it. In addition to structural features, future finds may include more examples of ritual artifact caches, two of which (including copper artifacts, mica sheets, and exotic flaked stone, including obsidian) have been discovered over the years in the vicinity of the course of the parallel walls.

One recent example of the sort of significant finds that may still remain undiscovered at enclosures turned up in 2005 in the North Fort. Remote sensing was being conducted across several areas prior to their traversal with heavy equipment to correct erosional problems in the embankments. In an open field located to the west of the museum a circular feature, almost 60 meters in diameter with an apparent entranceway gap to the south, was detected by magnetometry. Its archaeological investigation was begun in 2006 by the author and students from Wright State University. This work revealed two concentric rings of posts, the outermost of which consisted of posts set a meter deep using slip trenches, the trenches then each having been filled with 100 kilograms of rocks brought in for the purpose. The outer ring probably consists of over 200 such post features, spaced less than a meter apart. The inner ring contains smaller posts, and it may have consisted of sets of double posts. The posts from both rings appear to have been intentionally removed, with many of the postholes having been filled with rocks. At the approximate center of the circle (since named the Moorehead Circle, after the pioneering archaeologist) is a feature that yielded an exceptionally high magnetic response. It was found to be a pit or basin just over 4 meters in diameter and a half meter deep filled with burned soil. Postmolds and a prehistoric trench containing several probable posts are adjacent to the central feature, leading to the supposition that it may have been located within a structure. This area will be the subject of continued excavations. Radiocarbon dates for both the central feature and circle posts show them to be of Middle Woodland age. The way in which this assumed ceremonial feature was articulated with other elements of the earthwork is not yet understood.

The Ohio Historical Society, which administers Fort Ancient, built a new museum in the late 1990s inside the North Fort, which serves as the society's portal museum for all its prehistoric sites. The museum is open in late spring through early fall and is accessed via State Route 350, the old Chillicothe to Cincinnati road, which runs directly through the North Fort.

POLLOCK WORKS

The Pollock Works is located in Greene County, southwest Ohio, in the Indian Mound Reserve of the county's park system. It shares the park with a 30-foot-high Adena mound, the

Williamson Mound, and is situated along Massie's Creek, a tributary of the Little Miami River.

The Pollock Works consists of embankments built of earth and stone on the western and northern sides of an isolated limestone plateau. This 10–12-acre landform was created by the waters of the creek beside it and slopes about 33 feet downward from east to west; most of its circumference is composed of vertical limestone cliffs roughly 10 to 50 feet high. The sloping western approach to the plateau is blocked by embankment sections 10 feet high and penetrated by three gateway openings that span the 270 feet between the outcropping of the cliffs to the south and a steep, 22-foot-high bluff on the north. A 3-foot-high embankment then follows the sinuous course of the bluff until it reaches the outcropping cliff on the north side of the plateau. The Pollock plateau was formerly connected to the uplands adjacent to it, before the waters of the creek eroded the gaps between them; the Pollock plateau is, therefore, not elevated with respect to most of the surrounding topography, but it *is* a uniquely elevated limestone isolate.

Nineteenth-century plans of the site depict three mounds, one outside each of the gateways, with low earthen arcs between them just west of the enclosed plateau. These features have been effaced by modern limestone quarrying and possibly, in part, by the use of the plateau for farming until 1960.

In 1981 the author began the archaeological investigation of the site with student crews from Wright State University in Dayton, Ohio. During the years since, Pollock has been the centerpiece of summer field school excavations (with work also being conducted at several other prehistoric and historic sites). These years of steady work have produced evidence that the earthwork was built in five major construction stages that spanned over a century, between the first and early third centuries AD. Construction was at first concentrated on building up the embankments on the west that connected the cliff and bluff, closing off access to the plateau. Each of the first three stages employed soil heaped behind an exterior rubble face of limestone rocks, with the central and north gateways created by leaving spaces in the fill. The simple wall resulting from these efforts appears to have satisfied the needs of the people who enclosed the plateau for several decades, from sometime after AD 50 to 150–200. The use of the enclosed space is thought to have been ceremonial; it probably served as the place where the community met to conduct important rituals and to reinforce their social network.

Pollock has become best known for its fourth construction stage. Sometime in the middle to late second century AD a wooden stockade was built on top of the embankments, across the gateways, and east along the creek bluff to the cliff on the north side of the plateau. On top of the existing western embankment sections the stockade was about 6 feet high, while on the bluff it may have stood as high as 16 feet. Vertical support posts averaged about 9 or 10 inches in diameter and were placed about 3 feet apart, in holes chinked with limestone rocks. Other vertical members were placed between the supports, and branches were intertwined between them horizontally. A mud plaster is believed to have been daubed over the lower portion of the stockade, to a height of about 6 feet. Then, following the considerable effort required to erect this structure, the archaeological evidence suggests that within a few years it was burned down; burned wooden timbers have been found well preserved under the soils of the last major construction stage, on the western embankments as well as at the base of the 3-foot-high embankment built over the stockade's remains along the bluff overlooking the creek. Because the timbers from the stockade have been found so well preserved at many locations, it appears that they were covered with soil immediately after collapsing. Embankment construction, in other words, directly followed the burning. The destruction of the stockade is therefore believed to have been the purposeful act of its builders rather than the by-product of a hostile attack.

The construction of the stockade obviously has a great deal to do with the purpose the enclosure served late in its history. The reason for the abrupt and dramatic change in the way access to the plateau was controlled has not been identified to date in its archaeology. If hostilities arose and the plateau was suddenly perceived as an excellent natural defensive position, then conceivably the stockade may have been erected for defense. We know, for instance, that the wide opening of the central gateway, as it existed at the end of the third building stage and which constituted an open invitation to invaders, was securely closed off as part of the stockade construction effort. If the stockade *was* built for a defensive purpose, then its removal may have been triggered by a shift in the political climate, and the soil additions that covered it by a need to reconsecrate the hilltop. Despite the stockade's overtly defensive appearance, however, the logical objection to hilltop sites as defensive refuges or forts, due to the size of their perimeters versus the number of people it would have taken to make them secure, remains.

When our understanding of the social and political dynamics that operated in Hopewellian southwest Ohio improves, the history of whatever happened at hilltop enclosures will undoubtedly fit well into the larger puzzle. The debate over why the Hopewell enclosed certain hilltop and elevated places continues, as it has for more than a century. It is, however, only in recent years that considerable new information has been gleaned at both Fort Ancient and the Pollock Works, and from these efforts and others new interpretations may be forthcoming.

The Pollock Works is within Indian Mound Reserve, located off State Route 42 a mile west of the town of Cedarville in eastern Greene County. From the parking lot behind a log house that faces the road, the enclosure is reached by walking along a signposted trail 0.3 miles long. The site is undeveloped in wooded terrain, with no museum or interpretive displays.

Further Reading: Connolly, Robert P., and Bradley T. Lepper, eds., *The Fort Ancient Earthworks: Prehistoric Lifeways of the Hopewell Culture in Southwestern Ohio* (Columbus: Ohio Historical Society, 2004); Lepper, Bradley T., *Ohio Archaeology: An Illustrated Chronicle of Ohio's Ancient American Indian Cultures* (Wilmington, OH: Orange Frazer Press, 2005); Moorehead, Warren K., *Fort Ancient, the Great Prehistoric Earthwork of Warren County, Ohio* (Cincinnati: Robert Clarke & Co., 1890); Ohio Historical Society Web site, http://www.ohiohistory.org; Riordan, Robert V., "The Enclosed Hilltops of Southern Ohio," in *A View from the Core: A Synthesis of Ohio*

Hopewell Archaeology, edited by Paul Pacheco (Columbus: Ohio Archaeological Council, 1996), 242–257; Riordan, Robert V., "Boundaries, Resistance, and Control: Enclosing the Hilltops in Middle Woodland Ohio," in *Ancient Earthen Enclosures of the Eastern Woodlands*, edited by Robert C. Mainfort and Lynne P. Sullivan (Gainesville: University Press of Florida, 1998); Woodward, Susan L., and Jerry N. McDonald, *Indian Mounds of the Middle Ohio Valley* (Blacksburg, VA: McDonald & Woodward, 2002).

Robert V. Riordan

FLINT RIDGE STATE MEMORIAL

Near Newark, East Central Ohio
Ancient Flint Quarries and Workshops

Flint Ridge is a series of hills nearly 8 miles (13 km) long capped with a deposit of highly distinctive flint, or chert, located in east central Ohio. It is one of the most densely concentrated and intensively exploited sources of high-quality flint in eastern North America. The site also was recognized early by antiquarians as an important ancient quarry. In 1885 Charles Smith, writing in the annual report of the Smithsonian Institution, called Flint Ridge the "Great Indian Quarry of Ohio" and noted that "it is by all odds entitled to be called *the* 'Flint Ridge' not only of Ohio but of the whole country." Quarry pits and workshop sites occur in profusion across more than 2,000 acres (900 hectares [ha]), but they are most thickly concentrated within the limits of what is now the Flint Ridge State Memorial. Hundreds, if not thousands, of quarry pits occur along the ridge, ranging in size from 12 to 80 feet (4–25 m) in diameter. A few are as deep as 20 feet (6 m), although most are between 3 and 6 feet (1–2 m) in depth.

Flint Ridge flint is a very pure form of silica, but ironically, its popularity among ancient American Indians was based on the impurities it contained. Various trace elements in the silica ooze that collected in a shallow Paleozoic ocean basin produced the extravagant variety of colors that appear in this remarkable flint. The most common variety is white with light gray streaks and patches. A less common but more distinctive variety is made up of reds, yellows, blues, and greens in various combinations.

American Indians have used Flint Ridge as a quarry for over 15,000 years. Many of the flint tools found in the deepest layers of Pennsylvania's Meadowcroft Rockshelter were made from Flint Ridge flint. These layers have been dated to between 13,000 and 16,000 years ago and may be the remains of some of the earliest peoples in America. Large numbers of Ice Age Clovis spear points found in Ohio and

neighboring states are made from Flint Ridge flint, which continued to be an important source of raw material for stone tools for several thousand years. The popularity of this rainbow-colored flint reached its peak during the Early and Middle Woodland periods, 2,800 to 1,500 years ago. The Hopewell culture of central and southern Ohio, in particular, crafted a variety of tools from this material that were distributed through some kind of trade network or "interaction sphere" across much of eastern North America. The Newark Earthworks, the largest of the great Hopewellian earthwork centers, is located 9 miles (14 km) to the northwest. The proximity of Flint Ridge may have been one of the main reasons the Hopewell culture built the Newark Earthworks in this location, so far from its southern Ohio heartland.

William C. Mills, Curator of Archaeology for the Ohio Historical Society, intensively investigated Flint Ridge in 1920. He examined over thirty quarry pits and numerous workshop sites. He found that the Hopewell flint workers came to the site to make three kinds of tools: triangular bifacial preforms of varying size; small, blocky cores generally conical in shape; and the long, thin bladelets that they struck from these prepared cores. More recent investigations have confirmed that the Hopewell culture exploited the flint more intensively than other cultures. It is likely that they sent a specialized work force to Flint Ridge to quarry the flint and work it down into these basic forms; these could then be packed and carried to the Newark Earthworks where, presumably, they were exchanged or presented as gifts to visiting dignitaries or pilgrims. Most of the quarries and workshops on Flint Ridge are presumed to be the remains of this Hopewellian "industry."

After the Hopewell era, the use of Flint Ridge flint dropped off markedly. It is as if this distinctive material had become so closely associated with other Hopewellian elements that when the fabulous art and architecture of this culture were abandoned, the use of "Hopewell" flint was proscribed as well.

Along with the quarries that riddle the rugged hilltops constituting Flint Ridge are a number of earthen enclosures, mounds, and a few documented habitation sites. Hazlett Mound, located on the western end of the ridge but outside the boundaries of the State Memorial, is a Hopewell burial mound excavated by William C. Mills in 1920. At the base of the mound he discovered a "House of Flint." This was a rectangular structure about 37 feet square with walls averaging 6 feet in height constructed of rough blocks of Flint Ridge flint. The presence of such a structure within a burial mound suggests that Flint Ridge flint was more than just a source of raw material for tools. The Hopewell people may have believed it to be charged with great spiritual power, according tools (and houses) made from it a special value.

In historic times, European Americans quarried Flint Ridge flint to make "buhr stones." These were thick, circular stone wheels used for grinding flour. Flint Ridge flint also was used as road gravel. Today, Flint Ridge flint is honored as the state of Ohio's official gemstone.

Flint Ridge State Memorial is located 4 miles north of Interstate 70, 3 miles north of Brownsville, in Licking County, Ohio. Several trails wind through the myriad pits and around the masses of flint wastage. A small museum at the site is built around an excavated flint quarry pit. Artifacts recovered from excavations at Flint Ridge and Hazlett Mound are included in the exhibits. For more information, see the Ohio Historical Society Web site http://www.ohiohistory.org/places/flint/.

Further Reading: DeLong, Richard M., *Flint Ridge: Bedrock Geology of the Flint Ridge Area, Licking and Muskingum Counties, Ohio* (Map) (Columbus: Ohio Division of Geological Survey, 1972); Lepper, Bradley T., Richard W. Yerkes, and William H. Pickard, "Prehistoric Flint Procurement Strategies at Flint Ridge, Licking County, Ohio," *Midcontinental Journal of Archaeology* 26(1) (2001): 53–78; Mills, William C., "Flint Ridge," *Ohio State Archaeological and Historical Society Quarterly* 30 (1921): 90–161; Smith, Charles M., "A Sketch of Flint Ridge, Licking County, Ohio," in *Annual Report of the Smithsonian Institution for the year 1884* (Washington, DC: 1885), 851–873; Yerkes, Richard W., "Flint Ridge State Memorial," in *Ohio Archaeology: An Illustrated Chronicle of Ohio's Ancient American Indian Cultures*, by Bradley T. Lepper (Wilmington, OH: Orange Frazer Press, 2005), 58–59.

Bradley T. Lepper

SEIP MOUND STATE MEMORIAL

Ross County, South Central Ohio

Seip Earthworks and Mounds: Ancient Ritual Spaces

Seip Mound is located in the Seip Earthworks on Paint Creek, west of Chillicothe in southern Ohio. The Seip Earthworks are one of five tripartite geometric enclosures constructed by Ohio Hopewell people roughly 2,000 years ago. The others are Baum (also on Paint Creek), Frankfort on the North Fork of Paint Creek, and Works East and Liberty Works in the Scioto Valley. The earthworks at all five sites are referred to as tripartite because each of them consists of two conjoined circles and a square. These geometric embankments define ritual spaces in which Ohio Hopewell people prepared for and performed ceremonies and cremated, curated, and buried their dead.

The tripartite earthworks vary in the degree to which mounds were constructed within the circles. Whereas the squares at all five sites are uniform in size, construction, and the presence of small mounds just inside each entrance, only three of the tripartite earthworks (Seip, Liberty, and Frankfort) contain large mounds, all of which lie within the large circles. Seip Conjoined Mound, composed of three smaller mounds, also lay within the large circle at Seip. Seip Mound is the second-largest Ohio Hopewell mound, after Mound 25 at the Hopewell site.

Seip was first described by Caleb Atwater in 1820, who noted the elliptical Seip Mound as being 25 feet high, composed "mostly of stones," and containing human bone. Squire and Davis surveyed and mapped the earthworks and mound in 1845, noting that the mound at the time was 240 × 120 feet, with a surface of stones and pebbles. In 1931 Henry Shetrone and Emerson Greenman measured the dimensions as 250 × 150 feet, with its greatest height at 32 feet.

THE CHARNEL HOUSE

Emerson Greenman and Henry Shetrone, archaeologists from the Ohio State Museum (now the Ohio Historical Society), undertook excavations in Seip Mound from 1925 to 1928, after which the mound was restored. A portion of the large

Estimated floor plan of Seip Big House. Posthole plan of the major structure found at the base of Edwin Harness Mound superimposed upon the plan of the tombs and other floor features at the base of Seip Mound 1.   [From N'omi B. Greber 1983, Figure 10.1]

mound that was left intact in the 1920s was excavated in 1966 under the direction of Raymond Baby of the Ohio Historical Society. Together, these excavations revealed 123 burials as well as crematory basins, refuse pits, and caches of artifacts associated with a prepared clay floor.

Although over 200 post molds were encountered in the excavations, maps of their distribution, and thus evidence of the outline of a structure, are lacking. Further research has demonstrated that the excavators had encountered the floor of a charnel house. Based on her excavations in the Edwin Harness Mound at Liberty Earthworks, and William Mills's excavations in the Seip Conjoined Mound in the early 1900s, N'omi Greber of the Cleveland Museum of Natural History suggested that like these mounds, the Seip Mound covered a three-room, dismantled, possibly burned, charnel house. Three pieces of information substantiate Greber's inference. First, the burials beneath Seip Mound appeared to be spatially organized into three groups. Second, separate primary mounds had been constructed over each of the three groups, just as they had been at Seip Conjoined Mound and possibly the Edwin Harness mound. In fact, the Seip Conjoined Mound comprises three primary mounds that were never covered by a secondary mound to create a single entity. Third, when Greber superimposed the wall post outline of the Edwin Harness charnel house over the Seip Mound tomb and crematory basin clusters, she found a close correspondence between their distribution and the walls of the three structure segments of the Harness building.

Most of the burials in the charnel house were cremations, which occurred in both single and multiple graves. Eleven inhumations were also encountered. The Hopewell people who used this charnel house placed most of the burials on low rectangular clay platforms around which they constructed log tombs. They generally covered each tomb with a small earthen mound, 2 to 3 feet high. Offerings of well-crafted social valuables accompanied many of the burials or had been placed as separate deposits, or caches, in the charnel house. In addition, quantities of more prosaic materials, such as broken pottery, were found on the floor of the charnel house as well as in refuse pits and on platforms of several burials. Eighty-one individuals (66 percent) were buried with items made from copper (e.g., breastplates, ear spools, celts), the most frequent raw material included with the Seip Mound burials. One tomb contained only a cache of valuables with no associated burials. The cache included twelve copper breastplates, a large copper celt weighing 28 pounds, several large pearl beads, and three bear canines each set with a pearl.

One especially elaborate tomb was encountered at the western end of the charnel house. It contained six inhumations (four adults and two infants) on a large clay platform. The grave accompaniments were particularly lavish. Thousands of pearl beads had been used to outline the four adults. One adult had a necklace with grizzly bear canines suspended from it; the other three adults were each buried with a large copper breastplate. A depression in the platform's west end held a number of burned items, including bear claws, copper ear spools, flint and obsidian objects, mica cutouts, ceramics, shell beads, animal canines, pearl beads, fabric, Flint Ridge bifaces, and shell and chlorite plummet-shaped objects. In the primary mound above this burial, people had placed a cache of five very large stone animal effigy pipes (two birds, three mammals) similar to several pipes found at contemporaneous Copena sites in the Tennessee Valley.

Several researchers have analyzed the spatial and age/sex distribution of buried individuals with the valuables found in the graves associated with the Seip Mound. Greber, for example, noted that the number of artifacts per burial and the frequency of certain artifact types, such as copper breastplates, celts, and earspools, varied across the three rooms within the Seip Mound charnel house. Other objects, such as flint blades, shell beads, animal teeth, and pearls were not differentially distributed. Greber proposed that this variation reflected ranking among members of a single community. Christopher Carr, in a recent reanalysis of the Seip Mound grave goods information, however, has suggested that each room represented a different community. He proposes that the North Fork, Paint Creek, and Scioto Valley proper, the three areas where tripartite earthworks were built, constituted three different communities who expressed alliances with one another through the burial of some of their dead in different rooms within a single charnel house.

At some point in the life of the Seip Mound charnel house, people made the decision to close it. This decision may have coincided with the deaths of the inhumed individuals in the tomb at the western end of the charnel house. At that point, the structure was dismantled, and a mound was constructed over each of its three rooms. These mounds varied from 17.5 feet high on the west to 8 feet high on the east.

Sometime later, people covered the primary mounds with a layer of gravel 1/2 to 2 feet thick. This gravel extended 8 to 10 feet beyond the base of the primary mounds. Solid yellow clay was next laid over the gravel layer. Subsequently, layers of midden and earth and finally a thick outer layer of gravel (8 to 10 feet thick at the base) were added to the mound to create a single, rather than multi-lobed entity. Mortuary use of this space continued sporadically after the dismantling of the charnel house. Several burials were interred above the primary mounds, and a few had also been placed within the primary mounds but above the floor.

HOPEWELL CULTURE NATIONAL HISTORICAL PARK

Seip Mound State Memorial was established in 1930 to preserve Seip Mound and a portion of the circular embankment. The National Park Service's Hopewell Culture National Historical Park has recently acquired those portions of Seip that are not preserved by the State Memorial. The visitors' center for Hopewell Culture National Historical Park is located on State Route 104, a few miles north of Chillicothe. The center contains a recently updated, interactive introduction to the multiple sites protected by the park, displays of artifacts, and a film that helps put the Seip Earthworks and their associated mounds in the larger context of Ohio Hopewell archaeology.

Further Reading: Baby, Raymond, and Suzanne M. Langlois, "Seip Mound State Memorial: Nonmortuary Aspects of Hopewell," in *Hopewell Archaeology*, edited by D. S. Brose and N. Greber (Kent, OH: Kent State University Press, 1979), 16–18; Carr, Christopher, and D. Troy Case, eds., *Gathering Hopewell: Society, Ritual, and Ritual Interaction* (New York: Kluwer Academic/Plenum Publishers, 2005); Greber, N'omi, "Within Ohio Hopewell: Analysis of Burial Patterns from Several Classic Sites," Ph.D. diss. (Case Western Reserve University, 1976); Greber, N'omi, "A Comparative Study of

Site Morphology and Burial Patterns at Edwin Harness Mound and Seip Mounds 1 and 2," in *Hopewell Archaeology*, edited by D. S. Brose and N. Greber (Kent, OH: Kent State University Press, 1979), 27–38; Greber, N'omi, *Recent Excavations at the Edwin Harness Mound* (Kent, OH: Kent State University Press, 1983); Shetrone, Henry C., and Emerson F. Greenman, "Explorations of the Seip Group of Prehistoric Earthworks," *Ohio Archaeological and Historical Quarterly* 40 (1931): 343–509; Spielmann, Katherine A., Jarrod Burks, Steven L. De Vore, Scott Ingram, Sophia Kelly, Melissa Kruse, and Mason Scott Thompson, "Field Report for the Arizona State University Archaeological Field School Summer 2005 Excavations at Seip Earthwork (33Ro40)" (Report submitted to the Ohio Historical Society, Columbus, 2005); Squier, E. G., and E. H. Davis, *Ancient Monuments of the Mississippi Valley*, edited and with an introduction by David J. Meltzer (Washington, DC: Smithsonian Institution Press, 1998).

Katherine A. Spielmann

THE TREMPEALEAU LAKES MOUND GROUP

Upper Mississippi River Valley, Wisconsin
Hopewell Culture at Its Northwest Border

Trempealeau Lakes (47Tr31) is one of hundreds of mound groups that once dotted the bluffs and terraces of the upper Mississippi valley region. Untouched by glaciers, this region offers one of the most rugged and scenic landscapes in Wisconsin. The twenty-six mounds that make up the Trempealeau Lakes Mound Group occupy a narrow floodplain that separates the Mississippi River from the hills and ridges that rise to the east. Across this floodplain, the mounds cluster into three discrete groups, with the Second Lake group (mounds 7–16) and the Third Lake group (mounds 2–5 and 24–26) situated near lake shores, and the Nicholls group (mounds 1, 17–19, and 21–23) set farther back from the river. When originally mapped in the late 1920s, mounds 2 through 26 averaged 1.2 meters in height and 12.2 meters across. The Nicholls Mound (Mound 1) was one of the largest mounds in western Wisconsin, measuring 3.3 meters high, 28.3 meters long, and 25.9 meters wide. In addition to its exceptional size, this mound revealed some of the most impressive burials in the region.

Archaeological investigations at Trempealeau Lakes began in 1928 with W. C. McKern. During the 1928 and 1930 seasons, McKern supervised the excavation of eleven mounds and parts of two campsites. He published his findings the following year in *A Wisconsin Variant of the Hopewell Culture*, which remains the primary source for the

site. Investigations resumed in 1966 under the supervision of Joan Freeman of the Wisconsin Historical Society. Her excavations of two additional mounds and parts of both campsites sought to establish a relationship between the domestic and ritual aspects of the site. Unfortunately, much of this later work remains unreported. In 1974 the Trempealeau Lakes Mound Group and associated Second Lake Village were listed in the National Register of Historic Places. All subsequent studies have been based on these previously recovered materials, now curated in archaeological collections.

Interest in the Trempealeau Lakes site follows largely from its elaborate burial program and associated grave goods. Several of these practices and the artifacts found indicate participation in aspects of the Hopewell system or tradition, a distinctive set of rituals and symbols shared by many cultures of eastern North America approximately 2,000 years ago. A few key artifacts suggest ties with the Hopewell core area in Ohio, namely the plain copper celts, copper panpipes, plain copper breastplate, and silver buttons. Because of its location on the northwest fringe of the Hopewell system, Trempealeau Lakes is particularly valuable for an understanding of how materials and symbols entered the network and circulated among the participants.

Presumably, these exotic goods marked social differences among the deceased. The poor preservation of the bone,

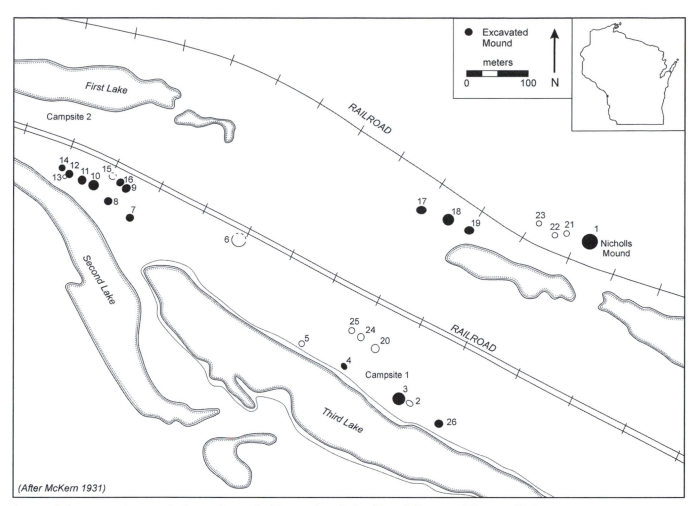

A map of the twenty-six mounds that make up the Trempealeau Lakes Mound Group.   [Shannon Fie]

unfortunately, prevents the systematic evaluation of grave goods in association with particular individuals. However, the frequency of artifacts in the Nicholls clusters suggests marked differences in social status. Individuals buried in this mound group were three times more likely to have associated grave goods than those in other mounds. Additionally, several distinctive Hopewell artifacts occurred exclusively in this cluster: copper ear ornaments, copper breastplate, copper tinklers, silver-covered buttons, a platform pipe and pipe bowl fragment, bear canines, and the few recovered pearls. This distribution suggests that some members of the community apparently maintained special access to valued Hopewell goods, probably as part of a local high-status group.

Although some of the grave goods suggest links with Ohio Hopewell, details of the burial program at Trempealeau Lakes indicate closer ties with Havana groups to the south in Illinois. Connections with the Illinois valley are most evident in the structure of several mounds, includ-

ing Nicholls Mound. Each contained a central bark-lined pit surrounded by a low embankment wall. In Nicholls mound, a thick layer of mixed bark also covered the central burial pit, which McKern interpreted as the remnants of a shelter that housed the dead prior to mound construction. Bodies were placed in the central tomb, and, following decomposition, the bones were bundled and placed to the side. Only the final tomb occupant(s) remained in place while basket loads of dirt covered the "full" tomb consisting of multiple extended and bundled burials. Except for the lack of log walls, these pit tombs correspond closely with those of the Illinois valley.

Not all mounds included a central burial crypt. In other mounds interments rested directly on a cleared floor at the base of the mound. While generally similar to pit burials, floor burials lacked the additional investment in a pit and surrounding embankment. Floor burials also included multiple internments. However, three mounds contained only bundled reburials, and one mound lacked a central burial of any kind.

Several mounds also included intrusive burials. In five instances, a simple pit contained between one and seventeen bundle burials. Unfortunately, the lack of associated artifacts prevented further identification. In contrast, the intrusive burial from Nicholls Mound consisted of a single extended burial and an associated object of copper and obsidian.

Of the many different burial goods recovered from the Trempealeau Lakes mounds, only two ceramics represent likely imports from the Illinois valley. The first is an unusually shaped, limestone-tempered Hopewell Zoned Rocker stamped vessel. The second is a bowl with a T-shaped lip and traces of red paint. The remaining four burial vessels correspond to local ceramic types.

Copper, and to a lesser extent silver, provides better evidence for exchange connections to the north. Like other Hopewell sites of the upper Mississippi valley, the Trempealeau Lakes mounds yielded a wealth of copper objects. The concentration of copper artifacts so near the Lake Superior source area suggests possible manufacturing in the region. Several unusual copper objects provide some support for a more localized exchange network, such as a curiously small (3.2 cm) gouge-like celt, five unicymbal ear ornaments, and some 400 rolled cylindrical copper beads strung like wampum.

The upper Mississippi valley also served as an important entry point for exotic stone originating as far west as Wyoming, Idaho, and North Dakota. At Trempealeau Lakes, evidence for such ties occurs in the form of both chipped-stone and polished-stone objects. While all are foreign imports, these materials likely arrived in the upper Mississippi valley region by way of different trade relationships.

Only three examples of obsidian occurred at Trempealeau Lakes: a knife and two scrapers. Chemical analysis determined that the knife came from the Obsidian Cliff source in Yellowstone Park, Wyoming, whereas one of the scrapers originated at the more distant Bear Gulch source in eastern Idaho. Perhaps local flint knappers acquired these few samples of obsidian from Ohio Hopewell traders who stopped at the site on their return trip east.

Excavation at Trempealeau Lakes also recovered several specimens of Knife River Flint from central North Dakota. These eight tools and twenty flakes represent the largest concentration of this material found at a Hopewell site. East of the Mississippi River, Knife River Flint occurs almost exclusively as large bifaces in burial mounds. Comparison of these forms with other plains artifacts suggests that the notched bifaces and ovoid knives originated with the Sonota complex of the central Dakotas. Similarly, several Sonota-style points of gray quartzite and one of speckled jasper originated in eastern Wyoming, arriving at Trempealeau Lakes in finished form.

An unusually tall red platform pipe from Nicholls Mound completes the list of exotic stone artifacts. Originally, McKern identified the material as red Ohio pipestone. However, recent mineral analyses trace this pipe to the catlinite quarries of southwest Minnesota. The only other examples of tall-bowl catlinite pipes occur at the Toolesboro mounds site in Iowa and the Tremper mounds in Ohio, which suggests the eastward and southward trading of finished western-style pipes.

More recent reexamination of the Trempealeau Lakes materials focused on the occupational debris recovered from the two associated campsites and beneath several of the mounds. Materials recovered from these excavations revealed little evidence of Hopewell exotics or ceremonialism. However, the materials indicated overlap between the different campsites and the construction of several mounds. Excavation of Campsite 1, for example, recovered a mix of Illinois valley–style Havana ceramics and shards representing the local Linn series. In contrast, excavations of the Second Lake habitation site yielded ceramics and radiocarbon dates (AD 350 ± 65) that post-date Hopewell mound construction. Together with neighboring assemblages, this material does not support an argument of sustained contact with other regional groups. Rather, it suggests that interaction consisted largely of sporadic visitation by groups from the Illinois valley. Thus some forty years after the last excavations, the Trempealeau Lakes Mound Group continues to play an important role in clarifying our understanding of the Hopewell presence in western Wisconsin.

Further Reading: Bernardini, Wesley, and Christopher Carr, "Hopewellian Copper Celts from Eastern North America," in *Gathering Hopewell: Society, Ritual, and Ritual Interaction*, edited by Christopher Carr and D. Troy Case (New York: Springer Science+Business Media, 2006), 624–647; Boszhardt, Robert F., "Wisconsin Radiocarbon Chronology—1976," *Wisconsin Archaeologist* 58 (1977): 87–135; Boszhardt, Robert F., "Additional Western Lithics for Hopewell Bifaces in the Upper Mississippi River Valley," *Plains Anthropologist* 43 (1998): 275–286; Boszhardt, Robert F., and James Gundersen, "X-Ray Powder Diffraction Analysis of Early and Middle Woodland Red Pipes from Wisconsin," *Midcontinental Journal of Archaeology* 28 (2003): 33–48; Clark, Frances, "Knife River Flint and Interregional Exchange," *Midcontinental Journal* 9 (1984): 173–198; Emerson, Thomas E., Richard E. Hughes, Kenneth B. Farnsworth, Sarah U. Wisseman, and Mary R. Hynes, "Tremper Mound, Hopewell Catlinite, and PIMA Technology," *Midcontinental Journal of Archaeology* 30 (2005): 189–216; Freeman, Joan, "Hopewell Indians," *Wisconsin Academy Review* 15 (1968): 5–7; Griffin, James B., Richard E. Flanders, and Paul F. Titterington, *The Burial Complexes of Knight and Norton Mounds in Illinois and Michigan*, Memoirs No. 2 (Ann Arbor: University of Michigan, Museum of Anthropology, 1970); Griffin, James B., A. A. Gordus, and G. A. Wright, "Identification of the Sources of Hopewellian Obsidian in the Middle West," *American Antiquity* 34 (1969): 1–14; Hughes, Richard E., "The Sources of Hopewell Obsidian: Forty Years after Griffin," in *Recreating Hopewell*, edited by Douglas K. Charles and Jane E. Buikstra (Gainesville: University Press of Florida, 2006), 361–375; McKern, W. C., *A Wisconsin Variant of the Hopewell Culture*, Bulletin of the Public Museum, Vol. 10, No. 2

(Milwaukee, 1931); Ruhl, Katharine C., "Hopewellian Copper Earspools from Eastern North America: The Social Ritual, and Symbolic Significance of Their Contexts and Distribution," in *Gathering Hopewell: Society, Ritual, and Ritual Interaction*, edited by Christopher Carr and D. Troy Case (New York: Springer Science+Business Media, 2006), 696–713; Schroeder, David L., and Katharine C. Ruhl, "Metallurgical Characteristics of North American Prehistoric Copper Work," *American Antiquity* 33 (1968): 162–169; Stoltman, James B., "Middle Woodland Stage Communities of Southwestern Wisconsin," in *Hopewell Archaeology: The Chillicothe Conference*, edited by David S. Brose and N'omi Greber

(Kent, OH: Kent State University Press, 1979), 122–139; Stoltman, James B., "Reconsidering the Context of Hopewell Interaction in Southwestern Wisconsin," in *Recreating Hopewell*, edited by Douglas K. Charles and Jane E. Buikstra (Gainesville: University Press of Florida, 2006), 310–327; Turff, Gina M., and Christopher Carr, "Hopewellian Panpipes from Eastern North America: Their Social, Ritual, and Symbolic Significance," in *Gathering Hopewell: Society, Ritual, and Ritual Interaction*, edited by Christopher Carr and D. Troy Case (New York: Springer Science+Business Media, 2006), 648–695.

Shannon M. Fie

EFFIGY MOUNDS NATIONAL MONUMENT AND OTHER SITES

Iowa, Wisconsin, and Minnesota

Effigy Mounds in the Upper Midwest

From around 1,500 to 1,000 years ago, the area of the upper Midwest now known as southern Wisconsin, northern Illinois, eastern Iowa, and southeastern Minnesota was home to a Native American tradition that archaeologists call the effigy mound culture. Why use the name "effigy mound" to refer to these particular groups of people? Like some of those before them, these people built thousands of earthen mounds across the landscape. However, unlike anyone before or since, this culture constructed many of these mounds in the distinct shapes of animals, including various types of mammals, birds, and reptiles. Unlike some of the earlier Hopewell mounds, effigy mounds tend to be relatively low in height although they can be very large in area; many are well over 100 feet (30 m) in length.

Effigy mound culture falls within what archaeologists call the Late Woodland stage, dating between about AD 650 and 1200. Late Woodland was a time of social, ideological, technological, and economic change. These people were beginning to rely on corn agriculture, and the bow-and-arrow was used for the first time. Most Late Woodland groups in this area lived in small villages, where houses were oval in shape and often built so that their bases were partly underground. The houses were relatively small, and most family activities happened outdoors. Although settled in villages, these people moved across the landscape regularly to take advantage of resources that were available in different locations at different times of the year.

MOUND LOCATIONS

Effigy mound groups tend to occur on high, flat places overlooking rivers and streams, especially where those rivers and streams intersect major wetlands and lakes. Mound groups are always located adjacent to zones of abundant and annually recurring food resources—ideal places for the congregation of people on a seasonal basis. The number and locations of effigy mound sites may indicate a seasonal aggregation-dispersal pattern of settlement by the Late Woodland people who created the mounds. Wetlands, and especially marshes, tend to have food available in the winter months, when it is hard to find elsewhere; deer tend to gather there, and a number of nutritional, storable plants can be collected there. With people dispersing for the winter to exploit the marshes and other wetlands, and then gathering again in villages in the spring and summer, groups may have met at these mounds just before the winter dispersal and/or the spring aggregation. The mounds may have served as a place to meet and keep track of who is where; in this way, their location can indicate a rich resource base and a logical place to wait for and meet others.

Many of these sites are tranquil and scenic, with mounds in complex arrangements and alignments. Thus, it is equally likely that mounds served a symbolic function, with their placement in these locations related to and representing peoples' views of the world and the cosmos, including distinctions between different clans and the upper and lower worlds, represented by the skies and the waters/wetlands.

MOUND CONSTRUCTION

Mounds are usually low, never more than 2 meters (6 ft) in height, but they are often of considerable length. Some linear mounds are more than 100 meters (325 ft) long, although most range from 20 to 50 meters (65–165 ft) in length.

Bird effigy mound.   [Lynne G. Goldstein]

Mounds generally occur in groups; it is rare to encounter only one mound. Groups may include as few as 3 mounds or more than 100, but most mound groups fall into one of three general categories: those with fewer than 10 mounds, those with around 25 to 40 mounds, and those with 60 to 80 mounds.

Mounds are often aligned parallel to the natural feature on which they are built or to other, similar landscape markers. There is no apparent pattern in terms of which mound types occur together. Conical mounds are the most common, with oval and linear mounds also appearing frequently. Birds, panthers, bear, buffalo, turtles, and lizards are among the most common effigy forms.

Construction of mounds is not uniform from site to site; rather, three different construction methods have been documented. In many instances, all or part of the topsoil is removed prior to mound construction, as if to define the areal extent of the mound. In other cases, a so-called intaglio foundation was used; the topsoil was removed, and then excavation was deepened to produce an intaglio or reverse cameo of the mound shape. The "hole" or large negative mound shape is then filled and the mound completed. Finally, in the third

method, the topsoil is not removed prior to construction; the mound is simply built on the original ground surface with no special preparation. This type of mound does not appear to be distinctive in any other way.

To create a mound, people dug and carried basket loads of soil from the nearby area, creating the mound all at one time rather than in stages. However, this does not mean that all of the mounds in a group were built at the same time. It is very likely that the mounds in a group were created over an extended period of time, with each mound constructed in a single season.

Mounds often contain one or more features or structures within them. The most common is what archaeologists have called a fireplace or altar, a feature that often shows evidence of fire and usually is made of stone. These structures can appear singly or in groups, and they are often near burials or in prominent parts of the effigy, such as the heart or head area of the "body" of the mound.

Burials are another common mound feature and include primary flexed interments, bundle reburials, and cremations. Treatment in any of these three forms may be single or multiple. Approximately 25 percent of the burials excavated have been primary (usually flexed) interments, about 61 percent

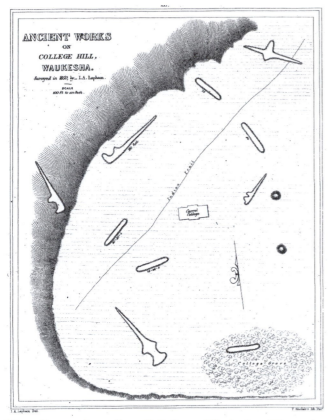

Map of mounds at Carroll College, Waukesha, Wisconsin. [The map was created by Increase A. Lapham, Antiquities of Wisconsin, 1855]

have been single or multiple bundle reburials, 2 percent have been cremations, and the remaining 12 percent consist of scattered bone in which the treatment of the body before burial is uncertain. Burials may be placed in pits excavated below the mound floor, they may be placed directly on the mound floor with no pit, or they may be in the mound fill with no pit. The type of burial does not seem to be correlated with the mound type.

Although nearly every effigy mound group that has been tested or excavated archaeologically has included at least one burial, it is *not* the case that every mound includes a burial. A number of mounds have yielded no evidence of human bone, and it is unusual for mounds to contain the remains of more than a few individuals. An exception is the presence of one or more sets of multiple (usually bundle) burials. Bundle reburial involves exposing the body until the soft tissue decays, after which the remaining bones are gathered and placed in the mound as a bundle. Smaller bones are often lost in the process. One or more individuals can be included in a bundle, and the individual(s) may or may not have been exposed at the same location where they are ultimately buried.

Although the number of burials in any mound is small, both adults and children may be present. There seems to be roughly equal representation of males and females, and all (including children) are prepared in each of the burial treatment types discussed above. Analyses of their skeletons indicate that they were well-nourished, healthy people. Grave goods, though rare, include an occasional ceramic pot, pipe, projectile point, bone artifact, or copper artifact. The pottery was thin walled, well made, and decorated with complex geometric designs. Artifacts are not necessarily directly connected with burials, but may be associated with the fireplaces or altars or found lying on the mound floor.

The spatial arrangement of features and burials within mounds is not random; burials and associated features are often placed at the "heart" or "head" of the animal represented, or are at the center of the mound.

THE MEANING OF MOUNDS

Many theories have been proposed concerning the meaning of the effigy mound forms. Some scholars and Native Americans think that the animal effigies represent the totems of various clans. Many effigy shapes are similar to Native American concepts of important spirit beings. A few researchers have suggested that the effigies relate to stars and constellations and may have been used to mark solar and astronomical events. While it is unlikely that we will ever know their complete meaning, archaeologists are certain that effigy mound groups were more than just places of burial. The mounds were probably multipurpose ceremonial places that were visited periodically by members of a family, band, or tribal group for a variety of social, religious, political, and economic activities. These activities served to integrate the group, reinforce its shared identity and beliefs, and reaffirm its links to the land and the supernatural world. Much of the ritual activity involved construction and use of the mounds, and the burial of at least some ancestors was an important part of these rituals. However, because some mounds do not contain human remains, and given that not everyone was buried there, it was apparently not mandatory to bury ancestors in the mounds. The mounds probably also functioned as territorial markers for the groups who built them.

Several scholars have suggested the possible use of the mound sites as aggregation centers. One idea is that people congregated at mound sites for ceremonial and funerary activities. Others have argued for a more complex model in response to seasonal availability of resources, where the mound group represents the territory of a number of loosely related families who seasonally merge into a larger corporate entity.

In summary, effigy mounds have been considered mortuary sites, astronomical markers, symbolic totems, and territory markers. It is likely that they may have represented all or some of these things in some way, but it is necessary to place them against the social and physical landscape to provide an overall context. In this sense, effigy mound sites can be seen

Table 1   Effigy Mound Sites That Are Open to the Public and Easily Accessible

County	Site Name	Location	Comments	Mounds
		State of Iowa		
Allamakee, Clayton	Effigy Mounds National Monument	Northeastern part of Iowa, on State Highway 76	Only National Park Service unit devoted to Effigy Mound culture	Over 200 mounds included in park; 31 bear and birds
		State of Wisconsin		
Calumet	Calumet County Park	Cty. Trunk Hwy. EE, off State Hwy. 55, Stockbridge	On east shore of Lake Winnebago, ca. 2 mi north of Stockbridge	6 panther effigies on top of an escarpment
	High Cliff State Park	State Hwy. 55, Sherwood	Along limestone cliffs, paralleling east shore of Lake Winnebago, south of Sherwood	6 panthers, several conical mounds, plus interpretive trail
Columbia	Kingsley Bend Mound Group	State Hwy. 16, Wisconsin Dells	In highway wayside, about 3 mi south of Wisconsin Dells	Originally at least 22 conical, linear, and effigy mounds; panther effigy, plus several linear and conical mounds preserved
Dane	Edgewood Mound Group	Edgewood College, Woodrow St., off Monroe Ave., Madison	12 mounds preserved on campus of Edgewood College	Linear and 6 conical mounds along Edgewood Dr.; remains of 2 linears near library, and large bird effigy on other side of library; 2 conicals near playground
	Forest Hill Cemetery	Regent St. and Speedway Dr., Madison	Established in 1858, Forest Hill Cemetery is final resting place of many of Wisconsin's most prominent citizens, including 8 governors	Among modern graves is effigy mound group that includes goose, 2 panthers, and linear
	Lewis Mound Group	Indian Mound Park, Burma Rd., McFarland	Located on hill overlooking Lake Waubesa	Includes bear effigy, 2 conicals, 2 linears, 1 oval, 1 "hook"-shaped mound
	Observatory Hill Mounds	Observatory, Univ. of Wisconsin, Madison	Due west of observatory on Madison campus, overlooking Lake Mendota	Bird effigy, unusual two-tailed panther effigy; plaque erected in 1914 is incorrect
	Univ. of Wisconsin Arboretum mound groups	McCaffrey Rd., Madison	On both sides of McCaffrey Rd.; map available at McKay Center at Arboretum	Two mound groups, including bird, panther, linear, conical mounds
Grant	Wyalusing State Park	Near Prairie du Chien	On the high bluffs overlooking confluence of Mississippi and Wisconsin rivers	21 mound groups recorded in park, once totaling >130 mounds, including bears, panthers
Jefferson	Jefferson County Indian Mounds and Trail Park	Koshkonong Mounds Rd., off State Hwy. 26, Fort Atkinson	Park represents southern part of General Atkinson Mound Group; designated walking trail around and between mounds	11 mounds—tapering linears, conicals, bird, "turtle" mounds, plus remnants of old documented Indian trail
	Panther Intaglio	On State Hwy. 106, west of downtown Fort Atkinson	On north side of Rock River, also on north side of road; State Historic Marker at site	This 125-ft intaglio is the only remaining of about 12 originally recorded in Wisconsin
Juneau	Indian Mounds Park	Indian Mound Rd., New Lisbon	On the Lemonweir River on south side of New Lisbon	Small group of effigy mounds; some have been reconstructed

Table 1   *(Continued)*

County	Site Name	Location	Comments	Mounds
Sauk	Devil's Lake State Park	State Hwy. 33, Baraboo	3 miles south of Baraboo; name is due to misunderstanding of original Ho-Chunk word	Number of effigy mounds on southeast shore of lake and on north shore
Sheboygan	Sheboygan Indian Mound County Park	South Ninth St., Sheboygan	Located to the south of Sheboygan; preserves what was known as the Kletzien Mound Group	Originally 33 mds.; 18 existing, 16 have been restored; there is a trail and a printed guide is available
Washington	Lizard Mounds County Park	½ mi east of intersection, State Hwy. 111 and Cty. Trunk Hwy. A, West Bend	Northeast of West Bend, on rise surrounded by springs and wetlands, but far from major rivers; there is interpretive trail with signs	60 mounds originally; now 5 conicals, 1 oval, 8 linears, 2 tapering linears, 2 symmetrically paired bird effigies, 11 panther effigies

as representing maps—not maps in the conventional sense of the word, but symbolic representations of form and space to the people who built and used the mounds. The different orientations of individual mounds, for example, may represent indicators or pointers to resources controlled by a particular group. The arrangement of mounds might represent intra- or intergroup relationships, but might also indicate directions to resources or types of resources. We may not be able to completely read the map with our Western orientations, but we can detect regularities. Within a mound group, the number of different types of effigy forms may represent not only clan or corporate groups, but also diversity of resources. The largest and most diverse mound groups are consistently located adjacent to the largest and most resource-diverse wetlands.

Effigy mounds undoubtedly served a variety of purposes. Their shapes and patterns, like the clan spirit symbols, also likely represented the world-view of the groups, with earth, sky, and underworld all represented. The act of constructing the mounds also reinforced social bonding through shared efforts, and it is probable that during these gatherings other social events, such as courtships and marriages, also occurred.

THE FATE OF THE EFFIGY MOUND PEOPLE

Current dating methods indicate that mound construction ceased or significantly decreased after about AD 1200. In northern Wisconsin and Minnesota, conical mounds were probably constructed right up to the time of European contact in the seventeenth century. Although mounds have not been constructed here for a very long time, historical and archaeological evidence, as well as the oral traditions of Native Americans, indicate that the Winnebago and other tribes occasionally used existing mounds for burial places as late as the nineteenth century. Contemporary Native Americans revere and honor mounds as ancestral burial places and spiritual centers. Visitors to mounds and mound groups should bear in mind that these places are considered sacred to many Native Americans.

At one time there were several thousand effigy mounds in this region (one estimate is that there may have been some 20,000), but farming, town and city development, and road building obliterated most of the mounds before laws were enacted to protect them in the late 1980s.

Effigy mound culture is likely ancestral to several midwestern tribes, and almost certainly to the Ho-Chunk (Winnebago), who continue to reside in this region.

VISITING EFFIGY MOUND SITES

One of the best places to visit an effigy mound site is the Effigy Mounds National Monument in northeastern Iowa, along the Mississippi River, almost directly across from Prairie du Chien, Wisconsin. This is the only National Park Service location devoted to the effigy mound culture. Mounds from three different contiguous sites are accessible in this one place. Over 200 mounds are preserved; 31 of these are effigies in the shapes of bears and birds. Table 1 is a list of other effigy mound sites that you can visit; most are state, county, or local parks that are easily accessible to the public. Other than Effigy Mounds National Monument, these are located in Wisconsin for two reasons: (1) a significant majority of effigy mounds were built in what is now Wisconsin, and (2) Wisconsin has managed to preserve more of their mounds in parks than have surrounding states.

The largest effigy mound in the United States is located in southern Ohio, far from the rest of these mounds, and is not part of the effigy mound culture. That mound is in the form of a serpent, is more than a quarter mile long, and is known as the Great Serpent Mound. It was once thought to pre-date effigy mounds, but new information suggests that this interpretation may be wrong, and the serpent may be more recent than most of the effigy mound culture constructions. The Great Serpent Mound is part of the Ohio Historical Society and is on State Route 73, 6 miles north of State Route 32 and 20 miles south of Bainbridge in Adams County.

Further Reading: Benn, David, "Some Trends and Traditions in Woodland Cultures of the Quad-State Region in the Upper Mississippi River Basin," *Wisconsin Archeologist* 60(1) (1979): 47–82; Birmingham, Robert A., and Leslie E. Eisenberg, *Indian Mounds of Wisconsin* (Madison: University of Wisconsin Press, 2000); Effigy Mounds National Monument, National Park Service Web site, http://www.nps.gov/efmo/ (online April 2007); Goldstein, Lynne, "Landscapes and Mortuary Practices: A Case for Regional Perspectives," in *Regional Approaches to Mortuary Analysis*, edited by Lane Anderson Beck (New York: Plenum Press, 1995), 101–121; Hurley, William M., *An Analysis of Effigy Mound Complexes in Wisconsin*, Anthropological Papers, No. 59 (Ann Arbor: University of Michigan, Museum of Anthropology, 1975); Mallam, R. Clark, *The Iowa Effigy Mound Tradition: An Interpretive Model* (Iowa City, IA: Office of the State Archaeologist, 1976); Mallam, R. Clark, "Some Views on the Archaeology of the Driftless Zone in Iowa," *Proceedings of the Iowa Academy of Science* 91 (1984): 16–21; Salkin, Phillip, "The Late Woodland Stage in Southeastern Wisconsin," *Wisconsin Academy Review* 33(2) (1987): 75–79; Storck, Peter L., "Some Aspects of Effigy Mound Subsistence and Settlement Patterns during the Late Woodland Period in Wisconsin," *Arctic Anthropology* 11 (1974): 272–279; Wisconsin Historical Society, *Effigy Mounds Culture*, www.wisconsinhistory.org/turningpoints/tp-004/ (online April 2007).

Lynne G. Goldstein

THE RANGE SITE

Near Dupo, Southwestern Illinois

Long Sequence of Communities in the American Bottom Area

The large, multi-component Range site is located on the American Bottom, a portion of the Mississippi floodplain, near the modern town of Dupo. The site covered more than 10 hectares and was situated on a point bar along an abandoned channel of the Mississippi River known as Prairie Lake. The inhabitants had access to the nearby uplands to the east and numerous aquatic habitats surrounding the site area. The present Mississippi River is 5 kilometers to the west.

The Range site excavations occurred between 1975 and 1981 as part of a large archaeological study done to mitigate the destruction of important sites in this area caused by the FAI-270 highway project. A remaining portion of the Range site was destroyed by construction of a subdivision in the mid-1980s. However, in the late 1990s an area of the site was preserved under a covenant prior to the construction of a new school. During the highway excavations over 10 hectares (about 25 acres) of the site was investigated, resulting in the identification of more than 5,000 prehistoric features that date from approximately 3000 BC to AD 1500. Of particular significance is the sequence of twenty-five identifiable ancient communities dating from the Late Woodland into the Early Mississippian times. Also of significance is the identification of two areas of Oneota habitation, the latest prehistoric occupation of the area. The following discussion summarizes the organization and significance of these communities.

Although older projectile point styles were recovered from later feature contexts and on the surface, the initial occupations of the Range site are linked to the Late Archaic period. These occupations were identified by scattered clusters of shallow pits left by intermittent seasonal encampments during this earliest period of site use. Evidence of subsequent Early and Middle Woodland utilization of the area is limited to scattered ceramics from later feature contexts. Again, this scattered material reflects the ephemeral nature of site occupation and use during these time periods.

The next major occupation dates to the Late Woodland Patrick phase (AD 650–850) occupation. Nearly 1,000 features including 80 houses were mapped and excavated. The Late Woodland occupation covers nearly 7 hectares (about 17 acres) of the site and consists of nine separate occupation areas representing a range of settlement types, including several villages. The most complete village identified consisted of thirty-three structures distributed in a series of spatially discontinuous clusters around a community square. This community and other Late Woodland villages reflect the fluid and dynamic nature of the egalitarian organization of the societies of that time. The distribution of houses suggests sociopolitical positions as well as the division of the village into two halves, which would be consistent with a moiety (basic tribal society subdivision) system characteristic of later eastern North American Indian groups. The subsistence focus is on a mixed economy of wild plants and animals, especially deer and aquatic species, but also a wide array of cultivated plants, including the suite of starchy seeds of

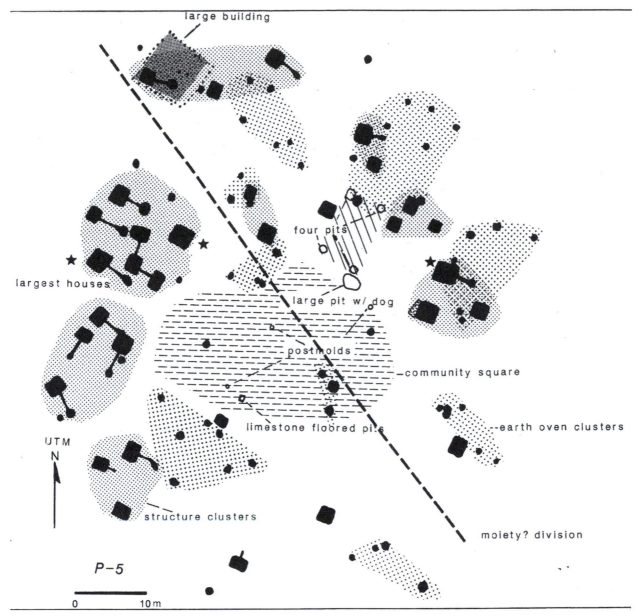

large building

four pits

largest houses

large pit w/ dog

postmolds

community square

limestone floored pits

earth oven clusters

UTM
N

structure clusters

moiety? division

P-5

0   10m

The most complete village identified consisted of thirty-three structures distributed in a series of spatially discontinuous clusters around a community square.   [John E. Kelly]

chenopodium, polygonum, maygrass, and little barley. Other cultivated plants included sunflower, marshelder, squash, gourd, and tobacco. Very little corn was present at this time, although it was already evident in the area by the Middle Woodland period. Ceramics are primarily grog tempered and cordmarked. Subconoidal jars dominate the assemblage. Other aspects of the material assemblage include small arrow points, gaming stones known as discoidals (the undoubted forerunner of the Chunky stone of the post-contact era), and small clay and stone pipes.

The next series of occupations were part of a transitional unit referred to as Emergent Mississippian. This term was introduced to characterize the shift from Late Woodland to Mississippian society in the American Bottom between AD 850 and 1050. This approximate 200-year period is characterized by rapid changes in the material culture manufactured and used, especially ceramics. Differences identified at the Range site and other Emergent Mississippian sites to the south of Prairie du Pont Creek are referred to as the Pulcher tradition. The area to the

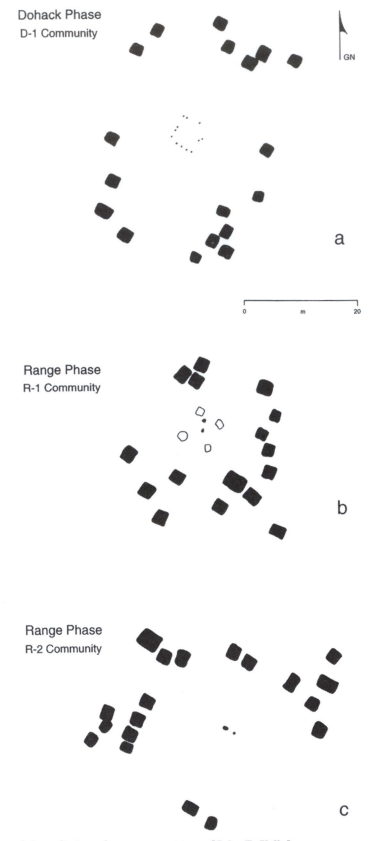

Dohack Phase
D-1 Community

a

Range Phase
R-1 Community

b

Range Phase
R-2 Community

c

A map showing the features of three distinct phase communities.   [John E. Kelly]

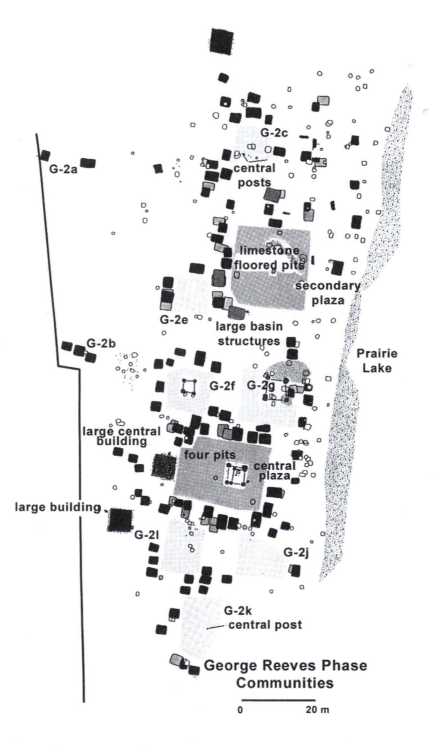

The George Reeves phase communities.   [John E. Kelly]

north, especially near a large oxbow lake, the Grand Marais, has been designated the Late Bluff tradition. Although earlier Late Bluff tradition occupations are evident at the site of Cahokia, by the end of the tenth century a substantial population of Emergent Mississip-

pian peoples had settled at Cahokia in areas covering up to 35 hectares (about 86 acres). Located a short distance north of the Range site, Cahokia ultimately was the largest settlement of its time and is often referred to as the capital of the Mississippian world.

At the Range site a series of small early Emergent Mississippian villages have been identified. Those from the initial two phases, Dohack and Range, are more Late Woodland in character, especially in terms of the ceramic assemblage, but also in structure type and size. The Pulcher tradition ceramics, while stylistically derived from the preceding Late Woodland, are primarily tempered with crushed limestone. The use of limestone is part of a tradition that extends into the northern Ozarks to the west. A total of eleven Dohack and Range phase communities have been identified. They are small villages similar to the Patrick phase community, with small (<4 m^2) houses distributed in a series of spatially discontinuous clusters around a community square. Of particular interest and significance is the presence of three separate types of central features. For two of the Dohack phase communities a large (ca. 16 m^2) single-post building is centrally located within two of the settlements. The remaining four Dohack phase communities have a quadripartite pit arrangement (cultural features organized into four parts) with a central pole. The subsequent Range phase settlements consist of the latter quadripartite configuration or simply a central pole. These centralized facilities and features are imbued with symbolism that embodies the community as a whole. These same central features are later incorporated into the later and larger Emergent Mississippian villages at the Range site.

The latter half of the Emergent Mississippian is more Mississippian in character, with a diverse ceramic assemblage in which plain and filmed surfaces are more prevalent. A variety of community types are evident throughout the region, but the primary settlement type is the large village consisting of over 250 houses. An analysis of this community indicates that it began in the George Reeves phase and was subject to numerous changes over its fifty to seventy-five years of occupation. Of particular interest is the presence of multiple plazas surrounded by the largest houses in the community. Beyond the plazas are small courtyards, some of which have central features similar to the earlier occupations. The earliest settlement of this period's community consisted of two distinct halves. In both halves the structures were distributed around two plazas. The center of the northern plaza had a large rectangular storage pit lined with limestone slabs. The southern half consisted of a large rectangular plaza with a quadripartite pit arrangement around a central pole at the east end. This complex was rebuilt on two occasions. At the west end was a large building. Paralleling the plaza to the north were two courtyards with a quadripartite pit arrangement and central pole in each. To the south were additional courtyards with the central pole. What is represented in the southern segment is the coalescence into a village of the three types of central features.

The next episode in the changes over time of the Range site settlements entails the slow abandonment of the southern half of the community. Although the plaza continued to be used along with the building to the west and the quadripartite pits at the opposing east end, the southernmost courtyards were abandoned. The large plaza to the north was maintained with a large central pit. Continuing changes in the evolution of this community resulted in a more semicircular village with a plaza fronting the lake and numerous courtyards, some of which have the quadripartite pit arrangement and central pole. Just prior to abandonment the village consisted of scattered structures distributed around a large oval plaza. Presumably, the population was drawn to the Pulcher site, a possible Emergent Mississippian mound center approximately 2 kilometers to the southwest. With the emergence of Cahokia 20 kilometers to the north, it is also possible that individuals were being incorporated into that community.

Although the Emergent Mississippian village was abandoned, subsequent occupations at the Range site are related to the onset of Mississippian culture in the region. However, it is important to emphasize the continuity of the older ceramic traditions well into the early Mississippian within the Pulcher tradition. Sometime early in the twelfth century both Range and the nearby mound center of Pulcher were abandoned as Cahokia reached its initial zenith.

The subsequent Mississippian component at Range consists of four separate areas of occupation indicative of farmsteads and a nodal settlement. These are restricted to the early Mississippian Lindhorst phase, a southern unit coeval with the Lohmann phase in the northern American Bottom. The Range site is reused during the later Mississippian as a mortuary area. The lack of any diagnostic ceramics makes it difficult to precisely assign these areas to a specific phase, although the use of limestone slab-lined graves is indicative of the Moorehead and Sand Prairie phases.

The final occupation of the Range site is represented by a brief Oneota, Vulcan phase farmstead. At least two oval, wigwam-style structures were identified in two separate areas of the site along with several deep bell-shaped pits and several large jar rims similar stylistically to Orr phase ceramics. The date for this occupation is approximately AD 1500.

Further Reading: Kelly, John E., "The Range Site Community Patterns and the Mississippian Emergence," in *The Mississippian Emergence*, edited by Bruce Smith (Washington, DC: Smithsonian Institution Press, 1990), 67–112; Kelly, John E., "The Emergence of Mississippian Culture in the American Bottom Region," in *The Mississippian Emergence*, edited by Bruce Smith (Washington, DC: Smithsonian Institution Press, 1990), 113–152.

John E. Kelly

GIANT CITY STATE PARK AND OTHER SITES

Southern Illinois
Ancient Stone Forts

"Stone fort" is a term often applied to prehistoric hilltop enclosures that are constructed primarily of stone. Although often termed "stone forts" or "hill forts" in nineteenth- and early-twentieth-century popular literature, these sites have been variously explained, but their interpretation as fortifications remains the most enduring in the public mind. These sites, which differ greatly in size and complexity, occur sporadically in the Eastern Woodlands, where they are broadly associated with the Middle and Late Woodland periods. Typically, these sites occur in widely scattered locations, but southern Illinois has an unusual concentration of them, with ten known examples located within the Shawnee Hills, a band of dissected uplands that extends across southern Illinois from the Mississippi to the Ohio River. They are some of the most intriguing archaeological sites in the lower Ohio valley. These sites occur over an east-west distance of about 50 miles and are situated on the margins of the most rugged portions of the hill country. Seven of the ten are located on the southern flanks of the hills, and all but one are in tributary drainages of the Ohio River. The distribution of sites within the east-west span is uneven, with seven of the ten located in the eastern hill country. No similar constructions are reported from the eastern Ozarks, to the west, and only one stone fort is reported in adjacent portions of western Kentucky, and it is not close to the Illinois examples.

The Illinois sites are simple constructions. Segments of stacked rock wall are built across the neck of a promontory, demarcating an area ringed by sandstone bluffs or steep, rocky slopes. One of the sites, Stonefort Bluff, is a semicircular wall abutted against the edge of near-vertical cliff. The Illinois sites are relatively small; they range in size from a little over an acre to over 30 acres, although most are less than 5 acres. Early accounts describe the walls as 6 feet high, but the accuracy of this is uncertain, given that all the walls were partially collapsed when first described. All of the southern Illinois sites are certainly defensible locations, but their remoteness, the generally poor access to water, and the large numbers of people that would actually be required to defend them make it unlikely that these were fortifications in any conventional sense. No Middle Woodland enclosures existed in this region, and the closest examples are substantial distances away, so the Shawnee Hills sites cannot be derived from older structures in the area.

These sites are noted in some early historical writings and briefly described in 1950s publications of a local amateur archaeologist, but the first important professional statement about them was not published until 1973, and that in a popular magazine, *Outdoor Illinois*. Small-scale excavations have been done on six of the sites, with the most extensive work carried out at Hog Bluff, Giant City, and Stonefort Bluff. The southern Illinois stone forts are definitely Late Woodland, dating to between AD 600 and 1000, based on both radiocarbon dates and artifact assemblages. Artifacts are usually sparse. Excavated assemblages contain small amounts of badly fragmented pottery but consist mostly of stone artifacts—especially projectile points and debitage, the stone debris and chips from making and resharpening points and other lithic tools. Except for one unusually large spear or knife point, no clearly exotic or ritual artifacts have been found. Rock hearths, earth ovens, and storage pits have been identified but in small numbers and with sparse contents. Carbonized plant remains from these pits contain abundant nut shell as well as some cultivated or harvested plant foods—small seeds of goosefoot (chenopodium), amaranth, maygrass, and erect knotweed—thought to be the remains of provisions brought to the site.

The sites exhibit no consistent orientation or topographic position. Some occupy commanding heights with grand vistas, whereas others are located within narrow valleys immediately surrounded by higher hills. Given the prevailing canopy forest around these sites, celestial observation would have been quite limited. No large habitation sites are located close to stone forts, although some rockshelter sites may exist nearby.

Many observers have noted that the walls of such sites demarcate space physically and symbolically, creating an area of restricted access that could have been used by certain people and not others. Although small, these barriers are lasting, visible alterations of the natural landscape that could have had major symbolic import. The walls represent a significant investment of labor, although one certainly within the means of small groups working for brief periods over a number of years. Estimates of the amount of sandstone contained in the original Giant City wall range from 225 to 370 tons, although this is one of the longer walls.

These bluff areas were clearly set apart for specific uses. The question is, for what and why? The site choices show that a remote or secluded location, an elevation above parts of the immediate terrain, and the ability to delimit the space with a stone barrier were major considerations. The prevailing professional view continues to be that these were seasonally

Ruins of one of the walls at the Giant City site. These barriers are lasting, visible alterations of the natural landscape that could have major symbolic import.   [Brian M. Butler]

Ruins at the Giant City site, the only one of these sites not located in the Ohio River drainage.   [Brian M. Butler]

used social aggregation and/or ritual spaces. They do not appear to be mortuary sites, although small stone mounds are documented near two of them. The prevalence of projectile points and evidence of their manufacture and maintenance suggest that preparation for hunting was an important activity at these sites, but that does not preclude a ritual function. The sites were largely abandoned at the onset of the Mississippian period. Only one site, Millstone Bluff, was used later, after a hiatus of several centuries, when a permanent Mississippian village was established on the hilltop.

Seven of the ten known sites are preserved on state or federal land, although none is in pristine condition. Two of the sites are readily accessible. The stone fort in Giant City State Park is one of the smallest sites, at a little over an acre, and it is the only one of these sites not located in the Ohio River drainage. The site occupies a small bluff projection within a narrow valley and is surrounded by higher ridges. The extant wall is a 1930s Civilian Conservation Corps reconstruction, although it was built on the original location. The wall has a gap in the center, which was created to admit a foot trail. The Pounds site, labeled Pounds Escarpment on newer USGS maps, is located on the Rim Rock National Recreation Trail in the Shawnee National Forest. Here, the headward erosion of ravines has nearly isolated a large hill overlooking the upper portion of Pounds Hollow. A stone wall, which is adjacent to the parking area, was built on a bedrock ledge extending across the narrow neck that joins this round-topped, 30-acre bluff to the adjoining uplands. A popular foot trail circles the bluff. Much of the rock wall has tumbled down the slope so that the wall is scarcely visible in some places, but there are signs, and a close look will reveal the structure. The Millstone Bluff site, near Robbs, Illinois, is another interpreted archaeological site in the Shawnee Forest, but its Late Woodland stone wall has been virtually obliterated, and the main attractions are the remains of the Mississippian village.

Further Reading: Brieschke, Walter L., and Frank Rackerby, "The 'Stone Forts' of Illinois," *Outdoor Illinois* 12 (1973): 19–26; Muller, Jon D., *Archaeology of the Lower Ohio River Valley* (Orlando, FL: Academic Press, 1986), ch. 5.

Brian M. Butler

ANGEL MOUNDS STATE HISTORIC SITE

Indiana

Angel Mounds

The Angel site is a large, fortified late prehistoric Mississippian civic-ceremonial center located on the north bank of the Ohio River 5 miles east of the town of Evansville, Indiana. It flourished between AD 1050 and 1450 and was home to an agricultural population of as many as 1,000 people. At its zenith, the Angel settlement covered approximately 40 hectares (nearly 100 acres) and comprised several hundred houses and other structures, four large platform mounds, and several lesser earthen mounds. The whole was enclosed by a palisade roughly 1.5 kilometers in length. This settlement was geographically and culturally central to what archaeologists have designated the Angel phase, a collection of sites and settlements found in the central Ohio valley between the mouths of the Wabash River to the west to the Anderson River to the east.

The Angel site, which bears the name of the family that owned the farm on which it was located, attracted attention of naturalists and archaeologists in the nineteenth and early twentieth centuries. When it became endangered by looting and urban development, Mr. Eli Lilly provided funds for the Indiana Historical Society to purchase the site in 1938. The historical society archaeologist, Glenn A. Black, began excavations at the site in 1939 and, with the exception of the years of World War II, conducted research at the site until his death in 1964. Between 1939 and 1941, with support from the Works Progress Administration, Black excavated 7,380 square meters in the southeastern portion of the site and an additional 4,090 square meters in the southwestern part of the site, which removed Mound F completely. The former excavation produced evidence of a village area of superimposed structures bounded on the north by multiple lined fortifications. The latter excavation, particularly the investigation of Mound F, yielded evidence of multiple building stages of the mound and the former existence of a large building on its summit. Black ran field schools at the site from 1946 to 1961, which cleared an additional 2,150 square meters and were dedicated to examining additional village areas and tracing the course of the palisade. Over the course of several years Black, with the assistance of Irwin Scollar and Richard Johnston, used proton magnetometry to examine 650 square

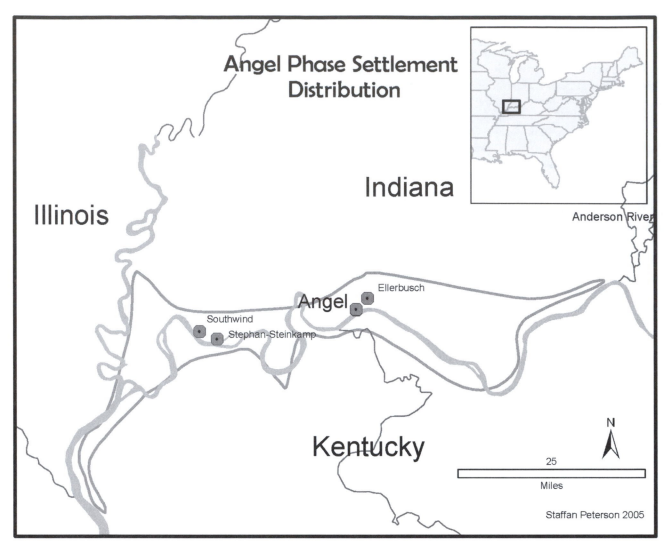

Angel Phase Settlement Distribution

Illinois

Indiana

Anderson River

Angel   Ellerbusch

Southwind
Stephan-Steinkamp

Kentucky

N

25
Miles

Staffan Peterson 2005

Distribution of Angel phase sites in Indiana and Kentucky.   [Christopher S. Peebles]

meters scattered across the site to trace additional segments of the palisade. Since Black's death, 800 square meters have been excavated near the location of Mound F prior to its reconstruction for display, and an additional 800 square meters have been excavated to answer specific questions about the development of the Angel settlement. Between 2000 and 2005 Staffan Peterson conducted a complete magnetometer survey of the site (some 3 million measurements), the results of which clearly show the location of hundreds of structures, multiple palisade lines, and other features that make up the archaeological remains of the site.

The vast majority (99.9 percent) of ceramics at the Angel site, and other sites of the Angel phase, comprise plain and cordmarked, shell-tempered bowls, jars, and plates. A small minority of vessels were decorated by painting a resist layer that contained the design and then washing the vessel with a mineral dye. After refiring, the removal of the resist layer left the lighter design elements—hence the name "Angel Negative Painted" pottery, the hallmark of the site and phase. Sherri Hilgeman has created a ceramic chronology for the Angel site that allows a basic understanding of its development between 1100 and 1450, the approximate time of its demise.

At its zenith, perhaps after AD 1200, household clusters were situated on most of the higher ground of the site. These residential groups seem to display continuity through time, and at death some individuals were buried within these houses. It remains an open question whether a structure was abandoned after an interment or if it continued in use. A few burials are located in the mounds; toward the later period in the history of the site, burials are clustered in areas that seem to be dedicated as cemeteries. Recent investigations have provided good evidence of craft specialization in pottery and stone tool manufacture.

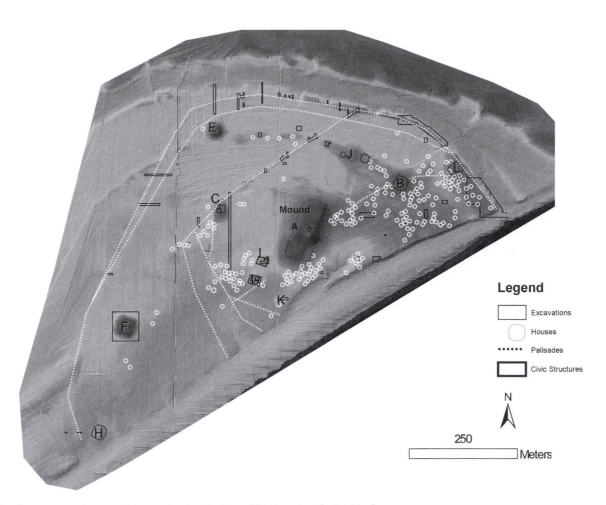

Major mounds, features, and excavations at the Angel site.   [Christopher S. Peebles]

Analysis of human remains shows that the Angel population were generally well nourished and that corn provided a substantial portion of their diet, though wild plants were also consumed. Macrobotanical remains included not only corn (the majority 8- and 10-row) but also squash, tobacco, and a variety of wild seeds such as goosefoot, little barley, and knotweed. Animals in the diet included deer, turkey, small mammals, and fish. As a whole, the Angel population had a typically Mississippian diet; however, this population relied on corn for basic calories to a greater extent than any similar population measured thus far.

Several sets of fortifications define the outer limits of the site, and there does not seem to have been a time that the Angel settlement was not protected by a stout palisade. One of the many questions about the development of the Angel site is the sequence in which these fortifications were constructed, and if the site layout was planned. Was the maximum area of the site as defined by the 1.5-kilometer palisade the earliest community? Did the area of settlement

then shrink to conform to the sequence of palisades that bisect the site? Or did the site begin at about half its maximum size and then expand to the whole 40-hectare settlement? In any case, most of the larger architectural features are aligned on a common axis, suggesting a planned community. Was such attention to layout a means of organizing social and economic activities? Current excavations at the Angel site by the staff of the Glenn A. Black Laboratory of Archaeology and Indiana University are dedicated to answering these questions and enhancing the interpretation of the site.

In 1947 Mr. Lilly and the Indiana Historical Society transferred interest in the surface of the site to the state of Indiana; he also built a museum to present the work that Glenn Black had undertaken at the site. This museum and the Angel site proper are open to the public Tuesday through Sunday throughout the year. It has become an important part of the Indiana State Museum and Historic Sites system. Many of the artifacts from excavations at the Angel site are on display in this museum; the bulk of the collections are curated at the Glenn A. Black

Laboratory of Archaeology, at the Indiana University in Bloomington.

Further Reading: Black, Glenn A., *Angel Site: An Archaeological, Historical, and Ethnographic Study*, 2 vols. (Indianapolis: Indiana Historical Society, 1967); Hilgeman, Sherri, *Pottery and Chronology at Angel* (Tuscaloosa: University of Alabama Press, 2000); Kellar,

James, *An Introduction to the Prehistory of Indiana* (Indianapolis: Indiana Historical Society, 1983); Lilly, Eli, *Prehistoric Antiquities of Indiana* (Indianapolis: Indiana Historical Society, 1937); Schurr, Mark, "The Relationship between Mortuary Treatment and Diet at the Angel Site," Ph.D. diss. (University of Indiana, 1989); Schurr, Mark, "Isotopic and Mortuary Variability in a Middle Mississippian Population," *American Antiquity* 57(2) (1992): 300–320.

Christopher S. Peebles and Staffan D. Peterson

AZTALAN STATE PARK

Between Milwaukee and Madison, Wisconsin
A Late Woodland and Mississippian Village

OVERVIEW

The Aztalan site, a Late Woodland and Mississippian (ca. AD 800–1300) village, is situated on the west bank of the Crawfish River, in the western portion of Jefferson County, Wisconsin. Aztalan is located between the modern cities of Milwaukee and Madison. Today the site is a state park managed by the Wisconsin Department of Natural Resources and open all year. Aztalan is the northernmost large Mississippian village recorded. It shares artifact styles with other Mississippian sites to the south, as well as displaying architectural features that are considered hallmarks of Mississippian culture, such as platform mounds with an associated plaza, conical mounds, and palisades. However, there are also features that set Aztalan apart from other Mississippian sites.

Although many other Mississippian villages have palisades or stockades around them, few are as massive or as extensive as Aztalan's. Aztalan also has several interior stockade walls, some of which are quite intricate. Interior walls at other Mississippian sites are simpler and less massive, often simply enclosing a platform mound or small ceremonial area.

Other large Mississippian villages are surrounded by a set of smaller, related sites. Towns like Aztalan tended to form the center of a complex and hierarchical social and settlement system. At Aztalan, however, there are no surrounding sites of the same culture. Aztalan appears to have been an isolated outpost. Because the Crawfish is not a major river, researchers initially thought that Aztalan was located in an unusual natural environment for an agricultural village, and the reasons for its placement on the landscape did not make sense. More recent work has demonstrated that the location is reasonable in terms of resource availability and landscape setting, although the site's physical location is unusual for a Mississippian village.

Mortuary practices at Aztalan also do not fit the standard Mississippian model. There have been few burials found and

no cemetery located, and while there is evidence of some of the kinds of burial treatment found at some other Mississippian sites, there is also extensive evidence of broken, scattered human bone across the site. This widespread distribution of human bone in pits led early researchers to conclude that these people practiced cannibalism. Some saw the bone evidence as so pervasive throughout the site that they argued that human flesh must have been a part of their daily diet, rather than a ritual practice. However, it is now known that Mississippian people regularly practiced extensive processing of human remains, and it is not unusual to find scattered human bone in non-burial contexts. Not every bone was considered important, so many were simply thrown away after processing. We have recovered only a portion of the remains of Aztalan's mortuary practices, but cannibalism is not the only, or the most likely, explanation for what has been found.

MAJOR SITE ACTIVITY AREAS
Palisaded Precinct

The bulk of activity took place within this approximate 21-acre (8.5-hectare) precinct within the outermost palisade. Early Aztalan visitors during the historic period wrote that they were impressed by what they thought were brick walls, but the walls actually represent the stockade with individual posts set in the ground. Bastions or watchtowers were constructed at regular intervals along the palisade line, and the walls were covered with clay plaster. What early European visitors saw as bricks were burned pieces of the plaster; such chunks of plaster (still ubiquitous) are known as "Aztalan brick."

In addition to the outer wall, there were several inner palisade walls. These inner walls functioned to divide the site into distinct areas, or perhaps to screen some activities from general view.

Examples of types of pottery found at Aztalan. Collared vessel on the left is earlier Late Woodland variety.   [Lynne G. Goldstein]

Within the outer palisade wall there are several important areas: The midden area was along the river bank, where garbage and debris were dumped. The habitation area was bounded by an inner palisade, the mounds, and the outer palisade. Some gardening probably also took place within this area. Houses were round or rectangular in shape and were built to withstand winter weather. Within the houses were pole frame beds, probably covered with tamarack boughs, and then deerskins and furs. In the center of the houses were fireplaces with a smoke hole above. Also inside were storage pits for corn, nuts, and seeds. Meat was stored outside, and much of the cooking also occurred outside. Each house was home to a single family. Residents grew corn and beans, but they also used many wild plants, including hickory nuts and acorns, and a variety of berries and other plant foods. They ate a lot of deer but also elk, raccoon, beaver, muskrat, and fox. Fish was common, and the people constructed a fish dam of rocks in the Crawfish River to improve their catch. Mussels were common, as were turtles and various birds, such as passenger pigeons, ducks, teals, turkey, goose, and swan. The only domesticated animal was the dog; four dog burials have been excavated.

Adjacent to the living precinct is the open plaza area. The plaza functioned as a public and/or ceremonial area that was generally kept free of debris by sweeping. Adjacent to the plaza precinct is the platform mound area. Each mound was constructed in stages, and each stage had a building on top. The buildings were ceremonial in nature, or they may have housed elite members of the society. The pyramidal mounds and the gravel knoll form a rectangle within which most of the site activity was concentrated. Given its location, the gravel knoll may have been used as a southeast pyramidal mound.

South of the northwest mound, archaeologists have discovered a large, rectangular surface that was sculpted into three terraces. At least seventy pits were excavated about 2 meters into bedded gravels after 1 meter or more of topsoil had been removed. Some pits may have been multipurpose; some were used for extended processing of human remains. Each terrace segment may have had a different function—food storage, secondary disposal of human remains, processing of human remains, and so on. This portion of the site was carefully planned, and the spatial arrangement of the pits is significant and tied to the terracing as well as to the northwest mound.

Conical Mound Line or Precinct

Along the western edge of the site was a linear group of about fifty conical mounds along the top of the ridge. These are not generally burial mounds. In the center of each mound was a large post set into a pit. This resulted in a row of large upright posts along the western edge of the site. Their function (at least in part) was to mark the site, and if one travels in almost any direction from Aztalan, these mounds remain in clear view. They may also have marked certain events—for example, to calculate solstices or other annual patterns.

The one exception to the use of these mounds as markers is one of Aztalan's most famous features—the so-called Princess burial. This individual was buried in an extended position with "belts" of shell beads around her shoulders, hips, and lower legs. She was placed in a conical mound at the very northern end of the conical mound line, near the present intersection of Highway B and Highway Q, outside the current state park boundaries but within the Pioneer Lake Mills–Aztalan Museum facility. It is unknown if she is associated with the Late Woodland or Mississippian period; Late Woodland burials often have shell beads associated with them, and no diagnostic Mississippian artifacts were recovered.

Agricultural Precinct

In addition to corn, beans, and squash, archaeologists have found other agricultural evidence at Aztalan. Immediately

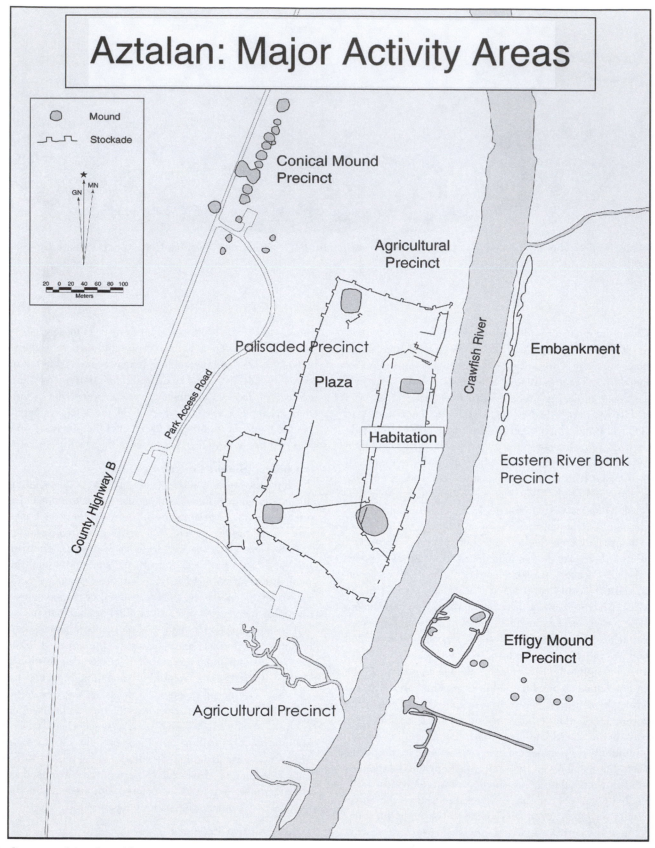

Aztalan: Major Activity Areas

Mound

Stockade

GN MN

20 0 20 40 60 80 100
Meters

Conical Mound
Precinct

Agricultural
Precinct

Palisaded Precinct

Plaza

Crawfish River

Embankment

Habitation

Eastern River Bank
Precinct

Park Access Road

County Highway B

Effigy Mound
Precinct

Agricultural Precinct

Outline map of Aztalan with major activity areas indicated. [Lynne G. Goldstein]

CRAWFISH RIVER

GRAVEL KNOLL

SOUTHWEST PYRAMIDAL MOUND

SCULPTED SURFACE

PALISADE   NORTHWEST PYRAMIDAL MOUND

CONICAL MOUNDS

Aerial view of Aztalan with important features noted.   [Lynne G. Goldstein]

north of the main palisade, there was a historically documented set of ridged fields that may be remnants of aboriginal agricultural fields. South of the palisade and south of the creek, archaeologists have found fragments of hoes with so-called hoe polish, suggesting another possible location of prehistoric agricultural fields. Hoe polish is a silica deposit that forms when plants are worked with chert hoes.

Eastern River Bank Precinct

The occupation on the eastern side of the river is primarily associated with the earlier Late Woodland period. The mounds date to the Late Woodland effigy mound culture, but recent excavations have identified a small Mississippian occupation here; in addition, a long "embankment," documented in the 1800s, has been shown to be made by humans.

HOW AZTALAN GOT ITS NAME

Aztalan has a Mesoamerican-sounding name, and many assume that such a connection exists. However, the name Aztalan was given to the site by Nathaniel Hyer in 1837. Hyer was the first European to publish a description of the site, and he named it Aztalan because he assumed that the site must be the location that Baron Alexander von

Humboldt described as the place the Aztecs talked about as the "country to the north" from where they had come. Humboldt and the Aztecs actually referred to that mythical place as Aztlan, but Hyer called it Aztalan, and the name stuck.

Further Reading: Aztalan State Park, Wisconsin Department of Natural Resources Web site, www.dnr.state.wi.us/org/land/parks/specific/aztalan/ (online April 2007); Baerreis, David A., *Aztalan: Exploration and Reconstruction,* special issue, *Wisconsin Archeologist* 39(1) (1958); Barrett, Samuel A., *Ancient Aztalan* (Milwaukee, WI: Milwaukee Public Museum, 1933); Goldstein, Lynne, "The Mysteries of Aztalan," *Wisconsin Academy Review* (Summer 1991): 28–34; Goldstein, Lynne, and Joan E. Freeman, "Aztalan: A Middle Mississippian Village," *Wisconsin Archeologist* 78(1/2) (1997): 223–248; Birmingham, Robert A., and Lynne G. Goldstein, *Aztalan: Mysteries of an Ancient Indian Town* (Madison: University of Wisconsin Press and Wisconsin Historical Society, 2005); Goldstein, Lynne, and Donald H. Gaff, "Recasting the Past: Examining Assumptions about Aztalan," in *Current Issues in the Archaeology of the Western Great Lakes: Problems and Progress,* edited by R. Jeske, *Wisconsin Archeologist* 83(2) (2002): 98–110; Mississippian Culture and Aztalan, Wisconsin Historical Society Web site, www.wisconsinhitory.org/turningpoints/tp-003/ (online April 2007).

Lynne G. Goldstein

CAHOKIA MOUNDS STATE HISTORIC SITE—WORLD HERITAGE SITE

Near St. Louis, Missouri, Southwestern Illinois
Center of the Mississippian World

Mississippian societies (AD 1050–1500) are characterized by the construction of large earthen monuments within residential communities whose populations numbered in the hundreds and in some cases the thousands. These communities were linked in political systems or polities referred to as chiefdoms. At the top of the social hierarchy were chiefs, who were the social and political elite. These polities were often located in areas where soils were suitable for the cultivation of crops. Centrally located within the midcontinent, the Cahokia site is the largest and one of the earliest Mississippian mound centers. Over one hundred earthen mounds are distributed within a 5–6-square-mile area of Mississippi River floodplain known as the American Bottom. The area across from St. Louis, Missouri, held some of the most productive soils, where Cahokia's inhabitants availed themselves of the cultivation of corn, squash, tobacco, and a variety of native cultigens such as chenopodium, maygrass, polygonum, little barley, sunflower, and marsh elder. Numerous aquatic habitats provided a rich suite of mammal, fish, and bird meats. The uplands to the southwest included the Ozarks, the primary source for lithic resources—especially cherts for tool manufacture and basalt for the manufacture of axe heads—plus other minerals, such as hematite and lead, for use in rituals. On the northern fringes of the Ozarks a bright red fireclay was procured from cavities or sinkholes in the earth's surface. This aluminum silicate was easily carved and was used to create some of the most elaborate ancient statuary ever produced. These statutes are found at sites near Cahokia and throughout much of the Mid-south and as far west as eastern Oklahoma.

The landscape of Cahokia site today is the product of heavy remodeling by Cahokia's residents of the ridge and swale landscape common in the American Bottom. The ancient planners modified the land to produce broad, level foundations on which plazas were laid out and around which platform mounds and large buildings were erected. This culturally modified landscape required precise planning to produce astronomically guided placement of the mounds. The result is a diamond-shaped configuration with the principal "boundary" mounds positioned symmetrically around the largest earthen platform, known as Monks Mound. Located at the geographic center of the Cahokia site, Monks Mound with its four terraces is 32 meters in height and covers 7 hectares.

In the early stages of the site's history, around AD 1050, four large plazas were created and flanked the four sides of a much smaller Monks Mound.

Throughout its 400 year history (AD 1000 to 1400), Cahokia was the ritual, social, and political seat of a polity that stretched at least 20 kilometers in all directions. Other large mound centers in St. Louis, East St. Louis, Dupo, Lebanon, and Mitchell were important satellites along with other, smaller mound centers, villages, and farms. These centers and other settlements have their own histories as communities; however, none was as enduring as Cahokia. The Cahokia polity, estimated at nearly 50,000 persons at its peak, was indeed a complex civilization with a population that carried on dynamic local and extra-regional interactions extending from the Gulf of Mexico to the western Great Lakes, and from the middle Missouri River of the plains to the lower Ohio River.

The history of this remarkable ancient American Indian community, referred to in the site's interpretive center as the City of the Sun, can be divided into four stages. The initial stage dates to AD 950–1050 and is known locally as Late Bluff, part of a larger period named the Emergent Mississippian. An area (between 17. 5 and 35 hectares [ha.], approximately 42 to 85 acres) of Emergent Mississippian occupation at the center of Cahokia extends nearly 1.75 kilometers east to west and 0.1 to 0.2 kilometers back from the edge of the natural levee overseeing an abandoned channel of the Mississippi River. The extent to which monumental architecture such as platform mounds and large buildings and plazas were part of this foundation has yet to be determined in part because of the selective and limited nature of excavations at the site. At other area Emergent Mississippian communities, however, there is some indication that small mounds were being constructed along with small (0.35 ha., a little less than 1 acre) plazas and large (64 m²) buildings.

Midway through the eleventh century a remarkable and dramatic change occurred in the site's cultural landscape, referred to by Timothy Pauketat as the "Big Bang," because of rapid changes in the overall scale of the site's central core. This disjuncture between what archaeologists in the region call Emergent Mississippian and Mississippian was recognized some twenty years ago by archaeologists such as George Milner for settlements outside Cahokia. Cahokia's ritualized

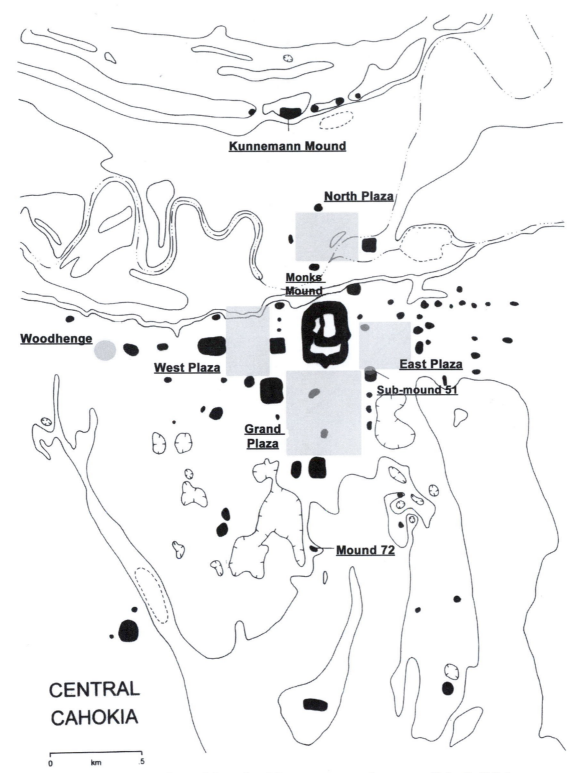

Kunnemann Mound

North Plaza

Monks Mound

Woodhenge

West Plaza

East Plaza

Sub-mound 51

Grand Plaza

Mound 72

CENTRAL
CAHOKIA

0   km   .5

A map of the Cahokia site, the largest and one of the earliest Mississippian mound centers.   [John E. Kelly]

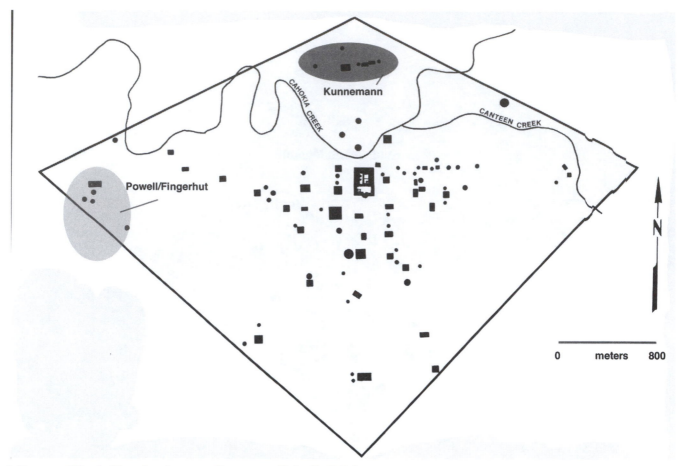

A diagram of Monks Mound and surrounding area.   [John E. Kelly]

core was characterized by a much smaller Monks Mound at the center of four large (6–21 ha., approximately 15 to 52 acres) plazas oriented to the cardinal directions. There is some indication that the Grand and West plazas were in the process of being created at the end of the Emergent Mississippian occupation.

Although mound building may not have required the labor of large numbers of people, other public works projects such as leveling the Grand Plaza most likely did. Most mounds were constructed in incremental stages over varying periods of time. The labor for large-scale projects may have been coordinated through large feasts. Evidence for community-wide feasts comes from a reclaimed borrow pit, sub-Mound 51, 150 meters southeast of Monks Mound on the northeast edge of the Grand Plaza and the south end of the East Plaza. Lucretia S. Kelly was the first to recognize the telltale signs of feasting, with the large quantities and selected portions of deer. The four public plazas in central Cahokia served as focal points or arenas for public gatherings including ritual and feasting activities, which in turned served to integrate and promote solidarity among the growing Cahokia population early in its history.

One aspect of early Cahokia is the widespread presence of craft activities. Raw materials, such as marine shell, chert, basalt, along with finished products, such as chert hoes, and finely crafted ceramics, made their way into Cahokia and the other settlements throughout the region. One of the major craft activities was the production of shell beads. The heaviest concentration of marine shell occurs to the east of Monks Mound. The tools employed in the cutting, grinding, and drilling of the shell are concentrated in two areas of Cahokia—one to the north (Kunnemann) of Monks Mound and the other at the western limits of Cahokia (Powell/Fingerhut)—which have extensive areas of a chert microlithic industry, including microdrills that were employed primarily in the creation of beads. The massive concentration of shell beads in Mound 72 illustrates the symbolic and social significance of these jewels.

Another craft activity represented at Cahokia is the production of basalt celts or axe heads. Evidence of the production of these woodworking tools has been documented at a village area on the west side of the site where the "wood-henges" (see later discussion) were eventually constructed. This production was actually initiated in the later Emergent

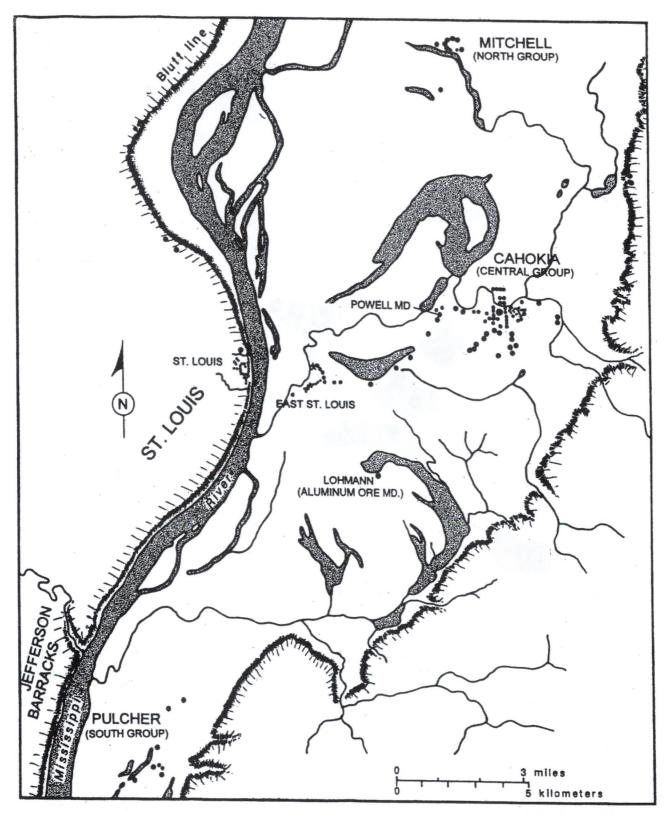

Throughout its 400-year history Cahokia was the ritual, social, and political seat of a polity that stretched at least 20 kilometers in all directions.   [John E. Kelly]

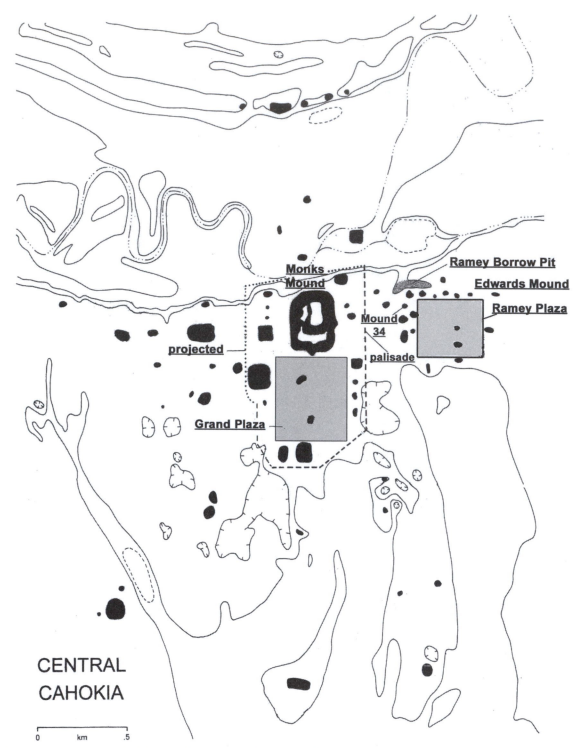

Monks Mound

Ramey Borrow Pit

Edwards Mound

Ramey Plaza

Mound 34

projected

palisade

Grand Plaza

CENTRAL
CAHOKIA

0   km   .5

The Cahokia area toward the end of the twelfth century.   [John E. Kelly]

Mississippian within an earlier episode of the village. Large blocks of basalt were imported from the Ozarks' St. Francis Mountains approximately 90 miles to the southwest. In contrast to the chert hoes that were imported as finished products from sources in southern Illinois, a considerable amount of effort was employed in the acquisition, transport, and manufacture of axe heads. Although they may be considered a utilitarian item used in the cutting and splitting of trees, they were undoubtedly at various times imbued with symbolic importance. Even in the millennia before Cahokia, axes, particularly those of copper, were also items of social power. Groups such as the Omaha recount the use of the axe to fell their sacred tree and reenact the killing of the tree as a man in other ceremonies. Historically, oral traditions such as these provide important analogues for insights into the way in which certain artifacts and elements in the archaeological record can be viewed and interpreted.

Other crafts, such as finely knapped projectile points, ceramic containers with intricate designs, and fireclay figurines, were produced at Cahokia and surrounding communities. The evidence for their production has yet to be identified; nonetheless, these carefully crafted items were undoubtedly the work of skilled artisans. Unlike the case for specialists in other areas of the world, the context of the production sequence may have parallels in the ethnographic record of the Midwest and plains, where important parts of ritual items were produced by different social groups. Societal cohesion was maintained by the involvement of different segments of the community.

Residential houses in the early, Emergent Mississippian years of Cahokia were rectangular, relatively small (about 10 m^2) and built using wooden poles with exterior thatching. They were generally excavated to a depth of 40–100 centimeters below the ground surface. Upright poles 10–15 centimeters in diameter were placed in individually excavated holes to a depth of 30 centimeters and spaced approximately 30 centimeters apart. The walls were interwoven with smaller wooden limbs and then thatched. It is not clear whether the structure roofs were bent-pole and arbor-like or whether they were pitched. While the use of single-pole construction continued into the Mississippian, a new technology was introduced in which the posts were set into a trench dug into the house floor. It is possible that the individual walls were prefabricated and then placed into the trench. Although the size of the residential houses continued to increase, the overall structures were much the same as in previous, pre-Mississippian times. The enlarged houses allowed the placement of interior pits, presumably for storage, and prepared hearths, which were rare to nonexistent during the Emergent Mississippian and early Mississippian occupations.

Cahokia's Stirling phase apogee occurred during the early part of the twelfth century with a significant increase in the construction of monumental architecture. In addition to smaller earthen mounds that supported large wooden buildings, construction included the completion of Monks Mound, with the largest (800 m^2) building placed on its summit. Immediately west of Monks Mound and at the north end of the West Plaza a series of large wooden buildings or enclosures were built. Four post pits aligned to the cardinal directions mark the center of this plaza. Of particular importance is the sequence of circular post monuments or "woodhenges" erected over 1 kilometer west of Monks Mound. It is during this era that crafting activities such as shell bead manufacture were at their height. It is also during this time that the seeds of the Southeastern Ceremonial Complex (SECC) were sown. As the iconographic and cosmologic manifestation of American Indian religion throughout the Mississippian world between AD 1200 and 1500, the artistic and symbolic elements of the SECC were being established in the midcontinent between AD 1000 and 1200.

During Cahokia's peak a distinctive ceramic vessel style known as Ramey Incised became the hallmark of Cahokia. These elaborate decorated jars were found at all levels of Cahokian society. These vessels were also distributed outside Cahokia, primarily throughout the upper Mississippi River valley, with some vessels also found at sites in the lower Mississippi River valley.

Contemporary Stirling phase centers within the Cahokia polity included the East St. Louis mound group and a series of smaller mound centers such as the Lohmann and Horseshoe Lake sites. Small villages were evident in the uplands to the east as part of the Richland complex that began in the late Emergent Mississippian and Early Mississippian episodes. Distributed in the area around Cahokia were numerous farmsteads and specialized ceremonial nodes.

Toward the end of the twelfth century another major disjuncture in the site's history, referred to by James Brown as the Moorehead Moment, occurred that marks the third stage. Mary Beth Trubitt has proposed that as part of the site's reorganization, Cahokia elite employed a new strategy, known as network, at this time. Four major events stand out. First is a noticeable drop in the population at the site and throughout the region. In part this can be linked to the expansion of Mississippian towns and polities in the lower Midwest and Southeast. Although Cahokia supports a smaller population, a large palisade surrounds the site's sacred core of Monks Mound and the Grand Plaza. William Iseminger over the last four decades has documented the extent of the palisade as being nearly 4 kilometers in length and constructed from 20,000 wooden poles. The creation of a new mound and plaza complex known as the Ramey plaza immediately outside of the wall to the east marks the second major event. Covering an area of 10 hectares (about 25 acres), it is the second largest plaza at the site. Of interest is the capping and symbolic burial of many of the mounds in the central portion of the site. Although reduced in size, Cahokia is still the largest Mississippian center, intricately wedded to the rest of the Mississippian world through the SECC.

Ongoing research within the Ramey Plaza has involved a reexamination of Mound 34, a small (less than 3 meter high) earthen edifice at the northwest corner of this complex. The mound is unique in its overall configuration, with a rectangular platform asymmetrically surrounded by four terraces. An unusual array of activities took place related to warfare and hunting, and it reflects an iconography linked to the SECC. Excavations by James B. Griffin and Albert Spaulding in 1950 recovered fragments of an engraved marine shell cup and a repoussé copper fragment. Beneath the mound, investigations by Gregory Perino later in the 1950s documented the presence of a copper workshop. Paul Parmalee, a zoologist, identified numerous animal species, with well over fifty species of birds including numerous raptors such as hawks, owls, and eagles recovered from Perino's work. The current work is in the process of documenting the older excavations and enhancing our understanding of the mound's construction sequence and the context of the materials recovered.

Although Cahokia continued to be occupied well into the fourteenth century, it shrunk steadily in size, with little evidence of mound or other monumental construction. It remained a large center but one more in line with the Mississippian world of the lower Midwest. The time of the site's abandonment as a center is still unclear; however, a concentration of Oneota sites to the southeast within the American Bottom may be the descendants of a mixed population. The region was probably depopulated sometime during the sixteenth century, only to be repopulated by the Illinois, whose homeland is generally considered to the eastern end of Lake Erie. Many Cahokian researchers now regard the Dhegihan-speaking groups such as the Osage as the contemporary descendants. Only time will tell as we try to unravel the mysteries that enshroud this sacred place known today as Cahokia Mounds Historic Site.

In the early twentieth century, efforts of local citizens resulted in the state of Illinois purchasing 144 acres of this site. More recently, additional areas of the site have been given to the park, which has become a World Heritage site and a National Historic Landmark. Today over half of the 5 to 6 square miles that encompass Cahokia is owned by the state of Illinois, including over 60 percent of the 105 mounds within the bounds of the site. Efforts are under way through the Cahokia Mounds Museum Society to augment the existing acreage. Under the former treasurer of Illinois, Judy Baar Topinka, a fund was established to assist in enhancing Cahokia as a World Heritage site through the purchase of additional properties and the formulation of a new Master Management Plan.

Further Reading: Brown, James, and John Kelly, "Cahokia and the Southeastern Ceremonial Complex," in *Mounds, Modoc, and Mesoamerica: Papers in Honor of Melvin L. Fowler*, edited by Steve R. Ahler, *Illinois State Museum Scientific Papers* XXVIII (2000): 469–510; Chappell, Sally A., *Cahokia: Mirror of the Cosmos* (Chicago: University of Chicago Press, 2001.); Dalan, Rinita, George R. Holley, William I. Woods, Harold W. Waters Jr., and John A. Koepke, *Envisioning Cahokia: A Landscape Perspective* (DeKalb: Northern Illinois University Press, 2003); Fowler, Melvin L., *The Cahokia Atlas: A Historical Atlas of Cahokia Archaeology*, rev. ed., Studies in Archaeology No. 2 (Urbana: University of Illinois, 1997); Iseminger, William R., "Mighty Cahokia," *Archaeology* 49 (1996): 30–37; Kelly, John E., "Redefining Cahokia: Principles and Elements of Community Organization," in *The Ancient Skies and Sky Watchers of Cahokia: Woodhenges, Eclipses, and Cahokian Cosmology*, edited by Melvin L. Fowler, *Wisconsin Archeologist* 77 (1996): 97–119; Kelly, John E, ed., "Introduction," in *Cahokia Mounds*, edited by Warren K. Moorehead (Tuscaloosa: University of Alabama Press, 2000), 1–57; Kelly, John E., "The Ritualization of Cahokia: The Structure and Organization of Early Cahokia Crafts," in *Leadership and Polity in Mississippian Society*, edited by Brian M. Butler and Paul D. Welch, Center for Archaeological Investigations, Occasional Paper No. 33 (Carbondale: Southern Illinois University, 2006), 236–263; Kelly, Lucretia S., "A Case of Ritual Feasting at the Cahokia Site," in *Feasts: Archaeological and Ethnographic Perspectives on Food, Politics, and Power*, edited by Michael Dietler and Brian Hayden (Washington, DC: Smithsonian Institution Press, 2001), 334–367; Milner, George R., *The Cahokia Chiefdom: The Archaeology of a Mississippian Society* (Gainesville: University of Florida Press, 2006); Mink, Claudia, *Cahokia: City of the Sun*, rev. ed. (Collinsville, IL: Cahokia Mounds Museum Society, 1999); Pauketat, Timothy R., *Ancient Cahokia and the Mississippians* (Cambridge: Cambridge University Press, 2004); Trubitt, Mary Beth D., "Mound Building and Prestige Goods Exchange: Changing Strategies in the Cahokia Chiefdom," *American Antiquity* 65 (2000): 669–690; Young, Biloine Whiting, and Melvin L. Fowler, *Cahokia: The Great American Metropolis* (Urbana: University of Illinois Press, 2001).

John E. Kelly

DICKSON MOUNDS MUSEUM

Central Illinois River Valley, Illinois

A Late Prehistoric Cemetery

Dickson Mounds is large, late prehistoric cemetery located near the confluence of the Spoon and Illinois rivers in the central Illinois River valley. The site featured a flat-topped, pyramidal, centrally located, charnel house mound surrounded by open cemeteries that were eventually covered over by at least ten individual burial mounds.

Portions of two of these mounds were excavated by chiropractor Don Dickson and relatives between 1927 and 1929, exposing the remains of 248 Late Woodland and Mississippian period burials. These were left in place along with their accompanying grave goods and displayed as part of a public museum under the protection of an enclosed museum building. Dickson and two uncles, who also had carried out pioneering archaeology in the Dickson Mounds area in the early twentieth century, provided daily tours of the excavation. The site was sold to the state of Illinois in 1945 and initially designated as a state park, and later a state memorial. In 1965 the property was transferred to the Illinois State Museum. Although the burial display continued to be the primary feature that brought visitors to the facility, changing public attitudes toward the treatment and display of human skeletal remains resulted in the covering of the burial site and cancellation of public viewing in 1992.

After the Illinois State Museum acquired Dickson Mounds, plans were begun for the construction of an expansive museum at the site that would include modern interpretive exhibits and a research and interpretive center to facilitate archaeological investigations throughout the region. Prior to construction in the late 1960s, archaeologists excavated those areas of the aboriginal cemetery to be covered by the museum. Over 800 burials were discovered, along with a wealth of new information about the people who had used the site. It was determined that the cemetery was first used by early Late Woodland people before AD 800, but that a majority of the estimated 3,000 burials at the site were made by Late Woodland and Mississippian occupations between AD 950 and 1275.

Two different Late Woodland cultural groups, referred to as Sepo and Maples Mill, occupied the Dickson Mounds area early in the history of the site when the primary use of the cemetery was begun. Although Mississippian culture influences, as indicated by certain styles and types of artifacts, had already reached these people by the eleventh century AD, several decades would pass before small numbers of Mississippian people began to spread northward from their great center of Cahokia, near present-day East St. Louis, and settle among the people of the central Illinois River valley. Initially, measurable differences in human cranial morphology (skull shapes and facial characteristics) allowed physical anthropologists to separate skeletal remains of the indigenous Woodland populations from those of the incoming Mississippian group. However, segregation of the cultures did not last. The new arrivals also began using the Dickson cemetery, and over the next three generations, all three groups would bury their dead there together. The common interchange of burial methods and blending of material culture items indicate that these groups readily shared ideas and probably intermarried, eventually forming their own variant of Mississippian culture called Spoon River.

Such rare examples of shared cultural activity and extended site use by succeeding generations provide archaeologists with unparalleled opportunities for documenting salient elements of social accommodation, cultural change, and continuity as indigenous Woodland populations came under the influence of the vibrant Mississippian culture. At first, the most recognizable local forms of this interchange were items of material culture used in daily living—new types of pottery, chipped-stone tools, horticultural equipment, and housing. Soon other elements of the strong Mississippian religious, political, and social organization began to appear and forever change the lives of local Woodland inhabitants. At Dickson Mounds, these changes are vividly reflected by new burial programs and the types of grave goods included with the dead.

Such accommodations indicate that Woodland lives became more structured as new levels of social order evolved in response to the presence of important persons in positions of power. With this social reorganization came a new concept of land ownership and population control. Local populations began to consolidate at larger habitation sites; protective fortifications were thrown up around major ceremonial centers; warfare began to increase; and human sacrifice came to the Illinois River valley. Stark examples of this latter practice appear among the earliest Late Woodland–Mississippian burial areas at Dickson Mounds.

Nonperishable artifacts and treatment of the dead provide the best evidence of how these early people viewed themselves and their positions within the community. An individual's importance in the developing Mississippian society was strongly measured in terms of tangible goods and public recognition. Somewhat surprisingly, important positions within the developing hierarchy were not closed to the indigenous Woodland population. Ceremonial equipment and items depicting status began to appear in the graves of important Woodland and Mississippian individuals. These items were dominated by marine shell pendants and bead necklaces, and beaded body ensembles consisting of forelocks, sashes, bracelets, garters, and anklets. Ear spools were also furnished to important personages, along with discoidals (ground-stone artifacts used in the chunky game), long-nosed god maskettes of marine shell, dance swords, bone hairpins, and various items fashioned from copper. Rather than representing simple ornamentation, these items served as badges of office to set their owners apart from others in the community and probably were in part obtained from Cahokia and other great Mississippian trade centers to the south.

How positions of authority were initially obtained or transferred at death is not fully understood. However, the inclusion of signature items as burial furniture suggests that neither the symbolic importance of the item nor its owner's special position were passed on to others. They obviously were retained for transport into the afterworld.

Certain insights into the achievement of social position within Mississippian society can be investigated by examining the age, sex, and general physical being of individuals buried with status items at Dickson Mounds. Most obvious is that females rarely if ever attained positions of power that rewarded them with important funerary objects. Such objects were reserved for males and male children. Among males, there is no indication that significant social position was ensured by advancing age or physical prowess. Old people received few burial offerings, and grave goods of the many young to middle-age warrior-class males tended to be dominated by simple weaponry and mundane tools. Rather, the interment of important ceremonial equipment with infants and children too young to have ever used them suggests that certain status positions may have been inherited at Dickson Mounds.

Complementing these analyses of cultural organization, detailed physical analyses of the well-preserved skeletal remains have been undertaken. They offer an unusually clear portrait of the physical existence of the Dickson Mounds people, revealing the difficulties they experienced in childbirth; surviving the weaning period and childhood diseases; undergoing periodic nutritional stress; combating chronic physical problems; and experiencing marked male/female differences in surviving to death, which occurred on average by the late 30s.

The studies provide unprecedented information about human adaptability, especially regarding population variability in skeletal shape and form and the examination of changes in health and patterns of diet and disease over time. Population-based studies of these pathological involvements, particularly arthritis and infectious diseases, continue to present researchers with opportunities to directly examine ways in which major changes in lifestyle and societal adjustment relate to these often debilitating conditions. Various trace element and microscopic analyses have provided evidence to support the conclusions generated by visual examination of the skeletal remains. From all of these studies, it became obvious that perceived advances in culture did not necessarily translate to healthier lives. Health deteriorated

over time in response to a variety of factors including, among others, inadequate diet as well as population growth and consolidation.

The diverse research opportunities provided by the Dickson skeletal samples have resulted in the publication of more than eighty substantial publications in a remarkable variety of outlets, from regional archaeological books and journals to volumes read primarily by dentists and physicians (cf. Buikstra and Milner 1989). The studies generated by the investigation of Dickson Mounds provide one of the best-documented records of human existence yet assembled and extend the significance of the site far beyond its base contribution to mid-continental prehistory.

Further Reading: Buikstra, Jane E., and George Milner, *The Dickson Mounds Site: An Annotated Bibliography*, Dickson Mounds Museum Anthropological Studies, Illinois State Museum Reports of Investigations No. 44 (Springfield: Illinois State Museum, 1989); Cobb, Dawn E., and Alan D. Harn, "Bioarchaeological Analyses of Special-Purpose Graves from Kingston Lake, Dickson Mounds, and Cahokia: New Perspectives on Programmed Death in Illinois," *Illinois Archaeology* 14 (2005): 41-72; Harn, Alan D., "Cahokia and the Mississippian Emergence in the Spoon River Area of Illinois," *Transactions of the Illinois State Academy of Science* 68(4) (1975): 414–434; Harn, Alan D., *The Prehistory of Dickson Mounds: The Dickson Excavation*, Dickson Mounds Museum Anthropological Studies No. 1 (rev. ed.), Illinois State Museum Reports of Investigations No. 35 (Springfield: Illinois State Museum, 1980); . Harn, Alan D., "The Eveland Site: Inroad to Spoon River Mississippian Society," in *New Perspectives on Cahokia: Views from the Periphery*, edited by James B. Stoltman (Madison, WI: Prehistory Press, 1991).

Alan D. Harn

THE CITY OF MOUNDS

East St. Louis, Illinois, and St. Louis, Missouri
Ancient Sites in the Center of America

Among the numerous Mississippian mound centers in the greater St. Louis metropolitan region two pre-Columbian communities, the St. Louis and East St. Louis sites, were on opposite sides of the Mississippi River. The East St. Louis mound group was located on the floodplain within a kilometer of the river and the St. Louis group was on the bluff above the river. Like the largest center in the Mississippian world, Cahokia, both the East St. Louis and St. Louis mound groups were composed of large earthen mounds. The mounds associated with

the St. Louis group were removed from the St. Louis landscape by the end of the nineteenth century by historic period development of this urban center. A similar fate awaited many of the mounds in the East St. Louis group; however, given the site's location on the Mississippi river floodplain and the nature of development, much of the site, including a number of mounds, survives today within an urban environment.

The St. Louis mound group was initially portrayed on the early maps of the region at the end of the eighteenth and

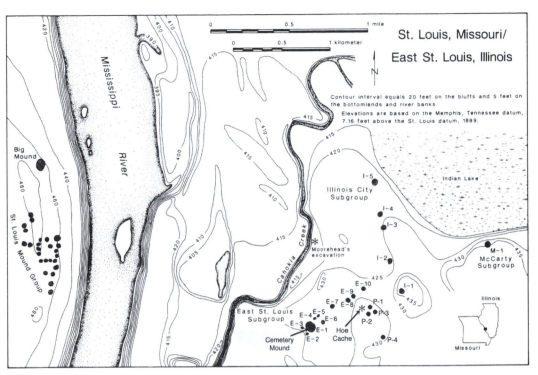

A map of the City of Mounds.   [John E. Kelly]

beginning of the nineteenth centuries as being located just north of the original French village. The first description of the group along with a description of Cahokia and East St. Louis was by Henry Marie Brackenridge in January 1811 as a series of unsigned newspaper articles in the *Louisiana Gazette*. Three years later the articles were published with some modification in Brackenridge's book *Views from Louisiana*. The first detailed map of any of the mound groups in the region was that of the St. Louis mound group and was completed in 1819 by Thomas Say and Titian Peale when they visited the city as part of the Stephen Long expedition. Using a compass and tape they recorded twenty-five mounds, measuring each mound's dimensions and distance from adjacent mounds. Fifteen mounds composed the central group, which defined a rectangular plaza covering 2.7 hectares (nearly 7 acres). In addition to the main group five mounds were located to the south, including a rectangular terraced earthen monument described as the "Falling Garden." Another four mounds were located just northwest of the main group. The largest mound associated with this complex was located nearly 600 meters north of the main group and was referred to as "La Grange de Terre" by the French inhabitants of St. Louis. Most of the information on the group was derived from a few artifacts recovered from this unique mortuary monument, known later as the "Big Mound." It was comparable in size and shape to two other large mortuary monuments, the Powell Mound at Cahokia and the Cemetery Mound in East St. Louis, measuring nearly 100 meters by 60 meters with a height of 13 meters.

Although efforts to preserve the mounds as a park in St. Louis were initiated in the 1830s and 1840s by local citizens, this did not happen. In part this was due to an ongoing debate within the St. Louis Academy of Science as to whether the mound was a natural feature or indeed constructed by the earlier Indian inhabitants. In the meantime a tavern was constructed on the mound's summit, lasting a few years before it burned. Regardless of the debate, by the 1850s the destruction of the Big Mound was under way. Thomas Easterly undertook documentation of the Big Mound's removal in the form of daguerreotypes. Toward the end of the mound's removal a large tomb with two individuals was uncovered. Among the few items recovered were two copper long-nosed god maskettes. These are linked to a Midwestern Siouan culture hero known as "He-who-wears-human-heads-as-earrings" or "Red-horn," and in turn are part of a horizon marker dating to the eleventh and twelfth centuries throughout much of the Midwest and Southeast. It is not clear how this mound is linked to the main mound group. We have little evidence in the form of artifactual materials from the main group that provides a date for the group.

Compared with the St. Louis group, the East St. Louis mound group has more information and is in part better preserved. Brackenridge noted that forty-five to fifty mounds were distributed in a semicircle over a mile in extent facing Cahokia Creek. A map of the group was produced by the Belleville, Illinois, dentist and collector Dr. John J. R. Patrick

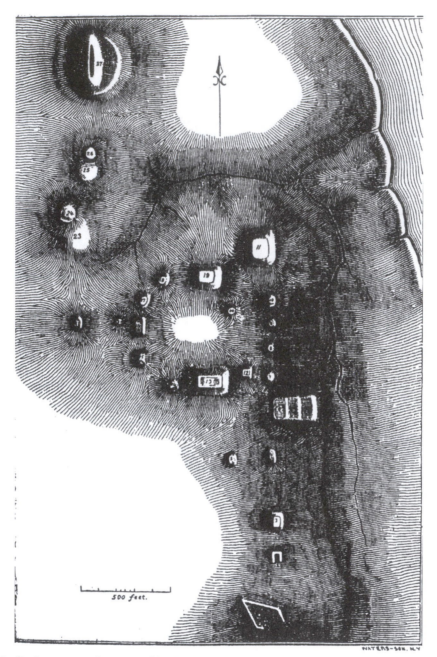

An early rendering of the St. Louis mound group.   [St. Louis Public Library]

shortly after the Civil War. At that time fifteen mounds were evident. Like St. Louis's Big Mound, the large Cemetery Mound was removed as part of the process of building the levees during the historic period in the newly incorporated city of East St. Louis. Again tombs were observed during the mound's destruction. Materials recovered suggest a date as late as the thirteenth century for the original construction of this ancient mound. Moorehead's investigations within the city in the 1920s documented intact deposits. This informa-

tion was ignored when the interstate highway began construction in the 1960s. It wasn't until the late 1980s and early 1990s that it became apparent that much of the site was intact, including mounds not on the Patrick map.

Investigations through the heart of the Mound group as part of a highway widening project in the 1990s have produced detailed information on a number of mounds not previously recorded as well as the remnants of others. At this time analysis indicates that construction of the main group of ancient

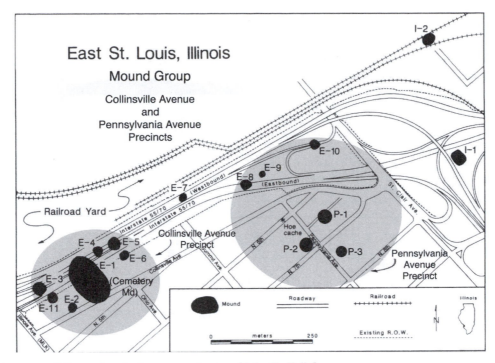

The Collinsview Avenue and Pennsylvania Avenue precincts.   [John E. Kelly]

mounds dates from the end of the eleventh century into the beginning of the thirteenth century. It has been possible to delineate at least three areas within the groups as distinct areas of occupation. The Collinsville Avenue precinct, an area where most of the investigations have taken place, includes the Cemetery Mound along with a plaza that extends across the interstate. Several of the mounds are low platforms with large buildings placed on their summits. Beneath the Cemetery Mound a number of unique buildings and enclosures have been documented, including the placement of square poles. Numerous (over thirty) large posts were placed in this area of the site as important symbolic markers. Toward the end of the twelfth century a palisade was erected complete with a ditch on the outside. Within the palisaded area numerous small rectangular structures were identified, many with evidence of burning and ceramic vessels and tools left behind.

Some 400 meters east of this area is another contemporary area of mounds and occupation, the Pennsylvania Avenue precinct. The mounds are relatively small, less than a meter in height. More limited excavations have revealed evidence of a borrow pit and a number of specialized structures involved in production of chert blades, presumably for the manufacture of arrow points. This area is near three pits uncovered during the grading of a street in the period following the Civil War and reported on by Charles Rau of the Smithsonian Institution. The pits consisted of a cache of over

seventy Mill Creek chert hoes. The dozen or so that have been examined to date are notched and show little evidence of use. The other pits consisted of marine shell and "greenstone" boulders.

Although the site is located in an urban environment at the intersections of interstate highways and railroads, significant portions remain intact. Those portions of the site still preserved include the undisturbed areas behind and between buildings and in the alleyways. When new buildings were constructed at the end of the nineteenth century, the spoil from digging the basement was often placed on the ground surface behind the building, often to a depth of nearly a meter. This has resulted in the covering over and preservation of large areas of the site. Efforts to preserve the site have been under way since the mid-1990s by the local groups, such as the Powell Archaeological Research Center, and the larger national group the Archaeological Conservancy. Portions of the Collinsville Avenue and Pennsylvania Avenue precinct are now preserved due to these modern efforts and these will hopefully one day provide the foundation for an area of green space that will extend from the downtown area of East St. Louis to the Katherine Dunham Museum.

Further Reading: Brown, James, and John E. Kelly, "Cahokia and the Southeastern Ceremonial Complex," in *Mounds, Modoc, and Mesoamerica: Papers in Honor of Melvin L. Fowler,* edited by Steve

R. Ahler, Scientific Papers Vol. XXVIII (Springfield: Illinois State Museum, 2000), 469–510; Chappell, Sally A., *Cahokia: Mirror of the Cosmos* (Chicago: University of Chicago Press, 2001); Dalan, Rinita, George R. Holley, William I. Woods, Harold W. Waters Jr., and John A. Koepke, *Envisioning Cahokia: A Landscape Perspective* (DeKalb: Northern Illinois University Press, 2003); Fowler, Melvin L., *The Cahokia Atlas: A Historical Atlas of Cahokia Archaeology*, rev. ed., Studies in Archaeology No. 2 (Urbana: University of Illinois, 1997); Kelly, John E., "Redefining Cahokia: Principles and Elements of Community Organization," in *The Ancient Skies and Sky Watchers of Cahokia: Woodhenges, Eclipses, and Cahokian Cosmology*, edited by Melvin L. Fowler, *Wisconsin Archeologist* 77(3–4) (1996): 97–119; Kelly, John E., "Introduction," in *Cahokia Mounds*, by Warren K. Moorehead (Tuscaloosa: University of Alabama Press, 2000), 1–57; Milner, George R., *The Cahokia Chiefdom: The Archaeology of a Mississippian Society*, (Washington, DC: Smithsonian Institution Press, 1998); Pauketat, Timothy R., *Ancient Cahokia and the Mississippians* (Cambridge: Cambridge University Press, 2004); Trubitt, Mary Beth D., "Mound Building and Prestige Goods Exchange: Changing Strategies in the Cahokia Chiefdom," *American Antiquity* 65(4) (2000): 669–690; Young, Biloine Whiting, and Melvin L. Fowler, *Cahokia: The Great American Metropolis* (Urbana: University of Illinois Press, 2001).

John E. Kelly

THE KINCAID SITE

Lower Ohio River Valley, Southern Illinois
A Political and Religious Mississippian Center

Kincaid is one of the two paramount centers of Mississippian culture in the lower Ohio valley from the period of around AD 1000 to 1450. The site consists of two major mound groups, associated plazas, and habitation areas that cover more than 150 acres. Kincaid was the political and religious center of a large Native American society based in the Black Bottom, an extensive alluvial bottomland of the Ohio River situated between the confluences of the Cumberland and Tennessee rivers with the Ohio. The site is just upstream from Paducah, Kentucky. The Kincaid political system also included numerous small villages and farmsteads dispersed in the surrounding bottomlands along the river and in the adjacent uplands.

The Kincaid site is situated on the north bank of Avery Lake, a narrow back channel remnant located about a half mile from the Ohio River. The site is divided by the north-south boundary between Massac and Pope counties, so different parts of the site have different county designations. The site has a central mound and plaza group with five major platform mounds surrounding a plaza of about 10 acres. The largest of these mounds by volume, Mx 8, measures roughly 370 by 250 feet at the base, and it also the tallest, at 30 feet. Mx 10, a long east-west mound that forms the north edge of the plaza, has the largest footprint, measuring roughly 500 by 216 feet at the base, but it is lower, with most of it being only 16 to 21 feet high. This mound is unusual in having a large conical addition at its west end, one of only a small number of Mississippian platform mounds to exhibit such a feature. About 600 yards to the east (in Pope County) is a group of six smaller mounds, whose largest (Pp 6) is 12 feet high. A number of additional small mounds exist within the site, but these

have not been investigated and most of them have been substantially reduced by plowing, making their identification uncertain.

The land surface is a subtle terrain of swales and low alluvial ridges, and some areas within the site are too low and wet to be inhabited. Large habitation areas extend west of the main plaza on the ridge crests and presumably also to the east, but that portion of the site is poorly known. At some point in time, large portions of the site were fortified with a wooden palisade with bastions; some portions of the wall were supported by an earthen embankment. The palisade ran along the rim of a deep swale that defines the limits of the site to the north and also extended along the lakefront to the south. Portions of the northern palisade are visible on pre-1937 aerial photographs, and a recent geophysical survey has verified its western side. The path of the palisade on the eastern side of the site is not clear, and current representations are speculative.

The Kincaid name comes from the family who owned portions of the site for over 100 years. The Kincaid house, erected around 1875, stood on Mx 8 until about 1950. The site is primarily known through the efforts of University of Chicago archaeologists, who worked at the site from 1934 to 1944. The Chicago work focused on the larger mounds and the village areas west of the main plaza. Little work was done in the eastern part of the site. In the 1970s and 1980s Jon Muller of Southern Illinois University at Carbondale (SUIC) documented the surrounding settlements in the Black Bottom in great detail but did not conduct formal excavations at Kincaid. In 2003 SIUC archaeologists Brian Butler and Paul Welch began new work at the site.

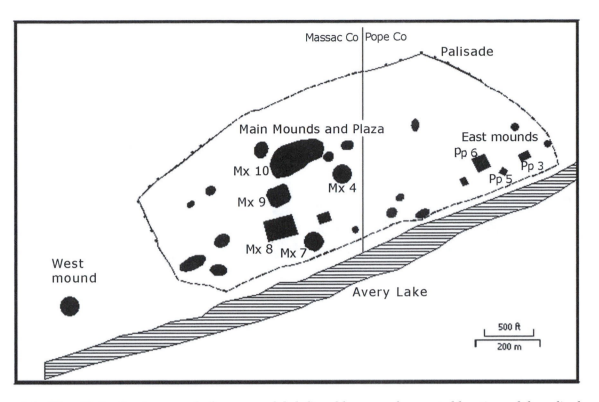

Plan map of the Kincaid site showing mounds (larger ones labeled) and known and suspected locations of the palisade. [Paul D. Welch]

Because most of the work at the site pre-dates reliable radiocarbon dating, the internal chronology of the site is poorly understood. Mound construction seems to have started on the main plaza around AD 1000, as the site developed rapidly from a cluster of terminal Late Woodland settlements around Avery Lake. The site reached its peak of complexity, and presumably political power, in the 1200s, which is also the period in which most of the Mississippian settlements in the Black Bottom around Kincaid flourished. Almost nothing is known of the eastern mound group, so its role in the site's history is unclear; but a burial mound the Chicago team excavated in this group does appear to have interments spanning most of the site's occupation.

Recent work has documented a mound and habitation areas west of the previously recognized site core, outside of the western palisade. A single low (ca. 3 ft) platform mound, called the West Mound, has now been identified about 1,100 yards west of the main plaza.

Although artifacts recovered from the site indicate contacts with groups in the American Bottom, including Cahokia to the north, the lower Mississippi valley to the south, and upstream in the Ohio Valley, Kincaid was an independent political center that sat astride important river routes for communication and trade. At its peak, Kincaid's political influence likely extended to near the mouth of the Ohio River and upstream to the Wabash confluence. The pottery styles at Kincaid are closely related to those further upstream at Angel site, in the lower Tennessee and Cumberland valleys, and in southeast Missouri, but they are not the same as those in the American Bottom.

Beginning around 1300, there are indications of important political and social changes in Mississippian society in the lower Ohio valley. Large-scale mound construction ceased, and Kincaid seems to have declined as a major center. Habitation areas appeared to shift location and decrease in size, and at some point, burials were placed in the tops of some of the platform mounds, something not previously done. A series of small mound centers emerged along the Ohio River, a process that may reflect the breakdown of centralized political authority at Kincaid. But not just at Kincaid. Mississippian culture over a large region, encompassing portions of the Ohio, Mississippi, Tennessee, and Cumberland valleys, was in decline. Kincaid and much of this region, sometimes called the Vacant Quarter, appear to have been largely abandoned between 1450 and 1500.

In 1975 the State of Illinois purchased most of the western part of the site, which is now managed by the Illinois Historic

A view northwest across the plaza at the Kincaid site showing geophysical survey work underway. Left to right, the mounds are Mx 7, Mx 8, and Mx 9.   [Brian M. Butler]

Preservation Agency and a local support group. The site is undeveloped and large parts of the state land are cultivated for crops, but there is a roadside viewing area with interpretive signage at the southern edge of the main plaza on the lakefront.

Further Reading: Clay, R. Berle, "The Mississippian Succession on the Lower Ohio," *Southeastern Archaeology* 16 (1997): 16–32; Cobb, Charles R., and Brian M. Butler, "The Vacant Quarter Revisited: Late Mississippian Abandonment of the Lower Ohio Valley," *American Antiquity* 67 (2002): 625–642; Cole, Fay-Cooper, Robert Bell, John Bennett, Joseph Caldwell, Norman Emerson, Richard MacNeish, Kenneth Orr, and Roger Willis, *Kincaid, a Prehistoric Illinois Metropolis* (Chicago: University of Chicago Press, 1951); Muller, Jon D., *Archaeology of the Lower Ohio River Valley* (Orlando, FL: Academic Press, 1986), chaps. 6, 7.

Brian M. Butler

THE MILL CREEK CHERT QUARRIES

Southwestern Illinois

Source of Widely Traded Mississippian Period Hoes

Stone hoes manufactured from Mill Creek chert were one of the most heavily traded items in the prehistoric Midwest. The raw material for these implements was procured through an extensive system of quarries found in southwestern Illinois in the mid-continental United States. Although the quarries have not been directly dated, the sites where the hoes made from this raw material have been found date to throughout the Mississippian period, or about AD 1000–1500. The prevalence of Mill Creek chert hoes at villages and towns throughout the lower Ohio and central Mississippi river valleys emphasizes the importance of these tools to the lifeways of Mississippian farmers. Furthermore, the scale of chert

Example of Mill Creek chert hoe. [Courtesy of the Center for Archaeological Investigations, Southern Illinois University, Carbondale]

extraction, and of stone tool manufacture and exchange, have often been taken as indicators of complex mechanisms of political and economic organization.

The Mississippian period in the eastern United States was marked by a dramatic increase in the size of Native American towns, the widespread construction of earthen mounds, and the adoption of maize agriculture. Many of the towns appear to have been gathered into larger political units, referred to as "chiefdoms," overseen by individuals or groups with some degree of authority and ritual power. The accounts of European explorers in the early 1500s described large fields of maize and other cultivated plants (in particular, beans and squash) supporting chiefdoms that included populations numbering in the thousands of individuals. These historical accounts also refer to Native Americans working their fields with hoes that were very similar to those used by Europeans. In contrast to metal European tools, however, Native American hoe blades in the east typically were made of large shells or stone. Although shell does not preserve as well as stone, the sheer abundance of the remnants of Mill Creek chert hoes suggests that this raw material was highly desired for digging implements. Hoes made

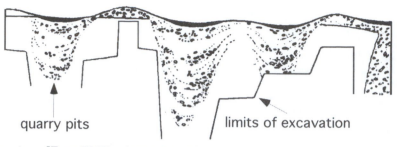

quarry pits   limits of excavation

Excavation profile of quarry pits.   [From Phillips (1900), Fig. 3]

from Mill Creek chert are relatively large, measuring up to 60 centimeters in length, and typically display a heavy gloss on the bit end. The gloss was likely caused by friction with the soil.

The Mill Creek chert quarries first came to widespread attention in the late nineteenth century. At that time, archaeologists from the Field Museum of Natural History and the Smithsonian Institution conducted excavations at the largest quarry in southwestern Illinois and at nearby workshop sites. Their reports reflect astonishment at the scale of the quarries and the amount of debris from tool manufacture dispersed across the landscape. The main quarry is characterized by hundreds of bowl-shaped depressions up to 3 meters in diameter. These extend over two ridge systems, covering an area of about 6 to 7 hectares. Excavations by the Field Museum through several of the quarry pits revealed that they ranged from 2 to 6 meters in depth. Although these are relatively deep, they do not seem to represent true shafts and the level of technological expertise associated with mining. Nevertheless, it is evident that prehistoric groups made a considerable effort to extract chert nodules from mantles of clay that capped the local ridge systems.

Eastern North America is extremely rich in cherts (stone primarily composed of silica whose extremely fine-grained structure allowed skillful stoneworkers to chip this raw material into a variety of shapes) that are amenable to the crafting of tools, but relatively few of these raw material types were selected for large digging implements. Of these, Mill Creek chert appears to have become popular for several reasons. First, the nodules are naturally found in large numbers throughout the upland ridges of a region covering about 10 kilometers in diameter. Second, the nodule itself is typically oval with a thin cross section; this shape makes it a natural preform for a hoe, requiring the removal of relatively little raw material to create a finished implement. Third, the large size of the nodules makes it possible to form similarly large digging implements. Finally, Mill Creek chert is a durable and grainy raw material. Although it is not as suitable as some other stone raw materials (such as obsidian) for creating tools with very sharp edges, it is a good choice for tools that can function well even with considerable battering.

While hoes were by far the primary product of the quarries, a variety of other tools were manufactured and traded as well. These included utilitarian forms such as chisels and picks, and prestige objects such as large Ramey knives, large spatulate celts, and maces.

For decades, the Mill Creek chert quarries were thought to be a prime example of the development of craft specialization, which reflected the emergence of highly complex forms of political and economic organization during the Mississippian period. The presence of a small mound center (the Hale site), about 1.5 kilometers southeast of the main quarry system, further supported the idea of some form of directed or centralized production. Excavations at the Hale site by the Smithsonian Institution in the 1800s recovered large amounts of hoe-manufacturing debris, leading to the idea that elites at the Hale site oversaw the extraction of chert at the quarry, and the subsequent production and exchange of stone tools.

Despite their recognized importance, no professional investigations were conducted in the vicinity of the quarries until the 1980s and 1990s. Archaeological reconnaissance demonstrated that there were several smaller quarries and at least one other sizable habitation in the region, known as Dillow's Ridge. Furthermore, a number of hoe manufacturing workshops were located in the floodplains of the local drainages, some of which also appeared to contain habitation debris. Excavations at Dillow's Ridge uncovered enormous amounts of hoe production debris around the village, but tool production estimates suggest that they could easily have been manufactured part-time by farming families. This evidence, in conjunction with a widespread rather than centralized distribution of source areas and workshops, has led archaeologists to argue that production and exchange of hoes were probably dispersed and autonomous, rather than monopolized by an elite segment of society. Nevertheless, the so-called main quarry is several times larger than the more recently discovered ones, suggesting that it was a preferred Mill Creek chert source for reasons that remain unknown. Local Mississippian communities continuously exploited the raw material from this location for four to five centuries, creating one of the more impressive quarry complexes in North America.

The primary Mill Creek chert quarries are located on private property and are not open to visitation.

Further Reading: Cobb, Charles R., *From Quarry to Cornfield: The Political Economy of Mississippian Hoe Production* (Tuscaloosa: University of Alabama Press, 2000); Muller, Jon, *Mississippian Political Economy* (New York: Plenum Press, 1997); Phillips, William A., "Aboriginal Quarries and Shops at Mill Creek, Illinois," *American Anthropologist* 2 (1900): 37–52; Winters, Howard D., "Excavating in Museums: Notes on Mississippian Hoes and Middle Woodland Copper Gouges and Celts," in *The Research Potential of Anthropological Museum Collections*, Vol. 376, edited by Anne-Marie E. Cantwell, James B. Griffin, and Nan A. Rothschild (New York: Annals of the New York Academy of Sciences, 1981), 17–34.

Charles R. Cobb

POWERS FORT AND OTHER MIDDLE MISSISSIPPIAN SITES

Southeastern Missouri

Social Organization Among Middle Mississippian Sites

Sites that belong to what archaeologists refer to as the Powers phase occur on low sandy ridges extending across 300 square kilometers of the Little Black River lowland of southeastern Missouri. Powers phase sites date to around AD 1250–1400, a time span referred to by archaeologists as the Mississippian period. At the top of the Powers phase settlement hierarchy was Powers Fort, which had an embankment and ditch enclosing an area of about 4.4 hectares (about 11 acres), a central plaza flanked by four mounds, and perhaps several hundred houses. At the second level were at least ten large villages that ranged in size from 0.6 hectares to over a hectare (one hectare equals 2.4 acres) and contained perhaps 40–130 houses. At the third level were smaller villages, or hamlets, each under 0.4 hectares in area and containing roughly a dozen houses. At the fourth level were small one- or two-house farmsteads and other resource procurement sites.

With the exception of Powers Fort, the communities in this area during this time period appear to have been occupied for short durations, perhaps on the order of five to ten years. Most Powers phase structures burned, either accidentally or through deliberate firing, and their remains subsequently were preserved in the shallow basins in which the structures were erected. Burned Mississippian houses are not unique to southeastern Missouri; what sets the Powers phase sites apart is the state of preservation of the structures and related artifact-bearing deposits. Locating the sites on large sand ridges connected with Pleistocene-age braided-stream channels of the Mississippi River—logical places for habitation and agriculture in a low-lying region susceptible to frequent flooding—ensured their survival. Coarse sediments, constantly reworked by wind and rain, spread over the sites from higher-elevation areas on the ridge network and created an effective barrier against erosion and destruction from historic period agricultural plowing and disking.

The University of Michigan conducted a study of the sites in the late 1960s and 1970s. Objectives of the project included locating all traces of settlement within a 15-kilometer radius of Powers Fort, defining the size of each community in the Powers phase hierarchy, and determining the range of activities carried out at each site. Sites in each size class were selected for either test excavation or large-scale block excavation. A key component of the project was the almost total excavation of two large villages, Turner and Snodgrass, which lie approximately 160 meters apart and 5 kilometers southeast of Powers Fort, and a two-house farmstead, Gypsy Joint, located approximately 3 kilometers south-southwest of Powers Fort.

Turner and Snodgrass contained forty-five and ninety-three structures, respectively, along with hundreds of pits inside and outside of the houses. Although the two villages looked similar in many respects, they differed in important ways. Snodgrass was surrounded by a fortification ditch and had what the excavators labeled an interior "white-clay wall" that divided the village into two segments, whereas Turner had no wall and no encircling ditch. Turner, however, contained a well-defined cemetery area containing 118 children and adults interred in 54 graves, whereas with a few exceptions the only burials at Snodgrass were those of infants placed beneath house floors.

The notion that Powers phase communities—and presumably the larger social group comprising the inhabitants of all the communities—were segmented has also been proposed for Mississippian societies throughout much of the eastern United States. At some sites, especially the larger ones, there are discernible differences in such things as burial treatment and the kinds of objects and foodstuffs to which households had access. At an even more visible level, the earthen mounds that are ubiquitous at Mississippian centers were not erected without concerted effort and direction: Someone had

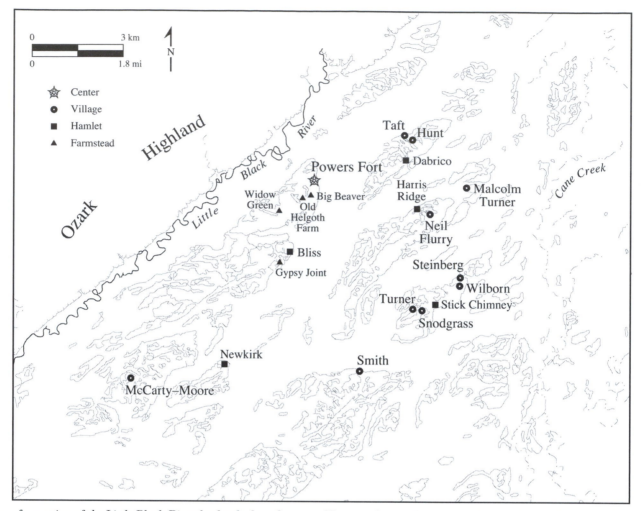

Map of a portion of the Little Black River lowland of southeastern Missouri showing locations of Powers Fort, villages, hamlets, and farmsteads.   [Michael J. O'Brien]

to coordinate the effort and ensure that the job was completed, and it is difficult to imagine that that someone was not of a different status relative to those whose efforts were being coordinated.

The difficulty lies in deciding what the precise nature of those status differences were. As yet there is no indisputable evidence for status differentiation at any Powers phase site. Certainly some individual leader, or several leaders, coordinated and oversaw construction of the mounds and fortification features at Powers Fort, but analysis of artifact distributions and burial treatment fails to highlight any differences that might reflect such differences in status. Analysis of artifacts that actually occurred on structure floors as opposed to artifacts that were deposited in structure basins after the houses burned shows that there was a tendency for structures located within the white-clay wall at Snodgrass—once proposed to be an elite segment of the village—to have disproportionately more artifacts than those located outside the wall,

but there is nothing in the distributions to suggest status differences.

Significantly, comparisons of artifact assemblages from all excavated Powers phase communities, including Powers Fort, demonstrate no significant differences in composition from one locality to another. Households at all levels were organized around activities such as cooking, food storage, and tool manufacture and maintenance, as evidenced in the repetitive nature of the artifact inventories. Pottery is ubiquitous in primary refuse from structure floors, as it is in secondary refuse originally deposited in open structure basins. The same applies to stone debris from the manufacture of arrow points, hoes, and other implements. Nor are there signs in animal remains that would indicate that foodstuffs were differentially distributed either among communities or among households within a community.

An intriguing question has to do with the place and date of origin of the people who built and occupied Powers Fort and

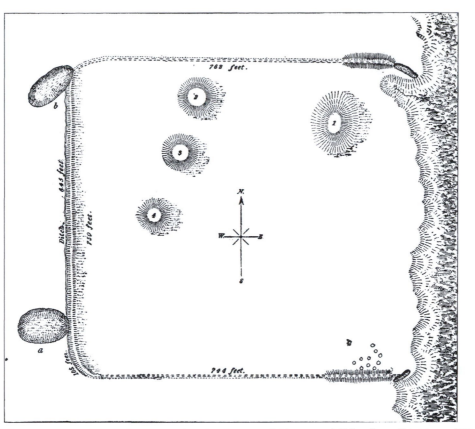

Plan map of Powers Fort, made by Col. P. W. Norris for the Bureau of (American) Ethnology, Division of Mound Exploration. Norris excavated in all four mounds, uncovering burials and artifacts. Although Thomas showed the embankments oriented to the cardinal directions, there is reason to believe the orientation is incorrect.   [Bureau of Ethnology]

its outlying communities. Were they colonizers from other parts of the central Mississippi River valley—perhaps the Malden Plain to the east—or were they the direct descendants of groups who had resided in and around the Little Black River lowland for generations? Few if any clues are provided by the archaeological assemblages from the lowlands of southeastern Missouri. In other words, when one compares the artifact assemblages from Powers phase sites to what appear to be contemporary assemblages from other sites in southeastern Missouri, few discernible differences are evident.

The most promising clue to the origin of the Powers phase phenomenon lies in a comparison of the chemical composition of raw clays and pottery from the eastern Ozark Highland to the west and clays and pottery from the Little Black River Lowland. Analysis demonstrates conclusively that between AD 700 and 1000 vessels made from clays found in the lowland were moving up into the Ozark highland valleys of the Little Black, Current, Jack's Fork, and Eleven Point rivers, in some cases over distances of up to 135 kilometers. If this kind of centuries-long connection existed between groups in the Ozark highland and those in

the Little Black River lowland, it is not much of a stretch to view the highland as contributing part of the population that built Powers Fort and the other Powers phase communities.

The reason for the population shift out of the Ozark highland sometime during the thirteenth century is unknown. By that time a number of fortified mound centers had begun to spring up in the lowlands to the east. At present, we do not know much about the social and political landscape of southeastern Missouri during the thirteenth century, but the settlement reorganization that took place—some degree of nucleation, presumably for defensive reasons—attests to the disintegration of the political climate. How one chooses to answer the questions of why the fortified centers arose and what the mound construction tells us in terms of how people organized themselves socially and politically is open, but it is clear that by at least AD 1250–1275 the landscape in southeastern Missouri had changed dramatically in terms of settlement organization.

All Powers phase sites are on private land, although Powers Fort is owned by the Archaeological Conservancy and can be visited with permission.

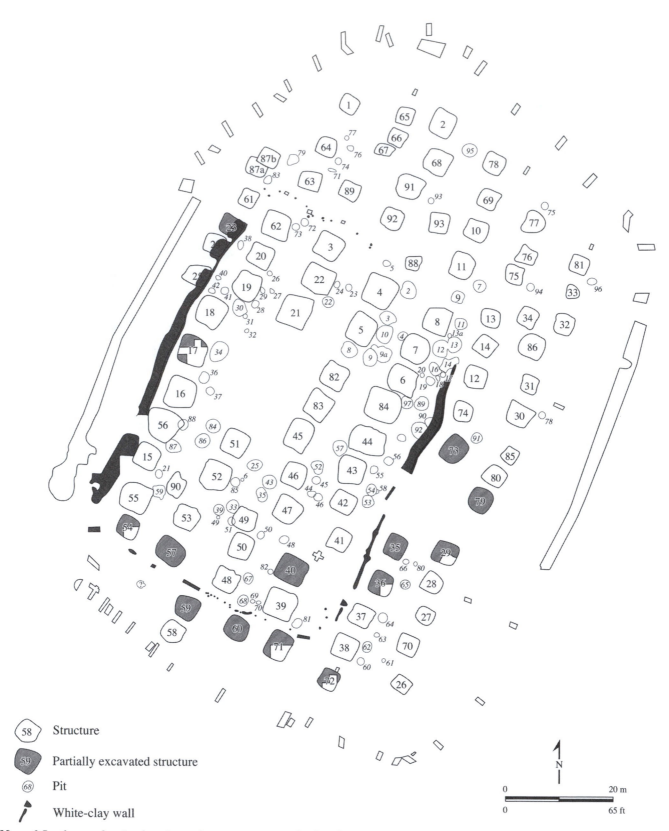

Structure

Partially excavated structure

Pit

White-clay wall

Map of Snodgrass showing locations of structures, pits, the fortification ditch, and what was identified during excavation as the "white-clay wall." [Michael J. O'Brien]

Further Reading: O'Brien, Michael J., *Mississippian Community Organization: The Powers Phase in Southeastern Missouri* (New York: Kluwer Academic/Plenum, 2001); Perttula, Timothy K., "Powers Fort: A Middle Mississippian-Period Fortified Community in the Western Lowland of Missouri," in *Changing Perspectives on the Archaeology of the Central Mississippi River Valley*, edited by Michael J. O'Brien and Robert C. Dunnell (Tuscaloosa: University of Alabama Press, 1998), 169–199; Price, James E., and James B. Griffin, *The Snodgrass Site of the Powers Phase of Southeast Missouri*, Anthropological Papers, No. 66 (Ann Arbor: University of Michigan, Museum of Anthropology, 1979); Smith, Bruce D., *Prehistoric Patterns of Human Behavior: A Case Study in the Mississippi Valley* (New York: Academic Press, 1978); Thomas, C., "Report on the Mound Explorations of the Bureau of Ethnology," *Bureau of Ethnology, Annual Report* 12 (1894): 3–742.

Michael J. O'Brien

TOWOSAHGY STATE HISTORIC SITE AND OTHER LARGE MISSISSIPPIAN SITES

Southeastern Missouri

Fortified Mississippian Villages in Missouri's Bootheel

The lowlands of southeastern Missouri have long been of interest to archaeologists and artifact collectors because of the hundreds of earthen mounds that dot the landscape and the beautifully crafted pottery they often contain. Mounds in southeastern Missouri were in use as burial structures since at least 600 BC and for use as building platforms since at least AD 600. Sometime after AD 900, and probably closer to AD 1100, a dozen or more large fortified centers appeared across the lowlands—at least eleven in the eastern lowlands and one (Powers Fort) in the western lowlands. The centers reached their zenith sometime between AD 1300 and 1350, after which they were abandoned.

Four of the centers—Sikeston, East Lake, Matthews, and Lilbourn—are located on Sikeston Ridge, a high deposit of ancient sediments that, prior to the beginning of the twentieth century, provided relief from the swampy terrain on either side. Three other fortified centers—Crosno, Sandy Woods, and Towosahgy (known historically as Beckwith's Fort)—are located on smaller, well-draining landforms in the Cairo lowland, a bulge of variously aged sediments that extends from the base of Sikeston Ridge east to the Mississippi River.

Excavation of the fortified sites began with the nineteenth-century work of Thomas Beckwith, George C. Swallow, and others and continued through expeditions by the Academy of Science of St. Louis under the direction of W. B. Potter and by Cyrus Thomas's Bureau of (American) Ethnography (at the time a part of the Smithsonian Institution) crews in the 1880s. It was Potter's work that tells us the most about the early state of the fortified sites, all of which have been highly modified by farming and modern construction. Potter's maps in some cases provide the only evidence that the communities were fortified, because erosion and agricultural activities have subsequently destroyed embankments and ditches. Potter also plotted locations of mounds, house basins, and larger depressions that resulted from the removal of soil for use in mound construction. Apparent in Potter's descriptions is the fact that mounds served different purposes—some were burial mounds and others were substructure mounds for buildings. For example, several of the larger mounds at Sandy Woods were said to contain nothing, whereas two of the mounds, both of which had been looted over a period of years, were estimated to have produced 800–1,000 ceramic vessels and 100–200 human skeletons.

More recent archaeological work has included major excavations at Crosno, Matthews, Lilbourn, and Towosahgy. Crosno was once represented by one large mound and three small mounds located within a rectangular embankment on the edge of a wide former channel of the Mississippi River. Archaeological excavations have shown that prehistoric houses at Crosno were similar to those at other Mississippian sites in southeastern Missouri. Rectangular to square houses were constructed in either shallow basins or on unmodified surfaces, and usually upright posts were driven into the bottom of a wall trench.

The Matthews site, almost no traces of which remain, was located on the western edge of Sikeston Ridge, a few kilometers south and on the opposite side of the ridge from the East Lake site. The walled-and-ditched settlement was the focus of numerous examinations over the years, and taken together the work gives us a fairly detailed picture of the internal arrangement of the 9-hectare site. There were at least seven mounds within the enclosure and, if Potter's count is anywhere near accurate, several hundred "hut rings." Croswell noted that 300 burials came from Mound B and that they were stacked in layers. At least one other mound contained burials. Later excavators cross-sectioned the defensive enclosure and found

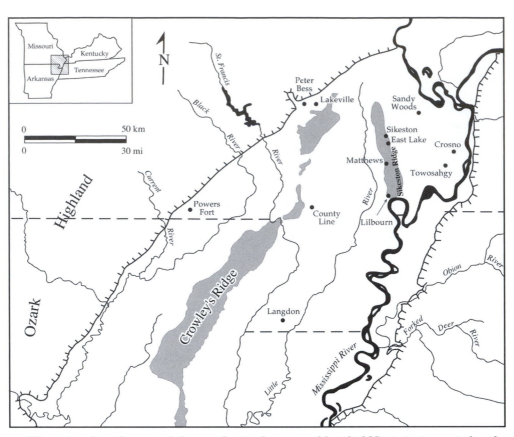

Map of southeastern Missouri and northeastern Arkansas showing locations of fortified Mississippian period settlements.   [Michael J. O'Brien]

a 2-meter-wide embankment of hard-packed clay containing a double row of post molds on top, surrounded by a half-meter-deep ditch.

Towosahgy lies at the eastern edge of Pinhook Ridge, a topographically high series of point bar deposits that were left when a former Mississippi River channel was increasing its northwestward curvature. Capping the deposits is a thin veneer of natural-levee sediments that was used as the building surface for the settlement. Cyrus Thomas, commenting in 1893 on the location of the site, noted that it was wisely selected, as it was the only point within an area of many square miles that was not covered by the great flood of 1882. Thomas's field party produced a sketch plan showing six mounds (there actually are seven), the earthen embankment and ditch that surrounded the settlement, and three low areas from which dirt was excavated during mound construction. Thomas's crew conducted excavations in several areas of the site, especially where there was evidence of "hut rings," which their map shows to have been ubiquitous across the site except for a large area at the eastern edge of the base of the largest mound. This "vacant" area was long suspected to be a plaza, but excavations undertaken in 1989 demonstrated that it contained structure basins and deep archaeological deposits.

Several hundred feet of fortification wall and accompanying bastions were excavated during various field seasons at Towosahgy. Excavations along the northern section of the large fortification ditch that was still evident in the late nineteenth century revealed that the system began as a simple log palisade around the site, constructed in a narrow, shallow wall trench. A second trench was later excavated, and palisade posts were set in it. This trench was followed by yet another palisade that consisted of single posts set into the ground without a trench. Then sediment from the ditch was piled up to create an embankment on its inner side. This event created a major palisade trench far larger than the earlier ones. It served as a wall for some time, after which the posts were removed and a large ditch was excavated.

The Lilbourn site is located at the extreme southern end of Sikeston Ridge. When the site was occupied, a wide slough (a former channel of the Mississippi River) bordered the western edge of the ridge and curved around the southern end of it. Potter mapped the site in 1878, although his sketch left out some interesting details that are visible on low-level aerial photographs. When the enclosed area was at its maximum extent, the fortification wall enclosed about 17 hectares (approximately 42 acres). The wall was composed of upright

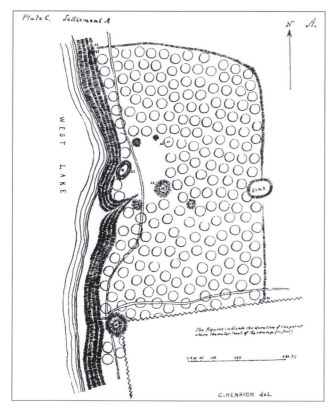

Map of the Matthews site, New Madrid County, Missouri, prepared by W. B. Potter in the 1870s. [Bureau of Ethnology, Smithsonian Institution]

timbers set into an earthen embankment that was approximately a meter high in 1878. A ditch encircled the wall on the outside. Potter described eleven mounds in and around the fortified area, the largest of which, Mound A, was said to be 270 feet by 140–210 feet at the base and to stand 21 feet high. Mound A had earlier been excavated by Swallow, who in December 1856 and January 1857 cut a 6-foot-wide trench through the mound. The trench was so large that its outline is still evident.

The house depressions at Lilbourn noted by Potter are not visible on aerial photographs, although excavations in the 1970s documented the presence of wall-trench houses set in shallow basins as well as non-wall-trench houses that had been erected on the original ground surface or in basins. Houses ranged in size from 4 to almost 8 meters on a side. The complicated manner in which structures were superposed made it impossible to determine how many houses might have been occupied at any one time.

Excavations in the 1970s produced nearly a hundred skeletons. In some cases grave goods, usually ceramic vessels, were placed alongside a body, but in other cases, especially those involving children, the bodies were unaccompanied by objects. There also appeared to be a few special burials of high-status individuals, who were interred with rare items. For example, one body had been interred with a large chipped-stone mace, or scepter; a circular copper disc; a bird bone projectile point; and a mollusk shell. The

Aerial photograph of the Lilbourn site, New Madrid County, Missouri, 1941 (north at the top). Mound 1 is in the grove of trees slightly below the center of the photograph, and the fortification walls and some of the house outlines are clearly evident in the crop marks. [Michael J. O'Brien]

chipped-stone mace was made of Mill Creek chert from a source in southern Illinois. It is 40 centimeters long and has a maximum width of 2.3 centimeters. It has been referred to as Missouri's most famous prehistoric artifact.

Towosahgy is a state park and can be visited year-round. Lilbourn is not open to the public, but Mound A is plainly visible on the west side of I-55, just south of Lilbourn, Missouri. Crosno is on private property and not open to the public, and Matthews has been almost completely destroyed by land leveling.

Further Reading: Chapman, Carl H., John W. Cottier, David Denman, David R. Evans, Dennis E. Harvey, Michael D. Reagan, Bradford L. Rope, Michael D. Southard, and Gregory A. Waselkov, "Investigation and Comparison of Two Fortified Mississippi Tradition Archaeological Sites in Southeast Missouri: A Preliminary Comparison," *Missouri Archaeologist* 38 (1977); O'Brien, Michael J., and W. Raymond Wood, *The Prehistory of Missouri* (Columbia: University of Missouri Press, 1998); Potter, W. B., "Archaeological Remains in Southeastern Missouri," in *Contributions to the Archaeology of Missouri, by the Archaeological Section of the St. Louis Academy of Science, Part 1: Pottery* (Salem, MA: Bates, 1880), 1–19; Price, James E., and Gregory L. Fox, "Recent Investigations at Towosahgy State Historic Site," *Missouri Archaeologist* 51 (1990): 1–71; Walker, Winslow M., and Robert M. Adams, "Excavations in the Matthews Site, New Madrid County, Missouri," *Academy of Science of St. Louis, Transactions* 31(4) (1946): 75–120.

Michael J. O'Brien

THE JONATHAN CREEK VILLAGE SITE

Marshall County, Western Kentucky

A Walled Mississippian Village

The Jonathan Creek site was a principal Mississippian community situated along the creek of the same name, a short distance from its confluence with the Tennessee River in western Kentucky. Between about AD 1000 and 1500, Mississippian peoples occupied many of these types of resource-rich, riverine settings of the southern Midwest and Southeast.

The Mississippian people transformed the terrain around their settlements by creating gardens and agricultural fields, in which they grew corn, squash, and numerous native domesticates and cultigens. They also gathered, hunted, and fished aquatic resources and terrestrial resources from nearby ecological settings that they sometimes actively managed, for example, by periodically burning off brush and dead wood in forests to keep them open and encourage large deer herd size. They crafted pottery, which typically was tempered with ground-up clamshell, in a wide variety of vessel forms that included jars, bowls, beakers, plates, pans, short- and long-neck bottles, hooded water bottles that resemble gourds, and restricted-orifice vessels called seed jars. Some vessel types were used predominantly for cooking and storage, while others were used to serve food and beverages.

These societies had hierarchical sociopolitical and settlement systems that have led many archaeologists to classify them as chiefdoms. The town in which the leader, or chief, lived often can be distinguished archaeologically from other communities by the presence of pyramidal earthen mounds with flat tops that form platforms, along with other monumental architecture, such as seen at the Jonathan Creek site. Smaller villages, hamlets, and farmsteads were distributed across the landscape around these mound centers, creating political systems that ranged in size from about 40 kilometers to 100 kilometers in diameter—and at times possibly growing even larger.

Architectural features indicate that the Jonathan Creek site was laid out like a typical Mississippian political center, with earthen platform mounds flanking an open plaza area. Radiocarbon dates for the site indicate that it reached regional eminence in the thirteenth century AD, about the time that other prominent sites nearby—particularly Cahokia, Wickliffe, and Kincaid—were in decline (Schroeder 2006). As at many other important and sizable Mississippian communities, a wooden wall, or palisade, around the site's perimeter protected the residents of Jonathan Creek. However, the site is unique for the number of these walls that were built during its occupation; at least six separate and sequential substantial wooden palisades studded with bastions were constructed around the community, and additional wall segments were added in some places. These features have provided archaeologists with the unprecedented opportunity to investigate physical variations in wall construction techniques as well as explore a range of social, economic, and political rationales for creating and sustaining a walled community.

The Jonathan Creek site first was described in the late nineteenth century by Robert Loughridge, a geologist, who

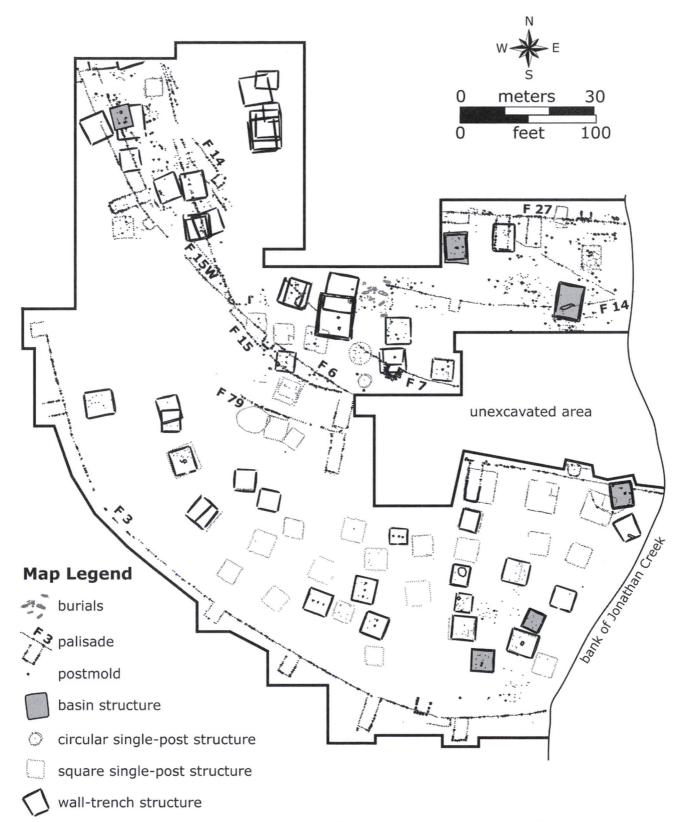

Map Legend

- burials
- F 3 palisade
- · postmold
- basin structure
- circular single-post structure
- square single-post structure
- wall-trench structure

F 14
F 15W
F 15
F 6
F 79
F 3
F 27
F 14
F 7

unexcavated area

bank of Jonathan Creek

0 meters 30
0 feet 100

Map of the Jonathan Creek Site showing structures, features, palisades, and the limits of excavation.   [Sissel Schroeder] described six earthen mounds arranged around an open plaza and a seventh mound in the nearby floodplain of Jonathan Creek. In 1914 and 1915, the site was visited by Clarence Bloomfield Moore, a prominent Philadelphian who explored numerous mound sites in the southeastern United States between 1891 and 1918. His short account of the site indicates that the mounds at that time had been affected by more than a century of plowing. Moore's limited testing failed to turn up any of the spectacular artifacts made of exotic raw material, such as marine shell and copper, that are associated with the Southeastern Ceremonial complex, prompting him to abandon his investigations at Jonathan Creek quickly and move on to other sites.

The mounds at the Jonathan Creek site, however, continued to attract attention, and in the fall of 1940, excavations were initiated at the site with Civilian Conservation Corps labor under the guidance of William S. Webb of the University of Kentucky in Lexington. This project ended in the spring of 1942, shortly after the bombing of Pearl Harbor, when the laborers and project supervisors were mobilized for World War II (Schroeder 2005; Webb 1952). Following World War II, a dam was completed across the Tennessee River that led to the site being covered by the waters of Kentucky Lake.

Although Webb's crew excavated less than half the site, enough was uncovered to reveal a substantial town surrounded by at least six sequentially constructed wooden walls studded with bastions. Excavations also uncovered eighty-nine structures, forty-fix of which were rectangular houses built of posts set into wall trenches. Of the remaining structures, six were semi-subterranean rectangular houses, thirty-four were square or rectangular houses built by setting support posts into individual holes in the ground, and three were circular or oval in shape and constructed with individually set posts. Five of the wall-trench houses were distinctive because of three large roof support posts that ran through the center of the structure.

Despite the range of construction techniques used to establish the framework of each building, all of them probably had walls built of a latticework of saplings and sticks that were covered with grass or reeds and then daubed with clay. Roofs, which would have varied in size, were made of saplings or more substantial wooden beams and then covered with thatch.

This degree of architectural diversity within one community, and the large number of walls, is unprecedented in the Mississippian world. Radiocarbon dates indicate that many of these different structure styles were roughly contemporaneous. Some of the architectural differences may be functional. For example, the more substantially built houses may have been occupied in winter, and some of the flimsier structures may have been used in summer. The circular buildings may have been used for storage of grain and other community resources, as sweat lodges, or for other special purposes. At least some of the distinctive architectural styles may represent ethnic differences among contemporaneous occupants of the site—people who joined the community to seek protection; wished to more closely ally themselves with the chiefly lineage; or were relocated as war captives, slaves, or remnants of a conquered (and now subordinate) group.

The three largest buildings at the site were erected, one after the other, on top of one of the platform mounds, which was situated at the southern end of the central community plaza. This small mound, which was built over dismantled walls and houses, was erected relatively late in the occupation history of the site. Interred in the mound in a cluster near these large buildings, archaeologists found more than a dozen burials (most with their skulls oriented to the west), leading them to classify the mound and the structures on top of it as a mortuary facility.

The final two structures built atop this mortuary mound were destroyed by major fires that possibly resulted from successful attacks against the settlement in which enemies intentionally disturbed the bones and symbolically important artifacts belonging to the community's most revered ancestors. This would have created a powerful symbol of the attacking enemy's defeat of the sanctity and authority of the leaders of the Jonathan Creek town. Alternatively, this building may have been burned upon the death of a particularly beloved leader, or demolished in anticipation of an attack to prevent the enemy from having the satisfaction of destroying the temple. At the very least, these conflagrations hint at a time of internal uncertainty and external instability in the lives of the residents of Jonathan Creek, which may also be reflected in the remarkable number of walls built around the town.

Mississippian walls, or palisades, were substantial constructions that necessitated access to large quantities of wood; they would have required advance planning and organization to build (Milner 1999). These enclosures are not found around all Mississippian towns, but tend to be more common at places (including the Jonathan Creek site), that were marked by earthen mounds—the presumed seats of regional leaders or chiefs. The most common reason given for why these wooden walls were built around certain Mississippian towns is that they were strategic defense initiatives to protect leaders and residents from raids and more serious attacks mounted by enemies (e.g., Milner 1999; Webb 1952).

However, at the Jonathan Creek site, variation in how the walls were built and the frequency with which they were repaired suggests that for the members of this community, the rationales for wall building were more complex and changed over time (Schroeder 2006). The earliest and innermost wall built at the site, Feature 27, appears to have been constructed in some haste, judging by the relatively small diameter of the timbers and the shallow depth to which they were set, probably in anticipation of an attack. Furthermore, this and the other early walls at the site were repaired frequently because of damage and decay, some of which may have resulted from assaults against the town.

In contrast, later palisades at the site appear to have been erected during times of relative peace, and the low rate of repair to these walls indicates that they were rebuilt from scratch, rather than repaired. This pattern suggests that the members of the community felt safe enough to leave the town to harvest timbers for the new wall or to live for a period of time without the full protection of the wall as they recycled logs from the old wall to build the new palisade. Under these conditions, palisades may have been constructed to spatially define the community and to control access—who was allowed into the town, who might be allowed to leave, and who participated in the social, political, and economic activities that connected those living inside the walled town with those living outside.

The final and outermost wall, Feature 3, is built around the town. The wall is of a much grander scale than any of the earlier stockades; it may have been a symbolic statement of splendor and status made by one of the final leaders at the site. The timbers used to construct this wall were larger in diameter than those associated with any of the other palisades at the site and are larger than typical for most Mississippian palisades in eastern North America. They were also set more deeply into the ground than was the case for any other walls at the site. This tall wall was studded with imposing bastions that towered over the town. The planning that went into this final wall built at the site, and the care with which it was built, are consistent with a scenario of construction during a time when the people of Jonathan Creek had the opportunity and resources to construct a monument of the community—a time when the threat of attack was unlikely. This palisade would have been a visually striking, impressive, awe-inspiring wall around the village. It would have made a statement of distinction, nobility, and preeminence, as well as a means of protecting and controlling access to the town and community events.

The town of Jonathan Creek appears to have been abandoned relatively rapidly not long after this monumental wall was built, and it was never reoccupied. The final wall was left to decay in place. It is tempting to speculate that the attacks upon the mortuary mound indicated a sudden escalation in regional violence, following a period of relative peace for the townspeople of the Jonathan Creek site. Despite the extraordinary strength of this fortification, the calculated attacks upon the ancestors whose remains reposed in mortuary mound created a sense of danger that must have been great enough to lead people to move elsewhere, perhaps joining together with members of other communities.

Further Reading: Milner, George R., "Warfare in Prehistoric and Early Historic Eastern North America," *Journal of Archaeological Research* 7 (1999): 105–151; Schroeder, Sissel, "Reclaiming New Deal Era Civic Archaeology: Exploring the Legacy of William S. Webb and the Jonathan Creek Site," *CRM: The Journal of Heritage Stewardship* 2 (2005): 53–71; Schroeder, Sissel, "Walls as Symbols of Political, Economic, and Military Might," in *Leadership and Polity in Mississippian Society*, edited by Paul Welch and Brian Butler (Carbondale: Southern Illinois University Center for Archaeological Investigations, 2006), 115–141; Webb, William S., *The Jonathan Creek Village*, Reports in Anthropology 7(1) (Lexington: University of Kentucky, 1952).

Sissel Schroeder

WICKLIFFE MOUNDS STATE PARK AND RESEARCH CENTER

Ballard County, Kentucky
The Wickliffe Site

The Wickliffe Mounds site is the best known of the Mississippian town sites of western Kentucky. Situated on the bluff overlooking the Mississippi River just a few miles below the mouth of the Ohio River, the Wickliffe site was well chosen for access to the trade and communications routes of the river system, as well as to the rich resources of the bottomlands and the Mississippi Flyway of migratory birds, including geese and ducks. First excavated in the 1930s, the Wickliffe site has been open to the public as a tourist attraction, then a university research center, and currently a Kentucky State Historic Site.

About AD 1100, a group of Native Americans belonging to the Mississippian culture founded a small town at the Wickliffe site. At first their wattle-and-daub houses clustered closely around an open plaza. Beginning about AD 1175, the townspeople began to build platform mounds—one on the north side and one on the west side of the plaza. By AD 1250, the mound on the west had become the larger one and supported a ceremonial building on its flattened summit, while a chief's residence stood atop the mound on the north.

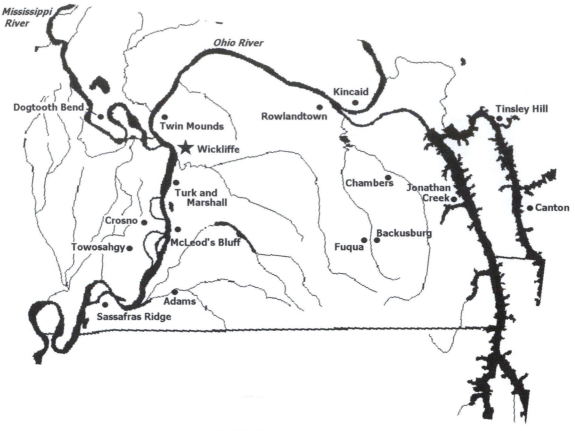

Wickliffe and nearby sites mentioned in the text.   [Kit W. Wesler]

In the same period, the boundaries of the town expanded, and the townspeople built a set of smaller mounds surrounding the platform-and-plaza complex. A pair of mounds on the east side of the plaza may have been burial places for chiefs. The functions of the other smaller mounds are still not clear, but one mound in the northeastern part of the site became the focus of a cemetery.

Artifacts from the same period attest to the townspeople's widespread trade contacts, including pottery and stone from the Cahokia region, a pot shard that probably came from northern Georgia, and ornaments of marine shell.

In the final century or so of the site's occupation, the village area continued to expand until it reached the edges of the bluff. Both of the platform mounds received their final caps of soil—perhaps in ceremonial burials, since it is not clear whether buildings stood on the highest summits. The townspeople apparently ate less fish, emphasizing land animals such as deer in their diet. The last burials in the cemetery occurred in the late AD 1200s, indicating that a new cemetery was established outside the town. The Wickliffe site was abandoned in the mid-1300s for reasons that are not clear.

Wickliffe is one of a number of Mississippian sites in western Kentucky and the surrounding region. The sites are found about every 5 to 8 miles (8 to 12 km) along the rivers, and it

is likely that a number of smaller village sites remain hidden in the creek valleys of the interior. South of Wickliffe, the Turk, Marshall, Adams, and Sassafras Ridge sites have been the subjects of investigations by the University of Illinois, while the University of Kentucky conducted minimal work at the McLeod's Bluff site in the 1930s. Along the Ohio River, University of Illinois teams also studied the Twin Mounds and Rowlandtown sites. Sites along the Clarks River include the Chambers, Backusburg, and Fuqua villages, while the lower Tennessee and Cumberland River valleys contain the Jonathan Creek, Tinsley Hill, and Canton sites. Nearby sites, such as Crosno and Towosahgy in Missouri, and Kincaid and Dogtooth Bend in Illinois, also have received archaeological attention.

While Wickliffe is the most extensively excavated of these sites, enough is known of the others to show that they were occupied in roughly the same period as the Wickliffe town. Some, like the Marshall site, were founded earlier, while others, such as the Adams Mounds and Dogtooth Bend sites, may have been occupied as late as the early 1400s. Recent excavations at the Rowlandtown Mound, on the west side of Paducah, Kentucky, indicate that the town was founded before AD 1000, and that the first construction of a platform mound began about AD 1000. On the other hand, the

Rowlandtown moundbuilders enlarged the mound numerous times in the later 1200s and early 1300s, during which time the Wickliffe platforms received only a single, final cap. In fact, a date from a house site at Rowlandtown suggests that the town was occupied into the early 1400s, a rather late date for the region.

It is clear that the Mississippian sites of western Kentucky and the surrounding region were a set of closely related communities, but that their chronology and interactions were complex. Whether the largest site in the region, the Kincaid site in southern Illinois, was a political center for the towns of the region is not clear. All of the sites will require much more detailed investigation before their full stories and interrelationships are known. Except for Wickliffe, all of the sites are privately owned and endangered by looting and agricultural uses of the land.

Excavations at Wickliffe began in 1932 as a result of the construction of a highway that cut through the southern end of the site. Fain W. King, a Paducah businessman and artifact collector, bought the site. Inspired by the opening of the Dickson Mounds (Illinois) to tourists, King—and later, his new wife Blanche Busey King—planned a similar display of excavated areas at Wickliffe. His early excavations were aided by the Alabama Museum of Natural History, while the University of Chicago consulted and assisted on Wickliffe excavations in the mid-1930s. Ultimately both institutions and the archaeological community at large withdrew their cooperation because of the Kings' commercialization and sensationalist interpretation of the site.

The Wickliffe site has been open to the public almost continuously since 1932. The Kings named the site the Ancient Buried City and operated under that name until 1946. Then the Western Baptist Hospital took over the site and kept it open to tourists under the same name until 1983. The hospital donated the site to Murray State University, which created the Wickliffe Mounds Research Center. From 1983 to 2004, the research center conducted new excavations and analysis, removed human remains from display, improved the educational quality of the exhibits, and conducted educational and training programs at the site.

In 2004 the site was transferred to Kentucky State Parks and became the Wickliffe Mounds State Historic Site. The parks system has invested in the facilities but maintains the archaeological focus of the education program. Three exhibit buildings still cover excavations created by the Kings in the 1930s and further analyzed by archaeologists from Murray State University and other institutions.

Further Reading: Lewis, R. Barry, "Mississippian Farmers," in *Kentucky Archaeology*, edited by R. Barry Lewis (Lexington: University Press of Kentucky, 1996), 127–159; Wesler, Kit W., *Excavations at Wickliffe Mounds* (Tuscaloosa: University of Alabama Press, 2001); Wesler, Kit W., "Excavating Wickliffe Mounds," Murray State University Web site, http://www.murraystate.edu/qacd/cos/geo/geos_fac/Wesler/Optimized%20WICKLIFFE%20MOUNDS_new_files/frame.htm (PowerPoint edition, online 2005) and http://www.murraystate.edu/qacd/cos/geo/geos_fac/Wesler/WickliffeMounds Notes.pdf (PDF edition, online 2005).

Kit W. Wesler

RIDGED AND CORN HILL AGRICULTURAL FIELDS

Wisconsin, Michigan, and Iowa

Examples of Late Prehistoric Agriculture in the Midwest

During the late prehistoric and historic periods in the upper Midwest, many Native American peoples relied heavily on a mix of crops such as maize, beans, squash, sunflower, and other plants. At some point in prehistory, perhaps around AD 900–1000, the cultivation of these crops began involving the construction of raised planting beds of one or more types. Most commonly, these beds were linear, curvilinear, or conical (circular) in shape.

Tracts of linear or curvilinear beds are usually referred to as either ridged fields or garden beds. These tracts most commonly included beds measuring approximately 3 to 6 feet across and 5 to 20 inches in height. The elongated beds were usually laid out in parallel rows measuring from 5 feet to more than 200 feet in length, arranged into plots of varying sizes.

Corn hills represent a somewhat different form of raised planting bed. They were constructed as circular hillocks that often measured 3 to 4 feet in diameter and had heights ranging from 5 to 15 inches or more. As is also true for the ridged fields, corn hills were commonly arranged into plats of various sizes—some with great regularity and others with no patterning whatsoever.

Whether they comprise corn hills, garden beds, or a combination of both, the extent of these ancient cultivation areas is quite variable. The smallest recorded sites total perhaps as

An excavation from one of the ridged field or corn hill sites within the western Great Lakes and upper Mississippi valley documenting the use of corn hills or other raised beds to cultivate crops.   [Robert F. Sasso]

little as a few hundred square feet. The largest, however, may have at one time covered several square miles, collectively. Such is the case for a set of sites near Winneconne, in eastern Wisconsin.

The raised planting beds represent a sizable investment of time and energy. It is not entirely clear why they were constructed, but archaeologists have proposed many possible functions, including moisture control, frost drainage, soil aeration, control of soil-dwelling insects, beneficial changes to soil structure, and mixing of soil nutrients. The beds warm more quickly in the spring because sunlight strikes them at a higher angle, and the soil within them tends to be drier in the spring than would be the case if it were flat. This translates to potentially earlier planting in the spring—and, effectively, a longer growing season. Such an increase in the growing season can make a difference between crop success and failure in the upper Midwest.

Some 400 sites with raised-bed features have been recorded in Wisconsin, where those features were associated with prehistoric or historic cultures. Several dozen sites have been recorded in Michigan, with far fewer reported for Iowa. Many of the recorded sites apparently were destroyed either by more recent human activities or the forces of nature, yet a number of these sites remain well preserved today. At some, ridges or corn hills remain obvious even to the untrained observer, though at most sites,

these features have been compacted, eroded, or are otherwise obscured by vegetation cover. They are easiest to observe during winter or early spring, before plants begin to put forth leaves.

The majority of the ridged field or corn hill sites within the western Great Lakes and upper Mississippi valley are believed to have been constructed and used by either Late Woodland culture peoples, Oneota (upper Mississippian) peoples, Mississippian peoples, or several historically known groups, including the Winnebago, Ojibwa, Potawatomi, Ottawa, Mascouten, Sauk, Fox, Menominee, Miami, Ioway, Oto, and Kickapoo. Some of these groups are documented as having utilized corn hills or other raised beds to cultivate their crops in Wisconsin, Michigan, and Iowa.

Most sites were recorded because archaeologists encountered ridges or corn hills on the ground surface, or because historic accounts indicate that Native Americans had cultivated a particular area at some known date. Occasionally, sites were recorded because raised beds were found preserved under sediments in low-lying areas, such as floodplains. Overall, archaeologists have excavated relatively few of these sites in the upper Midwest. Of those excavated, only a small number have been dated or yielded artifacts linking them definitively with any specific culture or group.

Excavation of the ridged fields found at the Sand Lake site in Wisconsin.   [Robert F. Sasso]

THE SAND LAKE SITE, ONALASKA, WISCONSIN

The most thoroughly investigated Native American agricultural site in the entire upper Midwest is the Sand Lake site, north of La Crosse, Wisconsin. Here a series of ridged fields were buried by sediments that accumulated quite rapidly while the fields were in use—approximately AD 1450. They were constructed and used by people of the Oneota culture, a society that occupied the La Crosse area and many other portions of the upper Midwest for several hundred years.

At Sand Lake, archaeologists found evidence of periodic rebuilding of the ridges many times as the sediments had accumulated. The rapid accumulation of sediments had a great benefit for archaeologists, as it quickly sealed in many contexts at the site, along with preserving many artifacts, plant remains, and related archaeological features. Among the artifacts recovered from agricultural contexts were fragments of bison and elk scapula hoes, as well as ceramic shards, stone tools, bone, and shell. Plant remains from the site included cultivated plants, such as corn kernels and cob fragments, squash, beans, and tobacco. Within the ridged-field settings were miniature corn hills, hearths, pits, and a few decomposed posts. The Sand Lake site excavations have revealed aspects of agriculture, economy, and technology that provide us with a far more complete understanding of life in a late prehistoric Oneota community. While this site survived for more than 550 years before being discovered and partly excavated, the development of a golf course on the site resulted in the apparent destruction of remaining portions of the ridged fields during the late 1980s.

OTHER AGRICULTURAL SITES IN THE UPPER MIDWEST

Beyond Sand Lake, several agricultural field sites are situated within places that may be visited by the public, or where remaining beds may sometimes be viewed from a passing auto. Aztalan, a well-known Mississippian village along the Crawfish River in southern Wisconsin, may still retain faint traces of what is believed to have been extensive tracts of ridged fields. An early-nineteenth-century site map shows features consistent with alternating tracts of garden beds. Some tracts are oriented east to west, while others run north to south. Based upon comparison to the 21-acre area of the walled village itself on the same map, these apparent fields would cover approximately 15 to 25 acres a short distance north of the village enclosure.

In Oconto County in northeastern Wisconsin, a few acres of well-preserved garden beds survive just southeast of White Potato Lake. These robust beds are preserved on a piece of land recently purchased by the Archaeological Conservancy and may be visited by the public. While the age of this site is not yet known, it is most likely either associated with a prehistoric Late Woodland or Oneota culture or the historic Menominee. The same may be said for an extensive series of beds running along the north side of the Menominee River at site 20ME61, west of the city of Menominee, in Menominee County, Michigan.

Surviving ridged areas are found in both Rocky Arbor and Mirror Lake state parks in the vicinity of Wisconsin Dells, in central Wisconsin. The beds at Rocky Arbor are situated around the north end of the park's camp area. Those at Mirror Lake lie along the Echo Rock hiking trail. At one time, these sites represented just a few of the many extensive prehistoric agricultural fields along the Wisconsin valley in this part of the state. Remnants of another extensive site may still be seen along nearby Hulburt Creek.

Relatively few corn hill sites are known to exist at the present time. Faint traces of a mere twenty-five corn hills may be seen on the front lawn of Carroll College along East Avenue in Waukesha, in southeastern Wisconsin. These are all that remain on the surface of the ground in an area where the Potawatomi cultivated as recently as the mid-1830s. Their fields within just the campus neighborhood alone are estimated to have totaled in excess of 165 acres.

In Iowa, a small number of ridged fields are known to exist. Those that survive are located on private lands and are not available for viewing by the general public. The best preserved is the Litka site, a Mill Creek culture site located along Waterman Creek in O'Brien County, Iowa.

Further Reading: Fox, George R., "Distribution of Garden Beds in Wisconsin and Michigan," *The Wisconsin Archeologist* 40 (1959): 1–19; Gallagher, James P., "Prehistoric Field Systems in the Upper Midwest," in *Late Prehistoric Agriculture: Observations from the Midwest*, edited by W. I. Woods, Studies in Illinois Archaeology No. 8 (Springfield: Illinois Historic Preservation Agency, 1992), 95–135; Gallagher, James P., and Robert F. Sasso, "Investigations into Oneota Ridged Field Agriculture on the Northern Margin of the Prairie Peninsula," *Plains Anthropologist* 32 (1987): 141–151; Gartner, William G., "Late Woodland Landscapes of Wisconsin: Ridged Fields, Effigy Mounds and Territoriality," *Antiquity* 73 (1999): 671–683; Sasso, Robert F., "Vestiges of Ancient Cultivation: The Antiquity of Garden Beds and Corn Hills in Wisconsin," *Midcontinental Journal of Archaeology* 28 (2003): 195–231.

Robert F. Sasso

THE NORRIS FARMS 36 CEMETERY SITE

Central Illinois River Valley, Illinois

A Fourteenth-Century Oneota Cemetery

The Norris Farms 36 Cemetery is a late prehistoric period, 700-year-old Bold Counselor phase Oneota site located on the Illinois River bluff top near the confluence of the Spoon and Illinois rivers. It is one of only five such sites known in the Central Illinois River valley and is the only Bold Counselor phase Oneota cemetery ever to be scientifically investigated.

Excavated by archaeologists from the Dickson Mounds Museum in the mid-1980s, the site yielded an unusually well-preserved burial population of 264 individuals. These burials in turn offered unprecedented information about this group of migrants who entered the Illinois River valley about AD 1300. Definitive Oneota artifact types, skeletons of the population, burial practices, and social relationships were documented by the excavation, which provided a vivid portrait of life during a period of widespread social disorder. Although apparently having established trading relationships with the already resident regional Mississippian groups, the Oneota were involved in frequent warfare. Nearly a third of the adults and some children at Norris Farms 36 met with violent deaths, and the population was further stressed by disease and inadequate food resources.

The Norris Farms 36 cemetery constitutes a substantial addition to the meager information available on Oneota social and ceremonial organization, and of relationships among warfare and subsistence activities, health, and mortality. The cemetery adds a unique temporal perspective to the study of late prehistoric adversity and accommodation. In addition, analysis of cranial dimensions, which indicate that these people were indeed new to the area, along with ancient DNA profiles created from the skeletal remains have begun to clarify late prehistoric genetic relationships across the mid-continent.

Researchers were unprepared for what they discovered at Norris Farms 36 when they began excavations there in advance of highway construction. Initially they found that the 264 Oneota burials in the cemetery were organized in a manner quite different than burials at other late prehistoric sites in the region. Rather than aligning bodies with respect to solar phenomena, the community had simply placed graves along the contour of the bluff crest, expanding outward in rows from a central starting point. Many of the graves were dug deeper than normal for burials of other contemporaneous groups—some exceeding 2 meters—and often the burials were roofed with wooden poles rather than backfilled at burial. Graves were later filled after roof collapse.

Bodies typically were extended on their backs, but ten flexed individuals were represented, along with eleven bundled burials of loose bones. Usually only one person was placed in each grave, but females with young children (assumed to be related) were sometimes included in the same grave, as were the remains of multiple victims of violent death. Sometimes graves were reopened for the inclusion of another, probably related, individual.

Items placed with the dead provided valuable information about the Oneota way of life and how Norris Farms 36 people viewed themselves. The presence of important artifacts with the oldest individuals may indicate that advancing age—and with it, accumulated wealth and social status—may have been important within the society. This kind of veneration of the elderly differs from that evidenced among local Mississippian groups.

Burial furnishings indicated that males were the most important members of Oneota society. Status-denoting ornamentation and ritualistic equipment were almost exclusively associated with males and (presumably) with male children. Only one female was distinguished by the presence of ritualistic paraphernalia: a rare spider gorget fashioned from marine shell. Although no adults were interred with extravagant grave goods, a number of infants and children were the recipients of important burial offerings apparently intended to set them apart from others. Four had elaborate ritualistic costuming indicating that they were from important families, which suggests that such status positions within the community may have been inherited rather than earned. This Oneota society probably was ranked, but featured a more egalitarian way of life than did contemporaneous Mississippian societies.

Other types of nonperishable items placed with the dead at Norris Farms 36 represent a cross section of domestic equipment, in particular, tools; eating utensils; hunting, fishing, and processing equipment; and weaponry. With the exception of weapons, such equipment occurred primarily with adults. The presence of disproportionate numbers of weapons with adult males, adolescents, and even young children indicates a population under substantial stress for which defensive equipment was seen as essential for day-to-day group survival.

The original homeland for the Norris Farms 36 Oneota group appears to have been the upper Mississippi River valley, but their sudden appearance in central Illinois at the beginning of the fourteenth century probably represented an attempt to escape severe social problems that must have existed there. Relocation gained them little peace, however. Severe traumas, unhealed wounds, decapitation, scalping, and postmortem dismemberment in evidence among the burials indicate that at least forty-three individuals met violent deaths. Two other women lived after being shot with arrows, and three survived being scalped. Both males and females met violent deaths, with the likelihood of being killed increasing with advanced age or deteriorated health.

These violent deaths reflect a pattern of warfare probably featuring both raids on the habitation site and opportunistic attacks on individuals and small groups isolated some distance from the protection of the village.

Those trying to determine the perpetrators of the killing continue to encounter intriguing questions. Did these violent episodes represent attempts by regional Mississippian populations to discourage or obliterate the new Oneota community, or are they corroborating evidence of the stressful situation that initially moved the Norris Farms 36 group out of its homeland? Most of the arrow points in the bones of victims are made from local cherts (flint) and are similar in appearance to Mississippian weapons, but excavation in the adjacent Oneota village site indicated that these people made use of Mississippian-like arrow points as well. Other identifiable arrow points embedded in victims were classic Oneota-style points, suggesting that Norris Farms 36 may in part represent an example of intra-group conflict.

The unusually well-preserved skeletons in the burials at Norris Farms 36 cemetery provided much information about the past lives of the people. The scientific examination and analyses identified several distinctive diseases that also significantly affected Oneota life. Yet, despite the risks of warfare and disease, group mortality profiles reveal that one of every five adults lived past age 50—an unusual success ratio, considering that only 2 of every 100 Mississippian people in nearby Dickson Mounds lived past their fiftieth year. However, such longevity does not accurately reflect the general low level of community health and poor quality of Oneota life.

One of the most striking aspects of the Norris Farms 36 population was the poor condition of their teeth. Dental decay was rampant, frequently contributing to complete tooth loss. Severe bone diseases also were common, often consisting of skeletal lesions dominated by periostitis and osteomyelitis. Thirty-two adults exhibited advanced lesions from a tuberculosis-like infection, and more than a dozen others exhibited lesions consistent with a treponemal infection (modern treponemal infections include venereal syphilis and yaws, among others). Nutritional deficiency was evident in nearly a third of the population in the form of bony lesions affecting the orbits and crania, and much of the post-childhood sample exhibited enamel hypoplasia—a measure of stress from poor diet or infectious disease experienced during the years when tooth crowns form. Although excavation in their habitation site revealed that the Oneota pursued a variety of planting and foraging activities, the high frequency of dental hypoplasia indicates that they often were subjected to periods of starvation. Perhaps this directly related to their inability to venture far from the protection of the village to plant crops or forage under the constant threat of violence.

All of the above factors contributed to lives of hardship for the Norris Farms 36 population. Whatever the reason for abandoning their Oneota homeland, these people purchased little peace or comfort by relocating in the Illinois River valley. With their population depleted and new village burned, the Oneota survivors moved several miles upriver, where they lived for an equally short period of time. In like manner, their descendants would move from place to place within the valley—all the while plagued by social conflict—until the valley was abandoned by the mid-fifteenth century AD.

Further Reading: Illinois State Museum, *Museumlink Illinois: Native Americans*, www.museum.state.il.us/muslink/nat_amer/index.htm

(2008); Milner, George R., Eve Anderson, and Virginia G. Smith, "Warfare in Late Prehistoric West-Central Illinois," *American Antiquity* 56 (1991): 581–603; Santure, Sharron K., Duane Esarey, and Alan D. Harn, "Archaeological Investigations at the Morton Village and Norris Farms 36 Cemetery," *Illinois State Museum Reports of Investigations* 45 (1990); Stone, Anne C., Mark Stoneking, A. J. Davidson, A. Millard, J. Bada, and R. Evershed, "Analysis of Ancient DNA from a Prehistoric Amerindian Cemetery [and Discussion]," *Philosophical Transactions: Biological Sciences* 354(1379) (Jan. 29, 1999): 153–159.

Alan D. Harn

THE LONZA-CATERPILLAR SITE

Central Illinois

Bison Hunting in the Midwest

The Lonza-Caterpillar kill site is located on the bank of the Illinois River near the mouth of the Mackinaw River, in Central Illinois. In the mid-1990s, rare bison bones discovered there by amateur archaeologist Rick Scott triggered a 10-year research project that would result in a major evaluation of bison in the mid-continent. The Dickson Mounds Museum and the Illinois State Museum performed a joint excavation at the site, producing semi-articulated skeletal remains of deer, elk, and bison that had been targeted by human hunters. The dozen or more bison individuals represented among the excavated bones constitute by far the largest collection of these animals available for study in Illinois and may represent the earliest Holocene age (within the last 10,000 years) bison kill site documented east of the Great Plains.

Prior to this discovery and investigation, bison were considered recent arrivals into the area that is now the state of Illinois. Their expansion across the Mississippi River was not thought to have occurred much before the mid-1500s. The first French explorers reported numbers of bison in the Illinois River valley by the late 1600s. A small number of bison remains have been reported in the scientific literature of the region, but these primarily represent food refuse from historic Native American villages, along with a few tools and ornaments from earlier late-prehistoric sites considered to be trade objects. Although other discoveries of bison bone have been reported by the public throughout Illinois, these rarely consist of more than a single specimen. Hence, the discovery of multiple bison bones in one location immediately attracted the interest of the scientific community.

The erosion of bison bones from the riverbank initially invited speculation that the remains could represent a Pleistocene age (the time period preceding the Holocene)

deposit or other natural accumulation, or evidence of a hunting or processing site. Although previous archaeological reconnaissance of the Lonza-Caterpillar site had not produced bison elements, it had documented evidence of an extended aboriginal occupation. In addition, several mid-1700s gun parts and lead musket balls found there were viewed as possibly pertaining to hunting activity during the three centuries bison traditionally were thought to inhabit Illinois before their extinction in the area in the early 1800s.

Archaeological investigation at the site located several concentrations of bones along the beach that were subsequently excavated, exposing partial skeletons of six bison and one elk. These remains were processed and examined at the Illinois State Museum, but failed to confirm an association between bison and human activity at the site. None of the bones had been burned by cooking or cracked to extract marrow; none exhibited evidence of butchering marks. Such negative evidence led researchers to surmise that the presence of so many bison in one location resulted from natural deaths that occurred at or near the site, perhaps representing a catastrophic drowning of the animals when too many attempted to cross the frozen river on thin ice.

Despite this speculation, the singular importance of the bison remains encouraged additional work and, over the next several years, Rick Scott continued to monitor the eroding beach and collect exposed bones after he had mapped their locations. Some seven years into the study, this diligence paid off with the discovery of a bison thoracic vertebra containing the tip of a chipped-stone projectile point, shattered by impact and embedded in the vertebra's transverse process. Although the projectile point was positioned in a location that would never have been fatal, no healing was evident around the wound, indicating that the animal was killed at the same time by other means.

This remarkable find prompted a major reevaluation of the site and a return for a more extensive excavation. A series of test trenches found only scattered animal remains, not the hoped-for bison bone bed. Most of these represented articulated legs and feet of deer and elk; only one partial bison skeleton was discovered. As in previous excavations, no evidence of human activity was associated with the newly excavated remains except for a few bits of charcoal and two chert (flint) flakes found in the vicinity of the bison.

However, when excavators returned to the site on the final day to collect the exposed remains and to backfill their trenches, they discovered that the river level had dropped significantly overnight, revealing the most complete bison skeleton to date. This large, 10-year-old bull soon would become the most important bison found in Illinois, for its skeleton featured a series of human induced wounds and a chipped-stone spear point still in place among the ribs. An impact cut to one rib indicated that the animal initially had been speared through its right side, the weapon traveling slightly forward into the lungs in what should have been a lethal wound. Yet, the bison did not immediately die and, lying on its right side, was speared again from the opposite side by the hunter. This time, the spear passed through the body and became lodged in the tenth right rib. There the blade portion remained after the spearhead snapped—probably when the hunter attempted to withdraw the weapon.

Surprisingly, the spear head proved to be a Dickson point, a weapon type used by Black Sand phase Early Woodland people who began inhabiting the Illinois River valley sometime after 500 BC. The implications of this find prompted investigators to immediately collect bone samples from both the bison skeleton and bison vertebra containing the shattered projectile point so that they could be radiocarbon dated. These samples yielded dates of 305 BC for the vertebra and 398 and 413 BC for two samples from the bison skeleton, precisely what was expected based on the type of stone point found in the rib bone. Finally, here was evidence that bison had made their way east of the Mississippi River and were being hunted by humans nearly 2,000 years earlier than previously thought.

Samples from other bison skeletons at the site were submitted for radiocarbon dating, and they also yielded surprising results. In all, seven dates ranged between 305 and 420 BC, and two were dated at 1316 and 1460 AD. None were of the era traditionally considered to represent the period of bison in Illinois (which began around AD 1550), although such remains may yet be found.

The particular hunting and processing patterns evidenced at the site, in conjunction with trace element analyses of the bison remains and reconstructions of ancient landforms, provide new insights into both bison behavior and aboriginal food procurement practices well back into prehistory. Although the bison remains were located on the north side of the Illinois River in a region that was heavily forested, the high carbon-13 values of their bone collagen indicate that most of their foraging was done in grasslands—probably the extensive prairies on the west side of the river. The factors that caused bison to repeatedly cross the Illinois River can only be partially addressed with the information presently available. The presence of these animals may in part represent natural biotic movement within a long-established round, perhaps bolstered on occasion by Native American hunting drives like those later recorded by the first Europeans.

Why animals crossed at this particular spot is clearer. An unusual combination of landforms created a virtual bluff-to-bluff passage across the wet Illinois River bottomland. This represented the only direct river access for miles upstream and down that was not impeded by backwater lakes, sloughs, and marshes. In addition, seasonally high river levels would have inundated the entire bottomland, leaving this site as the only viable access to easy crossing. All of these factors would have funneled animal traffic into this narrow land corridor, making them easy targets for human hunters.

Despite the presence of their skeletons on the riverbank, it is probable that most of the animals initially were not shot or speared there. Many probably were attacked in the water, perhaps from dugouts, or when slowed or bogged down at the water's edge. Those who died in the water were floated to the bank for processing, while wounded animals were finished off as they emerged.

From the examination of the physical remains, it can be postulated that Early Woodland processing of bison carcasses by the human hunters probably involved the salvage of all meat, including the tongue, and removal of rib sections to gain access to the organs. The absence of tool marks on the bones indicates the use of relatively delicate processing equipment in combination with hand separation of the meat from the bone. Skeletons were abandoned in place, where their remains probably were rearranged further by a combination of animal scavenging and fluvial action before becoming buried in river-edge muck.

Geological and archaeological assessments of the Lonza-Caterpillar site continue to provide valuable scientific information relating to the realms of past human behavior and natural settings that lie buried there. The antiquity of these animals especially holds important implications for early Native American subsistence studies in the eastern United States. These studies traditionally have not considered bison as a potential source of food. The database created by these excavations is extremely important to the study of bison throughout the mid-continent, for it allows researchers to analyze population dynamics and establish genetic (ancient DNA) and demographic profiles for Illinois bison, as well as obtain basic physical measurements of the bones and trace elements for expanded comparative analyses.

Despite the wealth of new data about bison derived from the Lonza-Caterpillar excavations, many questions remain. Were these animals actually available for human exploitation throughout the Holocene? This might be indicated by their extended presence at the Lonza-Caterpillar site, along with recent radiocarbon determinations on individual bison bones recovered from an Illinois peat bog, which place these animals here by at least 6000 BC. Or did the special landform crossing at Lonza-Caterpillar simply attract a disproportionate number of animals to one location, skewing potential demographic models? Also, did the site represent a location for the frequent and predictable exploitation of local bison that had maintained a population through the centuries, or do the skeletons represent opportunistic harvesting of transient animals on a seasonal—or even widely infrequent—basis? Further analysis of their DNA record may clarify if the entire spectrum of extant Illinois bison remains is biologically related or whether the sample represents periodic intrusions of unrelated populations into a given region.

Why are bison found at this site in numbers but not elsewhere in Illinois? And why do their bones almost never appear as the food discard of early Native Americans if these animals were widely available? While it is probable that bison hunting was more widespread than presently indicated by this singular archaeological occurrence, it is also probable that only limited evidence of this type of activity remains intact. Most bison hunting probably took place on Illinois prairies (the traditional habitat of these animals), and skeletal remnants of the hunt left there on the ground would have quickly deteriorated. Only in locations more favorable to preservation of bones, where such elements as water and alluvium could react in concert to quickly bury and seal the remains, might evidence of aboriginal hunting and processing be expected to survive.

The Lonza-Caterpillar kill site represents an unusual situation: A particular set of topographic features dictated animal behavior in a manner that exposed them to a type of human predation. This left an indelible signature in a setting that regularly buried and preserved these important remains.

Further Reading: McMillan, R. Bruce, ed., "Records of Early Bison in Illinois," *Illinois State Museum Scientific Papers*, vol. XXXI (Springfield: Illinois State Museum, 2006); Harn, Alan D., and Terrance J. Martin, "The Lonza-Caterpillar Site: Bison Bone Deposits from the Illinois River, Peoria County, Illinois," in *Records of Early Bison in Illinois*, edited by R. Bruce McMillan, Illinois State Museum Scientific Papers, Vol. XXXI (Springfield: Illinois State Museum, 2006).

Alan D. Harn

RED WING AREA ONEOTA SITES

Minnesota

The Late Prehistory of the Upper Midwest

The Red Wing locality is a dense concentration of late-prehistoric earthworks and village sites on both sides of the Mississippi River near the city of Red Wing, Minnesota. The area is best known as the location of the Silvernale phase (a Mississippian-like ceramic complex present at most of the major sites within the area); as one of the early loci of intensive maize horticulture in the upper Mississippi valley; and as a center of interaction with Mississippian, Plains, and other groups.

Humans have occupied the Red Wing region for perhaps 12,000 years, and classic Clovis, Archaic, and Woodland sites are present in the area. However, around AD 1050, a period of rapid population growth and cultural change occurred that lasted until around AD 1300. During this period, the Red Wing area became a vibrant location where local groups interacted with people from other cultures in the eastern Plains (western Minnesota, Iowa, and perhaps South Dakota), the northern Woodlands (central Minnesota, western and northwestern Wisconsin), and the Mississippi valley to the south. The Red Wing area served as a place of communication and exchange among the local inhabitants and people from these neighboring regions.

Cultural change during this time was both rapid and intense, encompassing four broad, interrelated themes. First, intensive corn horticulture was added to the traditional Woodland suite of hunting and gathering practices. Corn horticulture provided a larger and more stable source of food but also required new production and storage technologies (for example, hoes made of large animal scapulae for horticulture and bell-shaped storage pits). Second, ceramic technology and forms changed from the grit-tempered vessels of the Woodland period to those tempered with shell and displaying new vessel forms and decoration. Third, existing social structures were modified and elaborated. Although this may have been due in part to the seasonal requirements of maize horticulture, it also appears to be tied to local participation in and formation of specific groups or societies based, in part, on the Thunderbird.

Finally, during this cultural florescence, a complex process of ethnic-identity formation took place, and Red Wing appears to have been the crucible out of which the subsequent western Oneota cultural identity was forged. The principal social mechanisms involved in this process probably included seasonal aggregation of groups during the late spring and summer, ritual treatment of the dead and mound building during this time, and a complex pattern of ritual feasting associated with specific ritual societies. The Silvernale phase itself appears to be a direct product of this activity.

The peak of cultural activity at the locality appears to have occurred at the Bryan site around AD 1200. By 1300 or thereafter, the Red Wing area was largely abandoned and not permanently occupied again until the Mdewakanton Sioux established permanent settlements in the eighteenth century.

One of the critical issues at the Red Wing locality has been its relationship with the Mississippian cultures to the south. For many years, it was assumed that Red Wing was the product of interaction with Cahokia and the American Bottom of southwestern Illinois, and that some or all of the Red Wing sites were the product of direct site-unit intrusion from the south. It is now apparent that this was not the case.

Recent analysis of ceramics from multiple sites in the Red Wing area by George R. Holley indicates that Red Wing ceramics are distinctively different from those of Cahokia, although the two share certain traits. Holley suggests that two ceramic phases exist within Silvernale along with several subsequent ceramic phases, at least one of which is transitional into more familiar Oneota forms. Holley's analysis is consistent with a variety of other data and analyses that have been undertaken in recent years.

The most current interpretation is that the local Woodland populations selectively adopted specific aspects of Mississippian and Plains cultures and recast them into forms that fit within elements of their existing social and belief systems. The Silvernale phase itself emerged as a vehicle for specific types of interactions, display, and perhaps exchange. Although certain ceramic traits of Silvernale are Mississippian-like (Apple River, for example), the subsistence base and horticultural methods are notably Plainslike. It appears that during this period inhabitants of the Red Wing sites interacted with a wide variety of groups, and that the Plains influence on Red Wing is far stronger than previously assumed.

The logical candidate for Plains interaction is the Cambria complex, found in sites some 90 miles to the west. Although few unequivocal Cambria shards have been found at Red Wing, several wares and many shards that could easily be classified as Silvernale have been found at Cambria. One particularly interesting hypothesis that grows out of this connection is that sites in the Red Wing area represent some of the earliest examples of the classic Plains trade-fair centers,

which would make them similar in function to the much later Blood Run complex of northwestern Iowa.

SITE DESCRIPTIONS

The Red Wing locality encompasses about 60 square miles in both Goodhue County, Minnesota, and Pierce County, Wisconsin. Sites are usually situated on well-drained outwash terraces and are clustered near the confluence of the Cannon and Mississippi rivers (Minnesota) and the Trimbelle and Mississippi (Wisconsin). More than 3,500 mounds and earthworks, eight major village and mound complexes, at least a hundred smaller sites, a series of large rock towers (or cairns), and one petroglyph site associated with the period between approximately AD 1050 and AD 1300 have been identified.

Although all of the sites possess certain commonalities, distinct differences are apparent between the material culture of sites on the Wisconsin and Minnesota sides of the river. One explanation for this variation is that inhabitants of these sites interacted with different groups of widely distributed societies from the nearby regions. Thus, the Minnesota sites were more directly engaged with the Plains area (via the Cannon River), whereas the Wisconsin sites interacted both with Plains and with other Wisconsin cultures.

One site in the Red Wing locality is available for public visits (Energy Park), and others have been partly purchased and preserved. Collections from the sites have been consolidated and may be viewed at the Minnesota Historical Society (St. Paul), the Science Museum of Minnesota (St. Paul), and the Goodhue County Historical Society (Red Wing).

The Mero Terrace

The Mero Terrace is a large glacial outwash feature at the mouth of the Trimbelle River that extends for almost a mile from east to west. This terrace contains one of the densest concentrations of cultural material within the locality, and some of the earliest occupations have been found here. More than 400 mounds were mapped in 1887, and two large village sites associated with Silvernale and Oneota cultures are present. Both of these villages are surrounded by groups of mounds.

The best known of these village sites is the Diamond Bluff, or Mero site (47PIO2), on the western end of the terrace. This site has yielded the only unequivocal Mississippian artifacts in the Red Wing locality, including two copper maces and a shell long-nosed god maskette. Ceramics at the site include small fragments of Late Woodland ware, rolled-rim Silvernale forms, and later Oneota forms, including several classic Blue Earth–style vessels. Hundreds of pit features have been identified, as have two semi-subterranean houses. These houses are about 7.5 by 6.5 meters in size and extend to depths of 1 meter. One of these houses (excavated by Dobbs in 1990) contained multiple occupation zones. The lower zone (80–90 cm below the surface) contained rolled rim wares, while the upper zone (50–60 cm below the surface) contained typical

Oneota forms. Moreau Maxwell excavated six mounds at 47PI02 in 1948, and these are the largest controlled sample of mound excavations within the locality.

In addition to the Silvernale and Oneota materials, there is evidence of Late Woodland occupation on the terrace and buried in the adjacent floodplain.

The Mero site has been purchased and permanently preserved, although the remainder of the terrace remains in private hands. The site is not generally open to the public.

Adams (47P12)

The Adams site consists of at least ninety-seven mounds surrounding a village area overlooking the Mississippi River and Trenton Slough. Adams is distinctively different from other sites within the locality and appears to be principally Oneota.

There are no known trash pits at the site; the principal cultural features are large, shallow midden deposits. The debris profiles of these deposits indicate they were associated with specific resources, certain seasons, or both. Although small amounts of corn are present, the primary resources used at the site were freshwater mussels, deer and other game, and fish. Pieces of galena and chunky stones (used in the traditional chunky game) are more common than at other sites. Excavation at the site has been limited, and it has been extensively damaged by highway construction, cultivation, and wind erosion.

Silvernale (21GD03)

Silvernale is a large mound-and-village complex situated on a low terrace immediately adjacent to the Cannon River delta. Silvernale is the type site for the Silvernale phase and was most extensively excavated by Lloyd Wilford in the 1940s.

More than 400 mounds were present at this site complex and they surround a large village area. Hundreds of trash pits and midden deposits were present at the site. Although the dominant ceramic forms are Silvernale and initial Oneota, there is evidence of Late Woodland occupation along the margins of the site within the Cannon River floodplain.

Silvernale was largely destroyed in the 1970s. However, a small portion of the village site has been permanently preserved and is currently being investigated by Ronald C. Schirmer. This portion of the site is accessible to the public from the Cannon Valley Trail.

Energy Park (21GD52/158)

Energy Park consists of a group of sixty-four mounds surrounding a small village site and is situated on a high terrace overlooking the Cannon River floodplain. This site is best known for the presence of a flat-topped, pyramidal mound that was 4 feet high and 48 by 60 feet in diameter. The village portion of the site was discovered in 1984 and has been extensively studied using geophysical survey, controlled surface collection, and excavation. Ninety-eight pit features have been discovered to date, and thirty-eight of these have been

excavated. No houses or structures have yet been found, and the site appears to have been seasonally occupied, with a principal emphasis on corn horticulture. One of the most distinctive aspects of the site is the presence of complete horticultural tool kits found in several of the pit features.

Although the mound group at Energy Park has been largely destroyed by plowing, both the mounds and village area have been permanently preserved. The village site is accessible to the public from the Cannon Valley Trail.

Bryan (21GD4)

Bryan is situated on a high glacial outwash terrace overlooking the Cannon River several miles upstream from its mouth. This site represents the apogee of the cultural developments in Red Wing. In 1885, 173 mounds were mapped, and the village site was discovered in 1951 by Lloyd Wilford. Portions of the village site were excavated in the 1950s by Wilford, in 1983–84 by Clark A. Dobbs, and in the 1990s by Ronald Schirmer. The cultural deposits at the site are extremely dense; during the 1983–84 excavations, Dobbs discovered 557 pit features in an area measuring slightly over an acre.

The ceramic assemblage is dominated by Silvernale wares, but a variety of other forms, including Plains-like materials, have been found as well. Corn horticulture was an important focus of activities at Bryan, and dozens of bison scapula hoes, as well as pounds of carbonized maize, have been found in the excavations there. Wild rice also has been recovered and may have been an important food grain as well.

Multiple structures have been identified at Bryan. For at least a portion of its occupation, the site was surrounded by a large palisade that encompassed at least 5 acres. Multiple house forms are present, including round and square aboveground post structures; shallow, basin-shaped structures; and two possible community structures that were rebuilt on several occasions. The post-type structures were typically surrounded by clusters of deep pits. Burned human trophy or ancestor skulls were discovered in one of the shallow basin structures by Wilford.

Bryan is the best dated of the Red Wing sites. A high-precision radiocarbon study conducted by Dobbs (with M. Stuiver) dates the most expansive period of occupation at Bryan to between AD 1190 and 1223 (calibrated).

The Bryan site has been completely destroyed by gravel mining.

Stone Cairns

Among the unique features of the Red Wing landscape are a series of stone cairns situated on the remote high bluff tops overlooking Spring Creek in Minnesota. These cairns were first identified in the 1850s but were largely destroyed by collectors during the nineteenth century.

Early accounts of the cairns describe them as hollow structures made of stacked stone walls 8 to 12 feet high and 4 to 8 feet in diameter. Excavators reported finding little within the cairns except for a few fragments of human bone—and, in one instance, remnants of a cedar stake. The precise number and location of the cairns remains unknown, although it appears that there were at least two dozen of them. Ronald Schirmer is currently investigating several of these cairns, and it appears that they are often associated with small, presumably Oneota sites. All cairn sites are privately owned and are closed to the public.

Further Reading: Brower, J. V., *Minnesota: Discovery of Its Area 1540–1665* (St. Paul, MN: H. L. Collins Co., 1903); Dobbs, Clark A., *A Pilot Study of High Precision Radiocarbon Dating at the Red Wing Locality*, National Science Foundation Project No. BNS-9011744, Reports of Investigation No. 228, (Minneapolis: Institute for Minnesota Archaeology, 1993); Dobbs, Clark A., *The Archaeology of 21GD158: A 13th Century Native American Village at the Red Wing Locality*, Reports of Investigation No. 250 (Minneapolis: Institute for Minnesota Archaeology, 2000); *From Site to Story*, http://www.fromsitetostory.org; Schirmer, Ronald C., "Plant-Use Systems and Late Prehistoric Culture Change in the Red Wing Locality," Ph.D. diss. (University of Minnesota, 2002); Winchell, Newton H., *Aborigines of Minnesota* (St. Paul: The Pioneer Co., 1911), 143–172.

Clark A. Dobbs

THE SOUTH PARK VILLAGE SITE

Northeast Ohio

A Late Prehistoric Village

The Native American inhabitants of northeast Ohio arrived at the close of the Ice Age, 11,000 years ago, and departed perhaps only three generations before the arrival of Europeans in the early 1700s. In the closing centuries of this long expanse of time, from about AD 1200 to 1650, Native people in northern Ohio developed maize agriculture, consolidated their populations into permanent villages, and developed a tribal way of life.

And yet, because their last descendants departed the scene before meeting literate Frenchmen, we do not know the true name of these societies. So we name them for their archaeological remains, known as the Whittlesey tradition, named after Colonel Charles Whittlesey. Whittlesey, an accomplished citizen of Cleveland, Ohio, carried out extensive geological surveys across the state in the latter half of the nineteenth century. These forays inevitably led him to ancient mound and earthwork sites in the Cuyahoga and adjacent river valleys of northern Ohio, which he mapped with great precision and occasionally excavated.

Charles Whittlesey's most famous maps were of hilltop earthen enclosures (or "forts") and small concentrations of ancient mounds in the Cuyahoga Valley, which he attributed to a lost race of mound builders—a people he mistakenly believed to be unrelated to the Native Americans. By the early twentieth century, Ohio archaeologists no longer believed in such "mound builder myths" and recognized the hilltop forts to be the remains of Native American villages. One of these archaeologists was Emerson F. Greenman of the Ohio State Archaeological and Historical Society—who, beginning in 1929, set about exploring several of these important archaeological sites.

Greenman's most extensive excavations took place at two hilltop settlements in the lower Cuyahoga valley. One site was called Tuttle Hill after the original landowner but was actually the location of Whittlesey's Fort No. 3. The other settlement, named South Park by Greenman, was located just a few miles upriver on a high, mesa-like expanse of shale bedrock. South Park was apparently unknown to Whittlesey and may never have had an earthen wall enclosing a section of the hilltop, as did Tuttle Hill and the other forts. Still, initial excavations on both promontories produced abundant evidence of prehistoric habitation in the form of features, such as cooking and storage pits; post mold outlines from houses and other structures; human burials; and thick midden (trash) deposits containing thousands of pottery shards, flint arrow points, stone flakes from their manufacture, butchered animal bones, and the charred remains of maize and other plant foods.

As Greenman carefully studied the myriad artifacts and feature data he had accumulated, he realized that the stone tools and much of the decorated pottery, which had thick collars and incised, geometric designs, resembled "Iroquoian" material from western New York and northwestern Pennsylvania. Consequently he developed a new classification scheme for the archaeological remains from northeastern Ohio, which he called the Whittlesey Focus in honor of his illustrious predecessor.

Over the next several decades, Greenman's successors excavated additional sites across northern Ohio and refined the definition of pottery and stone-tool types. They mapped

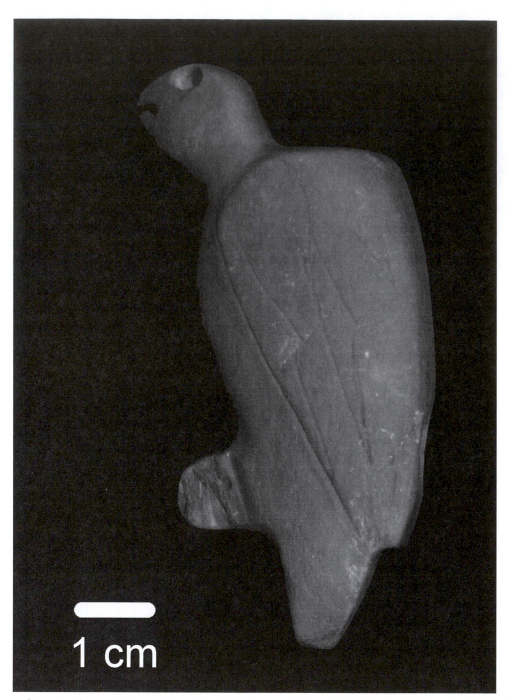

Stone bird effigy smoking pipe from the Reeve village site, Lake County, Ohio.   [The Cleveland Museum of Natural History]

the geographic distribution of these types of sites and even recorded burial styles. By the 1960s archaeologists in northern Ohio used radiocarbon dating to discover that the settlements of what became known as the Whittlesey tradition were occupied during the last few centuries before European contact, between about AD 1200 and 1650.

In 1968 archaeologist James Murphy of the Cleveland Museum of Natural History revisited the South Park site and carried out limited excavation across the plateau. The next year, work resumed under David S. Brose of Case Western Reserve University with support from the Cleveland Museum of Natural History. By late 1970 the site was threatened by industrial quarrying of the underlying shale deposits. At the same time, South Park was being slowly destroyed by a growing onslaught of illicit digging by local relic collectors. Consequently steps were taken to salvage what remained of the site through the use of mechanical excavating equipment, which succeeded in exposing a large sample of the remaining archaeological deposits of the village.

By 1971 the complete destruction of the site from commercial shale mining had been averted, although at least a third of the archaeological deposits were removed. Thus, the museum's crews were allowed to return to the site intermittently to salvage what they could until 1981, when work finally ceased. The land where South Park is located remains in trust to the Cuyahoga Valley National Park; however, very little of the site remains intact. Public access is not permitted, but in 2005, an Ohio historical marker was erected directly across the Cuyahoga River to commemorate this important site and to honor the Whittlesey-tradition inhabitants of the valley.

Today the South Park site remains the most thoroughly investigated Whittlesey-tradition village in the region. Brose and his colleagues' study of the thousands of artifacts and hundreds of domestic features and structures and other remains revealed a long-term occupation of the plateau by as many as three different populations of farmers, beginning as early as AD 1000 and lasting until about AD 1650. This sequence was marked by changes in pottery types from plain, cordmarked vessels through jars with intricately incised decorations to pots with distinctively notched collars and crushed-shell tempering. Stone artifacts were dominated by the simple and small Madison-style triangular arrow point but also included elaborately carved stone pipe bowls that were traded extensively throughout the region and beyond to Ontario, New York, and the Ohio valley.

Preserved food remains testify to an increasingly agricultural way of life based on the cultivation of maize, beans, and squash and supplemented by hunting and gathering of local animals and plants. Numerous large, cylindrical pits for storing the harvests were uncovered, along with the charred residues of crop plants. Abundant samples of butchered animal bones from the village middens and trash pits revealed the exploitation of numerous mammal and bird species, with elk, deer, raccoon, and wild turkey predominating. Bones from several species of riverine and Lake Erie fish were found, as were thousands of fragments from freshwater mussels. Finally, the carbonized shells of walnuts and hickory nuts revealed the importance of these autumnal foods.

The extensive excavation of South Park exposed numerous post mold patterns of dwellings and other structures that changed form over time. Some of the earliest deposits suggest that circular to oval houses, measuring 3 to 5 meters in diameter, were constructed for individual families in the original bluff top settlement. This architectural form gave way in the next phase of occupation to slightly larger dwellings with square or rectangular floor plans. Some of these houses were constructed with wall-trench foundations, an architectural innovation that may be derived from more populous and contemporaneous Mississippian societies in the Southeast or the

Mississippi valley. By the final occupation of the site, houses had been transformed into communal dwellings sheltering extended families or several nuclear families. These large, rectangular houses measured up to 10 meters in length and 5 meters in diameter. This evolution from single- to multiple-family dwellings reflects a significant increase in the population of the village settlement over time—and perhaps the development of formal lineages or clans. Such large formal kinship groups are well known among historically recorded Algonqian and Iroquoian tribal societies of the Great Lakes and the Northeast.

The most unusual kind of building uncovered during excavation at South Park was a single 5-meter-wide rectangular structure with a sunken floor and narrow entrance ramp. Such a building could have served as a ceremonial sweat bath or winter lodge. If it was the latter, then at least some of the villagers lived year-round at the site. Other families most likely traveled to the sheltered woods of interior creek valleys to hunt fur-bearing animals, such as bear, raccoon, beaver, and others, as recorded among eighteenth-century Wyandot and Ottawa families who eventually migrated to northern Ohio.

A surprisingly small number of human burials were found during professional excavations of the South Park site. Many more burials were very likely looted from the site and never recorded. Nonetheless no large cemetery area containing the remains of most of the village inhabitants has ever been found, which means that at least some funerals took place away from the village site, perhaps during winter stays in the interior.

A lingering mystery is the ultimate fate of the Whittlesey tradition people. Despite the collection of thousands of artifacts from South Park and other settlements, no verifiable European trade goods, such as glass beads or fragments of brass or iron implements, have ever been found. In contrast, small amounts of such materials have been recovered at late sixteenth- and early seventeenth-century settlements in northwestern and southern Ohio. Therefore, it seems that South Park was abandoned prior to the trade of such goods into the area, and its inhabitants moved on to parts yet unknown.

The impetus for the abandonment of the area may have been twofold. First, early historical sources describe devastating raids by Iroquoian societies in southern Ontario and New York state as part of the Beaver Wars in the early to mid-seventeenth century, which disrupted many native societies across the region. This aggression from the east may have forced the remaining Whittlesey societies out of their ancestral homeland. Second, we know that by the middle of the 1600s, the French began trading operations near Green Bay, Wisconsin. This attracted many of these dislodged peoples, who coveted the European metal implements and the symbolically important glass ornaments of the Europeans. Were the refugees from the Whittlesey tradition among the Algonquian-speaking tribes who moved northwest to meet and trade with the French? Continued archaeological work in their abandoned homeland will one day provide the answer to this important question.

Further Reading: Brose, David S., *The South Park Village Site and the Late Prehistoric Whittlesey Tradition of Northeast Ohio*, Monographs in World Archaeology, No. 20 (Madison, WI: Prehistory Press, 1994); Brose, David S., "Late Prehistoric Societies of Northeastern Ohio and Adjacent Portions of the South Shore of Lake Erie: A Review," in *Cultures before Contact: The Late Prehistory of Ohio*

and Surrounding Regions, edited by Robert Genheimer (Columbus: Ohio Archaeological Council, 2000), 96–122; Redmond, Brian G., "Before the Western Reserve: An Archaeological History of Northeastern Ohio," Cleveland Museum of Natural History Web site, http://www.cmnh.org/site/ResearchandCollections_Archaeology_Research_GeneralAudienceNontechnicall_HistoryNEOhio.aspx (online August 2006); Redmond, Brian G., and Katharine C. Ruhl, "Rethinking the 'Whittlesey Collapse': Late Prehistoric Pottery Migrations in Eastern Ohio," *Archaeology of Eastern North America* 30 (2002): 59–80.

Brian G. Redmond

MAMMOTH CAVE ARCHAEOLOGY

Kentucky

Ancient Uses of Caves in the Midwest

Mammoth Cave is the world's longest cave. Currently it has a mapped length of more than 580 kilometers. Historically and prehistorically, people have been fascinated with this cave. Humans explored Mammoth Cave as early as 5,500 years ago. Using only bundles of cane reeds or weed stalks and sticks for torches, prehistoric explorers penetrated several kilometers into the totally dark labyrinth of cave passages. Around 3,000 years ago, prehistoric cavers began mining several minerals that occur in the cave. This mining continued until 2,200 years ago, when interest in the cave appears to have abruptly ended.

Around AD 1800, Euro-American settlers rediscovered the cave. Early settlers knew that cave sediments often contained nitrates (or niter), a primary ingredient of gunpowder. The mining of niter dirt became a large industry at Mammoth Cave during the War of 1812. Following the end of the war, because of the cave's size and the prehistoric remains that had been found during the mining, travelers began coming to Kentucky specifically to see the *mammoth* cave. Cave tours have been in continuous operation at Mammoth Cave since 1816.

Located in south central Kentucky, Mammoth Cave's passages are formed within thick beds of limestone (approximately 100–110 m in thickness). The geology of the Mammoth Cave region is ideal for the formation of large, dry cave passages. Impermeable layers of sandstone and shale that act as a water-resistant cap or roof overlie the limestone cave passages, keeping them free of dripping water.

Perishable material, which in normal circumstances would quickly decay in the warm, wet climate of Kentucky, remains in a state of near-perfect preservation within the cave. It is this aspect of the prehistoric archaeology of Mammoth Cave that has made it famous. Items brought into the cave by the

first prehistoric explorers, such as torch remains, cordage, twined footwear, basketry, and wooden artifacts are preserved in the stable cave environment. In at least two instances, desiccated bodies of prehistoric explorers were also found in the cave. These so-called mummies created quite a sensation when they were discovered.

Although many artifacts were taken from the cave in early historic times and are now in private collections and museums, the first professional archaeologist to work at Mammoth Cave was Nels C. Nelson of the American Museum of Natural History in 1916. Nelson's interest, however, was not in the perishable remains found deep in the cave but rather in excavating the natural deposits and ancient occupation debris at the cave entrance. He excavated several trenches in the large cave vestibule, revealing stratified archaeological deposits from repeated ancient occupation of the entrance area. These deposits, which are typical in natural rock shelter and cave openings, date at least to 5,300 years ago, as determined by recent radiocarbon dates.

Alonzo Pond of the Smithsonian Institution spent several months at Mammoth Cave in 1935. He collected a number of perishable artifacts in the cave, but his primary purpose was to oversee the recovery of a desiccated prehistoric body that had been discovered during trail construction. The remains of this approximately 45-year-old man were found pinned under a large rock. Working in the cave at least 2,300 years ago, apparently he undermined a large rock on a ledge that rolled over and crushed him to death. After Pond removed the desiccated remains of this man from under the rock, they were on display in the cave for many years; however, they have been removed from display at the request of Native Americans who found the exhibit offensive.

The most thorough archaeological work in the Mammoth Cave system, however, has been performed by Patty Jo Watson and colleagues. Beginning in the 1960s and continuing to the present, Watson conducted excavations in Salts Cave (a portion of the Mammoth Cave system), collected various materials, and performed numerous analyses on these remains.

Watson's particular interest is in the remains of various plants found in the cave. Much of her analysis involves the study of domesticated plant remains found in desiccated human paleofecal specimens. The cave contains literally thousands of human paleofeces that date from 3,000 to 2,200 years ago. This is a critical period in the prehistory of eastern North America, when American Indians first began cultivating several native plants, including sunflower, marsh elder, goosefoot, and maygrass. Seeds of these plants were found in abundance in the human paleofeces, proving that indigenous plants were being cultivated nearly 1,500 years before non-native plants—corn and beans, arrived from Mesoamerica.

Prehistoric use of Mammoth Cave was very specialized. Working in the cave requires constant artificial light, and several plant stalks were used as torches. Dry river cane was the most common. Torch remains from several remote portions of the cave indicate that people began exploring Mammoth Cave to great depths by 5,500 years ago. These dates are consistent with evidence of early cave exploration in other parts of the southeastern and midwestern United States.

Most prehistoric remains in Mammoth Cave, however, date from 3,000 to 2,200 years ago; they result from the mining of several cave minerals. The mineral most commonly mined by prehistoric people was gypsum (calcium sulfate), which occurs in the dry passages as a crystal growth on the walls or as a fibrous or needle-like growth in the dry cave sediments. Digging of the sediments and scraping or battering of the walls by prehistoric miners to remove gypsum is apparent throughout several kilometers of cave passage. Tools used in this activity included digging sticks, mussel shell scrapers, hammerstones, gourd bowls, wooden bowls, and occasionally baskets and woven bags. Climbing poles were brought into the cave to reach upper ledges, and rock cairns were also built in locations to reach gypsum on the ceiling and upper ledges.

Two other minerals in the cave that were of interest to prehistoric people were epsomite (sodium sulfate) and mirabilite (magnesium sulfate). These sulfates occur as a soft, fibrous coating on the ceiling and walls of the cave under very special conditions. Both minerals have medicinal uses, the most significant being as an intestinal cathartic. Apparently, ingesting these minerals for their purgative effect was one purpose for entering the cave. The occurrence of sulfate minerals in the cave is much more limited in its distribution than the occurrence of gypsum; however, where it does occur, archaeologists have found the densest concentration of prehistoric remains, especially paleofeces.

The mining of gypsum and ingestion of medicinal salts by prehistoric people in Mammoth Cave continued throughout the Early Woodland period, but appears to have ended rather abruptly about 2,200 years ago. People may have continued to use the cave opening as a natural shelter after this time, but they no longer appear interested in exploring its deep recesses.

Euro-Americans began settling in this region of Kentucky after the American Revolution. By the early nineteenth century, reference to Mammoth Cave as a "saltpeter cave" occurs on the earliest land deeds. Saltpeter, the primary component of black gunpowder, was a valuable commodity on the American frontier.

Mining caves for niter (calcium nitrate), which can be turned into saltpeter (potassium nitrate), may have begun as a small cottage industry at Mammoth Cave. However, when the British blockaded America during the War of 1812, the value of saltpeter skyrocketed, and the mining of niter became a profitable industry at Mammoth Cave, as well as at other caves in the region. The saltpeter works at Mammoth Cave were quite elaborate and included a wooden pipeline to carry water into the cave from the entrance; numerous wooden vats to leach calcium nitrate from the sediment; a trough system to collect the niter solution; a tower and hand pump to raise the niter solution to a height where it would flow back out of the cave by gravity in a second pipeline; and then a system of troughs, filters, kettles, and a furnace near the cave's entrance to convert the calcium nitrate to potassium nitrate (saltpeter).

The 1812-era saltpeter works in Mammoth Cave are in a very good state of preservation, including most of the vats and portions of the pipeline. Saltpeter miners digging for niter dirt also significantly modified sections of the cave passage and built an oxcart trail that was used to ferry dirt from remote parts of the cave to the leaching vats. Many of these features are still visible in the cave.

The primary labor for producing saltpeter was provided by African American slaves. Later, as tourism increased at Mammoth Cave, African Americans also became some of the first tour guides, a tradition that continued for several generations. When not guiding visitors, the guides were responsible for building trails and exploring new passages. These explorers left their names in many remote portions of the cave that they discovered. It was also a common practice for cave visitors to write their names on the cave walls and ceilings. This was especially prevalent in the early nineteenth century. Thousands of names, dates, and places of origin have been inscribed onto some passage walls, providing a register of visitors from the early nineteenth century.

Mammoth Cave became part of the National Park system in 1941. The site is a National Historic Landmark and a World Heritage Site. The cave is open to the public but accessible by guided tour only. The saltpeter remains and the prehistoric archaeology are interpreted on several different tours, which change on a seasonal basis.

Further Reading: Crothers, George M., "Mineral Mining and Perishable Remains in Mammoth Cave: Examining Social Process in the Early Woodland Period," in *Fleeting Identities: Perishable Material Culture in Archaeological Research*, edited by Penelope B. Drooker, Occasional Paper No. 28 (Carbondale: Center for Archaeological Investigations, Southern Illinois University, 2001), 314–334; De Paepe, Duane, *Gunpowder from Mammoth Cave: The Saga of Saltpetre Mining Before and During the War of 1812* (Hays, KS: Cave Pearl Press, 1985); *Mammoth Cave*, National Park Service official Web site, http://www.nps.gov/maca/index. htm (online December 2005); Watson, Patty Jo, ed., *Archaeology of the Mammoth Cave Area*, reprinted ed. (St. Louis: Cave Books, 1997).

George M. Crothers

FORT ST. JOSEPH SITE

Niles, Michigan

An Early European Trade Site

Fort St. Joseph was one of the most important eighteenth-century frontier outposts in the western Great Lakes region. Initially established in the 1680s near a strategic portage linking the St. Joseph River and the Great Lakes basin to the Mississippi drainage, this complex, which served as mission, garrison, and trading post, was a hub of religious, military, and commercial activity for local Native American populations and European colonial powers for nearly a century.

Local historians collected artifacts from the site in the late nineteenth and early twentieth centuries; however, no systematic archaeological studies were conducted until 1998, when Western Michigan University (WMU) archaeologists began investigating the site. Subsequent excavations have identified undisturbed artifact deposits and features that are providing information on architecture, daily life, and social relations. Preliminary interpretations suggest that Fort St. Joseph was a multi-ethnic community in which the French and Native peoples were mutually dependent and freely shared information and ideas as they intermarried and created alliances along the frontier in the western Great Lakes.

HISTORICAL OVERVIEW

René-Robert Cavalier de La Salle visited the St. Joseph River valley in 1679 as the French sought to expand the fur trade and find a passage to the Far East. The following decade, the Jesuits were granted land by the French Crown for a mission along the river, and by 1691, an outpost had been established near the present-day southern boundary of Niles, Michigan. The post initially consisted of a palisade, a commandant's house, and a few other structures. It was authorized by Governor General Frontenac in an attempt to solidify relations with the Miami and Potawatomi Indians in the immediate vicinity of the fort; strengthen ties with other tribes farther west and north of the area; improve the fur trade in the region; and check the expansion and power of the Five Nations Iroquois Confederacy and their English allies.

Despite its religious origins, the French settlement on the St. Joseph River was known primarily for its commercial and military functions. It was a vital node in the colony's communications network and in the exchange of manufactured goods for furs obtained by the Natives. By the middle of the eighteenth century, it ranked fourth among all of New France's posts in terms of volume of furs traded. Fort St. Joseph played a prominent role in interactions between Native peoples and French and English colonial powers throughout the eighteenth century. It served as a central staging point and supply base for the French wars against the Fox Indians in the 1720s and 1730s, and later against the Chickasaws (1736–40). Commanders who had served at Fort St. Joseph and Natives from the region were key players in events leading up to, and during, the Seven Years' War that saw France lose Canada to the British. During Pontiac's Rebellion in the spring of 1763, supporters of the Ottawa leader attacked Fort St. Joseph in order to force the British from the area and encourage the return of the French.

The fort was not re-garrisoned after Pontiac's Rebellion, and in 1781 a small group of French and Native Americans from the Illinois country raided the fort. That expedition, which was supported by the Spanish governor at St. Louis, looted and occupied the fort for a day. The post was never reoccupied, although traders still frequented the valley into the early nineteenth century, when the area was part of America's Northwest Territory.

HISTORY OF INVESTIGATIONS

Although Fort St. Joseph has long been of interest to historians and antiquarians, systematic investigation of the site only began in 1998 with the initiation of the Fort St. Joseph

Students excavating a stone fireplace at Fort St. Joseph.   [Stephanie M. Barrante]

Several tinkling cones found at Fort St. Joseph.   [Fort St. Joseph Museum]

Archaeological Project. Early interest in the site was confined to collecting thousands of imported and locally produced eighteenth-century artifacts, many of which are now housed in local museums. The historian L. H. Beeson left a legal description of the location of the greatest concentration of materials.

Despite this documentation, subsequent searches, hindered by landscape changes, failed to relocate physical evidence of the fort. Beginning in the 1930s, George I. Quimby used the Niles collections to develop a chronology for post-contact artifacts in the western Great Lakes. In 1973 the site was listed on the National Register of Historic Places. The formation of Support the Fort Inc. (STF), a nonprofit organization dedicated to the identification, preservation, and interpretation of the remains of Fort St. Joseph, was critical to the discovery of the historic site's location. One of their members, New France scholar Dr. Joseph L. Peyser, had conducted extensive documentary research and determined that the fort was located on the east side of the river in Niles, contrary to some beliefs. This information narrowed the search for the fort to a 15-acre parcel owned by the city of Niles. WMU archaeologists conducted an archaeological survey there that led to the recovery of an assemblage of eighteenth-century artifacts, including gunflints, gun parts, brass kettle fragments, lead waste, glass trade beads, and European ceramics. They also found architectural remains, including hand-wrought nails and stones with traces of mortar, as well as many well-preserved animal food remains.

A geophysical survey, conducted to locate subsurface features and guide excavations, identified several circular and rectilinear anomalies that excavations have proven to be cultural in origin, demonstrating that the site of Fort St. Joseph had indeed been found.

DOCUMENTARY AND ARCHAEOLOGICAL FINDINGS

Documentary records in tandem with archaeological remains provide information on architecture, daily life, and the site's occupants. This information is useful for site reconstruction, public interpretation, and examination of the fort within broader comparative cultural, economic, historical, and political contexts. Written accounts indicate that Fort St. Joseph was constructed with entrances on the north and south palisade lines, and in 1691 it included a small commandant's house, a building that could accommodate twenty soldiers, a military storehouse, and some buildings to store trade goods and furs. In 1753 the post consisted of a jail and fifteen houses, though not all of these buildings were necessarily within the palisade.

Excavations have identified three stone fireplaces, a stone hearth, and a possible foundation wall. These features, together with the data from the geophysical survey, suggest the presence of one or more row houses oriented parallel to the riverbank. The recovery of numerous hand-wrought nails, *bousillage* (a mixture of clay and straw used to fill in the spaces between the upright posts in French buildings), *pierrotage* (a mixture of stones and mortar), and hardware (such as hinges) testify to the presence of multiple European-style structures at the site. Their size, methods of construction, age, and contents are currently being determined.

Numerous artifacts have been found in association with these architectural remains and elsewhere on the site. These artifacts and their spatial relationships are providing information on activity areas within the site, particularly in regards to production and exchange.

A broad range of artifact types are represented, reflecting the religious, military, and commercial functions of the site. These include crucifixes, religious medallions, military buttons, gun parts, domestic objects (ceramics, glass containers), objects of personal adornment (cuff links, finger rings), glass beads, lead seals used to identify and secure the contents of bales and bolts of cloth, and baling needles to wrap bundles of furs. One area of the site yielded a concentration of over 100 gun parts that has been interpreted as a gunsmith's repair kit. Documentary sources indicate that the French repaired Native guns as a service. Adjacent to one of the fireplaces were numerous glass beads, straight pins, and an awl, suggesting sewing in the fire's light and heat.

Other areas have yielded evidence for the production of musket balls or lead shot, as indicated by the waste that results from pouring molten lead into a mold. Numerous scraps of copper alloy derive from cutting sheet metal to produce patches and rivets to repair worn-out kettles and tinkling cones—cone-shaped ornaments used to decorate clothing or leather bags. Both burned and unburned bones have also been found, pointing to cooking and discard locations. Some artifacts made locally in the Native style, such as stone smoking pipes, bone tools, antler gaming pieces, and stone and metal projectile points, have also been recovered from excavations at the fort.

Faunal and floral remains are useful indicators of the fort residents' diets. Copious amounts of well-preserved animal bones indicate that predominantly wild animal species, such as deer, beaver, raccoon, and turkey, were being consumed at the fort. Relatively small amounts of pig, cow, horse, and chicken are among the domesticated animal bones found. Indian corn dominates the assemblage of plant remains, though only a limited amount of flotation has been conducted. Flotation is an archaeological technique used to recover small seeds and other organic material from soil samples, which are placed in water and stirred, after which the organic materials that float to the surface are collected and analyzed. The corn remains consist mostly of carbonized cobs that were found in a small pit feature. This feature has been interpreted as having been used originally used as a smudge pit used to tan hides in the Native fashion.

Ultimately the goal of archaeology at Fort St. Joseph is to gain a better understanding of the demographic composition of the fort and the identities of its occupants. Lists of commanders and soldiers reveal a military presence at the fort, as well as an interpreter to assist in dealings with Natives. In the early 1720s the garrison consisted of ten soldiers and eight officers, and by 1750 the fort supported about twenty families. Marriage and baptism records document the presence of French and Native women, some of the latter married to Frenchmen, and infants at the fort. The baptism records also indicate that Native American slaves and servants resided in the community, as did a master carpenter. Payment records reveal that a blacksmith capable of repairing guns lived at the fort.

Archaeological evidence is beginning to reveal the activities—and, by inference, the identities—of some of the fort occupants. For instance, the concentration of gun parts is evidence of the blacksmith. The presence of certain artifacts and practices, such as stone smoking pipes, antler gaming pieces, wild animal food remains, and smudge pits, suggest that the French had incorporated Native peoples into daily activities at the fort and begun to adopt Native practices, thus creating a new cultural identity on the frontier.

PUBLIC EDUCATION AND PUBLIC OUTREACH

Archaeological investigations of Fort St. Joseph have been conducted in partnership with the city of Niles. Local high school students, teachers, and adults continuing their education have participated in the field project, which culminates each season in an open house, during which the public is invited to witness ongoing excavations at the fort. In the off-season, the public can learn more about fort archaeology through publications, videos, Web sites, and a visit to the Fort St. Joseph Museum, which houses the collections and has current exhibits on the investigations.

Further Reading: Beeson, L. H., "Fort St. Joseph—The Mission, Trading Post and Fort, Located about One Mile South of Niles, Michigan," *Collections of the Michigan Pioneer and Historical Society* 28 (1900): 179–186; Hulse, Charles A., "An Archaeological Evaluation of Fort St. Joseph (20BE23), Berrien County, Michigan," *Michigan Archaeologist* 27(3–4) (1981): 55–76; Nassaney, Michael S., José António Brandão, William Cremin, and Brock A. Giordano, "Archaeological Evidence of Daily Life at an 18th-Century Outpost in the Western Great Lakes," *Historical Archaeology* 41(1) (2007): 1–17; Nassaney, Michael S., William Cremin, Renee Kurtzweil, and José António Brandão, "The Search for Fort St. Joseph (1691–1781) in Niles, Michigan," *Midcontinental Journal of Archaeology* 28(2) (2003): 1–38; Niles, Michigan, Fort St. Joseph Museum, *Archaeological Dig,* http://www.ci.niles.mi.us/Community/FortStJoseph Museum/ArcheologicalDig.htm (online March 2007); Peyser, Joseph L., ed., *Letters from New France: The Upper Country, 1686–1783* (Urbana: University of Illinois Press, 1992); Quimby, George I., *Indian Culture and European Trade Goods* (Madison: University of Wisconsin Press, 1966).

Michael S. Nassaney

THE NEW PHILADELPHIA HISTORICAL SITE

Southern Illinois

An Early Historic Free Black Townsite

New Philadelphia is the first town known to be established and platted by an African American, Frank McWorter. It is situated between the Illinois and Mississippi rivers in Pike County, Illinois. In 1836 McWorter subdivided 42 acres to form the town. He then used revenue from the sale of the lots to purchase his family's freedom (Walker 1983). African Americans and those of European descent moved to New Philadelphia and created a biracial community. The town serves as an important example of a farming community on the nation's midwestern frontier. Considering its origin, it is not surprising that the town also played a role in the Underground Railroad (Walker 1983).

The town's population peaked at about 160 people after the American Civil War. By the end of the century, however, the racial and corporate politics of America's gilded age tolled the death knell for the settlement. The new railroad line bypassed the town in 1869, and many of New Philadelphia's residents eventually moved away. By the early twentieth century, only a few families remained. Oral histories and newspaper accounts indicate that Ku Klux Klan activity, and the creation of sundowner towns and communities (places that warned blacks and members of other minorities that they had better leave before sundown) in the region, led to the dispersal of the remaining African American community to larger urban areas and west of the Mississippi (Loewen 2005).

Today most of the original 42 acres are planted in prairie grass or lay fallow. Only a few scattered house foundations are visible in the field. In the summer of 2002, the University of Illinois in Springfield and the New Philadelphia Association (NPA) initiated a long-term research project to study and celebrate the history of New Philadelphia. A collaborative archaeology project developed between the University of Maryland (UM), Illinois State Museum (ISM), University of Illinois in Urbana-Champaign (UIUC), and the New Philadelphia Association to undertake the archaeological investigation.

Many studies in African American archaeology and material culture have dealt with the pre-emancipation era (Epperson 1999; Ferguson 1992; Kelso 1986; Upton 1988; Vlach 1993). A research project at New Philadelphia allows archaeologists to examine the development of a biracial community on the western frontier during the pre- and post-emancipation eras.

The project began with a walkover survey that identified the spatial patterning and artifact concentrations. GIS overlays of the existing topography and the original town plan identified several house lots with discrete archaeological deposits associated with known owners (Gwaltney 2004). All of the occupation occurred in lots along the town's major roads, and a large portion of the town was not settled, even though lots throughout the town were bought and sold many times. The survey work and the GIS overlays provided a good basis for more in-depth archaeological fieldwork.

A geophysical survey at New Philadelphia was conducted to identify subsurface archaeological features such as pits, privies, cisterns, domestic architecture, and so on. Using two geophysical techniques—magnetic-field gradiometry and electrical resistance—the survey identified localized disturbances, potentially indicating archaeological deposits or features, to soils that would otherwise comprise relatively homogeneous, naturally developed soil deposits. Any human action that involves the localized disturbance of the soil is potentially detectable by geophysical techniques. In a geophysical map, cultural features (as well as other discrete disturbances) should appear as anomalies—that is, spatially discrete areas characterized by geophysical values that differ from those of the surrounding area.

The geophysical work focused on the areas where archaeologists had located large concentrations of artifacts in the walkover survey, and over two dozen anomalies were identified. These data helped develop an excavation strategy. Over the course of the next several seasons, field schools sponsored by the National Science Foundation Research Experiences for Undergraduates program and the UIUC Department of Anthropology ground-truthed several of the anomalies identified in the geophysical survey (i.e., they investigated them using excavation units to determine what was causing the anomaly).

Archaeological excavations demonstrated that undisturbed archaeological features exist below the plow zone, spanning the entire time period of the town's occupation. Several cellar features are associated with residents who lived in the town prior to the earliest known tax records. Subterranean features have been located throughout the townsite, some of which had been abandoned and filled by the end of the 1850s.

One cellar feature is associated with a single African American woman, Casiah Clark. She owned property in New

Philadelphia from 1854 onward The materials from the Clark cellar pit date to the 1850s–60s. A sewing assemblage from Casiah Clark's occupation furnishes a context for the domestic life of an African American family with a female head of household. By at least 1870, Clark had moved in with widowed Louisa McWorter and lived in that household until her death in 1888. Excavations revealed the foundations of this McWorter household. The identification of slate pencils close to the area where local accounts place a former segregated schoolhouse that served African American residents provides some evidence of the presence of this institution. Excavations on this location, referred to in documents as the "negro schoolhouse lot," uncovered the remains of a stone pier foundation that may be related to the building.

The artifact assemblages found at the different parts of the town also help to paint a different picture of the end of frontier Illinois. While a common perception exists of frontier life with little amenities, this was not the case as the town developed in the 1840s, 1850s, and after the American Civil War. Very early in the town's existence, the residents were well connected with regional and national markets. Refined earthenware ceramics from Great Britain found in contexts that date to the 1840s–50s provide notable evidence of the purchasing networks necessary to provision material items to this town, located over 20 miles from the Mississippi River. Agents from St. Louis traveled to eastern ports and ordered large quantities of ceramics to be shipped to St. Louis for eventual distribution to the city's hinterlands. By the 1850s, goods also flowed easily from Chicago.

It becomes clear upon comparing sites from the early nineteenth century in Illinois that material goods had become homogenized at domestic sites, and earlier cultural differences between households had become indistinguishable (Mazrim 2002, 268). A review of the material goods found at New Philadelphia shows that the types of material culture found at sites inhabited by members of different ethnic groups show little or no differences. All of the residents had the same types of material culture and could access local merchants for goods, such as refined earthenwares.

What distinguishes the different households from each other may be their dietary habits. Lack of access to some markets, because of economics, transportation, or racial discrimination, may have encouraged some families to continue the tradition through the nineteenth century of relying on foraging and hunting for a substantial amount of their protein intake (Mullins 1999).

Almost all of the nails found throughout the town are machine-cut nails. They were generally manufactured from about 1790 to about 1880. In the 1880s, wire nails became popular and are still manufactured today. The lack of wire-cut nails provides some perspective about the growth and eventual demise of the town. Little building occurred and very few repairs were made on existing buildings in New Philadelphia after the 1880s. While the residents of the former town left, people apparently did not build or renovate existing structures. The town suffered a slow decay as families moved away and buildings disappeared from the landscape.

The New Philadelphia story is about the quest for freedom, life on the frontier, confrontations with racism, and the struggle of a small rural town to survive. In August 2005, the town was listed on the National Register of Historic Places because of its archaeological potential to address questions related to the town's role in westward expansion, as a potential Underground Railroad site, and due to its multiracial composition.

The goal of the New Philadelphia archaeology project is to make data and interpretations available to the public as soon as possible. Democratization and transparency allow a diverse array of stakeholders, professionals, and members of the public to see how interpretations are developed based on the historical and archaeological evidence. A plurality of voices from the larger community helps build a better understanding of the town, more firmly placing it in America's national public memory.

Further Reading: Epperson, Terrance, "Constructing Difference: The Social and Spatial Order of the Chesapeake Plantation," in *"I, Too, Am America": Archaeological Studies of African-American Life*, edited by Theresa A. Singleton (Charlottesville: University Press of Virginia, 1999), 159–172; Ferguson, Leland, *Uncommon Ground: Archaeology and Early African America, 1600–1800* (Washington, DC: Smithsonian Institution Press, 1992); Gwaltney, Thomas, "New Philadelphia Project Pedestrian Survey: Final Report and Catalog, Phase I Archeology at the Historic Town of New Philadelphia, Illinois" (Bethesda, MD: ArGIS Consultants, LLC, 2004), http://www.heritage.umd.edu/CHRSWeb/New%20Philadelphia/NP_Final_Report_View (online July 2005); Kelso, William, "Mulberry Row: Slave Life at Thomas Jefferson's Monticello," *Archaeology* 39(5) (1986): 28–35; Loewen, James, *Sundown Towns: A Hidden Dimension of American Racism* (New York: The New Press, 2005); Mullins, Paul R., *Race and Affluence: An Archaeology of African America and Consumer Culture* (New York: Kluwer Academic/Plenum Publishers, 1999); Mazrim, Robert, *Now Quite Out of Society: Archaeology and Frontier Illinois, Essays and Excavation Reports*, Illinois Transportation Archaeological Research Program, Transportation Archaeological Bulletin No.1 (Urbana: Department of Anthropology, University of Illinois, 2002); Upton, Dell, "White and Black Landscapes in Eighteenth-Century Virginia," in *Material Life in America, 1600–1800*, edited by Robert Blair St. George (Boston, MA: Northeastern University Press, 1988), 357–369; Vlach, John M., *Back of the Big House: The Architecture of Plantation Slavery* (Chapel Hill: University of North Carolina Press, 1993); Walker, Juliet E. K., *Free Frank: A Black Pioneer on the Antebellum Frontier* (Lexington: University Press of Kentucky, 1983).

Paul A. Shackel, Michael L. Hargrave,
Terrance J. Martin, and Christopher C. Fennell

THE LINCOLN HOME ARCHAEOLOGICAL SITE

Springfield, Illinois
Lincoln Home National Historical Site

In 1972 the U.S. National Park Service assumed stewardship of President Abraham Lincoln's former residence in Springfield, Illinois, and thereupon established the Lincoln Home National Historic Site. The family home has been open for public tours since the late nineteenth century, when the president's first and only surviving son, Robert Todd Lincoln, deeded it to the state of Illinois. When the National Park Service took over management of the site, it sought to make the setting around the Lincoln Home more historically accurate. Accordingly, under provisions of a long-term management plan, the new administrators began acquiring the properties in the four-block area surrounding the featured domicile, removing intrusive modern structures, stabilizing historic structures, and conducting research that would assist in restoring the neighborhood to a semblance of its appearance during Lincoln's last full year of residency, 1860. Those efforts have included intensive archaeological investigation of the Lincoln Home site itself and at least a dozen other contemporary properties nearby.

In 1839 the Reverend Charles Dresser built the small cottage that Lincoln would eventually purchase from him. The future president had moved to Springfield only two years earlier from a small rural community west of the city—a reconstruction of which today is open to the public as Lincoln's New Salem State Historic Site. On November 4, 1842, Dresser performed the ceremony that united Lincoln in marriage with Mary Todd, and that may have been when the couple first became acquainted with the modest home situated at the corner of Eighth and Jackson streets. Indeed tradition has it that the wedding was originally supposed to be held in the reverend's house, but was later changed to a more prestigious venue: the nearby home of Ninian Edwards, who was the son of a former Illinois territorial and state governor, and whose wife, Elizabeth, was Mary's sister.

Dresser had advertised his house for sale or rent as early as July 7, 1841, but the Lincolns did not purchase it until January of 1844, a few months following the birth of Robert. By the spring of 1853, Mary had presented Lincoln with three more sons, though one of them, Eddie, died shortly before reaching his fourth birthday in 1850. With a larger family and growing social standing as an active circuit court lawyer and sometime politician, Lincoln initiated a series of renovations that would culminate in tripling the available space in their home by 1856, when the expanded story-and-a-half cottage gained a full second floor. That last major addition created the final

two-story house that the National Park Service would seek to recapture as part of its restoration efforts.

ARCHAEOLOGICAL INVESTIGATIONS

An early archaeological study of Lincoln's former residence was carried out in 1951 as part of a major site restoration project carried out by the state of Illinois. By that time, none of the original outbuildings still stood, and the excavators sought to gather information for their reconstruction. Archaeologist Richard S. Hagen led a small team in search of evidence relating to Lincoln's carriage house, woodshed, and privy, all of which had once been situated at the rear of the property near a service alley.

The Hagen investigations succeeded in finding the remains of those structures specifically mentioned in the insurance policy Lincoln took out on his Springfield property when he departed to assume the presidency in 1861. The team, however, also found two earlier privy pits, reflecting the fact that such facilities were occasionally moved in the days before their positions were fixed by use of brick-lined vaults, which were periodically maintained in accordance with a city ordinance of 1851. The archaeological team also discovered a large rubbish pit filled with a wide variety of domestic refuse, including tablewares and lamp chimneys as well as many personal items, such as fragments from combs and toothbrushes.

As part of the early planning process for the major 1987–1988 restoration of the Lincoln Home and surrounding neighborhood, the National Park Service contracted out for archaeological investigations at four properties within the park unit, including the Lincoln Home itself, in 1985. Directed by Floyd Mansberger for Northern Illinois University, the initial field project set out to determine whether archaeological deposits of potential significance survived in proximity to the historic structures scheduled for restoration in the initial development phase. This was indeed found to be the case, particularly at the Lincoln Home, where intact cultural features were discovered near the foundation, as well as beneath its side and rear porches.

In areas where additions had expanded the original house over once-open ground surfaces, the archaeological team found considerable evidence relating to both the Dresser and Lincoln occupations of the site. Beneath the side porch, for example, were remnants of the original brick walkway that once led from the doorway to the public sidewalk on Jackson Street. Additionally, removal of the back porch decking

Late nineteenth-century furnace remains found beneath the Lincoln Home basement floor.   [National Park Service]

Lincoln Home exterior after the 1987–88 restoration.   [National Park Service]

revealed an abandoned foundation from an earlier central L-shaped wing off the back of the house that Dresser had added. Most important was the discovery of the remains of a well that had served residents of the house before completion of the expanded rear section. Given the fact that Lincoln is known to have modified the backhouse in 1849, excavators concluded that the long-hidden well had been abandoned during Lincoln's occupation, and any archaeological materials deposited with the fill were likely to be artifacts used and discarded by the Lincoln family.

Because the feature would not be totally destroyed by restoration of the Lincoln Home, excavators only removed the upper 45 centimeters of fill from the well and preserved the remainder in place. Even that small sample, however, contained information about the diet, health, and lifestyle of the occupants. Among the items recovered were eggshells, peach pits, and bone from butchered animals, as well as the ground-glass stopper from a decanter and two fragmentary medicine vials. One of the latter still bore the distinctive mark of "Dr. Jayne's Carminative Balsam," a popular patent medicine of the mid-nineteenth century that was advertised as a "certain cure" for all manner of gastrointestinal ills. In addition the archaeologists found a pewter knob that probably once graced a coffeepot, a shell button and hard rubber garment stays, and even a badly mangled pewter spoon that one of the Lincoln boys may have used for digging in the yard.

While examining the exterior house foundation near the back porch in 1985, excavators also uncovered the edge of a large, domed cistern, which would have held rainwater for purposes such as laundering and bathing. The presence of a cistern at this location was no surprise, as a circa-1865 stereopticon slide taken from the Lincoln Home backyard clearly shows a downspout descending toward the ground just left of the porch and a hand pump in the yard a short distance from the house—indicating where the cistern's oculus should be located. The feature, however, was found to be in a remarkable state of preservation when the National Park Service archaeologist assigned to the 1987 restoration project examined it again, and the cistern was protected from damage while that work proceeded.

Throughout the demolition phase of Lincoln Home restoration work, NPS archaeologist Vergil E. Noble monitored all ground-disturbing activities to ensure that significant cultural resources associated with the site would not be inadvertently destroyed. In addition to demarcating the features first recorded in the preliminary Mansberger investigations for protection, Noble made a number of new discoveries related to the structural evolution of the nineteenth-century residence. The most notable of those discoveries occurred in the basement, following removal of a concrete floor poured in the early 1950s as part of the earlier state-funded restoration effort. A test unit, which excavated through the layer of fill that lay immediately below the concrete, revealed the original clay floor and even a few shards of window glass that had become embedded in its surface.

More remarkable, however, was the unearthing of an elaborate brick feature under the basement floor that comprised a barrel-vaulted tunnel and a circular chamber as distinct elements. Research into several nineteenth-century publications on house construction confirmed that the feature was part of a furnace base and air duct system associated with a gravity-feed furnace that heated by convection currents, and a search of administrative records revealed that a hot-air furnace was installed by the state of Illinois around 1890. This furnace was in use probably no more than a decade, however, as it is also known that steam heat was introduced to the Lincoln Home in 1902.

Only minor archaeological investigations have been carried out at the Lincoln Home since 1987, but to date archaeologists have conducted excavations on nine other house lots in the four-block National Historic Site prior to the restoration or reconstruction of period buildings on them. In each instance, the meticulous excavators have encountered significant archaeological deposits reflecting the use of Lincoln's contemporary neighbors. That research has yielded vast amounts of data related to urban life in the nineteenth-century Midwest while assisting National Park Service efforts to interpret Lincoln's life and times to the public.

Further Reading: Hagan, Richard S., "Back-Yard Archaeology at Lincoln's Home," *Journal of the Illinois Historical Society* (Winter 1951); Noble, Vergil E., "Archaeology's Contribution to Lincoln Home Restoration," *Historic Illinois* 12(2) (1989): 4–7; Temple, Wayne C., *By Square and Compasses: The Building of Lincoln's Home and Its Saga* (Bloomington, IL: Ashlar Press, 1984).

Vergil E. Noble

PEA RIDGE NATIONAL MILITARY PARK AND WILSON'S CREEK NATIONAL BATTLEFIELD

Northwest Arkansas and Southwest Missouri
Civil War Battlefields in the Southern Midwest

The rolling hills of the western Ozark uplands of Missouri and Arkansas were the scene of some of the earliest armed clashes of the American Civil War. The second major battle was fought in Missouri on August 10, 1861, when Union troops under the command of General Nathaniel Lyon were defeated in a hard-fought battle with Southern forces led by Major General Sterling Price and General Ben McCulloch. Lyon was the first Union general officer killed in the war, and the battle was significant because it helped to determine whether the North or South would gain control of Missouri.

The fight for control of Missouri, and its commercial hubs and riverine transportation systems (the Mississippi and Missouri rivers), was essentially settled in 1862 with the defeat of Confederate forces under the command of Major General Earl Van Dorn by Union General Samuel Curtis at the early March battle of Pea Ridge, Arkansas.

Wilson's Creek National Battlefield is located near Republic in southwest Missouri, about 15 miles from Springfield, and Pea Ridge National Military Park is located in the northwest corner of Arkansas, near Bentonville; both are part of the U.S. National Park System. Park managers had long realized that history alone could not tell the complete story of either battle and sought the aid of battlefield archaeologists to help tell the story through physical evidence.

War, time, and agricultural practices literally buried the physical evidence of these moments of history that archaeologists began to unearth in 2001. Over the years, storms and plowing brought some items to the surface that were found, picked up, and sold in curio shops and makeshift museums near the battlefields. But there were still artifacts below the surface, waiting to be detected by systematic archaeological surveys using advanced equipment, such as metal detectors and the global positioning system (GPS), and techniques such as geographic information systems (GIS) to locate and study them. Agriculture, road building, and home construction disturbed some soil, but 6 inches to a foot below the surface, there were thousands of artifacts still arrayed in their patterns of deposition, waiting to be detected and recorded so they could offer a fuller understanding of the battles.

In archaeology it is not enough to know where artifacts are to be found, but also where artifacts are not to be found. A primary research goal of the Wilson's Creek and Pea Ridge Battlefields Archeological Project was to define the limits of the battlefields, as well as recover evidence of the ebb and flow of the battles.

The first requirement, then, was to develop field procedures capable of examining the entire extent of the battlefield. Faced with examining a large area, and assuming that most

A team of archaeologists and metal detectors sweep a portion of Wilson's Creek National Battlefield seeking physical evidence of the battle.   [Douglas D. Scott]

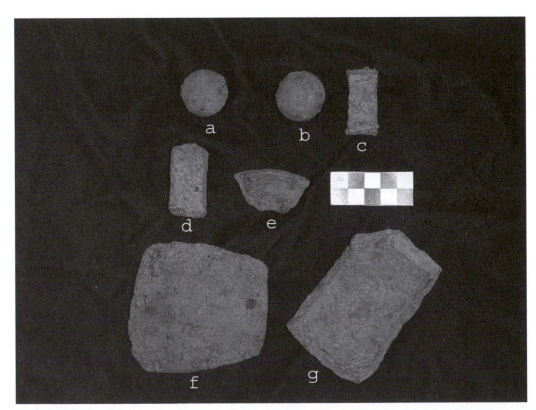

Finds of fragments of artillery shell and expedient canister helped identify the location of cannon positions using GIS terrain analysis functions.   [Douglas D. Scott]

An open field at Pea Ridge National Military Park was the site of archaeological finds that aided in reinterpreting the fighting that took place here in 1862.   [Douglas D. Scott]

surviving artifacts of war were either metallic or associated with metal, researchers employed metal detectors as an inventory tool based on the success of the technique at Little Bighorn Battlefield National Monument. The systematic archaeological survey using metal detectors operated by knowledgeable people has overwhelmingly proven its value in numerous battlefield and historic-site investigations.

Locational control was accomplished through the use of GPS units. Each item or location recorded on the data recorder was identified by unique coordinates, as well as a previously established identification code. All collected provenience information and analytical information regarding different artifact types was processed using a GIS.

The archaeological record confirms the documentary sources of intense firefights scattered about both battlefields. Expedient canister made from wrought-iron bar and rod—so-called bar shot—was found; it could have been used by only one specific Confederate Missouri artillery unit. This confirmed each side's position on both fields of battle.

That precise locational information coupled with a reassessment of historic documents allowed specific units that fought on their flanks as well as their opposing forces to be more accurately located on the landscape. With this new information, more complete reconstruction of the battle lines was undertaken. It became clear that traditionally interpreted artillery positions at the southern end of the Wilson's Creek battle were not correct. Using GIS terrain analysis based on the artifact patterning allowed investigators to pinpoint artillery fieldpieces on the landscape more accurately and then reinterpret the accounts of various officers and recollections of other participants. It became clear that both Northern and Southern commanders exaggerated the intensity of the firefights in order to rationalize the failure of their inexperienced men to stand up to intense, but short, artillery barrages.

On the western portion of the Pea Ridge battlefield, the archaeological artifact pattern turned the battle on its side. Historical accounts suggest the Union artillery had command of the field but fired blindly across a grove of trees into a

Bullets from Pea Ridge, simple common artifacts, were key elements in determining who fought where, what guns were actually used, and when properly recorded unit organization can be deduced from the data.   [Douglas D. Scott]

Confederate column. Artillery artifact distributions indicate that this did occur, but at least one Confederate artillery unit moved much farther south than documentary sources note, and there was a short but intense artillery duel between these units before the Confederate guns were silenced.

Clashes between opposing infantry during the last part of the fighting between Confederate and Union units in a wooded area was chaotic and disorganized, according to Union reports of their victory. Artifact patterning suggests this was not quite the case. The wooded area did cause individual unit maneuvering difficulty, but Confederate forces made a determined infantry assault on an artillery battery, nearly breaking the Union line. Fired and lost bullets were found in linear patterns, indicating that Union troops fired volleys in organized ranks; but due to the Confederate onslaught, the

Northern ranks became disorganized and fell back. But command and control was re-established, the line reorganized, and the Confederate assault broken.

The real surprise pertains to the orientation of the respective lines of soldiers. The traditional view of the infantry battle involved a Confederate charge from the north or northeast toward Union lines, on the south side of a farm field. The archaeological artifact pattern shows this to be an inaccurate view; rather, the Union line pivoted or completed an oblique movement from an east-to-west array to one that was on a north-to-south alignment, then met the Confederate assault coming from the east through the wooded area. The Union accounts give short shrift to this part of the story, perhaps glossing over a near defeat to make the general officers appear as if they had matters in hand all along. It now appears that the Confederates'

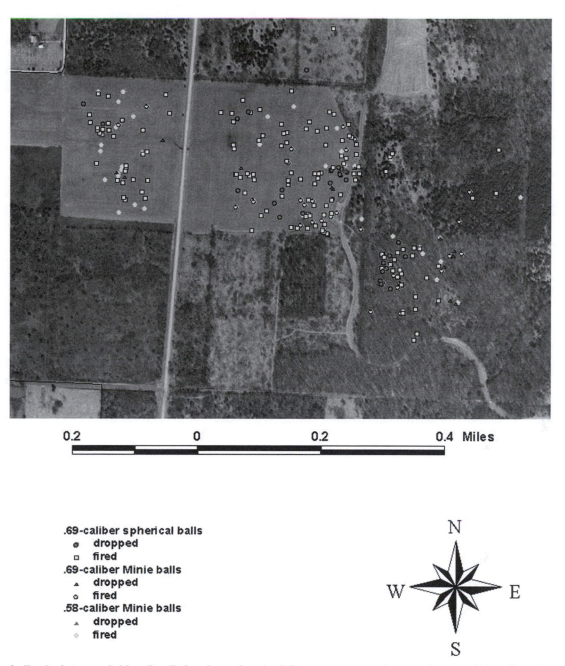

0.2   0   0.2   0.4 **Miles**

.69-caliber spherical balls
- ø dropped
- □ fired

.69-caliber Minie balls
- ▲ dropped
- ○ fired

.58-caliber Minie balls
- ▲ dropped
- ✦ fired

N
W — E
S

A plot of the bullet finds in one field at Pea Ridge shows that the fighting was not north to south, as traditionally believed, but that the soldiers fought a battle flowing east to west. The battlelines are approximated by the locations of fired and impacted bullets as well as bullets dropped in the melee. [Douglas D. Scott]

eastward flanking move was in reality a surprise that nearly wrecked a Union victory. The tenacious Union company commander perhaps deserves more credit than the senior officers chose to mention in the official reports of the day.

It might be said the historical record is accurate in recording the events, but perhaps not precise in its description or detail. Taking into account the fact that these were first battles for most participants, it is not unreasonable to expect some distorted views of the fights to occur. In both battles,

Union and Confederate commanders and their men were surprised. Neither likely wanted to place too harsh a critical light on those episodes of the engagement. Rather, it seems likely that commanders and their subordinates would focus on the positive aspects as well as, perhaps, exaggerate the intensity of the firefight to justify their actions and reactions at different points in the battle.

Regardless of the depositional contexts at both battlefields, the archaeological data is the physical evidence of those tumultuous events of 1861 and 1862. Systematic investigation of the archaeological record provided a new and independent means of assessing and evaluating the disparate historical record of those events. It certainly does not alter the outcome, but it does provide a physical link, and an interpretable body of data, to significant episodes in the history of the American Civil War. The results of these archaeological studies provide new insight into elements of each battle that was not recorded in the historic documents. While the archaeological record may not directly reflect the commanders' personalities, the patterned artifact distributions do provide us with a glimpse into how effectively or ineffectively military commanders spurred their men on at the battle of Wilson's Creek and Pea Ridge.

Coupling the archaeological data with historic accounts garnered a greater understanding of the events at a level of precision on the landscape that was not previously available. The battlefields are taking on a whole new look as cannons are placed where they once were. Some vegetation is being thinned or removed to aid in re-creating, as much as is possible, a landscape that resembles what the participants saw.

Perhaps the greatest value of these investigations is not the artifacts that were found, nor even the interpretations of their patterning. Rather, it is the experience of having historians, archaeologists, natural resource managers, and park management working as a team to assess and reassess all the information to create a more accurate and better interpretive experience for the park visitor.

Further Reading: Bearss, Edwin C., *The Battle of Wilson's Creek* (Washington, DC: U.S. Department of the Interior, National Park Service, 1960); Carlson-Drexler, Carl G., Douglas D. Scott, and Harold Roeker, *"The Battle Raged . . . with Terrible Fury": Battlefield Archeology of Pea Ridge National Military Park* (Lincoln, NE: National Park Service, Midwest Archeological Center, 2005); Scott, Douglas D., "'A Stirring Effect on the Enemy': Civil War Archaeology of Sharp's Cornfield at the 1861 Battle of Wilson's Creek, Missouri," *Missouri Archaeologist* 66 (2005): 77–92; Scott, Douglas D., Harold Roeker, and Carl Carlson-Drexler, *"The Fire Upon Us Was Terrific": Battlefield Archeology of Wilson's Creek National Battlefield, Missouri* (Lincoln, NE: National Park Service, Midwest Archeological Center, 2005); Shea, William L., and Earl J. Hess, *Pea Ridge: Civil War Campaign in the West* (Chapel Hill: University of North Carolina Press, 1992).

Douglas D. Scott

Great Plains/Rocky Mountains Region

KEY FOR GREAT PLAINS/
ROCKY MOUNTAINS REGIONAL MAP

1. Head-Smashed-In Buffalo Jump
2. Alibates Flint Quarries National Monument
3. Crow Creek
4. Grand Teton and Yellowstone National Parks
5. Knife River Indian Villages National Historic Site
6. Osage Village State Historic Site
7. Blackwater Draw
8. Folsom
9. Steed-Kisker
10. Fort Union Trading Post National Historic Site
11. Fort Clark State Historic Site
12. Steamboat Bertrand site and cargo collection
13. Bent's Old Fort National Historic Site
14. Fort Larned National Historic Site
15. Sand Creek Massacre National Historic Site
16. Pipestone National Monument
17. Fort Union National Monument
18. Fort Scott National Historic Site
19. Red River War sites
20. Double Ditch Village State Historic Site
21. Lindenmeier
22. Stewart's Cattleguard
23. Dent
24. Horner
25. Barton Gulch
26. Mill Iron
27. Ray Long
28. Agate Basin
29. Hell Gap
30. Signal Butte
31. Plainview
32. James Allen
33. Medicine Lodge Creek
34. Caribou Lake
35. Chance Gulch
36. Cooper
37. Lubbock Lake
38. Jones Miller
39. Olsen-Chubbuck
40. Hudson-Meng Bison Kill
41. Ulm Pishkun State Park
42. Vore Buffalo Jump
43. Old Women's Buffalo Jump
44. Huff Indian Village State Historic Site
45. Fay Tolton
46. Biesterfield
47. Like-a-Fishhook Village
48. Little Bighorn Battlefield National Monument
49. Washita Battlefield National Historic Site
50. Pawnee Fork
51. Writing-on-Stone Provincial Park
52. Pictograph Cave State Park
53. Bear Gulch
54. Legend Rock Petroglyph Historic Site
55. Mujares Creek
56. Buried City sites
57. Lake Theo

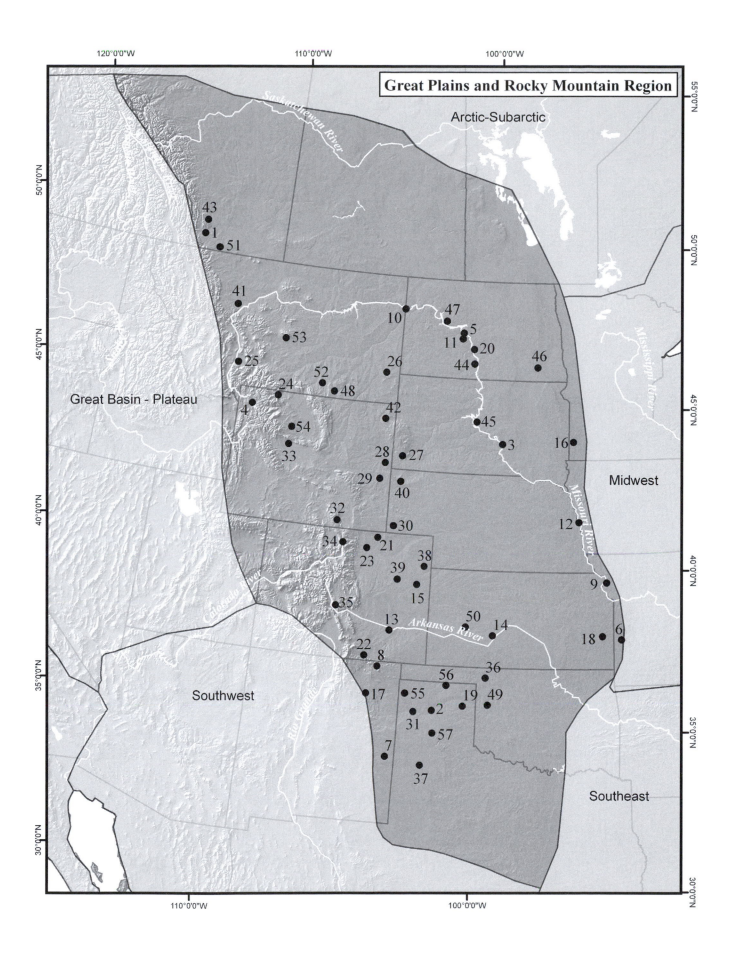

Great Plains and Rocky Mountain Region

Arctic-Subarctic

Great Basin - Plateau

Midwest

Southwest

Southeast

INTRODUCTION

This section of *Archaeology in America* includes essays about archaeological sites in the Great Plains and the Rocky Mountains. The eastern boundary for this large region can be imagined as a line running from the east central Texas coast roughly north through eastern Oklahoma, central Kansas, western Iowa and Minnesota, and into Manitoba. On its western side, the region's border runs north from west Texas through eastern New Mexico, clips eastern Utah, includes much of Colorado and all of Wyoming, includes southeastern Idaho and much of Montana, and runs into western British Columbia. Included within this west central slice of North America, in addition to those states already listed, are Nebraska, South Dakota, and North Dakota, plus the southern portions of the Canadian provinces of Saskatchewan and Alberta.

The dominant large-scale geomorphological features of the region are the wide swath of low and high plains from central Texas to southern Canada, and the rugged mountains and high-altitude plateaus along the western boundary of these plains. Running through these dramatic landscapes, which tend to be arid, is a network of rivers. These rivers have been used by people throughout the 15,000 to 20,000 years that human populations have inhabited this portion of North America. From the beginning of human occupation and use of the land and resources, the rivers have provided, and still do provide, essential pockets of well-watered land and corridors for travel and transport.

The western portion of the Great Plains and adjacent front range sections of the Rocky Mountains contain some of the earliest dated archaeological sites in North America. Two of these sites—Blackwater Draw near Clovis, New Mexico and the Folsom site near Folsom, New Mexico—have provided the names for the two earliest Paleoindian traditions recognized by archaeologists. Readers will find examples of Clovis tradition projectile points covered in one or two essays in each section of *Archaeology in America*. The distinctive projectile points associated with these traditions and with several of the traditions or cultures that derived from them are quite widespread.

From the earliest period to historic times, inhabitants of the Great Plains–Rocky Mountains region have looked to large game animals for an important portion of their sustenance. The projectile technology utilized is described in several essays. The essay about "Head-Smashed-In" buffalo jump, a World Heritage Site in Canada, describes the common sites where herd animals, in particular the buffalo and its now extinct ancestors, were cornered on or stampeded off a cliff. Ancient settlements and sites along rivers throughout the region also are described. Rivers were an important focus of human settlement both for natural resource utilization and in late prehistoric times for providing water for agriculture. A number of sites along the Missouri River are described to depict the aspects of life in the region before and following the contact with Europeans and Euro-Americans from the seventeenth century onward.

Archaeological sites described in the essays also record aspects of the historic period in the Great Plains and Rocky Mountains, including nineteenth-century warfare between pioneer and settler Euro-Americans and the Indian tribes fighting to retain their traditional ways of life. The entry on the shipwreck *Bertrand* and its collection of equipment, provisions, and supplies intended for nineteenth-century settlers along the Missouri River provides a fascinating view of this period.

These essays focus on the most important and interesting archaeological sites and topics in the Great Plains–Rocky Mountains region. Readers can learn more about these sites, and others as well, by referring to the additional sources of information and references listed at the end of each essay. More articles, books, Web sites, information on museums, and other sources are available to those who wish to learn more about these fascinating places and subjects. In many cases, the sites can be visited as parts of national, state, local, or other public parks.

The articles in the Great Plains–Rocky Mountains section of *Archaeology in America* include seven general essays on various topics that cover the ancient and historic time periods. The general essays are followed by fifteen essays on specific archaeological sites or related groups of sites in a particular region. These more specific essays are arranged in roughly chronological order.

ENTRIES FOR THE GREAT PLAINS/
ROCKY MOUNTAINS REGION

ARCHAEOLOGY OF THE GREAT PLAINS AND ROCKY MOUNTAINS

HISTORY OF RESEARCH

The history of archaeological research in the Great Plains and Rocky Mountains began over a century ago. Much of this early work was limited in scope and often focused on the description of individual sites—especially those with architectural remnants visible on or above the ground surface, such as the Medicine Wheel in the Bighorn Mountains of Wyoming. The development of a focus on the archaeology of the region began in the 1930s, ushered in with the professionalization of the discipline and the formation of avocational (amateur) archaeological societies.

Several important research projects of the 1930s include E. B. Renaud's multi-year reconnaissance surveys of the western Plains, which laid the foundation for a regional chronology based on projectile point and ceramic styles. These efforts were strengthened by excavation of ancient sites, such as Frank H. H. Roberts's work at the Lindenmeier site in northern Colorado, where many aspects of the Folsom Paleoindian culture were unearthed from the late Pleistocene period. William Duncan Strong's excavation of the Signal Butte site in western Nebraska established a chronological sequence based on stratified archaeological deposits dating back to the Middle Holocene period, about 6,000 years ago. Working in the more recent past, Waldo R. Wedel explored the origins of the Pawnee through excavation of village sites in Nebraska and Kansas.

The quantity of work expanded exponentially following World War II, with the creation of the River Basin Survey program, led by the Bureau of American Ethnology, the Smithsonian Institution, and the National Park Service. Extensive archaeological surveys and excavations were conducted to rescue artifacts, along with other remains and data about their contexts, before they could be destroyed by dam construction or submerged beneath the extensive system of new reservoirs. The archaeological investigations were done in advance of a massive federal water control public-works program, with a particular focus on the Missouri River basin. Large prehistoric and historic Native American agricultural villages and early historic period Euro-American trading posts were excavated along the Missouri River in North and South Dakota, providing invaluable information about the density and types of sites now inundated by reservoirs.

Archaeological research flourishes today, in academic investigations as well as cultural resource management (CRM) studies, much of it conducted in advance of energy extraction (primarily coal, oil, and natural gas). The vast majority of CRM work is conducted in those states containing large tracts of federal land holdings, such as Colorado, Montana, and Wyoming.

The establishment of the annual Plains Anthropological Conference was also important to the professional development of Great Plains archaeology. First convened in 1931, the conference met only intermittently until World War II. However, the conference has met annually since 1947 at locations across the Great Plains, in both the United States and the prairie provinces of Canada. The conference serves to inform students and archaeologists about the latest fieldwork and trends in the region. The Rocky Mountain Anthropological Conference (RMAC) is a more recent development that has provided a mountains-specific regional meeting. Founded in 1993, the RMAC meets biannually at locations throughout the Rocky Mountain west. The *Plains Anthropologist* serves as the principal peer-reviewed journal for the professional archaeological literature of the Great Plains and Rocky Mountains. Established in 1955, the journal remains strong today, publishing four issues a year, along with periodic topical memoirs.

Amateur archaeological societies, formed to channel public interest in the popular science, have played and continue to play important roles in Great Plains and Rocky Mountain archaeology. For example, the Texas Archaeological Society was formed in 1929, followed by the Colorado Archaeological Society (1935), the Oklahoma Anthropological Society (1952), and the Wyoming Archaeological Society (1959). These societies are successful at publishing state-level research, through both newsletters and journals such as *Southwestern Lore* (Colorado Archaeological Society) and the *Bulletin of the Texas Archaeological Society*. Many society members volunteer in various kinds of archaeological projects. The contributions of avocational archaeologists cannot be overstated, as many of the notable sites examined in the twentieth century were discovered by non-professionals.

REGIONAL INTERPRETIVE SYNTHESES

The archaeological record of the Great Plains and Rocky Mountains contains evidence documenting two basic forms of human organization, based on subsistence patterns and social complexity. The primary form of organization is one based on foraging, which involves hunter-gatherers who are dependent on wild plant and animal products for their livelihood. Foragers usually are mobile populations, moving between different food source locations on seasonal cycles. Archaeological sites associated with foraging societies tend to be spatially small and are occupied for short periods—probably no more than several consecutive weeks to months at any one time. This pattern dominates the archaeological record, spanning 13,000 years from the earliest Clovis Paleoindian sites in the Late Pleistocene period until as recently as, in some areas, the late nineteenth century.

The second major form of human organization found in this region includes those groups reliant upon domesticated plant foods, which correlates with decreased mobility, village formation, the use of pottery, and large-scale farming. Archaeological sites associated with this type of economic and social organization were occupied for long periods—sometimes on the scale of years—and the associated archaeological deposits are often extensive and complex. This form of organization is a relatively recent transition, occurring in the Late Holocene period and with greatly increasing social complexity during the last thousand years. Village life came to dominate large portions of North America in the last millennium, including the Southwest, Midwest, and many parts of what is now the eastern United States. In fact, these regions serve as possible sources for the organizational complexity that spread to the Great Plains

These two basic forms of organization are used as simplified frameworks for studying past cultures. They do not represent stages of cultural development. Both forms existed simultaneously in the past 2,000 years, depending on the location within the Great Plains and Rocky Mountain region. Environmental conditions (e.g., climate and ecological carrying capacity) strongly influence many aspects of human economic and social organization. Thus, farming is not possible in all portions of the Plains and Rockies, flourishing primarily east of the 100th meridian, where rainfall supports dry-land farming. Also, ancient farmers were probably seasonally mobile, moving away from their villages on hunting-and-gathering trips during portions of the year.

Both of these macro-forms of human organization were transformed during the protohistoric, or contact, period (after AD 1500). The European introduction of horses, diseases, and trade goods radically altered indigenous ways of life. Some groups that were once sedentary became mobile, others moved into new territories, and still others coalesced and formed new groups.

These forms of human organization have been encapsulated into four simplified cultural periods spanning the prehistory of the Great Plains. These include the Paleoindian, Archaic, Woodland, and Plains Village periods. "Paleoindian" refers to hunter-gatherer populations occupying the region during the Pleistocene and Early Holocene periods, approximately 11,000–8000 BC. Early Paleoindian remains (associated with Clovis-style projectile points) are sometimes found with extinct megafauna (e.g., mammoths, horses, camels), suggesting that humans played at least a minor role in the megafaunal extinction at the end of the last Ice Age. Later Paleoindian foragers are often interpreted as specialized bison hunters.

The Archaic period follows, from 8000 to 1000 BC. During the Archaic, human populations increased slowly and diet breadth increased, incorporating a wider range of plants and animals. Subterranean earth houses appeared in large numbers, suggesting at least seasonal sedentism, with stone grinding implements and thermal earth ovens introduced for processing wild plant foods.

The following Woodland period (1000 BC to AD 1000) represents early village formation, especially on the eastern Plains, with the introduction of domesticated plant foods, pottery, and cemeteries. Finally, large villages dependent on agriculture were formed during the Plains Village period (AD 1000–1800), with extensive settlement along the major waterways of the eastern Plains, including the Missouri River and other rivers stretching south into modern-day Texas. Population movement was also seen during this period, with migration to the Plains from the Midwest and eastern Woodlands. Trade networks were expanded with the increased cultural complexity of the Plains Village period.

RESEARCH QUESTIONS BEING ADDRESSED

Today there is great diversity in the types of archaeological research questions addressed in the Great Plains and Rocky Mountains. Most of the early archaeological work was descriptive in scope, focused on determining the age and function of individual sites or a small number of sites. This attention was not unexpected, given the historical trends of the day, and certainly provides the spatial-chronological framework (often referred to as "culture history") that exists today and is necessary for addressing more complex questions related to ancient human behavior, social interactions, and human ecology. With the development of new theoretical and methodological approaches (known as processual and postprocessual archaeology) over the last 40 years, several additional research themes have emerged.

For example, the archaeological record is no longer taken at face value. Site artifacts have undergone a complex transformation from when they were originally used and discarded until the time of their eventual recovery hundreds or thousands of years later by archaeologists. The study of taphonomy seeks to explain how the archaeological record is formed and modified by natural and cultural forces, such as how bones weather and erode, how artifacts are altered by stream flow, and how intense fires can modify stone tools. This middle-range research is of fundamental importance in interpreting the past as archaeologists strive to understand the fragmented record based on the artifacts they locate and excavate.

Reconstruction of past environments remains an important focus of regional archaeology. Excavation of stratified sites is often completed within a geoarchaeological framework to recover information about past climates through fossil pollen, phytolith, gastropod, and faunal records. For instance, major advances have improved the exploration of bison health, migration, and evolution through the study of carbon and oxygen isotopes obtained from teeth and bones recovered from paleontological and archaeological sites.

Another important theoretical framework has emerged: behavioral ecology, a subset of evolutionary ecology. Behavioral ecology is useful for exploring prehistoric decision processes. For example, optimal foraging is an explanatory model used for examining dietary choices made by past human groups. In many studies, faunal remains are quantified in regards to species and element to detect whether the highest-utility (most valuable in regards to meat, bone grease, etc.) bones and associated meat units were selected for disarticulation and processing. Models seek to explain why some species and elements were selected over others, as well as explore to what degree human behavior operated in the most efficient ways possible.

The study of gender has also taken on increased importance. Countless hours of past research have focused on specifics of hunting technology, such as the manufacture and use of projectile points. This weaponry was thought (or assumed) by some researchers to represent the realm of men and boys. Gender (as well as age and class) differences have also been explored through mortuary analysis, where researchers study the differences or similarities among the types of grave goods buried with females versus males. Rock art provides another valuable forum for examining gendered relations. Additionally, camp layout (site structure) has been compared against the ethnographic record to explore whether certain tasks, tools, and features were used exclusively by females as compared to males.

Research within the Great Plains and Rocky Mountains continues its evolution toward more complex forms. The coming century is certain to witness continued growth, refining the historical sequence as well as developing more robust explanatory models.

Further Reading: Duke, Philip, and Michael C. Wilson, eds., *Beyond Subsistence: Plains Archaeology and the Postprocessual Critique* (Tuscaloosa: University of Alabama Press, 1995); Frison, George C., *Survival by Hunting: Prehistoric Human Predators and Animal Prey* (Berkeley: University of California Press, 2004); Kornfeld, Marcel, and Alan J. Osborn, eds., *Islands on the Plains: Ecological, Social, and Ritual Use of Landscapes* (Salt Lake City: University of Utah Press, 2003); Schlesier, Karl H., ed., *Plains Indians, A.D. 500–1500: The Archaeological Past of Historic Groups* (Norman: University of Oklahoma Press, 1994); Thiessen, Thomas D., *Emergency Archeology in the Missouri River Basin: The Role of the Missouri Basin Project and the Midwest Archeological Center in the Interagency Archeological Salvage Program, 1946–1975*, Midwest Archeological Center Special Report No. 2 (Lincoln, NE: Midwest Archeological Center, National Park Service, 1999); Wood, W. Raymond, ed., *Archaeology on the Great Plains* (Lawrence: University Press of Kansas, 1998).

Jason M. LaBelle

EARLIEST INHABITANTS AND SITES IN THE PLAINS AND ROCKY MOUNTAINS

INTRODUCTION

Paleoindian archaeologists study the earliest non-disputed human occupants of the New World. On the Great Plains and in the Rocky Mountains, most view the Paleoindian time frame as extending from approximately 11,500 radiocarbon years before present (rcybp) to 8,000 rcybp. Radiocarbon years—the raw values archaeologists obtain from radiocarbon labs when they submit prehistoric organic samples for dating—are for this time frame a bit younger than regular calendar years. When corrected using established calibration curves, the Paleoindian period dates from about 13,500 to 9,000 calendar years ago.

In addition to representing a discrete chronological interval, archaeologists conceive of the term "Paleoindian" as describing the period during which North and South America's earliest hunter-gatherers co-existed with now-extinct, often very large Pleistocene (Ice Age) and Early Holocene animals. During the Late Pleistocene, the animals on the Plains and in the Rockies included, among many others, mammoths, mastodons, camels, horses, and giant subspecies of bison. After the Pleistocene waned and transitioned to the Holocene around 11,000 rcybp, only giant forms of bison—*Bison antiquus* and *Bison occidentalis*—persisted, and then only until about 8,000 rcybp, at which point modern *Bison bison* came to dominate the paleontological and archaeological records. After 8,000 rcybp, Great Plains and Rocky Mountain faunas on the whole assumed a modern character,

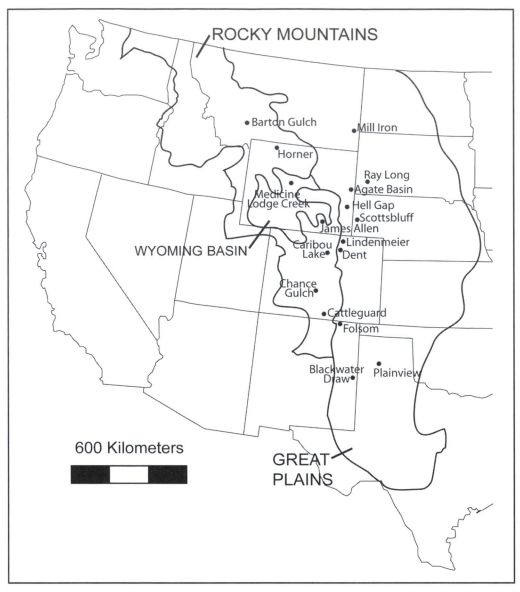

Map showing the location of the Great Plains, Rocky Mountains, and key Paleoindian sites mentioned in the text. Sites depicted are a representative sample of the hundreds of Paleoindian sites documented on the Great Plains and in the Rocky Mountains.   [Map drafted by Sara Lundberg, Utah State University Museum of Anthropology]

and archaeologists refer to subsequent hunter-gatherers of the region not as Paleoindians, but as Archaic peoples.

HISTORICAL CONTEXT

The Great Plains have played a starring role in the history and evolution of Paleoindian archaeology in the Americas for nearly a century, while the Rocky Mountains have only in the last 25 years or so been recognized as important to the story of how the first Americans populated North America.

From the moment Europeans first reached the New World in the sixteenth century, they and their successors pondered who the indigenous populations they encountered could be,

where they originated, and how long they had occupied the Americas. A point of particular interest for centuries was whether the earliest residents had once shared the landscape with Ice Age animals. Most sixteenth- through early-twentieth-century European Americans—laypersons and scientists alike—doubted that the people they called "Indians" could have occupied the New World for so long. However, a crucial find on the high plains of northern New Mexico in the 1920s changed the archaeological and public mind-set on this point.

In 1908 George McJunkin, a former slave who had purchased his freedom, was working as a ranch foreman. He discovered and reported giant bison bones protruding from the

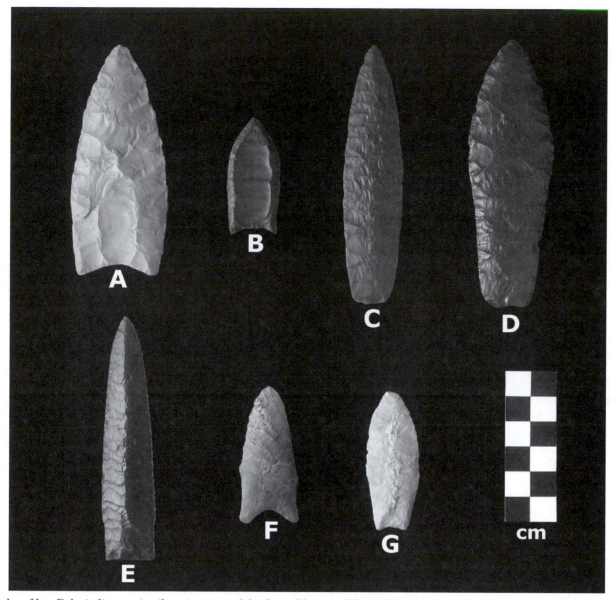

Examples of key Paleoindian projectile point types of the Great Plains and Rocky Mountains: *A*, Clovis (Dent site, Colorado plains); *B*, Folsom (Lindenmeier site, Colorado plains); *C*, Agate Basin (Hell Gap site, Wyoming plains); *D*, Hell Gap (Casper site, Wyoming plains); *E*, Eden (Horner site, Bighorn basin, Wyoming); *F*, James Allen (Middle Park, Colorado Rockies); *G*, Angostura (Middle Park, Colorado Rockies). [Photograph of casts of original specimens by Sara Lundberg, Utah State University Museum of Anthropology]

walls of a draw known as Wild Horse Arroyo, near the small town of Folsom, New Mexico. Nearly two decades later, scientists from the Colorado Museum of Natural History (now the Denver Museum of Nature and Science) excavated the site and discovered slender, fluted (basally thinned) spear points embedded in the rib cages of Ice Age bison remains. The projectiles came to be known as Folsom points in recognition of the nearby town, and the Folsom site earned a place in archaeological history as having definitively demonstrated the co-existence of humans and Pleistocene fauna.

The Folsom find spawned a gold rush–style search for more archaeological sites dating to the Pleistocene and early Holocene. These efforts yielded a host of important finds of Great Plains Paleoindian localities, including the seminal sites of Lindenmeier, Dent, and Blackwater Draw. Lindenmeier, located on the plains of northeastern Colorado, was discovered by Claude C. Coffin in 1924, two years before excavations began at the Folsom site. However, archaeological excavations at Lindenmeier did not commence for another decade, at the time Smithsonian Institution archaeologist Frank H. H. Roberts initiated his study that recovered what is now one of the best-known Folsom assemblages in North America. Had excavations begun at Lindenmeier just a bit sooner, the famous Folsom points of today might instead have been forever known as Lindenmeier points.

The Dent and Blackwater Draw sites share a similarly ironic history and relationship. Dent, not far from Lindenmeier on the northeastern Colorado plains, was excavated in the early 1930s. Rather than producing giant bison bones and slender spear points, though, it yielded mammoth bones—among them, larger, much more robust stone projectiles. In 1933 Jesse Figgins, who had excavated the Folsom site a few years earlier, studied the Dent bones and artifacts and characterized the spear tips as Folsomoid, based on their abbreviated, yet Folsom-esque flutes.

In the meantime, excavations began in 1932 at a site called Blackwater Draw, located on the southern plains of east central New Mexico. Like Dent, Blackwater Draw yielded mammoth and other Pleistocene mammal bones together with spear points like the Folsomoid points found with the Dent mammoths. This time, however, excavators also recovered a stratigraphically higher occupation containing massive bison bones and true Folsom points. This demonstrated that the spear points associated with the mammoths were older than Folsom, and were not just a stylistic variant of that point type. The older spear points were thenceforth named Clovis (again, after a nearby New Mexican town), and one of the best-known cultures of New World archaeology was christened. Just as Lindenmeier narrowly missed serving as the type locality for what came to be known as Folsom, so did Dent narrowly miss serving as the type locality for the oldest documented culture of North America.

PLAINS AND MOUNTAIN PALEOINDIAN CHRONOLOGY AND SUBSISTENCE

Since the heady discoveries of Folsom, Lindenmeier, Dent, and Blackwater Draw in the 1920s and 1930s, archaeologists have learned a great deal about Clovis and Folsom and a host of other Paleoindian groups of the Great Plains and Rocky Mountains. They know, for example, that in those regions, as in others, spear point styles changed throughout the Paleoindian time frame. Clovis, now securely dated at a number of localities to between about 11,500 and 10,800 rcybp, remains the oldest documented Paleoindian point type of the Great Plains, and it remains the only Paleoindian point type definitively associated with Pleistocene megafauna other than *Bison antiquus* and *Bison occidentalis*.

A more recently recognized spear point style, called Goshen, best defined at the Mill Iron site on the plains of southern Montana, may overlap Clovis (and, in fact, Folsom) chronologically, but it has been found thus far only with ancient forms of bison. Goshen has also been documented in Middle Park, a very large southern Rocky Mountain grassland park prehistorically popular with the Ice Age bison favored by Goshen hunters. Some confusion surrounds the relationship between Goshen on the northern Plains and the technologically identical but significantly younger Plainview point type

of the southern Plains, named for the Plainview site in northern Texas. Resolving the association between the two types, if there is a relationship, is an issue for future investigation.

Folsom sites, like Goshen but occurring with greater frequency, have been found throughout the Great Plains and in the Rocky Mountains, occasionally at elevations of 10,000 feet or higher. Folsom sites date to between 10,500 and 10,000 rcybp, and they occur where Early Holocene bison congregated, and at places on the landscape where bison herds could have been readily monitored.

The Wyoming basin and Colorado's Middle Park, Gunnison basin, and San Luis Valley—all expansive mountain parks with grassland or shrubland vegetation communities—have yielded Folsom localities. The most carefully interpreted may be the San Luis valley's Cattleguard site, excavated by the Smithsonian Institution's Margaret (Pegi) Jodry, which has revealed a great deal about Folsom use of the local and regional landscape. Folsom groups exploited a variety of plant and animal resources, but like Goshen hunter-gatherers, they clearly specialized in and excelled at bison hunting.

After 10,000 rcybp, the Paleoindian record of the Great Plains and Rocky Mountains diversified—a function of burgeoning populations, constricting territory sizes, and a resource base changing with the emergence of the arid Early Holocene. Plains-based Paleoindians adopted new bison hunting strategies tailored to exploit shifting herd structures, and the average number of bison slain per kill episode increased through time.

People also moved into the Rockies on a full-time, year-round basis at approximately 10,000 rcybp, following in the footsteps of their Folsom predecessors (who favored high mountain parks) but now also exploiting all Rocky Mountain niches, from the lowest foothills to the highest alpine zones. Paleoindian spear point styles dating to the time frame between 10,000 and 8,000 rcybp—known as the Late Paleoindian period—reflect the diversification of resource use and reduction of territory sizes on the plains and in the mountains.

On the Great Plains, the post-Folsom Paleoindian projectile point chronology includes—from oldest to youngest—Agate Basin, shown recently at the stratified Hell Gap site of southeastern Wyoming to overlap Folsom in time; Hell Gap, named for its first recognized occurrence at the same rich site; Cody Complex—including Eden, Scottsbluff, and Cody Knives; and James Allen.

The term "Agate Basin" traces its roots to a bison kill in east central Wyoming, "Cody Complex" to the Horner bison kill and processing center of northwestern Wyoming, "Scottsbluff" to a bison kill in west central Nebraska, and "James Allen" to a bison kill in southern Wyoming. Great Plains late Paleoindian point types vary significantly in shape and manufacturing technique. However, all were used to hunt bison, and all are either lanceolate (leaf-shaped) or stemmed, rather than exhibiting the side or corner notching characteristic of post-Paleoindian projectile points on the plains and elsewhere. All, too, are spear points, launched with an *atl atl* (spear thrower), and not with the much later bow and arrow, which used smaller point tips.

All of the classic Great Plains, Late Paleoindian point types are at least occasionally recovered in the Rocky Mountains. However, research over the past quarter century has shown that once Paleoindians moved into the mountains full-time, those populations developed the unique projectile point types by which they now are recognized archaeologically.

The consummate Late Paleoindian point type of the southern Rocky Mountains, for example, is called Angostura, after its first occurrence at the Ray Long site in the Black Hills. Angostura points are found in all southern Rocky Mountain settings, and specimens reminiscent of the type have also been documented at middle and northern Rocky Mountain sites, such as Wyoming's Medicine Lodge Creek and Montana's Barton Gulch. In contrast to the close association of all post-Clovis Plains Paleoindian point types and early Holocene bison, mountain hunter-gatherers used their projectiles to procure bison, elk, deer, bighorn, and other mountain species.

For instance, at the Caribou Lake site, a short-term hunting camp at an elevation of 11,800 feet west of Boulder, Colorado, blood residue analysis of a spear point confirmed that it had contacted an elk 8,000 radiocarbon years ago.

In addition to procuring a variety of large game animals, mountain Paleoindians used a wider array of plant resources than did their Plains counterparts, because the mountains offered many more choices of plant species edible to humans than did the grass-dominant plains. The Chance Gulch site, an 8,000-radiocarbon-year-old Angostura site in Colorado's Gunnison basin, is a good example, in that the site's Late Paleoindian assemblage included not only two dozen Angostura projectile point bases (apparently broken off during hunting and brought back to camp for maintenance, resharpening, or replacement) and a variety of chipped-stone processing tools, but also several pieces of ground stone for preparing vegetable resources.

In addition to Angostura, one other Late Paleoindian point type occurs with particular frequency in the southern Rocky Mountains, and perhaps farther north as well: James Allen. This type also occurs with some frequency on the southern and central Plains—the James Allen type site, recall, is in southeastern Wyoming. The distribution of the James Allen point type within the Rockies is intriguing in that it occurs primarily at the very high elevations of the subalpine and alpine zones and in large mountain parks. The mountain parks attracted bison, and like Folsom before them, the makers of James Allen points, who are known to have hunted bison on the plains, likely also spent part of the year hunting bison at higher altitudes. The very high-altitude settings in which James Allen points occur, including the Caribou Lake site, were accessible only in late summer and early fall, when late-lying snow had melted. The people who left behind James

Allen points may have sought refuge from the hot, dry plains by migrating into the mountains to seasonally hunt elk, bighorn, and other high-altitude game.

CURRENT AND FUTURE RESEARCH QUESTIONS

Despite the fact that archaeologists have focused intensively for over three-quarters of a century on the Paleoindian archaeology of the Great Plains and for a quarter century on Paleoindian archaeology of the Rocky Mountains, many questions remain unanswered.

Such questions, of course, will guide research in the years to come. Of particular interest now to both Great Plains and Rocky Mountain Paleoindian archaeologists is precisely how both Early and Late Paleoindian groups moved across the Great Plains and Rocky Mountain landscapes.

Conventional thinking suggests, for example, that early Paleoindians (Clovis and Folsom in particular) often traveled very long distances—sometimes hundreds of kilometers—to pursue megafauna, stone for tools, and other resources. New research, however, suggests that this may have been the case only under certain circumstances. Recent Plains undertakings are also focusing on expanding understanding of the resource base of early Plains-based hunter-gatherers. While nearly a century's worth of evidence illustrates the heavy reliance of Great Plains Paleoindians on now-extinct bison, new recovery methods are revealing use of a far broader array of animal, bird, and plant resources than previously documented.

Rocky Mountain archaeologists, for their part, would like to unravel with greater resolution how mountain-based Paleoindians utilized the complex landscapes of the high country. A key difference between the Great Plains and the Rocky Mountains lies in the horizontal structure of the plains versus the vertical structure of the mountains. The short- and long-grass prairies of the plains extend for hundreds of kilometers east to west and north to south. The bison that converted the grass to food edible by humans ranged across those grasslands in vast herds, and the Paleoindians who hunted them made foraging decisions based in large part upon the locations of this bread-and-butter resource.

The Rocky Mountains, on the other hand, contain an enormous range of resources in a geographically circumscribed area. Paleoindian hunter-gatherers of the Rockies based foraging decisions on their intimate knowledge of when particular plant, animal, and other resources would be available in a given mountain environmental zone (for example, bighorn in the subalpine and alpine zones in late summer, pinyon nuts in the foothills in autumn, and bison in parklands in the winter months). They undoubtedly faced challenging logistical choices when they needed or wanted to obtain different resources in different areas at once—choices that likely led to great flexibility in group membership as families or task groups split up to take advantage of the varied resources the mountains offered.

SITES AND RELEVANT MUSEUMS ACCESSIBLE TO THE PUBLIC

A range of museums and interpretive centers throughout the Great Plains and Rocky Mountains can help interested members of the public learn more about Paleoindians of those regions. Many small-town museums showcase Paleoindian sites excavated in the vicinity or collections of Paleoindian artifacts donated by local farmers and ranchers.

For example, the Wray History Museum in Wray, Colorado, located about 10 miles from the Nebraska border, features a Smithsonian Institution–created display on Paleoindians of the Colorado plains.

Larger educational facilities open to the public include the following:

- The Mammoth site of Hot Springs, South Dakota (1800 West Highway 18), where visitors can tour a paleontological excavation of Ice Age fauna and see mammoth bones in place in the ground.
- The Hudson-Meng Museum and Archaeology Research Center (Crawford, Nebraska), which maintains summer hours and interprets what some archaeologists argue is an early Cody Complex bison kill (others view it as a natural die-off event).
- The Denver Museum of Nature and Science (2001 Colorado Boulevard, Denver, Colorado), which serves as the repository for many key Paleoindian collections from Colorado and beyond.
- The Blackwater Draw Site and Museum (42987 Highway 70, 7 miles northeast of Portales, New Mexico), which

offers self-guided tours and interpretations of the Clovis type site, a National Historic Landmark.
- The Lubbock Lake Landmark and the Museum of Texas Tech (Lubbock, Texas), an archaeological preserve and collection of associated museum exhibits that interpret nearly 12,000 years of prehistory at the Lubbock Lake National Historic Landmark.

Further Reading: Bamforth, Douglas B., "High-Tech Foragers? Folsom and Later Paleoindian Technology on the Great Plains," *Journal of World Prehistory* 16(1) (2002): 55–98; Brunswig, Robert H., and Bonnie L. Pitblado, *Frontiers in Colorado Paleoindian Archaeology: From the Dent Site to the Rocky Mountains* (Niwot: University Press of Colorado, 2007); Frison, George C., "Paleoindian Large Mammal Hunters on the Plains of North America," *Proceedings of the National Academy of Sciences* 95 (1998): 14,576–14,583; Holliday, Vance T., *Paleoindian Geoarchaeology of the Southern High Plains* (Austin: University of Texas Press, 1997); Jodry, Margaret A., "Folsom Technological and Socioeconomic Strategies: View from Stewart's Cattle Guard and the Upper Rio Grande Basin, Colorado," Ph.D. diss. (American University, 1999); Kornfeld, Marcel, and George C. Frison, "Paleoindian Occupation of the High Country: The Case of Middle Park, Colorado," *Plains Anthropologist* 45(172) (2000): 129–153; Pitblado, Bonnie L., *Late Paleoindian Occupation of the Southern Rocky Mountains* (Niwot: University Press of Colorado, 2003); Seebach, John D., "Drought or Development? Patterns of Paleoindian Site Discovery on the Great Plains of North America," *Plains Anthropologist* 51(197) (2006): 71–88; Waguespack, Nicole M., and Todd A. Surovell, "Clovis Hunting Strategies, or How to Make Out on Plentiful Resources," *American Antiquity* 68(2) (2003): 333–352.

Bonnie L. Pitblado

"BUFFALO JUMP" SITES

For millennia Native Americans targeted a variety of large animal species. They devised special procurement techniques for hunting these gregarious herd animals. Successful hunts resulted in multiple kills per hunting episode. Bison were a favorite target, especially on the Great Plains. Bison are unique to North America. Their distant Old World cousins are buffalo, a term often used for the American bison and in describing Native American relationships with the species, extinct and modern.

BISON PROCUREMENT

Bison procurement techniques on the Plains included the use of various topographic features, resulting in a variety of bison-kill site types. Three main types are recognized: ambushes, traps, and jumps. Ambush kill sites are found in narrowly constricted areas along bison paths. Animal traps are recognized in various landscape features—arroyos, bogs, sinkholes, and dunes. For winter kills, snow drifts and (icy) ponds can be

added to the list. Occasionally archaeologists find traces of artificial pounds (corrals) into which bison were driven.

Traps typically restricted or immobilized animals, thereby facilitating the kill. Bison jumps (or "falls")—precipitous landforms like cliffs and chasms, sharp inclines and steep talus slopes, or some combination thereof—killed, maimed, or (less commonly) temporarily disoriented animals. Some bison-kill sites, especially jumps, were used repeatedly, resulting in multiple bone beds (the result of butchering the dead bison). Multiple-episode bison jumps signal strategic locations—for example, along seasonal migratory routes—selected on the basis of predictability. Some single-episode jumps are likely similarly sited, but others probably resulted from opportunistic moments.

COMMUNAL BISON JUMPING

Communal bison jumps are most common. Successful bison procurement using jumps involved a series of activities including, the drive, the approach, the jump, and the kill, followed by butchering and processing. In prehistoric times, all members of human groups that hunted bison likely participated in one or more of the jump activities, perhaps in the manner recorded historically for Blackfoot bands (Siksika, Kainai, Aapatohsipiikani, and Aamsskaapipiikani) and preserved in their oral traditions.

Scouts watched for the right conditions and reported back. The community mobilized, sending out a runner. The honor usually fell to a young, unmarried man. Disguised as a buffalo, he found the lead cows and started them moving. The herd followed. Others stationed along the predetermined drive lane hazed the animals using robes, keeping the herd on course.

During approach, drivers stampeded the animals; mass momentum prevented them from turning away. If all went well, the runner preceded the herd to the jump, where he safely hid. The animals hurtled over. Hunters waiting below dispatched surviving bison that were unable to escape. Women and children waiting in the nearby camp then descended upon the kill site to help with butchering and initial processing. Processing continued in the camp(s) for days afterward (Schaeffer 1978, 243–248). The people processed many animal parts, including meat and marrow for food; hair and sinew for cordage and string; bones and horns for tools; and hides for clothing, shelter, and paraphernalia.

Preparation for a jump also required communal effort, frequently in the construction and maintenance of drive lanes. The Blackfoot built lanes using stone cairns, brush markers, lodge poles, and even piles of bison dung. Lane markers capitalized on the tendency of bison to shy away from landscape protrusions (Barsh and Marlor 2003, 575). Markers were particularly effective when combined with hazers.

At jump sites, drive lanes are recognized archaeologically by the cairns, sometimes numbering in the many hundreds. Lanes narrow at or before the approach. At a few multiple-episode jumps, cairns define lanes up to 40 kilometers long. At Head-Smashed-In, a multiple-episode cliff jump near Fort McLeod, Alberta, numerous drive lanes extend up to 12 kilometers in various directions from the precipice. Historical accounts report Blackfoot drives that lasted for several days before reaching the jump (Barsh and Marlor 2003, 573–576).

BISON JUMPING RITUAL

For the historic Blackfoot, and presumably ancient hunters, bison jumping was intimately tied to ritual. In one Blackfoot account, ritual centers on the *iniskim* (buffalo stone), a marine fossil bearing rough resemblance to a bison. In ancient times, the traditional story relates, the *iniskim* gave a Blackfoot woman songs that ensured successful drives. Thereafter, Blackfoot bands prepared for drives by appointing a husband and wife, who were joined by others, to perform the songs as they danced through the night. The next morning a runner, now ritually prepared, left the ceremony to begin the drive (Schaeffer 1978, 245). In other stories, Blackfoot people

learned to hunt bison communally from wolves—animals that do indeed hunt large game, including bison, in packs (Barsh and Marlor 2003, 581–583).

Little evidence for bison hunting ritual is known archaeologically, but a few hints exist. At the Jones-Miller site (near Wray, Colorado) archaeologists found a bird-bone whistle and butchered dog remains. They had been placed next to a post centrally located in the butchering area (Hoffman and Graham 1998, 121). At the Cooper site, in northwestern Oklahoma, excavations produced a bison skull bearing a lightning bolt painted in red on the forehead. The skull had been placed atop piled skeletal remains (Bement 1999). Both sites are traps, not bison jumps, but there is no reason to differentiate between site types in considering spiritual and ritual connections between man and beast.

JUMPING AND BISON ETHOLOGY

As important as ritual was, ancient hunters also depended on sophisticated understandings of bison behaviors. That knowledge was as essential to success as preparation and cooperation. The multi-episode jump sites clearly demonstrate that knowledge. Ancient hunters knew where and when success was likely. They also knew bison capabilities, habits, and probable responses to noise or scent.

While bison are susceptible to herd instincts, they are also clever, wary, agile, and fast. The latter characteristics make it very difficult to herd bison to a predetermined spot. Cowhands today know that such behaviors are best overcome by working bison in large groups—up to a hundred or more (Frison 1991, 234–237). Ancient hunters also knew this. To improve the chance of success, they often jumped more bison than needed. Archaeology and history bear witness: bone beds at various jump sites contain fully articulated, unbutchered bison skeletons, sometimes in the hundreds. On May 29, 1805, Meriwether Lewis passed by the Madison cliff jump near Three Forks, Montana, observing in his journal "an immence [*sic*] pile of slaughter[ed carcasses]" (in Thwaites 1904, 5).

THE ANTIQUITY OF BISON JUMPING

Bison hunting in North America dates at least to Clovis times (ca. 11,500 to 11,000 BC) in the terminal Pleistocene. Clovis bison jumps, however, are not known, nor are mass kills of any type (at least with certainty). Rather, Clovis people, apparently using the surround technique, closed in on bison (and other Pleistocene fauna, including horse, mammoth, tapir, and more)—typically a lone animal or perhaps a few—at watering holes. Bison in Clovis kills are extinct Pleistocene forms (*Bison antiquus* and *B. occidentalis*) from which much smaller Holocene bison (*B. bison* spp.) probably evolved. Perhaps post-Pleistocene climate instability reduced carrying capacities, selecting for the smaller form.

Surrounds were used into historic times. After Clovis other bison kill sites appeared, principally the arroyo trap. The

Olsen-Chubbuck site (southeast of Limon, Colorado) is a prominent arroyo kill (Wheat 1972). Excavations revealed nearly 200 bison (*B. antiquus*). The animals died in a single event somewhere between 8000 and 7500 BC, accumulating atop each other. The uppermost exhibited rather thorough butchering, the lowest little to none. These circumstances indicate the bison came from above, spilling over the arroyo banks. Archaeologists usually assume hunters purposefully drove them to the pitfall. However, material evidence at Olsen-Chubbuck, along with mass kills of similar and later age, does not speak to how the bison got there. Perhaps storm or fire caused stampedes, after which local bands took advantage.

Natural events aside, there is little reason to suspect ancient hunters did not drive bison now and then, but incontrovertible evidence is lacking until Middle Archaic times. The oldest recognized and agreed-upon bison jumping episodes date to about 4000 BC to about 3500 BC. The setting for these jumps typically matches the traditional image: towering cliffs or high, steep bluffs. During this period, certain jumps were used repeatedly, and communal bison jumping appeared. Thereafter communal jumping flourished, becoming most common after about 1000 BC and continuing into historic times. Hundreds of known jump sites date to this period. Most sites exhibit some or all of the topographic and cultural elements recognized by archaeologists as signs of purposeful, planned jumping: a landscape suitable for gathering, driving, and jumping, plus drive lane markers, sometimes a modified approach, bone bed(s) with culturally modified bone, and nearby processing area(s) and/or campsite(s).

Traditional views regarding the antiquity of jumping have been challenged. Two sites that figure in the debate are Hudson-Meng (near Crawford, Nebraska) and Bonfire Shelter (near Langtry, Texas). Using radiocarbon dating and projectile-point chronologies, both are touted as evidence of an early origin for driving bison to jumps.

Bone beds at Bonfire Shelter (Bement 1986; Dibble and Lorrain 1968) are near what once was a frequently inhabited rockshelter. Clear human-bison associations are present at two of the three bone beds. The older of the two (Bed 2; MNI 27 *B. antiquus*) dates to approximately 9680 BC (carbon-14 wood charcoal); it yielded a projectile point characteristic of the Folsom culture (ca. 10,900 to 10,000 BC). The bed's early age, the precipice above, and the suitable landscape (but without drive lanes) prompts some to consider Bonfire Shelter as the oldest known bison jump. Others say that Bed 2 did not result from jumping. Citing a paucity of low-yield elements (for example, lower limb bones with less meat and marrow), they argue that choice cuts removed from bison killed elsewhere were brought to the shelter vicinity for processing (Binford 1978, 475; Byerly et al. 2005; see also Bement 2007, Byerly et al. 2007).

Hudson-Meng (Agenbroad 1978) contains remains of some 500 animals. The bone bed is located just west of a now

buried bank where the bison were allegedly jumped. Several carbon-14 assays date the bed to approximately 8000–7500 BC. Claims for human involvement are in part based on alleged contextual associations between the bones and artifacts, including Late Paleoindian (ca. 10000 to 8000 BC) Alberta projectile points. The artifacts, however, may be from a subsequent occupation stratigraphically above the bison. If so the bison likely died naturally, perhaps stampeded by natural phenomena (Todd and Rapson 1995). Also, original faunal analyses attributed bone modification to humans. Later taphonomic studies support the natural-cause hypothesis (Koch 2000, 8–9).

Hudson-Meng and Bed 2 at Bonfire Shelter are dated at 4,000 to 6,000 years earlier than the jump sites recognized and agreed upon by most archaeologists who have studied this type of site. Accepting them as bison jumps creates an awkward temporal gap. Cultural loss and reinvention (per Dibble 1970, 252) may or may not explain the problem. In any case, rejecting them need not, given the very ancient human-bison connection, preclude early bison jumping, but in light of the archaeological record as currently known, such early bison jumps probably were opportunistic, rare, small-scale events rather than the carefully planned and executed procurement activities known from later times. Without the kind of evidence that indicates planned, communally organized jump kills, distinguishing these early sites from human scavenging at natural kills is difficult, especially in exceedingly broken country.

BISON JUMPING: SPATIAL DISTRIBUTIONS

Not only is Bonfire Shelter removed in time from the undisputed material evidence for bison jumping, but the site is also 1,800 kilometers distant from other jump sites. Bison jump sites, many of them communal, abound on the northern Plains, principally east of the continental divide on the high plains of Alberta, Montana, and Wyoming. A few outliers are situated in Idaho, the western Dakotas, and extreme northern Colorado. Nearly 300 jumps are known for Montana and some 150 for Alberta.

Alberta's Head-Smashed-In (see Reeves 1983), a UNESCO World Heritage site, is perhaps the most prominent communal jump site. Hunters here repeatedly drove bison over 18-meter cliffs served by several drive lanes. The cliffs face east, opposite prevailing winds. Downwind siting, found at most multiepisode jumps, heightened success. Bison possess a keen sense of smell. The winds had to be just right, lest the driven bison catch the scent of previous kills. If they did, they would invariably turn away at the critical moment, only to waste days of driving.

Excavations at Head-Smashed-In revealed bone beds 11 meters deep (deeper deposits exist). The lowest radiometrically dated beds accumulated around 3700 BC. Bison jumping at Head-Smashed-In continued into historic times, and was used by Blackfoot bands. Indeed, the name comes from the Blackfoot *estipah-skikikini-kots*, or "where he got his head smashed in." Tradition has it a young man wanted to watch from below as the buffalo fell. Alas, cascading animals knocked him against the cliff face, crushing his skull.

The Blackfoot word for "bison jump" (or "bison pound") is *pisskan* (often seen as *pishkun* or *piskun*), meaning "deep blood kettle." Ulm Pishkun, near Great Falls, Montana, is one of the largest jump sites (Holmes 1999). Cliffs here stretch for nearly a mile; bone beds below are as deep as 4 meters. Ulm Pishkun was used repeatedly between approximately AD 900 and AD 1500.

The Vore site (see Reher and Frison 1980) does not match the traditional image of driven bison plummeting over a cliff. Instead hunters drove bison along cairn-lined drive lanes into a precipitous sinkhole. Now some 15 meters deep, bone beds below the sink's floor extend to depths of just over 5 meters. Archaeologists estimate that the sink, located in the Wyoming Black Hills, contains remains of at least 10,000 bison. Various dating techniques, including radiocarbon, indicate the entire bone deposit dates from around AD 1500 to around AD 1800. Stratigraphic sections suggest the sink at times was used annually.

WHY COMMUNAL JUMPING?

The dearth of evidence for communal jumping prior to the Middle Archaic has nothing to do with capabilities. Archaeological evidence throughout the Plains, and through time, demonstrates sophisticated and varied human adaptive strategies—in some places and times without much emphasis on bison, if any. Probably the explanation lies in socioeconomic adjustments concomitant with the onset of a modern climate.

Many archaeologists correlate the emergence of communal jumping with the sub-Boreal climate episode (ca. 3000 to 700 BC), when wetter conditions generally prevailed on the Plains. Bison populations undoubtedly increased during this period; human populations almost certainly did as well. By 1000 BC, local human hunter-gatherer groups filled the Plains, as suggested by a proliferation of projectile point styles, site type variety, and site density data. Local groups may have been forerunners of band-tribal societies encountered historically; the concept is at least analogous. In any case, population packing tended to restrict mobility, in turn encouraging maximum use of available local resources.

Though not all local groups adopted communal jumping, all enjoyed access to bison, the most prolific of Plains resources. By sub-Boreal times, tens of millions were spread widely through many Plains herds. Animals in these numbers are, to potentially stressed human populations, risk reducers on the hoof simply because they can be taken en masse. Mass kills, combined with mobile storage technology (jerking, drying, etc.), provided the capability to offset seasonal risks when necessary. This may help explain why communal jumping originated in and did not spread beyond the northern Plains. Over the long run, risks were probably greater in the north, where seasonal differences are most pronounced and where seasonal conditions, especially during winter, can be comparatively harsh.

SEASONALITY

Sexing and aging bison bone assemblages help determine the kill season. A preponderance of fetal remains, for example, points to late winter; mostly adult cows indicate a pre-rutting season kill. Dental analysis is most common, simply because assemblages always contain maxillae and mandibles. The focus is on tooth eruption stages in calves and yearlings. Most calves are born within a few weeks during middle to late winter. Using comparative dental data from modern herds, age at death (in months) can be determined for kill site assemblages. Dental studies indicate bison jumping occurred year-round, even in the dead of winter, but more commonly in spring, early summer, fall, and early winter. Some bone beds at the Vore site, for example, exhibit kills that alternated between late fall and late spring or early summer (Frison 1991, 275–278).

What seem to be favored times of the year correlate with tribal practices known historically. A tribe's bands—self-sufficient socioeconomic units that operated independently much of the year—typically amalgamated at these times (as did small groups of friendly tribes on occasion). Band members shared goods and information, established and bolstered alliances, arranged marriages, performed joint ceremonies, organized hunting expeditions, and so on.

For these hunters and gatherers, larger group size was likely very attractive. Not that bands could not jump bison; some campsites associated with jumps suggested fewer than a hundred people. Rather, more people probably increased chances of a successful jump. But that may not be all; very likely there was another attraction. The spiritual reverence in which tribal folks held bison is well known historically and is exemplified in ancient rock art. In prehistoric times, communal bison hunting during band amalgamation provided communities the opportunity to share widely a worldview. In the dim past, ideology must have worked hand in hand with material causes to produce the sophisticated, complex procurement technique known as *pisskan*, or bison jumping.

THE END OF BISON JUMPING

Bison jumping came to an end in the later nineteenth century. The Blackfoot and Crow conducted some of the last jumps. At some sites, like Old Women's buffalo jump (near High River, Alberta), archaeologists have found reminders of the recentness of jumping: remnants of flesh, hide, and hair clinging to the bones.

At the end, horses were sometimes used to jump bison, and they had been used where available for perhaps a century and a half prior. By far, though, most jumping episodes on the Great Plains took place prior to the reintroduction of the horse in early historic times—the times Blackfoot elders call the dog days. Thinking of bison jumping this way tends to shock the senses. At the very least, it conjures thoughts of the high degree of skill, planning, and cooperation required for successful jumping—especially in light of the magnitude some jump episodes reached, involving many hundreds of bison at a time.

The magnitude is underscored by what happened next. Just decades after Crow, Blackfoot, and other tribes stopped adding to the bone beds, entrepreneurs began digging them up (see Davis 1978). Commercial miners, principally in Montana and Alberta, mined the bones (including traps and other kinds of kills), sometimes using mechanized equipment. The enterprise began around the turn of the twentieth century and continued into the 1940s. One of the "mines" was Ulm Pishkun.

The ground bones were used in fertilizer, sugar refining, munitions, and other nitrogen- and phosphorous-based applications. In 1942 in Alberta, bison bones brought $20 per ton; a dozer could extract 20 tons a day. The bones, raw and ground, were transported east by rail, sometimes a dozen or more carloads at a time. With the trains went untold knowledge forever lost.

Further Reading: Agenbroad, Larry D., *The Hudson-Meng Site: An Alberta Bison Kill in the Nebraska High Plains* (Washington, DC: University Press of America, 1978); Barsh, Russel Lawrence, and Chantelle Marlor, "Driving Bison and Blackfoot Science," *Human Ecology* 31(4) (2003): 571–593; Bement, Leland C., *Excavation of the Late Pleistocene Deposits of Bonfire Shelter, 41VV218, Val Verde, Texas, 1983–1984* (Austin: Texas Archeological Survey, the University of Texas at Austin, 1986); Bement, Leland C., *Bison Hunting at Cooper Site: Where Lightning Bolts Drew Thundering Herds* (Norman: University of Oklahoma Press, 1999); Bement, Leland C., "Bonfire Shelter: A Jumping Off Point for Comments for Byerly et al.," *American Antiquity* 72 (2007): 366–372; Binford, Lewis R., *Nunamiut Ethnoarchaeology* (New York: Academic Press, 1978); Byerly, Ryan M., Judith R. Cooper, David J. Meltzer, Matthew E. Hill, and Jason M. LaBelle, "A Further Assessment of Paleoindian Site-Use at Bonfire Shelter," *American Antiquity* 72 (2007): 373–381; Byerly, Ryan M., Judith R. Cooper, David J. Meltzer, Matthew E. Hill, and Jason M. LaBelle, "On Bonfire Shelter (Texas) as a Paleoindian Bison Jump: An Assessment Using GIS and Zooarchaeology," *American Antiquity* 70 (2005): 595–629; Davis, Leslie B., "The 20th-Century Commercial Mining of Northern Plains Bison Kills," *Plains Anthropologist Memoir* 14 (1978): 254–286; Dibble, David S., "On the Significance of Additional Radiocarbon Dates from Bonfire Shelter, Texas," *Plains Anthropologist* 15 (1970): 251–254; Dibble, David S., and Dessamae Lorrain, "Bonfire Shelter: A Stratified Bison Kill Site, Val Verde County, Texas," in *Texas Memorial Museum*, Miscellaneous Papers No. 1 (Austin: University of Texas, 1968); Forbis, Richard G., Review of "Bonfire Shelter: A Stratified Bison Kill Site, Val Verde County, Texas," *American Antiquity* 34 (1969): 90–91; Frison, George C., *Prehistoric Hunters of the High Plains* (San Diego, CA: Academic Press, 1991); Hoffman, Jack L., and Russell W. Graham, "The Paleo-Indian Cultures of the Great Plains," in *Archaeology on the Great Plains*, edited by W. Raymond Wood (Lawrence: University Press of Kansas, 1998), 87–139; Holmes, Krys, "Ulm Pishkun: World of the Early Plains Bison," *Montana: The Magazine of Western History* 49(2) (1999): 86–87; Koch, Amy, *High Plains Archaeology*, Explore Nebraska Archaeology, No. 5 (Lincoln: Nebraska State Historical Society, 2000), http://www.nebraskahistory. org/archeo/pubs/highplains5.pdf (online May 2007); Reeves, Brian O. K., "Six Millenniums of Buffalo Kills," *Scientific American* 249 (October 1983): 120–135; Reher, Charles A., and George C. Frison, "The Vore Site, 48CK302, a Stratified Jump in the Wyoming Black Hills," *Plains Anthropologist Memoir* 16 (1980); Schaeffer, Claude E., "The Bison Drive of the Blackfeet Indians," *Plains Anthropologist Memoir* 14 (1978): 243–248; Thwaites, Reuben G., *Original Journals of the Lewis and Clark Expedition 1804–1806*, vol. 2 (New York: Dodd, Mead and Co., 1904); Todd, L. C., and D. J. Rapson, "Excavations at Hudson-Meng Bonebed," a paper presented at the symposium "Bison Subsistence through Time: From Middle Paleolithic to PaleoIndian Times," Toulouse, France (1995); Wheat, Joe Ben, "The Olsen-Chubbuck Site: A Paleo-Indian Bison Kill," *American Antiquity Memoir* 26 (1972).

Richard A. Fox

MISSOURI RIVER NATIVE AMERICAN VILLAGE SETTLEMENTS

The region of the Great Plains known as the "Middle Missouri" corresponds generally to the valley of the Missouri River and immediately adjacent areas within the states of North and South Dakota; the archaeology of this region is closely linked to adjacent areas of Nebraska and Iowa. In this area, the Missouri River has cut a well-defined drainage that in some areas is over 5 miles wide and 100 meters deep—referred to as the "Missouri Trench"—into the surrounding plains. In sharp contrast to the level, grassy uplands adjacent to it, the Missouri Trench is marked by steep and heavily dissected edges, terraces of varying widths above its floor, and a broad floodplain containing the bed of the Missouri itself; throughout most of the area, the terraces and floodplain are fairly heavily wooded. This area was the home of Plains farmers—primarily, but not exclusively, the ancestors of the modern Mandan, Hidatsa, and Arikara—for nearly a millennium prior to

European and Euro-American contact. Literally thousands of archaeological sites richly document the history of these ancient and historic period farmers.

ARCHAEOLOGICAL RESEARCH IN THE MIDDLE MISSOURI

Perhaps more than in any area of North America, the archaeological understanding of the Middle Missouri is conditioned by the development of government land-use and water-control policies. Systematic investigation of ancient and early historical period horticultural sites in North and South Dakota dates back to the early twentieth century, reflecting the interests of local colleges and state organizations as well as of outside universities. However, the U.S. government's decision in the mid-1940s to dam the Missouri in several places produced an enormous amount of archaeological fieldwork carried out to salvage artifacts and contextual information from the archaeological sites that these dams were going to inundate.

The archaeological salvage work along the Missouri has profoundly structured what we know about the indigenous farmers of the Middle Missouri. For one thing, it largely limited the process of site discovery and excavation to the main stem of the river; little is known about sites that are not located on the Missouri itself. Because almost all of the archaeological work was overseen by two centralized government agencies, the Smithsonian Institution and the National Park Service, it was characterized by standardized field procedures, modes of analysis, and report organization and content. By providing most of the fieldwork opportunities in the region for decades, it passed these standards and the intellectual framework that went with them along to almost all archaeologists working there. This work also produced an enormous backlog of unanalyzed artifacts and records derived from unreported field projects. Archaeologists can excavate faster than they can analyze and write, and no area of the world illustrates this better than the Middle Missouri region.

The end result of the Middle Missouri excavations has been an extraordinarily rich but incompletely understood and published body of work conducted with a clear, consistent, and largely unchanging set of emphases over a period of roughly fifty years. The primary emphasis of this work was to understand the relations among the sites being excavated—that is, to search for patterns of similarity and difference in the archaeology of the region in space and time. Chronology building and regional comparison have thus been at the center of archaeological work in the Middle Missouri region since this project was initiated, and these topics continue to dominate research there to a greater extent than they do in other areas. As the rest of this discussion shows, archaeologists know a lot about the agricultural populations of the Middle Missouri region, but there are enormous portions of the region that remain largely unexplored, huge collections of artifacts that remain largely unanalyzed, and many important research questions that remain unasked.

AN ARCHAEOLOGICAL HISTORY

The archaeology of the Middle Missouri region documents the history of many horticultural groups, particularly in the centuries after Euro-American contact. Prior to contact, however, two major groups appear to have occupied the region: the ancestors of the modern Siouan-speaking Hidatsas and Mandan and of the Caddoan-speaking Arikara. The languages of these groups fairly clearly document distinct long-term connections to areas outside of the Middle Missouri; the Mandan and Hidatsa languages are related to languages spoken in the upper Midwest and Mississippi valley, and Arikara is related to languages spoken on the central and southern plains and adjacent areas of the Southeast. Archaeologically, occupations linked to these groups are distinguished most clearly by house form and less clearly by pottery and stone tool styles, all of which mirror these linguistic patterns.

The earliest horticultural occupation in the region appeared in northwestern Iowa and southwestern Minnesota in approximately AD 900. This occupation is marked by long rectangular houses with extended entryways and by unambiguous evidence for cultivation of corn, squash, and a variety of indigenous North American domesticates, along with exploitation of a diverse array of wild plants and animals. These early communities appear to have been small and show limited evidence of house remodeling and trash accumulation, presumably reflecting relatively short periods of site occupation. During the eleventh century, however, settlement data indicates an increase in site size and permanence as well as the establishment of some form of connections with the great Mississippian center of Cahokia, near modern-day St. Louis and the junction of the Missouri and Mississippi rivers.

At the same time, sites with the same basic house form spread up the Missouri valley, reaching central North Dakota within a century or so. Archaeologists debate whether this expansion represents a migration or in-place change; probably it represents a complex mix of both in different areas. Collectively, sites showing long rectangular houses are grouped together as the Middle Missouri Tradition (MMT) and represent the ancestors of the Siouan-speaking groups in the region. MMT sites dated prior to the fourteenth century are not all the same. For example, sites father to the south tend to be larger (averaging twenty to thirty houses per site) than those in the north (averaging roughly twelve to eighteen houses per site), and many sites in South Dakota are fortified by ditch and palisade defenses, which are virtually, and perhaps entirely, absent farther north. However, the archaeology of these sites is sufficiently homogeneous that it is reasonable to interpret them as the remains of a single cultural group.

Identifying a single culture is important because the fourteenth century shows the appearance in South Dakota of a second group of sites, once again marked particularly by distinctive architecture. These new sites show square houses with four center posts, a central fireplace, and an extended entry—a floor plan that is found prior to this time on the central and southern plains. Pottery and some stone tools also link these sites to more southern regions of the plains. Sites with these square houses (or other diagnostic artifacts) are collectively grouped together as the Coalescent Tradition (CT) and represent the ancestors of Caddoan speakers in the region, who appear to have migrated into the Middle Missouri from the central plains. A limited number of early Coalescent sites have been investigated, but those that are well documented are large and fairly heavily fortified. The presence of fortifications along with geographic overlaps in the distributions of Coalescent and Middle Missouri groups have generally been seen as evidence of conflict between these groups, and it is clear that Middle Missouri populations abandoned the Missouri valley in South Dakota by the middle to late 1400s, leaving only Coalescent sites. However, small and undefended Coalescent sites are well known, and there is good evidence for geographic intermingling of these sites with similar MMT sites in some areas prior to the mid-1400s; similarities in some aspects of ceramic decoration between CT and MMT sites also implies social interactions.

There is good evidence that environmental problems contributed significantly both to variation within MMT and CT sites and to changing relations between the social groups these sites represent. Multiple climatic indicators (including tree rings and detailed studies of lake sediments) indicate that the plains experienced severe, long-term, and widespread droughts many times during the period of interest here; particularly severe and well-documented droughts are evident from the late 1200s to the early 1300s and during the mid-1400s and late 1500s. Matching radiocarbon-dated sites against drought intervals indicates that human groups along the Missouri River tended to build fortified communities during droughts and to build unfortified communities during non-drought intervals. It has long been recognized that the migration of Coalescent/Caddoan populations into the Middle Missouri was likely driven by the abandonment of the western parts of the central plains in response to the drought of the late 1200s.

The presence of fortified and unfortified sites in the region prior to the appearance of Coalescent populations thus appears to reflect alternating periods of peace and war between MMT communities. Direct evidence of violence at the Fay Tolton site in South Dakota graphically documents the form such conflict can take: the bodies of the victims of an attack were found sprawled on the floor of a burned house at this site. Expansion of MMT populations into North Dakota may date primarily to the relatively drought-free period during earlier parts of the thirteenth century. The in-migration of a culturally distinct population, perhaps in the midst of a particularly severe drought or perhaps just after it (the radiocarbon data is unfortunately not precise enough for this interval to be sure), however, may have shifted conflict away from culturally related neighbors to culturally unrelated migrants. If so, the absence of drought for most of the 1300s and the first

half of the 1400s likely helped to foster an extended period of peace. Sites dated to this interval are almost always small and unfortified, and there is good evidence for settlement of Coalescent populations in the midst of areas that were otherwise occupied by Middle Missouri groups. Neighboring sites of these different groups also show substantial similarities in ceramic style, attesting to some combination of trade among communities of pots, of sharing of pottery-making techniques and designs, or even of movement by potters themselves.

The return of drought in the mid-1400s corresponds to a major change in the archaeological record. Sites dated from approximately 1450 onward show a dramatic separation of populations into a northern Middle Missouri group and a southern Coalescent group, with a largely unoccupied stretch of river between them. Many of these sites are very large (the Middle Missouri Huff site in North Dakota, for example, contains over 100 houses) and heavily fortified; even small Coalescent sites were at least partially surrounded by defenses if they were at the northern end of Coalescent territory. The exact date of the well-known Crow Creek massacre, in which the entire population of a large CT site in central South Dakota was slaughtered (including at least 500 individuals of all ages and both sexes), is not clear, but there are good reasons to suggest it dates to this interval. Ceramic assemblages dated to this period show far more distinctly regional patterns than before, suggesting a significant decrease in social interaction. By the end of the 1400s the overall pattern in the archaeological data suggests that the post-contact pattern of occupation of South Dakota by the Arikara and of North Dakota by the Mandan and Hidatsa had been set.

The period from the sixteenth to the eighteenth centuries was marked by an increasing homogenization of the archaeological record of these groups and by increasing evidence for incursions of outside groups, both Native American and Euro-American, into the Middle Missouri. Within the Middle Missouri region, the architectural distinctions that so clearly marked Caddoan and Siouan groups disappeared during the 1500s; from this time onward, houses in the region were round, with four center posts and a covering of earth and sod, like those in use when explorers such as Lewis and Clark passed through the area. In North Dakota, communities of these lodges were often very large and almost invariably fortified, and many of these sites remained in place for most of this period. Fortifications were very common in South Dakota as well.

By this time, hostilities likely involved additional groups. MMT populations had been replaced in Iowa and Minnesota during the 1300s by the ancestors of other Siouan speakers, known archaeologically as the Oneota. The modern descendants of the Oneota include the modern Omaha, Ponca, and other groups occupying the margins of the eastern plains in the 1700s and 1800s. Evidence of Oneota presence on the eastern plains goes back to the mid-1200s, but these groups appear to have expanded into this area permanently only after

1500. Omaha oral histories record conflict with the Arikara, and similar Arikara histories confirm this.

The appearance of Europeans on the northern plains, and particularly the expansion of the European fur trade, ultimately had more profound consequences for the indigenous people of the Middle Missouri region than did the Oneota. Recovery of small numbers of glass beads and metal artifacts as early as AD 1600 indicates that farmers all along the Missouri were at the end of trading chains extended back to Europe. Indirect access to European goods seems to have been the rule in the Middle Missouri until at least 1700, although isolated European traders may have been on the river by this time (and one probable European skeleton has been identified in an Arikara cemetery of this age). Trade goods increase in sites dated to the early 1700s and begin to include gun parts. By 1740, the Missouri River towns had substantial access to both horses and guns, and they thrived as regional trade centers. One measure of the influence these communities had in the region is that refugee groups moving west often adopted the architecture, community organization, and material culture of the existing Missouri River groups almost wholesale; for example, ethnohistoric information indicates that the Biesterfeld site is an earth lodge town occupied during the 1700s by the Cheyenne, but the archaeology of this site is almost indistinguishable from that of any number of Arikara sites.

Increased contact with whites brought epidemic disease by the late 1700s, dramatically reducing populations in these towns. At the same time, trade with whites was intensifying, both through formal expeditions of traders and through the efforts of individual traders who settled in native towns. The nineteenth century saw increasing efforts on the part of whites to control trade, including great increases in the numbers of white trappers and, by the 1820s, establishment of trading posts along the Missouri itself. During this time, increasing pressure on tribes to the east of the plains forced many groups westward, and inter-tribal conflict increased. Archaeologically, this period is marked by dramatic declines in the number and size of communities as well as by at least one graphic example of a massacre of an Arikara community, probably by the Lakota. Decimated by warfare and disease, the farmers of the Middle Missouri region concentrated northward into a handful of towns in northern South Dakota and North Dakota. By 1862, the Mandan, Hidatsa, and Arikara were living together in a single town in central North Dakota—Like-a-Fishhook Village. The descendants of these groups live on the Fort Berthold reservation in the area around this site today.

Further Reading: Ahler, Stan, and Marvin Kay, *Plains Village Archaeology: Bison Hunting Farmers in the Central and Northern Plains* (Salt Lake City: University of Utah Press, 2007); Ahler, Stan, Thomas Thiessen, and Michael Trimble, *People of the Willows: Prehistory and Early History of the Hidatsa Indians* (Grand Forks: University of North Dakota Press, 1991); Bamforth, Douglas B., "Climate, Chronology, and the Course of War in the Middle Missouri Region of the North American Great Plains," in *The Archaeology of Warfare: Prehistories of Raiding and Conquest*, edited by Elizabeth Arkush and Mark Allen (Gainesville: University of Florida Press, 2006), 66–100; Lehmer, Donald, *Middle Missouri Archaeology* (Washington, DC: Department of the Interior, 1971).

Douglas B. Bamforth

NINETEENTH-CENTURY INDIAN WARS ARCHAEOLOGICAL SITES

The story of the battle of the Little Bighorn has assumed legendary, if not mythical, proportions in American culture, as have many western Indian battles. One of the most interesting and little-known facets of those stories is the role army tactics played in the battles, which has been revealed through new historical research and archaeological investigations. The study of war and its results has occupied historians and scholars for centuries. There are literally shelves of books that delve into the reasons people fight and die for a cause. Those who fight rarely do so without some knowledge, whether formally gained or learned by practical experience, of strategy and tactics. Custer is often criticized for dividing his command in the face of the enemy during his last battle. Often those critical of his tactics of June 25, 1876, see only that day and are unaware that Custer's troop deployments were completely consistent with his previous fights with Indians of the west, and more important, it was consistent with generally accepted U.S. Army practice for the period.

George Custer did not invent the divided command attack concept that he employed at his last fight, the battle of the Little Bighorn. He was, however, influenced by its historically successful application in other Indian War engagements and by his own successes with this tactic in earlier fights. Recent archaeological and historical research at Custer's earliest Indian war conquest, an 1867 Cheyenne and Sioux village on Pawnee Fork (Kansas), at the 1868 battle of the Washita

Hancock burning the village on Pawnee Fork, Kansas.   [*Harpers Weekly*, November 1867]

(Oklahoma), as well as at the 1876 battle of the Little Bighorn (Montana) demonstrate Custer's continued reliance on a proven tactical approach that failed him only once and that moved his story from its place in history to the realm of American myth.

U.S. ARMY TACTICS IN THE
NINETEENTH CENTURY

The Napoleonic Wars and the United States' war with Mexico (1846–48) heavily influenced tactical doctrine during the early years of the Civil War. Custer and most officers of the Indian wars learned this approach to warfare during their West Point education and in the field during the Civil War. Custer learned one manner of fighting at West Point—close-order infantry assaults with bayonets gleaming, cavalry charges with sabers flashing, and direct fire by smoothbore artillery placed to the front of the line—which gave way to more discreet tactics by 1863. Both Union and Confederate commanders saw appalling casualty rates using these tactics against the commonly used rifled musket. Smoothbore artillery was no longer able to mass to the front of an infantry line and pound the enemy. The range of the rifled musket was equal to that of the smoothbore artillery, allowing the infantryman to pick off gun crews at will. The time-honored cavalry charge to break the infantry line was no longer feasible, again due to the long range and accuracy of the rifled musket; the

infantrymen could easily decimate a cavalry charge before it was well underway. Finally, the infantryman armed with the rifled musket could destroy a close-order infantry charge well beyond the traditional 100-yard firing range of the old smoothbore musket.

By the last years of the Civil War tactics had adapted to the effectiveness of modern rifled arms. Infantry tactics were modified to open-order skirmish lines with available cover used whenever possible. Defensive positions were usually fortified with extensive entrenchments. Prepared rifle pits, picket posts, and videttes usually protected even short-term camps.

Although used extensively throughout the war, artillery, by 1863, became a defensive rather than an offensive weapon, as it had been in 1861. Artillery was required to move behind the line of defense to be effective due to the increased range of the rifled musket. Artillery tactics of the Civil War always used direct fire. Indirect fire would not be developed for another forty years. The direct-fire concept relegated the artillery to a defensive role throughout the Civil War and for many years to come, although rifled artillery was common in the later years of the Civil War and into the third quarter of the nineteenth century.

Of the three combat branches, cavalry made the greatest adaptation during the latter part of the Civil War, continuing these tactics during the Indian wars. In battle it moved from the close-order charge meant to break or outflank a line to a mobile unit that could move quickly to the scene of action

The August 11, 1873, battle site on the Yellowstone River in Montana.   [Douglas D. Scott]

then dismount and fight as light infantry. With the advent of breechloading single-shot and repeating carbines, cavalry firepower increased dramatically. This increased firepower and mobility allowed the cavalry to regain usefulness on the battlefield, which it had lost with the introduction of the rifled musket. Cavalry was also used extensively throughout the Civil War and Indian wars as a fast and efficient scouting and intelligence-gathering arm. Its mobility allowed units to range far and wide around larger columns to protect the marching columns and scout opponent movements. Custer and most senior officers of the Indian wars learned these lessons by very real and practical experience during the Civil War.

The U.S. Army was downsized and reorganized in 1866 to reflect a change in mission at the end of the Civil War. During the late 1860s and into the early 1870s the army began to assess and develop new tactical doctrine in response to their role of frontier protector. One officer, Emory Upton, is credited with developing a new system of tactics for the army during this era. However, Upton only headed a board of officers that, for the first time, studied all three combat branches and developed a compatible system of tactics for all branches. This system, an outgrowth of both experience in the Civil War and a study of European armies, focused on two major changes in the way the army went into battle, and that information was widely available in the army by 1867. First, companies were reorganized so the men marched and maneuvered in columns of four.

Groups of four could then be combined into units of eight, twelve, or larger numbers for specific tasks. Upton and his board also introduced a second concept, open-order skirmishing. As a direct result of their Civil War experiences of facing rifled musket fire in massed lines and witnessing large numbers of killed and wounded, the board recognized the necessity of opening the line to minimize casualties caused by the more effective range and greater firepower of the breechloading firearm.

Two other tactics developed as a direct result of Indian fighting. First was the recognition that the most effective time to score a victory over the mobile warrior was during his moments of least mobility. The army high command, building on its frontier experiences in the years preceding the Civil War, saw that the Plains Indians were the most vulnerable during the winter when the lack of good forage and raw weather prevented movement of the various bands. Second was the concept of a multi-pronged or column attack on a band or village. This concept involved splitting commands, whether wings of battalions, battalions of regiments, or even whole regiments of larger forces into elements that would maneuver to encircle the subject of the action. For the most part the tactic was successfully employed on numerous instances. It failed on certain occasions, in particular at the Little Bighorn.

Although neither of these concepts was ever codified as formal army doctrine, in the modern sense it is clear that as a body of theory there was an Indian fighting strategy

Metal detecting operations at the Little Bighorn Battlefield National Monument, Montana.   [Douglas D. Scott]

recognized and practiced by the frontier army. Officers of the Indian wars, including Custer, were no strangers to this body of theory and practice; in fact, they embraced it and used it throughout their encounters with the tribesmen of the northern and southern plains.

There are many examples of the encirclement strategy available in the literature of the Indian-fighting army. The divided command and encirclement tactic has a long history of use by field commanders in their engagements with the tribesmen of the West. The encirclement tactic did not develop in response to the post–Civil War Indian warfare, but has a much longer history than many would suppose.

Sand Creek Massacre: Attack at Dawn

Near dawn on November 29, 1864, the camp of Black Kettle's Cheyenne was visible to the northwest of Colonel John M. Chivington's Colorado Volunteer Cavalry. Advancing slowly from the south, the citizen soldiers gained a ridge overlooking Sand Creek from which they could clearly see the camp. Horse herds grazed on either side of the intermittent stream. Details of the Sand Creek Massacre and its associated archaeological evidence are told elsewhere in this volume; however, a recapitulation is given here to place the story in the context of army combat tactics during the Indian wars in the West.

The site of the Sand Creek Massacre was relocated using battlefield archaeological investigation techniques in 1999. The archaeological record contains abundant lines of evidence to support the conclusion that this is Black Kettle's village attacked by Colonel Chivington's forces.

The firearms artifact distribution is particularly striking in one respect—that is, the absence of bullets or other weaponry evidence of resistance in the camp itself. Bullets representing weapon types that can be reasonably associated with the Cheyenne and Arapaho are singularly absent from the artifact

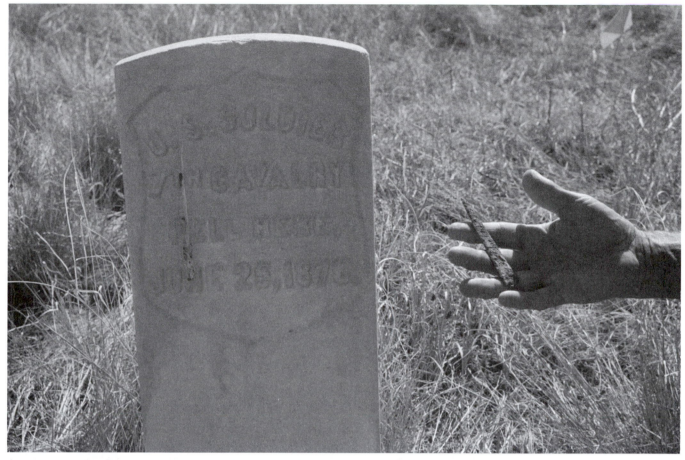

An iron arrowhead recovered near one of the soldier's markers at Little Bighorn Battlefield National Monument, Montana. [Douglas D. Scott]

collection from the campsite. The absence of definitive artifacts of resistance supports the Native American oral tradition that the attack came as a complete surprise.

The archaeological data is consistent with the historical accounts of a multi-sided attack on the village. However, the archaeological data suggests that the attack, although initially well coordinated, became disorganized, and the troops became intermingled early in the fray, suggesting that command and control was at a minimum during the attack.

CUSTER IN COMBAT

Custer's First Engagement with Indians:
The Indian Camp on Pawnee Fork, Kansas

General Winfield Scott Hancock's spring 1867 expedition to negotiate peace treaties with the central Plains tribes was Lt. Col. George Custer's introduction to Plains warfare. The expedition was essentially a failure and may very well have left an indelible impression on Custer, who was fresh from victory after victory on the battlefields of the Civil War. Hancock met with some Sioux and Cheyenne tribal leaders in early April at Fort Larned, Kansas, but these encounters were

disappointing in their results as far as Hancock was concerned. He decided to take the army to the Indians and meet them in the field. Whether he intended to provoke a confrontation or achieve goals of peace is still widely debated.

On the afternoon of April 14, 1867, Hancock encountered a large body of mounted warriors arrayed across his line of march some 30 miles west of Fort Larned, Kansas. A meeting with the tribal leaders ended with the Indians agreeing to meet with General Hancock the next morning at his camp. Hancock camped that evening about 1 mile from the Indian camp, which was composed of around 111 Cheyenne and 140 Sioux tepees.

During the late afternoon hours the villagers, apparently fearing another affair like Sand Creek, quietly slipped away, leaving behind their tepees and most of their camp possessions. Hancock, upon learning that the Indians had fled, roused his command around 8:00 pm and marched to the village. He deployed his cavalry to encircle the camp in single file in order to prevent any escape, although he was too late. Hancock also positioned his artillery on either side of the camp, which sat on a series of terraces on the meandering

Pawnee Fork. Hancock then sent Custer and scout Edmund Guerrier forward to reconnoiter. Custer found the camp abandoned, with most possessions still lying about and three people—an old man, an old woman, and a young girl—the only inhabitants.

Upon confirming the reports, Hancock redeployed his troops, with infantry surrounding the village. He had Custer prepare to give chase to the Indians, while Hancock and the remainder of the troops inventoried and destroyed the tepees and the camp goods left behind. This much-ado-about-nothing event was Custer's rather ignominious introduction to Plains Indian warfare.

The Pawnee Fork village site is now owned by the Archaeological Conservancy, and a rich archaeological record of the camp and its destruction was recently reported. Hancock's destruction of the camp and camp goods is comparable to that described in the archaeological record of the Sand Creek Massacre of 1864. In fact, many of the Cheyenne who fled Hancock and Custer were in the Sand Creek camp and were to be in the Washita village as well.

Custer's First Real Indian Combat: The Washita Battle of 1868

Aside from the Little Bighorn battle, Custer's fight with the Cheyenne on the Washita River in western Oklahoma is one of the better-known engagements on the southern plains. On a cold November morning Custer put into motion one of the classic divided-command attack tactics that epitomizes the Indian wars. As with many other fights that employed this tactic, this attack was successful.

For the dawn November 27 attack Custer divided his Seventh Cavalry into four separate attacking forces. With the main body of cavalry, he moved from the northwest toward the sleeping village. Major Joel Elloitt's command attacked the village from the northeast while Captain Edward Myers came in from the west with his company. Captain William Thompson was ordered to sweep around the other commands and attack from the south, essentially encircling the village and its inhabitants. The troops did achieve their objective of surprise and captured the village in good order. The story is familiar enough that the details need not be repeated here, but it suffices to note that this was Custer's first real combat experience with Indians, and he carried the day with his encircling tactic.

Recent archaeological investigations of the Washita battlefield, prior to its becoming a National Park Service site, met with mixed results. The village site itself has been destroyed by the movement of the Washita River back and forth across the valley and by modern agricultural practices. Archaeological evidence of the attacks from the surrounding terraces or bluffs above the river are still partially intact, particularly that of Thompson's attack from the south. The archaeological data is minimal at best at this time, but all the evidence is consistent with the historical accounts of the method and manner of Custer's attack tactics.

Custer Surprised: The Fight on the Yellowstone in 1873

Custer's August 11, 1873, fight on the Yellowstone is not so well known as his other engagements, but the tactics he employed in a defensive fight are instructive as to Custer's overall tactical concepts. Custer's command, as part escort party for the Northern Pacific Railroad survey under the overall command of Colonel David Stanley, was encamped on the Yellowstone River near its confluence with the Big Horn River on the night of August 10. Sioux tribesmen took position across the river from the camp and around 4:00 am began firing into the sleeping soldiers.

Custer immediately rallied his command and, gathering a group of sharpshooters, including himself, moved to a wooded island on the river and began a determined return fire. Lieutenant Charles Baden from a high terrace along the river spotted warriors trying to cross the river and attack from the flanks. Custer ordered Captain Thomas French, commanding his right wing, to move out and protect his downriver flank, and Captain V. K. Hart, commanding the left wing, to do the same on the upriver side. Custer divided his command with two elements to protect the flanks and his central element to stand and fight, firing at warriors as far as 450 yards across the river.

After being informed that some warriors had indeed crossed the river, Custer further divided his command and sent Captain George Yates up the bluffs to command a high point above the river from where he could engage and halt the warriors' advance. Some warriors succeeded in obtaining a good field of fire on Custer's center from a ravine near the center of the line. Custer had Captain Owen Hale and his brother, Captain Tom Custer, charge the ravine and drive out the warriors. Custer further divided his command as the pressure from the warriors waned by sending French's Company M to guard a river crossing and Lieutenant Donald McIntosh up the valley to prevent further crossing upstream. The warriors finally dispersed as an artillery piece in the remainder of Stanley's column arrived and went into action.

Even on the defensive, Custer employed well-proven tactics at the Yellowstone. The division of the command to protect the flanks and carry the attack to the enemy was neither new to the Indian wars nor particularly innovative. It was a tried and proven method of defense in a surprise attack to secure the flanks and, above all, to reverse the situation by putting the enemy on the defensive, thus blunting their ability to achieve their objective.

C. Vance Haynes of the University of Arizona has conducted extensive archaeological investigations on the site of the August 11 fight, which is on privately owned land. Haynes reports that the areas of fighting on the bluffs are very well preserved. Custer's troops were armed by companies with a variety of experimental carbines during the engagement. The Seventh Cavalry was field-testing weapons for the army, and the distribution of unique cartridge cases and bullets allowed

Haynes to follow the movement of Custer's troops and locate Indian positions with ease. The fighting ranged over more than 1 mile around the valley camp, thus making it somewhat comparable to the Little Bighorn battle in size and maneuver. Custer's division of command and troop movement is clearly reflected in the archaeological record, and that record indicates that the movements of the companies was far more extensive than attested to in the historical records.

Little Bighorn Battle: Custer's Twilight

In the spring of 1876, a three-pronged campaign was launched to shepherd the Sioux and Cheyenne back to the reservation. The first column, under General John Gibbon, marched east from Fort Ellis (near present-day Bozeman, Montana). The second column, led by General Alfred Terry (and including Custer), headed west from Fort Abraham Lincoln near Bismarck, North Dakota. The third column consisted of General George Crook's men moving north from Fort Fetterman, Wyoming, into Montana. These three columns were to meet near the end of June in the vicinity of the Little Bighorn.

Unknown to Terry and Gibbon, Crook encountered the Indians near the Rosebud Creek in southern Montana and was defeated by them about a week before Custer's battle. After this, his force withdrew to Wyoming, breaking one side of the triangle. Meanwhile, Terry was moving west up the Yellowstone River to the Little Bighorn. The Seventh Cavalry, under Custer, was to scout ahead and departed Terry's command on June 22. On the morning of June 25, the Seventh Cavalry was at the divide between the Rosebud and Little Bighorn rivers. From a spot known as the Crow's Nest, they observed a large Indian camp.

Worried the Indians might escape, Custer decided to attack and descended into the valley of the Little Bighorn. Captain Frederick Benteen was ordered to travel southwest with three companies to block a possible southern escape route. A few miles from the Little Bighorn, Custer again divided his command, as Major Marcus Reno was ordered to take three companies along the river bottom and attack the Indian village on its southern end. The remaining five companies would follow Custer in support of Reno.

Custer took the remaining five companies along the east side of the river to an ephemeral tributary of the Little Bighorn. He must have finally realized the gravity of the situation as the north end of the village came into view. From here, he sent a message back to Benteen: "Benteen, Come on. Big village, be quick, bring packs. P.S. Bring pacs [sic]. W. W. Cooke." The messenger, bugler John Martin, was the last to see Custer and his command alive.

In the meantime, the Indian warriors had forced Reno and his men to retreat across the river and up the bluffs to a defensible position. Reno and the men on the hilltop were joined by Benteen's forces and the pack train, both moving along Custer's line of march in order to bring up the ammunition packs. The Indians pinned down all until June 27, when the village retreated as the combined column under Generals Terry and Gibbon arrived. For that day and a half, Reno, Benteen, and the men fought to keep their defensive position and wondered when Custer would relieve them. Reno sent two men to meet the advancing column, and they found Terry and Gibbon near the abandoned Indian village. Here, a scout brought the news: Custer and his men lay dead on a ridge above the Little Bighorn.

Archaeological investigations at the site of the battle of the Little Bighorn in Montana yielded thousands of artifacts. Spatial patterning analysis of the physical evidence of the 1876 battle revealed new insights into the movements of individual combatants as well as overall Indian and soldier positions. The archaeological investigations at Little Bighorn Battlefield National Monument have provided a new perspective on the various elements of the battle of the Little Bighorn. Combatant positions have been identified, firearms have been identified and quantified, and the sequence of events has been elucidated and history enhanced—and in some areas revised.

A FOUNDATION FOR THE PRESENT

Today's military is driven by the combined-arms concept. Within that concept is a highly refined set of operational objectives that are based on a body of theory and practice. Whenever army forces are called to fight, they fight to win. Army forces in combat seek to impose their will on the enemy. Victory is the objective, no matter the mission. Nothing short of victory is acceptable. The fundamental tenets of army operations doctrine describe the characteristics of successful operations. In and of themselves, they do not guarantee victory, but their absence makes it difficult and costly to achieve. Even though not codified like today's standards, the same principles and tenets were, in essence, used by the frontier army and by Custer.

Although army campaigners of the Indian wars did not have the benefit of modern tactical and strategic analysis, they did employ the basic concepts. It is clear in both the historical and archaeological record that they, perhaps unknowingly, did use the concepts that are codified in today's tactical prescriptions for successful operations. Suffice it to say that modern practice, built on nearly 200 years of army combat experiences, can be used as a model to evaluate past battle tactics.

Applying the model of modern tactical prescriptions and comparing Custer's actions at the Little Bighorn shows that what he did as a commander was not new in his experiences fighting Indians on the plains, nor was it a new tactic applied for the first time in a desperate situation. Rather, the historical and archaeological data ably demonstrates that Custer had ten years of experience with the divided-command approach in attacking and subduing hostile Indian villages. The record also shows that the tactics he employed at Little Bighorn were well known in army circles, and that this type of attack had been used for over twenty years by many officers in their confrontations with tribesmen of the West. Custer's failure was not a result of the tactics used, per se, but was simply due to the particular circumstances that he faced on June 25, 1876. He was simply outnumbered, outgunned, and outfought on that day, and he paid the ultimate price for his command decisions.

Further Reading: Farrow, Edward S., *Mountain Scouting: A Handbook for Officers and Soldiers on the Frontier* (Norman: University of Oklahoma Press, 2000, reprint of 1881 ed.); Fox, Richard A., Jr., and Douglas D. Scott, "The Post–Civil War Battlefield Pattern," *Historical Archaeology* 25(2) (1991): 92–103; Griffith, Paddy, *Battle Tactics of the Civil War* (New Haven, CT: Yale University Press, 1989); Hoig, Stan, *The Sand Creek Massacre* (Norman: University of Oklahoma Press, 1961); Hoig, Stan, *The Battle of the Washita* (Lincoln: University of Nebraska Press, 1976); Jamieson, Perry D., *Crossing the Deadly Ground: United States Army Tactics, 1865–1899* (Tuscaloosa: University of Alabama Press 1994); Jones, Bruce A.; "Historical Archeology at the Village on Pawnee Fork, Ness County, Kansas," Midwest Archeological Center Technical Report No. 86 (Lincoln, NE: National Park Service, Midwest Archeological Center, 2002); Lees, William B., Douglas D. Scott, and C. Vance Haynes, "History Underfoot: The Search for Physical Evidence of the 1868 Attack on Black Kettle's Village," *Chronicles of Oklahoma* 79(2) (2001): 158–181; Scott, Douglas D., "Battlefield Archaeology: Patterns of Combat in the American Indian Wars," in *Fields of Conflict: Progress and Prospect in Battlefield Archaeology*, edited by P. W. M. Freeman and A. Pollard, British Archaeological Reports International Series No. 958 (2001): 177–200; Scott, Douglas D., Richard A. Fox Jr., Melissa A. Connor, and Dick Harmon, *Archaeological Perspectives on the Battle of the Little Bighorn* (Norman: University of Oklahoma Press, 1989).

Douglas D. Scott

NATIVE AMERICAN PERSPECTIVE ON GREAT PLAINS AND ROCKY MOUNTAINS ARCHAEOLOGY

The relationship between American Indians and archaeology (historic preservation, more generally) is tenuous at best and confrontational at worst. With the publication of Vine Deloria's book *Custer Died for Your Sins*, in 1969, the relationship between archaeologists and American Indians took a decided turn. Prior to the book's publication, there was little indication of American Indian distrust and discontent with the discipline of archaeology, but following its publication, American Indians became openly critical of the actions of archaeology and archaeologists. The excavation of the burials of individuals of American Indian descent has been a primary point of concern between both American Indians and archaeologists, and American Indian protests for the period from 1969 to 1979 showed that their distrust of archaeology and archaeologists did revolve primarily around the perceived threat to their ancestors and human remains. Articles published in American Indian newspapers and magazines presented the general attitudes of the more radical Indians in the 1970s. The American Indian Movement's disruption of excavations at Welch, Minnesota, and the occupation of the Southwest Museum in Los Angeles aimed at getting American Indian human remains and sensitive material out of public displays in 1971 exemplified the physical actions taken to confront the issue. At the same time, tribal groups increased efforts at regaining human remains and artifacts from museums and federal repositories. Published American Indian opinions tended to view this as a conflict between Indian and non-Indian spiritual or religious values, whereas most archaeologists tended to view the problem as a conflict between scientific and nonscientific values.

It is difficult to broadly generalize regarding American Indian relationships with archaeology because each tribe negotiates its relationships with a myriad of archaeologists and organizations wishing to conduct archaeological research on its tribal land or its tribal heritage. Tribal perspectives on the practice of archaeology range from outright distaste for the field to recognition of archaeology as necessary for compliance with the federal regulations that impact tribal members and projects.

Two important questions consistently appear when one considers the relationship between the indigenous people and archaeologists: To whom does the past belong? Does anyone have the right to control access to the evidence of the past, or should access to that archaeological record be open to anyone and everyone? These rhetorical questions revolve around very concrete issues about control over the resources that exist in the present, as well as the construction or interpretation of the past.

Because of American society's emphasis on formal education and the role of science within it, archaeologists are generally seen to possess knowledge that is somehow beyond the understanding of nonscientists; they are the keepers of that knowledge. With their training in the scientific method, archaeologists believe that they consider information objectively. As the "recognized" authority on the scientific record held within archaeological and heritage sites, archaeologists have substantial power over resources associated with the cultural history of indigenous peoples; thus members of descendant communities often feel powerless about what happens to the archaeological sites associated with them. Because of this power differential, archaeologists often are perceived to be arrogant and insensitive by Native people, while Native people often are perceived to be antagonistic toward archaeological research.

The United States government recognizes American Indian tribes as domestic dependent nations that retain sovereign powers, except as divested by the United States. Indian sovereignty is a key issue defining the interaction between Native Americans and archaeologists on Indian-owned land. Indian sovereignty means that all archaeological research undertaken by non-Indians on Indian land requires the approval of the tribal government, and that a tribe retains the right of ownership of all cultural materials found on their land.

Native peoples and scholars often have different concepts of heritage resources and their relation to the past. Archaeologists conceptualize the archaeological record as inanimate deposits of artifacts and sediments that offer information about a long-dead past. Many indigenous peoples, however, view archaeological sites as places where ancestors and spirits still live and continue to have a profound influence in contemporary life. In many indigenous cultures, the boundary between the past and present is not as clearly demarcated as it is in the scientific worldview. For archaeologists, the principal values of the archaeological record are derived from its ability to yield scientific data about past human behavior. Although some indigenous people might appreciate the scientific values of the archaeological record and the information it can offer about the past, indigenous values for archaeological sites are primarily derived from their association with ancestors, tribal history, and traditional values that transcend scientific data. The desire to preserve archaeological sites in situ as monuments that attest to tribal history is often more important to indigenous people than the information that can be gained through archaeological excavation.

Given the cultural and spiritual importance of ancestors, some indigenous people want all ancestral graves threatened with destruction to be located and moved, and many indigenous communities allow nondestructive analysis and documentation of osteological material as part of the process of excavation and reburial. The Wichita Tribe of Oklahoma, for example, has worked with biological anthropologists to develop a database of human remains that have been found within their ancestral homeland so that biological and cultural information about their ancestral populations can be saved.

To their credit, more and more archaeologists are trying to accommodate American Indian cultural values in the practice of archaeology. This is being done in a variety of ways, including focusing on the identification and study of archaeological sites using nondestructive survey techniques; excavating only those sites that are threatened by land development, vandalism, or some other form of destruction; providing training to native students in an archaeological field school situation; and involving Native communities in excavations of cultural sites.

Balancing scientific and tribal values within archaeology is a difficult and challenging task. More archaeologists are recognizing that professional responsibilities to scholarship and science need to be balanced with ethical responsibilities to indigenous peoples, and that this is not an easy or straightforward task. Different values, sometimes hard to reconcile, are involved in this balancing act. For instance, archaeologists are taught that the dissemination of knowledge through scholarly publication of research is an ethical responsibility, yet this often conflicts with the desire of indigenous people to maintain the confidentiality of esoteric cultural information. Additionally, assertion of intellectual property rights by indigenous communities is often seen to be at odds with academic notions giving scholarly authors ownership over their written works.

In addition to tribally operated archaeology programs, some governmental agencies such as the United States Department of Agriculture Forest Service offer programs that provide training to indigenous people in archaeological techniques and subsequently employ them as cultural resource technicians on Forest Service projects. Some programs combine academic and on-the-job training as a means of providing indigenous people with opportunities to participate more fully in the archaeological enterprise. In the southern Great Plains, the Forest Service has provided training to various tribes to help develop Tribal Heritage Resource Technicians who can work within tribal land managing agencies to conduct preliminary heritage inventories to protect heritage sites.

In spite of such training programs, however, there still exists a dichotomy between the wishes of North American archaeologists and American Indians, perhaps as an unintended byproduct of the reality of the current situation. Archaeologists and indigenous peoples are often working toward the same goal of protecting archaeological sites, even though their motives for protecting those sites (as well as their idea of what constitutes "protection") might be different. Archaeologists may be intent on protecting a nonrenewable database that holds a part of the record of human adaptive evolution, while tribal groups might be more intent on saving integral and irreplaceable parts of their cultural identity and history as a people.

Additionally, although most archaeologists hold that information on the past should be supplemented by information from documentary history when available, many American Indian groups know or understand the past through traditional histories transmitted by oral performances, ritual observances, dances, and other means. Traditional histories can provide important sources of interpretative data about archaeological sites, but the fact that oral traditions are some-times embedded in ritual or esoteric knowledge make it impossible for some tribal groups to allow their oral traditions to be used in scientific research. This ritual and esoteric foun-dation of oral traditions is a two-edged sword, and perhaps one of the reasons why archaeologists do not use oral traditions in scientific research.

North American archaeologists have made a concerted effort to integrate American Indian perspectives into the everyday practice of the discipline. In the United States, major strides in legislative equality were made in the last decade of the twentieth century. The passage of the National Museum of the American Indian Act of 1989, the Native American Graves Protection and Repatriation Act of 1990, and the 1992 amend-ments to the National Historic Preservation Act expanded the role of American Indians in the regulation of the archaeologi-cal enterprise. These laws gave tribal authorities the opportu-nity to consult with archaeologists concerning their cultural heritage, to communicate their wishes to the broader anthropo-logical community, and to coordinate intercultural programs aimed at increasing American Indian involvement in the dis-cipline. Tribal groups were granted legal standing to partici-pate in the regulatory processes concerning the protection of cultural resources on tribal and federal land from impacts resulting from federally sponsored or federally funded proj-ects. Additionally, they were able to take over responsibility for protection of cultural resources on their tribal lands from state officials under certain circumstances. American Indian human remains were finally afforded protection under the law equal to that of non-Indian human remains, and procedures were initiated to return human remains, burial objects, sacred items, and items of cultural patrimony—items that cannot legally be alienated by an individual within a culture.

Yet, at the same time, under the same circumstances, American Indian perspectives have had minimal impact on the practice of archaeology. The regulatory "concessions" made in recent times to North American indigenous groups are those that should have been the right of those groups as sovereign nations all along; they still are limited in their rights to control their own heritage and still have to rely upon archaeologists to protect their heritage and that of their ances-tors. They must continue to justify their definitions of cultural resources within a framework foreign to them and must also struggle to protect certain areas from disturbance, while being unable to prevent the wholesale destruction of cultural and heritage sites on private (and sometimes federal) property.

Thus, although advances have been made toward integrating the wishes of American Indians into the practice of archaeology, those advances are often seen as lateral ones rather than forward ones. Concessions have been made toward allowing North American indigenous groups to become more involved in the protection of their heritage, but such concessions generally have been made within a framework that allows scientists and archae-ologists the ultimate decision concerning heritage resources.

In order to broaden American Indian acceptance of archae-ology as a valid and useful tool in protecting tribal cultural heritage, archaeologists must recognize that stewardship, the first principle in the Society for American Archaeology's Prin-ciples of Archaeological Ethics, must be shared between themselves and American Indian tribes. It makes good eco-nomic and professional sense for archaeologists to protect and conserve archaeological sites because, without the archaeo-logical record, archaeologists would soon run out of resources that they could study. However, this failure to include American Indians more fully within that stewardship effectively removes American Indians from the cultural resource protection sphere, forcing them to compete with archaeologists for the right to pro-tect their own heritage. Archaeologists must integrate North American indigenous groups more effectively into their attempts to conserve and protect the cultural heritage that is the focus of their study if they are to remove the competitive "us versus them" atmosphere that has developed.

THE TRIBAL HISTORIC PRESERVATION OFFICER PROGRAM

Even while most Indians do not trust the system supposedly designed to protect their heritage, more and more tribal groups are adapting archaeological practices and methodol-ogy to protect cultural resources on their reservations. In fact, as a result of the 1992 amendments to the National Historic Preservation Act, in July 1996, twelve American Indian tribes took over a portion of the historic preservation duties from State Historic Preservation Officers. As of November 17, 2006, there are sixty-six American Indian tribes who have taken over the formal responsibility for managing the federal process regarding tribal heritage under the National Historic Preservation Act; it is estimated that by 2008 there will be seventy-three tribal historic preservation offices.

As of this writing, only seventeen tribes within five of the Great Plains and Rocky Mountain states have formally estab-lished tribal historic preservation offices. Visit the National Association of Tribal Historic Preservation Officers (THPOs) Web site (http://www.nathpo.org/map.html) and click on each state to view a listing of the THPOs and their contact informa-tion. These offices operate under the authority of the National Historic Preservation Act and serve to offer tribal perspectives on the compliance procedures established by federal laws. They implement several federal laws that protect cultural her-itage resources and work closely as a liaison between tribal organizations and federal and state agencies. And while there are other tribal groups that operate to provide tribal perspec-tives and input on heritage sites and heritage issues, these pro-grams have gone through a rigorous process to formally take over the roles of the state historic preservation officers within their states on projects that impact their tribal lands.

However, funding has not kept pace with the growth of the program. Funding for each tribal historic preservation office has slid from an all-time high of slightly more than $155,000 per program in 2001 to an estimated funding of approximately $50,000 for fiscal year 2007. With the increased demand on the tribal offices by a growing number of federal and private projects, tribal programs continue to bear the brunt of protecting tribal heritage.

Although there are only seventeen tribal historic preservation offices within the eleven states that make up the Great Plains and the Rocky Mountain portions of the United States, other tribes participate within the process to some extent. The Pawnee Tribe of Oklahoma has been an active participant in being involved in the repatriation of human remains from archaeological sites in Colorado, Kansas, Oklahoma, and Nebraska, seeing it as their responsibility to return what they perceive to be ancestral human remains to the earth. In some ways this may be seen as antithetical to archaeology, but the Pawnee in general recognize that there are some answers archaeology can provide while there are others that only tribal histories can provide.

SUMMARY

The hopes for archaeology rest on groups who know how to use the system to get the results they want as well as on those who will push to modify that system to better fit the beliefs of indigenous people. By determining the path of the programs that study early populations of an area, indigenous populations can influence not only the outcomes of archaeology but also the extent and quality of knowledge obtained. Through their influence, the discipline of archaeology can rise beyond the image it currently carries as an esoteric discipline producing data of benefit to no one other than archaeologists.

This discussion has focused on some of the differences between American Indian perspectives on archaeology and those of non-Indigenous practitioners of the discipline. These perspectives concerning archaeology have had an impact on its practice in the United States, but there are other possibilities that archaeologists should address as a means of further improving and cementing positive relationships with American Indians.

Further Reading: Deloria, Vine, Jr., *Custer Died for Your Sins: An Indian Manifesto* (London: Macmillan, 1969); Watkins, Joe, *Indigenous Archaeology: American Indian Values and Scientific Practice* (Walnut Creek, CA: Alta Mira Press, 2000).

Joe Watkins

ROCK ART SITES IN THE PLAINS–ROCKY MOUNTAINS REGION

The Great Plains, abutting the Rocky Mountains from Calgary, Alberta, to northwestern New Mexico, comprise an incredible diversity of landscapes. Extending from the Continental Divide to the Eastern Woodlands, the region is often misconceived as a nearly featureless plain, but it is better characterized as a land of extremes, where stretches of seemingly endless prairie are suddenly broken by towering mountains with peaks far above timberline, or badland deserts whose eroded buttes and arroyos were aptly named Hell's Half Acre by early pioneers.

In the north, Pleistocene glaciers sculpted rolling prairies and left deep meltwater channels and house-sized glacial erratics. Between the Yellowstone and South Platte rivers are pine parklands whose broad, open valleys and low tree-covered ridges supported immense herds of bison, elk, and antelope and provided pasture for the largest historic herds of Indian horses. To the south lies the canyon country of southeastern Colorado and the Llano Estacado of the Texas panhandle.

Like its landscape, plains climate is equally harsh and variable. Long, cold winters follow hot, dry summers. Thunderstorms typify the summer, and blizzards occur anytime from late September to May. Temperatures can rise and fall dramatically—in 1916 the temperature on Montana's Blackfoot rose 100°F (−56 to +44) in twenty-four hours, and in March 1980 the temperature in Great Falls, Montana, rose from −32°F to +15°F in just seven minutes!

The plains are watered by several major river systems, including the South Saskatchewan, Missouri, Yellowstone, Platte, Arkansas, Canadian, and upper Rio Grande. Born as rushing streams in the Rocky Mountain foothills, these flow eastward through broad valleys flanked by hundreds of miles of cliffs and buttes, providing an almost endless rock art canvas.

Plant communities are as varied as the landscapes. Dense fir and pine forests cover the Rocky Mountain foothills and outlying mountain ranges while sagebrush and prickly pear deserts occupy Wyoming's Bighorn and Green River basins. But above all, the plains are grass country, and the lush grassland carpeting the rolling prairies, river valleys, and extensive foothill basins provided prime grazing grounds for millions of American bison that fed Plains Indians for more than 11,000 years.

Plains cultures, representing nine different language families, can be classified into two basic patterns—nomadic hunter-gatherers and sedentary farmers. Plains Indians have been hunter-gatherers since Paleoindian times, and many tribes maintained that lifestyle into the 1870s. These hunters exploited North America's richest terrestrial fauna—mainly bison, but also elk, deer, antelope, and mountain sheep. Bison, antelope, and mountain sheep were often hunted communally by driving herds over cliffs or into constructed corrals. Hunters lived in hide tepees and followed the bison herds from season to season. Many tribes regularly traded with or raided village farms in the eastern and southern parts of the region—originally to acquire corn, beans, and squash, but in historic times to obtain European trade goods.

Some Plains tribes were farmers—occupying semi-subterranean pit houses clustered in villages along the Missouri River and streams from Iowa south to eastern Oklahoma. Villages were occupied year-round by some people, but every year large groups left seasonally to hunt bison.

Leaders in all Plains groups were charismatic individuals who formed a council of respected elders, and a Plains man rose to a leadership position through military, hunting, and religious accomplishments. Rock art indicates that both hunting and religious accomplishments have a history stretching back more than 5,000 years, but military prowess seems to have become more valued after about AD 900. By historic times tribal leaders were required to have performed a specific set of brave deeds in combat—a system known as "coup counting."

Plains rock art derives primarily from religious life and coup counting. Religion was based on power obtained through the vision quest. As religious specialists, shamans had more comprehensive powers acquired through more frequent contacts with the supernatural. Images painted or carved as rock art or on shields and tepees represent supernatural beings and vision experiences of men and women.

From about AD 1600 to 1900, rock art images indicate that a man's war record had supplanted his supernatural contacts as the key to determining his tribal status. During this period most rock art scenes are narrative compositions showing fighting figures or tallies of war booty, stolen horses, or vanquished enemies.

Plains rock art is second only to rock art of the American Southwest in complexity and diversity of content. Ranging from finely drawn polychrome paintings as aesthetically pleasing as masterpieces from anywhere in the world to crudely pecked curvilinear abstracts, images illustrate hunting scenes, war exploits, visions, supernatural beings, and family portraits. Some examples show the most sophisticated portraiture done anywhere in North American rock art, but other images are hurried scratches, now barely recognizable as a horse or human. Many sites are small clusters of images from a single art tradition, but every part of the region has sites showing hundreds of figures from as many as five separate traditions. Among these are the most famous sites, including Writing-On-Stone, Pictograph Cave, Bear Gulch, Legend Rock, Petroglyph Canyon, and Mujares Creek.

Scholars currently recognize fifteen different Plains rock art traditions, and more are being discovered every decade. Plains rock art is primarily petroglyphs—only the Columbia Plateau, Foothills Abstract, Vertical Series, Purgatoire, Ceremonial, and Biographic traditions commonly have pictographs. Petroglyphs are usually pecked or incised, and most traditions show a strong preference for one or the other technique. Only the Ceremonial and Purgatoire traditions do not show such marked preferences, and only Ceremonial art has significant numbers of incised, pecked, and painted images.

Given this diversity it is not surprising that more than thirty animal species are portrayed, several by their characteristic track. Most common are horse, deer, and elk, but many mountain sheep, bear, bison, and birds are also shown. Mythical animals include Thunderbird, Horned Serpent, and an underwater monster with oversized teeth and claws, antlers, and dragon spines down its back. One large Hoofprint tradition boulder, named the Sleeping Buffalo, has ribs, eyes, nose, mouth, and horns carved to accentuate its natural shape, which resembles a reclining bison. Although twelve traditions regularly illustrate animals, only Hoofprint, Early Hunter, and Pecked Representational art have a marked preference for them over humans.

Humans are a major component of nine Plains rock art traditions and range from the simplest stick figures through stylized V-neck humans to masks. Sophisticated lifelike portraits characterize the latest Biographic drawings. Humans frequently participate in action scenes (e.g., hunting, sex, combat, horse riding, and dancing) in five traditions, but other traditions more often show humans as handprints or vulvaforms. Humans are sometimes identified as male or female by genitalia, but more often by clothing or weaponry. Early Hunter, Ceremonial, Biographic, and Rio Grande art traditions often show humans associated with clothing, weapons, or ceremonial paraphernalia such as masks, headdresses, or ritual implements.

Material culture items are shown frequently in five traditions and occasionally in three others. Most common are weapons, horse tack, and clothing (more than ten different items from each category), but wagons, tepees, buildings, a boat, and even a gallows and an automobile occur in Biographic art. The prevalence of material culture items is largely due to the narrative aspects of Biographic art, where minute details were necessary to illustrate a story.

Spirit beings—anthropomorphic and zoomorphic—characterize the Dinwoody and Foothills Abstract traditions. Many Dinwoody petroglyphs are therianthropic (part human, part animal) beings with fantastic combinations of human and animal characteristics—for instance, a human head and body, but insect or bird wings or claws rather than hands or feet. Others are recognizable ghosts, trolls, or supernatural monsters with human heads but oversized hands and strangely proportioned bodies. Some have multiple heads, Siamese twin bodies, or smaller beings growing within them.

Others are tethered to dogs or hold bows or arrow points representing the malevolent "ghost arrows" they used to cause disease. Such spirits are often surrounded by wavy lines or streams of dots, and ethnography tells us that shamans saw just such beings during their vision quests at rock art sites. Foothills Abstract tradition pictographs also include spirit beings. These strangely stylized figures show elaborated body parts or maze-like internal organs. Some are so abstract that they are recognizable only by eyes, a head, or arms sprouting from a maze.

Three Plains rock art traditions are primarily nonrepresentational, and two others have significant nonrepresentational components. Plains Grooved art spans the region with several local, recently recognized styles. The grooves, deeply abraded in large clusters, are obviously structured; some clearly served to sharpen various bone tools, but others are put in special locations indicating ritual behaviors. Some long series of vertical marks are connected by a horizontal line on top or bottom, and some connected series have a dot on each vertical line. Ethnographic references suggest several ritual functions for these grooves. The most compelling is the women's vision quest among Siouan tribes, where supplicants formed and sharpened various bone hide-working implements to ensure their futures as respected women.

Pecked Abstract rock art comprises complex asymmetrical maze compositions pecked onto hard sandstones, sometimes with associated human figures, handprints, or footprints. These designs are best explained as entoptic patterns (images that may derive from effects within the central nervous system, e.g., spirals, dots, wavy lines, and similar elements) characteristic of shamans' visions. Their extremely individualistic, almost frenetic, structure is apparently the product of individual ecstatic trance.

Vertical Series rock art is the most enigmatic on the Plains, consisting exclusively of repeated sequences of highly conventionalized geometric shapes (e.g., crescents, triangles, crosses) and letter-like symbols (e.g., I, H, L, U, C, E, T). This art may be the beginning of an ideographic notation system, but the "letters" are often oriented upside down, sideways, or backward from their normal position and frequently have small serifs in odd positions. Whether this rock art was influenced by Plains Indians seeing true writing of early explorers and traders is unknown, and more sites must be studied before it can be better understood.

Columbia Plateau and Foothills Abstract traditions also include significant nonrepresentational images. Columbia Plateau art, with numerous geometric abstracts, is best characterized by tally marks. Ethnography indicates that tallies were vision quest mnemonics indicating number of days spent fasting, site visits, spirit helpers obtained, and proper rituals conducted. Foothills Abstract art has numerous geometric mazes (some possibly abstract humans and animals) and finger lines, paint spatters, and paint-smeared walls. In combination with the numerous handprints at many Foothills Abstract sites, the smearing and spattering of paint hints at rituals whose purpose was group participation and cohesion.

Plains rock art spans the last 6,000 years. The oldest is Early Hunter art, dated by cation ratio (a technique for relative dating of the "varnish" that forms over surface pecking or incisions in some stone and thereby determining how long ago the alternation was made) and AMS radiocarbon techniques to between 11,000 and 2,500 years ago, but the earliest of these dates (before 4000 BC) have yet to be confirmed. Eight other Plains rock art traditions (Columbia Plateau, Dinwoody, Pecked Abstract, Plains Grooved, Foothills Abstract, En Toto Pecked, Pecked Representational, and Eastern Woodlands) began during the Archaic period and all extended into the late prehistoric period. Columbia Plateau, Dinwoody, Plains Grooved, and Eastern Woodlands art lasted even into historic times. Various dating studies using several methods have provided strong support for this chronology. Hoofprint, Ceremonial, Purgatoire, and Rio Grande traditions began in the late prehistoric period, and all but Purgatoire extended into historic times. Finally, Biographic and Vertical Series rock art was added in the historic period.

Thus, on the plains, the late prehistoric period saw the greatest florescence of rock art. At least eleven separate traditions were in development about 1,000 years ago, and 800 years later there were still eight different active rock art traditions in the region. By any measure, the last millennium on the plains was a time that showcased some of the most magnificent rock art ever created in North America. Combined with the heroic exploits of historic Plains tribesmen who fought the U.S. cavalry to a standstill for more than thirty years, it is no surprise that Plains warrior rock art has come to represent Plains Indians in both popular culture and scholarly writing.

The incredible variety of Plains rock art has examples that functioned in four major themes: vision questing, shamanism, hunting magic, and status determination. Vision quest imagery occurs in most Plains rock art traditions, but the best examples are Columbia Plateau and Ceremonial tradition art. Most easily identified by simple juxtaposed compositions showing a human acquiring power from a spirit animal or displaying the power thus acquired, these images often have associated symbols such as celestial imagery (e.g., "sun" circles, "stars," zigzag "lightning" lines) or geometric abstracts. In the Columbia Plateau tradition such compositions are often associated with tally marks, and ethnography provides dozens of references that document these as vision quest records.

A few Ceremonial and Eastern Woodlands compositions are similar to those identified as Columbia Plateau vision quest records. More important, many Ceremonial and Eastern Woodlands rock art compositions are duplicated in identified vision imagery painted on historic tepees, war shields, and ceremonial regalia. These images show animals and people with heart lines, genitals, and kidneys interacting with

Thunderbirds, underwater monsters, and other supernatural beings. Often they are associated with celestial imagery and zigzag lines. Given such strong parallels, it is clear that many Ceremonial tradition images represent vision quest art.

Extensive study of woman's puberty rituals and associated metaphors has enabled archaeologist Linea Sundstrom to recently demonstrate that much Hoofprint and Plains Grooved rock art is the product of women's vision quests, done by female supplicants seeking the virtues of Buffalo Woman and Double Woman.

Shamans also made and used Plains rock art. Pecked Abstract, Dinwoody, Ceremonial, and Foothills Abstract imagery each have strong shamanic associations, and several other traditions hint at a shamanic origin. Pecked Abstract tradition mazes are entoptic designs whose highly individual-istic structure and composition indicate production associ-ated with shamanic trance. Some Foothills Abstract tradition mazes may also be entoptic in origin.

Dinwoody art, characterized by bizarre anthropomorphs juxtaposed with numerous entoptic designs, is clearly attrib-utable to shamans. Many Dinwoody figures are supernatural beings described in Wind River Shoshone folklore as shamans' familiars, and ethnographic references document shamans seeking just such beings as spirit helpers by fasting at petroglyphs. Composite figures and small beings carved within the main figure are exactly what Shoshone shamans reported their spirit helpers to be. Given the preponderance of entoptic designs and excellent ethnographic documenta-tion, Pecked Abstract and Dinwoody art best fit the neuropsy-chological model for rock art interpretation.

Although Foothills Abstract rock art pre-dates ethno-graphic sources, the use of analogy enables archaeologists to interpret that this art was the product of shamans. An empha-sis on bears, turtles, and lizards mirrors historic ethnography that indicates these were shamans' familiars. Additionally, handprints, masks, transformation images, and stick figure humans in "flying" postures distinguish this art from simple vision quest compositions in other traditions. Very abstract humans and bears and handprint/bear tracks that cannot be distinguished from one another provide a visual metaphor that indicates transformation of shamans into bears.

Some Ceremonial tradition images are also probably shaman-istic. These include images of both humans and animals show-ing heart lines, ribs, kidneys, and genitals, as if exposed by X-rays. In these images humans also wear elaborate head-dresses and clothing and carry ceremonial regalia feather fans. All of these imply shamanism, and some scenes show shamanic control of animals. A few ethnographic references document the use of rock art by historic Plains shamans who used the images to read the future and predict success in war. Almost certainly other Plains rock art was made and used by shamans (e.g., Rio Grande, En Toto Pecked, Hoofprint, and Eastern Woodlands tra-dition images), but in-depth study has not yet been done.

Hunting magic occurs in two Plains rock art traditions and may exist in two others. Most striking is Early Hunter tradi-tion imagery, which illustrates a wide range of hunting tech-niques and animal behaviors suggesting that this art was drawn to exercise shamanic control over prey animals and to instruct novice hunters in the rituals and practices associated with communal hunting. Cougars, possibly associated as shamans' helpers, and ritual dance scenes also imply a shamanic aspect to this art. Columbia Plateau rock art has several strong ethnographic references to hunting magic, and similarly some Hoofprint tradition images (bison tracks pecked at or near bison kill sites) and Pecked Representa-tional images of deer and bison may also document hunting magic rock art.

Plains Biographic tradition compositions are the best-developed narratives in North American rock art. Painted and carved to document and validate a man's social status before both sacred and secular audiences, these action scenes are true picture writing, able to communicate a detailed story a century after they were drawn. Relying on a standardized lex-icon of symbols, postures, conventions, and equipment, these narratives occur throughout the plains. Images depicting pitched battles, horse raids, dances, sex acts, tallies of war booty, and the coming of white men attest to the value of coup counting for Plains tribes. This rock art documents that a man's position depended not only on performing such brave deeds but also on recounting them. A man would paint his tepee, war shirt, and buffalo robe, but he also depicted his deeds at sacred rock art sites where the spirits dwelled. Unin-tentionally, these scenes also document Plains Indian history, recording changes in warfare strategy and tactics, the coming of the horse, the gun, and eventually white men.

Finally, the last of these images shows life after tribes were confined to reservations and intertribal wars had ended. The words of Southern Cheyennes Laird and Colleen Cometsevah, although commenting on a particular ledger book, are equally appropriate with respect to Biographic rock art in general:

> The drawings . . . depict the history of our people. . . . [They] represent real people and real events . . . a record of coups and combat . . . against traditional ene-mies as well as the White newcomers who now invaded our homeland. . . . [This was] the beginning of our strug-gle to exist as a free people. (Afton et al. 1997, x)

Further Reading: Afton, Jean, David Fridtjof Halaas, and Andrew E. Masich, *Cheyenne Dog Soldiers: A Ledgerbook History of Coups and Combat* (Boulder: University Press of Colorado, 1997); Keyser, James D., "A Lexicon for Historic Plains Indian Rock Art: Increas-ing Interpretive Potential," *Plains Anthropologist* 32(115) (1987): 43–71; Keyser, James D., and Michael A. Klassen, *Plains Indian Rock Art* (Seattle: University of Washington Press, 2001).

James D. Keyser

BLACKWATER DRAW

Near Clovis, New Mexico
The Type Site for Clovis Paleoindian Points

Blackwater Draw is an extinct riverbed in eastern New Mexico's Llano Estacado that once drained a series of spring-fed lakes, marshes, and intermittent streams into the Brazos River. These rare aquatic resources attracted animals and humans throughout prehistory, resulting in a series of archaeological sites including a deeply stratified archaeological complex known as Blackwater Draw Locality 1. This locality is the type site for Clovis projectile points, which were associated with mammoth remains from the sites excavated from the deepest cultural strata. The type name is derived from the town of Clovis, New Mexico, which is located 14 miles northeast of the site. The importance and extent of the cultural remains at Blackwater Draw have ensured the operation of nearly continuous research projects in the area by multiple institutions since its discovery.

Ridgely Whiteman, a local collector who found fluted points exposed in sand dune blow-outs along with mammoth and bison bone fragments, brought Blackwater Draw to professional attention in 1929. However, little fieldwork was conducted until after 1932, when A. W. Anderson, another artifact collector, along with Whiteman, showed the exposed bones and artifacts to E. B. Howard of the Academy of Natural Sciences of Philadelphia and the University of Pennsylvania Museum. During the following two summers Howard surveyed several locations in the area, but it wasn't until a gravel quarry pit was opened up that in situ bone and artifacts were found. John Cotter, Howard's assistant, focused his attention on the gravel pit between 1936 and 1937. Cotter found two fluted points, a beveled-base bone projectile point, and other artifacts in direct association with mammoth bone, proving for the first time that humans hunted mammoths in North America.

The gravel pit was designated Blackwater No.1 (LA3324) by E. H. Sellards, who, along with Glen Evans, a geologist from the Texas Memorial Museum, conducted research at the site in 1949 and 1950. Evans mapped six geological strata containing archaeological material above the basal gravel deposits. This study provided for the first time a stratigraphic sequence to assess the Paleoindian chronology before the introduction of radiocarbon dating. Clovis artifacts were found in ascending order in two strata: the gray and brown sands. In a later reevaluation of the stratigraphy, Vance Haynes Jr., a geologist from the University of Arizona, suggested that the artifacts found in gray sand deposits were intrusive, likely trampled down from the brown sand by the activities of mammoths and humans. Folsom artifacts associated with *Bison antiquus* bones were found in the diatomaceous earth strata above the level of the Clovis points. Agate Basin points were also recovered from the diatomaceous earth and appear to be coeval with Folsom, but they also occurred above the Folsom occupation. This pattern has been observed at the Hell Gap site in Wyoming and suggests that Agate Basin and Folsom were co-traditions. Stemmed points variously called Portales, Scottsbluff, Firstview, and San Jon, along with indented stemmed points, were found in the carbonaceous silt level. A variety of archaic point styles were found in a dark brown jointed sand deposit, and a mixture of late prehistoric artifacts were in the upper tan eolian sand.

During gravel quarrying operations in 1962 a cache of seventeen prismatic blades were collected from the gray sand layer by Dr. Earl Green of Texas Tech University after they were exposed by earthmoving equipment. This discovery provided proof that Clovis people had a true blade technology and suggested continuity with the Old World Upper Paleolithic. A second cache of five Clovis blades was found in 1990 by Joanne Dickenson when a section of the west bank wall of the gravel pit collapsed.

Ongoing gravel quarrying in the 1960s uncovered at least five mammoths and many artifacts. Salvage work was conducted ahead of the bulldozers by a local group known as El Llano Archaeological Society under the direction of Jim Warnica, a competent amateur from Portales, New Mexico. Earl Green and George Agogino of Eastern New Mexico University were also involved in salvaging the Paleoindian remains. At the same time, Fred Wendorf of Southern Methodist University and Jim Hester of the Museum of New Mexico were conducting the High Plains Ecology Project. This project was the first multidisciplinary study of the geology, paleoecology, and archaeology of any region in the Americas.

During the 1964 salvage work an enigmatic circular pit feature was found. It was roughly 60 centimeters in diameter and extended some 140 centimeters below the Clovis level. A nearby hearth contained the roasted remains of six turtles, so the feature was purported to be a holding tank for turtles. The feature was relocated in 1993 by C. Vance Haynes and Dennis Stanford from the Smithsonian. The pit was a nearly vertical shaft, excavated through a caliche deposit down into the permeable gravel below. Pick scars, roughly the size of a mammoth rib, were noted in the caliche walls. A spoils pile of caliche mixed with sediments reflecting those strata encountered during excavation of the hole was found nearby. It is likely that this feature was intended to be a water well excavated by Clovis people, and as such would have been the oldest well in the New World. However, it was probably a dry hole since there was no rounding of the pit lip, as would be expected if water had been drawn from the well. Also, the permeable gravels were not collapsed, as would be expected if water had been flowing into the pit. Indeed, this failed attempt at producing water would suggest that surface water was scarce and drought conditions were being endured by Clovis people.

A project directed by Stanford and Pegi Jodry of the Smithsonian, along with Vance Haynes, consisted of drilling a pattern of cores across a shallow tributary, known as Spring Draw, which drained the overflow discharge from the springs of the pit area into Blackwater Draw proper. Many of the cores along Spring Draw contained bone fragments in various strata, suggesting that additional archaeological features are buried between the south wall of the gravel pit and Blackwater Draw.

In 1979 gravel quarrying operations were suspended and Blackwater Draw Locality 1 came under the management of Eastern New Mexico University. The site finally achieved National Historic Landmark status in 1982. A museum was built along the Clovis–Portales highway, and the Blackwater Draw Research Center is now located at the site. A large portion of the south wall with a complete stratigraphic profile has been excavated in a stairstep fashion with bones and artifacts left in situ. A protective building and on-site lab covers the excavation. The museum and site are open to the public, and future excavations will no doubt produce more important data on the earliest peoples of the Americas.

Further Reading: Boldurian, A. T., and J. L. Cotter, *Clovis Revisited: New Perspectives on Paleoindian Adaptations from Blackwater Draw, New Mexico* (Philadelphia: University of Pennsylvania, University Museum, 1999); Haynes, C. V., D. Stanford, M. Jodry, J. Dickenson, J. Montgomery, P. Shelley, I. Rovner, and G. Agogino, "Clovis Well at the Type Site, 11,500 B.C.: The Oldest Prehistoric Well in America," *Geoarchaeology* 14 (1999): 455–470; Hester, J. J., *Blackwater Locality No. 1: A Stratified Early Man Site in Eastern New Mexico* Fort Burgwin Research Center, Publication No. 8 (Ranchos de Taos, NM: Southern Methodist University, 1972); Sellards, E. H., *Early Man in America* (Austin: University of Texas Press, 1952); Stanford, D., C. V. Haynes Jr., J. Saunders, and G. Agogino, "Blackwater Draw Locality 1: History, Current Research and Interpretations," in *Guidebook to the Archaeological Geology of Classic Paleoindian Sites on the Southern High Plains, Texas and New Mexico*, edited by V. T. Holliday (College Station: Texas A&M University Press, 1986), 82–113; Warnica, J. M., "New Discoveries at the Clovis Site," *American Antiquity* 31 (1966): 345–357; Wendorf, F., and J. J. Hester, *Late Pleistocene Environment of the Southern High Plains*, Fort Burgwin Research Center, Publication No. 9 (Ranchos de Taos, NM: Southern Methodist University, 1975).

Dennis Stanford

FOLSOM, LINDENMEIER, AND OTHER SITES

West Texas, Oklahoma, New Mexico, and Colorado

Ancient Bison Hunters of the Plains

The Folsom culture is named after the village in northeast New Mexico near where the first exquisitely crafted ancient projectile points were found with the remains of now extinct large bison. The demise of the mammoth and other large Late Pleistocene animals sought by the earlier Clovis hunters prompted a new hunting adaptation targeting the expanding herds of ancient bison (*Bison antiquus*). Although precise ages are known for less than two dozen Folsom sites, the culture is dated at 10,200 to 10,900 radiocarbon years ago.

Folsom hunters crafted projectile points similar in outline to Clovis points, but considerably smaller and thinner. The channel flake or flute flake used to thin the Folsom projectile point extends nearly the full length from base to tip on each side. A great deal of skill is needed to successfully remove such flakes. The Folsom flint knappers are thought to have been among the most accomplished and skillful of any North American culture. The special design of the projectile point facilitated its use on a spear thrown with great force by use of an *atl atl* (spear thrower). It is possible that the exquisite craftsmanship held ritual significance in addition to being functional.

Folsom flint knappers preferred high-quality, lustrous, or colorful stone for making stone tools. The source areas for many of these materials are often several hundred kilometers from where the artifacts are found by archaeologists. In addition to projectile points, the Folsom tool kit includes scrapers, very thin knives, perforators, hammer stones, and objects of bone and antler, including very thin-eyed bone needles for sewing. The widespread distribution of finished tools made from stone obtained from great distance suggests

Channel Flake

a.
Clovis

b.
Folsom

0 cm 5

This comparison of a Clovis (*a*) and Folsom (*b*) projectile point illustrates overall size differences and the length of channel flaking. [Leland C. Bement]

these people were highly mobile, moving across the sparsely inhabited Great Plains and Rocky Mountains. Such mobility is consistent with the migratory behavior of their favorite prey—bison.

The mainstay of Folsom life was bison. Bison kill sites have been found from Texas to North Dakota. Kills range in size from two or three animals ambushed near water, as seen at Lubbock Lake and Blackwater Draw, to thirty to sixty animals in planned large kills utilizing natural traps such as those proposed at Cooper and Stewart's Cattle Guard, as discussed later. The large kills were conducted mainly during the late summer and early autumn, whereas smaller kills occurred during all seasons of the year. This seasonal dichotomy is probably linked to bison behavior as well as seasonal changes in human group size. The larger kills required more people for a successful hunt. These larger groups probably reflect several smaller family bands joining for communal bison kills as well as social reasons. A painted bison skull found at the Cooper site reflects ritual activity associated with large-scale hunts on the southern plains.

Folsom hunters also acquired deer, pronghorn antelope, wolf, rabbit, and birds. Although some camel and horse bones have been found, it is not clear whether these bones were from animals killed by Folsom hunters or simply bones scavenged from animals gone extinct during earlier times. In addition, they collected turtles and rodents. Plants are not preserved in Folsom sites, but undoubtedly nuts, fruit, and roots were important foods.

Bison kill sites are often accompanied by short-term camps where inhabitants butchered the bison and refurbished their hunting equipment. Some large kill sites are not accompanied by camps, suggesting a large encampment was some distance away. In such situations, special task groups visited the kill to remove meat and other products for processing and consumption at the distant camp. These larger camps display more activities than their smaller counterparts. They may represent longer stays. One such camp is the Lindenmeier site in northeast Colorado.

Large camps are also found near the highly sought stone sources. Here, large quantities of stone chipping debris and tool manufacturing failures, accumulated over repeated visits, dominate site assemblages. These sites provide evidence of the technological stages of tool manufacture. At a regional scale, mapping the distribution of tools made from a particular source provides an idea of the size of the territory traversed by these mobile hunters.

COOPER SITE, NORTHWEST OKLAHOMA—LARGE BISON KILL

The Cooper site consists of three bison kills in a gully feeding the North Canadian River. The remnant of the ancient gully contained between twenty and thirty animals in each of three kill events. Each kill is thought to represent less than half of the total number of animals killed; the remainder of each kill was lost to erosion by the river. All three kills occurred during the late summer or early fall, and each herd consisted of cows, calves, and young bulls. Folsom points made from central Texas and Texas panhandle cherts indicate these hunters obtained their tool stone from sources to the south and west. Tools recovered from the site are limited to projectile points and large flake knives. Butchering procedures in each kill targeted the highly desirable portions along the hump, back, and ribs, leaving large amounts of meat on the legs untouched. No camp was found near this site. A painted bison skull at the base of the second kill event indicates that a pre-kill ritual transpired at this site. The design consists of several zigzag lines painted in red ochre. At 10,530 years old, this skull is the oldest painted object in North America.

FOLSOM SITE, NORTHEAST NEW MEXICO—LARGE BISON KILL

The Folsom site is historically famous as the first site to positively associate human tools with Ice Age animals in the New World, thereby establishing an early occupation of North

America. The site is similar to the Cooper site in that it is a large bison kill area in a gully; has no associated camp; contains cows, calves, and young bulls; has a limited tool assemblage of projectile points and flake knives; and is an autumn kill site. The stone tool kit is made of lithic material from sources as far south as the Texas panhandle and others along the foothills of the Rocky Mountains.

LINDENMEIER SITE, NORTHEAST COLORADO—LARGE CAMP

The Lindenmeier site is a large camp where a wide range of activities was carried out, including cooking, meat processing, tool manufacture, hunting equipment refurbishing, hide processing, and bone tool manufacture and utilization. Multiple discrete activity areas suggest the site saw repeated use probably by several different groups. Red ocher is abundant and is found in a wide variety of contexts. Recovery of bison bone suggests a kill area is located nearby. In addition to bison, animal remains including deer, pronghorn, rabbit, duck, turtle, and rodent round out a rather eclectic or broad-base subsistence pattern. This site may be a base camp where multiple family groups congregated for lengthy stays. The rarity of camps of this size baffles archaeologists, who expected to find a dichotomy of camp sizes ranging from small family habitations to multi-family base camps.

LUBBOCK LAKE, WEST TEXAS—SMALL BISON KILLS

The Lubbock Lake site contains Paleoindian through historic cultural deposits in vertically stratified contexts. The horizontal distribution of discrete kill areas suggests multiple uses of the area during Folsom times. Its Folsom age component consists of at least five bison bone beds. Each bone bed consists of the butchered remains of between two and six animals.

Complete skeletal disarticulation is the normal butchery pattern. None of the kills provide evidence for a trap. Instead, the animals were ambushed along the marshy waterway. Stone tool material is dominated by cherts from central Texas.

STEWART'S CATTLE GUARD SITE, CENTRAL COLORADO—BISON KILL AND CAMP

The Stewart's Cattle Guard site consists of a bison kill area in a sand dune trap and a nearby camp where meat processing and hunting gear refurbishing occurred. Distinct work areas interpreted as family activity loci suggest at least five families joined forces at this site. The use of a sand dune trap illustrates the innovative aptitude of the Folsom hunting adaptation. In addition to projectile points and flake knives associated with the killing and butchering of the bison, this site assemblage also contained a highly specialized meat-slicing knife thought to have been invented for preparing muscle masses for meat drying. This tool form may have been a women's knife, indicating a division of labor along gender lines.

Further Reading: Bement, Leland C., *Bison Hunting at Cooper Site: Where Lightning Bolts Drew Thundering Herds* (Norman: University of Oklahoma Press, 1999); Jodry, Margaret A., "Folsom Technological and Socioeconomic Strategies: Views from Stewart's Cattle Guard and the Upper Rio Grande Basin, Colorado," unpublished diss. (American University, 1999); Johnson, Eileen, *Lubbock Lake: Late Quaternary Studies on the Southern High Plains* (College Station: Texas A&M University Press, 1987); Meltzer, David J., *Folsom: New Archaeological Investigations of a Classic Paleoindian Bison Kill* (Berkeley: University of California Press, 2006); Wilmsen, Edwin N., and Frank H. H. Roberts Jr., *Lindenmeier, 1934–1974*, Concluding Report on Investigations, Smithsonian Contributions to Anthropology No. 24 (Washington, DC: Smithsonian Institution, 1978).

Leland C. Bement

HEAD-SMASHED-IN BUFFALO JUMP AND INTERPRETIVE SITE

Southwestern Alberta, Canada

A 6,000-Year-Old Buffalo Jump Site

INTRODUCTION

Imagine the sights, sounds, and smells at a buffalo jump on the high plains in the final moments of a bison drive. A thundering herd stampedes down toward a sheer cliff. Hunters line both sides of a V-shaped chute leading toward the cliff,

shouting and waving hides to keep the animals on track. Yet more hunters circle behind the herd, keeping up the pressure, ensuring the herd does not attempt a retreat. The lead bison reach the precipice and finally see the deadly trap, but it is too late. Dozens of bodies sail through the crisp air of autumn. The first of the lot hit the earth with a sickening thud, silenced moments later by the arrival of yet more bodies on top, crushing those beneath. Wounded animals bellow as they roll off to the sides of the ever-increasing pile—buffalo with broken backs, legs, and ribs and some miraculously unscathed, stunned, and trying to stand and run for freedom. The hunters yell as they scurry to kill the wounded animals and avoid being killed themselves. A dark red color seeps into the parched prairie soil; the dust swirling beneath the cliff carries the scent of feces and a strong metallic smell of blood. It was, no doubt, a precious moment.

For raw, unbridled drama there is little in the prehistory of any continent or any culture that can match the excitement that must have transpired in the final moments of a buffalo jump. There is also little or nothing that can match the amount of food and supplies that was instantly available at the conclusion of a successful jump. Bison are the largest land mammal in North America. Males weigh in around 900 kilograms, females about 500 kilograms. Buffalo jumps involved large numbers of animals; a herd of 100 was likely typical. When 100 dead bodies of bison lay at the bottom of a cliff, aboriginal hunters had just procured something in the range of about 60,000 kilograms of meat, fat, hide, and bone. Over millions of years of evolution as hunters, there is nothing in human history where a comparable amount of food was obtained at one time. Much larger animals were hunted—mammoth, rhinos, giraffes, elephants—but always singly or in small numbers. Even the killing of a huge bowhead whale by Inuit of the Arctic, the largest animal ever hunted by indigenous people, would yield less meat and fat than an average buffalo jump. Mass killing of bison on the Great Plains of North America, using jumps and wooden corrals, was the most productive food-getting enterprise ever devised by human beings.

Bison and human beings coexisted on the Great Plains for at least 12,000 years (Frison 1991). Over that vast span of time all manner of traps were designed to kill buffalo singly, in small groups, and in huge herds (Verbicky-Todd 1984). Foremost among the latter were buffalo pounds, where herds were driven into large wooden corrals, and jumps, where a herd was stampeded over sheer cliffs and steep drops.

There are hundreds of mass bison kill sites known in the western United States and Canada, more yet to be discovered, and still more swept from the land by erosion and settlement. And of all the buffalo jumps known, there is perhaps none more imposing, more perfectly designed, more consistently executed, more lethal than Head-Smashed-In. It is estimated that more than 100,000 bison died during the 5,800 years of use of the jump (Brink et al. 1985, 1986). A United Nations Educational, Scientific, and Cultural Organization (UNESCO) World Heritage Site, it is the premier example of a bison jump in North America.

THE SITE

Head-Smashed-In Buffalo Jump is located in southwestern Alberta, Canada, about 160 kilometers south of the city of Calgary, and some 20 kilometers west of the town of Fort Macleod. It lies at the southern terminus of the Porcupine Hills; the Rocky Mountains are directly to the west, the immense edge of the northern Plains to the east. At the edges of the Porcupines the sandstone is exposed, where it fractures forming many sheer cliffs. The rolling, broken country is ideal for rounding up and moving herds of grazing animals. Finding herds of bison on the flat, open prairie must have always been a daunting and tenuous exercise. Locating herds of bison in the Porcupine Hills solved many of these problems.

The total area of land that figured into the Head-Smashed-In Buffalo Jump complex is staggering in size. Aspects of the landscape, as well as human-made features, can be found over an area of some 40 square kilometers. This includes a massive natural basin of the Porcupine Hills that lies to the west side of the jump, dozens of individual lines of small stone cairns (rock piles) that formed the drive lanes along which the bison were herded, the cliff and the kill site below, and an extensive prairie below the kill where the spoils were butchered and processed.

The Basin

There is a single huge collecting basin located directly to the west of the jump-off. It extends toward the mountains about 10 kilometers before the land finally rises and you climb out of the bowl. A small stream drains the main basin, providing water for hunters and bison alike. The almost perfectly formed natural gathering basin at Head-Smashed-In—ideal for finding, stalking, and moving bison—was the single most important factor in making this site perhaps the most productive of all known buffalo jumps.

The Drive Lanes

Drive lanes are the long lines of rock piles that were used at many bison kills to steer the animals in the desired direction. More than two dozen lanes have been identified and mapped at Head-Smashed-In, most in the vicinity of several different jump-off points (Reeves 1978, 1985; Rollans 1987). The lanes today consist of simple small clusters of five to ten rocks, seldom extending more than a decimeter or two above the surface (Brink et al. 1986). It is believed that the function of the lanes in directing stampeding herds of bison was derived from the addition of other materials to the rock piles: stacks of buffalo chips (dung), hunks of overturned sod, and branches of trees and brush that were probably wedged between the rocks (Brink and Rollans 1990). The primary purpose of the rock piles may have been twofold: to serve as a permanent marker for the proper direction of the drive to the cliff, and as a place to anchor brush and branches that made the structures more imposing, more visible, and perhaps an imitation of human hunters.

The Cliff

The cliff that formed the jump-off faces east, away from the prevailing winds. It is essential that the kill site be located downwind from the direction of the drive so as to hide the smell of the huge group of people waiting at the camp and kill site. The cliff at Head-Smashed-In is about 10 meters high, but wind-blown soil, bedrock topple, decayed vegetation, and bones of bison have gradually accumulated on the narrow bench below the cliff. The deepest excavations at the kill site recovered artifacts and bison bones nearly 10 meters below the current surface (Reeves 1978, 1983). Thus, when the site was first used, some 5,800 years ago, bison were falling nearly 20 meters to their death.

The Kill Site

Slump and topple of the sandstone bedrock has formed a narrow bench that parallels the north-south trend of the cliff. This is the surface on which the falling bison slammed into the hard earth, and where the initial butchering of the carcasses took place. With an average jump of 100 animals, an enormous task lay ahead for the hunters. The carcasses would begin to spoil quickly if steps were not taken to butcher and cool down the meat and fat. The incredibly insulating hides of the bison were removed, the stomachs opened to spill out the heat-generating gastric fluids, thus allowing the carcasses to cool down. The bison were then butchered into manageable-sized pieces for transport to the lower prairie.

The Butchering and Processing Site

Moving east from the bench that forms the jump-off at Head-Smashed-In, the ground levels off in a broad prairie. This region of the lower flats served as an immense butchering area (Brink et al. 1985, 1986). Most likely, disarticulated pieces of the bison carcasses were piled onto fresh hides and dragged downslope to the prairie. Here they were rendered into a variety of food products, the critical element of which was preservation meat through drying in thin sheets and by smoking. Not only would dry meat last for months, it was also much lighter to carry away from the site.

A great deal of cooking was conducted at the Head-Smashed-In butchering site. A favorite technique was to cook in earthen pits, dug into the prairie soil, lined with a fresh bison hide and filled with water. Rocks heated in a nearby fire were placed in the pits, and the water was brought to a boil. Roasting meat in deep rock-lined pits was also popular. Archaeological studies of the butchering area have uncovered countless fireplaces, literally tons of stones used for boiling, and dozens of roasting and boiling pits. Thousands more are estimated to remain at the site (Brink and Dawe 1989, 2003).

ARCHAEOLOGY AT HEAD-SMASHED-IN

Head-Smashed-In Buffalo Jump is the most intensively studied archaeological site in Alberta. It was visited by Junius Bird in 1938 (Bird 1939). In 1949 a pioneer of western Canadian archaeology, Boyd Wettlaufer, excavated at both the kill and butchering site (Wettlaufer 1949). In 1965 Richard Forbis organized a major dig at Head-Smashed-In, put under the direction of Brian Reeves. This work, continued in 1966 and 1972, led to the deepest excavations at the kill site, where the full age and cultural use of Head-Smashed-In were defined (Reeves 1978, 1983). With the decision to develop the site for the public, additional studies were directed at exploring the little-known butchering area (Brink et al. 1985, 1986; Brink and Dawe 1989). In addition, there have been individual studies of select features of the site, including the drive lanes (Brink and Rollans 1990; Reeves 1985; Rollans 1987), a nearby vision quest site (Hughes 1986), and a series of petroglyphs located above the jump (Brink et al. 1986).

In 1989 Brian Kooyman returned to the Head-Smashed-In kill site to continue excavations in an area near where Reeves had left off (Kooyman et al. 1992; Newman et al. 1996). His excavations were aimed at recovering more of a sample of the oldest use of the jump, assigned to the Mummy Cave Complex (Reeves 1978, 1983), and to obtain high-fidelity records of the sequence of bison butchering and processing.

Excavations at the kill site revealed a long, stratified, discontinuous record of bison killing beginning about 5,800 years ago and ending in about the middle of the nineteenth century (Reeves 1978, 1983). Depending on who you believe, Head-Smashed-In may be the oldest evidence of the use of a buffalo jump. One site, Bonfire Shelter, in Texas, is much older and has been described as a buffalo jump (Dibble and Lorraine 1968). The site is well dated at 10,000 years old, but there is some debate as to whether the site was actually a buffalo jump (Byerly et al. 2005).

DEVELOPMENT AND INTERPRETATION AT HEAD-SMASHED-IN

Opened in 1987, Head-Smashed-In Buffalo Jump has a year-round 2,400-square-meter interpretive center built into the cliff. By 2007 the site had welcomed 2 million visitors. The striking architecture of the interpretive center was intended to hide and blend the building with the local bedrock. Visitors can walk along the cliff face, or on trails below the kill area, with almost no intrusion of the modern world. The building has a total of seven levels with display themes including the plains environment, Native people of the plains, the operation of a buffalo jump, the end of the buffalo hunting days, and the archaeology of the site. The signature display in the building is a replica of the sheer cliff, with bison poised at the top and a replica archaeological dig at the bottom.

Most of the staff, and all of the interpreters, at Head-Smashed-In are members of the Blackfoot Nation. This group, especially the Piikani (Peigan) and the Kainai (Blood), were certainly the primary users of the jump in late pre-contact times, that is, about the last 1,000 years. Fittingly, the Blackfoot were involved in planning and development of the site. They were consulted on the initial proposal, reviewed all displays and text, provided oral history that is used in the building, were important members of the archaeological digs, and continue to advise on the operation of the site (Brink 1992; Slater 2006). Despite being a government-owned facility, the Head-Smashed-In Interpretive Center has become a focus for Blackfoot culture, a place they have adopted as their own.

Equally important, it has become a place for the general public to learn about the grand buffalo-hunting traditions of the Blackfoot, and to do so in the context of respect for the achievements of this culture. If there is a single core message the center tries to convey, it is that of respect and understanding. It was built to celebrate the astonishing skill, ingenuity, knowledge, sophistication, and spiritual power that went into a successful buffalo jump. Two million people have heard this message.

The Head-Smashed-In interpretive center is open year-round. For information see the Web site at http://www.head-smashed-in.com/ or call (403) 553-2731.

Further Reading: Bird, Junius, "Artifacts in Canadian River Terraces," *Science* 89(2311) (1939): 340–341; Brink, Jack, "Buffalo Jump," *Horizon Canada* 89 (1986): 2120–2125; Brink, Jack, "Blackfoot and Buffalo Jumps: Native People and the Head-Smashed-In Project," in *Buffalo*, edited by John Foster, Dick Harrison, and I. S. MacLaren (Edmonton: University of Alberta Press, 1992), 19–43; Brink, Jack, "An Example of In Situ Preservation of Archaeological Resources, A UNESCO World Heritage Site, Head-Smashed-In Buffalo Jump," in *Archaeological Remains In Situ Preservation*, Proceedings of the Second ICAHM International Conference (Montreal, QC: ICOMOS International Committee on Archaeological Heritage Management, 1996), 5–12; Brink, Jack, and Bob Dawe, *Final Report of the 1985 and 1986 Field Season at Head-Smashed-In Buffalo Jump, Alberta*, Archaeological Survey of Alberta Manuscript Series No. 16 (Edmonton: Archaeological Survey of Alberta, 1989); Brink, Jack, and Bob Dawe, "Hot Rocks as Scarce Resources: The Use, Re-Use and Abandonment of Heating Stones at Head-Smashed-In Buffalo Jump," *Plains Anthropologist* 48(186) (2003), 85–104; Brink, Jack, and Maureen Rollans, "Thoughts on the Structure and Function of Drive Lane Systems at Communal Buffalo Jumps," in *Hunters of the Recent Past*, edited by L. B. Davis and B. O. K. Reeves (London: Unwin Hyman, 1990), 152–167; Brink, Jack, Milt Wright, Bob Dawe, and Doug Glaum, *Final Report of the 1983 Season at Head-Smashed-In Buffalo Jump, Alberta*, Archaeological Survey of Alberta Manuscript Series No. 1 (Edmonton: Archaeological Survey of Alberta, 1985); Brink, Jack, Milt Wright, Bob Dawe, and Doug Glaum, *Final Report of the 1984 Season at Head-Smashed-In Buffalo Jump, Alberta*, Archaeological

Survey of Alberta Manuscript Series No. 9 (Edmonton: Archaeological Survey of Alberta, 1986); Byerly, Ryan M., Judith R. Cooper, David J. Meltzer, Matthew E. Hill and Jason M. LaBelle, "On Bonfirre Shelter (Texas) as a Paleoindian Bison Jump: An Assessment Using GIS and Zooarchaeology," *American Antiquity* 70 (2005): 595–629; Darragh, Ian, "The Killing Cliffs," *Canadian Geographic* 107 (1987): 55–61; Dibble, D. S., and D. Lorrain, *Bonfire Sherlter: A Stratified Bison Site, Val Verde County, Texas*, Miscellaneous Papers No. 1 (Austin: Texas Memorial Museum, 1968); Fagan, Brian, "Bison Hunters of the Northern Plains," *Archaeology Magazine* (1994): 37–41; Frison, George C., *Prehistoric Hunters of the High Plains*, 2nd ed. (San Diego, CA: Academic Press, 1991); Hughes, Cristopher C., "DkPj-21: A Description and Discussion of a Vision Quest Site in the Porcupine Hills, Alberta," in *Final Report of the 1984 Season at Head-Smashed-In Buffalo Jump, Alberta*, by J. Brink, M. Wright, B. Dawe, and D. Glaum, Archaeological Survey of Alberta Manuscript Series No. 9 (Edmonton: Archaeological Survey of Alberta, 1986), 364–403; Kooyman, Brian, M. E. Newman, and H. Ceri, "Verifying the Reliability of Blood Residue Analysis on Archaeological Tools," *Journal of Archaeological Science* 19 (1992): 265–269; Newman, M. E., H. Ceri, and B. Kooyman, "The Use of Immunological Techniques in the Analysis of Archaeological Materials: A Response to Eisele, with Report of Studies at Head-Smashed-In Buffalo Jump," *Antiquity* 70 (1996):677–682; Pringle, Heather, "Boneyard Enigma," *Equinox* (1988): 87–103; Pringle, Heather, "Killing Fields: Head-Smashed-In Buffalo Jump, Alberta," in *In Search of Ancient North America*, by Heather Pringle (New York: John Wiley and Sons, 1996), 149–167; Reeves, Brian O. K., "Head-Smashed-In: 5500 Years of Bison Jumping in the Alberta Plains," in *Bison Procurement and Utilization: A Symposium*, edited by L. B. Davis and M. Wilson, *Plains Anthropologist Memoir* 14 (1978): 151–174; Reeves, Brian O. K., "Six Millenniums of Buffalo Kills," *Scientific American* 249(4) (1983): 120–135; Reeves, Brian O. K., "The Head-Smashed-In Drive Lane/Kill Complex," unpublished manuscript on file at the Royal Alberta Museum (Edmonton, AB: 1985); Reid, Gordon, *Head-Smashed-In Buffalo Jump* (Calgary, AB: Fifth House Ltd., 2002); Rollans, Maureen, "Interpreting the Function of Bison Drive Lanes at Head-Smashed-In Buffalo Jump, Alberta," unpublished master's thesis, Department of Anthropology (Edmonton: University of Alberta, 1987); Slater, Byron, "Blackfoot Consultation and Head-Smashed-In Buffalo Jump Interpretive Centre," master's thesis, International Centre for Cultural and Heritage Studies (Newcastle, UK: University of Newcastle, 2006); Sponholz, E., "Head-Smashed-In Buffalo Jump: A Center for Cultural Preservation and Understanding," in *Buffalo*, edited by J. Foster, D. Harrison and I. S. MacLaren (Edmonton: University of Alberta Press, 1992), 45–59; Thomas, D. H., "Head-Smashed-In Buffalo Jump," in *Exploring Native North America*, by D. H. Thomas (Oxford: Oxford University Press, 2000), 52–61; Verbicky-Todd, Eleanor, "Communal Buffalo Hunting Among the Plains Indians," Archaeological Survey of Alberta Occasional Paper No. 24 (Edmonton, AB: 1984; Wettlaufer, Boyd, "Manuscript and Field Notes of 1949 Archaeological Survey and Excavations at the Maclean Site (Head-Smashed-In)," unpublished manuscript on file, Archaeological Survey (Edmonton: Provincial Museum of Alberta, 1949).

Jack W. Brink

ALIBATES FLINT QUARRIES NATIONAL MONUMENT AND BATTLE SITES OF THE RED RIVER WAR

The Texas Panhandle

Ancient and Historic Archaeology on the Southern Plains

The vast expanse of the southern Great Plains has been the home to various indigenous groups for more than 13,000 years. As such, the region has a substantial archaeological record. Although scientific excavations began early in the twentieth century and have continued to the present, the region remains one of the most sparsely documented and poorly understood archaeological areas. It has only been within the last quarter century that enough data has been gathered to enable researchers to appreciate fully the archaeological diversity and complexity of the entire region.

The panhandle of Texas received informal archaeological attention during the course of the mid-nineteenth century by U.S. Army expeditions. In 1845 Lieutenant J. W. Abert described the Alibates flint quarries along the Canadian River as the "Agate Bluffs." Lieutenant A. W. Whipple documented the major rock art site of Rocky Dell in 1853, and Lieutenant T. M. Woodruff conducted the first subsurface excavation of an Indian ruin on the Canadian River in 1876. These investigations were done more out of curiosity, however, than a desire to systematically learn about past cultures.

In 1907 T. L. Eyerly and his students from the Canadian Academy conducted archaeological excavations at the Buried City ruins on Wolf Creek in Ochiltree County, Texas. These investigations were soon followed by a host of other researchers who studied sites in the Buried City area and in the Canadian River Valley in the 1920s and 1930s.

Other early archaeological work in the region began primarily out of an interest in early man. In 1923 the Colorado Museum of Natural History investigated the Lone Wolf Creek site near Colorado City, Texas. Although little publicized, this investigation provided proof of the association of projectile points and extinct bison three years before similar evidence was discovered at the now famous Folsom site in New Mexico.

Throughout time, the various cultural groups that occupied the southern Great Plains depended on the massive herds of bison in the region for food, clothing, and shelter. Another important resource for the prehistoric inhabitants was the outcrop of silicified or agatized flint along the Canadian River in the Texas panhandle.

ALIBATES FLINT QUARRIES NATIONAL MONUMENT IN FRITCH, TEXAS

The Alibates flint quarries along the canyon rims of the Canadian River valley near Fritch in the Texas panhandle were highly valued and extensively utilized as a lithic resource by prehistoric inhabitants of the southern plains. Large quarry pits (some 736 pits have been located within the monument boundaries) and literally tons of stone manufacturing debris bear testimony to thousands of years of quarrying the brilliantly colored stone known as Alibates agate. Projectile points and other tools made of Alibates agate have been found in sites as far south as central Mexico, east to the Mississippi River, as far north as Montana, and to the west in southeastern New Mexico and west Texas, indicating that the stone was highly prized and was traded over great distances.

Alibates agate is a beautiful, multicolored stone. Colors range from white to pink, maroon, and vivid red, to orange-gold, pale grey, and an intense purplish blue. Bands of alternating color create stripes and a marbled effect.

Prehistoric peoples throughout the millennia have used Alibates agate to make tools and weapons. Paleoindian hunters tipped their weapons with the stone to kill now-extinct large game animals and fashioned knives and scrapers to process meat and hides. Alibates agate projectile points were found at the Blackwater Draw site in eastern New Mexico, where mammoths were killed about 13,000 years ago.

From AD 1150 to 1450, villagers of the Antelope Creek phase settled along the Canadian River and built complex slab-houses. In exchange for Alibates chert and bison products, Antelope Creek people received painted pottery, turquoise, and obsidian from groups to the southwest and to the north.

Today, many of these important village ruins and quarry sites are protected as the Alibates Flint Quarries National Monument, the only such site in Texas. Petroglyphs and house ruins are located in remote areas of the monument, but these are not normally accessible to visitors. A new visitors' center is currently under construction, and the public may contact park headquarters to inquire about touring the monument.

Alibates agate flakes from a Late Plains Village site in the Texas panhandle.   [Patricia A. Mercado-Allinger]

LUBBOCK LAKE LANDMARK
IN LUBBOCK, TEXAS

Another location with a long history of use and occupation is the Lubbock Lake Landmark site on the outskirts of Lubbock, Texas. The Lubbock Lake site is located in Yellow-house Draw, which once contained a major spring that flowed out of the Ogallala aquifer. The abundant water and sheltered draw was a haven for plants and animals, which drew humans, beginning with Paleoindian hunters, and continuing up into historic times. The archaeological record at Lubbock Lake is unparalleled in the southern high plains, and archaeologists and other scientists have been studying the site for over sixty-five years.

In the late 1930s, a project to dig out and renew the springs turned up Folsom projectile points and other evidence of Paleoindian peoples. This led to the first archaeological digs

A Buried City house feature at the Kit Courson site.   [Patricia A. Mercado-Allinger]

in 1939 and 1941 under the sponsorship of the Works Progress Administration (WPA) and directed by Joe Ben Wheat. During the late 1940s and the 1950s, the Texas Memorial Museum carried out additional excavations at the site. These excavations were able to document a complex sequence of natural and cultural deposits, including bone beds associated with Folsom artifacts.

Since 1972, archaeologist Dr. Eileen Johnson and students at Texas Tech University have investigated the Lubbock Lake Landmark. The site is now a part of a 336-acre preserve and is a state and federal historic landmark. In addition to the site, the park contains an interpretive center and a research center operated by the Museum of Texas Tech University.

LAKE THEO SITE, CAPROCK CANYONS STATE PARK, IN QUITAQUE, TEXAS

The importance of bison to Paleoindian occupants of the southern plains is also evident at the Lake Theo site, situated on the south bank of Holmes Creek in the canyonlands a few kilometers east of the Eastern Caprock Escarpment. The site is located in Caprock Canyons State Park and Trailway, north of Quitaque, Texas.

Investigations conducted in 1974 and 1977 by Panhandle-Plains Historical Museum personnel under the direction of Billy R. Harrison revealed three cultural components. Excavations exposed a sparse amount of campsite debris in association with two bone beds containing the butchered remains of extinct bison. Scattered Archaic period materials, indicative of camp activities of short duration, overlay these deposits.

The bone beds are separated horizontally and temporally, with one found in the northern site area and containing Folsom points. The second bed, detected in trench excavations conducted in the southern site area, yielded Late Paleoindian (Eden and Plainview) period projectile point types. These occupations are believed to have occurred on the same land surface, suggesting either utilization of the same surface at different times or deflation of later deposits.

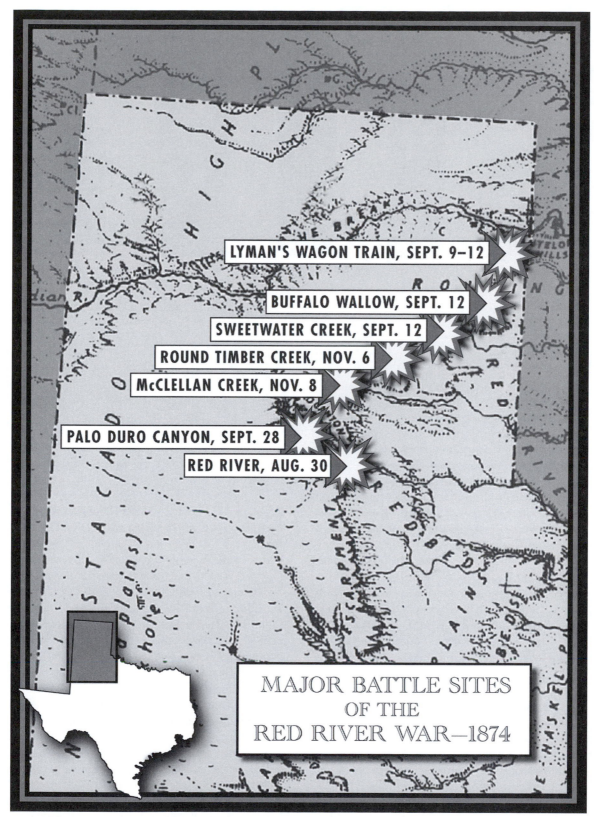

LYMAN'S WAGON TRAIN, SEPT. 9–12

BUFFALO WALLOW, SEPT. 12

SWEETWATER CREEK, SEPT. 12

ROUND TIMBER CREEK, NOV. 6

McCLELLAN CREEK, NOV. 8

PALO DURO CANYON, SEPT. 28

RED RIVER, AUG. 30

MAJOR BATTLE SITES
OF THE
RED RIVER WAR—1874

Major battle sites of the 1874 Red River War.   [Patricia A. Mercado-Allinger]

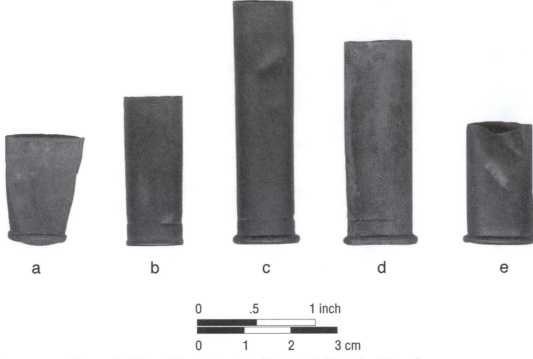

Spent cartridges recovered from a Red River War battle site.   [Patricia A. Mercado-Allinger]

No bison skulls and few articulated bone elements were encountered in either of the bone beds.

During the 1974 excavations at Lake Theo, a Folsom projectile point was found in direct association with the lower bone bed. It was decided that the section of the bone bed containing the point would be jacketed with plaster and removed for future exhibition. This led to the discovery of a unique feature composed of a circular arrangement of bison bones purposefully embedded below the Folsom bone bed. The feature, containing three mandibles, two tibiae, one femur, and a dorsal spine from a thoracic vertebra, has undergone laboratory restoration and is among the exhibits in the Paleontological Hall at the Panhandle-Plains Historical Museum in Canyon, Texas. The significance of this feature remains an intriguing question for researchers.

In spite of the abundant availability of knappable stone such as Ogallala gravels and Tecovas jaspers and quartzites in the immediate vicinity, prehistoric inhabitants of the Lake Theo site utilized Alibates agate to manufacture lithic tools, including several of the Paleoindian and Archaic projectile points. The Alibates quarries are about 120 miles (193 km) distant, suggesting that either raw materials or finished implements were acquired through trade.

The Lake Theo site is located at Caprock Canyons State Park and Trailway, part of the Texas Parks and Wildlife Department park system. The park features interpretive exhibits on the natural and cultural history of the area. The park is also the home of the official Texas State Bison Herd, made up of descendants of the last free-ranging bison of the southern plains.

PLAINS VILLAGERS OF THE TEXAS PANHANDLE AND WESTERN OKLAHOMA

From AD 1150 to 1450, inhabitants of the southern Great Plains began to settle in permanent villages along the Canadian and Washita rivers and their tributaries in the Texas panhandle and western Oklahoma. It is generally believed that the villagers from the Antelope Creek and Buried City phases in the Texas panhandle and villagers from the Custer, Paoli, and Washita River phases in Oklahoma developed from indigenous Plains Woodland groups.

During the Plains Village period on the southern plains, cultural groups became more settled, planting small fields of corn, beans, and squash, making pottery, and trading within large interregional networks. The southern plains villagers were still heavily dependent on bison, but horticulture became increasingly important.

One concentration of Plains Village period sites is the so-called "Buried City" located along Wolf Creek in Ochiltree County, Texas. Buried City is not, in fact, the remains of a city, but it is one of the most densely settled archaeological districts in the southern plains. The area's rich natural resources attracted generations of villagers who gathered wild plant foods and hunted bison, deer, and smaller game. Within a few

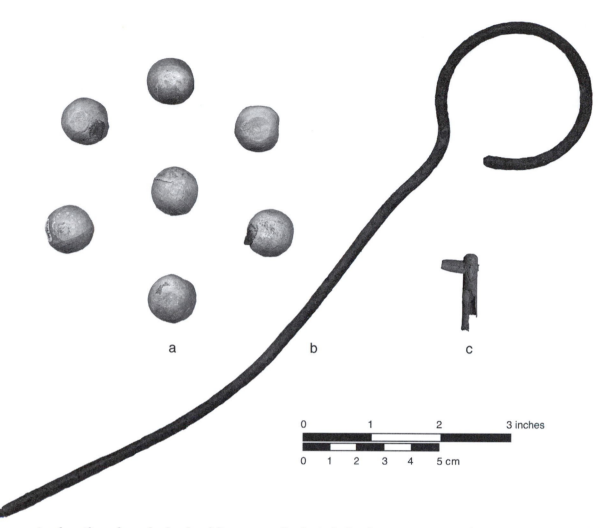

Artillery-associated artifacts from the battle of Sweetwater Creek, including howitzer canister shot, priming wire, and friction primer.   [Patricia A. Mercado-Allinger]

miles along Wolf Creek are more than 100 known habitation sites with the remains of houses built between about AD 1200 and 1400.

Although not of the scale of the multiple-apartment dwellings of the southwestern pueblos and the sizable earth lodges the Pawnee used to house large extended families on the central plains, Buried City houses were nonetheless substantial. Some houses measure 8 by 10 meters with an interior floor space of about 63 square meters. The typical Buried City house appears to have been constructed using the jacal technique, with the walls formed of closely spaced upright pickets woven together with thin vines or sticks and then plastered over. Double-pen walls were constructed with two parallel rows of pickets, which were anchored by caliche boulders and slabs and covered with mud plaster. The roofs were most likely capped with a thick layer of grass thatch. A depressed

floor "channel" typically ran the length of the structure with a hearth located in the center. An extended, covered entry typically opened to the east.

The people of the Buried City were horticulturalists, hunters, and foragers. They raised corn and probably other crops such as beans, squash, and peppers. Crops were probably planted in the low-lying swales between houses and along the valley floor. The primary gardening tool was the digging stick with a bone tip made from a bison tibia. Bison scapulae may also have been used to move loose dirt or as hoes. The abundant bison bone at Buried City sites shows that buffalo hunting was important.

By about AD 1400, Buried City and the other southern plains village sites were abandoned. The precise cause of the abandonment is not clear, but it was likely due to climate change, depletion of resources, and/or warfare. What happened to the Buried City and other southern plains villagers? Most researchers now believe they are the likely ancestors of the Plains Caddoan peoples: the Wichita, Pawnee, Arikara, Kitsai, and others whose names are lost in time.

The Museum of the Plains in Perryton, Texas, features exhibits on the Buried City settlements.

RED RIVER WAR BATTLE SITES, TEXAS PANHANDLE

After AD 1700, various historic tribes invaded and settled into the southern plains. These included the Kiowa, Comanche, Southern Cheyenne, and Arapaho. Although initially in conflict with one another, by 1830 the tribes were allies against the ever-increasing Anglo and Texan settlers. As Indian attacks on westward-bound settlers escalated, Congress pressured the U.S. Army to protect the settlers and control the Indians. During the summer of 1874, the U.S. Army launched a campaign to remove the Indian tribes from the southern plains and enforce their relocation to reservations established in the Indian Territory (Oklahoma). The campaign against the Indians, known today as the Red River War, led to the end of an entire way of life for the southern plains tribes and brought about a new chapter in the history of the southern plains.

During the Red River War, as many as twenty engagements between the U.S. Army and the southern plains Indians may have occurred across the Texas panhandle region. The well-equipped army kept the Indians on the run until eventually they could not run or fight any longer. The war officially ended in June 1875 when Quanah Parker and his band of Quahadi Comanche entered Fort Sill, Oklahoma, and surrendered. The Indians were defeated, and they would never again freely roam the buffalo plains.

From 1998 to 2003, archaeologists with the Texas Historical Commission investigated and documented six of the better-known Red River War battle sites: the battle of Red River, the battle of Lyman's wagon train, the battle of Buffalo Wallow, the battle of Sweetwater Creek, the battle of Palo Duro Canyon, and the battle of Round Timber Creek.

More than 3,000 battle-related artifacts were recovered during the investigations. Most of the artifacts are cartridge cases and bullets, but other items such as buttons, horse tack, canteen parts, harmonica pieces, and wagon parts were also recovered. Numerous domestic-use items from the Indian village sites were found, including knives, spoons, thimbles, scissors, scrapers, buttons, tinklers, jewelry, pots, and pans.

Detailed firearms analysis of the recovered cartridge cases and bullets from the sites suggests the Indian combatants were not as well armed as the army reports indicated. If the army accurately reported the number of Indians present at each battle, then the archaeological evidence suggests that only about 30–35 percent of the Indians had firearms of any type, and many of these were older, even obsolete, models.

Today, most of the Red River War battle sites are on private property and are not accessible to the public. Two sites, however, are owned by the Panhandle-Plains Historical Society and can be visited by the public. These are the sites of the battle of Buffalo Wallow and the battle of Adobe Walls, which were not investigated by the Texas Historical Commission. Several museums in the region have displays and information about the Red River War. The primary museums include the Panhandle-Plains Historical Museum in Canyon, Texas; the White Deer Land Museum in Pampa, Texas; the Old Mobeetie Jail Museum in Mobeetie, Texas; and the visitors' center at Palo Duro Canyon State Park near Canyon, Texas.

Camp Supply in Indian territory served as an important supply point for the Red River War. It was reclassified as Fort Supply in 1878, functioning as a hub for transportation and communication for the southern Great Plains until late 1893. The Oklahoma Historical Society has since assumed responsibility for the army period buildings. The facility, located east of the community of Fort Supply in northwestern Oklahoma, is now known as Fort Supply Historic Site.

Located north of Lawton, Oklahoma, Fort Sill was a key U.S. Army post of the Red River War campaign. Now a National Historic Landmark, Fort Sill continues to serve as an active military installation, specializing in field artillery training. The Fort Sill Museum occupies over twenty historic structures on the base, where collections and archival documents are housed and exhibited.

Further Reading: Cruse, J. Brett, *Battles of the Red River War* (College Station: Texas A&M University Press, in press); Harrison, Billy R., and Kay L. Killen, *Lake Theo: A Stratified, Early Man Bison Butchering and Camp Site, Briscoe County, Texas* (Canyon, TX: Panhandle-Plains Historical Museum, 1978); Hughes, David, "Investigations of the Buried City, Ochiltree County, Texas," *Bulletin of the Texas Archeological Society* 60 (1991): 107–148; Johnson, Eileen, *Lubbock Lake: Late Quaternary Studies on the Southern High Plains* (College Station: Texas A&M University Press, 1987); Lintz, Christopher, *Architecture and Community Variability within the Antelope Creek Phase of the Texas Panhandle*, Studies in Oklahoma's Past No. 14 (Norman: Oklahoma Archeological Survey, 1986); Museum of Texas Tech University, Lubbock Lake Landmark Web site, http://www.depts.ttu.edu/museumttu/lll/visitus.html; National Park Service, Alibates Flint Quarries National Monument Web site, http://www.nps.gov/alfl/index.htm; Texas Parks and Wildlife Department, Caprock Canyons State Park and Trailway Web site, http://www.tpwd.state.tx.us/spdest/findadest/parks/caprock_canyons/; University of Texas at Austin, *Texas beyond History*, http://www.texasbeyondhistory.net.

J. Brett Cruse and Patricia A. Mercado-Allinger

OSAGE VILLAGE STATE HISTORIC SITE

Vernon County, Southwestern Missouri
Early Historic Period Native American Village Site

Osage Village State Historic Park is located in Vernon County in southwestern Missouri and represents one of the few documented villages of the Osage during historic times. It is also the only village site of the Osage Nation established as a state park. The site, originally known as Carrington Osage Village (Missouri state archaeological file number 23VE001), was placed on the prestigious National Historic Landmarks listing in 1964 while still private property. Carrington Osage Village was acquired by the state of Missouri in 1984 and established as a state park covering approximately 100 acres. The park is located northeast of Nevada, Missouri, and contains walking trails and narrative exhibits on Osage history.

The village site is strategically situated on a high, open hilltop overlooking the headwaters of the Osage River valley to the north. This setting places it on the western edge of the Green Valley Prairie. Inhabitants of the village would have been in a highly desirable location: adjacent to water, between the woodland and prairie habitats, and with a great vista of the surrounding countryside.

Despite the noteworthiness, this Osage Indian village never received major attention as the focus of professional archaeological investigations but instead gained its prominence through historic documentation. The village was occupied from approximately AD1775 to 1825. This makes Carrington Osage Village the last occupied settlement of the "Big or Grand Osage" in southwestern Missouri prior to their removal to Kansas in 1825–36. A number of historic explorers passed through this settlement on their journeys.

Carrington Village may be one of the Osage settlements on the Osage River mentioned by Marquette in his 1673 journal. It is thought that the Frenchman Dutisné stopped here on his journey across the Kansas prairies in 1719. There is much better documentation for the village being visited by Major Zebulon Pike in his exploration into Spanish territory in 1806. Pike kept excellent records of his journey, including an account of his visit with the Osage. Based on the physical description, his narrative must refer to Carrington Village.

The village in Pike's records was described as having some 214 lodges with about 12 feet of space between the structures. The chief at the time of Pike's visit in August 1806 was Cheveau Blanc, or the White Hair Chief. His French name, or title, alludes to an enduring (and sometime conflicting) relationship between the French and the Osage. Pike or his men also conducted a rough village census and recorded 502 men, 341 boys, and 851 women. Unfortunately, Pike did not stay with the Osage long enough to provide a detailed account of village life; he does, however, speak of two classes of males: warriors/hunters and doctors/cooks. The men who were cooks were apparently warriors who were not needed or for some reason were unable to become members of the war party.

The only archaeological references to Carrington Village was a very brief summary of artifact collections made at the site in the 1920s and 1930s, and limited archaeological trenching was conducted at the site by the University of Missouri in 1942. The report in the 1930s described the village as being about 200 yards long and oval shaped, with the long axis oriented north-south. Because the village was only abandoned about 100 years prior to the initial collections at the site, it was still possible to discern the location of lodges spaced about 40 feet apart. Materials collected from the village were gunflints, brass arrow points, axes, beads, and many gun parts. The subsequent work in the 1940s recovered essentially a similar record of material remains. With so little available archaeological information, much of the common knowledge on the Osage inhabitants of this village is drawn from ethnographic and historic sources.

The Dhegihan Siouan-speaking Osage are known as the *Wa-zha-she*, or the Children of the Middle Waters. This may also reflect a clan or moiety name among the Osage. The name is derived from their oral history in which an all-powerful god, *Wakonda*, created and ordered the universe into air, land, and water, creating the "Middle Waters." Because little research has focused on Osage cultural history prior to extensive contact with the French, the tribe's origins are somewhat ambiguous. Oral histories among the Osage have them living in the Ohio River valley in prehistoric times, perhaps in association with other Dhegihan-speaking groups such as the Missouri, Kansa, and Quapaw. They were driven from this homeland by the frequent raids of the Iroquois Nation. Osage groups moved down the Ohio River to its confluence with the Mississippi, where they crossed over into present-day southeastern Missouri. They slowly moved west and slightly north following the Missouri upstream. They eventually moved farther west and south, arriving at the headwaters of the Little Osage River by the late seventeenth century. This history is accepted by a number of cultural historians and parallels the oral history of the Quapaw, a closely related tribe.

What little can be discerned from the patchy record of aboriginal material culture of the Osage differs from this portrayal, instead linking the tribe to prehistoric Oneota culture

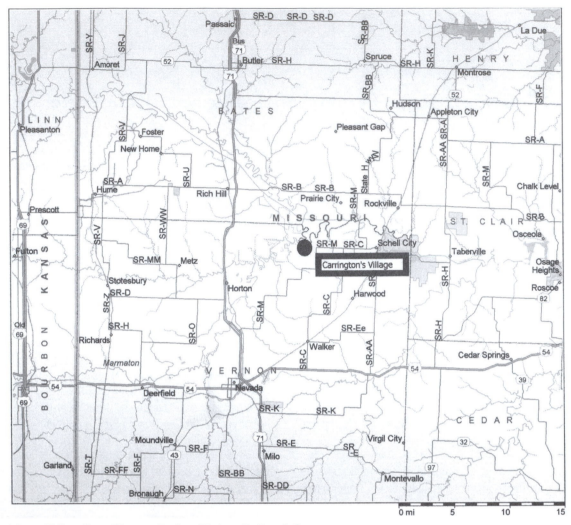

Location of Osage Village State Historic Park.   [Robert L. Brooks]

from northern areas (e.g., Iowa and Minnesota). Without evidence from prehistoric sites that can be clearly identified as culturally affiliated with the Osage, their origins and movements remain obscure. It is known that the Osage were living on the headwaters of the Osage River by the late 1600s–early 1700s. Prior to their arrival in southwestern Missouri, the Osage functioned as a single group or society. However, they soon split into two groups. As a result of internal political disagreements, one group of Osage moved northeast along the Missouri River and established relationships with the Missouri tribe. These became known as the "Little Osage." Other tribal members remained in residence along the Osage River and are referred to as the "Grand or Big Osage." Despite their separation, the two groups of Osage maintained very similar lifestyles, although the Little Osage may have been slightly affected by their close ties to the Missouri.

The Osage adopted their economic and social ways of life to a transitory existence between the woodlands to the east and

the prairies/plains to the west. Subsistence needs were met by small-scale farming of family plots consisting of corn, beans, squash, and pumpkins. They also collected persimmons in the fall and water lilies in the summer. This diet was supplemented by the hunting of local game around the village and more extended bison and deer hunts periodically during the year. Late winter marked the time of bear and beaver hunts. In April, fields were cleared and planted, with much of this work done by the women and children. Once the crops were planted, most of the villagers went on extended hunts for deer and bison. The Osage returned to the village in late summer to harvest the crops. After crops were harvested and the corn shelled and stored, they would again leave for a more extended hunt for bison and deer, which lasted until late winter.

Villages such as Carrington consisted of numerous lodges sometimes arranged in rows and alleys. The lodges were rectangular, measuring roughly 30–40 feet long by 15 feet wide. The walls consisted of upright posts covered with rush mats.

Center posts supported a ridge pole from which other poles were bent to form the roof. Doorways were typically on the long side of the dwelling, facing east. Chiefs' houses were generally somewhat larger than those of other tribal members. Inside the houses were hearths (fireplaces), storage pits, smudge pits for hide smoking, and sometimes low benches where goods were stored. The Osage used more temporary housing during their extended hunting trips. These were reminiscent of the tepees found on the plains at this time, although either skins or mats might have covered the Osage dwellings.

By the time the Osage were living at Carrington Village (ca. AD 1725–1830), their material culture had been profoundly affected by trading relationships with the French. The Osage had a lucrative trading relationship with the French at Fort Orleans, exchanging deer, buffalo, beaver, and other fur-bearing mammals' pelts for Limbourg cloth, mirrors, brooches, bracelets, and vermillion. Domestic items such as brass or iron pots and kettles were also highly desired by the Osage. However, the most prestigious trade items were guns. The trading of guns with the French was the source of considerable conflict between the Osage and French, since the Osage did not want the French trading guns to other tribes and thus disrupting their dominance over nearby groups.

Some aboriginal technology remained by the early eighteenth century at settlements such as Carrington Village. Included were bows made from the bois d'arc (Osage orange) tree, sandstone sharpeners, bone needles, awls, and beads; antler and bone handles; deer bone arrow-shaft straighteners; and catlinite pipes. Clothing remained predominantly animal skins, although cloth from trade with Europeans, including wool, was increasingly used. Items of aboriginal manufacture that were mainly used in hunting and hide processing included flint (chert) knives, scrapers, and arrow points.

European goods consisted of domestic as well as ornamental items. Again, guns were a dominant aspect in the French trade with the Osage. Gun barrels, frizzens, mainsprings, trigger plates, and gunflints were in abundance. There were also iron kettles, saws, hoes, axes, and files. Some domestic goods, such as iron kettles, were refurbished into triangular flat and conical rolled arrow points. There were also ornaments such as brass and cooper hawks bells, ear dangles, buttons, medals, and silver crucifixes. Like most Native Americans in contact with Europeans, glass beads were obtained in mass quantities. Among the Osage, white and blue seem to be favored colors.

The social lives of the Carrington Village inhabitants were focused around the clan. In fact, the village layout was probably arranged by some sort of clan order. Most political and ceremonial events also had a clan order based on rank and function. Clans were patrilineal with exogamous marriage rules. Two moieties, each represented by a chief, crosscut clan and family divisions. Although there are exceptions, one moiety typically assumed the leadership role in "war/sacred" functions (*Hon-ga*), whereas the other would be the "peace/household" moiety (*Tsi-zhu*). The governing political body of the Osage was made up of the "Little Old Men," who represented a special society of village elders who advised the chiefs. Chiefs generally obtained office through hereditary relationships, although there was sufficient fluidity to this system that a poor leader among the war moiety could be passed over for someone more qualified. Even in these circumstances, there were probably only certain families from which the chief could be selected. As with any society of this size, among the men there were warriors, hunters, and doctors or medicine men. Women's roles were generally focused around domestic activities such as gardening, cooking, and making and repairing clothing.

Intersocietal conflict or warfare was a constant companion to the residents of Carrington Village in the eighteenth and early nineteenth centuries. The Osage defended an expansive territory, raiding and being raided by the Choctaw, Cherokee, Quapaw, Pawnee, and Wichita. Their constant raids eventually forced the Wichita living in northern Oklahoma south to the Red River. They even had disagreements with other Siouan-speaking groups, such as the Kansa and the Missouri. Even with firearms supplied by the French, the Osage were faced with too many adversaries and eventually agreed to a treaty in 1825, relinquishing their lands in Missouri for lands in eastern Kansas. This treaty resulted in an uneasy truce between the Osage and their Plains adversaries. Following the Civil War, the Osage were relocated again to northern Oklahoma, where many tribal members currently reside and they have their tribal headquarters.

Further Reading: Bailey, Garrick A., "Osage," in *Handbook of North American Indians: The Plains*, edited by Raymond D. DeMallie (Washington, DC: Smithsonian Institution Press, 2001), 476–496; Berry, Brewton, Carl Chapman, and John Mack, "Archaeological Remains of the Osage," *American Antiquity* 10 (1944): 1–11; Chapman, Carl H., *Osage Indians III: The History of the Osage Tribe* (New York: Garland Press, 1974); Chapman, Carl H., "Osage Indians in Missouri and Oklahoma A.D. 1796–1825," in *Pathways to Prehistory*, edited by Don G. Wyckoff and Jack L. Hofman, Oklahoma Anthropological Society Memoir No. 3 and Cross Timbers Heritage Association Contribution No. 1 (1982): 19–28; Chapman, Carl H., and Eleanor F. Chapman, *Indians and Archaeology of Missouri* (Columbia: University of Missouri Press, 1983); Din, Gilbert C., and A. P. Nasatir, *The Imperial Osages: Spanish-Indian Diplomacy in the Mississippi Valley* (Norman: University of Oklahoma Press, 1983); Harner, Joe, "The Village of the Big Osage," *Missouri Archaeologist* 5 (1939): 19; Mathews, John Joseph, *The Osage: Children of the Middle Waters* (Norman: University of Oklahoma Press, 1961); Rollings, William H., *The Osages: An Ethnohistoric Study of Hegemony on the Prairie Plains* (Columbia: University of Missouri Press, 1992); Rollings, William H., "Osages," in *Encyclopedia of the Great Plains*, edited by David J. Wishart (Lincoln: University of Nebraska Press, 2004), 587; Wedel, Mildred Mott, "Claude—Charles Dutisné: A Review of His 1719 Journeys," *Great Plains Journal* 12 (1973): 146–173; Wiegers, Robert, "The Little Osage Village," *Missouri Archaeologist* 43 (1982): 43–111.

Robert L. Brooks

THE CROW CREEK SITE

South Dakota

Site of a Fourteenth-Century Massacre

People have lived in the northern Great Plains for at least 10,000 years. Hunting animals such as the mammoth in the earliest times, they gradually focused on bison (buffalo) hunting when the mammoth and other large game disappeared. From that time on, all the Plains tribes hunted bison as an important part of their diet. By AD 800, some people began cultivating domesticated crops, the "three sisters" of maize (corn), beans, and squash, on the fertile, well-watered floodplains of the rivers and streams of the region. Most of these gardeners lived in large permanent villages but also went on seasonal bison hunts. Located along the east bank of Missouri River in central South Dakota, Crow Creek village was one of largest of these villages. The 1978 discovery of the mutilated remains of nearly 500 villagers in the village's fortification ditch changed the way archaeologists understood the nature of village life, and especially the level of warfare on the plains before European contact.

Crow Creek fortification ditch snakes along the top. Remains in the ditch at the top left. Dark spots inside the ditch are collapsed lodges. [Larry J. Zimmerman]

Partially excavated bone bed.   [Larry J. Zimmerman]

Crow Creek village (site number 39BF11) sits on a roughly triangular point of land that is formed by the confluence of Crow Creek and Wolf Creek as they enter the floodplain of the Missouri River. The site has archaeological evidence of all but the earliest inhabitants, containing a deeply buried Archaic tradition (ca. 6000–1000 BC) occupation and Woodland tradition (ca. 500 BC–AD 1000) burial mounds slightly northeast of the village. The village itself contains two different cultural complexes. The earliest is the Initial Middle Missouri culture (ca. AD 1000–1200), which is ancestral to the historic Mandan people, located downslope of the Initial Coalescent culture (ca. AD 1200–1400) and ancestral to the Arikara people. A small post-contact Coalescent (AD 1475–1600) settlement is just across Wolf Creek. The Crow Creek village became a National Historic Landmark in 1955.

Two sides of the point of land are steep, providing natural defense from intruders. On the side away from the river, villagers dug dry moat fortifications for protection. Within the fortifications, people lived in earth lodges that were slightly rectangular for the earlier group but circular for the later. The lodges were semi-subterranean houses, usually with four massive central support posts supporting the roof and side walls made of smaller trees interwoven with saplings and covered in

daub. Earth partially or completely covered the exterior. A central fire hearth sat below a smoke hole in the roof, and an extended entryway opened to the rising sun. Archaeologists have mapped more than fifty lodges on the site, many of them still visible as donut-like depression from the collapsed lodges.

The most impressive feature of the site is the large Initial Coalescent fortification ditch dug across the open side of the triangle. The ditch is about 370 meters long with at least ten bastions protruding at regular intervals along the ditch. The ditch was 3.5 meters wide at the top and about 1.75 meters deep. The builders piled the excavated earth on the inside and on top placed posts interwoven with brush, which created a formidable barrier. Evidence of another ditch inside this large one suggests that either the earlier Initial Middle Missouri village had been fortified or that the Initial Coalescent peoples outgrew their first ditch and built a new one. The interior ditch was filled with village debris, whereas the exterior had almost no village materials in it.

In a 1950s project, the Nebraska State Historical Society (NSHS) conducted limited excavations at Crow Creek in advance of construction of several dams along the main channel of the Missouri River. On the Crow Creek Sioux

Reservation, the site is located just downstream from Ft. Thompson, South Dakota, along the east side of the Missouri. Wave action from Lake Francis Case, formed by the Ft. Randall Dam about 170 kilometers downstream, heavily eroded and destabilized the site. A 1978 archaeological survey found that waves and looters had damaged one end of the fortification ditch, exposing and breaking parts of at least forty-seven human skeletons. Many skull fragments showed cut marks consistent with the practice of scalping.

Archaeologists excavated the bottom and sides of the end of the ditch, which uncovered a pile of skeletons that had been thrown into the ditch. The pile was a rough pyramid, about 3 meters on a side and 1 meter thick, containing at least 486 individuals. The remains were a jumble and not in their normal skeletal positions. Bodies had partially decomposed before being buried. Archaeologists found more evidence of scalping and other mutilations that often accompany warfare. The pile included everyone from children to elders. Consistent with small-scale society warfare, skeletons of women of child-bearing age mostly were absent; the women probably were taken captive. Archaeologists could not get permission to test the ditch for additional skeletons, but they believe that the village population may have been as many as 1,000 people.

The Initial Coalescent villagers had been attacked and at least some of them massacred. Skull fractures indicated that they had been clubbed, suggesting killing at close quarters. Many lodges had been burned, as the 1950s excavations had discovered and reported. The massacre and burial probably happened during cold months, and the remains of the dead lay exposed for some time, where they partially decomposed. There was evidence of gnawing on the ends of many of the exposed bones, probably by dogs, wolves, or coyotes. Eventually someone returned, gathered up the remains, dumped them into the ditch, and covered them with a thin layer of earth brought from the stream valley below. Remains of a small fire atop this layer were radiocarbon dated to AD 1325. This is consistent with dates from the NSHS excavations, but some archaeologists think the date is too early and are reexamining the dates.

The reasons for the massacre and who did it are unclear. Many archaeologists believe that conflict resulted because Initial Coalescent peoples moved in from the south, displacing Initial Middle Missouri peoples, but some believe that unknown outsiders attacked the village from some distance away. Another hypothesis stems from skeletal evidence. Most skeletons showed protein, iron, and vitamin C deficiency, indicating a level of malnutrition. Regional climatic instability at a time when population seems to have grown rapidly may have caused competition for land needed to plant crops, which brought conflict. That such disagreement could lead to massacre and mutilation seems difficult to comprehend, but similar consequences are known from disputes in other cultures. Unusual bone growth over parts of several skulls showed that individuals had been scalped and lived, while bone grown over arrowheads indicated healed wounds. Such healing would take at least three months, which suggests that there was an ongoing conflict. Unfortunately, who carried out the massacre and why probably will remain unknown.

The significance of the Crow Creek site and massacre stems from the fact that archaeologists had no idea that such violence was taking place on the Great Plains prior to the arrival of Europeans and Euro-Americans. They had assumed that life was relatively peaceful, but Crow Creek's evidence of the largest known prehistoric massacre in North America demonstrates otherwise. Although nothing at this level of warfare has been discovered since, excavations in other sites suggest that conflict may have been more common at the time than archaeologists had suspected.

The site also is significant because one of the earliest large-scale repatriations and reburials in the United States occurred there, well ahead of enactment of the Native American Graves Protection and Repatriation Act of 1990. Part of the agreement with the Crow Creek reservation tribal council was that the massacre remains could be studied, but only if they were repatriated for reburial. In late 1981, the skeletons were buried on the site on which the people had lived and died. Reburial services included traditional Lakota and Christian rituals, and a day later, the Arikara conducted private ceremonies. Since the reburial, the Corps of Engineers (COE) has erected a commemorative marker and worked to stabilize the eroding banks along the Crow Creek site.

Although the site is on public land, both the COE and the Crow Creek Sioux Reservation tribal council are reluctant to mark the site in any way that is visible from South Dakota Highway 50, which runs closest to the site a few miles north of Chamberlain. There is no interpretation at the site. The COE and the tribe are extremely protective of Crow Creek because site looting is common, and the tribe considers the site to be sacred. They patrol the site often. Permission from the COE should be sought before one attempts to enter the site.

Further Reading: Bamforth, Douglas, "Indigenous People, Indigenous Violence: Prehistoric Warfare on the North American Great Plains," *Man* 29(1) (1994): 115–125; Willey, P., *Prehistoric Warfare on the Great Plains* (London: Routledge, 1990); Zimmerman, Larry J., *Crow Creek Massacre*, http://www.usd.edu/anth/crow/crow1.html (online January 2007); Zimmerman, Larry J., and Richard Whitten, "Mass Grave at Crow Creek in South Dakota Reveals How Indians Massacred Indians in 14th Century Attack," *Smithsonian* 11(6) (1980): 100–109.

Larry J. Zimmerman

SITES IN GRAND TETON AND YELLOWSTONE NATIONAL PARKS

Wyoming and Montana
Rocky Mountain Archaeology

Archaeology is the scientific study of past human culture, technology, and behavior based on the analysis of remains that people have left behind. Archaeologists propose, evaluate, and undertake research projects to learn how specific ways of life developed and how they changed over time. They use careful methods to record and excavate sites and examine material remains.

Archaeologists study remains from the historic period as well as from more distant, ancient, or prehistoric times. For the Yellowstone National Park (NP) area, the historic period (and written records) begins in the late eighteenth century. Historic archaeological sites in the area include the remains of early tourist hotels, soldier stations, and historic period Native American sites. The U.S. Army managed the park from 1886 to 1918 (the National Park Service was established in 1916). Archaeological investigations at the Fountain Soldier Station and the Tower Soldier Station have improved our understanding of the army activities. Organic materials (e.g., wood, bone, basketry, clothing) are only rarely preserved in the park's environment, so stone artifacts compose the majority of evidence of pre-contact (with Europeans) or prehistoric (before written records) lifeways in sites. "Pre-contact" and "prehistoric" are synonyms, with "pre-contact" considered more appropriate because these early people had history before contact with Europeans.

Unfortunately, archaeologists do not know how earlier peoples referred to themselves, so they often name different ancient cultures after the first location where they were identified or a distinctive artifact or "diagnostic tool" found at the site. A diagnostic tool is one that has a unique and recognizable form that is associated only with a particular culture. In the Rocky Mountains and adjacent Great Basin and Plains, most diagnostic tools are projectile points. Different shapes and sizes of projectile points were manufactured at different times to conform to the technology used to propel them. Over time, this technology changed from thrusting spear to *atl atl* (or throwing stick) to bow and arrow.

Many myths exist about Yellowstone; none of which is more persistent than the notion that American Indian groups rarely ventured into the area because of their fear of the numerous geysers. Archaeological study has shown, however, that this is not the case. Our current understanding indicates Native Americans visited the area that was to become Yellowstone National Park seasonally for almost 12,000 years. Furthermore, many thermal areas contain evidence that early people camped there.

Archaeologists have only recently begun to investigate and understand how prehistoric groups used upland and mountain environments like Yellowstone and Grand Teton. Currently, archaeologists believe that early people used the park area primarily during the warmer months and did not stay in the center of the park (which is above 7,000 feet) during the winter. Their diets depended primarily on hunting the same animals you can see in the park today, with little emphasis on plants. The Little Ice Age (AD 1450–1850) was a worldwide period of cooler weather, and evidence of its effect can be seen in the narrowing of Douglas fir tree rings. During the Little Ice Age, there was a major shift in human activities in the park. Families stayed at lower elevations elsewhere, while work parties came to the park to hunt bighorn sheep, collect obsidian, and carry out other specific short-term tasks. The few archaeological sites dating to the Little Ice Age are small and contain few artifacts, reflective of their short duration of stay.

Contemporary archaeological investigations use a number of methods and techniques from various related disciplines to piece together the puzzle of prehistoric societies. Palynology, the study of plant pollen, is important for understanding the various plant communities that occupied the region in the past, and it helps archaeologists understand how the climate has changed through time. Geomorphology, the study of past landforms, provides information on how landforms such as terraces have changed through time, usually in relation to shifting climatic patterns. This helps archaeologists understand better where people would prefer to live. Paleoethnobotany provides an understanding of what plants were used by prehistoric groups. Through the results of these studies, archaeologists are beginning to piece together a story of a very dynamic relationship between humans and their environments. People adapt to changing and different environmental conditions through their culture. Understanding these adaptations is a major focus of archaeology. One example is that throughout most of Yellowstone's human past, fish were not considered to be food. Only during the short period of about

AD 400–900 did people eat fish. Although archaeology borrows from zoology, botany, and geology, archaeology can also help those scientists determine the ages of landforms and what animals and plants were in the park at different times in the past.

THE PALEOINDIAN PERIOD (8,000–12,000 YEARS AGO)

In the Yellowstone region, the last major ice age ended about 14,000 years ago. The valleys became ice-free, and vegetation had recolonized the area by about 13,000 years ago. The post-glacial environment dried and warmed gradually, and the animals that were adapted to the cooler glacial environment—for example, the mammoths, mastodons, camels, short-faced bears, and horses—all disappeared. The Pleistocene bison, *Bison antiquus*, which stood about 8 feet at the shoulder, was replaced by the modern bison, *Bison bison*, which is about 5–6 feet high at the shoulder. People during this early period, referred to as Paleoindians, used large (compared to later samples) points hafted to spears, which were propelled by thrusting and short throws.

The form of the projectile points changed as people adapted to different environmental conditions and as technology changed. The earliest points are lanceolate and fluted. "Lanceolate" refers to a point that is slender in comparison to the length. "Fluting" refers to the removal, from the base toward the tip, of a flake, which thins the base and creates a concave channel up the long axis of the point. The fluting probably made hafting these points to the wooden spear shafts easier. These early fluted lanceolate points often are referred to as Clovis points after the location in New Mexico where their ancient temporal context was first confirmed. Late Paleoindian points have shoulders, contracting stems, and concave bases. Paleoindian people hunted bison, bighorn sheep, rabbit, deer, and bear.

The earliest evidence of humans living in the Yellowstone area is a Clovis point that was found near Corwin Springs, 12 miles north of the park. This artifact is made from Obsidian Cliff obsidian, a stone that is found only in Yellowstone National Park. Archaeologists know the obsidian came from Obsidian Cliff in the park because the point has the same composition as the obsidian that is found at Obsidian Cliff according to chemical analyses. Obsidians from different rhyolite lava flows can be chemically fingerprinted using X-ray fluorescence, a nondestructive analytical technique. Some sixteen different sources of obsidian in the greater Yellowstone ecosystem have been identified in prehistoric tools found in the park. Nevertheless, each year archaeologists find evidence of obsidian sources not previously known. Obsidian Cliff is the remnant of the Obsidian Cliff rhyolite flow 180,000 years ago and is the predominant obsidian for tool manufacture in the park.

The next people or culture in western North America is known as Folsom. An Obsidian Cliff obsidian Folsom point dating to about 10,900 years ago was discovered in the Bridger-Teton National Forest south of the park. A second Obsidian Cliff Folsom point was found about 15 miles northwest of the park. More substantial evidence of occupation and increasing population is provided by numerous point types, such as Agate Basin and Hell Gap, dating to about 10,000 years ago.

The earliest intact cultural deposits in the park are related to the Cody complex, which dates to 9,400–9,600 years ago. The Cody complex is named for a *Bison antiquus* kill site near Cody, Wyoming. It is believed that these Paleoindians visited the park during the summer to hunt and collect obsidian for tools. The Osprey Beach site is a 9,400-year-old camp at nearly 7,300 feet, where several families spent time on Yellowstone Lake repairing and manufacturing tools. They used blocks of local sandstone to shape their wooden shafts. The large number of obsidian tools found at this site is changing the view that Paleoindians did not use obsidian.

About 9,000 years ago, a mountain-oriented lifestyle developed. This archaeological tradition is characterized by lanceolate spear points with contracting stems and concave bases. Outside the park, there is evidence that these people utilized more plants as well as large and small mammals for food. It has been suggested that a climatic shift to warmer and more arid conditions on the plains may have caused this increased utilization of the mountain environment, or possibly the increasing population expanded from the plains into the mountains on a summer seasonal basis.

THE ARCHAIC PERIOD (1,800–8,000 YEARS AGO)

Continuation of the broad-based economy begun during late Paleoindian times is a hallmark of the Archaic cultures. Outside the park in the plains and Great Basin, there was increased use of plants and a wide array of animals from bison to rabbits. However in the park, hunting continued to be emphasized, with little evidence for use of plants. Analysis of the animal bones from sites shows little change in the animals that were hunted through time. A change in projectile point technology from spear to dart and *atl atl* marks the beginning of the Archaic period, and the projectile points become smaller and change from the Late Paleoindian lanceolate form to stemmed, side notched, and corner notched. This terminology refers to the manner in which these points were hafted or attached to the dart or shaft.

The Archaic period is quite lengthy (6,500 years) and is broken into three divisions: the Early, Middle, and Late Archaic periods. These are differentiated by environmental changes and technological developments. The Early

Archaic period, which lasted about 2,000 years, was generally hot and dry and is known in the park only from surface finds, although there are many buried camps associated with the Middle and Late Archaic occupations (4,500 BC–AD 200). This suggests increased use of the park area or exploitation of the food and stone tool resources in the area during the last two-thirds of the Archaic period. The climate changed to cooler and wetter to warmer and drier (although not as warm or dry as the Early Archaic) and back to cooler and wetter about every 500–1,500 years. During the Middle Archaic period, people began to cook using stone boiling technology. In this style of cooking, rocks were heated in a fire and then transferred into a water-filled hide. Heat from the rocks was rapidly transferred to the water, and water could rapidly be brought to boiling. Campsites contain quantities of rocks fractured through rapid cooling that occurred when the rocks were placed in water after being heated. These are called fire-cracked rocks.

There are more sites with thicker cultural deposits, radiocarbon dates, and projectile points from the Middle and Late Archaic periods than from any other time during the almost 12,000 years of human visitation to the park. This evidence is interpreted as indicating intensive use of the park. Campsites of the Middle and Late Archaic periods are often large base camps where a whole family or groups of families stayed in the park during the summer. They spent significant lengths of time at these locations carrying out a variety of activities, including manufacturing and repairing tools, tanning hides, and cooking. These activities are represented by broken and whole tools, flakes from tool maintenance, fire-cracked rocks and hearths, charcoal, and animal bones.

THE LATE PREHISTORIC/
PROTOHISTORIC-HISTORIC PERIOD
(100–1,500 YEARS AGO)

The late prehistoric period is sometimes also called the pre-contact period, indicating the time before contact between Native people and Europeans. This period is best characterized by the development of the bow and arrow (ca. AD 250), which replaced the earlier *atl atl*, or spear thrower. Other innovations in hunting include the use of wooden bighorn sheep traps in the mountains. The use of steatite (soapstone) vessels and the addition of pottery probably also increased the efficiency of these groups in preparing and storing food.

There is evidence that, for a few hundred years during the beginning of this period, people from the Great Basin/southern Idaho area came to the park. Identified by the Rose Spring corner-notched points, these people ate fish and constructed roasting pits that functioned like prehistoric crock pots.

Many forces acted upon Native peoples of the west from about AD 1523 onward. The Spanish arrived in Mexico City in AD 1523 and brought seven infectious diseases with them. The North American natives had no resistance to these diseases and lost perhaps 80 percent of their populations over the next 350 years. The Spanish brought horses to the New World, and as these got loose and became wild, Indians learned how to capture, train, and use horses. Horses provided the means to change from killing buffalo by running them over jumps to chasing herds on horseback. More goods could by carried by horses, and people could travel longer. Raiding increased over longer distances, especially raiding for horses. The cold of the Little Ice Age appears to also have discouraged long visits to the park, with people preferring to occupy lower-elevation sites. The fur trade flourished, and more goods had to be produced to be traded for European manufactured items, requiring more of the women's time to tan more buffalo hides and to grow more garden produce. These factors resulted in changes in the daily activities, such as where people went and for how long.

In Yellowstone, archaeologists see major differences in the ways of life followed by people in the park between about 4500 BC–AD 200 and the years after AD 1100. Earlier, whole families and groups came to the park and stayed during the summer months and created many campsites. These sites contain animal bones from food, fire-cracked rock from cooking, and much stone debris from manufacturing and repairing tools. Such sites are common. Those after AD 1100 are rare and contain only a few scraps, indicative perhaps of an overnight stay. Archaeologists know people were still coming to the park because Obsidian Cliff obsidian has been found in sites outside the park, but the interpretation now is that instead of family groups coming to the park, small, specialized work parties were dispatched to obtain obsidian, to hunt bighorn sheep, or to carry out some other specialized activity.

The protohistoric period indicates that time when European manufactured goods such as beads, axes, knives, and kettles were traded into an area but before there were any historic records. To date, no sites containing trade beads are known from the park. No sites can be identified with a particular historic tribe.

Although there are over 1,700 sites documented in about 2 percent of the park, there are no sites interpreted for the public in Yellowstone National Park. Archaeological understanding of past lifeways in this high mountain environment is still rudimentary.

Further Reading: Dougherty, John, *A Place Called Jackson Hole: A Historic Resource Study of Grand Teton National Park* (Moose: Grand Teton National Park, 1999); Janetski, Joel, *Indians in Yellowstone National Park*, rev. ed. (Salt Lake City: University of Utah Press, 2002).

Ann M. Johnson

KNIFE RIVER INDIAN VILLAGES NATIONAL HISTORIC SITE

Along the Middle Missouri River, North Dakota
Ancient and Historic Native American Villages

For thousands of years Indian people have lived along the Missouri River and on the vast plains landscape that the river channel cuts through as it runs from the northern Rocky Mountains to its juncture with the Mississippi in the center of the continent. The portion of the Missouri that runs through the area today covered by South and North Dakota is sometimes referred to as the "middle Missouri." This region of the river valley consists of a wide floodplain, within which the river channel lies, flanked by river terraces. This dynamic river system fits within a wide trench (more than 5 miles wide in some portions of the middle Missouri) that cuts through the overall regional prairie topography of the Great Plains.

Horticulture as a major part of economy and subsistence began to the east of the middle Missouri region about a thousand years ago in parts of the Midwest region, but within a century or two farming villages of ten to thirty households had spread up the Missouri River.

There is a cluster of ancient and historic archaeological sites near the junction of the Knife River and the Missouri, some within a unit of the National Park Service known as Knife River Indian Villages National Historic Site (NHS). Archaeological investigations have identified over fifty archaeological sites within the NHS (e.g., Thiessen 1993). The archaeological sites that are interpreted actively there date to the late prehistoric and early historic periods. The Lewis and Clark expedition spent the winter of 1804–5 in a fort they constructed close to the Indian villages, which were occupied by members of the Hidatsa tribe, descendants of the early horticultural village settlers, and the Mandan, relatively recent settlers at the mouth of the Knife River, having moved upriver from the Heart River area, where they had experienced a terrible smallpox epidemic in 1781.

The earliest archaeological evidence for human activities in the Knife River area dates to between 11,000 and 6,000 years ago and includes artifacts associated with the Paleoindian period. The site also includes archaeological evidence of occupation and use during the subsequent Archaic and Woodland time periods when a semi-sedentary way of life, including limited involvement in growing, or fostering the growth of, native wild food plants was common. About 1300 AD, the descendants of the Indians who occupied the villages in 1804 arrived. They constructed permanent earth lodge dwellings, domestic, dome-shaped structures made of logs and packed soil. The men usually decided how large an earth lodge would be, and the women did most of the building. First, a wooden framework

was erected, and it was then covered with layers of willow branches, grass, and finally earth. It is reported that 150 trees were needed to build one lodge. The structures were from 20 to 65 feet in diameter and housed individual extended families of eight to twenty people. They were built close together, with no geometric pattern of pathways or trails among them. Today, at archaeological sites where the remnants of earth lodges have not been disturbed, their arrangement and precise locations are identifiable as circular depressions on the ground surface.

The villagers followed an economy that combined horticulture in rich floodplain fields, collecting of wild plant foods, fishing in the rivers, and hunting of bison, deer, and smaller game on the river terraces and the nearby plains. Domesticated plants included maize, beans, squash, and sunflowers; wild berries and root crops were collected in season. The people also engaged actively in trade with nomadic groups, who lived mainly on the plains. The farmers exchanged their horticultural surplus for hides and skins, dried meat, and catlinite (a soft stone used for carving that is particularly abundant in quarries east of the Knife River area in present-day western Minnesota). The villagers also had access to deposits of Knife River flint or chert nearby and must have exchanged it with the nomadic groups. Knife River flint is a stone with physical characteristics that make it exceptional for shaping into sharp chipped-stone points and other cutting and scraping tools. Artifacts of this material are found in archaeological sites throughout North America.

Trading activity was the first context in which these villages and others along the entire Missouri River system encountered Europeans during early historic times. At first only the trade goods were transported along the river, but eventually European and Euro-American fur trappers and traders themselves appeared, making contact with the Missouri River tribes. The decade preceding the Lewis and Clark expedition witnessed increasing awareness of the Mandans and Hidatsas by British interests from the north and east, and the Spanish regime from St. Louis. By 1797, the five villages at the Knife River confluence, comprising two southern Mandan and three northern Hidatsa settlements, had become known to British and Spanish authorities. Lewis and Clark encountered these same villages in October 1804 during the first leg of their epic journey to the Pacific coast.

The Knife River village sites are well known today as the location where the Lewis and Clark expedition spent the winter of 1804–5. This is where the expedition added the French-Canadian trader Toussaint Charbonneau and his young wife, the indispensable Sakakawea (Sacagewea), as members. Much of what is known historically about the Mandans and Hidatsas between 1804 and 1806 and their five primary villages at the Missouri-Knife confluence are found in the documents written by the "Corps of Discovery." These reports by the expedition's leaders and members on matters cultural, historic, and scientific are a treasury of information about this period in the American West. The years following 1806 witnessed increasing contacts from the south via the Missouri River. Another smallpox epidemic in 1837 again reduced the Indian population substantially. By 1845 the Mandan and Hidatsa had moved away from their Knife River villages up the Missouri and settled at another village, known today as the Like-A-Fishhook site. In 1885 the federal government forced the Indian tribes still living at this village to abandon it and move to the Fort Berthold Indian Reservation, where their descendants reside today.

It is possible to visit the Knife River Indian Villages NHS, which is near Stanton, North Dakota, about 60 miles north of Bismarck. The park has a visitors' center with displays and exhibits about the Missouri River tribes and the archaeological record at the site and in the region. Trails at the site allow visitors to see the surface indications of lodges, and an earth lodge has been reconstructed to provide the public with interpretation of this type of structure. The states of North and South Dakota also have preserved archaeological sites of the late prehistoric and early historic periods at a variety of state historic sites. One of these, Double Ditch Indian Village State Historic Site, is located about 7 miles north of Bismarck, North Dakota. It contains the remains of a large Mandan earth lodge village. This is probably the site of one of the villages abandoned after the 1780–81 smallpox epidemic. Mandan from this site resettled at the Knife River Mandan village sites. The earth lodge remains and two fortification ditches, as well as interpretive signs, can be seen by visitors to the Double Ditch historic site.

Further Reading: Ahler, Stanley A., Thomas D. Thiessen, and Michael K. Trimble, *People of the Willows: The Prehistory and Early History of the Hidatsa Indians* (Grand Forks: University of North Dakota, 1991).; Beckham, Stephen Dow, *The Literature of the Lewis and Clark Expedition: A Bibliography and Essays* (Portland, OR:

Lewis and Clark College, 2001); Biddle, Nicholas, and Paul Kane, *History of the Expedition under the Command of Captains Lewis and Clark, to the Sources of the Missouri, Thence Across the Rocky Mountains and Down the Columbia to the Pacific Ocean. Performed During the Years 1804-5-6* (Philadelphia: Bradford and Inskeep, 1814); Cutright, Paul Russell, *A History of the Lewis and Clark Journals* (Norman: University of Oklahoma Press, 1976); Gurney, George, and Therese Thau Heyman, *George Catlin and His Indian Gallery* (Washington, DC: Smithsonian American Art Museum and W. W. Norton, 2002); Jackson, Donald, *Thomas Jefferson and the Shining Mountains: Exploring the West from Monticello* (Urbana: University of Illinois Press, 1981); *The Knife River People*, Knife River Indian Villages National Historic Site Web site, www.nps.gov/archive/knri/people.htm (online May 2008); Libby, Orin Grant, *The Mandans and Grosventres*, Collections of the State Historical Society of North Dakota, Vol. 1 (Bismarck: State Historical Society of North Dakota, 1906); McDermott, John Francis, "Up the Wide Missouri: Travelers and Their Diaries, 1794–1861," in *Travelers on the Western Frontier* (Urbana: University of Illinois Press, 1970); Moulton, Gary E., *Atlas of the Lewis and Clark Expedition* (Lincoln: University of Nebraska Press, 1983); Moulton, Gary E., *The Journals of the Lewis and Clark Expedition* (Lincoln: University of Nebraska Press, 1983–2001); Ronda, James P., *Lewis and Clark among the Indians* (Lincoln: University of Nebraska Press, 1984.); Ronda, James P., *Finding the West: Explorations with Lewis and Clark* (Albuquerque: University of New Mexico Press, 2001); Stewart, Frank Henderson, "Hidatsa," in *Handbook of North American Indians*, Vol. 13, Pt. 1: *Plains* (Washington, DC: Smithsonian Institution, 2001); Thiessen, Thomas D., ed., *The Phase I Archeological Research Program for the Knife River Indian Village National Historic Site*, Vols. I–IV, Occasional Studies in Anthropology, No. 27 (Lincoln, NE: Midwest Archeological Center, National Park Service, 1993); Wood, W. Raymond, "David Thompson at the Mandan-Hidatsa villages, 1797–1798: The Original Journals," *Ethnohistory* 24(4) (1977): 329–342; Wood, W. Raymond, *Prologue to Lewis and Clark: The Mackay and Evans Expedition* (Norman: University of Oklahoma Press, 2003); Wood, W. Raymond, and Lee Irwin, "Mandan," in *Handbook of North American Indians*, Vol. 13, Pt. 1: *Plains* (Washington, DC: Smithsonian Institution, 2001); Wood, W. Raymond, and Thomas D. Thiessen, *Early Fur Trade on the Northern Plains: Canadian Traders Among the Mandan and Hidatsa Indians, 1738–1818* (Norman: University of Oklahoma Press, 1985).

Francis P. McManamon and Paul Picha

CENTRAL PLAINS TRADITION SITES

Missouri, Kansas, Iowa, and Nebraska

Late Prehistoric Village Farmers

The Central Plains tradition dates from AD 900 to 1450, varying by geographic region. It includes the Upper Republican, Solomon, Smoky Hill, Initial Coalescent, St. Helena, Nebraska, and Steed-Kisker subcategories, known as phases, in southeastern Iowa, northeastern Missouri, northern Kansas, and southern Nebraska. The Central Plains tradition represents the earliest people on the Great Plains, people that were committed to farming. They grew maize, squash, and beans but also domesticated native plants that today are considered weeds, including sunflower, goosefoot, little barley, and marshelder. Tobacco also was grown. They were more settled, building and living in large houses that could last for several years. The increase in food production and settled lifestyle may have supported larger populations, explaining the increase in the number of sites at this time and the general increase in archaeological debris. Although bison was a significant source of meat for the Upper Republican phase, evidence of a wide range of animal species in Central Plains tradition sites shows that these people focused their hunting toward animals near their residential sites. There are a number of sites on the high plains in Wyoming and Colorado that lack earth lodges but have typical Central Plains tradition artifacts, with the noteworthy exclusion of horticultural tools. These sites date to between AD 1000 and 1300 and thus are coeval with the early and middle time periods of the tradition. At these high plains sites, the focus was primarily on bison. These sites appear to be more than just seasonal hunting camps and instead may be a western non-farming extension of the tradition.

Central Plains tradition sites often consist of the remains of substantial earth lodges built on the edges of terraces on soil surfaces stripped of sod. Four central posts supported them, branches and brush interwoven between outer wall posts were covered with clay, and the covered house entrances typically faced to the east or south. Earth lodges were typically square to rectangular, but some were round or had rounded corners. Floor areas ranged between 650 and 800 square feet. Inside, a central fireplace was used for warmth and cooking, and interior cylindrical or bell-shaped pits were dug to store food and supplies. These substantial dwellings are a departure from earlier times, during which the structures were small saucer-shaped depressions of packed soil with few or no post molds, suggesting less permanence. Most Central Plains tradition settlements were small, containing only one or two lodges; others had over twenty. In these larger sites, the houses may represent repeated small-scale occupations, although house floors rarely overlapped, indicating that they may all have been standing at the same time.

Stone tools are fairly consistent across the tradition's phases. Arrow points consistently are small and triangular, and may have side or basal notches. Other chipped-stone tools include drills; scrapers; diamond-shaped, beveled-edge "Harahey" knives; chipped and polished axe-like tools called celts; ground and pecked stone tools that include flat grinding stones paired with handheld stones used to grind seeds; hammer stones; pipes (made of materials other than the soft red stone catlinite, which became popular later); and paired sandstone pieces used to smooth arrow shafts. There is a well-developed bone tool kit. Hoes made of bison scapulae (shoulder blades) are common; other bone tools include awls, gouges, fishhooks, and ornamental beads. Shell hoes are found at some sites

Burial practices varied. Burials are found in cemeteries, ossuaries (pits containing large numbers of burials), in natural mounds and in mounds built over burials, and in residential sites, with the latter two being most common. Secondary burials—those in which the body is left out to decompose and the remaining bones then buried—are more common than primary (in-the-flesh) burials, and grave goods, when they are present, most typically are ceramic vessels but also may include bone or shell beads, projectile points, or other artifacts. The Whiteford site (14SA1, also known as the Salina Burial Pit) is a large, organized cemetery containing at least 151 individuals. The cemetery was excavated with the burials left in place and was open for decades as a tourist attraction. It was closed in 1989 and reburied in 1990 as a result of the indignation of American Indians.

Trade is indicated by turquoise and obsidian from the Southwest and several species of marine shell from the Southeast. Small amounts of copper and freshwater snails from the Midwest have been recovered. Alibates agatized dolomite, a high-quality tool stone from the Texas panhandle, also is found. Caddoan Crockett Curvilinear shards from southeastern Texas were recovered from the Whiteford site.

The pottery is distinguishable from that of the earlier Plains Woodland in that the vessels are thinner and rounder and have a more constricted orifice. Cord-marked vessel surfaces, when present, are finer than the coarse cord marking of Plains Woodland pottery. Pottery varies widely but is characterized by jars with a generally globular shape and a restricted orifice, often characterized by a substantial thickened collar. The clay is often tempered with gritty crushed rock, but sand-, bone-, grog-, and shell-tempered wares are well documented. Occasionally there are handles or lugs. Vessel exteriors may exhibit fine cord impressions; decoration is restricted to the shoulder, rim, and lip. Bowls are rare, and small cord-marked pots referred to as coconut vessels (the shape is similar to a coconut with the upper third removed) occasionally are recovered.

Pottery decoration, along with the geographic location of sites, is a primary means of delineating Central Plains tradition phases. Differences in pottery between phases includes decoration styles, the type and location of decoration, rim height and thickness, the presence of thickened "collared" or uncollared rims, the percentage of cord-marked versus smooth ware, and the type of temper used in the clay body. Phase designations continue to be a matter of debate, but these variations suggest different social groups within the tradition.

THE STEED-KISKER PHASE

Steed-Kisker phase sites serve as an example of the differences between phases. They are among the more distinctive Central Plains tradition sites, so much so that they have been interpreted as representing colonists from the east. They are found from Clay County in northwestern Missouri, along the

Missouri River between Kansas City and St. Joseph, to as far west as the Delaware River in Leavenworth County, Kansas. Steed-Kisker phase sites are distinctive because of the presence of decorated pottery nearly identical to the Ramey Incised style of pottery found at the Mississippian tradition Cahokia site, 250 miles to the east. This pottery typically has burned, crushed shell mixed with the clay and often has tabs, loop handles, and incised line decorations. Occasionally Steed-Kisker pottery has decorations from the Southeastern Ceremonial complex, a set of icons representing warfare, the sun, and humans with bird-like features, more typical of Mississippian sites. Other Mississippian similarities include a Steed-Kisker house that had its outer wall posts in a trench, a common design at Cahokia. Finally, a possible solstice shrine, similar to a structure at Cahokia known as Woodhenge, was found at a Steed-Kisker site at Smithville Lake, north of Kansas City, Missouri. Still, outside of a small set of Mississippian traits, Steed-Kisker sites are typical of the Central Plains tradition. Furthermore, some of these traits, such as shell-tempered pottery and Southeastern Ceremonial complex decorations, also appear in other Central Plains tradition phases. This is not to say that Cahokian influence is not present—it clearly is. But instead of Steed-Kisker sites representing settlements of Cahokian immigrants, it is more likely that ideas and techniques common to Cahokia spread upriver along trade routes and influenced an indigenous Central Plains tradition occupation.

THE BEGINNINGS AND THE END OF THE CENTRAL PLAINS TRADITION

The origins of the Central Plains tradition are not clear. One assertion is that it has an eastern origin out of the Steed-Kisker and Nebraska phases; the second proposes an origin in the Plains Woodland leading to the Solomon phase, with a subsequent spread of the tradition to the north and east. The end of the tradition is better documented, with radiocarbon dates showing that the more northern Loup River, St. Helena,

and Initial Coalescent phases are more recent, suggesting northward movement of Central Plains tradition people. The number of houses at sites of these phases is larger. The northward movement may be the result of the intrusion of Oneota populations into the plains from the northern Midwest beginning about AD 1250. Climate change also has been postulated as a factor.

For decades researchers have asserted that the Central Plains tradition evolved, directly or indirectly, into the Pawnee. Although this issue still is being discussed, it seems clear that the Central Plains tradition was involved to some degree in the beginnings of the Pawnee. The Pawnee Indian Museum (http://www.kshs.org/places/pawneeindian/index.htm) contains the excavated remains of a Pawnee earth lodge from around 1820 and is open to the public. Pawnee earth lodges are round but otherwise share a number of architectural characteristics with the Central Plains tradition.

Further Reading: O'Brien, Patricia J., "Steed-Kisker: A Western Mississippian Settlement System," in *Mississippian Settlement Patterns*, edited by Bruce D. Smith (Orlando: Academic Press, 1978), 1–19; Roper, Donna C., "The Central Plains Tradition," in *Kansas Archaeology*, edited by Robert J. Hoard and William E. Banks (Lawrence: University Press of Kansas, 2006), 105–132; Roper, Donna, *The Whiteford Site, or Indian Burial Pit: A Smoky Hill Phase Cemetery in Saline County*, Anthropological Series No. 18 (Topeka: Kansas State Historical Society, 2006); Scheiber, Laura L., "The Late Prehistoric on the High Plains of Western Kansas: High Plains Upper Republican and Dismal River," in *Kansas Archaeology*, edited by Robert J. Hoard and William E. Banks (Lawrence: University Press of Kansas, 2006), 133–150; Steinacher, Terry L., and Gayle F. Carlson, "The Central Plains Tradition," in *Archaeology of the Great Plains*, edited by W. Raymond Wood (Lawrence: University Press of Kansas, 1998), 235–268; Wedel, Waldo R., *Archeological Investigations in Platte and Clay Counties, Missouri*, United States National Museum Bulletin No. 183 (Washington, DC: Smithsonian Institution, 1943).

Robert J. Hoard

PIPESTONE NATIONAL MONUMENT

Pipestone County, Minnesota

Ancient and Historic Pipestone (Catlinite) Quarries

Historic stone quarries near the town of Pipestone in Pipestone County, Minnesota, are the source of an easily carved argillite that Native Americans have used to make pipes and other artifacts for at least two millennia. This material is called

catlinite, after the artist George Catlin, who was the first to publicize the quarries in art and in a narrative travel account based on his personal visit in 1836. He was also the first to bring samples of the stone with him when he returned east.

Native Americans working one of the catlinite quarry pits around the turn of the twentieth century.   [Photograph by Samuel Calvin, Iowa State Geologist. The Calvin Photographic Collection, Department of Geoscience, The University of Iowa]

Catlinite is an argillite or clay stone that originated as mud deposited on riverine floodplains during major flooding episodes during Early Proterozoic times, about 1.5 to 1.75 billion years ago. It occurs as relatively thin beds ranging from about an inch to 2 feet in thickness, sandwiched between massive beds of Sioux quartzite. Today catlinite occurs in at least six discontinuous beds exposed in a line of Native American quarry pits that extends in a north-south direction for more than a half mile through Pipestone National Monument, a park administered by the National Park Service. The beds dip toward the east at approximately 5 to 10 degrees from horizontal and extend in that direction for several hundred feet.

Though its color may vary from dark maroon to nearly white, catlinite is normally reddish in color, often speckled with white spots due to partial leaching of the hematite that colors the stone. Catlinite resembles argillites found at a number of other places in the United States, ranging from Ohio to Wisconsin to Arizona. Argillites of generally similar appearance but from different geographic source locations can be distinguished from one another on the basis of mineralogical composition. Analytical methods for identifying their

mineralogical characteristics include x-ray powder diffraction and neutron activation analysis. One drawback of both methods is that they require small amounts of powdered stone, which can result in the destruction of a small part of any artifact which is sampled for analysis. Recent experimentation with an instrument called a portable infrared mineral analyzer (PIMA) offers promise of an efficient, non-destructive method to distinguish between different argillites in the future.

Catlinite samples from the beds at Pipestone National Monument share sufficiently distinctive mineralogical attributes to be collectively referred to as catlinite. However, artifacts made from argillitic stone from other source locations are often incorrectly assumed to be made of catlinite. In light of this, former Wichita State University geologist James N. Gundersen, who has extensively studied catlinite and other argillitic pipestones, has urged that the name "catlinite" be reserved exclusively for stone from Pipestone National Monument and that the term "pipestone" be applied in a generic sense to stone from source locations other than the monument.

The ability to identify the source locations of stone used for the production of Native American artifacts offers immense potential for the study of prehistoric trade patterns through

A Native American craftsman making a pipe from catlinite at Pipestone National Monument, Minnesota, around 1965.   [Photograph by John S. Sigstad. Courtesy of the National Park Service, Midwest Archeological Center, Lincoln, Nebraska]

time and geographic space. Catlinite artifacts, largely in the form of pipes, have been confirmed from more than forty archaeological sites in ten states (Alabama, Illinois, Iowa, Kansas, Nebraska, North Dakota, Ohio, Oklahoma, South Dakota, and Wisconsin) as well as the Canadian province of Manitoba, attesting to widespread use and trade of the material through a long span of prehistoric and historic time. Catlinite artifacts from Wisconsin and Ohio, and possibly Iowa, are believed to date to Early and Middle Woodland times (approximately 500 BC to AD 500), suggesting that use of the material may have begun perhaps as early as 2,500 years ago. Catlinite as a trade commodity appears to be most abundant at Late Prehistoric sites dating after about AD 1100 and was commonly used by many Plains tribes into late historic times. Catlinite continues to be actively quarried today at Pipestone National Monument, whose enabling legislation authorizes quarrying of the stone by Native Americans of all tribes. Quarrying is conducted on a permitted basis, and only non-mechanized hand tools may be used. Contemporary Native Americans of many tribal affiliations quarry the stone and make it into pipes and other articles that are traded and sold to Indians and non-Indians alike.

Catlinite plays an important role in the cosmology of many Plains tribes. The stone, quarries, and pipes in general figure prominently in many Native traditions. These traditions often illuminate themes that portray the catlinite quarries as (1) the origin place of humankind; (2) the place where the people received the gift of the pipe from the Great Spirit; (3) a place where peace prevails among visiting tribesmen, even those

otherwise hostile to one another; (4) a place where a great flood or an epic intertribal battle killed off the people, who colored the stone with their blood; and (5) the place where the thunderbird dwells, and which is often visited with thunder and lightning as a result. Most of these stories are poorly documented, and many may be traced to Catlin's rather romantic renditions of them. The often-repeated theme of the quarries as a place of peace among the tribes has substantial time depth, as the earliest mention of it in recorded literature occurs in Jonathan Carver's 1778 book, which is based on his 1766–67 travels and the writings of contemporary authors.

Near the southern end of the quarry line, within the monument lie a group of six huge, glacially deposited erratic boulders, commonly known as the Three Maidens. Varying accounts say that they are the home of the spirits of two or three old women who guard the quarries and who must be propitiated by offerings and prayers before the stone is quarried. The boulders lie on Sioux quartzite bedrock that once featured dozens of petroglyphs (designs and images pecked into the stone) depicting anthropomorphic, zoomorphic, and other motifs observed and commented on by early visitors to the quarries. However, these petroglyphs were removed on slabs of quartzite late in the nineteenth century as the result of a misguided early effort at historic preservation (they were beginning to be defaced by graffiti). Many of the slabs were lost over the years following their removal, but at least seventeen of them are presently on display in the monument's visitor center.

The quarries and archaeological features near them, such as the rock art mentioned above and mounds observed by visitors, attracted early attention from scientists. The petro-glyphs were recorded by the Minnesota state geologist in the late 1870s and again by Theodore Lewis of the Northwestern Archaeological Survey in 1889, and several mounds were dug into by Smithsonian Institution archaeologist Philetus Norris in 1882 as part of Cyrus Thomas's survey of ancient mounds in the United States. In 1892 another Smithsonian researcher, William Henry Holmes, drew a detailed and accurate map of the quarries, mounds, and hundreds of stone circles presumed to be the remains of weights for hide and cloth tepee covers used by Native Americans who camped near the quarries.

Following Holmes's visit, the quarries received little attention from archaeologists until after the monument was established in 1937. National Park Service archaeologist Paul Beaubien excavated several of the quarry pits in 1949 and assessed the overall importance of the local archaeology for the future development and interpretation of the new monument. The monument's archaeological resources were inventoried by archaeologists from the universities of Colorado and Missouri in 1965 and 1966, and from the National Park Service's Midwest Archeological Center in 1997 and 1998. Today, over forty locales within the monument's boundary have been identified as being important to the story of past use of catlinite by Native peoples of the Plains.

Further Reading: Boszhardt, Robert F., and James N. Gundersen, "X-Ray Powder Diffraction Analysis of Early and Middle Woodland Red Pipes from Wisconsin," *Midcontinental Journal of Archaeology* 26 (2003): 33–48; Catlin, George, *Letters and Notes on the Manners, Customs, and Conditions of North American Indians*, 2 vols. (New York: Dover, 1973); Gundersen, James N., "The Mineralogical Characterization of *Catlinite* from Its Sole Provenance, Pipestone National Monument, Minnesota," *Central Plains Archeology* 9 (2002): 35–60; Holmes, William Henry, "The Red Pipestone Quarry," in *Handbook of Aboriginal American Antiquities, Part I*, Bureau of American Ethnology Bulletin No. 60 (Washington, DC: Smithsonian Institution, 1919), 253–265; Murray, Robert A., *Pipestone: A History* (Pipestone, MN: Pipestone Indian Shrine Association, 1965); Scott, Douglas D., and Thomas D. Thiessen, "Catlinite Extraction at Pipestone National Monument, Minnesota: Social and Technological Implications," in *The Cultural Landscape of Prehistoric Mines*, edited by Peter Topping and Mark Lynott (Oxford: Oxbow Books, 2005), 140–154; Upper Midwest Rock Art Research Association, *The Pipestone Petroglyphs*, http://www.tcinternet.net/users/cbailey/PipeTom.html and http://www.tcinternet.net/users/cbailey/pipestone.html (both online December 2005).

Thomas D. Thiessen

FORT UNION TRADING POST NATIONAL HISTORIC SITE

Montana–North Dakota Border

Historic Trading in the Rocky Mountains

Fort Union Trading Post is located on the Montana–North Dakota border, with the park straddling the Missouri River about 2 miles above its confluence with the Yellowstone River. The post was constructed in 1828 as the American Fur Company's major trade distribution and collection center in the upper Missouri region and served in that capacity for almost four decades through 1867. The post and its subposts served the Assiniboin, Blackfoot, Crow, Cree, Sioux, and other northern Plains tribes. During its existence, the fort was visited by many Euro-American explorers, priests and preachers, traders, artists, and other travelers who recorded their impressions of the trading post in letters, journals, paintings, sketches, and photographs. Among the visitors to the post were the western artist George Catlin, the naturalist John J. Audubon, and the Jesuit priest Father Pierre DeSmet. Aside from its economic importance, the post contributed significantly to the history of exploration, anthropology, and transportation of the American frontier. In 1961 the old fort site was designated a National Historic Landmark. In 1965 Congress created Fort Union Trading Post National Historic Site and placed it within the National Parks system. As with many other historic sites placed in its keep at the time, the National Park Service's primary means of interpreting the trading post was through an attempt to reconstruct the historic structures that once existed at the site.

Reconstruction plans were initiated in 1968 with historical and archaeological research on the structural history of the fort. From 1968 through 1972, the National Park Service's Midwest Archeological Center conducted excavations on the manager's house, trading house, blacksmith shop, bastions, and a host of the post's minor historic structures and open areas. As that work was completed, however, philosophical changes turned the National Park Service away from reconstruction as an appropriate treatment and toward preservation of the site. In the process, funding was halted for analysis of the archaeological data and the tens of thousands of artifacts recovered during that work.

Despite this change, continued public interest in the reconstruction eventually led to a 1985 congressional mandate that required the National Park Service to reconstruct Fort Union on the actual site. Recognizing that on-site reconstruction would completely destroy Fort Union's historic foundations and other deposits, the Midwest Archeological Center was directed to re-initiate excavations at the site. The investigations that followed became one of the largest excavations undertaken by the National Park Service, with 3,716 square meters (39,892 square feet) of the site excavated between 1986 and 1988. Because reconstruction took place simultaneously with the archaeological excavations, fieldwork emphasized acquisition of information relating to architecture and the historic site plan. This work resulted in recovery of detailed information for 32 fort era structures and over 900 lesser features. Architectural plans for reconstruction drew on archeological data and historical images to develop plans for replicas of the Bourgeois (manager's) House, palisades, bastions, Indians' and Artisans' (trading) House, and main gate. Construction was begun in 1986, and reconstruction was completed in 1991.

In addition to architectural information, National Park Service excavations produced an immense collection of artifacts and excavation records. By the end of the 1988 field season, approximately 800,000 objects had been recovered, creating one of the foremost assemblages of fur trade era artifacts in North America. In addition, archaeologists recorded the progress of their work with thousands of frames of photographs and 31 linear feet of excavation forms, notes, and maps. By the end of the project, analyses of the excavation data and artifacts had produced twelve excavation reports, thirteen artifact analyses, three master's theses, one dissertation, and fifteen articles published in magazines and books. In addition, information about the project and its results was presented through thirty-eight public presentations and pages on the Midwest Archeological Center Internet Web site (http://www.cr.nps.gov/mwac/).

Although the park commemorates one of the pre-eminent nineteenth-century American trading posts, archaeologists have discovered the location had also been occupied in late prehistoric times. In fact, the area around Fort Union has had a long history of human occupation. The upper Missouri region was intensively occupied from the Plains Archaic period (3000 BC–AD 500) through the historic era, although there is some evidence that humans have intermittently occupied the area as long ago as the Paleoindian period (6000–9000 BC). The prehistoric occupation at the trading post site is represented by small pits and hearths, burned and unburned animal bones, a variety of worked stone (projectile points, scrapers, and byproducts of stone tool manufacture), and ceramic shards common to the late prehistoric (AD 500–1800) or contact period (post-1800). Artifacts and features indicate that people camping here pursued such activities as hunting, butchering, cooking and roasting, tanning hides, refuse disposal, and perhaps ritualistic usage of sweat lodges. Calibrated radiocarbon dates from several of the burn features ranged from AD 1525–1560 to 1740–1810. Together, the artifacts and dated features suggest an association with a prehistoric complex known as the "Mortlach aggregate." Many prehistorians attribute this phase to pre-contact Siouan speakers, either Assiniboine- or Hidatsa-related groups. Since the Fort Union site is located within the traditional hunting grounds of the "Southern Assiniboine," it seems likely that the prehistoric component of the site is associated with that cultural group. Many of the Assiniboine still live in the region today, residing at the Fort Peck Reservation in northeastern Montana.

Historic documents indicate Fort Union was built in late fall of 1828. After their arrival on site, traders dug large pits to temporarily store their trade goods until a storehouse could be built. The most important task at hand, however, was to build shelters to protect themselves from attack by Indians and to shelter themselves from the hard northern plains winter. The first post was small, and its palisade was built in the traditional manner by digging a trench and inserting upright "pickets" or posts of split timbers. Little is known about the buildings erected inside this fence because they lay outside the excavation zones established by reconstruction demands. Variations in this first palisade's construction combined with the late season in which it took place have led archaeologists to believe that the fort's builders may have been faced with an early onset of winter weather and had to rush the fort to completion by taking shortcuts in construction. As a result, the new trading post was poorly built and had to be replaced within a few years.

Fort Union was totally rebuilt in the 1830s, and archaeologists found it had been greatly expanded in size. This second post, built over several years, was far sturdier than the first construction. Its massive palisade and all interior buildings were set upon stone foundations. Instead of building the fort's corner bastions (blockhouses) of timber, they built massive, two-story fortifications of stone at the northeast and southwest corners. Over the course of its forty-year occupation, Fort Union's buildings were repaired and rebuilt. The trade house, for instance, was rebuilt at least twice. The range of storage buildings and the dwelling range of the workers were rebuilt at least once. The Bourgeois (manager) House was rebuilt once and heavily remodeled in 1851–52 to change its appearance from a traditional French style of building common to the upper Mississippi and northern plains regions to the (then) more modern Greek Revival style.

Fort Union was like a small western company town, and its multi-ethnic employees were drawn from western Europe, Canada, Mexico, the eastern United States, and, of course, the Indian tribes of the American prairies. These residents pursued all the activities one might expect in such a community. Among these were building fires, hide smoking, gardening, hunting, tending to domesticated animals, cooking food, disposing of trash, maintaining sanitation, controlling drainage and mud, housekeeping, manufacturing and repairing tools and firearms, tearing down buildings and constructing new ones, quarrying stone, and manufacturing lime to make mortar for construction. An analysis of the faunal material (animal bones) from the site indicated that the post residents hunted and ate a wide variety of wild animals including bison, elk, antelope, beaver, and waterfowl. Fishing commonly produced large catches of catfish. Through time, however, over-hunting devastated the populations of larger species such as elk and bison, and hunters were forced to focus on smaller species such as antelope and rabbits. By the last decade of the post's occupation, a large percentage of the meat eaten at the fort was from domestic cattle and pigs.

Artifacts recovered from the site reflect activities pursued by the fort's occupants as well as items sought by Native American traders who came to the post for goods from the United States and European industrial areas. A whole host of clay pipes from Germany, Britain, and France reflect the common activity of smoking tobacco. Buttons from rough and refined clothing were recovered. Beads from Italy and Bohemia were traded to visiting Native Americans and used on clothing and moccasins worn by company employees. Among the myriad goods traded and used at Fort Union were guns and ammunition from England, the United States, and Belgium; knives and ornaments from England; wines from France and Spain; and cloth from the industrial looms of England and France.

The onset of the Sioux wars in the 1860s created an environment where it was increasingly difficult to continue the trade. In 1864–1865, the traders at Fort Union were joined by soldiers of the U.S. Army. A military button recovered at the site indicates that at least some of these men were "galvanized yankees," that is, Confederate prisoners of war forced to serve on the American frontier as the Civil War played out. Soldiers at the post had a printing press and published the *Frontier Scout*, the first newspaper known to have been published in northern Dakota Territory. Archaeological discovery of printing type established the location of the printing office just inside the south palisade. Other vestiges of military occupation include large latrines behind the store and dwelling ranges, a small latrine (probably for officers) behind the Bourgeois House, spent cartridges from military rifles and pistols, and uniform insignia and buttons.

The history of Fort Union ends in 1867, when the dilapidated old trading post was sold to the U.S. Army. Soldiers quickly razed much of the fort, recycling its building materials to construct a new infantry post, Fort Buford, at the confluence of the Yellowstone and Missouri rivers. The remaining wooden structures were torn down by steamboat crews carrying men and supplies to upriver goldfields in Montana.

Further Reading: Barbour, Barton H., *Fort Union and the Upper Missouri Fur Trade* (Norman: University of Oklahoma Press, 2001); Chittenden, Hiram M., *The American Fur Trade of the Far West*, 2 vols. (New York: Press of the Pioneers, 1935; repr., Lincoln: University of Nebraska Press, 1986); Denig, Edwin T., *Five Indian Tribes of the Upper Missouri*, edited and introduction by John C. Ewers (Norman: University of Oklahoma Press, 1961); Denig, Edwin T., *The Assiniboine*, edited with notes and biographical sketch by J. N. B. Hewitt (Norman: University of Oklahoma Press, 2000); Hunt, William J., Jr., "Origins of Fort Union: Archeology and History," in *The Fur Trade Revisited: Selected Papers of the Sixth North American Fur Trade Conference, Mackinac Island, 1991*, edited by Jennifer S. H. Brown, W. J. Eccles, and Donald P. Heldman (East Lansing: Michigan State University Press, 1994), 377–392; Hunt, William J., Jr., "At the Yellowstone . . . to Build a Fort: Fort Union Trading Post, 1828–1833," in *Fort Union Fur Trade Symposium Proceedings* (Williston, ND: Friends of Fort Union, 1994), 7–21; Jameson, John H., Jr., and William J. Hunt, Jr., "Reconstruction versus Preservation-in-Place in the U.S. National Park Service," in *The Constructed Past: Experimental Archaeology, Education and the Public*, edited by Peter G. Stone and Philippe G. Planel (New York: Routledge, 1999), 35–62; Larpenteur, Charles, *Forty Years a Fur Trader on the Upper Missouri: The Personal Narrative of Charles Larpenteur, 1833–1872*, introduction by Milo M. Quaife (Chicago: R. R. Donnelley & Sons, 1933; repr., with introduction by Paul Hedren, Lincoln: University of Nebraska Press Bison Book, 1989); Mattison, Ray M., "The Upper Missouri Fur Trade: Its Methods of Operation," *Nebraska History* 42(1) (1961): 1–28; Mattison, Ray M., "Fort Union: Its Role in the Upper Missouri Fur Trade," *North Dakota History* 29 (1962): 1–2; Matzko, John, *Reconstructing Fort Union: An Administrative History of Fort Union Trading Post National Historic Site, North Dakota–Montana* (Lincoln: University of Nebraska Press, 2001); Thompson, Erwin N., *Fort Union Trading Post: Fur Trade Empire on the Upper Missouri*, 2nd ed. (Medora, ND: Theodore Roosevelt Nature and History Association, 1994).

William J. Hunt, Jr.

FORT CLARK SITE

Central North Dakota

Early Historic Trade Along the Missouri River

Fort Clark State Historic Site is located in central North Dakota about 60 miles north of Bismarck. The site uniquely incorporates archaeological remains of a Mandan-Arikara earth lodge village (ca. 1822–61) and two mid-nineteenth-century American fur trade posts: Primeau's Post (ca. 1858–1861) and Fort Clark (ca. 1830–1860).

The story of Fort Clark began in 1822 when the Mandan built a village of earth-covered homes on the bluffs of the west bank of the Missouri River at the confluence of Chardon

Creek and Clark's Creek. They called their new home *Mitu'tahakto's*, (pronounced "me-toot-a-hank-tosh"), meaning "first (or east) village." Mandan and Hidatsa communities of the upper Missouri River were centers of intertribal trade for centuries before Europeans arrived on the scene. Every fall in the historic period, nomadic Indians from the Rocky Mountains, the southern and eastern plains, and what is now Canada traveled to exchange goods with these corn-growing village Indians. Thus, it is not surprising that a succession of American trading posts was established near Mitu'tahakto's. In 1830 the American Fur Company built Fort Clark, naming it in honor of explorer William Clark, who was Superintendent of Indian Affairs at the time. It was built for trade with the Mandans but also served visiting tribes such as the Hidatsas, Crow, and Dakota Sioux. After a tragic smallpox epidemic in 1837 virtually destroyed the Mandans, the Arikaras moved into the village and became Fort Clark's primary trading partner. In 1860 Fort Clark burned and was abandoned. The company purchased the opposition Primeau's Post located nearer the earth lodge village and continued to trade for another year until the Arikara moved to Star Village near present-day Garrison, North Dakota.

Three archaeological investigations have taken place at the site. The first two, in 1973 and 1974, were conducted by State Historical Society of North Dakota archaeologist C. L. Dill. Dill identified elements of the perimeter palisades (a fence of massive stakes forming an enclosure for defense) and a number of interior structures. Dill's work was followed in 1985–86 by a mapping project directed by noted University of Missouri–Columbia archaeologist and historian W. Raymond Wood. That project combined aerial photography and transit mapping to produce detailed maps of more than 2,200 surface features, including 86 earth lodges, hundreds of storage and burial pits, two trading posts, and Euro-American and Native American roads and trails.

The most intensive investigation at Fort Clark was the 2000–2003 interdisciplinary Fort Clark Interpretation Project. This research incorporated experts and students from the universities of Arkansas, Kansas, Missouri, Nebraska, and Tennessee; the U.S. National Park Service's Midwest Archeological Center; the State Historical Society of North Dakota; Arizona-based PaleoCultural Research Group; and the Smithsonian Institution's National Museum of Natural History.

These investigations began with a large-scale geophysical survey, which identified unusually strong areas in the earth's magnetic field and locations of high electrical conductivity that could be caused by subsurface features such as pits, hearths, and trenches. This data was used to guide excavations at the Fort Clark site. The investigation of a midden area north of the fort, for example, determined that magnetic anomalies identified during the geophysical survey were caused by large fort era ash and trash deposits.

Inside the trading post, excavations focused on clarifying Fort Clark's structural evolution. Contemporary historical

journals and illustrations of the post suggest its configuration changed radically through time. These physical alterations were apparently accompanied by changes in the size of the post. Archaeological data demonstrated that Fort Clark was expanded at least twice, with bastions (blockhouses) rebuilt each time, sometimes on different corners of the post. Based on historic accounts and artifacts recovered from the site, these expansions probably occurred around 1843–47 and sometime in the late 1850s. The last blockhouse on the west corner was fairly small, with exterior dimensions of only 4.4 meters (14 ft). Documentary evidence and artifacts from the structure suggests this bastion was built in the mid- to late 1850s but was removed within a few short years. Excavations also demonstrated that a magnetic anomaly in the center of the fort courtyard was caused by a large rectangular pit containing the base of a massive pole. This was interpreted to be the remnant of the fort's flagpole.

From 1973 onward, about 1,000 artifacts other than beads and bone were recovered at Fort Clark. Their recovery locations suggest variations in activity patterns within the trading post. Domestic structures or living areas occur at the front (northeast side) and right (northwest side) quarters of the post. Low densities of personal items suggest that the north and west interior corners of the post were used as work or storage areas. A building on the right side of the fort's front gate may have been the employees' dining area. Gun parts, horseshoes, and tools from the fort's west interior corner indicate the location of a blacksmith and artisans shop. Activities in the shop included small-scale metal fabrication, woodworking, gun repair, ammunition manufacture, wagon repair, and horseshoeing. A few objects provide information about how people passed their personal time at Fort Clark. Small ceramic discs made from dinner plates suggest checkers or a version of the plum-pit gambling game. Bottle fragments dating from the last years of the fort's occupation indicate that some employees, most likely those of higher status, consumed such bottled beverages as whiskey, ale, wine, and champagne. Of course, the indulgence most commonly used by trading post employees was tobacco. Fragments of kaolin (white clay) pipes from England, France, Germany, and Belgium were the most common artifact recovered at Fort Clark. A few terracotta pipes are probably from the eastern United States, although one specimen was made in Bohemia, in Eastern Europe. A few fragments of lead-inlaid red stone pipes were also recovered. This kind of pipe was often made and generally used by Native Americans. Historic accounts indicate, however, that Euro-Americans quarried stone at what is now Pipestone National Monument, Minnesota, manufacturing large numbers of pipes and pipe blanks for the trade by the late 1850s.

Food is always an important item, and workers in the bison robe trade were well known for prodigious appetites. Bone remains from Fort Clark indicate its residents ate bullhead catfish, ducks, geese, sandhill cranes, and trumpeter swans from the river and meander loop lakes; cottontail rabbits, deer, elk, and passenger pigeons from the woody margins of the river; and jackrabbit, sharptail grouse or prairie chicken, antelope, and bison from the upland prairies. Dogs were common at the post and were eaten by traders upon occasion. Other domestic animals at Fort Clark included cattle, pigs, and chickens. Recovery of two nested milk pans indicates the presence of milk cows at Fort Clark, an activity supported by entries in the post manager's journal. Traders grew a variety of vegetables including peas, corn, beans, and potatoes. They also traded with Indian neighbors for beans, squash, and corn. Wild plant foods eaten at the fort included chokecherry, wild plum, wild grape, wild rose hips, and snowberry. Among artifacts used for storing, cooking, and eating food are stoneware storage jars, tin milk pans, yellow ware ceramics, a metal skillet handle, tinware bowls and cups for the tables of the common workers, and china dishes from Staffordshire, England, for the higher-status employees. A small two-pronged fork from the fort midden is probably typical of eating utensils one would find at the fort's dining tables.

American trading posts on the upper Missouri River appear to have been dirty, unsanitary places in general. Archaeological data suggests that outhouses were rarely provided at American posts. Privies at Fort Clark's sister post, Fort Union, for instance, were created only in the 1860s during a short military occupation of that post. No military occupation occurred at Fort Clark, and there is no evidence for privies there to date. The lack of sanitation is substantiated by historic accounts of large numbers of Norwegian rats infesting this post and the neighboring Indian village. The archaeological record clearly reflects this abundance of rats, with 54 percent of the micromammal bones from the site being Norwegian rat remains. With poor sanitation often comes disease, and Fort Clark saw its share. The most infamous event was the 1837 smallpox epidemic.

The means of transportation used by fort occupants varied. Travel to and from "civilization" at St. Louis was generally by water, through the use of dugout canoes, keel boats, and steamboats. At the fort, most typically one would see people moving about on foot, by horse- or oxen-drawn cart, or on horseback. In the winter, one might witness travel by dogsled. A few artifacts associated with land-based transportation were recovered. Not surprisingly, all are related to the use of the horse. These include a harness snap and roller buckle, harness trace chains, and trace hook. Iron terrets (loops that guide the path of the harness or reins) were probably elements of a cart harness or single harness (used on a horse for drawing a wagon). A pair of metal bars recovered from the bastion are from a wagon of the type used prior to the Civil War. In fact, most recovered objects suggest use of carts or wagons. Of course, the animals had to be fed and maintained and, appropriately, fragments of scythes, hay forks, and horseshoes were recovered.

Numerous tool fragments reflect woodworking at the post. Logging and rough shaping of timber or large pieces of wood is suggested by the recovery of a lightweight to extra-lightweight Kentucky pattern axe. Smaller-scale woodworking is reflected by a variety of worn and broken tools, including wood chisels, files, a wood auger, a gimlet, awls, screwdriver, and a homemade wedge.

The Fort Clark site was listed on the National Register of Historic Places as an archaeological district in 1986. Visitors are welcome to walk the site's earth lodge and palisade depressions. There are no facilities at the site, however, and interpretation is limited to recently updated signage.

Further Reading: Abel, Annie H., ed., *Chardon's Journal at Fort Clark, 1834–1839* (Pierre: South Dakota Historical Society, 1932); Catlin, George, *Letters and Notes on the Manners, Customs, and Conditions of the North American Indians* (New York: Dover Publications, 1973; originally published in London in 1844); Chittenden, Hiram M., *The American Fur Trade of the Far West*, 2 vols. (New York: Press of the Pioneers, 1935; repr., Lincoln: University of Nebraska Press, 1986); Heidenreich, Virginia L., ed., *The Fur Trade of North Dakota* (Bismarck: State Historical Society of North Dakota, 1990).

William J. Hunt, Jr.

THE *BERTRAND* SHIPWRECK SITE AND COLLECTION

Western Iowa
DeSoto National Wildlife Refuge

The *Bertrand* archaeological site features an 1865 steamboat that was excavated on the grounds of DeSoto National Wildlife Refuge during 1968 and 1969. The ship was en route from St. Louis, Missouri, to Fort Benton, Montana, carrying passengers and over 200 tons of cargo. The excavation of the ship yielded over 500,000 artifacts, many types of which had never previously been recovered from an archaeological site. This cargo has given us a unique glimpse into the material culture of late Civil War America and has provided type specimens for innumerable categories of artifacts. Although the

Steamboat *Bertrand*

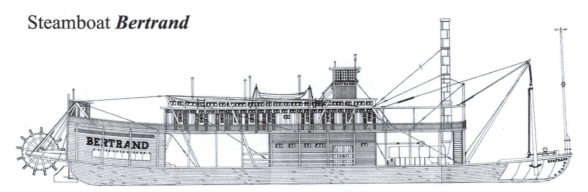

Drawing of the *Bertrand* by Jerry Livingston.   [Courtesy of DeSoto NWR, U.S. Fish and Wildlife Service]

structural remains of the *Bertrand* were reburied in place, these artifacts form the core for exhibits and an extensive research collection at the DeSoto visitors' center.

The cargo of the steamboat *Bertrand* provides us the physical remains of the changing nature of American culture during the mid-nineteenth century. Much of the cargo consisted of supplies destined for mining operations in the goldfields of Montana, which included such typical mining equipment as hundreds of picks and shovels, blasting powder and fuse, mercury for processing gold ore, and dredge materials. Less obvious examples of mining culture from the collection were clothing, canned and bottled foodstuffs, and matches and candles. The thousands of bottles of alcoholic beverages from the cargo also speak to the boomtown nature of the Montana goldfield settlements. The excavators had anticipated whiskey in the cargo, but instead they found hundreds of bottles of champagne and thousands of bottles of medicinal bitters. The large numbers of bitters may be a reflection of taxation during the Civil War. During the war whiskey was taxed, but medicinal drinks, such as bitters, were not. Medicinal or not, the alcohol content of many bitters exceeded that of commonly available whiskey in 1865.

The cargo of the *Bertrand* also reflects the growing number of farming communities along the Missouri River. These are represented in the cargo by a number of massive plows, butter churns, rakes and hoes, and other necessities of farm life.

The year 1865 was also a time of great stress for many of the Siouxan tribes of the Missouri River valley. The growing number of farming and mining communities along the river, the Minnesota Uprising of 1862 and its reprisals, and the Sand Creek Massacre just a year before in southeastern Colorado had led many of the Lakota and Dakota to see armed resistance as the most viable method of survival along the Missouri River. Perhaps a reflection of this coming struggle, the amount of Indian trade goods on the *Bertrand* was rather small in comparison with the howitzer, rifle, and pistol ammunition carried in her cargo. Prior to departure, the passengers and crew had drawn rifles and a small cannon from

the St. Louis Arsenal for protection during the voyage. Viewed from this perspective, the cargo of the *Bertrand* provides us with the physical remains of a very turbulent time in American history.

At 3:00 pm on April 1, 1865, the steamboat *Bertrand* was approximately 20 miles north of Omaha, Nebraska, on the Missouri River, when it hit a submerged tree, or sawyer. Within five minutes the ship and over 200 tons of cargo settled to the bottom of the river in shallow water. Companies insuring the cargo of the *Bertrand* conducted salvage operations on the wreck in the following weeks, but they met with only limited success.

In 1968 two amateur salvors, Sam Corbino and Jesse Pursell, from nearby Omaha, Nebraska, discovered the possible location of the wreck through archival research. After conducting test drilling on DeSoto National Wildlife Refuge, they found the wreck beneath 20 feet of dirt, several hundred feet from the water. The changing course of the Missouri River had shifted the wreck location from river bottom to cornfield. The site was located on the interior bend of an oxbow on the Missouri River.

In 1968 the salvors reached an agreement with the U.S. Fish and Wildlife Service and began excavations on the site. The agreement stipulated that all excavations would be supervised by a government archaeologist and assisted by refuge personnel. By agreement, all mercury, gold, and whiskey recovered would become property of the salvors, while all artifacts remained under government ownership.

The excavation was supervised by government archeologist Jerome Petsche and lasted until October 1969. Soon after the excavation began, a high water table caused flooding at the site. A pioneering system of well points was emplaced, which dewatered the site and allowed for excavation. Petsche, Corbino, and Pursell conducted the excavation with assistance from the refuge, National Park Service, and contractor personnel. Over 500,000 artifacts were recovered, most very well preserved. The combination of soil type, cool temperatures, and lack of oxygen resulted in the preservation of all

Photograph of the excavated *Bertrand*. [Courtesy of Woodmen of the World, taken by Leland A. Larson]

types of materials, with the notable exception of cotton. Shovels appeared as if new, labels on shipping crates were clear and easily read, butter and lard were preserved, and most of the artifacts looked as if they had been buried the day before.

This level of preservation was unique. Hundreds of glass bottles were recovered, most still filled with preserved fruit and vegetables. Case after case of full bitters and champagne bottles were also excavated. Tins of canned meat still rested in wooden shipping crates. Cans of strawberries, oysters, peaches, essence of coffee, and others still held their contents. This has provided archaeologists with a unique opportunity to study the actual food of the mid-nineteenth century.

After being stripped of its cargo, main deck, and fittings, the ship was covered in plastic sheeting and reburied. Soon

after, the well points were removed, and the excavation pit rapidly turned into a water-filled pit. The site is now accessible by a short walking trail from a nearby parking lot.

The artifacts from the ship were transported to the refuge headquarters for treatment and storage. While this took place in an eight-stall garage initially, by 1969 the *Bertrand* Building was created to house the *Bertrand* Conservation Lab and staff. The National Park Service provided a staff of conservation and museum professionals to preserve and process the collection. The collection presented many conservation challenges that had never been faced before, and the staff pioneered many new treatments. The initial intensive degree of conservation established a level of documentation and conservation excellence that continues today. Few archaeological collections are as well documented or preserved as the *Bertrand* collection.

In 1981 the *Bertrand* Conservation Lab and collection were relocated to the new visitors' center at the DeSoto National Wildlife Refuge. The new building featured display galleries and an extensive visible storage area highlighted by 165 feet of glass walls.

The steamboat *Bertrand* and its collection have provided a very important resource for those researching the material culture of mid-nineteenth-century America. To date, it has been the subject of four books, forty-five periodical articles, and nine unpublished articles. Common research topics include nineteenth-century glassware, preserved foods, farming implements, pocket knives, Stanhope lenses, bitters and champagnes, Ironstone ceramics, mining equipment, early canned foods,

mountain howitzer ammunition, Goodyear patent buttons and slickers, Maynard cartridges and primers, historic textiles, and steamboat construction. To supplement the collections, the visitors' center also includes a substantial research library.

Further Reading: Corbin, Annalies, *The Material Culture of Steamboat Passengers: Archaeological Evidence from the Missouri River*, Springer Series in Underwater Archaeology (New York: Plenum Press, 2000); Peterson, Leslie Perry, *The Bertrand Stores*, 2nd ed. (Missouri Valley, IA: Friends of Boyer Chute & DeSoto NWR, 2005); Petsche, Jerome, *The Steamboat Bertrand: History, Excavation and Architecture* (Washington, DC: National Park Service, 1974); Switzer, Ronald, *The Bertrand Bottles: A Study in 19th Century Glass and Ceramic Containers* (Washington, DC: National Park Service, 1974).

Marshall D. Owens

FORT LARNED, BENT'S OLD FORT, AND OTHER SITES

Missouri, Kansas, Colorado, and New Mexico
Archaeological Sites along the Santa Fe Trail

For sixty years the Santa Fe Trail operated as a major commercial wagon route connecting the United States to northern Mexico. Later the trail served as a military road tying the American Southwest to the rest of the country. The route extended for about 1,200 miles, with trail remnants and other associated sites now found in five states from Franklin, Missouri, to Santa Fe, New Mexico. The trail remained in use in whole or in part until 1880, at which point the Atchison, Topeka, and Santa Fe Railroad reached the Santa Fe area, effectively ending the trail's function as a commercial cargo route.

Congress recognized the significance of the trail by proclaiming it a National Historic Trail in 1987. The National Park Service administers the Santa Fe National Historic Trail in partnership with other federal, state, and local agencies; nonprofit organizations; and private landowners.

The history of the trail begins with Lieutenant Zebulon Pike's 1806 expedition to explore the Arkansas and Red rivers and evaluate the possibilities of trade with New Mexico. With the 1810 publication of Pike's journals, the possibility of using this as a commercial route to Santa Fe immediately became apparent to the American public. While Spain prohibited commerce with the Americans for the next decade, Mexican independence in 1821 established an opportunity for trader William Becknell to open the trail to Santa Fe from Old Franklin, Missouri. During the next five years, the eastern

trailhead moved west to Independence, Missouri, with traders moving in both directions from Mexico and the United States.

In western Kansas the trail divided into two major routes, the more direct being the Jornada Route or Cimarron Cutoff. In many places this portion of the trail lacked access to firewood, water, or grass for the animals. It also passed through territories occupied by Native American tribes hostile to encroachment of their territories. Nevertheless, this shorter route, requiring only sixty-two days to travel from Independence to Santa Fe, carried up to 75 percent of the trail's traffic. A more northerly route, the Mountain or Long Route, had access to water and supplies and was less prone to attack by hostiles but added 230 miles requiring ten additional days to get to Santa Fe.

The Santa Fe Trail was an important American military road. In the 1820s the United States established Fort Leavenworth to protect the eastern end of the route. Later forts Union and Marcy in New Mexico anchored the west end of the line, and the Army garrisoned more than twenty new forts from the 1840s through 1870s. The trail was first used to project American military power in 1846, when American General Stephen W. Kearny moved his "Army of the West" to secure the New Mexico capital, Santa Fe. The trail also witnessed what is generally considered the major Civil War battle in the western theater when Federal forces met and fought the

Confederates at Glorieta Pass in New Mexico. The destruction of Southern supply wagons during the battle forced Rebel forces back into Texas.

There are literally hundreds of archaeological sites relating to the trail between Franklin, Missouri, and Santa Fe. Although a few have been investigated archaeologically, most such projects are reported only in research reports of limited distribution.

In Missouri the most prominent Santa Fe Trail sites are Fort Osage and the villages of Franklin and Arrow Rock. Fort Osage, originally a trading post, was used at the end of its existence as a military depot. The only site with ties to the trail that has seen considerable archaeological investigation is Arrow Rock. Missouri Valley College archaeologist Timothy E. Baumann has worked at this site since 1996, focusing on African American culture before and after the Civil War (i.e., generally well after Arrow Rock was an integral part of the trail).

The greatest extent of the Santa Fe Trail lies in Kansas, and as a consequence the state contains the largest number of associated sites. Among the more noteworthy are Fort Leavenworth/Cantonment Leavenworth (established 1827); the McGee-Harris Stage Station; 110-Mile Creek Crossing; Havana Stage Station; Dragoon Creek Crossing; Soldier Creek Crossing; the Cottonwood Creek Crossing and Campground; Fort Riley (established 1853); Allison's Ranch, a trader's store from 1855 to 1868; Fort Zarah (1864 to 1867), at the Walnut Creek crossing; Page Ranch (1864), a trader's store and mail station; and Fort Ellsworth (1864 to 1867), established to protect the Smoky Hill Trail and the Fort Zarah Road. Most of these sites have been subjected to minimal archaeological testing. Two Kansas military sites have been extensively investigated by the National Park Service (NPS) in anticipation of restoration or reconstruction. After the razing of a large swath of commercial and residential buildings, John D. Reynolds excavated at the Fort Scott National Historic Site between 1968 and 1972. All major structural elements that remained extant were exposed and documented. This was followed by extensive excavations at the Fort Larned National Historic Site by Douglas D. Scott from 1972 to 1974. The fort's major structures (1859–78) had been modified in the late nineteenth century as a ranch complex, and Scott's groundbreaking work at the site helped clarify elements that were associated with the earlier military era. In 1986 NPS archaeologist Jan Dial-Jones and NPS historical architect Alan W. O'Bright excavated the fort blockhouse in anticipation of its reconstruction.

In Colorado there are a number of sites and numerous trail elements relating to the Santa Fe Trail's Mountain Branch. While several sites have witnessed minor investigations (e.g., the 1853–59 Bent's New Fort/Big Timbers trading post, the 1860–67 military post of Fort Fauntleroy, and the 1860–67 Fort Wise/Fort Lyon army post), only a few have been subject to intensive or long-term investigations. Among these are

three sites (Bent's Old Fort, Boggsville, and the Lockwood Stage Station) representing mercantile, early settlement, and commercial transportation eras in the history of the trail.

Bent's Old Fort was the only major supply point for travelers on the Mountain Branch from 1834 to 1849. It also participated in Native American trade and had a prominent role in the American expansion into the Southwest. This site has experienced a large number of investigations of varying scale beginning in 1954 with Herbert Dick's exploratory investigations. After its acquisition by the National Park Service, Jackson W. "Smokey" Moore conducted large-scale excavations from 1963 to 1965 to gather data to facilitate reconstruction of the trading post. In the process he was able to clarify the construction history of the post and identify the location of associated dumps outside the enclosure. Douglas Comer followed up on Moore's investigations in 1976 with excavations at post dump sites threatened by landscaping and construction. Comer's report provided the foundation for his later book that considers the fort's role in the Southwest, its symbolism, and the importance of ritual in the interactions of the post's occupants and visitors.

William G. Buckles and Richard F. Carrillo's ongoing work at Boggsville, Colorado, represents an unusual example of broad, ongoing research at a specific Santa Fe Trail site. Boggsville was established during the Civil War as the first unfortified town on the Santa Fe Trail in Colorado. By the 1870s the town had grown into a small, multi-ethnic community. Initial archaeological work at Boggsville gathered information for building preservation and reconstruction. Later research focused on the broader settlement and included research on the earlier riverbank settlement and identifying elements of the Santa Fe Trail at the site.

The Lockwood Stage Station was operated from the mid-1860s through 1876 by the Barlow and Sanderson stage line at a time when railroads were making huge inroads on traditional Santa Fe Trail commercial traffic. The site is located at the U.S. Army's Pinyon Canyon Maneuver Site near Trinidad, Colorado, and was excavated by Richard Carrillo. Subsequent analysis of archaeological data by Carrillo and others served to clarify the occupational history of the site and the role of stage transport in southern Colorado.

New Mexico has the second longest assemblage of Santa Fe trail segments, with elements of both the Mountain and Cimarron routes. Given this extensive trail network, it is not surprising that New Mexico contains a very high number of related cultural sites. A few small projects have focused on inventorying trail-related sites. Three locations have witnessed more intensive archaeological work. Fort Marcy is a star-shaped fort and blockhouse built in 1846 by General Stephen W. Kearny's troops in Santa Fe, New Mexico, as a symbol of the American occupation. An extensive complex of structures was later constructed as administrative headquarters for scattered Army units throughout New Mexico. The post was officially decommissioned in 1895. Extensive archaeological investigations have been undertaken by Stephen Post, Matthew Barbour, and Stephen Lentz, Office of Archaeological Studies, Museum of New Mexico. Excavations have exposed the hospital's foundations, officers quarters, parade ground, enlisted men's quarters, the livery, and associated wells, privies, and cisterns. Two distinct cultural horizons were distinguished, the first dating from about 1846 to circa 1880 and reflected by materials transported to the fort over the Santa Fe Trail by military supply wagons. The second, later horizon dates to post-1880 and encompasses goods brought to Santa Fe by the railroad.

Fort Union was an Army post established in 1851 to protect travelers on the Santa Fe Trail. It was decommissioned in 1891 after the railroad had reached Santa Fe and within a few years after the Apache Wars. Fort Union National Monument, created in 1954, encompasses three forts. The most visually prominent are the second (1861) star-shaped fort and the adobe third fort (1863–91). This last complex was the largest military installation in the American Southwest, incorporating a military garrison, territorial arsenal, and military supply depot. The largest visible network of Santa Fe Trail ruts may also be seen here. Major archaeological work by the National Park Service at Fort Union took place between 1956 and 1961. This work was largely directed toward stabilization and preservation of extant fort structures, and largely ignored recovery of artifacts that would provide information about the fort's development and everyday life on the post. The National Park Service also conducted an archaeological inventory of the park in the early 1990s.

Glorieta Battlefield, in the Pigeon's Ranch sub-unit of Pecos National Historical Park, is the location of the decisive 1862 Civil War engagement on the Santa Fe Trail. The battle effectively marked the end of the Confederate campaign in the Southwest. Several archaeological investigations have occurred at this site. In 1986–89, Museum of New Mexico archaeologist Yvonne R. Oakes conducted excavations at Pigeon's Ranch, a site occupied by Confederate forces during the battle, which resulted in the documentation of several historic features, including an 1850s well and an 1880s saloon. Oaks also directed the 1987 excavation of a Confederate mass burial. Thirty-one individuals and associated artifacts were recovered, with subsequent analyses targeted at illuminating the nature of injury and disease among the troops. DNA and archival research was conducted prior to reburial in an attempt to identify the individuals. In 2005 NPS archaeologist Douglas Scott directed a metal detection inventory in the Pigeon's Ranch sub-unit. This work demonstrated that despite considerable and long-term impact by private collectors, battle lines may still be discerned and much data remains at the site that can shed new light on the battle's history.

The Oklahoma panhandle contains a short segment of the Cimarron Route and the terminus of the Aubrey Cutoff. The Cimarron Route through Oklahoma passes by the rock fortifications of Camp Nichols, built in 1865 by Colonel Kit Carson

to help protect caravans from Indian raids. Another famous site in Oklahoma, Autograph Rock, is at the Cold Springs campsite. This rock cliff is marked with the names of hundreds of Santa Fe travelers and others dating as early as 1826. A third and very unusual complex of sites is associated with an 1860s gang of outlaws led by Captain William Coe. Coe built a stone fortress a few miles off the trail and, a short distance away, set up a blacksmith shop where stolen horses and mules were pastured. None of these locations has undergone archaeological investigation.

INTERNET RESOURCES

USGS aerial photographs and Terra Server links for most major sites and trail ruts on the Santa Fe Trail, from Franklin, Missouri, to Santa Fe, New Mexico, may be found at *Santa Fe Trail Sites*, a Web site by Larry and Carolyn Mix at http://www.stjohnks.net/santafetrail/spacepix/aspacelinkpage.html.

The same Web authors have created *Santa Fe Trail Research Site*, at http://www.stjohnks.net/santafetrail/, which provides a plethora of information about trail sites, trail and trail site histories, touring the trail by auto, books to read, and other Santa Fe Trail Web sites.

The events surrounding the discovery, excavation, and reinterment of Confederate soldiers found in a mass grave at Glorieta Pass are described at "The Second Battle of Glorieta" by Cheryle Mitchell on the *Civil War in New Mexico* Web site at http://www.nmculturenet.org/heritage/civil_war/essays/4.html.

The National Park Service makes information available about the trail and NPS sites (Fort Union National Monument, Bent's Old Fort National Historic Site, Fort Larned National Historic Site, Fort Scott National Historic Site) that may be accessed online at www.nps.gov. Information on the Santa Fe National Historic Trail at http://www.nps.gov/safe/ is a good starting point for exploring the trail and its myriad associated sites through its partner organizations. An excellent online map of the trail is available at this Web site, though it is difficult to navigate to. It may be found at http://www.nps.gov/safe/planyourvisit/maps.htm.

Further Reading: Alberts, Don E., *The Battle of Glorieta: Union Victory in the West* (College Station: Texas A&M University Press, 1998); Boyle, Susan Calafate, *Los Capitalistas: Hispano Merchants and the Santa Fe Trade* (Albuquerque: University of New Mexico Press, 2000); Comer, Douglas C., *Ritual Ground: Bent's Old Fort, World Formation, and the Annexation of the Southwest* (Berkeley: University of California Press, 1996); Dickey, Michael W., *Arrow Rock: Crossroads of the Missouri Frontier* (Arrow Rock, MO: Friends of Arrow Rock, 2004); Gardner, Mark L., *Fort Union National Monument* (Tucson, AZ: Western National Parks Association, 2005); Gardner, Mark L., and Ron Foreman, *Santa Fe Trail National Historic Trail* (Tucson, AZ: Western National Parks Association, 1993); Lavender, David, *Bent's Fort* (Lincoln: University of Nebraska Press, 1979); Levine, Fran, William Westbury, and Lisa Nordstrum, *A History of Archeological Investigations at Fort Union National*

Monument, Southwest Cultural Resources Center Professional Papers, No. 44 (Santa Fe, NM: National Park Service, 1992); Moore, Jackson W., Jr., *Bent's Old Fort: An Archeological Study* (Boulder, CO: Pruett, 1973); Utley, Robert M., *Fort Union National Monument, New Mexico* (Washington, DC: Government Printing Office, 1962); Utley, Robert M., Michael Henry, and T. J. Priehs, *Fort Scott National Historic Site* (Tucson, AZ: Western National Parks Association, 1991); Utley, Robert M., Fred Hirschmann, and J. C. Leacock, *Fort Larned National Historic Site* (Tucson, AZ: Western National Parks Association, 1993); Whitford, William C., *The Battle of Glorieta Pass: The Colorado Volunteers in the Civil War, March 26, 27, 28, 1862* (Glorieta, NM: Rio Grande Press, 1971).

William J. Hunt, Jr.

SAND CREEK MASSACRE NATIONAL HISTORIC SITE

Southeast Colorado

Finding and Interpreting the Site of an American Tragedy

The Sand Creek Massacre is one of the most significant and tragic events in American history. On November 29, 1864, Colonel John M. Chivington led a group of approximately 700 soldiers of the Colorado First and Third Volunteers from old Fort Lyon (near present-day Lamar, Colorado) to an Indian village of more than 100 lodges on Sand Creek, which was then also known as the Big Sandy. Approximately 500 Cheyenne and Arapaho Indians were camped at this village under the general leadership of Black Kettle, the Cheyenne peace chief. They believed they were under U.S. Army protection. As instructed by Colorado Governor John Evans, the Indians had earlier presented themselves to the U.S. Army at Fort Lyon, at which time they were told to remain at their Sand Creek camp. The Indian camp was at the edge of the Cheyenne and Arapaho reservation that had been established by the 1861 Treaty of Fort Wise. Nevertheless, volunteer troops led by Colonel John Chivington launched a surprise attack upon the village. The strike began at dawn, when the soldiers fired upon the Cheyenne and Arapaho encampment with small arms and cannon. Many of the villagers who survived this initial attack fled to the north, upstream. Approximately 1 mile above the village, according to most accounts of the massacre, the Indians sheltered themselves in hastily dug trenches along the banks of the creek. This area, known as the sandpits, was one of the areas of fiercest fighting. The army troops brought at least two 12-pound mountain howitzers to the sandpits area.

By day's end, at least 150 Indians—mainly women, children, and elderly people—had been killed. On the army's side, 10 soldiers died and 38 were wounded. Although Chivington's troops returned to a heroes' welcome in Denver, the Sand Creek Massacre was soon recognized for what it was—a national disgrace—and investigated and condemned by two congressional committees and a military commission.

Chivington lost his command, and territorial Governor John Evans was forced to resign. The event also loosed a pent-up anger among the Cheyenne and Arapaho that erupted in nearly a full-scale war on the central plains for several years.

Sand Creek remains to this day an important sacred site to the Cheyenne and Arapaho peoples. The site embodies the disenfranchisement and loss of life they suffered due to U.S. government policy toward them in the nineteenth century. The precise location of the Sand Creek Massacre was lost to memory, although Cheyenne and Arapaho oral traditions identified a specific bend on Sand Creek as the site of the village. Privately owned by several different landowners, the Sand Creek site could not always be visited and memorialized by tribal members as they desired.

Through a series of rather involved steps and actions, the Northern and Southern Cheyenne tribes and the Northern and Southern Arapaho tribes moved to have the site acquired by the National Park Service as a National Historic Site. In 1998 Senator Ben Nighthorse Campbell introduced Senate Bill 1695. The bill passed the Senate on July 21, 1998; passed the House of Representatives on September 18, 1998; and was signed by President Bill Clinton on October 6, 1998, as Public Law 105-243. Known as the "Sand Creek Massacre National Historic Site Study Act of 1998," the legislation directed the National Park Service—in consultation with the State of Colorado, the Cheyenne and Arapaho tribes of Oklahoma, the Northern Cheyenne tribe, and the Northern Arapaho tribe—to complete two tasks. First, the act directed the National Park Service to "identify the location and extent of the massacre area and the suitability and feasibility of designating the site as a unit of the National Park Service system." The location was designated a National Historic Site on November 7, 2000, after an extensive multidisciplinary team investigation that included Cheyenne and Arapaho

Sand Creek archaeological team members, including Arapahoe and Cheyenne tribal members, wait to excavate a metal detected target at the village site. [Douglas D. Scott]

consultants, historians, aerial photography specialists, soil scientists, remote sensing specialists, and archaeologists. Each team element had different tasks and research objectives, but all were aimed at the same goal: to locate and identify the site of the Sand Creek Massacre.

The primary research question to be answered with archaeological data was whether any evidence of the village attacked by Chivington existed in the study area. An archaeological project was undertaken in May 1999 with great success. The artifacts, their distribution on the landscape, and the context in which they were recovered provided the answers.

Artifacts of the 1864 period were found scattered all along the Sand Creek drainage beginning with the location traditionally associated with the village site and continuing northerly for several miles along Sand Creek. There was only one significant concentration of artifacts in that 3.5-mile length of the creek, and that is on the eastern side of the creek about 1 mile north of the traditional village site.

The Sand Creek South Bend, the traditionally acknowledged village site, yielded only about a dozen 1864 period artifacts. Those artifacts indicate some activity or activities occurred in this bend of Sand Creek about 1864, but the number and sparse distribution of artifacts did not constitute evidence of the large campsite that was attacked.

The more northerly areas of Sand Creek yielded only a few artifacts of the 1864 era as well. That evidence was found in the form of bullets fired from Civil War–era small arms and spherical shell and case shot cannon projectile fragments. These combat-related materials were found along either side of the creek and were widely scattered. There is no definitive evidence of camp debris of the 1864 period; however, the scattered period artifacts do indicate that these lands played a role in the 1864 event.

The largest concentration of 1864-era artifacts (about 400) was found on the eastern side of Sand Creek about 1 mile north of the traditional site. The artifact concentration, situated on an eastern terrace above Sand Creek, is about 450 meters long, trending southeasterly to northwesterly and about 160 meters wide. The artifacts found in the concentration include tin cups, tin cans, horseshoes, horseshoe nails,

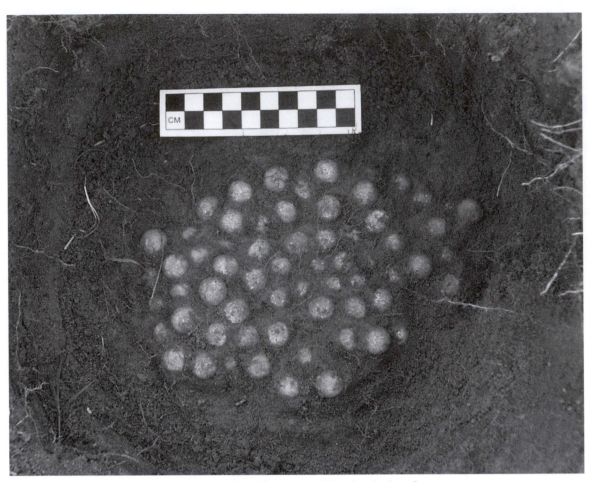

A cache of .50-caliber spherical rifle bullets found at the village site.   [Douglas D. Scott]

plates, bowls, knives, forks, spoons, barrel hoops, a coffee grinder, a coffee pot, iron arrowheads, bullets, and cannonball fragments (Scott 2000, 2003).

The concentration includes artifacts that are usually considered unique to Native American camp or village sites of the nineteenth century. Besides the arrowheads, some of which are in an unfinished state, are a variety of iron objects modified for Native American uses. These artifacts include knives altered to awls, iron wire altered to awls, fleshers or hide scrapers, strap iron altered by filed serrations as hide preparation devices, and several iron objects altered by filing to serve an, as yet, unidentified cutting or scraping purpose.

The presence of a Native American campsite with artifacts dating to about 1864 prompted the question, was this, rather than the traditionally designated area, the correct location for the Cheyenne and Arapaho village of Black Kettle and his followers? Short of finding an item with a known 1864 camp resident name glyph scratched on it, other lines of evidence were used to make the identification. There is a wealth of comparative data from Cheyenne and Arapaho annuity requests, annuity lists, and other correspondence that provides a set of comparative data. The Cheyenne and Arapaho were parties to several treaties with the U.S. government, which obligated the government to supply the tribes with a variety of goods. These annuity payments were made to the tribes beginning in the 1850s and continued until well after 1864.

The annuity lists, requests, and correspondence were researched and clearly demonstrate that most of the artifact types found are the same types as listed for the Cheyenne and Arapaho. Tin cups, bowls, plates, coffee grinders, coffee pots, kettles, pans, knives, forks, spoons, fleshers, axes, butcher knives, horse tack, guns, lead, and bullets are consistently listed. These are the durable goods, the ones that can be expected to survive in the archaeological record, and indeed were found during the field investigations.

Ideally, there should be a list of goods captured and destroyed by the Colorado Volunteer Cavalry at Sand Creek compiled after the attack on the village. But given the unit's laxity of military protocol on any number of fronts, it is not surprising that no such list was found during the documentary research.

Other comparable sources were consulted, including lists of captured and destroyed goods from three other Cheyenne

A fragment of a 12-pound spherical shell fired into the Sand Creek village by the Colorado Volunteers.   [Douglas D. Scott]

camps dating to within five years of the Sand Creek event. Two of those sites had also been archaeologically studied. The lists and archaeological data show a remarkable degree of correspondence.

It is abundantly clear from comparisons with the available annuity lists, lists of captured and destroyed goods, as well as the other archaeologically studied Cheyenne sites that the concentration of artifacts found at Sand Creek are consistent with a Native American camp of the 1860s era.

Another issue addressed was whether there is evidence in the archaeological record that this is the village attacked by the Colorado Volunteer Cavalry. The archaeological record contains abundant lines of evidence to support the conclusion that this is Black Kettle's village attacked by Colonel Chivington's forces.

Present in the site area are two lines of evidence that this village was attacked and destroyed. First is the evidence of arms and munitions. The village site yielded bullets for various calibers and types of firearms. The weapon types and calibers were used during the American Civil War and can be readily dated and identified. Lists of ordnance used by the First and

Third Colorado Volunteer Cavalry units during late 1864 exist. The concordance of the archaeological munitions finds and the lists of weapons in the volunteers' hands is quite remarkable. They match exceedingly well. In addition, there has been some limited archaeological investigation of one of the Colorado volunteer campsites in eastern Colorado at Russellville. The Russellville archaeological collection and the Sand Creek collection also show a very high degree of similarity.

Perhaps the single most important artifact types that can definitively identify this village as being attacked are cannonball fragments. The Colorado Volunteers employed four 12-pound Mountain Howitzers during their attack. Cannonball fragments of this type were found in and around the site and are nearly unequivocal evidence in their own right that this is the campsite site of the Sand Creek Massacre.

The firearms artifact distribution also adds to the story. There are two concentrations of firearms artifacts and several widely dispersed bullets. The first concentration consists of bullets found in the village site. These bullets are both fired and unfired items. Almost all calibers associated with the Colorado Volunteer units are present. A 12-pound howitzer case fragment was also found in the village. It provides mute testimony to the fact the camp was shelled by the artillery.

The second concentration of firearms artifacts was found on the west side of Sand Creek and about 1,000 feet directly opposite the village. The firearms artifacts were found along a line about 1,000 feet long. Civil War–era bullets were found as were three 12-pound case shot fragments. These bullets and cannonball fragments probably represent rounds that overshot their intended targets in the camp or were simply ricochets from the firing on the camp. This artifact distribution probably reflects firing along nearly the entire length of the camp, and as such is another strong indicator that the camp was attacked and fired upon.

The other widely dispersed firearms artifacts are quite literally found east of the camp ranging from 300 to 600 meters and north of the camp ranging from a few tens of meters to well over 2.5 miles. Among the bullets closest to the camp are also mingled bits of village items, such as the coffee grinder, that may reflect attempts to salvage a treasured item at the time the Cheyenne and Arapaho fled the attack on the camp. The distribution of these fired bullets and other privately collected cannonball fragments clearly show the line of the flight for survival by the fleeing villagers and the pursuit by the Colorado troops.

The firearms data is particularly striking in one respect, and that is the absence of bullets or other weaponry evidence of resistance in the camp itself. Bullets representing weapon types that can be reasonably associated with the Cheyenne and Arapaho are singularly absent from the artifact collection from the campsite. The absence of definitive artifacts of resistance supports the Native American oral tradition that the attack came as a complete surprise. Other evidence of combat or armed resistance is not great, but more compelling, as seen in the firearms artifacts found along the flight for survival route.

The final bit of evidence that identifies this site as Black Kettle's village is the condition of the artifacts found in the camp. Every spoon, a fork, all tin cups, plates, bowls, and containers (i.e., buckets, pots, and kettles) have all been crushed and flattened. Even the tin cans are crushed. The cast iron pieces—kettles, pots, and a skillet—are broken. The patterns of crushing and breakage point to the intentional destruction of the camp equipage so as to make it unserviceable to its owners.

Through a multidisciplinary approach that included historical research, tribal oral histories and traditional methods, and archaeological investigations, the National Park Service Sand Creek Massacre Site Location Study resulted in the definitive identification of the massacre site. For the first time, there is conclusive physical evidence of the Sand Creek Massacre, as over 400 massacre-related artifacts have been located and identified. In addition, the site location study brought together the most comprehensive research to date regarding the massacre's location, including original maps,

diaries, congressional testimony, newspaper articles, interviews, and aerial photographic analysis. Moreover, the project also resulted in the recording of numerous Cheyenne and Arapaho oral histories on the Sand Creek Massacre.

As with any historical event, archaeologists' understanding of the Sand Creek Massacre is still limited and obscured through time. Thus, although the length and extent of the Sand Creek Massacre site have been conclusively identified, there are differing views regarding some of the specifics of the massacre within that boundary.

The National Park Service, based on a preponderance of evidence, believes that the Indian village that was attacked by Chivington's troops on November 29, 1864, is definitively identified. Completed prior to the archaeological survey, a review of historical documents, which included an 1868 map of the Sand Creek Massacre area drawn by Lieutenant Samuel Bonsall, indicated that an area north of the traditional site was the likely site of the village. The archaeological survey uncovered approximately 400 artifacts in a concentrated area within this section.

The Northern Arapaho tribe concurs with the National Park Service on the location of the village and sandpits. The other tribes disagree with those conclusions. Those tribes believe there are several lines of evidence that support another conclusion. George Bent, a mixed-blood Cheyenne survivor of the Sand Creek Massacre, had drawn several diagrams that show the Sand Creek Massacre camp. Two of the diagrams show the village within the crux of a 90-degree bend of Sand Creek. The tribes believe Bent's diagrams match the configuration of the traditional South Bend location and are significant evidence that the village was located in that area. Cheyenne oral histories and traditional tribal methods also indicate that the South Bend was the village site. Moreover, the Cheyenne Arrow Keeper, who is the tribe's highest spiritual leader, blessed the South Bend as "Cheyenne earth" in 1978, thereby designating it as the Sand Creek Massacre site. For the Cheyenne, there may be no more powerful evidence that the South Bend is the Sand Creek Massacre site than that designation bestowed upon it by the Arrow Keeper.

Thus the power of oral tradition takes precedent over historical and archaeological data sets in this case. Although the tribes accept the study area as containing the massacre site, the historical and archaeological identification of the village is rejected because the data do not fit neatly with oral tradition.

The Sand Creek Massacre study provides an interesting juxtaposition on the cultural meaning ascribed to place and the role of "objective" scientific study of past events and places. The Sand Creek case provides a jarring example of the reality that not everyone shares the same cultural values or ascribes the same weight to disparate lines of evidence. To those trained in scientific methods of analysis the answer seems simple. Three lines of evidence—historical documentation, archaeological data, and oral tradition—are evaluated and a conclusion drawn. Where one line of evidence, oral tradition, diverges from the others, it can be explained as the failure of memory to be passed accurately through three to five generations. Thus the preponderance of scientific evidence is accepted with a reasonable and scientifically defensible conclusion. In this case the failure was to consider the deep-seated cultural values and meanings placed on the traditional site by traditional Native American religious and cultural practitioners.

The lesson to be drawn is neither earthshaking nor a leap forward in theoretical explanation. Rather it is a reminder to those trained in and practicing the scientific method that not all people share the same viewpoint of the infallibility of the deductive method. The National Park Service's plans for public interpretation of the site include the intention to present the various points of view of specific site location but emphasize that the parties share a sense that the Sand Creek Massacre site is preserved and memorialized within the agreed-upon boundaries.

Further Reading: Afton, Jean, David Fridtjof Halaas, Andrew W. Masich, and Richard N. Ellis, *Cheyenne Dog Soldiers: A Ledgerbook History of Coups and Combat* (Niwot: Colorado State Historical Society and University of Colorado Press, 1997); Craig, Reginald S., *The Fighting Parson: The Biography of Colonel John M. Chivington* (Los Angeles: Westernlore Press, 1959); Greene, Jerome A., and Douglas D. Scott, *Finding Sand Creek: The History and Archaeology of the 1864 Massacre* (Norman: University of Oklahoma Press, 2004); Grinnell, George Bird, *The Fighting Cheyennes* (New York: Charles Scribner's Sons, 1915; republished Norman: University of Oklahoma Press, 1956); Hoig, Stan, *The Sand Creek Massacre* (Norman: University of Oklahoma Press, 1961); National Park Service, *Sand Creek Massacre Site Location Study* (Denver: Intermountain Regional Office, National Park Service, 2000); Scott, Douglas D., *Identifying the 1864 Sand Creek Massacre Site through Archaeological Reconnaissance: The Sand Creek Massacre Site Location Study* (Denver, CO: Intermountain Regional Office, National Park Service, 2000); Scott, Douglas D., "Oral Tradition and Archaeology: Conflict and Concordance Examples from Two Indian War Sites," *Historical Archaeology* 37(3) (2003): 55–65.

Douglas D. Scott

GLOSSARY

Accelerator Mass Spectrometric (AMS) Dating. A method of radiocarbon dating precise enough to count the proportion of carbon isotope (carbon 14) atoms directly and reducing the size of the sample of material required for accurate dating dramatically.

Anasazi (Ancestral Puebloan) Cultural Tradition. A well-known ancient cultural tradition that existed in the "Four Corners" area of the Colorado Plateau, around the common corners of Colorado, Utah, Arizona, and New Mexico, beginning about AD 900 and lasting until about AD 1300. Anasazi is the older and more traditional term used by archaeologists to refer to Ancestral Puebloan people. Many well-known sites are associated with this tradition, for example, the ancient architectural sites of Mesa Verde, Chaco Canyon, and Canyons of the Ancients National Monument (see the essays by Steve Lekson, Wirt Wills [on Shabik'eschee Village site], Paul Reed [Overview of Chaco Canyon], Jill Neitzel, Tom Windes, LouAnn Jacobson, John Kantner, Cathy Cameron, and Mark Varien in the Southwest section).

Archaic. A general term used to refer to a time period that encompasses the early Holocene from about 10,000 to 3,000 years ago, but varying in different regions. Developments during the Archaic included the manufacture of ground stone tools, the beginnings of food cultivation, and initial settled life. In some parts of North America this time period is divided into three sub-periods: the Early, Middle, and Late portions.

Assemblage. A group of artifacts recurring together at different places or times. Assemblages may be associated with particular activities or with a cultural tradition.

Atl atl. A spear-, arrow-, or dart-throwing tool. These are composite tools usually with several parts, including an antler or wood handle, a weight, and a hooked end. The atl atl works as a lever to propel the projectile for greater distance and with greater force.

Avocational archaeologist. Individuals with a serious interest in archaeology, but who do not engage in the discipline as their profession. Many avocational archaeologists have made important archaeological discoveries and contributions to our understanding of the ancient or historic pasts.

Basketmaker. A term used to refer to the early portion of the Ancestral Puebloan cultural tradition. Early Basketmaker people relied on hunting and gathering for much of their food, but during this period, domesticated plants, such as corn, beans, and squash, were added to the diet. During this period, ways of life became more settled and more permanent houses, called "pithouses" because they were dug partly below ground became common. Coiled and twined basketry also is common, and people began to make plain pottery for the first time.

Biface. A stone tool that has been chipped on both sides to shape and thin it.

Blade tool manufacture and technology. Blade manufacture is a quite different method of making flaked stone cutting and piercing tools than that employed in making chipped stone tools, such as a bifacial point or knife. The latter involves shaping, thinning, and sharpening a single piece of stone. In blade manufacture, a nodule of stone is carefully prepared to form a core so that multiple, long, narrow, parallel-sided flakes with very sharp edges can be struck. These "blades" then are used as knives for cutting, or snapped into segments that can be inserted into slots on the sides of antler or wooden points to form the cutting edges. Knives can also be made this way. One advantage of this technique over biface manufacture is that large cutting and piercing tools can be made using small pieces of stone when large pieces are not available.

Cation ratio dating. Cation ratio dating is used to date rocks that have a modified surface such as prehistoric rock carvings (petroglyphs). This is a relative dating technique that is not considered an accurate method of dating by some professional archaeologists.

Rocks are covered by a kind of varnish, a chemically-changed layer caused by weathering that builds up over time. The change in the rock varnish is due to calcium and potassium seeping out of the rock. The cation ratio is determined by scraping the varnish from the carved or petroglyph surface back to the original rock surface and making a comparison of the two. The technique relies on change due to weathering of the stone over long periods of time, so geographically distinctive patterns are needed to compare the original surfaces with the modern suface that show the results of weathering.

Chert. A type of very fine-grained stone rich in silica. It is often found in or weathered from limestone deposits. It was shaped into chipped stone tools, and sometimes for blade tools, using stone and bone or antler hammers.

Chipped Stone tools. Tools shaped and thinned by systematically flaking exterior portions off. Typically this manufacturing technique is used with very fine-grained stone (e.g., obsidian, chert, or flint) that can be flaked relatively easily because it fractures smoothly in a way that can be controlled manufacturing techniques skillfully applied.

Clovis. Clovis is a term used to name an archaeological culture, a time period, and a particular variety of fluted stone spear points or knives. The name derives from Clovis, New Mexico, near which is located the type site, Blackwater Draw. Clovis spear points have been found in direct association with extinct megafauna in ice age gravel deposits The Clovis culture is known to have occupied many parts of North America during the Paleoindian period. The distinctive Clovis spear point has a vertical flake scar or flute on both faces of the point that extends about 1/3 its length. Sites containing Clovis points have been dated across North America to between 13,500 and 10,800 years ago. In western North America Clovis points have been found with the killed and butchered remains of large animals like mammoth or mastodon. As a result, Clovis peoples are assumed to have targeted large game animals, although how much of their diet actually came from hunting, much less from large game, is unknown (see the essays by David Anderson in the Southeast section and Bonnie Pitblado and Dennis Stanford in the Great Plains and Rocky Mountain section).

Component. A culturally homogenous stratigraphic unit within an archaeological site.

Core. A lithic artifact used as the source from which other tools, flakes, or blades are struck.

CRM (Cultural Resource Management). This activity includes archaeological investigations done as part of public project planning required by federal or state laws to ensure that important archaeological sites are not wantonly destroyed by public undertakings. CRM also includes the long term management of archaeological resources that are on public lands and for which legal protections and preservation is required of the public agencies that administer these lands (see the general introduction for more details abut contemporary CRM in North America).

Dalton. Term used to refer to an archaeological culture dating to the end of the Paleoindian period and the beginning of the Archaic time period. Dalton artifacts and sites are recognized in the Midwest, Southeast, and Northeast of North America. The point distribution shows that there was a widespread Dalton lifeway oriented toward streams and deciduous forests. Dalton culture people were hunters and gatherers using a variety of wild animal and plant foods over the course of each year. Timber and nuts were important as raw materials and food. Like Paleoindians, Dalton groups probably consisted of families related by kinship and mutual dependence (see the essay by Dan Morse in the Southeast section).

Debitage. Stone debris from chipped-stone tool manufacturing or maintenance activities.

Desert Culture. Ancient cultural groups that occupied the present-day Great Basin and Plateau regions. They created a distinctive cultural adaptation to the dry, relatively impoverished environments of these regions. The Cochise or Desert Archaic culture began by about 7000 BC and persisted until about AD 500.

Earthfast foundation. Earthfast (also known as "post-in-the-ground") architecture was the most prevalent building tradition of 17th-century Virginia and Maryland. At its core, the typical "Virginia House" (as dwellings of this type were sometimes called) consisted of pairs of hewn wooden posts set into deep, regularly-spaced holes dug into the ground. Once set in the ground and backfilled, these posts were either pegged on nailed together with cross beams to form the sides and gables of a rectangular, A-framed structure. The exterior "skins" of such earthfast structures varied. Some were both roofed and sided with riven wooden clapboards. Others were sided in wattle-and-daub and roofed with thatch. Irrespective of their construction, earthfast structures tended to be rather impermanent, lasting no more than perhaps a decade or two at most in the hot, humid Chesapeake region.

Effigy pipes. A variation on the plain stone tube pipe carved in the likeness of an animal. A wide variety of animal images—birds, mammals, and reptiles—are used for these pipes which are frequently associated with the Adena and Hopewell cultures in the Midwest region.

Feature. Usually refers to types of archaeological deposits related to a particular focused activity or event. For example, hearths, garbage or trash pits, storage pits, and foundations or other architectural remnants are referred to generally as features.

Flotation. A technique for recovering very small organic remains, such as tiny pieces of charcoal, seeds, bone, wood, and other items. A soil sample is placed in a drum of water, sometimes mixed with other liquids. The liquid is agitated to loosen any soil from the organic material. This material, being lighter than water, floats to the surface and can be skimmed off using a fine mesh screen. The organic materials can be used in a variety of analyses, for example, to interpret diet, subsistence activities, for dating, and to determine use of wood for tools or structures.

Gorgets. Made of copper, shell or polished or smoothed stone these thin, often oval artifacts were often perforated by two or more holes and worn around the neck.

Hohokam Cultural Tradition. Hohokam refers to the Sonoran Desert region of Phoenix and Tucson in southern Arizona and further south. The Hohokam region witnessed remarkable cultural developments beginning about AD 900. In this general area, about 200 sites with large oval, earthen features (interpreted as local expressions of Mesoamerican ball courts) have been found. A distinctive cluster of large sites in the area of modern Phoenix clearly represent the Hohokam center. Hohokam had red-on-buff pottery, large towns composed of scores of courtyard groups (three to five single-room thatch houses facing inward into a small courtyard or patio), and ball courts. There were regular markets for the exchange of goods supported by canal-irrigated farming (see Steve Lekson's essay on the classic period ancient Southwest).

Holocene. The most recent geological epoch, which began about 10,000 years ago. The period after the last glaciation in North America.

Hopewell Cultural Traditon. An archaeological tradition of the Midwest dated to the Middle Woodland period (about 50 BC to AD 400). The Hopewell tradition is known for a distinctive burial patterns and a wide-ranging exchange among communities. Communities hundreds, even thousands, of miles from one another participated in this exchange system and raw materials, as well as finished products were exported and imported. The Hopewell tradition also is known for the mounds that they built for ceremonial and burial purposes. It is known to be one of the most considerable achievements of Native Americans throughout the ancient past. These mounds, especially in the Ohio River valley are large complexes incorporating a variety of geometric shapes and rise to impressive heights (see essays in the Midwest section by George Milner, Douglas Charles, N'omi Greber, William Dancey, and Bradley Lepper).

Horizon. A set of cultural characteristics or traits that has a brief time depth but is found across multiple areas or regions.

Kiva. Among modern Pueblo Indian communities in the Southwest, a kiva is a nonresidential structure or room that is owned and used by specific social groups, such as clans or religious societies. The activities that take place in kivas are different than the daily, domestic activities—such as food preparation and pottery manufacture—that occur in dwellings. Because of this historic affiliation of sociopolitical functions with kivas, archaeologists use this term to refer to large pit structures lacking evidence for domestic functions that may have been used as public buildings, rather than household dwellings.

Lithic. Stone.

Loess. Fine-grained windblown sediment deposited as soil layers on areas not ice-covered during the last glaciation.

Megafauna. Large mammal species, such as mammoth, mastodon, bison, giant beaver, giant ground sloth, and stag elk that lived in North America during the late glacial and early post-glacial time periods. Many megafauna species have become extinct.

Midden. The archaeological remains of a human settlement's garbage and trash deposits. Middens typically are an accumulation of decomposed organic refuse usually very dark colored that frequently also contains thousands of discarded pieces of stone artifacts and ceramics, animal bones, nutshells, and other remains.

Mimbres Cultural Tradition. The Mimbres cultural development occurred in the Mogollon region of western New Mexico between about AD 900 and 1150. It is most famous for its remarkable black-on-white pottery. While the majority of Mimbres bowls are painted with striking geometric designs, images include depictions of people and events using an artistic style that merits inclusion in the world's major art museums. Images also show Mimbres' wide interests: Pacific Ocean fish, tropical birds from western Mexico (and, perhaps, monkeys from the same area), and armadillos (see essays by Steve Lekson [Classic Period Cultural and Social Interaction], Karen Schollmeyer, Steve Swanson, and Margaret Nelson, and J. J. Brody in the Southwest section).

Mississippian Cultural Tradition. A widespread tradition centered on Midwestern and Southeastern North America beginning about AD 1000 and lasting in some places until AD 1600. Typically societies that were part of this cultural tradition had chiefdom level political organizations, had subsistence systems based on intensive agricultural production of corn, beans, squash, and other domesticated plants, and built settlements that incorporated earthen architecture, typically various kinds and sizes of mound architecture. Mississippian chiefdoms flourished across much of the Eastern Woodlands: as far north as Illinois and southern Wisconsin; as far west as eastern Oklahoma; as far east as the Carolinas and Georgia; and south to Florida and the Gulf Coast (see essays by Robin Beck in the Southeast section and Mary Beth Turbot in the Midwest section).

Mogollon Cultural Tradition. An ancient Southwestern cultural tradition dating between about A.D. 200 and 1450. The tradition is found in a vast, ecologically diverse geographic area in southwestern New Mexico, southeastern Arizona and northwestern Mexico. Mogollon takes its name from the mountain range and highlands that separate the Anasazi and Hohokam regions. The Mogollon area witnessed remarkable cultural development referred to as the Mimbres after the river in southwest New Mexico where this development was centered (see essays by Steve Lekson [Classic Period Cultural and Social Interaction] and Wirt Wills [the SU site] in the Southwest section).

Paleoindian (Paleoamerican) Cultural Tradition. The Paleoindian time frame extends from approximately 13,500 to 9,000 BC and is found in almost all parts of North America. It is the earliest widely recognized archaeological cultural tradition in North America. The Clovis culture is the earliest Paleoindian culture, but there are increasing numbers of investigations of sites that are purported to be older than the Clovis or Paleoindian tradition.

Pit. A hole in the earth constructed and used for cooking, storage, or garbage or trash disposal. Pits are a common kind of archaeological feature.

Pithouse. Pithouses typically are single room dwellings, although some have antechambers. Pit-houses are semi-subterranean dwellings in which some portions of the walls consist of the sides of an excavated pit. They are constructed by excavating a large hole or pit, building a timber framework inside the pit, then covering the framework with the excavated dirt, resulting in a house that is very thermally efficient, but prone to rapid deterioration, depending on the climate, from the effects of moisture, as well as vermin infestation.

Pleistocene. The geological epoch dating from 1.8 million to 10,000 years ago. During the last part of the Pleistocene human populations began to migrate into North America. The end of this epoch is a period of repeated glaciations in North America. It is succeeded by the Holocene era.

Postmolds. The archaeological remains of timbers, posts, saplings, or other wood structural elements of former buildings or dwellings. Depending on the age and soil conditions, posts placed in the ground ultimately will decay into fragments or mere stains indicating where these portions of buildings once existed.

Prehistory, prehistoric. Regarded by some as a demeaning term indicating primitive, but, most often used simply to refer to the general period of time prior to written records. As such, the length of the prehistoric period for different parts of North America varies according to when written records are available, generally associated with the beginning of European contact with aboriginal cultures.

Radiocarbon Dating (also known as Carbon-14 [^{14}C] Dating). An absolute dating method that measures the decay of the radioactive isotope of carbon (^{14}C) in organic material.

Steatite (Soapstone). A metamorphic rock, composed largely of the mineral talc and relatively soft. Steatite has been used as a medium for carving for thousands of years. Steatite also was carved out in ancient times to create bowls, in particular in places and at times before pottery had begun to be produced.

Taphonomy. The study of the process of fossilization. Used in archaeology to examine the human and natural changes that produce the archaeological record. For example, changes to organic materials after the death of the organism, such as how bone is changed by chemical, mechanical or animal processes after burial.

Tradition. An archaeological concept indicating a consistent set of cultural characteristics and traits that has great time depth and covers a recognized area.

Wattle-and-daub construction. A building technique using poles placed vertically in the ground and then plastered over with mud to construct the walls. Usually structures of wattle and daub were topped with thatched roofs.

Woodland Time Period. A time period term used mainly in the eastern North America south of Canada between roughly 1000 BC and AD 1000. In the Midwest region the Woodland period is regarded as the centuries between Archaic times and the Mississippian period. During this long period, the technology of pottery developed and spread, social and political complexity increased, cultivated plants changed from a supplemental part of diet to dietary staples, and settlements grew from small groups of residences to some of the largest cities in the world at that time.

Younger Dryas. A cold climatic event that took place from 12,900–11,600 years ago. It was a rapid return to glacial conditions during the longer term transition from the last glacial maximum to modern climatic conditions.

Sources used for definitions: The definitions in this glossary are derived from a number of sources, including essays in this encyclopedia, and the following texts:

Renfrew, Colin and Paul Bahn (2000). *Archaeology: Theories, Methods, and Practice*, third edition. Thames and Hudson, London and New York.

Thomas, David Hurst (1991). *Archaeology: Down to Earth*. Harcourt Brace Jovanovich College Publishers, Fort Worth and New York.

INDEX

A page number followed by *i* indicates an illustration; *m* indicates a map; *t* indicates a table.